NO LONGER PROPERTY Of
SEATTLE PUBLIC LIBRARY

RECEIVED

AUG 1 6 2018

WALLINGFORD LIBRARY

D1024472

SOMETHING NEW

TALES FROM A MAKESHIFT BRIDE

BY LUCY KNISLEY

First Second
New York

First Second

Copyright © 2016 by LUCY KNISLEY

Published by First Second
First Second is an imprint of Roaring Brook Press,
a division of Holtzbrinck Publishing Holdings Limited Partnership
175 Fifth Avenue, New York, New York 10010
All rights reserved

Library of Congress Control Number: 2015944392
ISBN: 9781626722491

Our books may be purchased in bulk for promotional, educational or
business use. Please contact your local bookseller or the Macmillan Corporate
and Premium Sales Department at (800) 221-7945 ext. 5442 or
by e-mail at MacmillanSpecialMarkets@macmillan.com.

First edition 2016

Book design by GORDON WHITESIDE

Printed in China by Toppan Leefung Printing Ltd.,
Dongguan City, Guangdong Province

1 3 5 7 9 10 8 6 4 2

Dedication

For all the other makeshift, and *not-so-makeshift*, brides and grooms out there. It doesn't matter if your wedding is impending or happened fifty years ago, or may someday happen in the future... Whether it's big or small or borrowed or blue... We're all joined in this matrimonial bond of

occasional utter cluelessness.

And for Johnny, who was game to marry into the dubious position of husband-to/fodder-for an autobiographical cartoonist spouse, and whose sweet handsome face I so love to draw.

And for my mom, who makes stuff happen. MOB: Thank you, I'm sorry, I love you.

Love,
The ∧ Bride
MAKESHIFT

TABLE OF CONTENTS

PART THREE: THE PUFF, THE PLACE, THE PLATE, AND THE PLAYLIST

PART FOUR: THE PRETTY

PART FIVE: THE BIG DAY

MARRIED LIFE GOES ON

Of all the unfamiliar roles in which I've found myself as an adult, this has been one of the strangest...

Despite hundreds of years of traditions and expectations, familiar rituals and ancient promises...

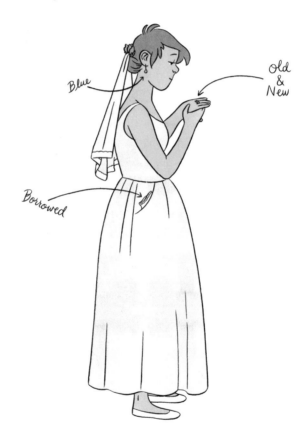

Blue

Old & New

Borrowed

A year ago, I couldn't have even _imagined_ myself as a _bride_.

A year ago, I was single.

I didn't know a thing about weddings...

I couldn't imagine all the planning that went into this day.

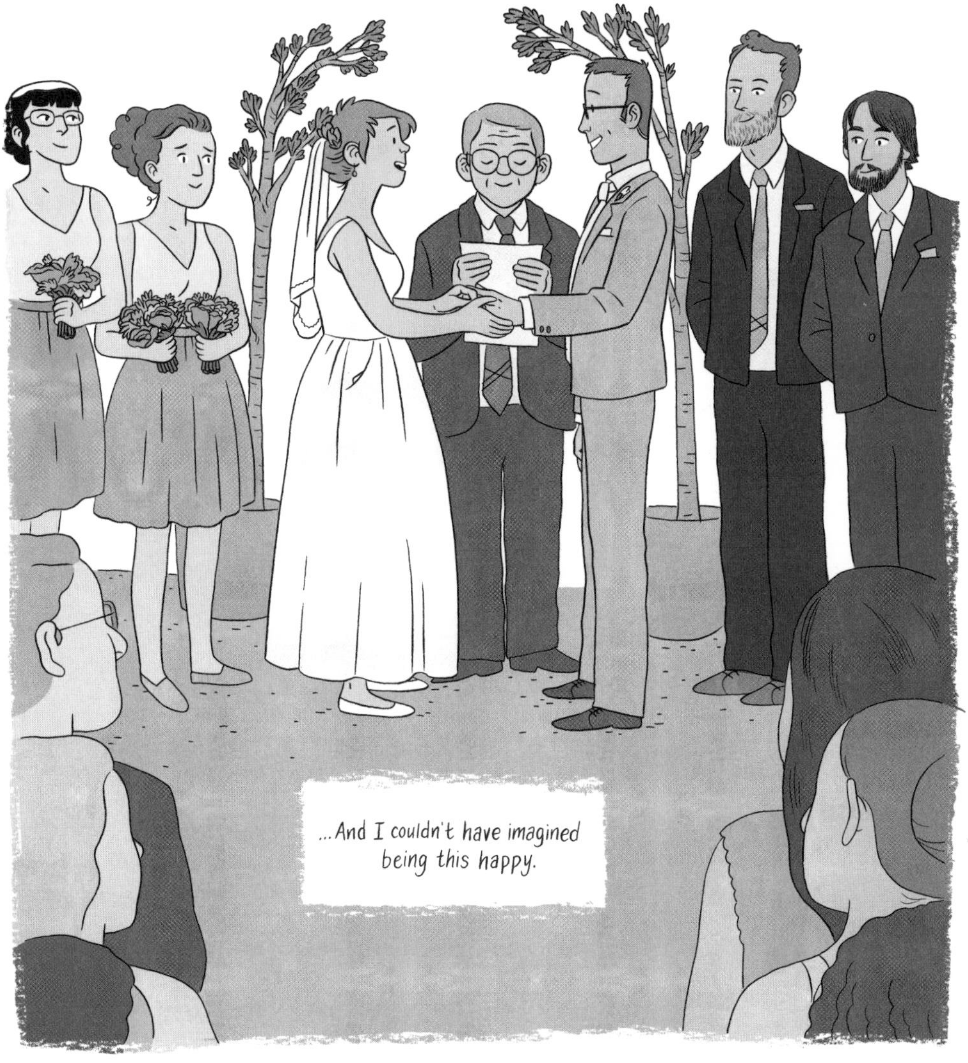
...And I couldn't have imagined being this happy.

SOMETHING OLD,
SOMETHING NEW,
SOMETHING BORROWED
& SOMETHING BLUE

Introduction

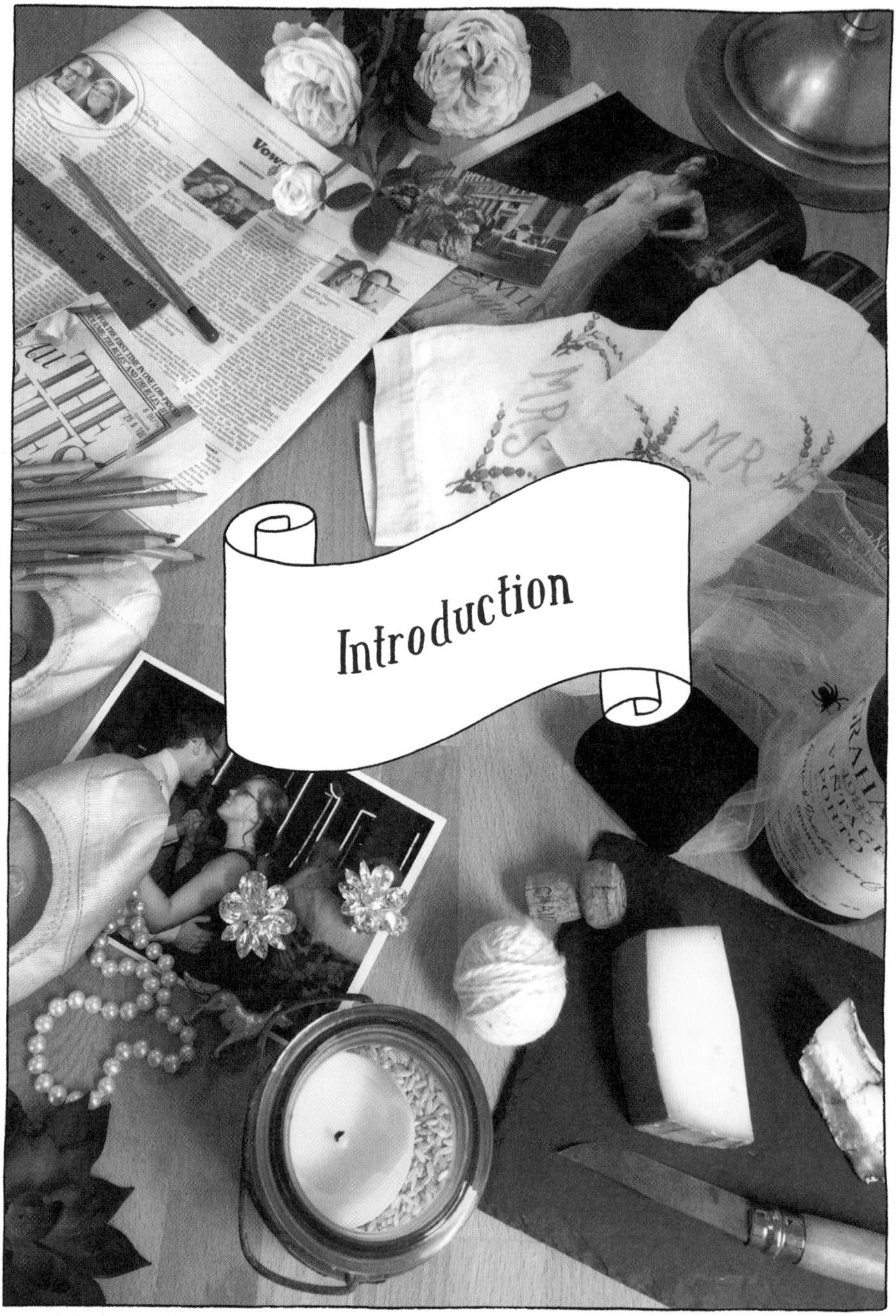
MRS
MR

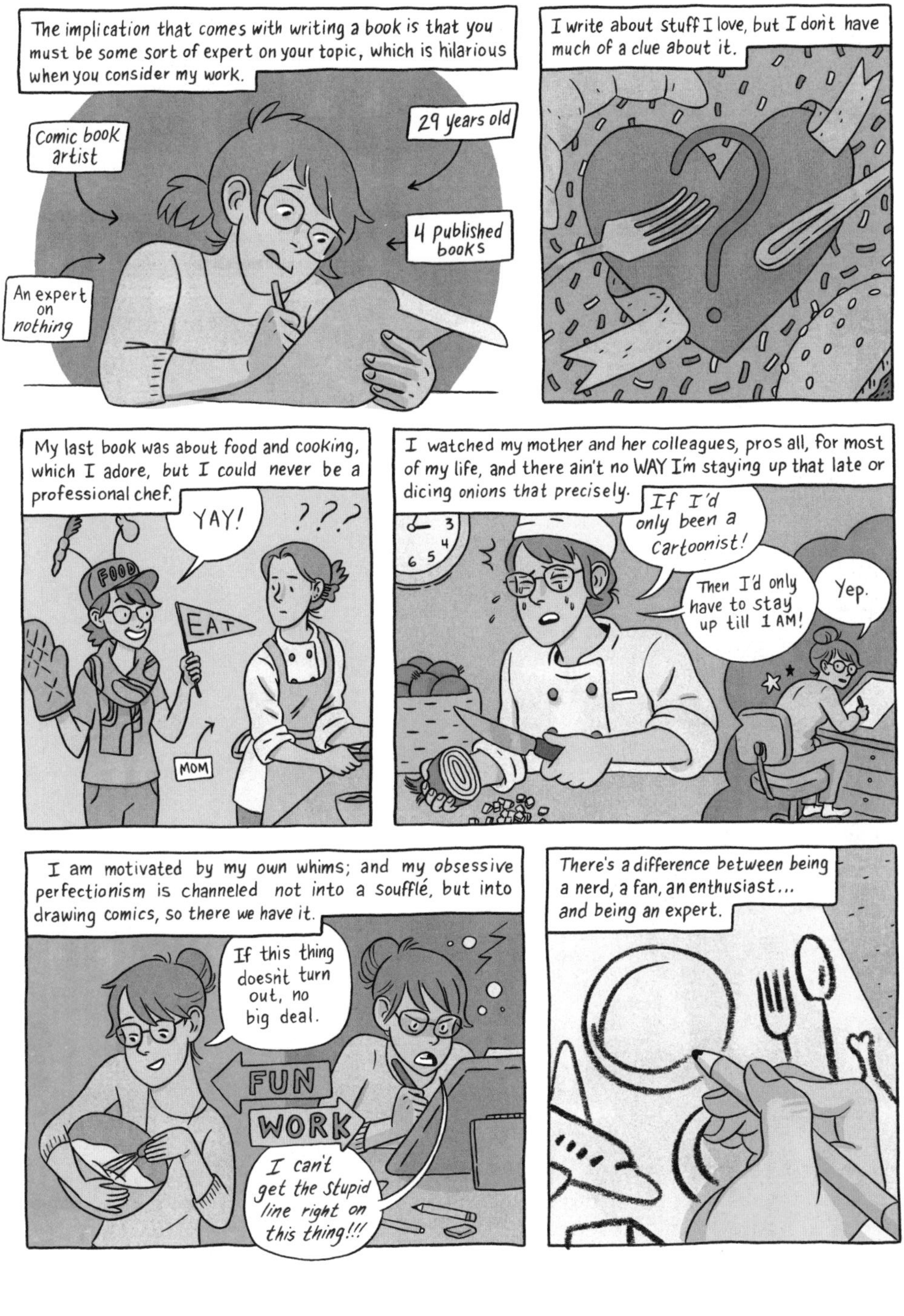
The implication that comes with writing a book is that you must be some sort of expert on your topic, which is hilarious when you consider my work.
Comic book artist
29 years old
4 published books
An expert on *nothing*
I write about stuff I love, but I don't have much of a clue about it.
My last book was about food and cooking, which I adore, but I could never be a professional chef.
YAY!
???
FOOD
EAT
MOM
I watched my mother and her colleagues, pros all, for most of my life, and there ain't no WAY I'm staying up that late or dicing onions that precisely.
If I'd only been a cartoonist!
Then I'd only have to stay up till 1 AM!
Yep.
I am motivated by my own whims; and my obsessive perfectionism is channeled not into a soufflé, but into drawing comics, so there we have it.
If this thing doesn't turn out, no big deal.
FUN
WORK
I can't get the stupid line right on this thing!!!
There's a difference between being a nerd, a fan, an enthusiast... and being an expert.

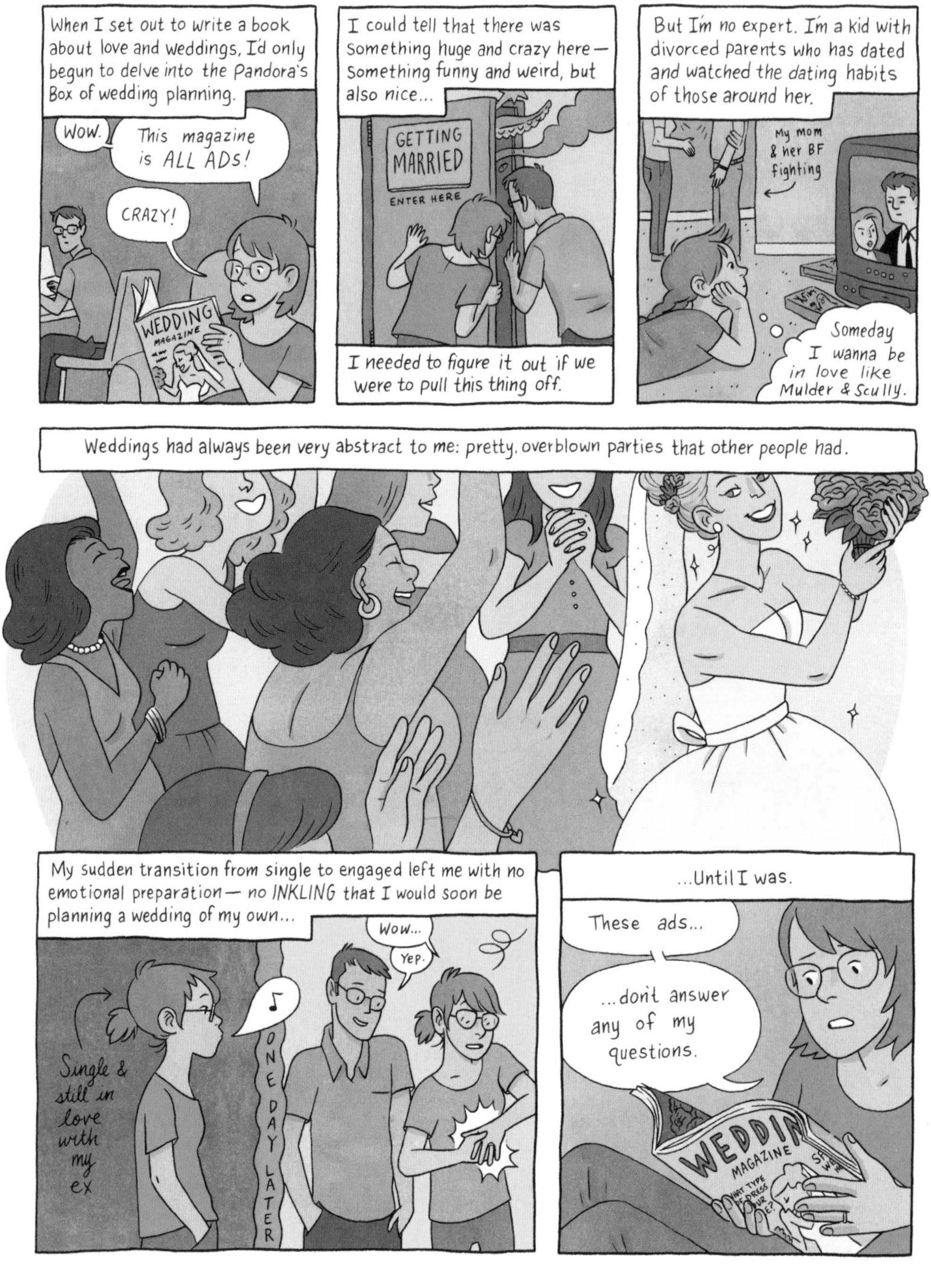
When I set out to write a book about love and weddings, I'd only begun to delve into the Pandora's Box of wedding planning.
WOW.
This magazine is ALL ADS!
CRAZY!
WEDDING MAGAZINE
I could tell that there was something huge and crazy here— something funny and weird, but also nice...
GETTING MARRIED
ENTER HERE
I needed to figure it out if we were to pull this thing off.
But I'm no expert. I'm a kid with divorced parents who has dated and watched the dating habits of those around her.
My mom & her BF fighting
Someday I wanna be in love like Mulder & Scully.
Weddings had always been very abstract to me: pretty, overblown parties that other people had.
My sudden transition from single to engaged left me with no emotional preparation— no INKLING that I would soon be planning a wedding of my own...
Single & still in love with my ex
ONE DAY LATER
Wow...
Yep.
...Until I was.
These ads...
...don't answer any of my questions.
WEDDIN
MAGAZINE

I came to this new obsession as a bridal newborn — aghast and impressed with the significance and pageantry of it all.

BRIDE

Jeez.

Like all brides, I wanted to

MAKE IT MY OWN

Huh?

And with a lot of help, and a steep learning curve, I think I did.

Lucy! Come to bed — it's 1 AM!

RmRmRmRmRm

It wasn't so hard, in the long run.

FINISH!

CONFETTI CANNON

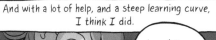

Just hold on to the speeding locomotive and try to enjoy the ride.

HOW MUCH LONGER?

ONLY A YEAR!

THE WEDDING PLANNING EXP

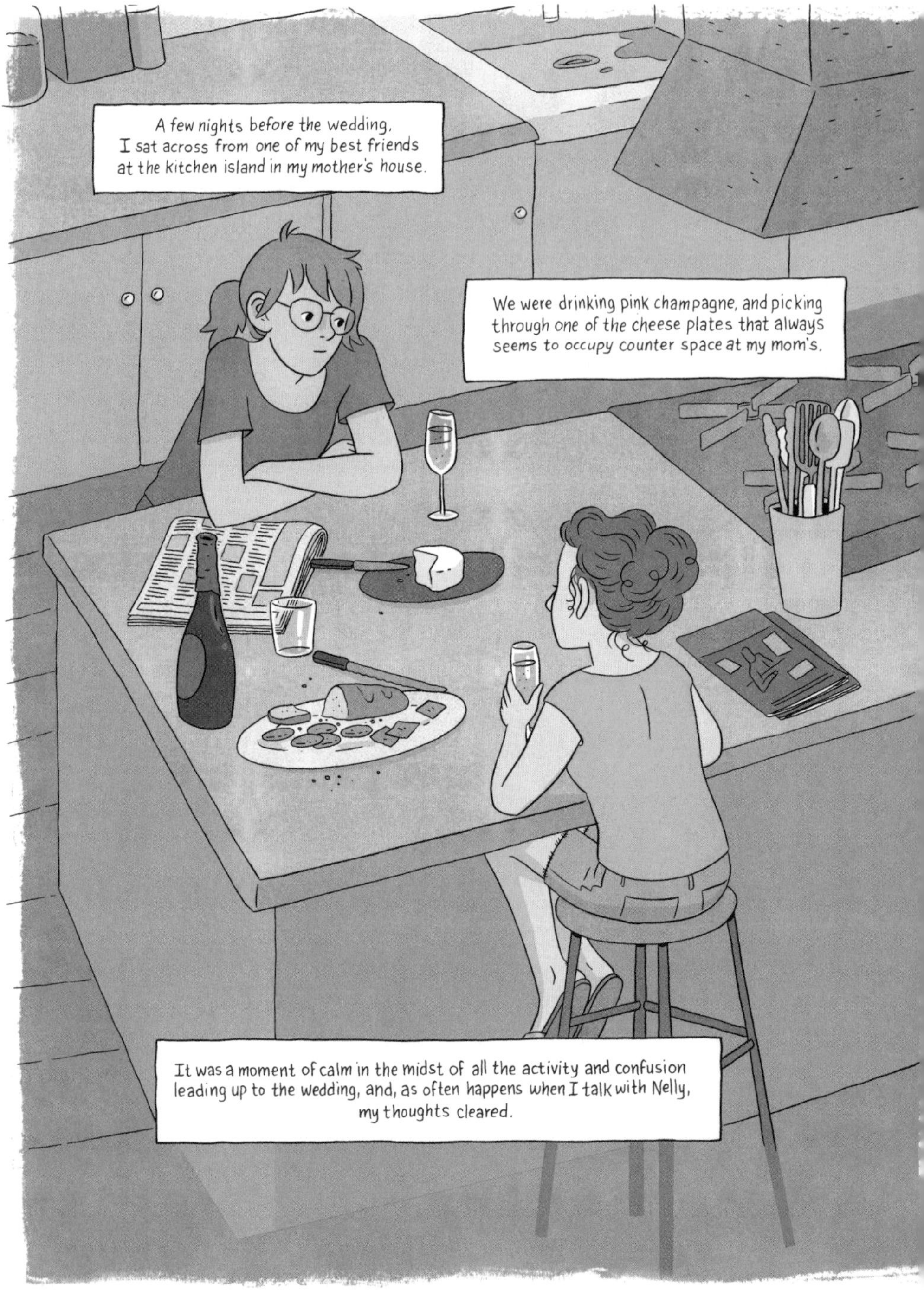
A few nights before the wedding, I sat across from one of my best friends at the kitchen island in my mother's house.
We were drinking pink champagne, and picking through one of the cheese plates that always seems to occupy counter space at my mom's.
It was a moment of calm in the midst of all the activity and confusion leading up to the wedding, and, as often happens when I talk with Nelly, my thoughts cleared.

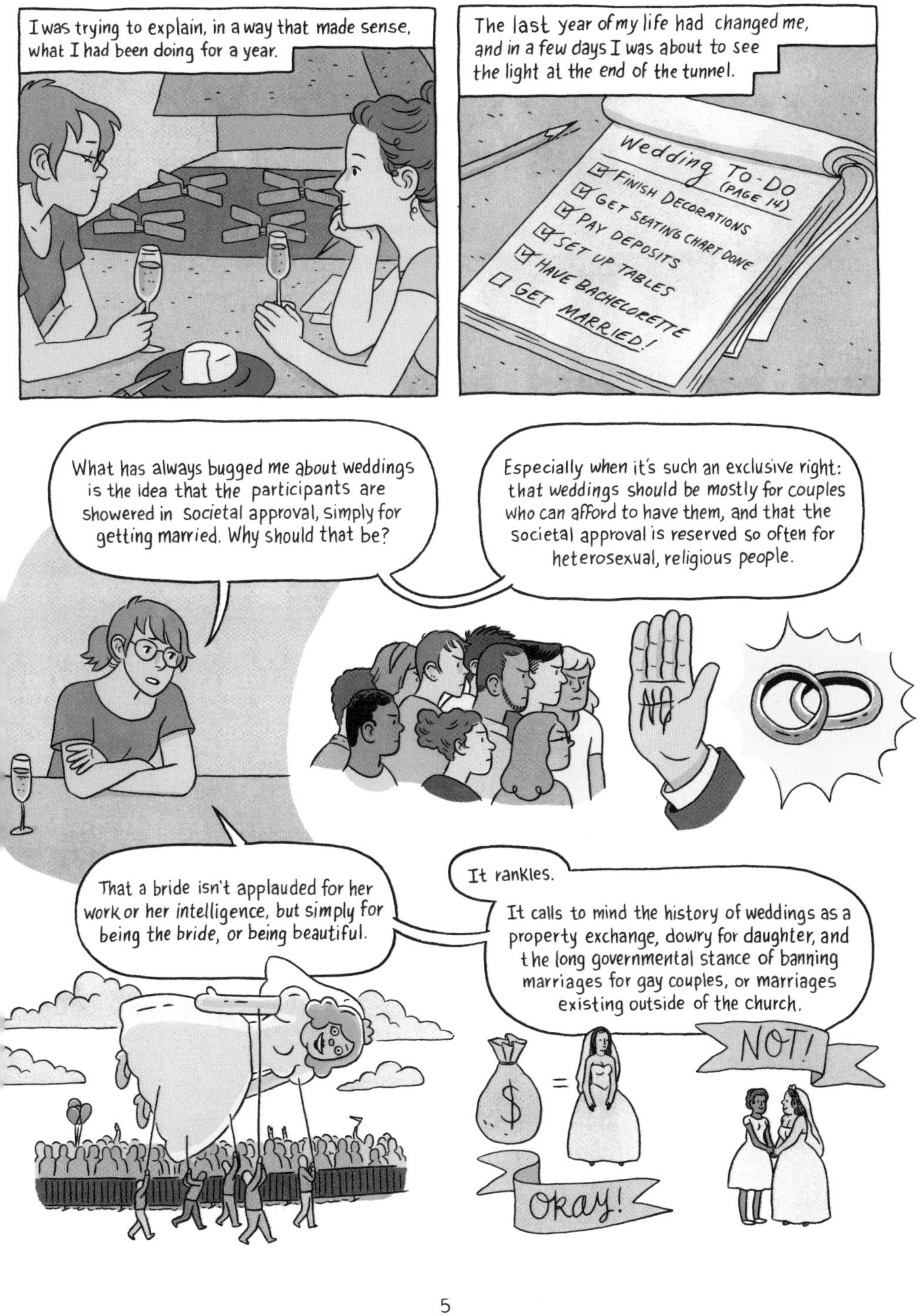

I was trying to explain, in a way that made sense, what I had been doing for a year.
The last year of my life had changed me, and in a few days I was about to see the light at the end of the tunnel.
Wedding To-Do (PAGE 14)
FINISH DECORATIONS
GET SEATING CHART DONE
PAY DEPOSITS
SET UP TABLES
HAVE BACHELORETTE
GET MARRIED!
What has always bugged me about weddings is the idea that the participants are showered in societal approval, simply for getting married. Why should that be?
Especially when it's such an exclusive right: that weddings should be mostly for couples who can afford to have them, and that the societal approval is reserved so often for heterosexual, religious people.
NO
That a bride isn't applauded for her work or her intelligence, but simply for being the bride, or being beautiful.
It rankles.
It calls to mind the history of weddings as a property exchange, dowry for daughter, and the long governmental stance of banning marriages for gay couples, or marriages existing outside of the church.
$
=
OKAY!
NOT!

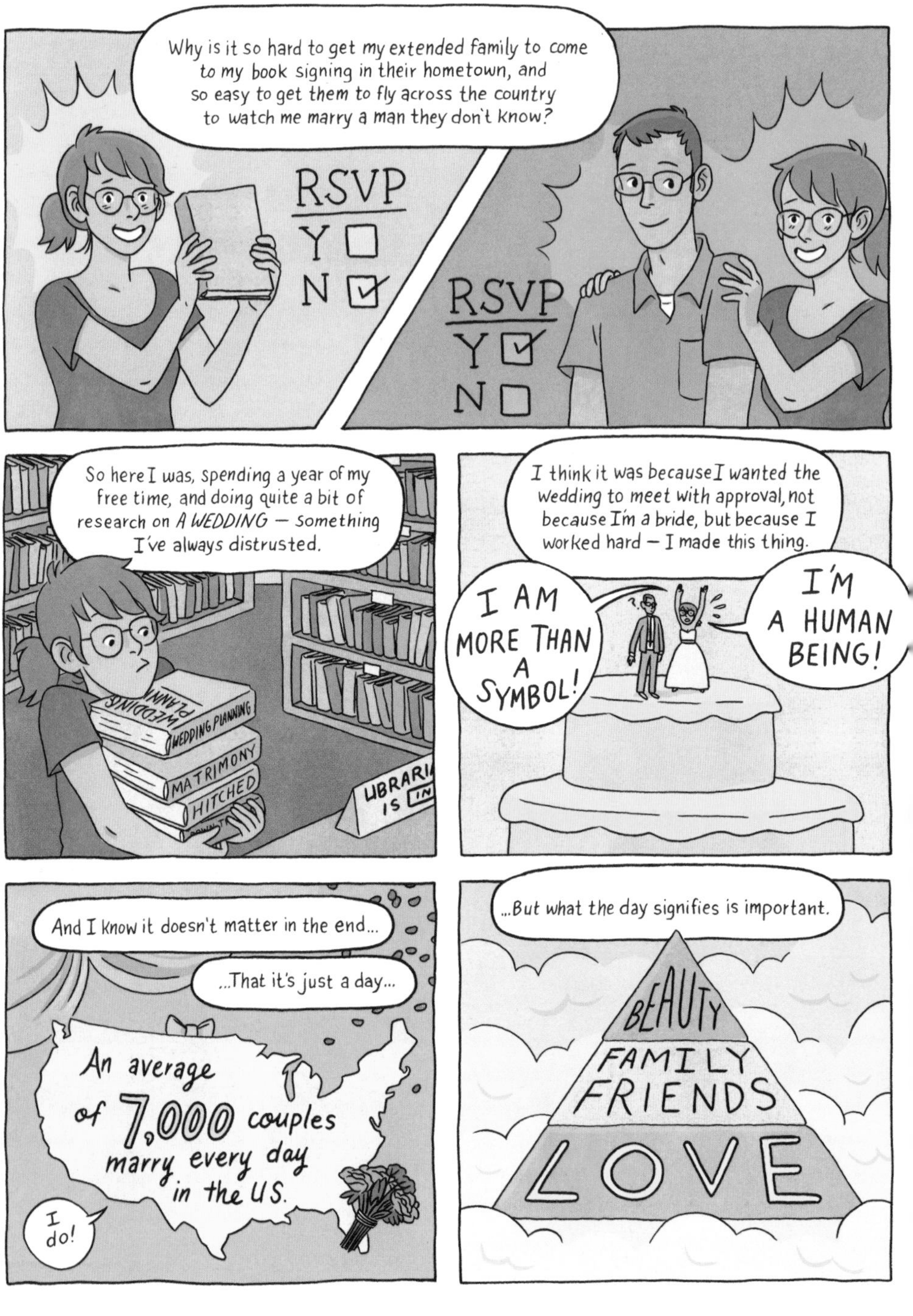
Why is it so hard to get my extended family to come to my book signing in their hometown, and so easy to get them to fly across the country to watch me marry a man they don't know?
RSVP
Y
N
RSVP
Y
N
So here I was, spending a year of my free time, and doing quite a bit of research on *A WEDDING* — something I've always distrusted.
WEDDING PLANNING
WEDDING PLANNING
MATRIMONY
HITCHED
I think it was because I wanted the wedding to meet with approval, not because I'm a bride, but because I worked hard — I made this thing.
I AM MORE THAN A SYMBOL!
I'M A HUMAN BEING!
And I know it doesn't matter in the end...
...That it's just a day...
An average of 7,000 couples marry every day in the US.
I do!
...But what the day signifies is important.
BEAUTY
FAMILY
FRIENDS
LOVE

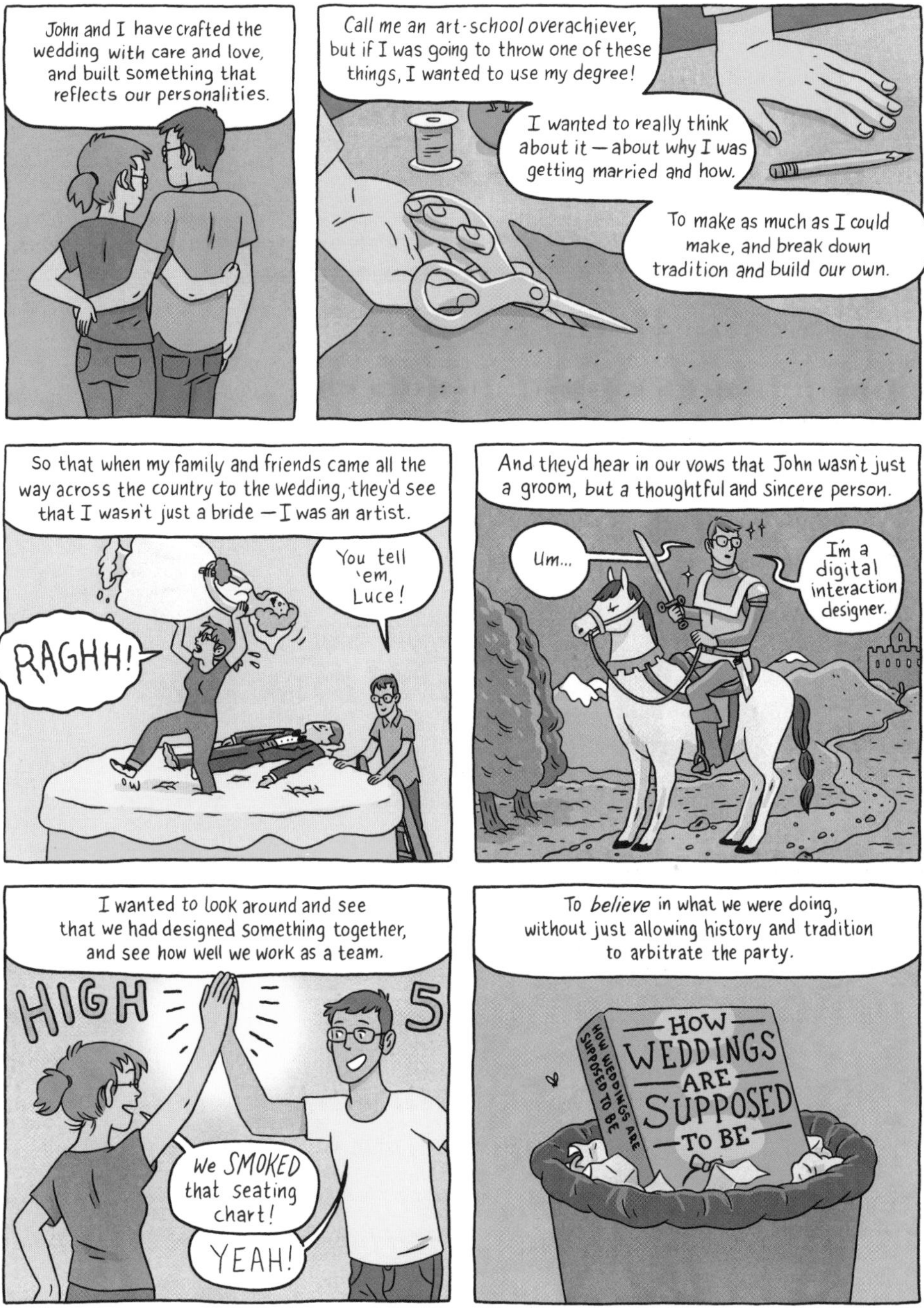

John and I have crafted the wedding with care and love, and built something that reflects our personalities.
Call me an art-school overachiever, but if I was going to throw one of these things, I wanted to use my degree!
I wanted to really think about it — about why I was getting married and how.
To make as much as I could make, and break down tradition and build our own.
So that when my family and friends came all the way across the country to the wedding, they'd see that I wasn't just a bride — I was an artist.
RAGHH!
You tell 'em, Luce!
And they'd hear in our vows that John wasn't just a groom, but a thoughtful and sincere person.
Um...
I'm a digital interaction designer.
I wanted to look around and see that we had designed something together, and see how well we work as a team.
HIGH 5
We SMOKED that seating chart!
YEAH!
To *believe* in what we were doing, without just allowing history and tradition to arbitrate the party.
HOW WEDDINGS ARE SUPPOSED TO BE
HOW WEDDINGS ARE SUPPOSED TO BE

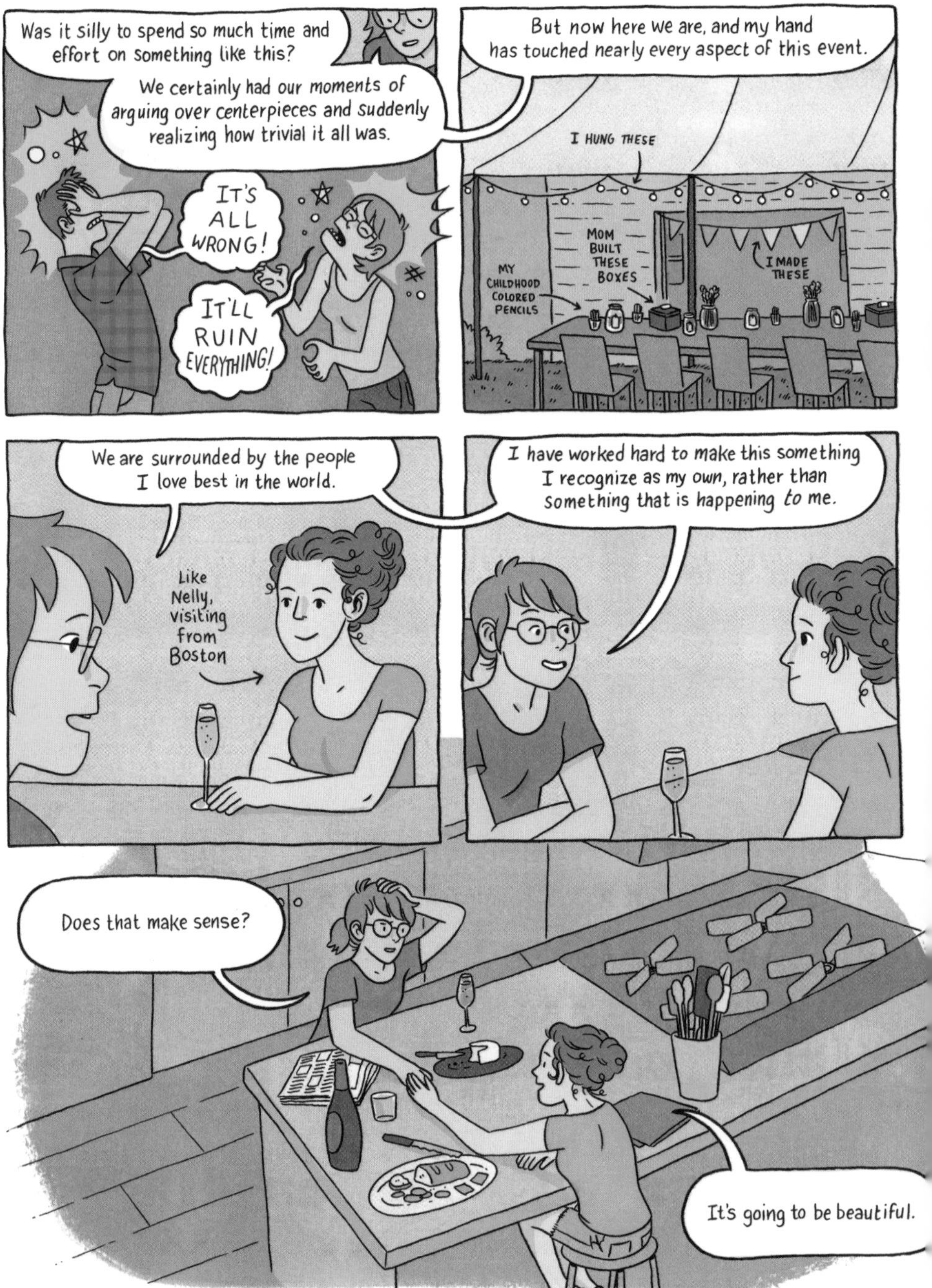
Was it silly to spend so much time and effort on something like this?
We certainly had our moments of arguing over centerpieces and suddenly realizing how trivial it all was.
IT'S ALL WRONG!
IT'LL RUIN EVERYTHING!
But now here we are, and my hand has touched nearly every aspect of this event.
I HUNG THESE
MOM BUILT THESE BOXES
MY CHILDHOOD COLORED PENCILS
I MADE THESE
We are surrounded by the people I love best in the world.
Like Nelly, visiting from Boston
I have worked hard to make this something I recognize as my own, rather than something that is happening *to* me.
Does that make sense?
It's going to be beautiful.

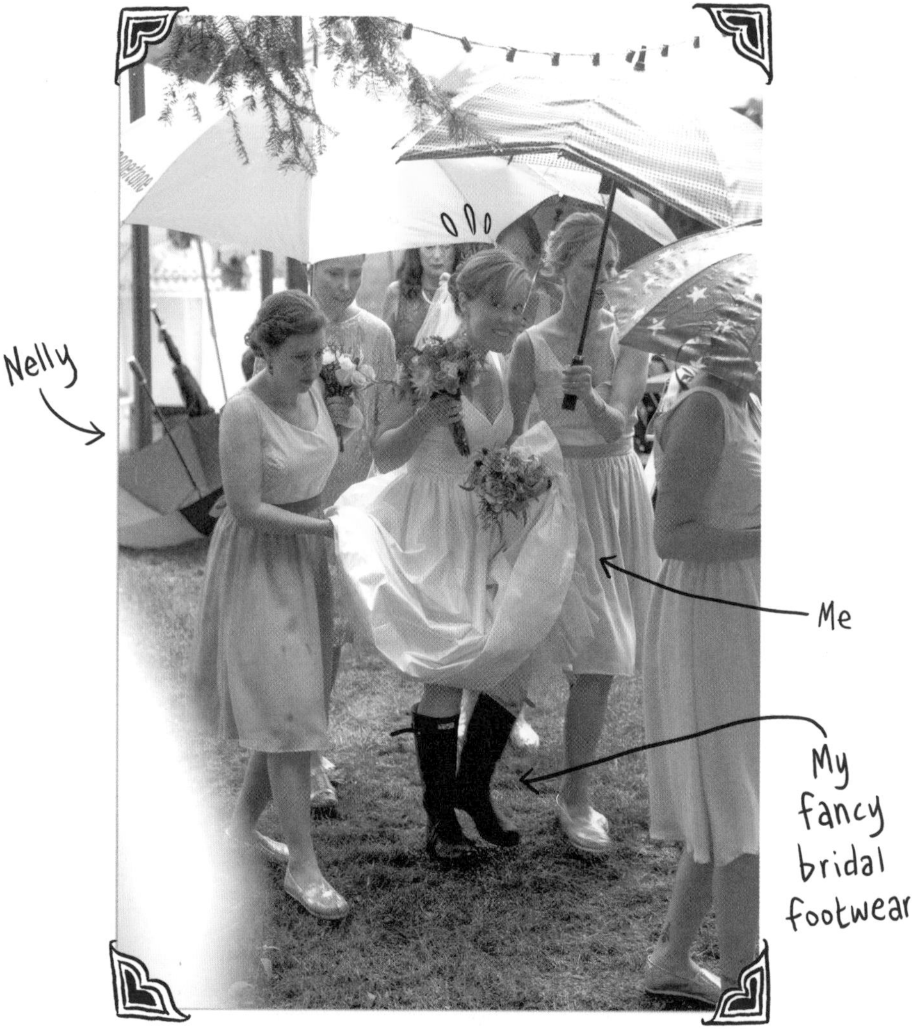
Nelly
Me
My fancy bridal footwear

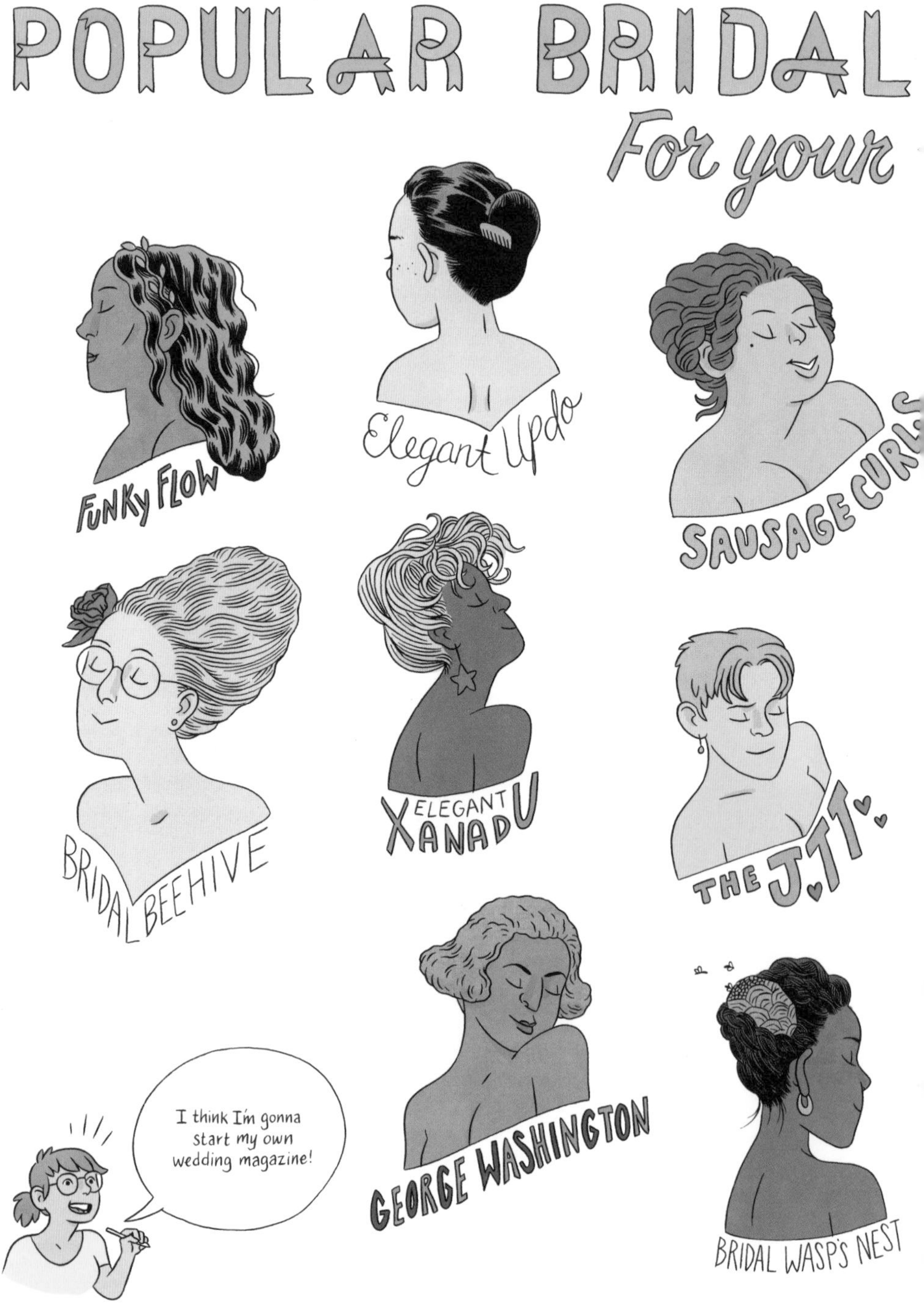

POPULAR BRIDAL
For your
Funky Flow
Elegant Updo
Sausage Curls
Bridal Beehive
Elegant Xanadu
The J.T.T.
George Washington
Bridal Wasp's Nest
I think I'm gonna start my own wedding magazine!

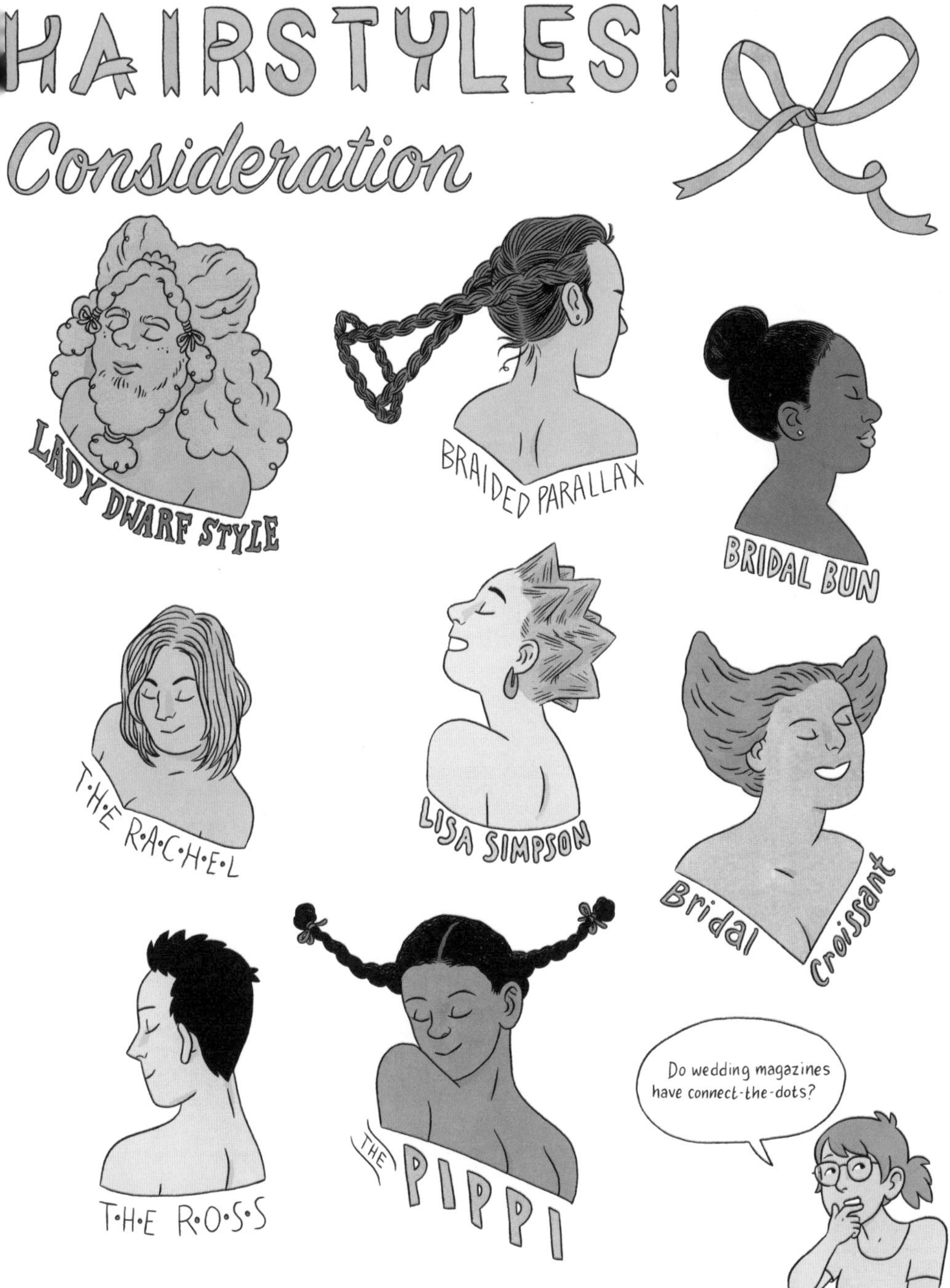
HAIRSTYLES!
Consideration
LADY DWARF STYLE
BRAIDED PARALLAX
BRIDAL BUN
THE RACHEL
LISA SIMPSON
Bridal Croissant
THE ROSS
THE PIPPI
Do wedding magazines have connect-the-dots?

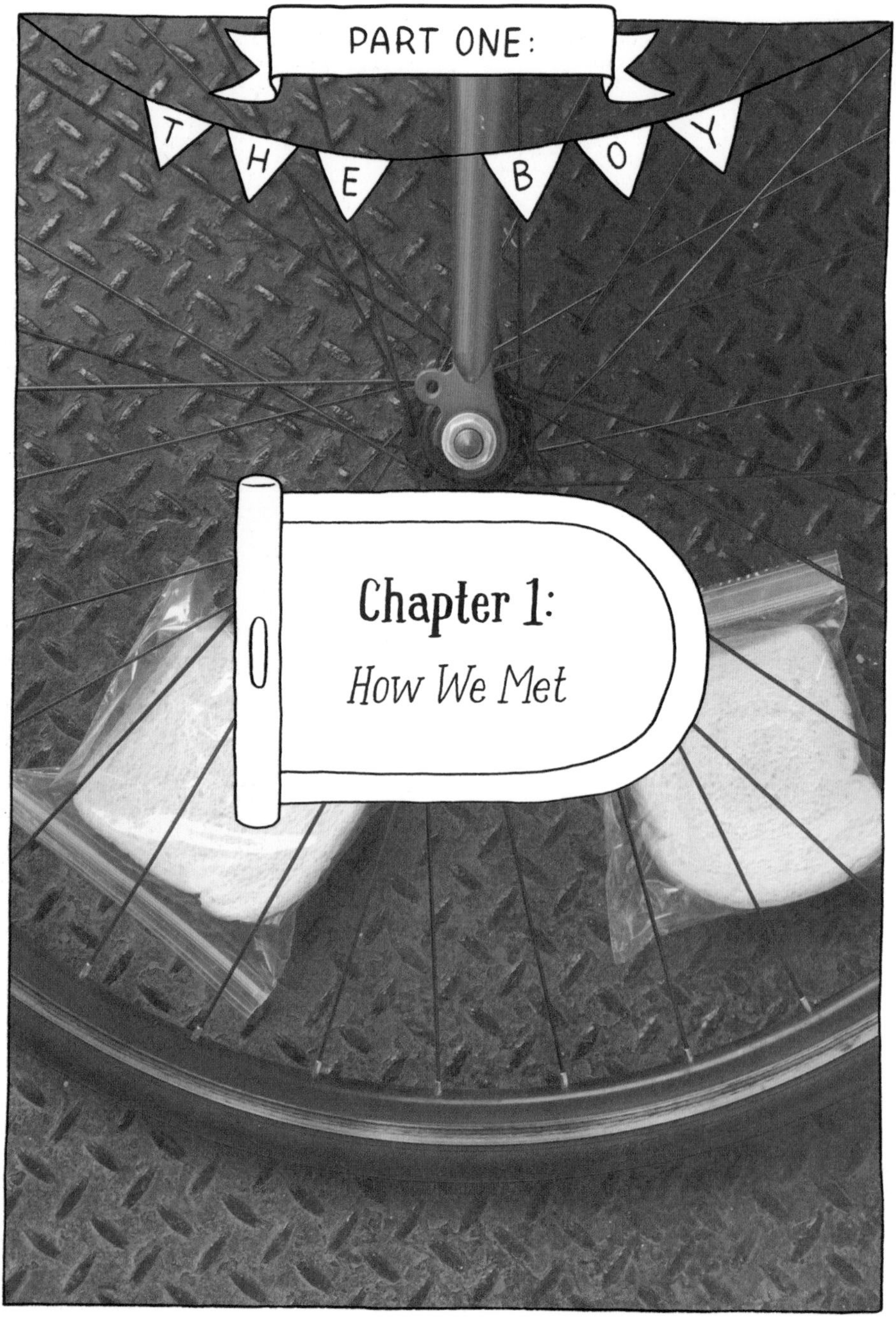
PART ONE:
THE BOY
Chapter 1:
How We Met

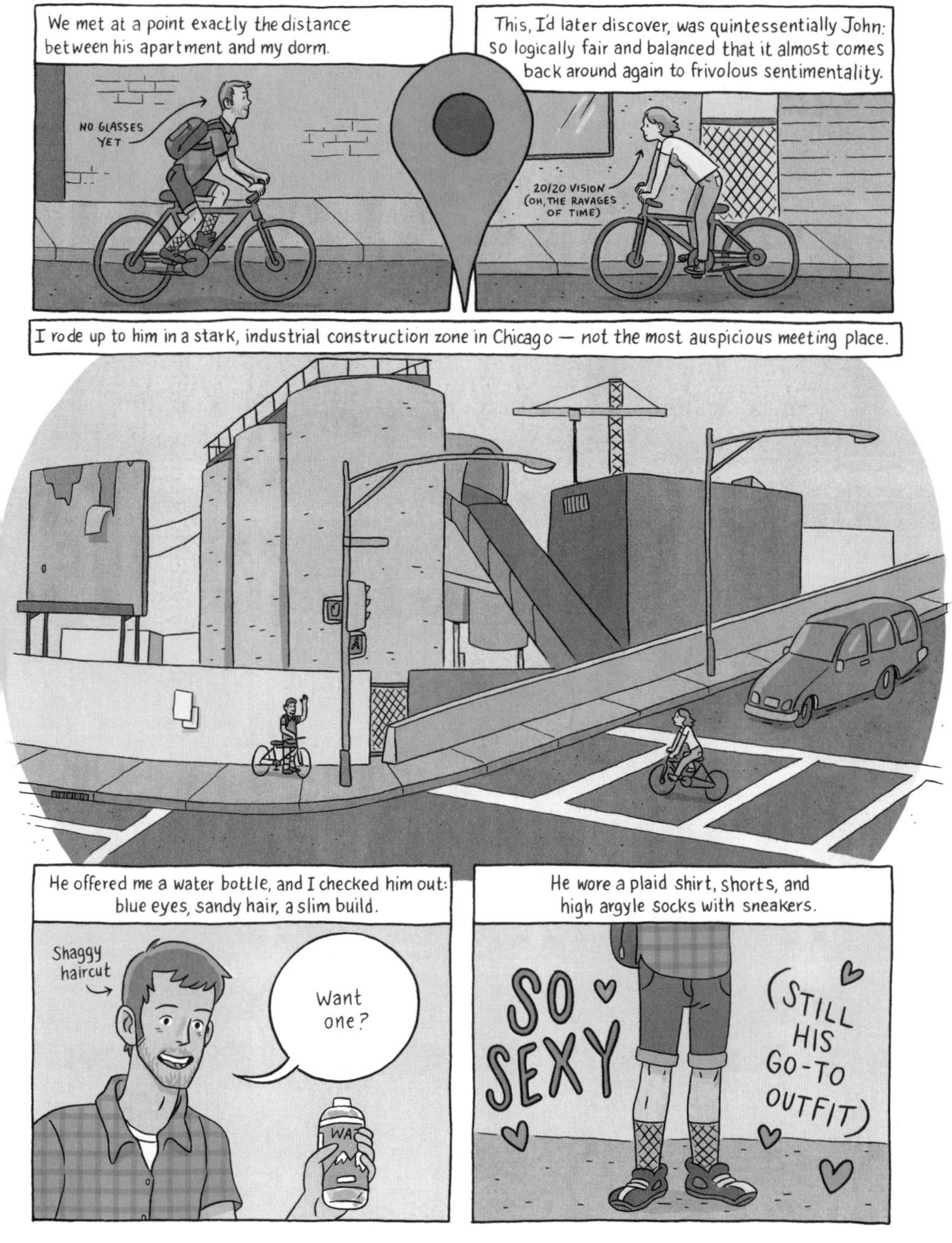
We met at a point exactly the distance between his apartment and my dorm.
NO GLASSES YET
This, I'd later discover, was quintessentially John: so logically fair and balanced that it almost comes back around again to frivolous sentimentality.
20/20 VISION (OH, THE RAVAGES OF TIME)
I rode up to him in a stark, industrial construction zone in Chicago — not the most auspicious meeting place.
He offered me a water bottle, and I checked him out: blue eyes, sandy hair, a slim build.
Shaggy haircut
Want one?
WA
He wore a plaid shirt, shorts, and high argyle socks with sneakers.
SO SEXY
(STILL HIS GO-TO OUTFIT)

Chicago was still fairly new to me.

I'd spent the first year of art school shuffling between classes and the loft bed where I worked, slept, and ate, ensconced in my Rapunzel tower of shyness.

My aunt and uncle had offered me an old bike from their garage in my second year, and perched on that blue Schwinn, I'd begun to venture outside of my urban campus into the surrounding neighborhoods.

No helmet
yet, because
YOUNG & Dumb

Having grown up in New York, city neighborhoods were, to me, fairly similar, demarcated by numbered streets and subway stops.

W 23 ST
7 AV

Chicago's neighborhoods are so different, and each new one I explored would totally change my impression of the city.

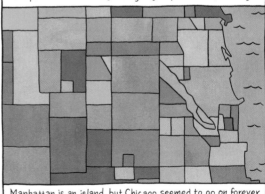

Manhattan is an island, but Chicago seemed to go on forever.

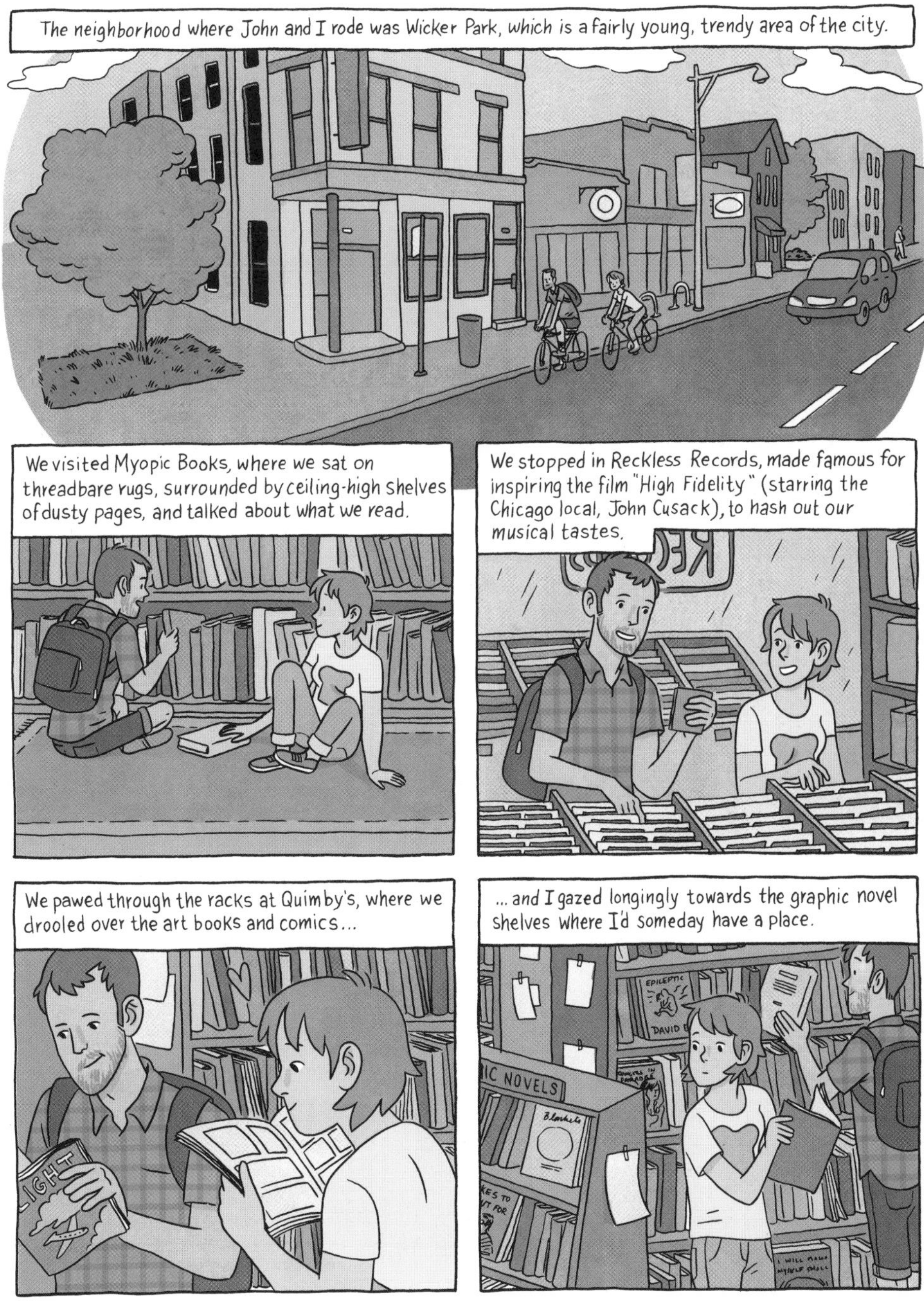
The neighborhood where John and I rode was Wicker Park, which is a fairly young, trendy area of the city.
We visited Myopic Books, where we sat on threadbare rugs, surrounded by ceiling-high shelves of dusty pages, and talked about what we read.
We stopped in Reckless Records, made famous for inspiring the film "High Fidelity" (starring the Chicago local, John Cusack), to hash out our musical tastes.
We pawed through the racks at Quimby's, where we drooled over the art books and comics...
LIGHT
...and I gazed longingly towards the graphic novel shelves where I'd someday have a place.
EPILEPTIC
IC NOVELS

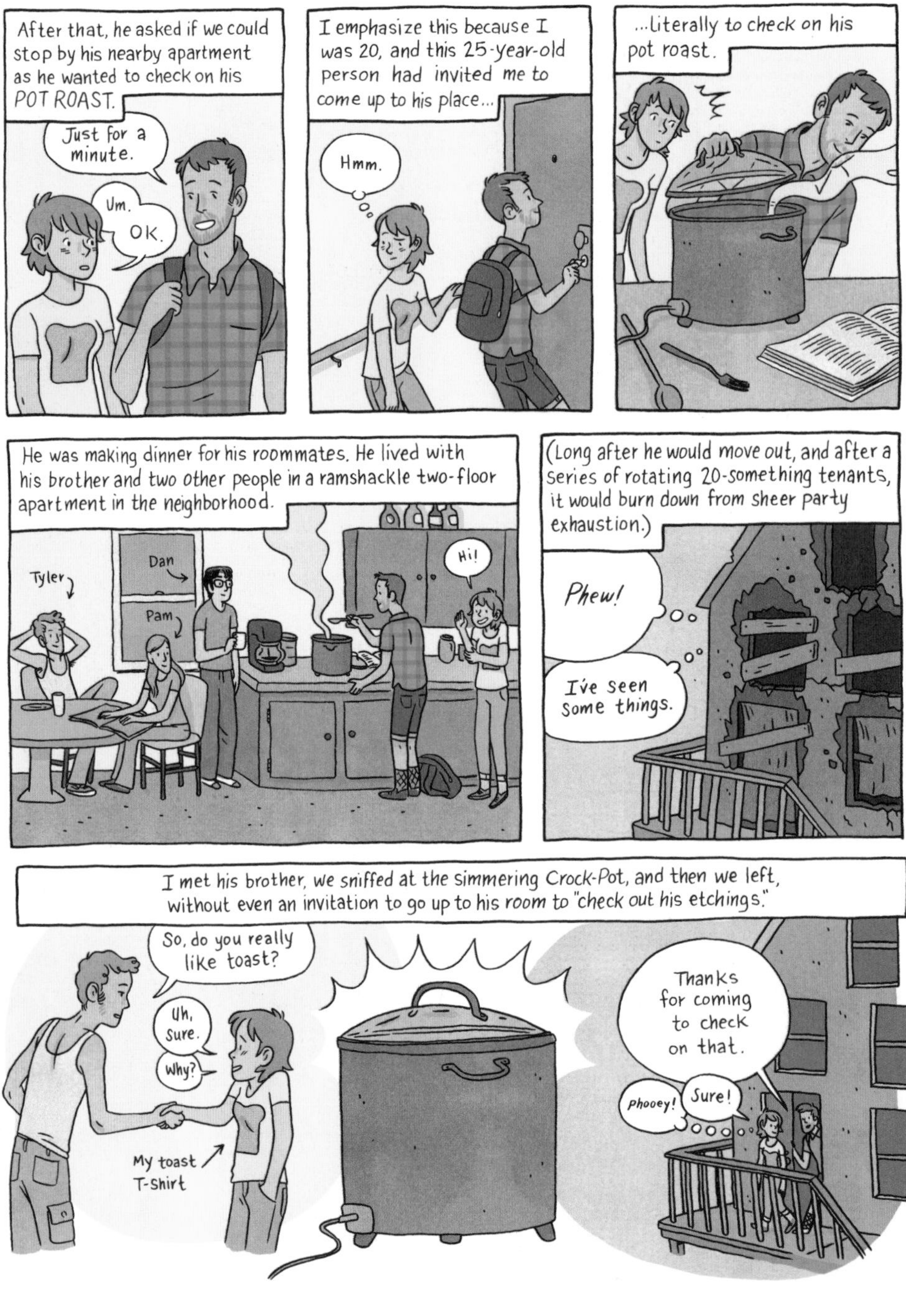
After that, he asked if we could stop by his nearby apartment as he wanted to check on his POT ROAST.
Just for a minute.
Um.
OK.
I emphasize this because I was 20, and this 25-year-old person had invited me to come up to his place...
Hmm.
...literally to check on his pot roast.
He was making dinner for his roommates. He lived with his brother and two other people in a ramshackle two-floor apartment in the neighborhood.
Tyler
Dan
Pam
Hi!
(Long after he would move out, and after a series of rotating 20-something tenants, it would burn down from sheer party exhaustion.)
Phew!
I've seen some things.
I met his brother, we sniffed at the simmering Crock-Pot, and then we left, without even an invitation to go up to his room to "check out his etchings."
So, do you really like toast?
Uh, sure.
Why?
My toast T-Shirt
Thanks for coming to check on that.
Phooey!
Sure!

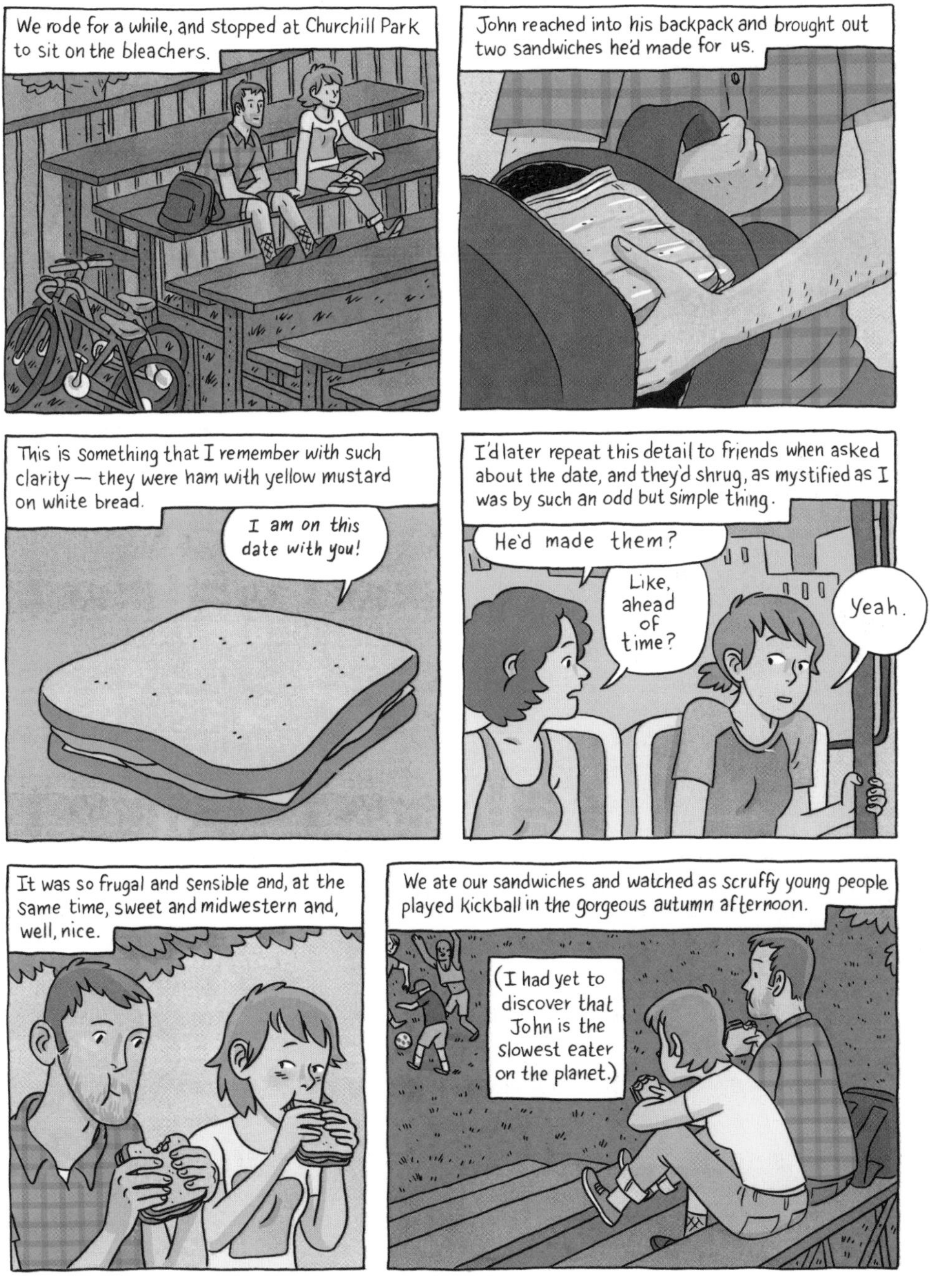

We rode for a while, and stopped at Churchill Park to sit on the bleachers.
John reached into his backpack and brought out two sandwiches he'd made for us.
This is something that I remember with such clarity — they were ham with yellow mustard on white bread.
I am on this date with you!
I'd later repeat this detail to friends when asked about the date, and they'd shrug, as mystified as I was by such an odd but simple thing.
He'd made them?
Like, ahead of time?
Yeah.
It was so frugal and sensible and, at the same time, sweet and midwestern and, well, nice.
We ate our sandwiches and watched as scruffy young people played kickball in the gorgeous autumn afternoon.
(I had yet to discover that John is the slowest eater on the planet.)

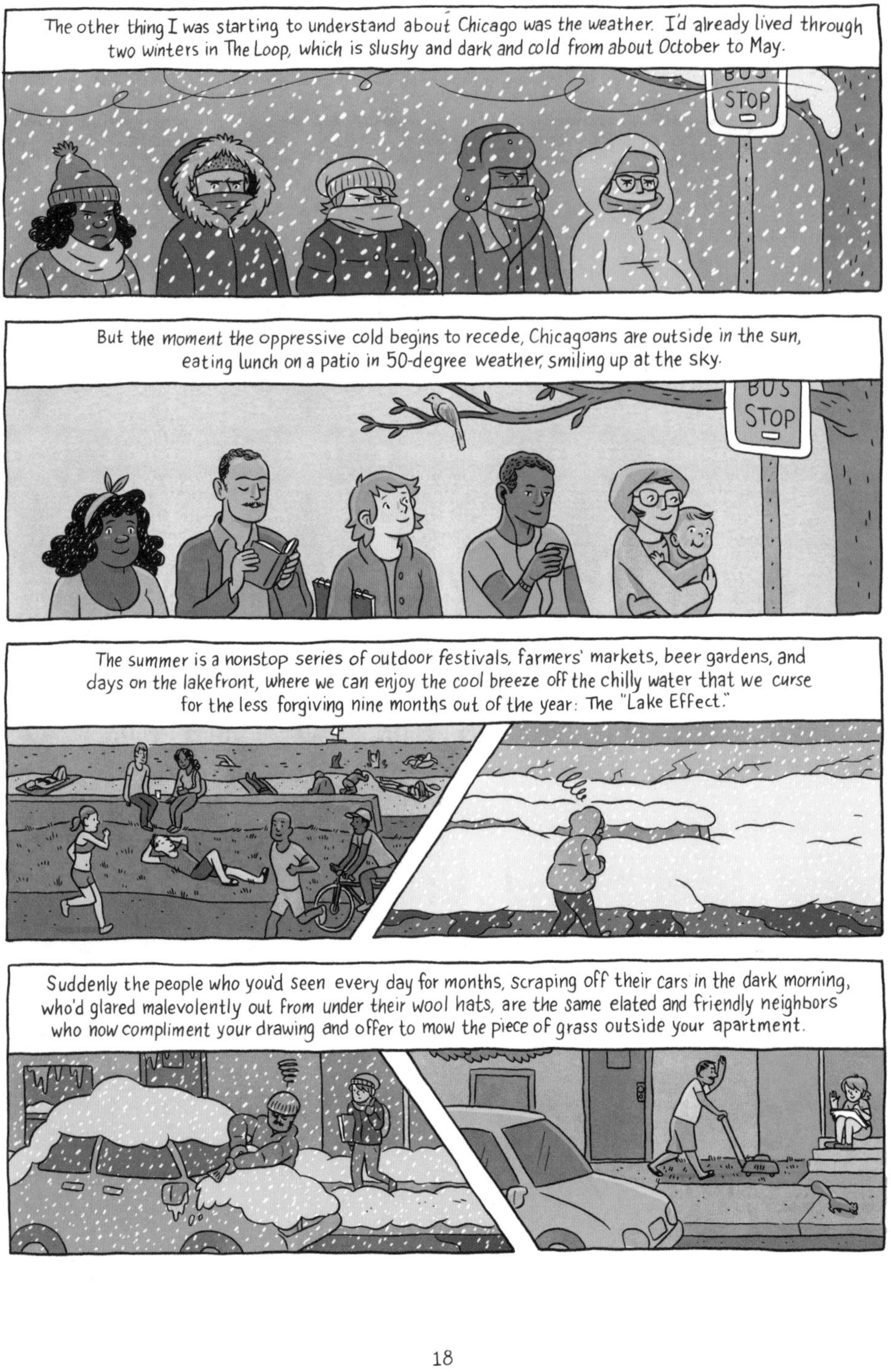
The other thing I was starting to understand about Chicago was the weather. I'd already lived through two winters in The Loop, which is slushy and dark and cold from about October to May.
STOP
But the moment the oppressive cold begins to recede, Chicagoans are outside in the sun, eating lunch on a patio in 50-degree weather, smiling up at the sky.
BUS
STOP
The summer is a nonstop series of outdoor festivals, farmers' markets, beer gardens, and days on the lakefront, where we can enjoy the cool breeze off the chilly water that we curse for the less forgiving nine months out of the year: The "Lake Effect."
Suddenly the people who you'd seen every day for months, scraping off their cars in the dark morning, who'd glared malevolently out from under their wool hats, are the same elated and friendly neighbors who now compliment your drawing and offer to mow the piece of grass outside your apartment.

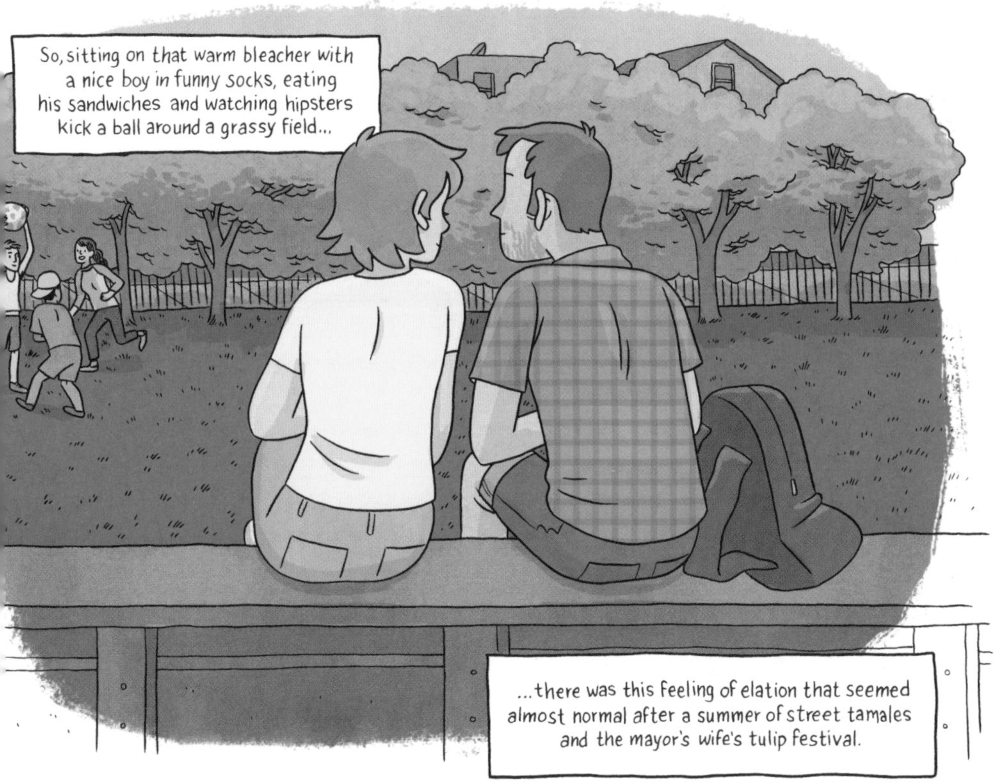
So, sitting on that warm bleacher with a nice boy in funny socks, eating his sandwiches and watching hipsters kick a ball around a grassy field...
...there was this feeling of elation that seemed almost normal after a summer of street tamales and the mayor's wife's tulip festival.

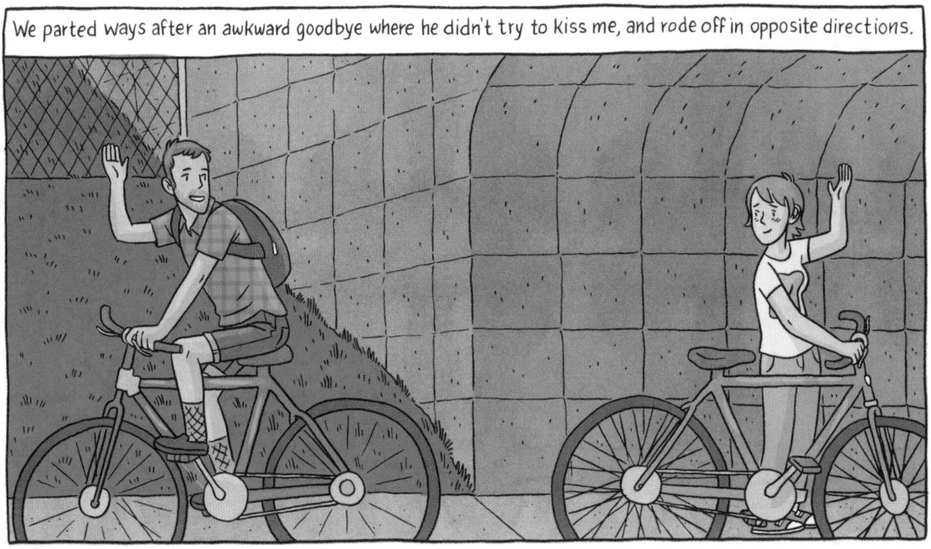
We parted ways after an awkward goodbye where he didn't try to kiss me, and rode off in opposite directions.

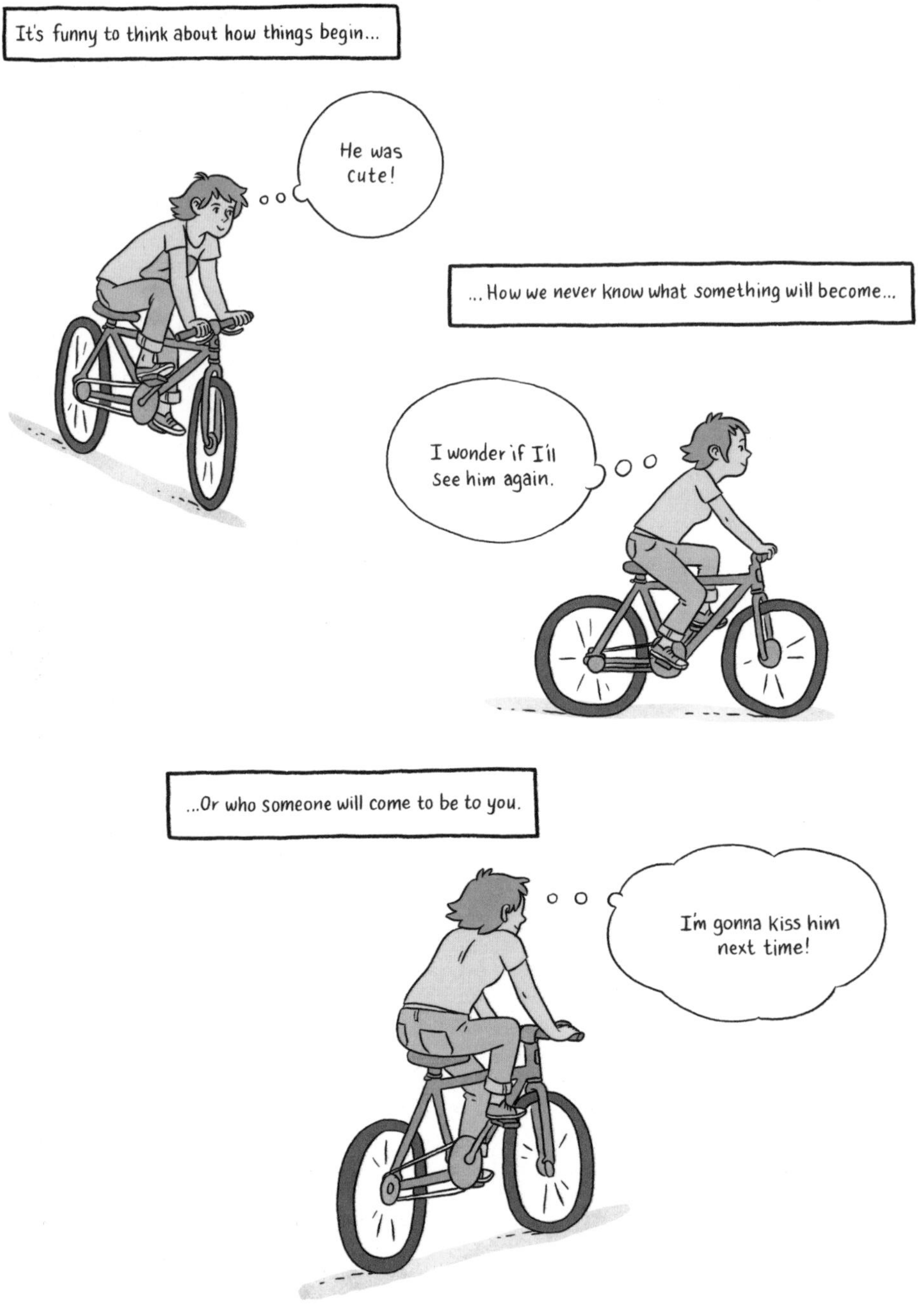
It's funny to think about how things begin...
He was cute!
...How we never know what something will become...
I wonder if I'll see him again.
...Or who someone will come to be to you.
I'm gonna kiss him next time!

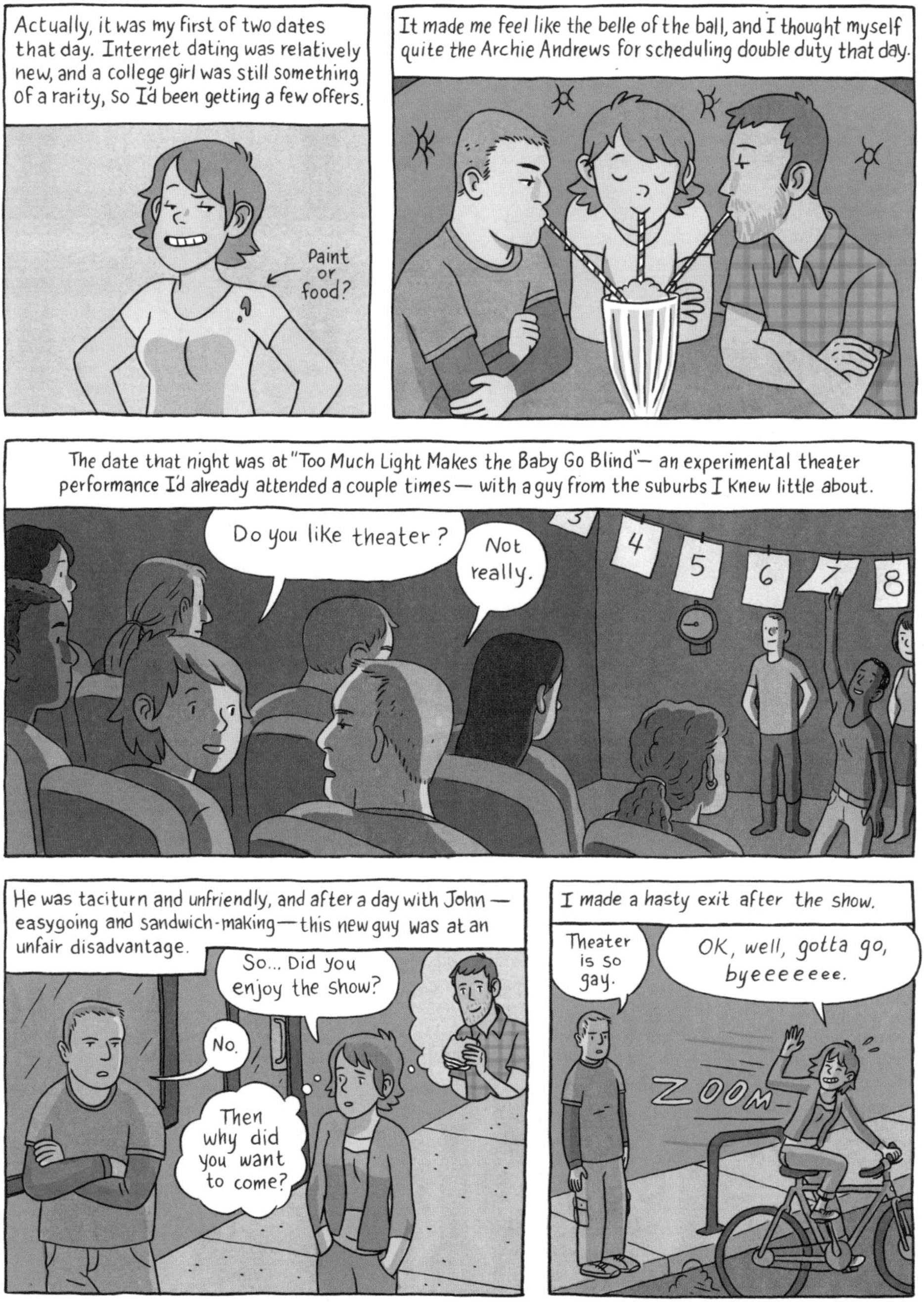
Actually, it was my first of two dates that day. Internet dating was relatively new, and a college girl was still something of a rarity, so I'd been getting a few offers.
Paint or food?
It made me feel like the belle of the ball, and I thought myself quite the Archie Andrews for scheduling double duty that day.
The date that night was at "Too Much Light Makes the Baby Go Blind"— an experimental theater performance I'd already attended a couple times— with a guy from the suburbs I knew little about.
Do you like theater?
Not really.
3
4
5
6
7
8
He was taciturn and unfriendly, and after a day with John— easygoing and sandwich-making— this new guy was at an unfair disadvantage.
So... Did you enjoy the show?
No.
Then why did you want to come?
I made a hasty exit after the show.
Theater is so gay.
OK, well, gotta go, byeeeeeee.
ZOOM

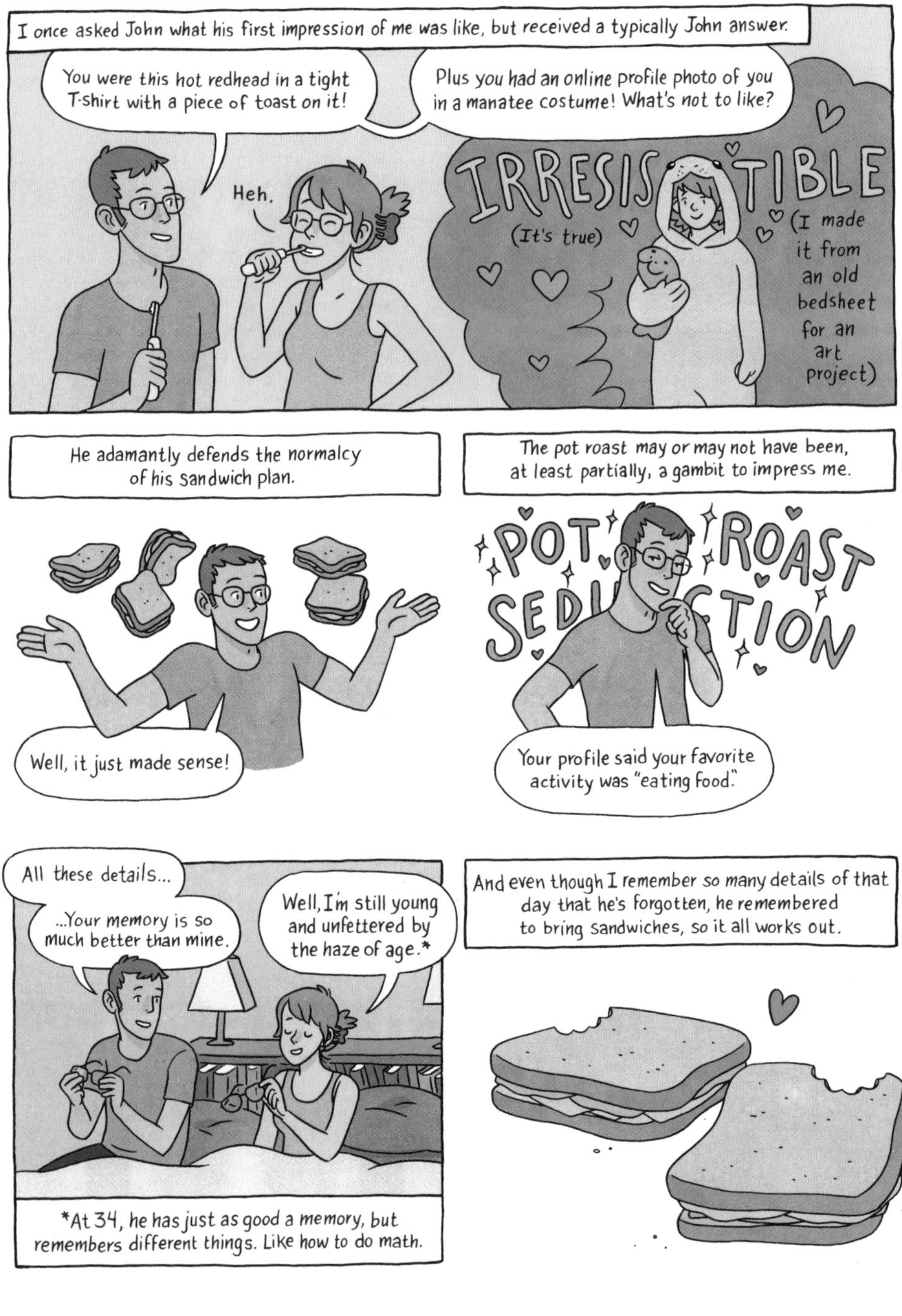
I once asked John what his first impression of me was like, but received a typically John answer.
You were this hot redhead in a tight T-shirt with a piece of toast on it!
Plus you had an online profile photo of you in a manatee costume! What's not to like?
Heh.
IRRESISTIBLE
(It's true)
(I made it from an old bedsheet for an art project)
He adamantly defends the normalcy of his sandwich plan.
Well, it just made sense!
The pot roast may or may not have been, at least partially, a gambit to impress me.
POT ROAST SEDUCTION
Your profile said your favorite activity was "eating food."
All these details...
...Your memory is so much better than mine.
Well, I'm still young and unfettered by the haze of age.*
*At 34, he has just as good a memory, but remembers different things. Like how to do math.
And even though I remember so many details of that day that he's forgotten, he remembered to bring sandwiches, so it all works out.

(2005)

A RUNDOWN OF HIGHLIGHTS OF

The 6th-grade love of my life, Gareth, who liked Dave Matthews Band. First kiss at a concert.

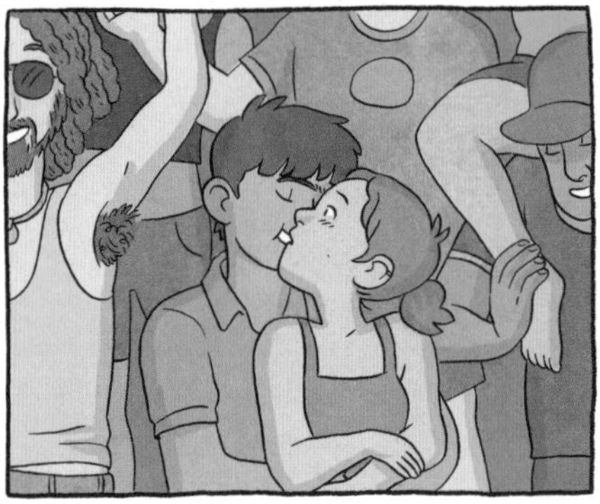

I was extremely sunburned and the air smelled like pot and his mouth was wet and my neck was cricked, but it was still pretty cool.

Cuddling in a dark dorm room with my "partly platonic" girlfriend in freshman year of high school...

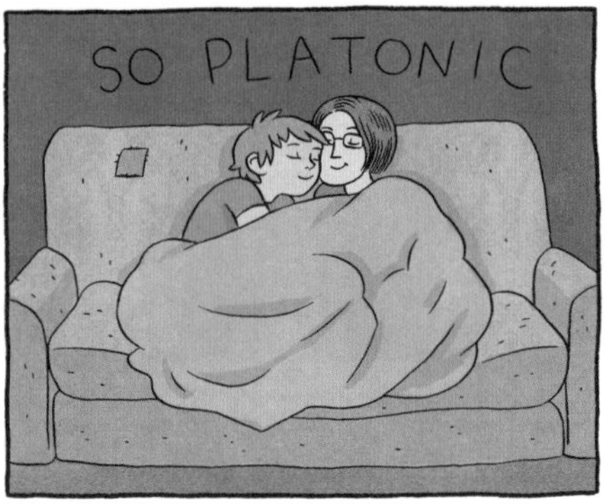
SO PLATONIC

...while watching "Better Than Chocolate" and skipping class.

That time I was *goth* and it was simultaneously the only time more than one person has wanted to date me and I wanted to date nobody so that I wouldn't lose my friends.

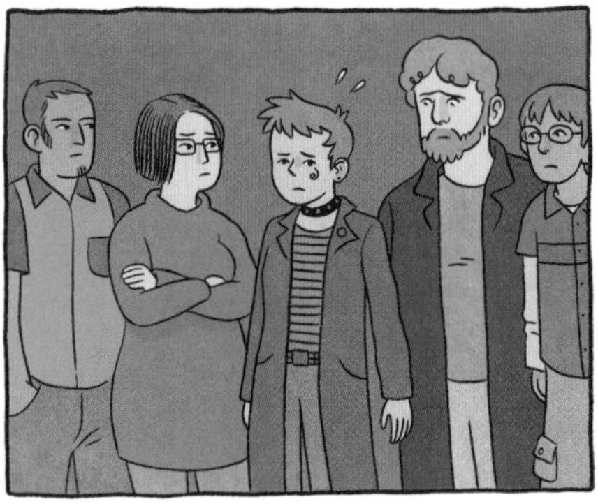

Did I mention that I was *goth?*

The guy who was not very nice to me, but he had a car and could therefore take me away from school...

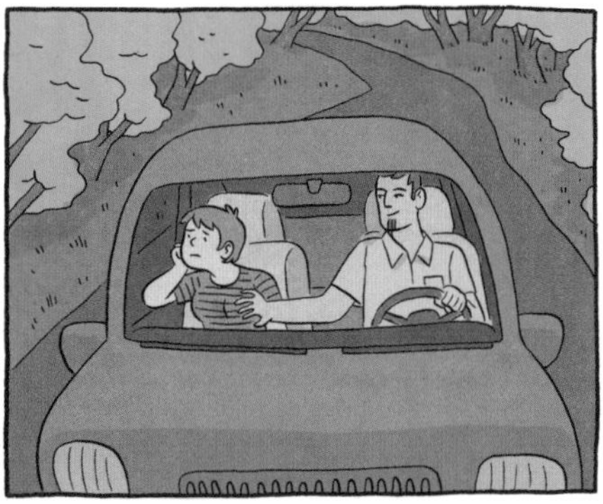

I hated school more than I hated having a mean boyfriend.

MY ROMANTIC LIFE, PRE-JOHN

The adorable altar boy who used to get mad at me for leaving hickies on his neck on nights before he had to serve in church.

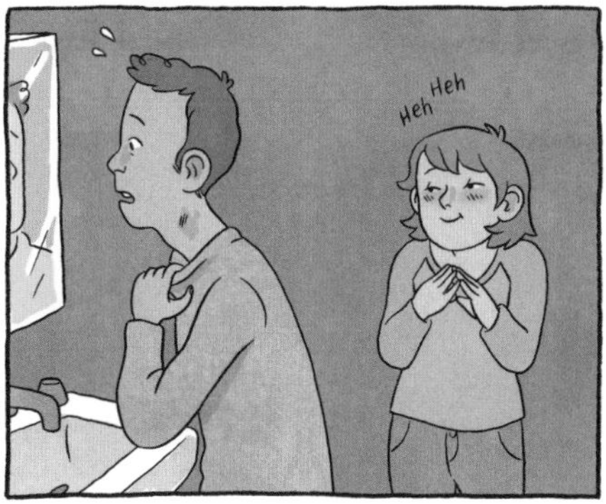

Heh Heh

Heh heh...

The time I completely lost myself in a romantic/artistic relationship that transcended identity and gender and ownership of creative energies...

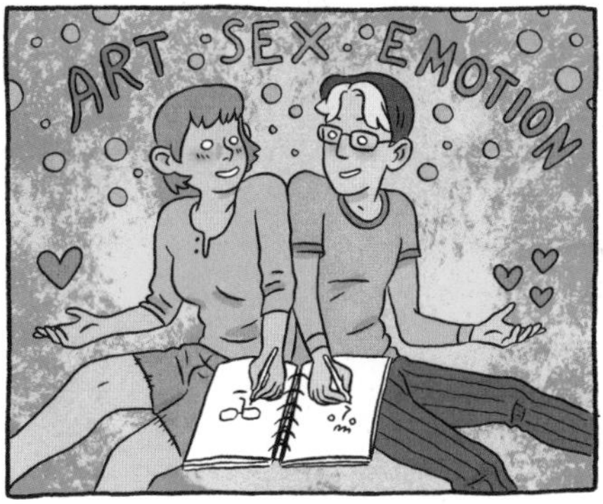

ART
SEX
EMOTION

...and entirely blew up in my inexperienced face when we became fundamentally incompatible.

The poor girl I dated in the aftermath of that romantic flash flood.

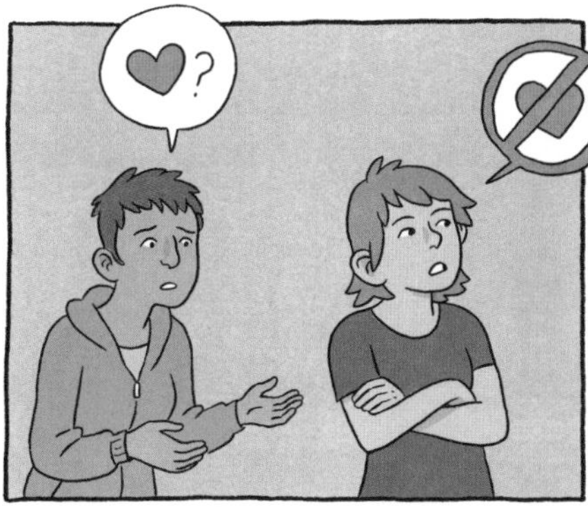

?

Yikes.

Various ill-advised but fondly-remembered college short-term things and hookups.

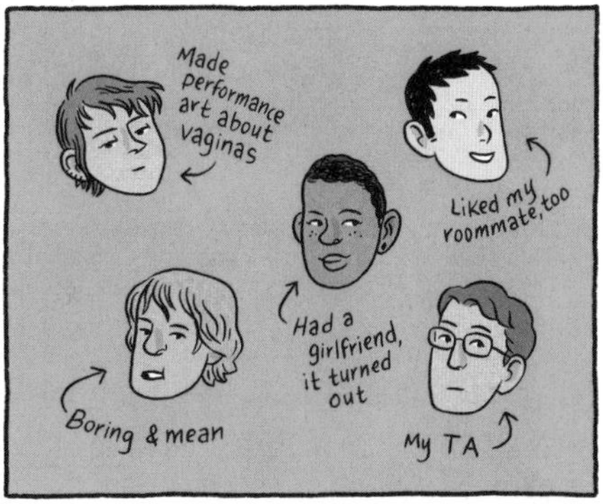

Made performance art about vaginas
Liked my roommate, too
Had a girlfriend, it turned out
Boring & mean
My TA

AND THEN JOHN.*

* This is not comprehensive, nor is it the end of this list, alas, but no spoilers!

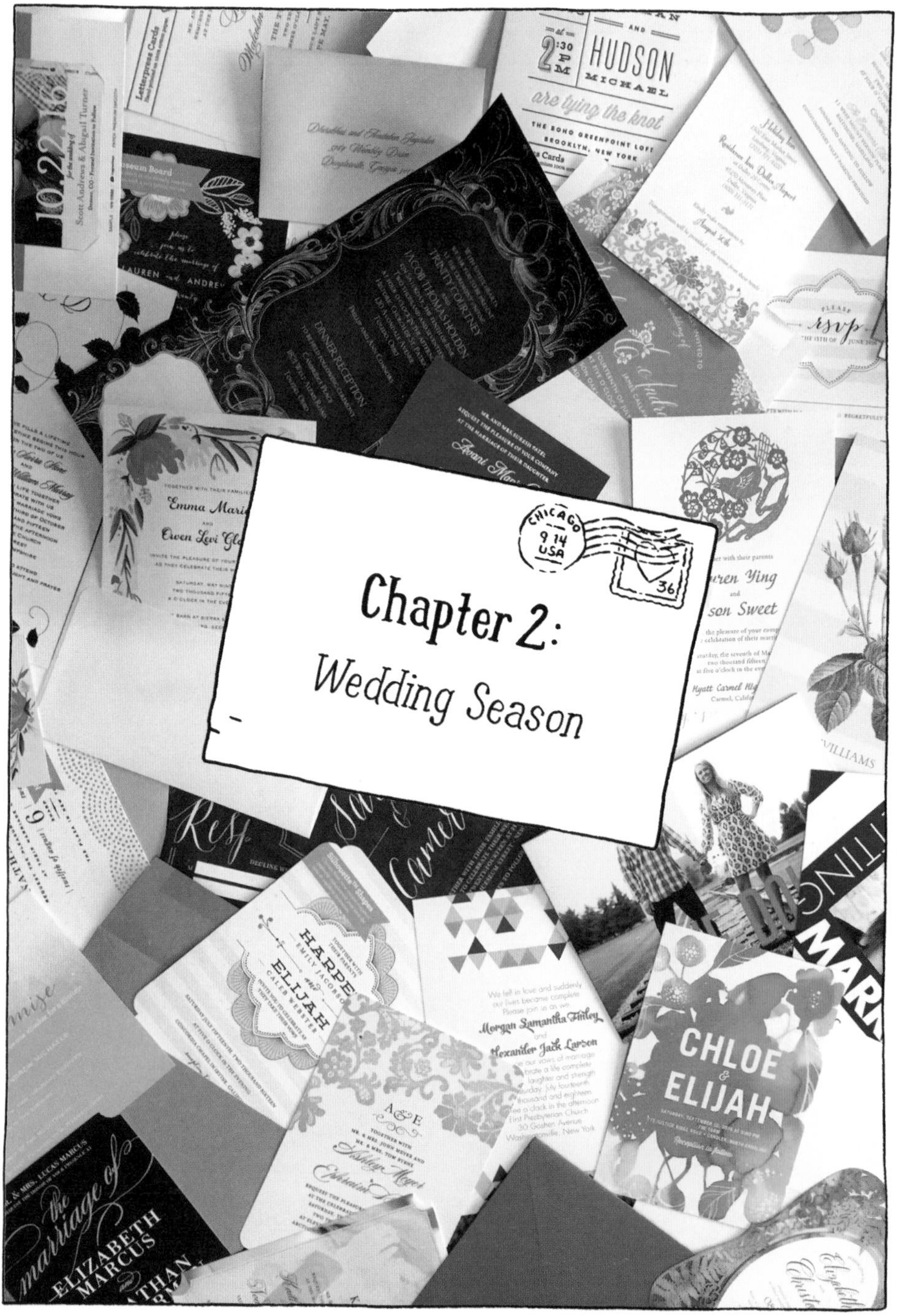
CHICAGO 9 14 USA
36
Chapter 2:
Wedding Season
HUDSON
MICHAEL
are tying the knot
THE BOHO GREENPOINT LOFT
BROOKLYN, NEW YORK
CHLOE
&
ELIJAH
HARPER
ELIJAH
Morgan Samantha Finley
Alexander Jack Larson
ELIZABETH
MARCUS

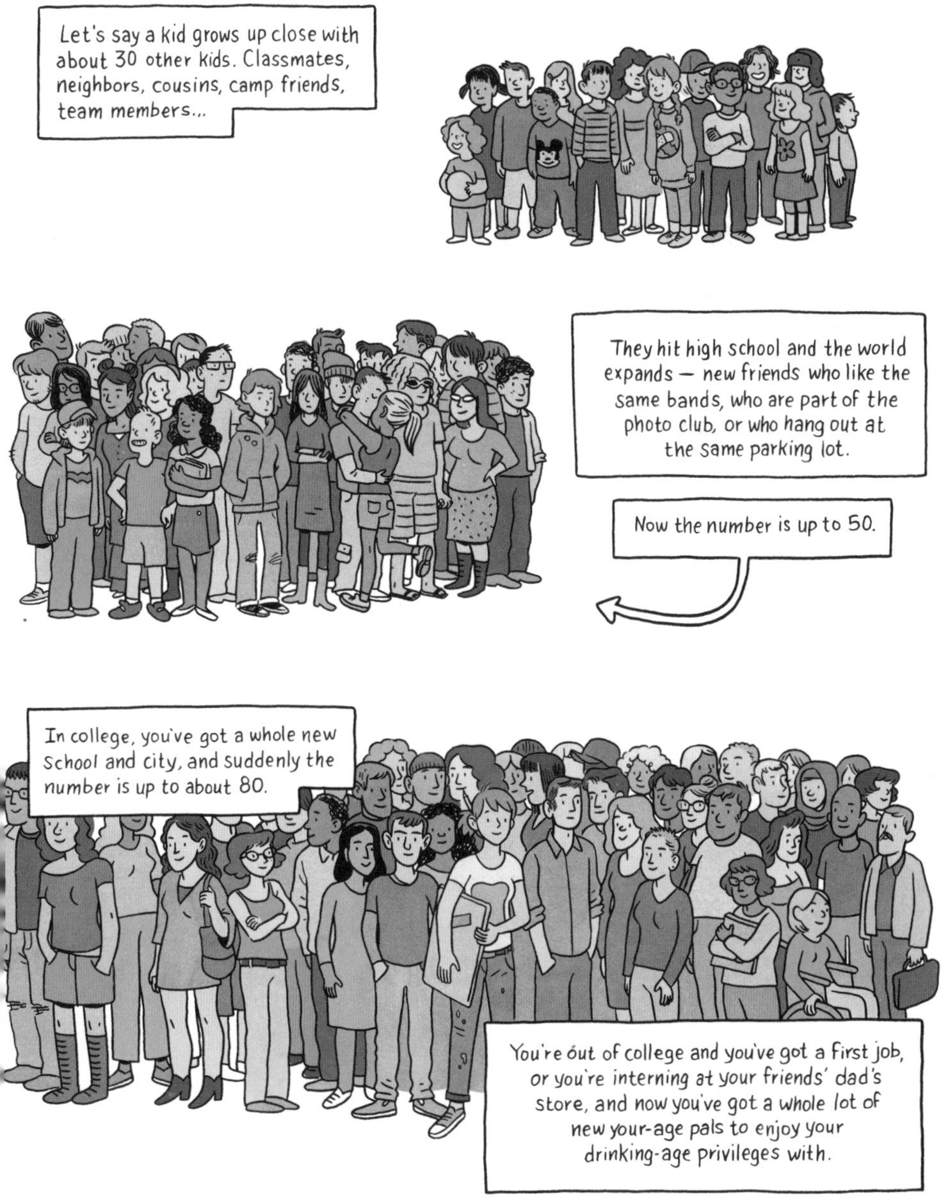
Let's say a kid grows up close with about 30 other kids. Classmates, neighbors, cousins, camp friends, team members...
They hit high school and the world expands — new friends who like the same bands, who are part of the photo club, or who hang out at the same parking lot.
Now the number is up to 50.
In college, you've got a whole new school and city, and suddenly the number is up to about 80.
You're out of college and you've got a first job, or you're interning at your friends' dad's store, and now you've got a whole lot of new your-age pals to enjoy your drinking-age privileges with.

That means that by the time you're in your twenties, you've got about 100 friends from growing up who are navigating their own twenties alongside or far from you.

If you fall in love, you and your new partner have a combined force of potentially around *200 PEOPLE*, who could put your names on a guest list.

If even a fifth of these peeps get hitched in the next decade, you have the potential of spending a good chunk of your warm-season weekends doing the electric slide in celebration of their newfound matrimony.

Break out the finery...

It's Wedding Season

Together with their parents you are invited

US

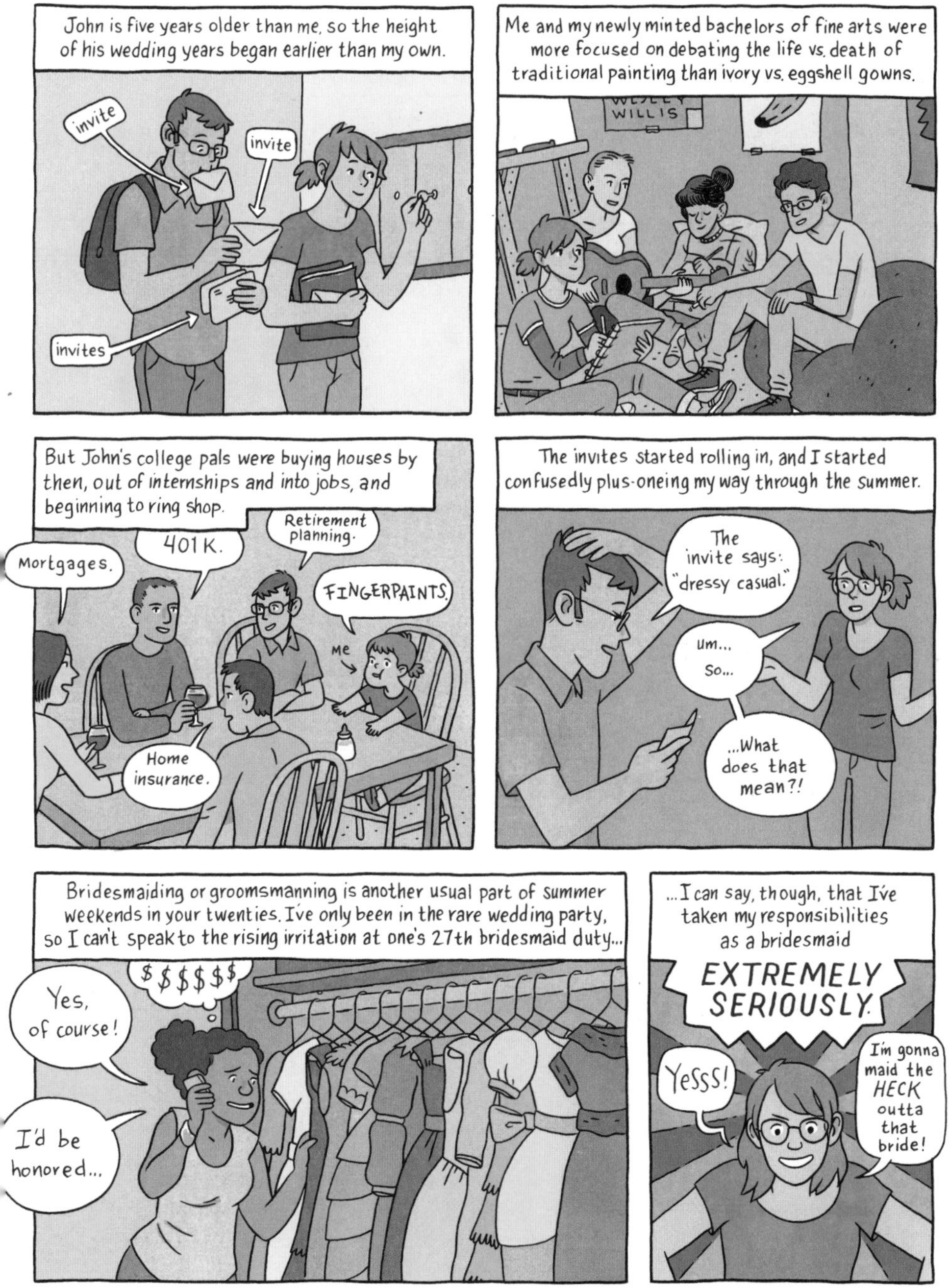
John is five years older than me, so the height of his wedding years began earlier than my own.
invite
invite
invites
Me and my newly minted bachelors of fine arts were more focused on debating the life vs. death of traditional painting than ivory vs. eggshell gowns.
WILLIS
But John's college pals were buying houses by then, out of internships and into jobs, and beginning to ring shop.
Mortgages.
401K.
Retirement planning.
FINGERPAINTS.
Me
Home insurance.
The invites started rolling in, and I started confusedly plus-oneing my way through the summer.
The invite says: "dressy casual."
um... so...
...What does that mean?!
Bridesmaiding or groomsmanning is another usual part of summer weekends in your twenties. I've only been in the rare wedding party, so I can't speak to the rising irritation at one's 27th bridesmaid duty...
$$$$$
Yes, of course!
I'd be honored...
...I can say, though, that I've taken my responsibilities as a bridesmaid
EXTREMELY SERIOUSLY.
Yesss!
I'm gonna maid the HECK outta that bride!

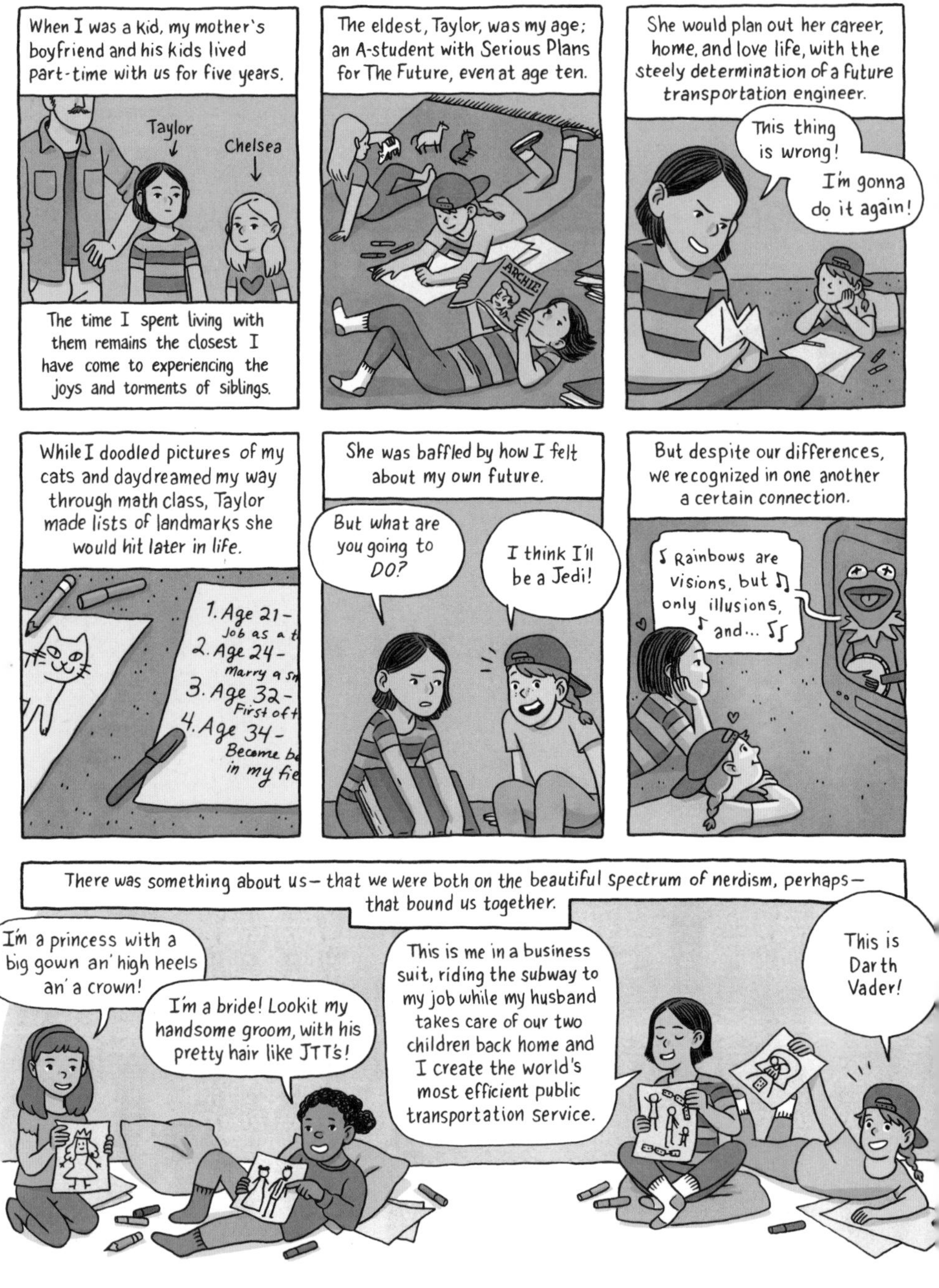
When I was a kid, my mother's boyfriend and his kids lived part-time with us for five years.
Taylor
Chelsea
The time I spent living with them remains the closest I have come to experiencing the joys and torments of siblings.
The eldest, Taylor, was my age; an A-student with Serious Plans for The Future, even at age ten.
ARCHIE
She would plan out her career, home, and love life, with the steely determination of a future transportation engineer.
This thing is wrong!
I'm gonna do it again!
While I doodled pictures of my cats and daydreamed my way through math class, Taylor made lists of landmarks she would hit later in life.
1. Age 21-
Job as a t
2. Age 24-
Marry a s
3. Age 32-
First of
4. Age 34-
Become b
in my fi
She was baffled by how I felt about my own future.
But what are you going to DO?
I think I'll be a Jedi!
But despite our differences, we recognized in one another a certain connection.
♪ Rainbows are visions, but ♫ only illusions, ♪ and... ♫
There was something about us— that we were both on the beautiful spectrum of nerdism, perhaps— that bound us together.
I'm a princess with a big gown an' high heels an' a crown!
I'm a bride! Lookit my handsome groom, with his pretty hair like JTT's!
This is me in a business suit, riding the subway to my job while my husband takes care of our two children back home and I create the world's most efficient public transportation service.
This is Darth Vader!

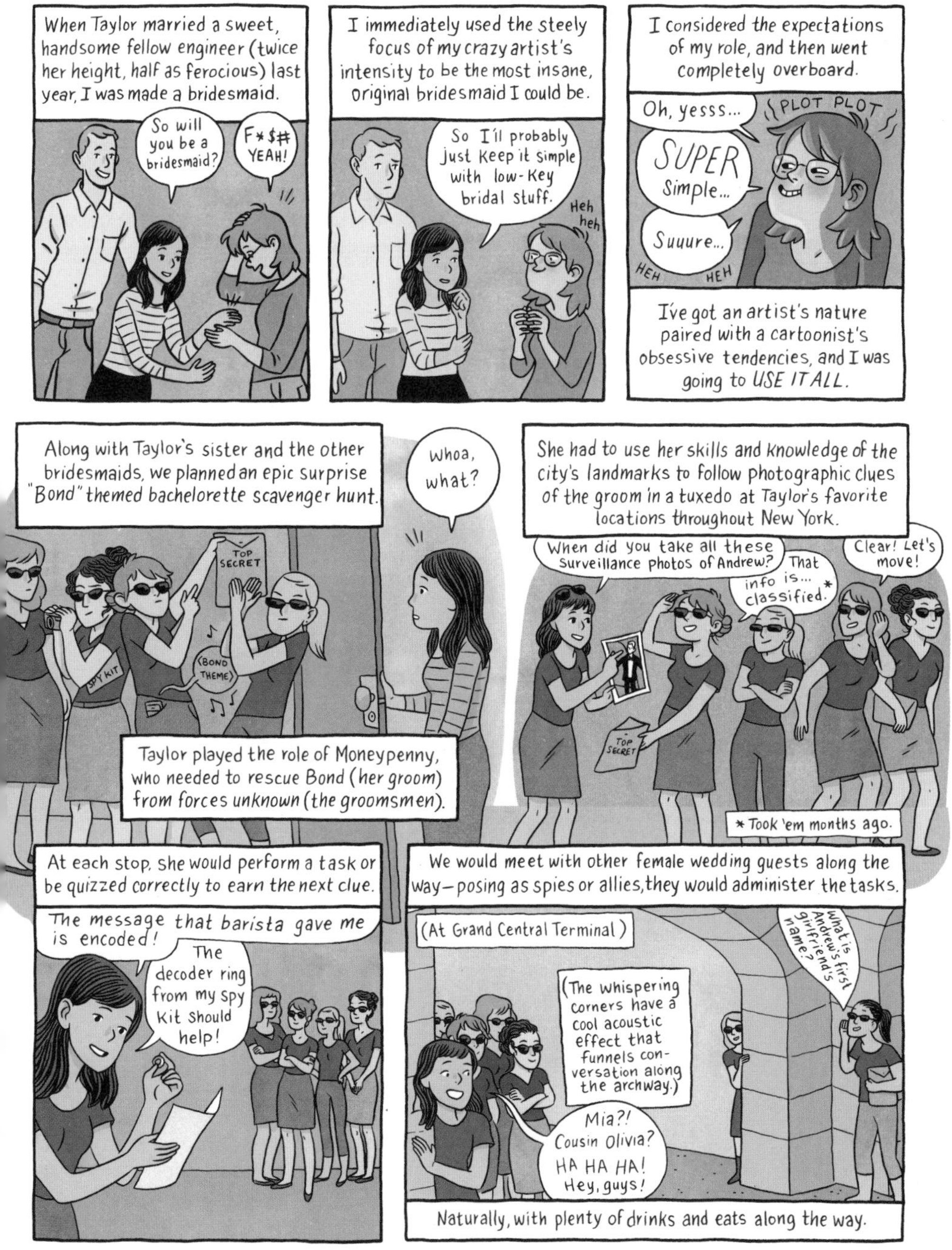

When Taylor married a sweet, handsome fellow engineer (twice her height, half as ferocious) last year, I was made a bridesmaid.
So will you be a bridesmaid?
F*$# YEAH!
I immediately used the steely focus of my crazy artist's intensity to be the most insane, original bridesmaid I could be.
So I'll probably just keep it simple with low-key bridal stuff.
Heh heh
I considered the expectations of my role, and then went completely overboard.
Oh, yesss...
PLOT PLOT
SUPER Simple...
Suuure...
HEH HEH
I've got an artist's nature paired with a cartoonist's obsessive tendencies, and I was going to USE IT ALL.
Along with Taylor's sister and the other bridesmaids, we planned an epic surprise "Bond" themed bachelorette scavenger hunt.
Whoa, what?
TOP SECRET
SPY KIT
(BOND THEME)
Taylor played the role of Moneypenny, who needed to rescue Bond (her groom) from forces unknown (the groomsmen).
She had to use her skills and knowledge of the city's landmarks to follow photographic clues of the groom in a tuxedo at Taylor's favorite locations throughout New York.
When did you take all these surveillance photos of Andrew?
That info is... classified.*
Clear! Let's move!
TOP SECRET
* Took 'em months ago.
At each stop, she would perform a task or be quizzed correctly to earn the next clue.
The message that barista gave me is encoded!
The decoder ring from my spy kit should help!
We would meet with other female wedding guests along the way—posing as spies or allies, they would administer the tasks.
(At Grand Central Terminal)
What is Andrew's first girlfriend's name?
(The whispering corners have a cool acoustic effect that funnels conversation along the archway.)
Mia?! Cousin Olivia? HA HA HA! Hey, guys!
Naturally, with plenty of drinks and eats along the way.

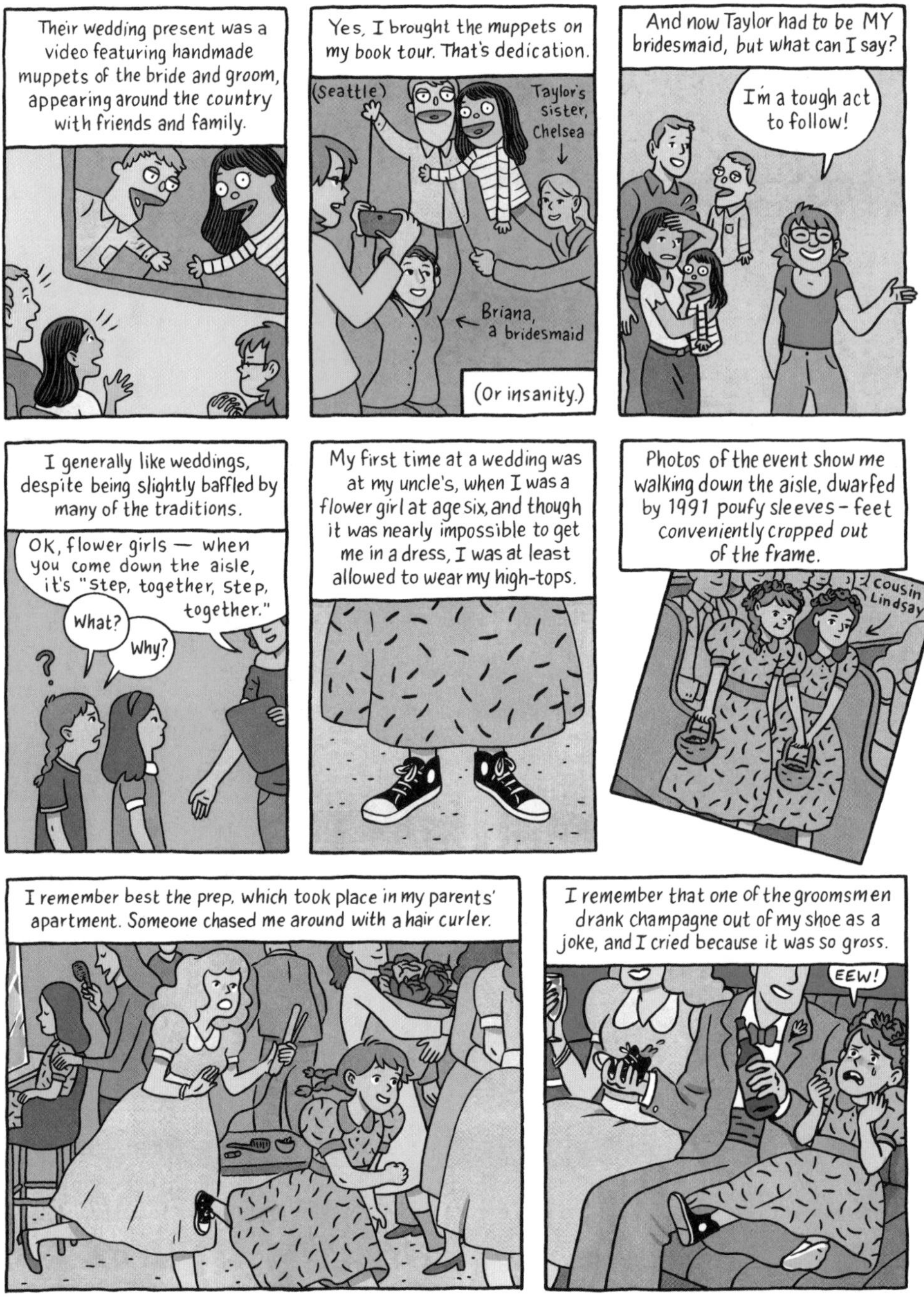

Their wedding present was a video featuring handmade muppets of the bride and groom, appearing around the country with friends and family.
Yes, I brought the muppets on my book tour. That's dedication.
(Seattle)
Taylor's sister, Chelsea
Briana, a bridesmaid
(Or insanity.)
And now Taylor had to be MY bridesmaid, but what can I say?
I'm a tough act to follow!
I generally like weddings, despite being slightly baffled by many of the traditions.
OK, flower girls — when you come down the aisle, it's "step, together, step, together."
What?
Why?
?
My first time at a wedding was at my uncle's, when I was a flower girl at age six, and though it was nearly impossible to get me in a dress, I was at least allowed to wear my high-tops.
Photos of the event show me walking down the aisle, dwarfed by 1991 poufy sleeves - feet conveniently cropped out of the frame.
Cousin Lindsay
I remember best the prep, which took place in my parents' apartment. Someone chased me around with a hair curler.
I remember that one of the groomsmen drank champagne out of my shoe as a joke, and I cried because it was so gross.
EEW!

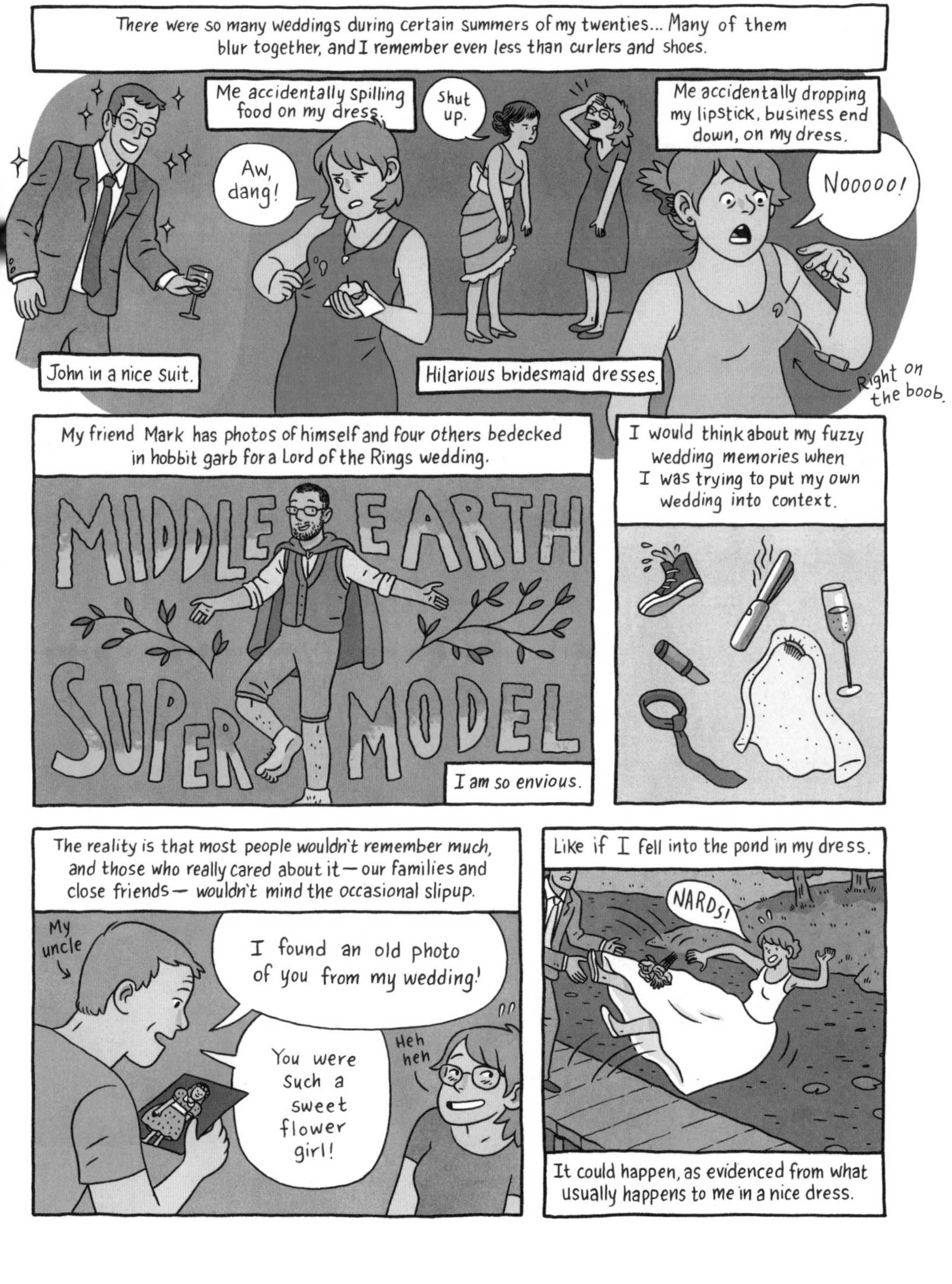
There were so many weddings during certain summers of my twenties... Many of them blur together, and I remember even less than curlers and shoes.
John in a nice suit.
Me accidentally spilling food on my dress.
Aw, dang!
Shut up.
Hilarious bridesmaid dresses.
Me accidentally dropping my lipstick, business end down, on my dress.
Nooooo!
Right on the boob.
My friend Mark has photos of himself and four others bedecked in hobbit garb for a Lord of the Rings wedding.
MIDDLE EARTH SUPER MODEL
I am so envious.
I would think about my fuzzy wedding memories when I was trying to put my own wedding into context.
The reality is that most people wouldn't remember much, and those who really cared about it — our families and close friends — wouldn't mind the occasional slipup.
My uncle
I found an old photo of you from my wedding!
You were such a sweet flower girl!
Heh heh
Like if I fell into the pond in my dress.
NARDS!
It could happen, as evidenced from what usually happens to me in a nice dress.

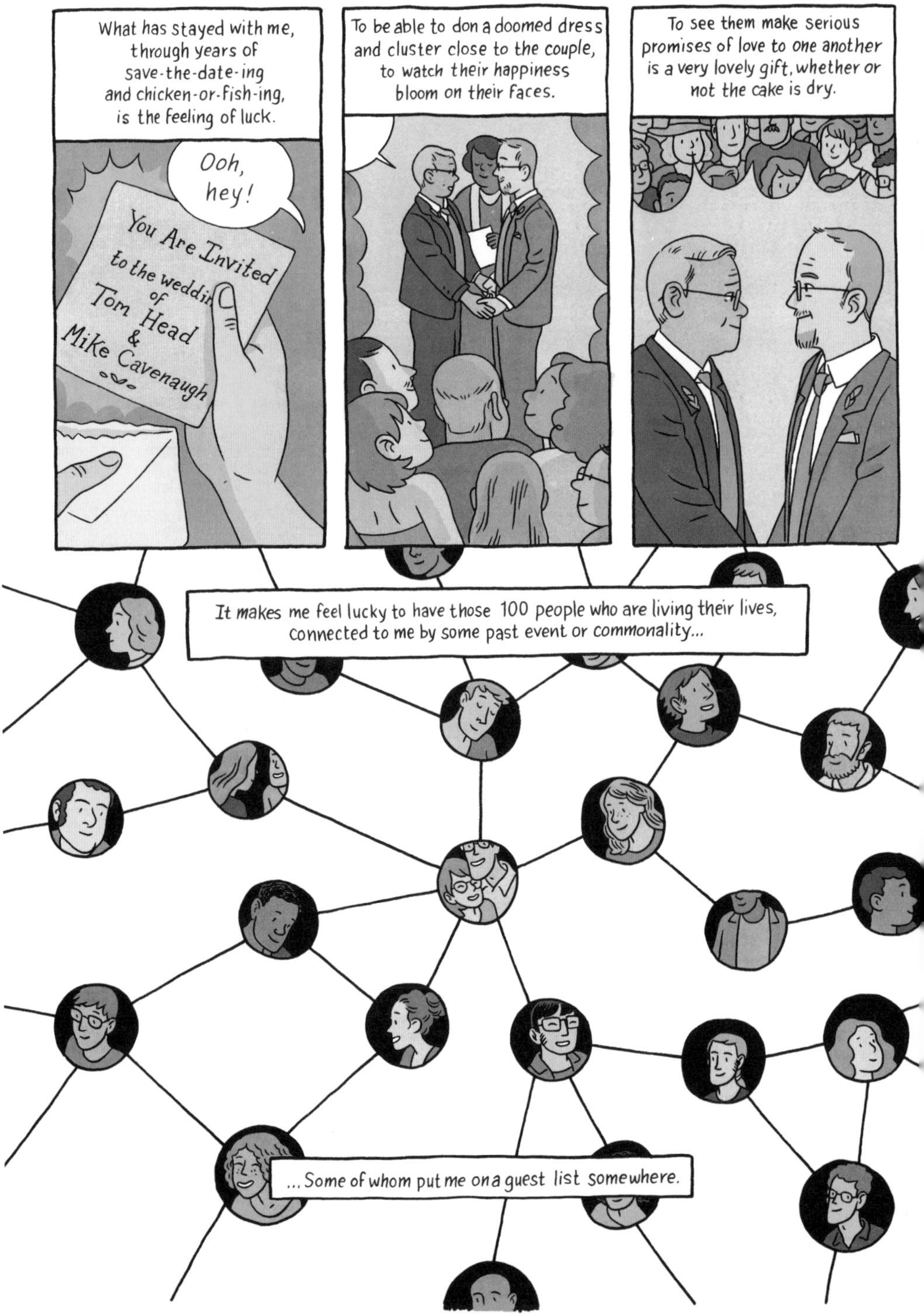
What has stayed with me, through years of save-the-date-ing and chicken-or-fish-ing, is the feeling of luck.
Ooh, hey!
You Are Invited to the weddi[ng] of Tom Head & Mike Cavenaugh
To be able to don a doomed dress and cluster close to the couple, to watch their happiness bloom on their faces.
To see them make serious promises of love to one another is a very lovely gift, whether or not the cake is dry.
It makes me feel lucky to have those 100 people who are living their lives, connected to me by some past event or commonality...
... Some of whom put me on a guest list somewhere.

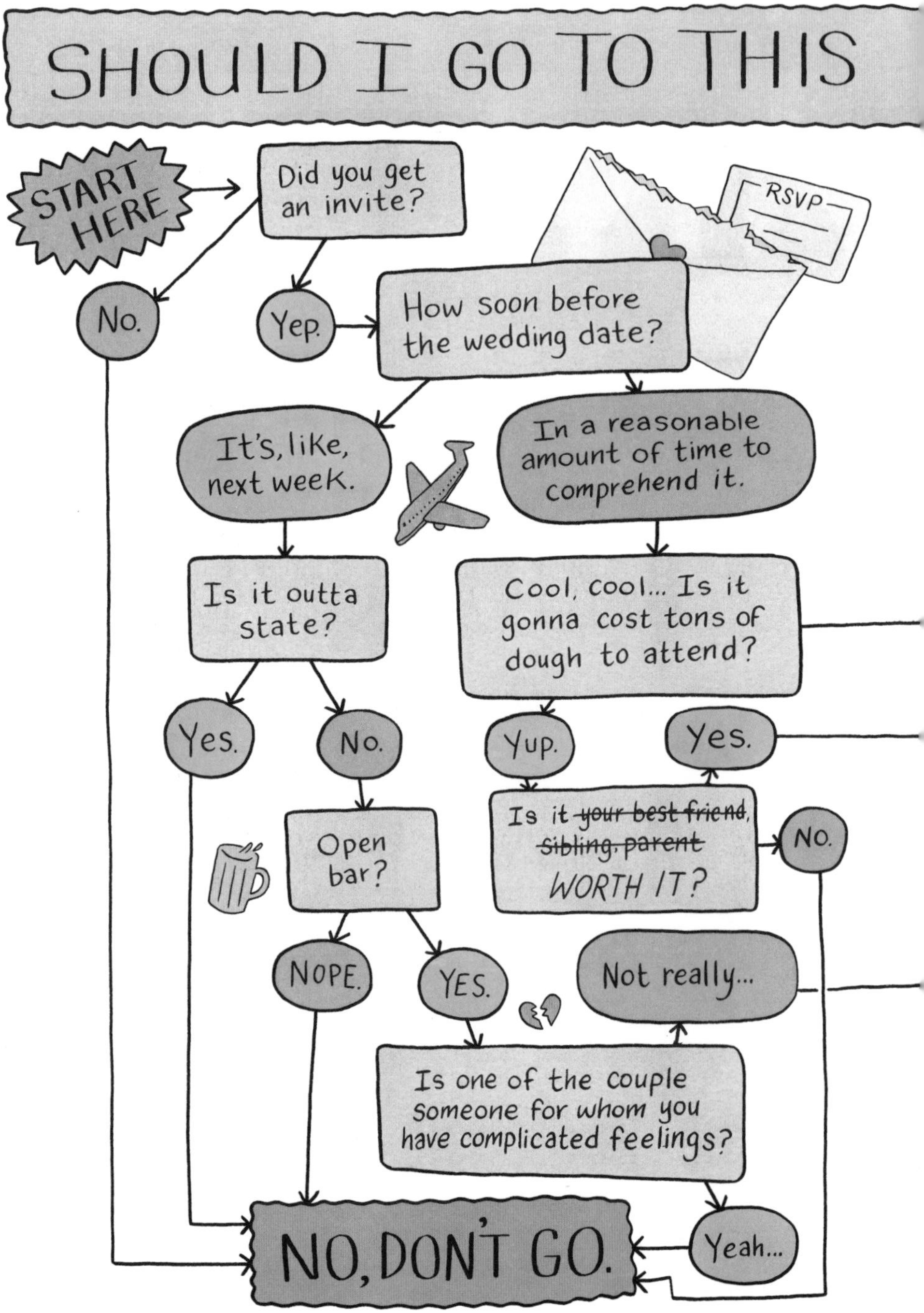

SHOULD I GO TO THIS
START HERE
Did you get an invite?
No.
Yep.
RSVP
How soon before the wedding date?
It's, like, next week.
In a reasonable amount of time to comprehend it.
Is it outta state?
Cool, cool... Is it gonna cost tons of dough to attend?
Yes.
No.
Yup.
Yes.
Open bar?
Is it ~~your best friend, sibling, parent~~ WORTH IT?
No.
NOPE.
YES.
Not really...
Is one of the couple someone for whom you have complicated feelings?
Yeah...
NO, DON'T GO.

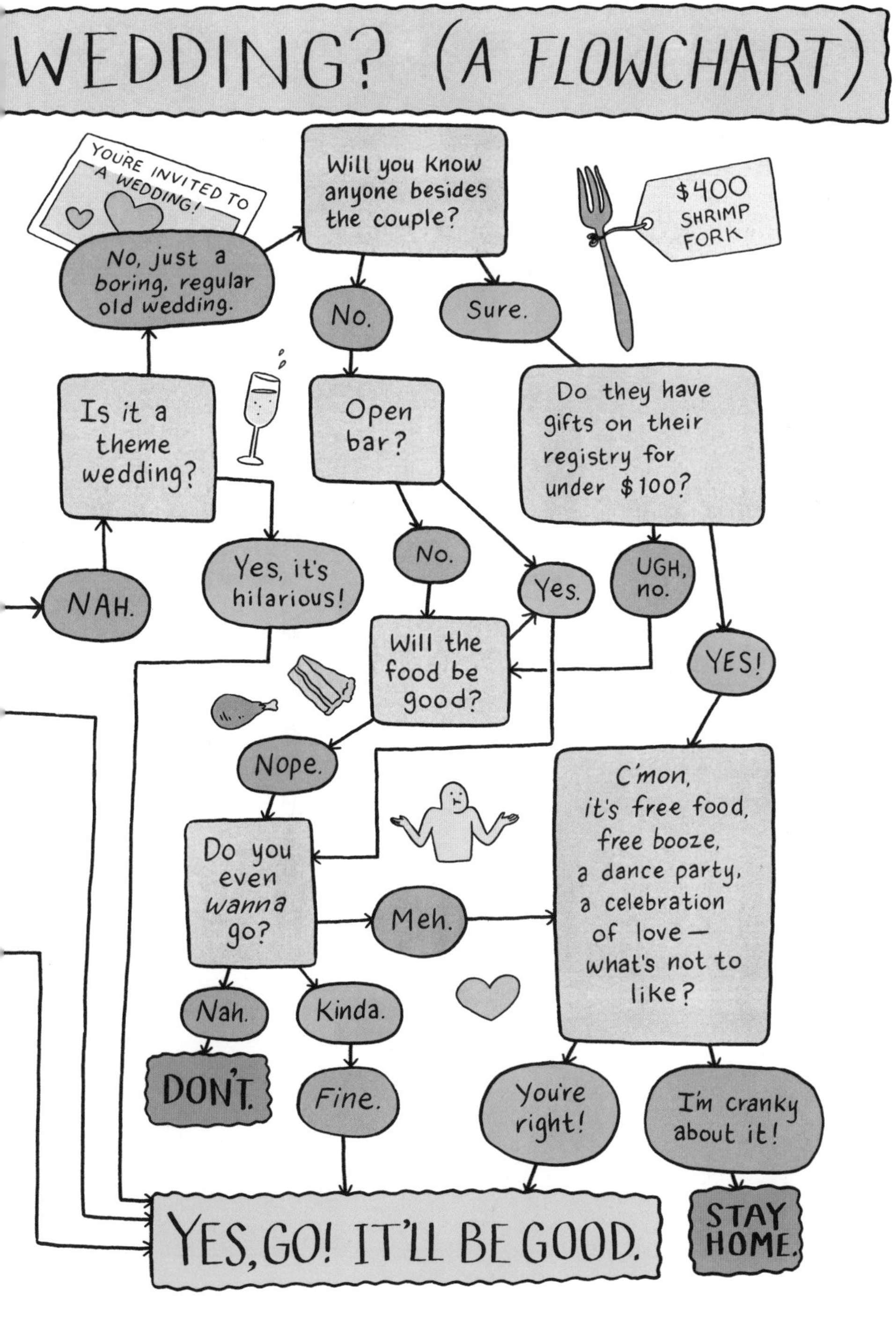
WEDDING? (A FLOWCHART)
YOU'RE INVITED TO A WEDDING!
No, just a boring, regular old wedding.
Will you know anyone besides the couple?
$400 SHRIMP FORK
No.
Sure.
Is it a theme wedding?
Open bar?
Do they have gifts on their registry for under $100?
No.
Yes, it's hilarious!
Yes.
UGH, no.
NAH.
Will the food be good?
YES!
Nope.
C'mon, it's free food, free booze, a dance party, a celebration of love— what's not to like?
Do you even wanna go?
Meh.
Nah.
Kinda.
DON'T.
Fine.
You're right!
I'm cranky about it!
YES, GO! IT'LL BE GOOD.
STAY HOME.

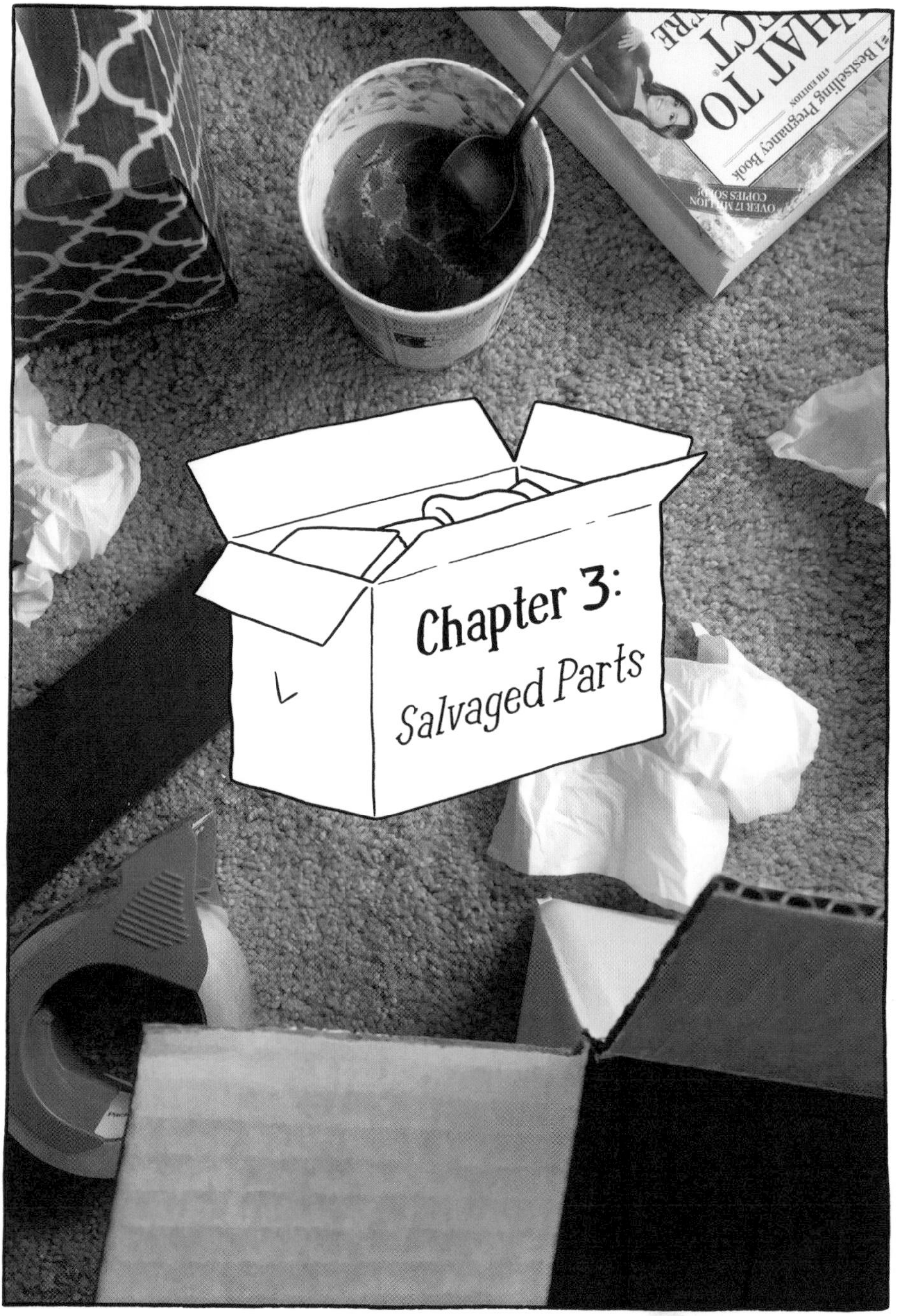
Chapter 3:
Salvaged Parts

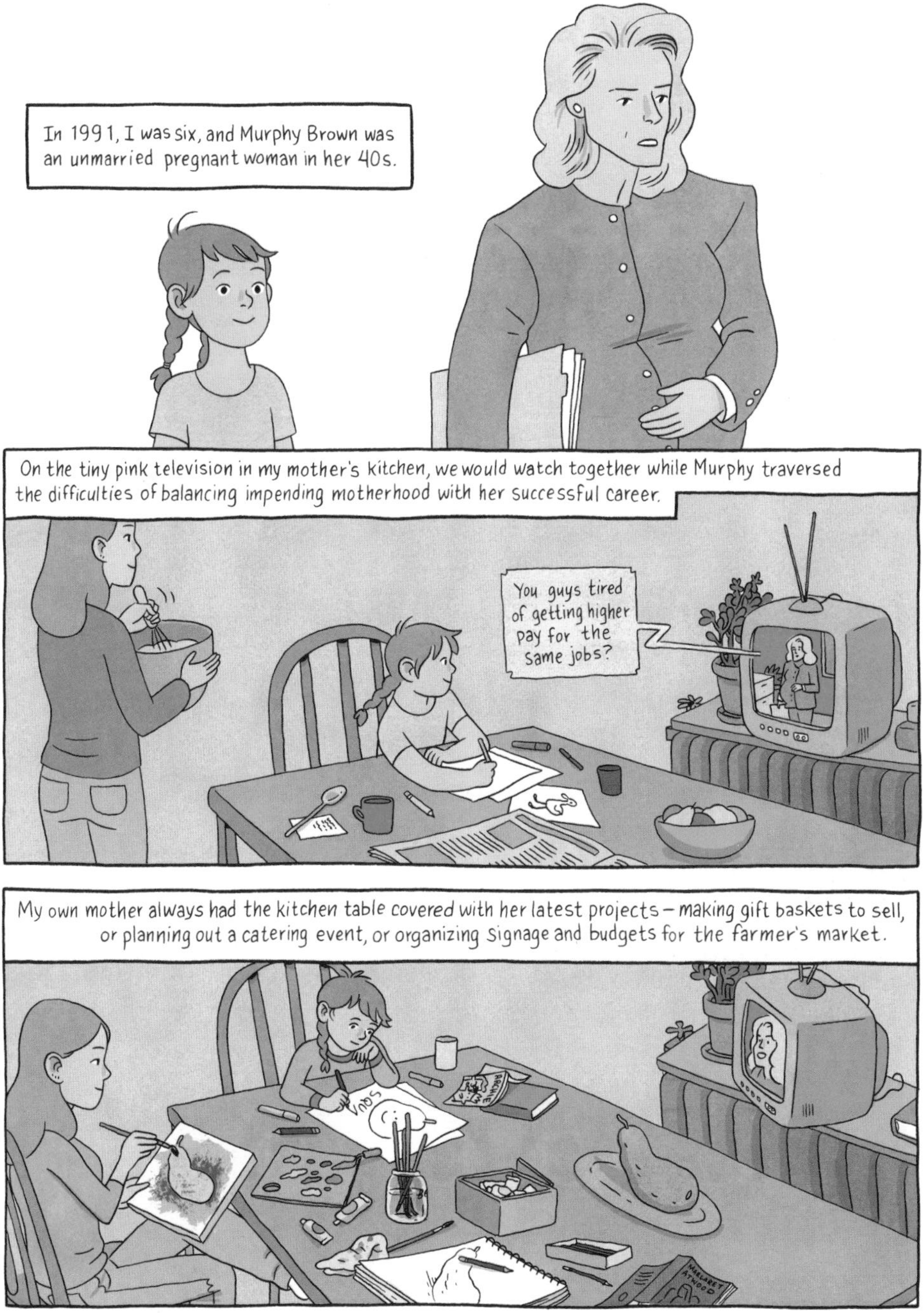
In 1991, I was six, and Murphy Brown was an unmarried pregnant woman in her 40s.
On the tiny pink television in my mother's kitchen, we would watch together while Murphy traversed the difficulties of balancing impending motherhood with her successful career.
You guys tired of getting higher pay for the same jobs?
My own mother always had the kitchen table covered with her latest projects – making gift baskets to sell, or planning out a catering event, or organizing signage and budgets for the farmer's market.

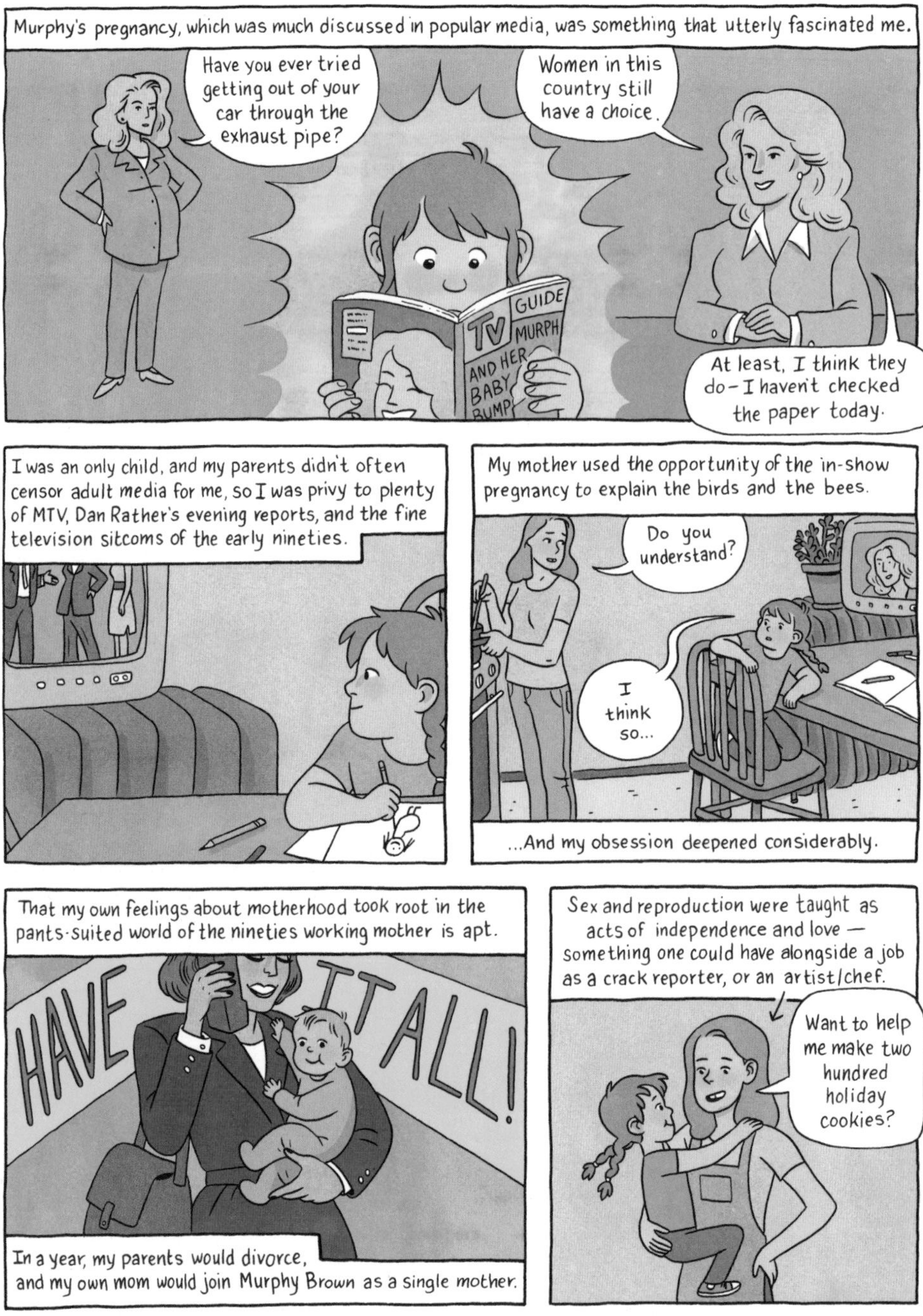
Murphy's pregnancy, which was much discussed in popular media, was something that utterly fascinated me.
Have you ever tried getting out of your car through the exhaust pipe?
Women in this country still have a choice.
TV GUIDE MURPH AND HER BABY BUMP
At least, I think they do – I haven't checked the paper today.
I was an only child, and my parents didn't often censor adult media for me, so I was privy to plenty of MTV, Dan Rather's evening reports, and the fine television sitcoms of the early nineties.
My mother used the opportunity of the in-show pregnancy to explain the birds and the bees.
Do you understand?
I think so...
...And my obsession deepened considerably.
That my own feelings about motherhood took root in the pants-suited world of the nineties working mother is apt.
HAVE IT ALL!
In a year, my parents would divorce, and my own mom would join Murphy Brown as a single mother.
Sex and reproduction were taught as acts of independence and love — something one could have alongside a job as a crack reporter, or an artist/chef.
Want to help me make two hundred holiday cookies?

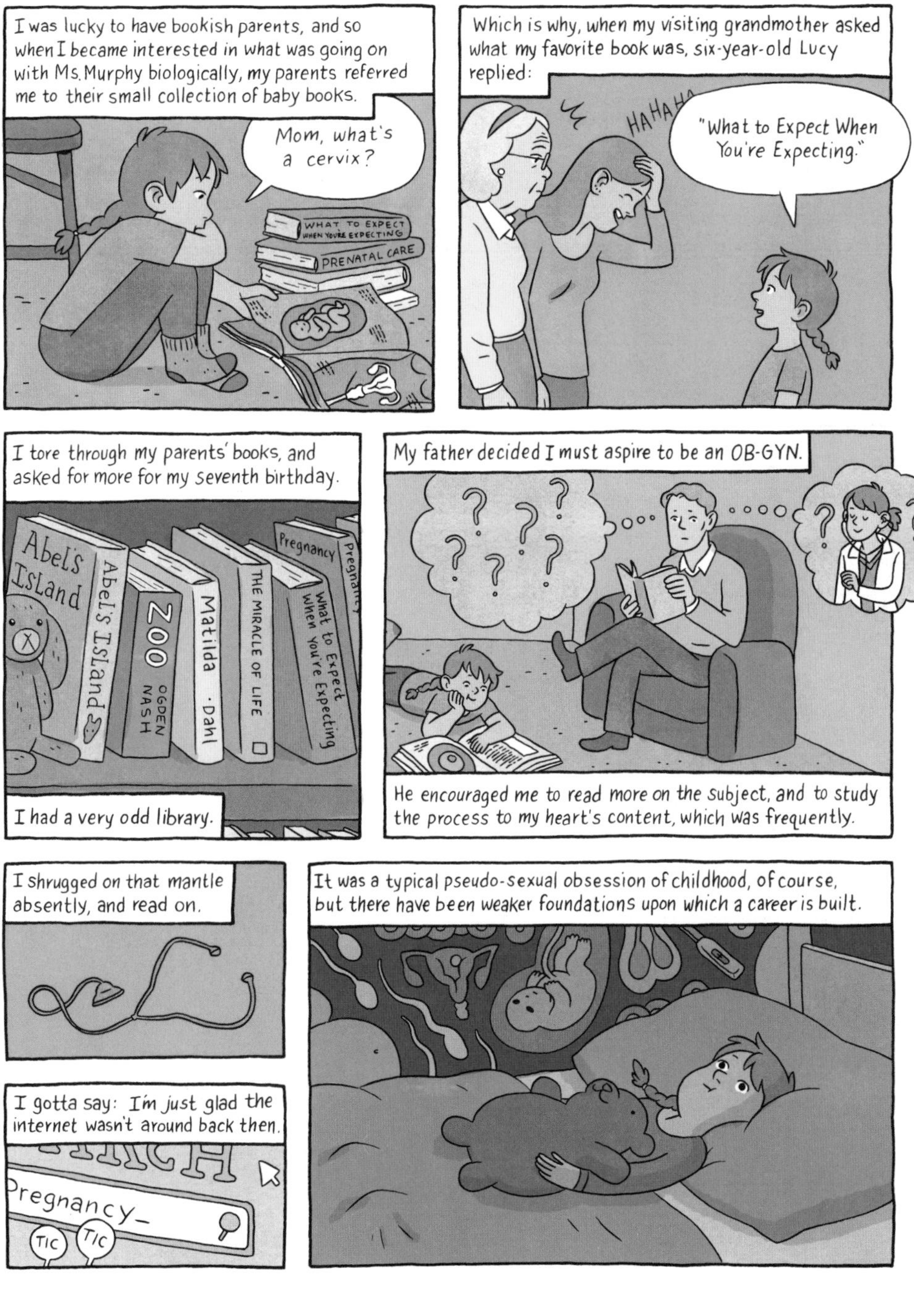
I was lucky to have bookish parents, and so when I became interested in what was going on with Ms. Murphy biologically, my parents referred me to their small collection of baby books.
Mom, what's a cervix?
WHAT TO EXPECT WHEN YOU'RE EXPECTING
PRENATAL CARE
Which is why, when my visiting grandmother asked what my favorite book was, six-year-old Lucy replied:
HAHAHA
"What to Expect When You're Expecting."
I tore through my parents' books, and asked for more for my seventh birthday.
Abel's Island
Abel's Island
ZOO OGDEN NASH
Matilda ·Dahl
THE MIRACLE OF LIFE
Pregnancy
What to Expect when you're Expecting
Pregnancy
I had a very odd library.
My father decided I must aspire to be an OB-GYN.
He encouraged me to read more on the subject, and to study the process to my heart's content, which was frequently.
I shrugged on that mantle absently, and read on.
I gotta say: I'm just glad the internet wasn't around back then.
Pregnancy_
TIC
TIC
It was a typical pseudo-sexual obsession of childhood, of course, but there have been weaker foundations upon which a career is built.

Obviously I did not become an OB-GYN, or a midwife (which I switched to sometime in middle school, when I found out that it requires fewer years of medical training).

What do you want to be when you grow up?

I wanna deliver babies!

A midwife.

I dunno.

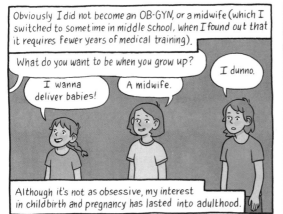

Although it's not as obsessive, my interest in childbirth and pregnancy has lasted into adulthood.

At some point, discussing these things became embarrassing, and confessing to this fascination seemed to imply that I was what people termed:

BABY CRAZY

It took me a while to learn that everyone makes their own rules, and that wanting or having or not wanting kids has no bearing over whether or not you are a feminist, or a strong person.

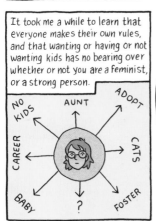

NO KIDS
AUNT
ADOPT
CAREER
CATS
BABY
?
FOSTER

"Baby crazy" is an unkind term made up by men to villainize women and domesticity.

D.Q.

Bearing babies irresponsibly is simply wrong.

People will always pick on ladies about their reproductive choices (see Dan Quayle's 1992 speech in which he bitched out Murphy for single-parenthood).

It's rad that women can 3D-print human beings, so why would you ever deem wanting to do that as "weak" or "irrational"?

So where do you see yourself in ten years?

Don't say "a parent," or you'll spoil everything!

Date or job interview?

My mother (and Murphy Brown) worked hard as moms, but never gave up their jobs or their social lives.

My mother carted me around to professional restaurant kitchens, and put me to work helping her cook for catering events.

My parents perched my baby seat in restaurant booths, airplanes, and even the occasional bar, where the bartender would give me a lemon to suck.

We were lucky that they could afford to travel and dine out, and that they had a baby who was content to suck on a lemon (still my favorite thing to do in a bar).

The truth is, for me, the baby part of parenthood is great and all, but it's always astonished me that my body has the potential to do such an insane, amazing thing!

My body could do this, someday...

So cool...

I have the ability to create someone who will sit at the kitchen table and watch Murphy Brown with me while we draw.

I was lonely a lot as an only child, and switched schools so often that making lasting friends was hard.

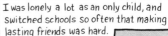

You wanna go to the park?

Imaginary Kid

Wanting to someday have kids has always been this part of who I was — to create more people who could be my family.

So what was I doing, dating a man who

NEVER WANTED KIDS?

It just seems like there are enough people in the world.

Why make more?

Fortunately, I was twenty, and I had tons of time to figure it out.

Oh well...

He's so cute.

It probably won't last, so I might as well enjoy it.

FLASH FORWARD FIVE YEARS:

DAMMIT! He's just gotten cuter!

John and I had lived together for two years, and that made it much harder to face this question.

Like two dogs who had heedlessly twined their leashes, our lives were all the more painful to untangle.

Ruh roh...

Beside that, there was that familiar embarrassment.

I know he's RIGHT.

There's too many people in the world already...

I can't imagine ever being able to afford a kid as a cartoonist.

And everyone says you totally lose all freedom...

I know.

Trying to explain to my mostly childfree friends

43

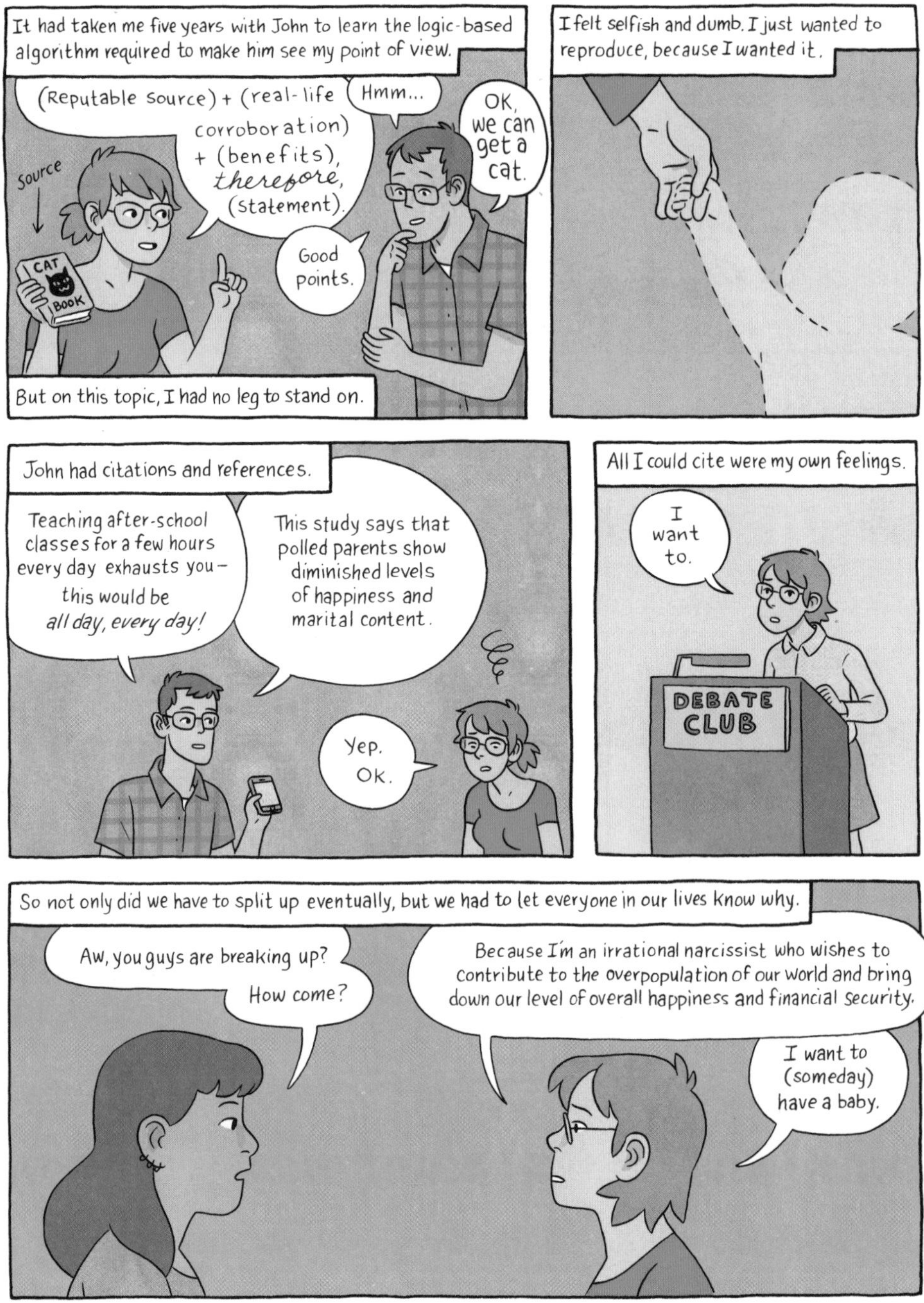
It had taken me five years with John to learn the logic-based algorithm required to make him see my point of view.
(Reputable source) + (real-life corroboration) + (benefits), *therefore*, (statement).
source
CAT BOOK
Hmm...
Good points.
OK, we can get a cat.
But on this topic, I had no leg to stand on.
I felt selfish and dumb. I just wanted to reproduce, because I wanted it.
John had citations and references.
Teaching after-school classes for a few hours every day exhausts you — this would be *all day, every day!*
This study says that polled parents show diminished levels of happiness and marital content.
Yep. Ok.
All I could cite were my own feelings.
I want to.
DEBATE CLUB
So not only did we have to split up eventually, but we had to let everyone in our lives know why.
Aw, you guys are breaking up?
How come?
Because I'm an irrational narcissist who wishes to contribute to the overpopulation of our world and bring down our level of overall happiness and financial security.
I want to (someday) have a baby.

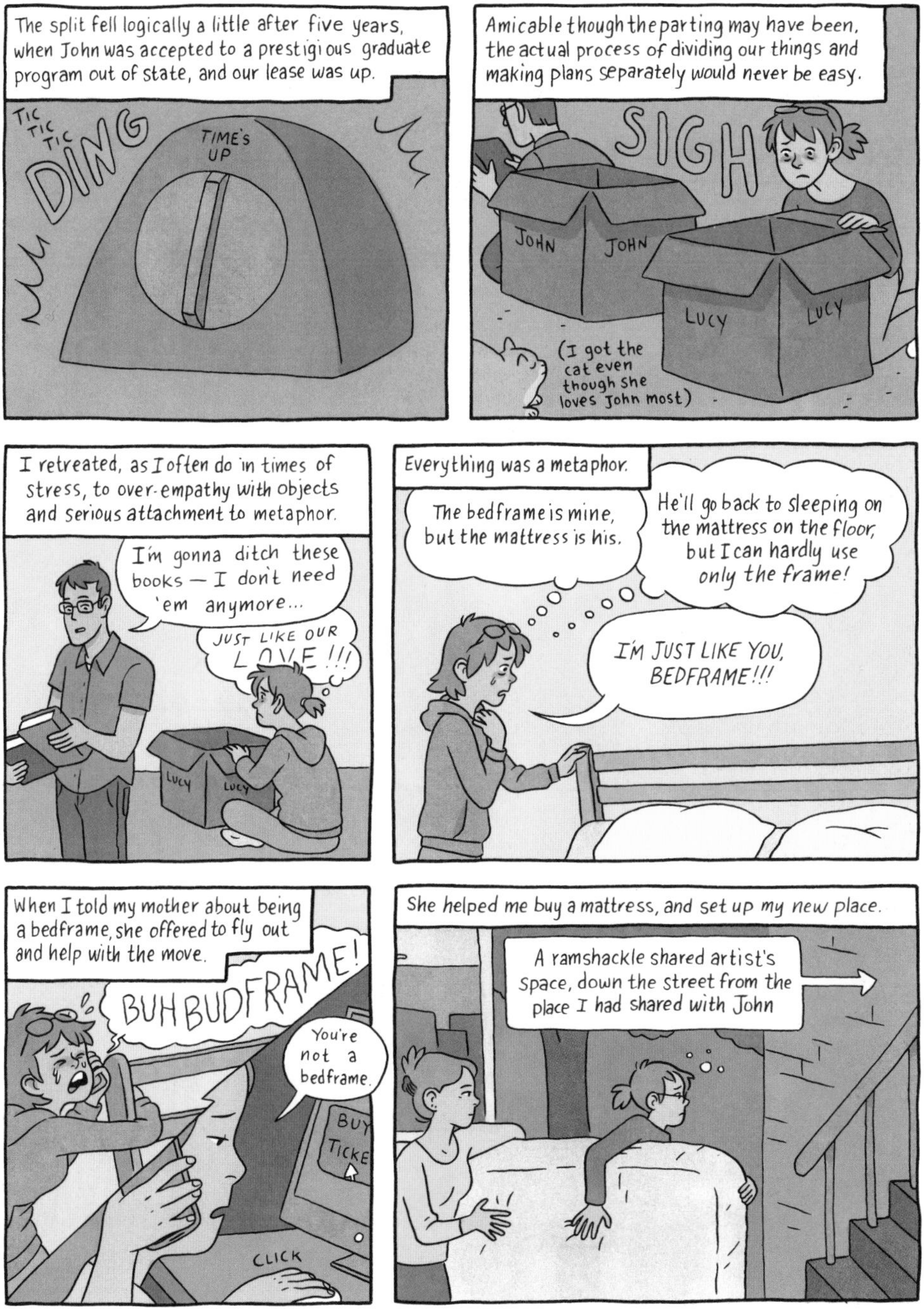
The split fell logically a little after five years, when John was accepted to a prestigious graduate program out of state, and our lease was up.
TIC TIC TIC
DING
TIME'S UP
Amicable though the parting may have been, the actual process of dividing our things and making plans separately would never be easy.
SIGH
JOHN
JOHN
LUCY
LUCY
(I got the cat even though she loves John most)
I retreated, as I often do in times of stress, to over-empathy with objects and serious attachment to metaphor.
I'm gonna ditch these books — I don't need 'em anymore...
JUST LIKE OUR LOVE!!!
LUCY
LUCY
Everything was a metaphor.
The bedframe is mine, but the mattress is his.
He'll go back to sleeping on the mattress on the floor, but I can hardly use only the frame!
I'M JUST LIKE YOU, BEDFRAME!!!
When I told my mother about being a bedframe, she offered to fly out and help with the move.
BUH BUDFRAME!
You're not a bedframe.
BUY TICKE
CLICK
She helped me buy a mattress, and set up my new place.
A ramshackle shared artist's space, down the street from the place I had shared with John

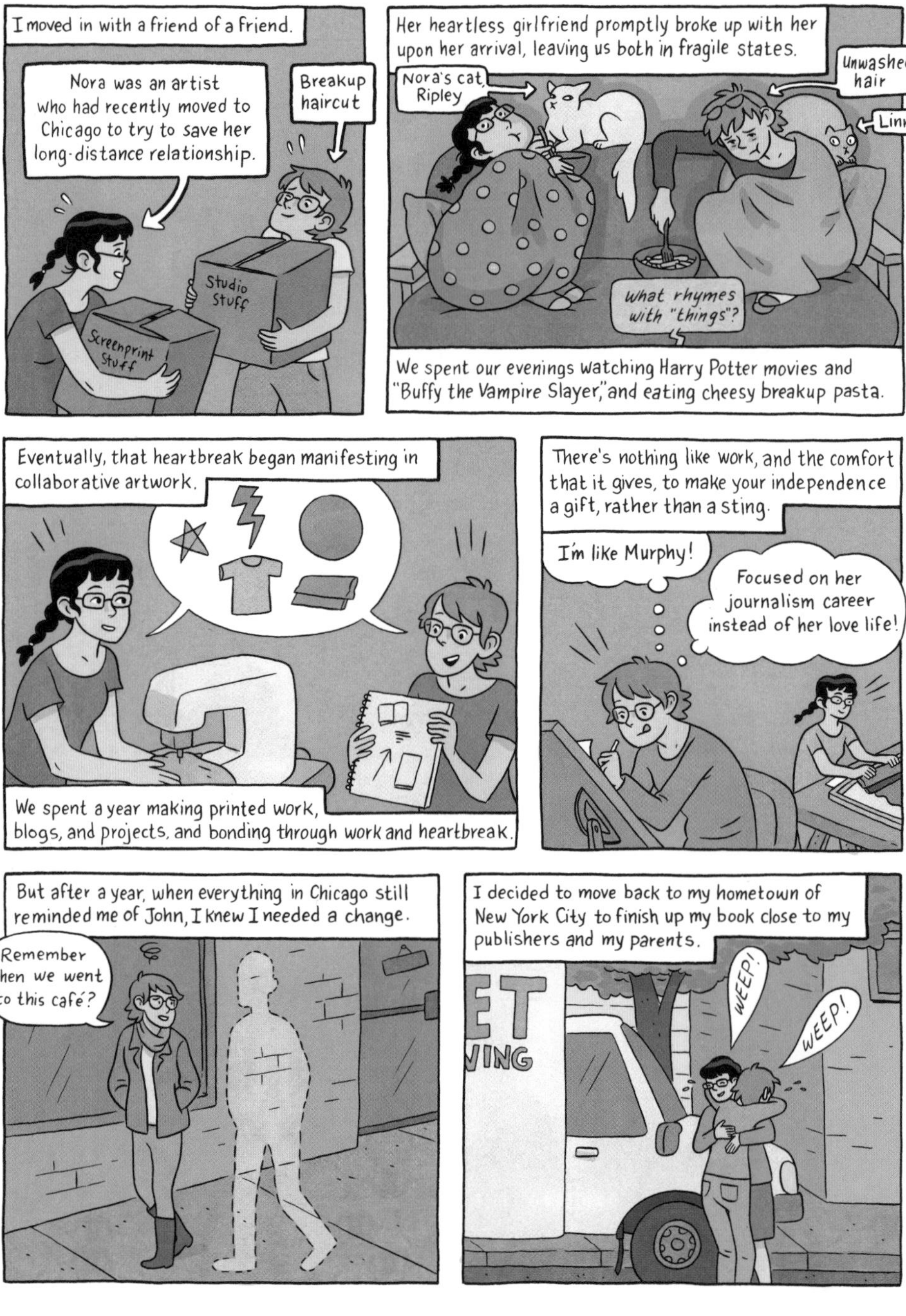
I moved in with a friend of a friend.
Nora was an artist who had recently moved to Chicago to try to save her long-distance relationship.
Breakup haircut
Studio Stuff
Screenprint Stuff
Her heartless girlfriend promptly broke up with her upon her arrival, leaving us both in fragile states.
Nora's cat, Ripley
Unwashed hair
Linney
What rhymes with "things"?
We spent our evenings watching Harry Potter movies and "Buffy the Vampire Slayer," and eating cheesy breakup pasta.
Eventually, that heartbreak began manifesting in collaborative artwork.
We spent a year making printed work, blogs, and projects, and bonding through work and heartbreak.
There's nothing like work, and the comfort that it gives, to make your independence a gift, rather than a sting.
I'm like Murphy!
Focused on her journalism career instead of her love life!
But after a year, when everything in Chicago still reminded me of John, I knew I needed a change.
Remember when we went to this café?
I decided to move back to my hometown of New York City to finish up my book close to my publishers and my parents.
WEEP!
WEEP!

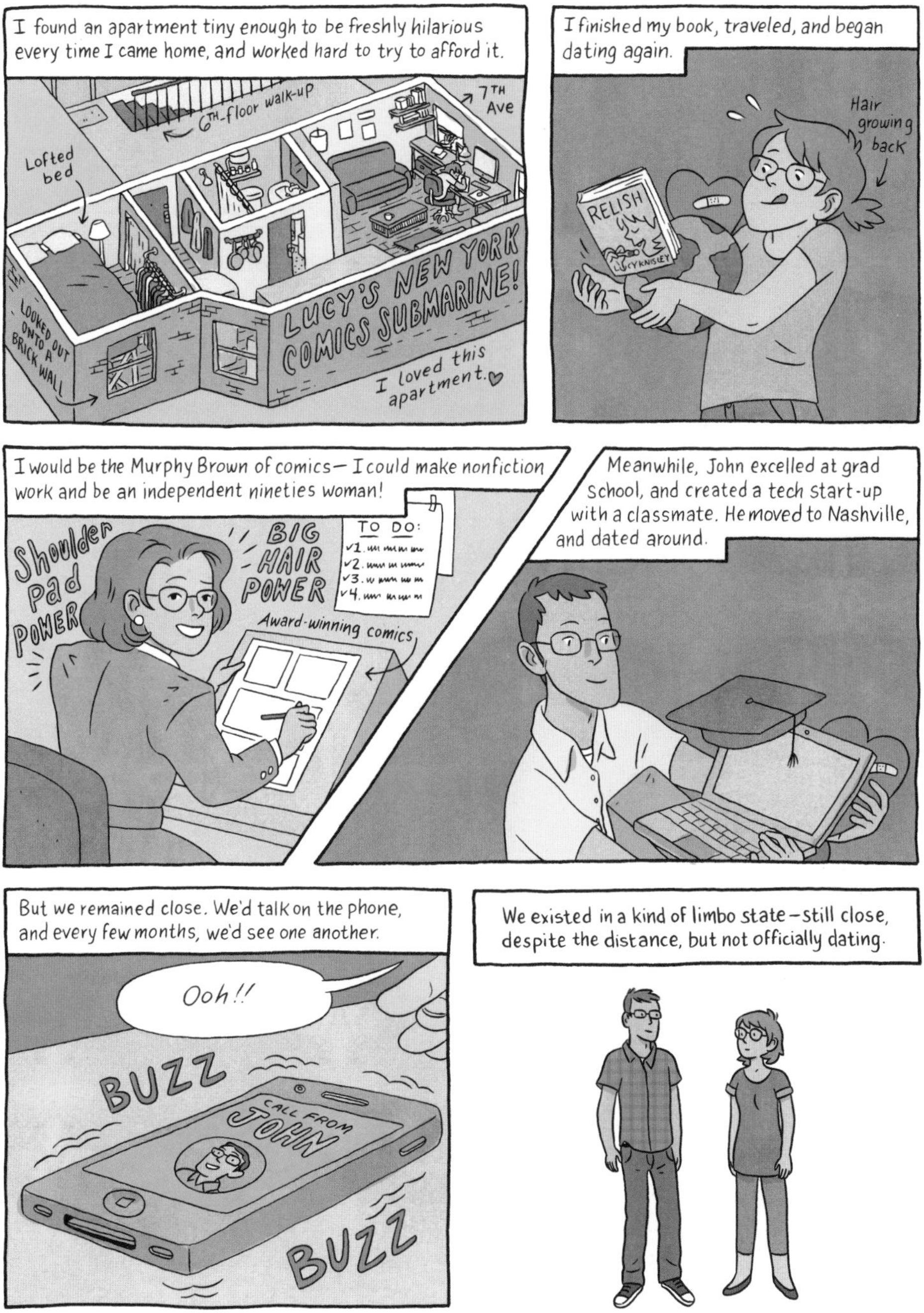
I found an apartment tiny enough to be freshly hilarious every time I came home, and worked hard to try to afford it.
6TH-floor walk-up
7TH Ave
Lofted bed
LOOKED OUT ONTO A BRICK WALL
LUCY'S NEW YORK COMICS SUBMARINE!
I loved this apartment.
I finished my book, traveled, and began dating again.
Hair growing back
RELISH
LUCY KNISLEY
I would be the Murphy Brown of comics— I could make nonfiction work and be an independent nineties woman!
Shoulder pad POWER
BIG HAIR POWER
TO DO:
Award-winning comics
Meanwhile, John excelled at grad school, and created a tech start-up with a classmate. He moved to Nashville, and dated around.
But we remained close. We'd talk on the phone, and every few months, we'd see one another.
Ooh!!
BUZZ
CALL FROM JOHN
BUZZ
We existed in a kind of limbo state—still close, despite the distance, but not officially dating.

This went on for three years.

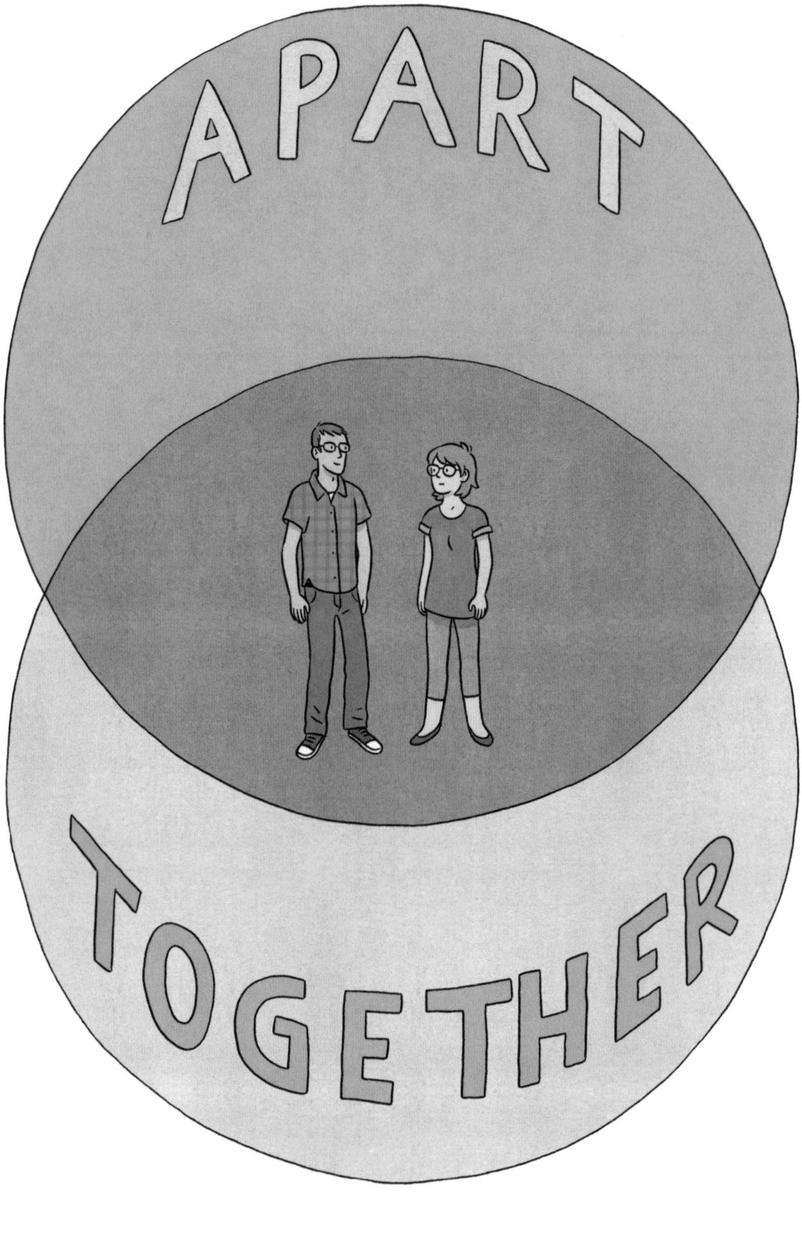
APART
TOGETHER

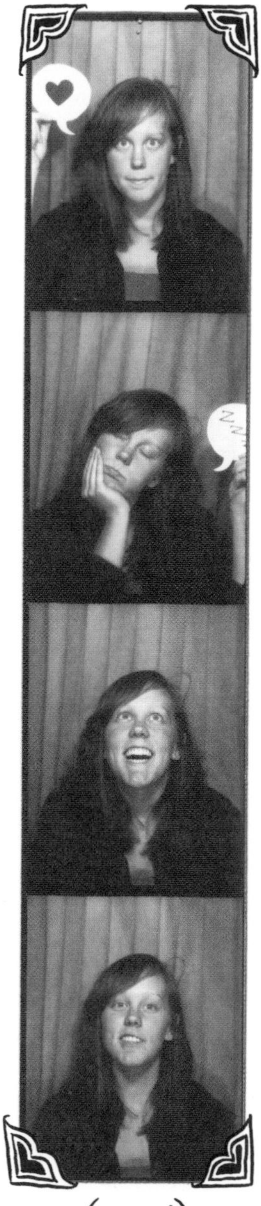
Z
Z
Z

(2011)

Lucy's Handy Dandy

BLANKET BURRITO

DEAR DIARY

Boo hoo!

A LIVING THING TO POUR ALL YOUR EXCESS LOVE INTO

ACTUAL BURRITO

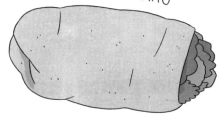

NORA'S TECHNIQUE: ALL 8 HARRY POTTER MOVIES

INTERNET FRIENDS (low contact, high yield of digital support)

Bad-Breakup Kit!

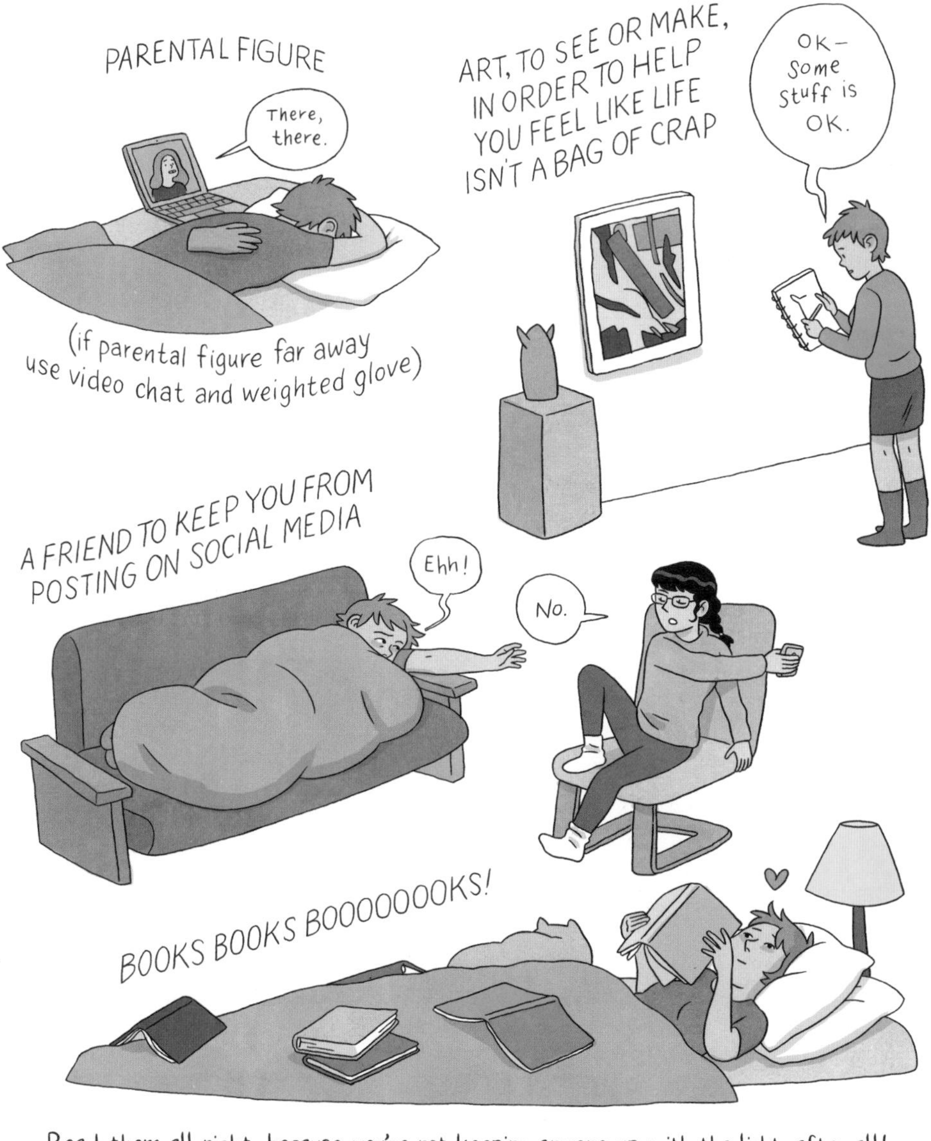
PARENTAL FIGURE
There, there.
(if parental figure far away use video chat and weighted glove)
ART, TO SEE OR MAKE, IN ORDER TO HELP YOU FEEL LIKE LIFE ISN'T A BAG OF CRAP
OK– Some stuff is OK.
A FRIEND TO KEEP YOU FROM POSTING ON SOCIAL MEDIA
Ehh!
No.
BOOKS BOOKS BOOOOOOOKS!

Read them all night, because you're not keeping anyone up with the light, after all!

Chapter 4:

How He Asked; or, A Light That Never Goes Out

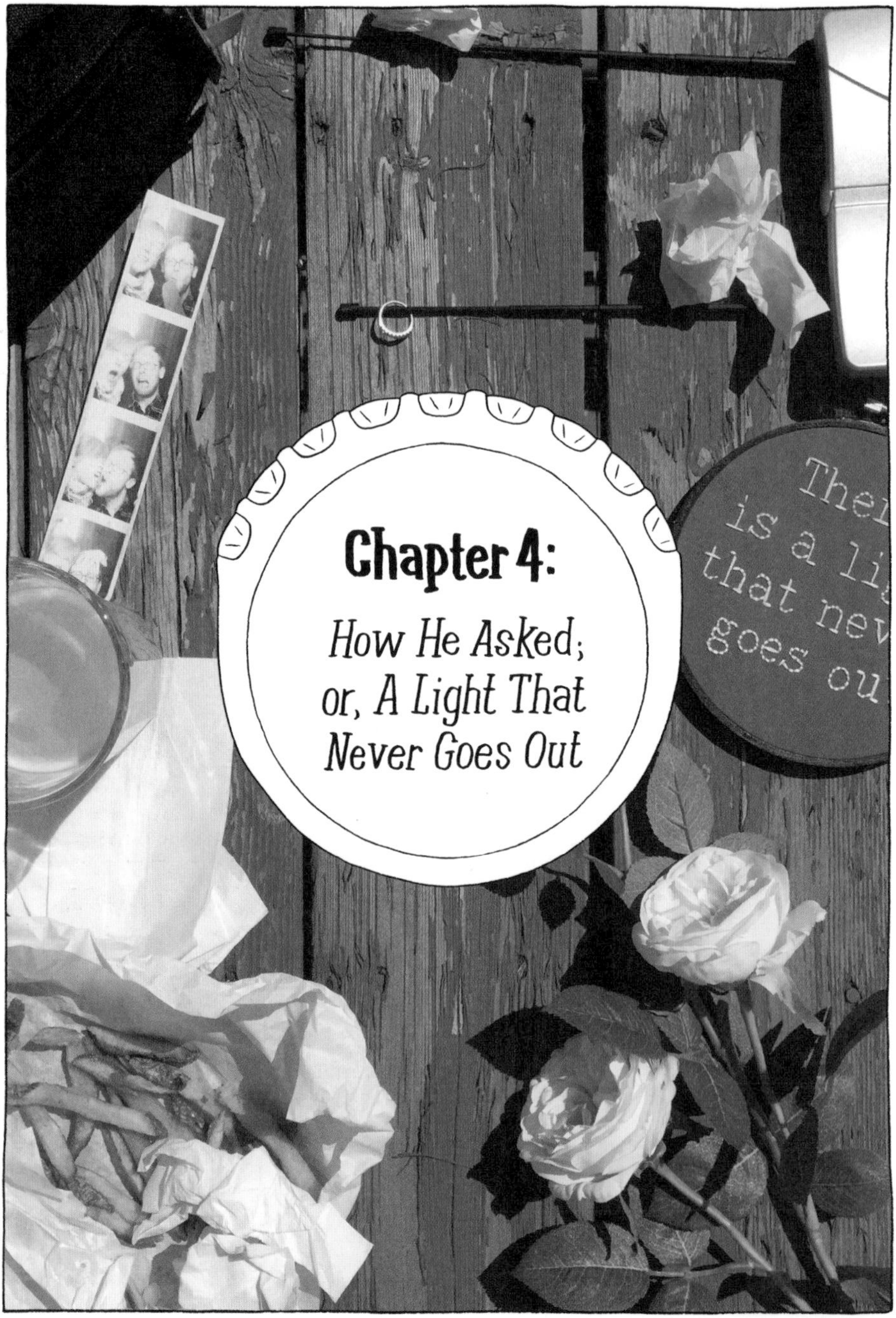
Ther
is a li
that nev
goes ou

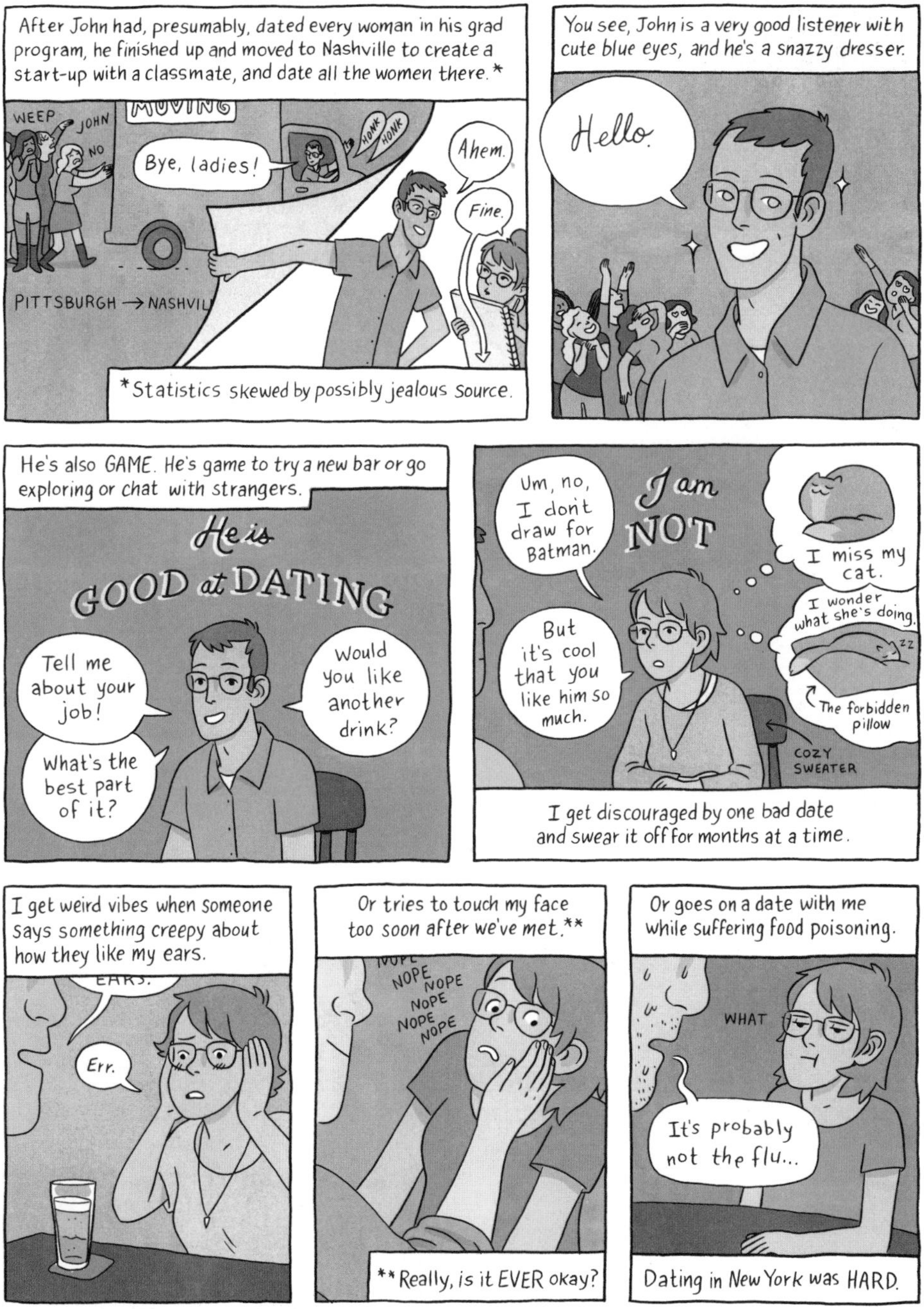
After John had, presumably, dated every woman in his grad program, he finished up and moved to Nashville to create a start-up with a classmate, and date all the women there.*
MOVING
WEEP
JOHN
NO
Bye, ladies!
HONK
HONK
Ahem.
Fine.
PITTSBURGH → NASHVIL
*Statistics skewed by possibly jealous source.
You see, John is a very good listener with cute blue eyes, and he's a snazzy dresser.
Hello.
He's also GAME. He's game to try a new bar or go exploring or chat with strangers.
He is GOOD at DATING
Tell me about your job!
What's the best part of it?
Would you like another drink?
Um, no, I don't draw for Batman.
I am NOT
But it's cool that you like him so much.
I miss my cat.
I wonder what she's doing.
ZZ
The forbidden pillow
COZY SWEATER
I get discouraged by one bad date and swear it off for months at a time.
I get weird vibes when someone says something creepy about how they like my ears.
Err.
Or tries to touch my face too soon after we've met.**
NOPE
NOPE
NOPE
NOPE
NOPE
**Really, is it EVER okay?
Or goes on a date with me while suffering food poisoning.
WHAT
It's probably not the flu...
Dating in New York was HARD.

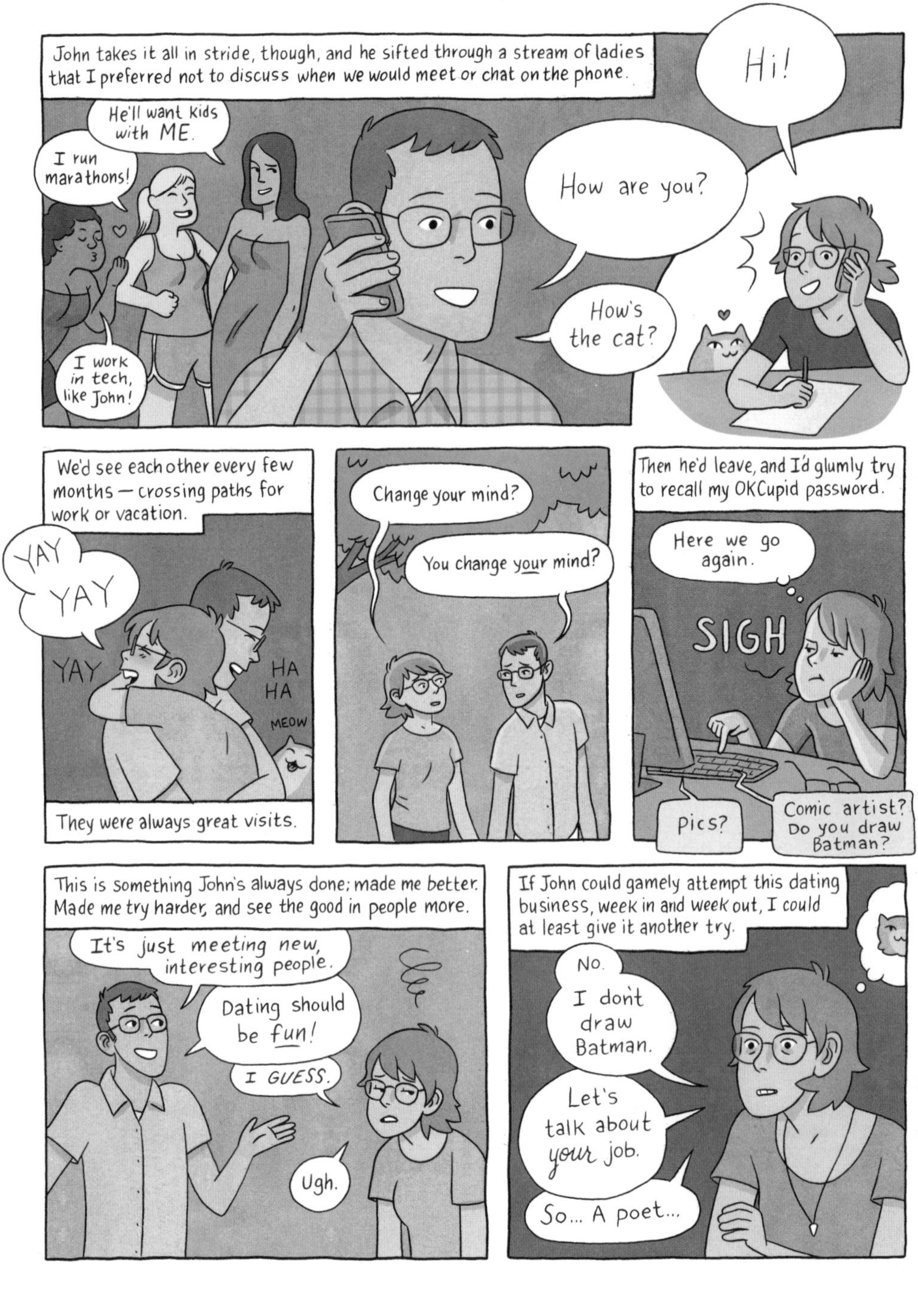
John takes it all in stride, though, and he sifted through a stream of ladies that I preferred not to discuss when we would meet or chat on the phone.
He'll want kids with ME.
I run marathons!
I work in tech, like John!
How are you?
Hi!
How's the cat?
We'd see each other every few months — crossing paths for work or vacation.
YAY YAY
YAY
HA HA
MEOW
They were always great visits.
Change your mind?
You change your mind?
Then he'd leave, and I'd glumly try to recall my OKCupid password.
Here we go again.
SIGH
Pics?
Comic artist? Do you draw Batman?
This is something John's always done; made me better. Made me try harder, and see the good in people more.
It's just meeting new, interesting people.
Dating should be fun!
I GUESS.
Ugh.
If John could gamely attempt this dating business, week in and week out, I could at least give it another try.
No.
I don't draw Batman.
Let's talk about your job.
So... A poet...

I wonder... if I'd known that we'd wind up together in the end, would there have been less pressure and misery associated with dating?

I was unaware that we were on a dating walkabout, wherein we'd see what was out there before we sweetly reunited.

Perhaps if I'd known, I'd have had a few more casual dates, though I doubt it. I'm not comfortable with the early intimacy of romance.

Mental shield

It seems strange to me to let someone you met online last week into your apartment, and I don't really like holding hands while walking, because I prefer to hold a sandwich.

PLUS IT BLOCKS THE WHOLE SIDEWALK!

UNCOUPLE OR WALK FASTER!

I get uncomfortable when someone, especially a man, pays for my drinks or food before I know him well. I don't like the sexist gender-role paradigm of expected expenses in exchange for female company.

Allow me, little lady.

No, thanks.

This all makes me sound like a heartless and frigid person, and my failures at dating were beginning to convince me that was the case.

DISPENSE OCCUPATION ANECDOTE

Um.

WHAT WAS WRONG WITH ME, that I didn't like making out with someone on a public corner, or felt panicked at the thought of someone walking me home to find out where I lived?

Heading in opposite direction of home...

KAYBYE.

...to get away.

WAS THE ROMANCE INSIDE ME **DEAD?**

HISS!

Just leave us alone!

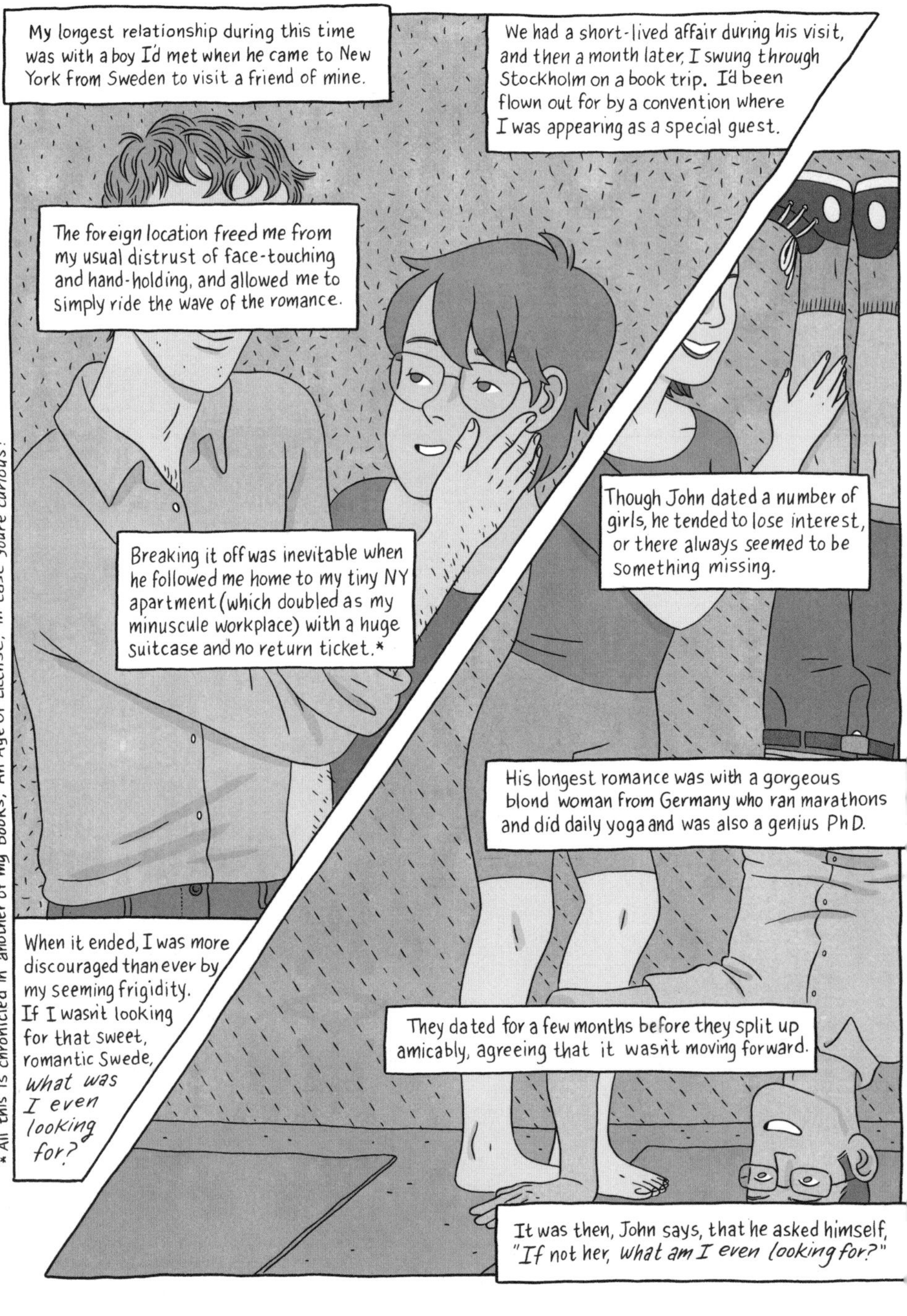
My longest relationship during this time was with a boy I'd met when he came to New York from Sweden to visit a friend of mine.
The foreign location freed me from my usual distrust of face-touching and hand-holding, and allowed me to simply ride the wave of the romance.
Breaking it off was inevitable when he followed me home to my tiny NY apartment (which doubled as my minuscule workplace) with a huge suitcase and no return ticket.*
When it ended, I was more discouraged than ever by my seeming frigidity. If I wasn't looking for that sweet, romantic Swede, *what was I even looking for?*
We had a short-lived affair during his visit, and then a month later, I swung through Stockholm on a book trip. I'd been flown out for by a convention where I was appearing as a special guest.
Though John dated a number of girls, he tended to lose interest, or there always seemed to be something missing.
His longest romance was with a gorgeous blond woman from Germany who ran marathons and did daily yoga and was also a genius PhD.
They dated for a few months before they split up amicably, agreeing that it wasn't moving forward.
It was then, John says, that he asked himself, "If not her, *what am I even looking for?*"

* All this is chronicled in another of my books, "An Age of License," in case you're curious!

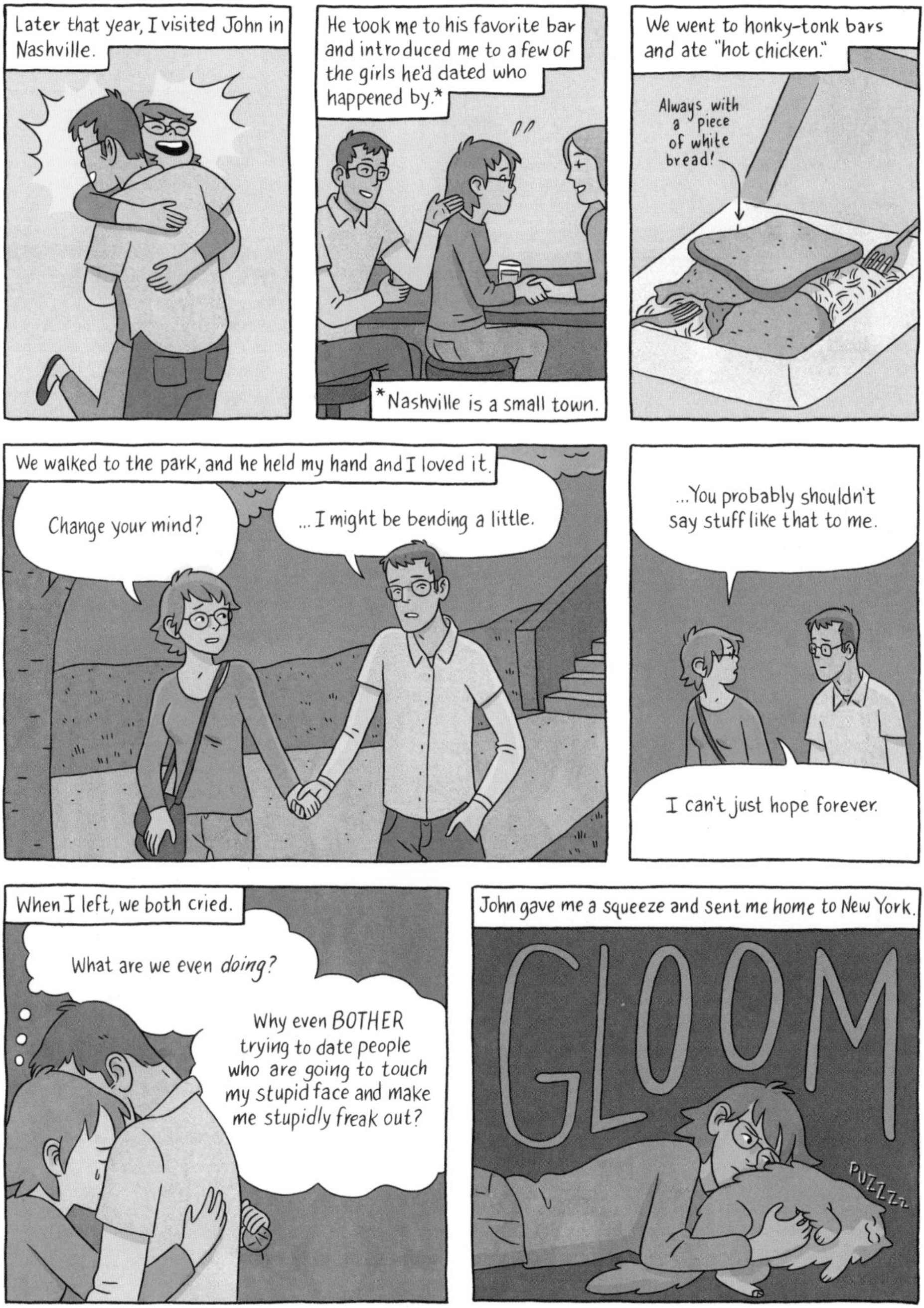
Later that year, I visited John in Nashville.
He took me to his favorite bar and introduced me to a few of the girls he'd dated who happened by.*
*Nashville is a small town.
We went to honky-tonk bars and ate "hot chicken."
Always with a piece of white bread!
We walked to the park, and he held my hand and I loved it.
Change your mind?
...I might be bending a little.
...You probably shouldn't say stuff like that to me.
I can't just hope forever.
When I left, we both cried.
What are we even doing?
Why even BOTHER trying to date people who are going to touch my stupid face and make me stupidly freak out?
John gave me a squeeze and sent me home to New York.
GLOOM
PUZZZzz

And then John visited his parents for a few days at their home in a Chicago suburb.

John's mom
John's pop

As much as I loved John, during our relationship, I had also loved his family.

John's sister
John's brother
John's great aunt and stand-in grandma

His parents and great-aunt were incredibly nice to me, always fed me to the gills, and his siblings were all interesting, lovely people.

John likely spent his visit eating and couch-basking, as he usually did.

And waiting for everyone to go to bed.

Then he snuck into his family's secret stash of keepsakes, which his mother had shown him years ago.

He picked out a ring she'd mentioned back then (his grandmother's wedding band), which she'd offered to him.

She'd said: "Use it to propose, someday."

I think about this a lot — about the trust of his family, that well-loved ring, the meaning of this act, and how he told no one.

He hid it in a pocket of his toiletry bag, where it stayed for a few months.

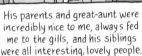

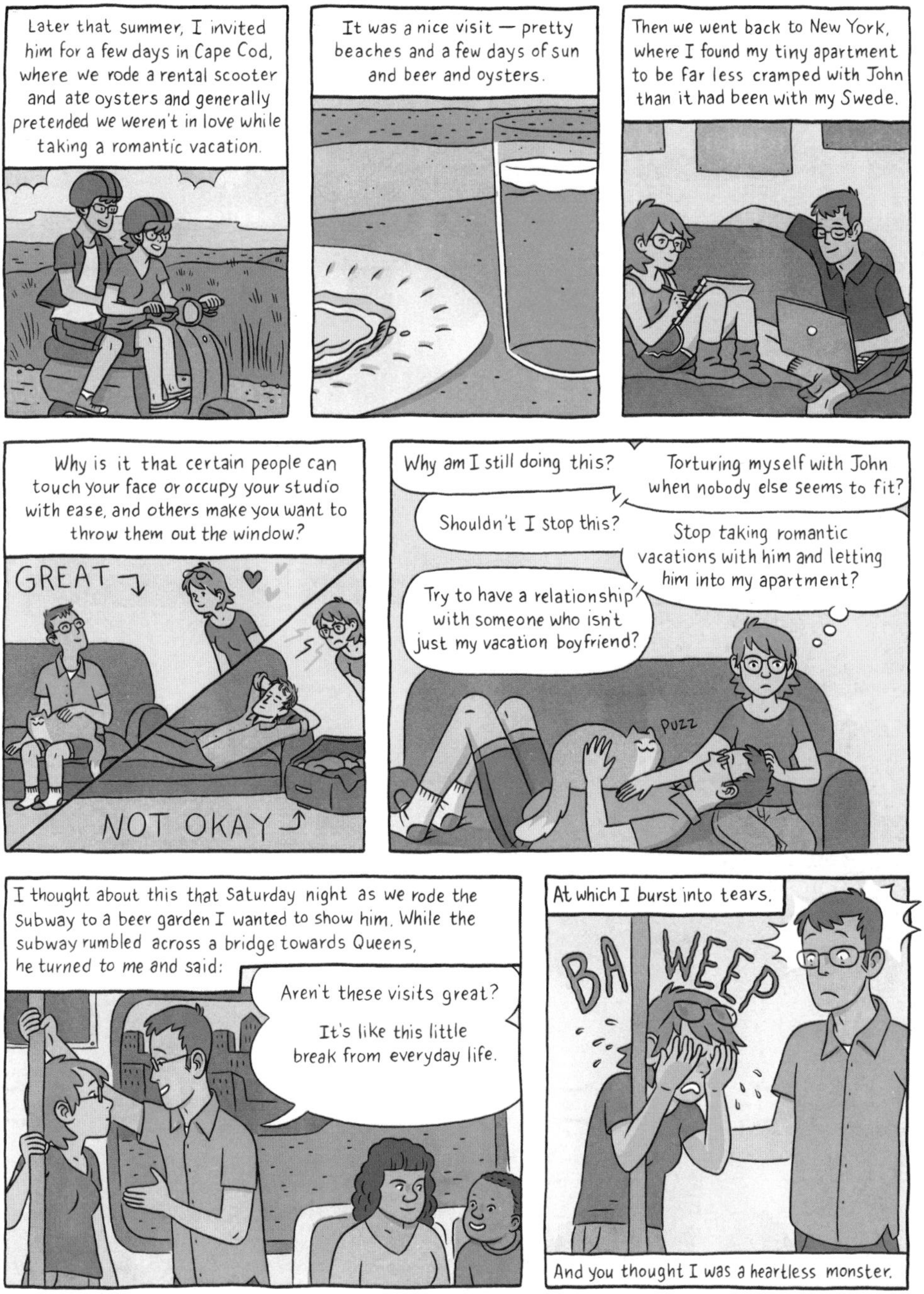
Later that summer, I invited him for a few days in Cape Cod, where we rode a rental scooter and ate oysters and generally pretended we weren't in love while taking a romantic vacation.
It was a nice visit — pretty beaches and a few days of sun and beer and oysters.
Then we went back to New York, where I found my tiny apartment to be far less cramped with John than it had been with my Swede.
Why is it that certain people can touch your face or occupy your studio with ease, and others make you want to throw them out the window?
GREAT
NOT OKAY
Why am I still doing this?
Torturing myself with John when nobody else seems to fit?
Shouldn't I stop this?
Stop taking romantic vacations with him and letting him into my apartment?
Try to have a relationship with someone who isn't just my vacation boyfriend?
PUZZ
I thought about this that Saturday night as we rode the subway to a beer garden I wanted to show him. While the subway rumbled across a bridge towards Queens, he turned to me and said:
Aren't these visits great?
It's like this little break from everyday life.
At which I burst into tears.
BA WEEP
And you thought I was a heartless monster.

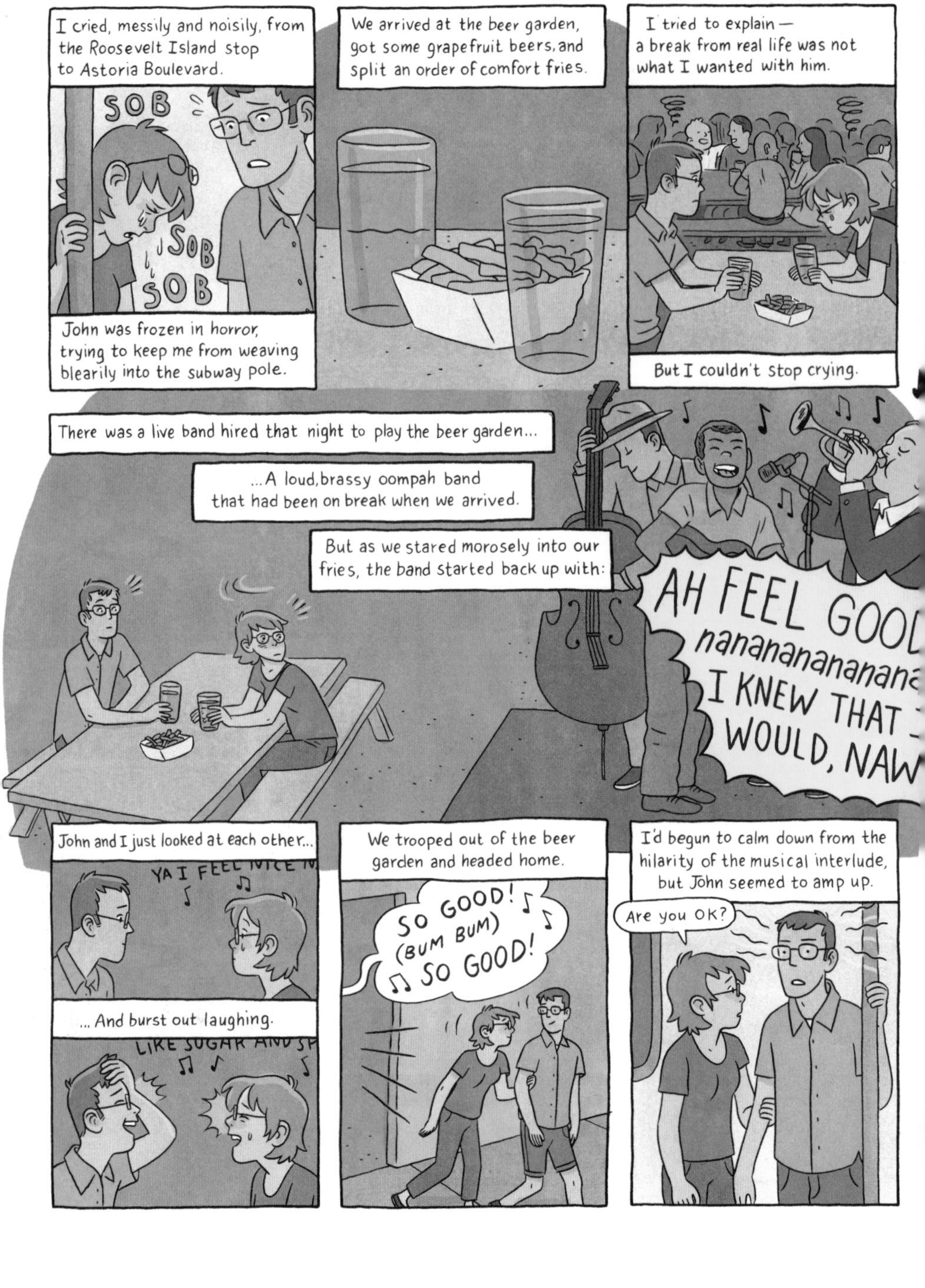

I cried, messily and noisily, from the Roosevelt Island stop to Astoria Boulevard.
SOB
SOB
SOB
John was frozen in horror, trying to keep me from weaving blearily into the subway pole.
We arrived at the beer garden, got some grapefruit beers, and split an order of comfort fries.
I tried to explain— a break from real life was not what I wanted with him.
But I couldn't stop crying.
There was a live band hired that night to play the beer garden...
...A loud, brassy oompah band that had been on break when we arrived.
But as we stared morosely into our fries, the band started back up with:
AH FEEL GOOD
nananananananana
I KNEW THAT
WOULD, NAW
John and I just looked at each other...
... And burst out laughing.
We trooped out of the beer garden and headed home.
SO GOOD! (BUM BUM) SO GOOD!
I'd begun to calm down from the hilarity of the musical interlude, but John seemed to amp up.
Are you OK?

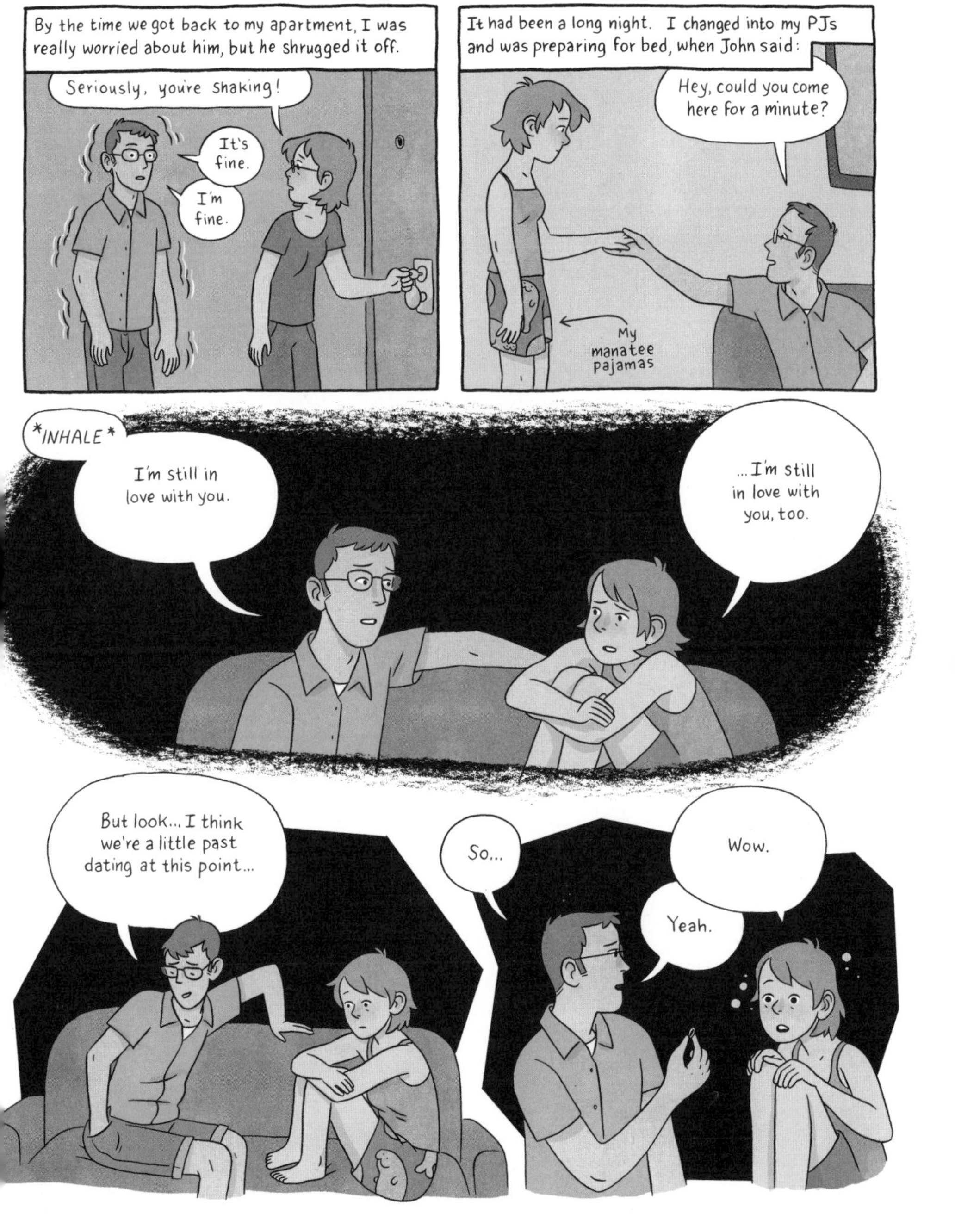
By the time we got back to my apartment, I was really worried about him, but he shrugged it off.
Seriously, you're shaking!
It's fine.
I'm fine.
It had been a long night. I changed into my PJs and was preparing for bed, when John said:
Hey, could you come here for a minute?
My manatee pajamas
INHALE
I'm still in love with you.
...I'm still in love with you, too.
But look... I think we're a little past dating at this point...
So...
Wow.
Yeah.

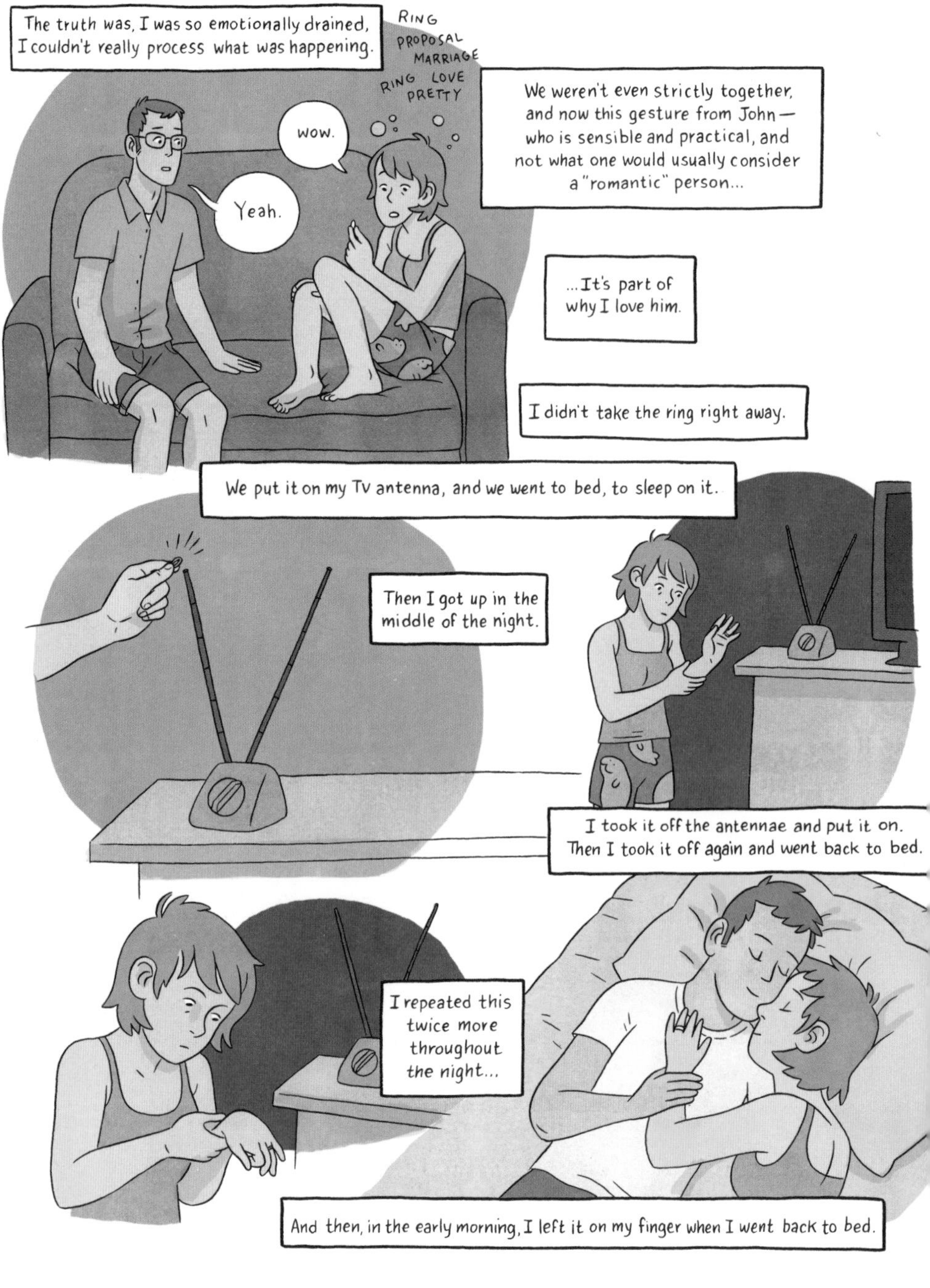

The truth was, I was so emotionally drained, I couldn't really process what was happening.
RING
PROPOSAL
MARRIAGE
RING LOVE
PRETTY
WOW.
Yeah.
We weren't even strictly together, and now this gesture from John — who is sensible and practical, and not what one would usually consider a "romantic" person...
...It's part of why I love him.
I didn't take the ring right away.
We put it on my TV antenna, and we went to bed, to sleep on it.
Then I got up in the middle of the night.
I took it off the antennae and put it on. Then I took it off again and went back to bed.
I repeated this twice more throughout the night...
And then, in the early morning, I left it on my finger when I went back to bed.

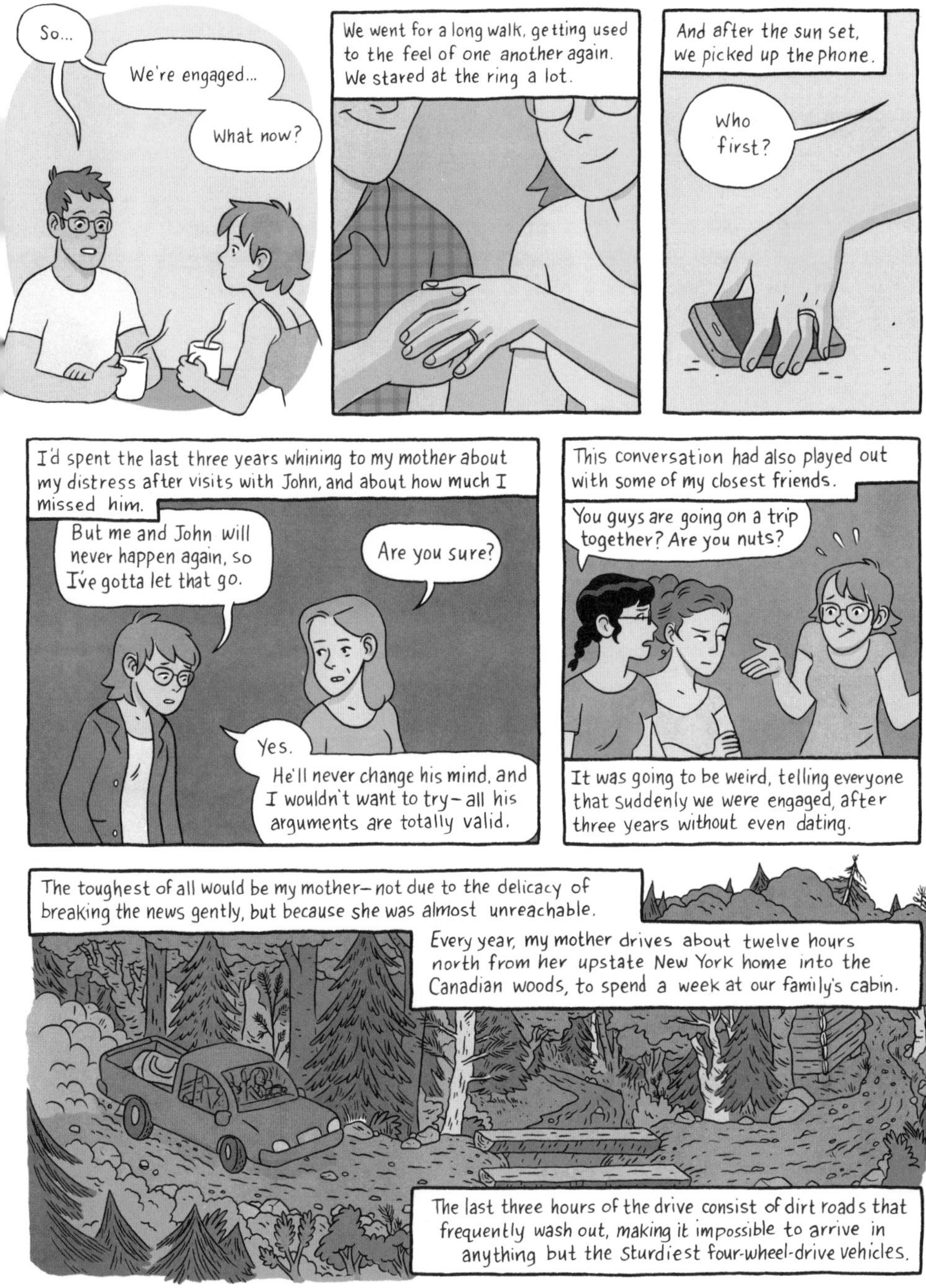
So...
We're engaged...
What now?
We went for a long walk, getting used to the feel of one another again. We stared at the ring a lot.
And after the sun set, we picked up the phone.
Who first?
I'd spent the last three years whining to my mother about my distress after visits with John, and about how much I missed him.
But me and John will never happen again, so I've gotta let that go.
Are you sure?
Yes.
He'll never change his mind, and I wouldn't want to try— all his arguments are totally valid.
This conversation had also played out with some of my closest friends.
You guys are going on a trip together? Are you nuts?
It was going to be weird, telling everyone that suddenly we were engaged, after three years without even dating.
The toughest of all would be my mother— not due to the delicacy of breaking the news gently, but because she was almost unreachable.
Every year, my mother drives about twelve hours north from her upstate New York home into the Canadian woods, to spend a week at our family's cabin.
The last three hours of the drive consist of dirt roads that frequently wash out, making it impossible to arrive in anything but the sturdiest four-wheel-drive vehicles.

Mom taught me to drive along this road to the cabin — first sitting on her lap and steering...

(Age five)

...Then navigating the steering and pedals myself...

(Age seven)

...And once, when I was nine or so, without *any* influence from the passenger's seat.*

* My mom was going through a divorce...

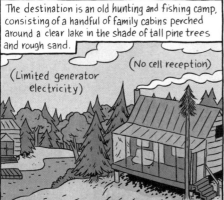

The destination is an old hunting and fishing camp, consisting of a handful of family cabins perched around a clear lake in the shade of tall pine trees and rough sand.

(Limited generator electricity)

(No cell reception)

Breakfast and dinners at the camp are still served at a dining hall, where everyone in the cabins gather to eat pancakes or ham.

There's also a phone. Yes, *one* phone for everyone.

It's a satellite phone, which has the faraway sound of calling someone in outer space. It's reserved, mostly, for emergencies.

CRACKLE
CRACKLE

I had to wait until dinner began at the camp to make my call.

Je voudrais parler à Georgia, sil vous plait!

Ne quittez pas!

CRACKLE CRACKLE CRACKLE

She answered from outer space, breathless with panic and expected disaster.

WHO DIED?!
WHAT'S WRONG!?

64

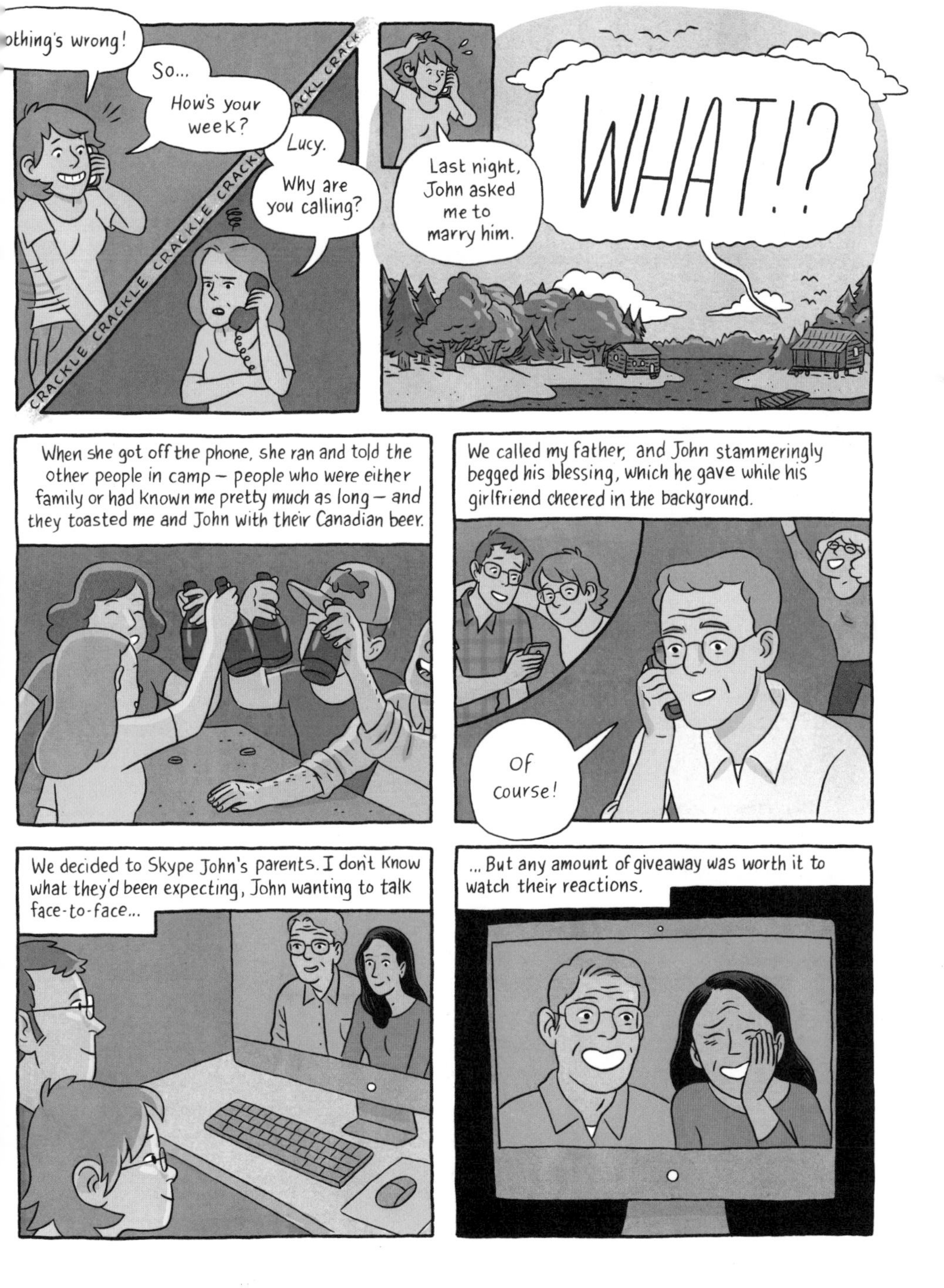

othing's wrong!
So... How's your week?
CRACKLE CRACKLE CRACKLE CRACKLE CRACKL CRACK
Lucy. Why are you calling?
Last night, John asked me to marry him.
WHAT!?
When she got off the phone, she ran and told the other people in camp – people who were either family or had known me pretty much as long – and they toasted me and John with their Canadian beer.
We called my father, and John stammeringly begged his blessing, which he gave while his girlfriend cheered in the background.
Of course!
We decided to Skype John's parents. I don't know what they'd been expecting, John wanting to talk face-to-face...
... But any amount of giveaway was worth it to watch their reactions.

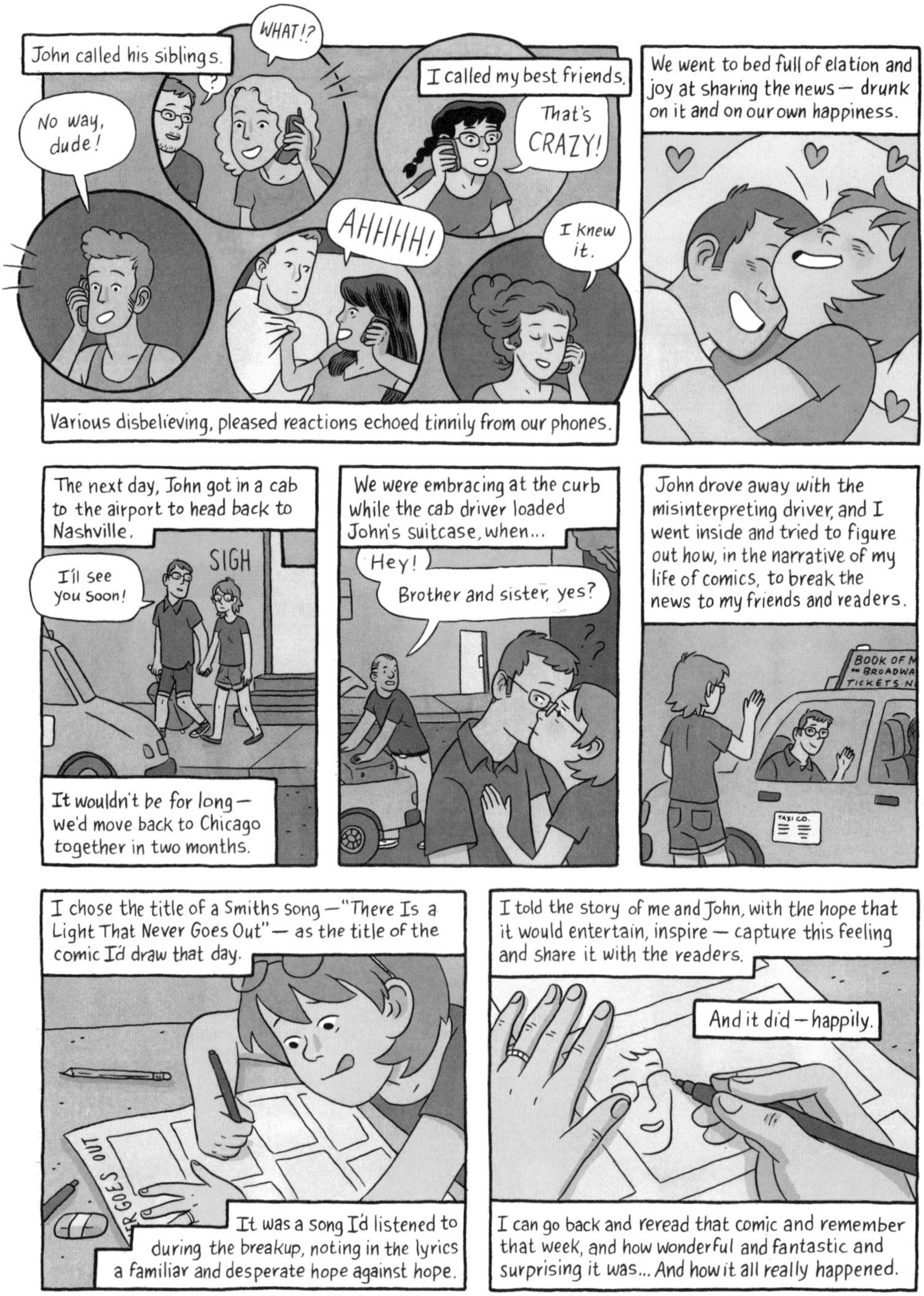
John called his siblings.
WHAT!?
?
No way, dude!
I called my best friends.
That's CRAZY!
AHHHH!
I knew it.
Various disbelieving, pleased reactions echoed tinnily from our phones.
We went to bed full of elation and joy at sharing the news — drunk on it and on our own happiness.
The next day, John got in a cab to the airport to head back to Nashville.
I'll see you soon!
SIGH
It wouldn't be for long — we'd move back to Chicago together in two months.
We were embracing at the curb while the cab driver loaded John's suitcase, when...
Hey!
Brother and sister, yes?
??
John drove away with the misinterpreting driver, and I went inside and tried to figure out how, in the narrative of my life of comics, to break the news to my friends and readers.
TAXI CO.
I chose the title of a Smiths song — "There Is a Light That Never Goes Out" — as the title of the comic I'd draw that day.
GOES OUT
It was a song I'd listened to during the breakup, noting in the lyrics a familiar and desperate hope against hope.
I told the story of me and John, with the hope that it would entertain, inspire — capture this feeling and share it with the readers.
And it did — happily.
I can go back and reread that comic and remember that week, and how wonderful and fantastic and surprising it was... And how it all really happened.

Sometimes I still can't believe

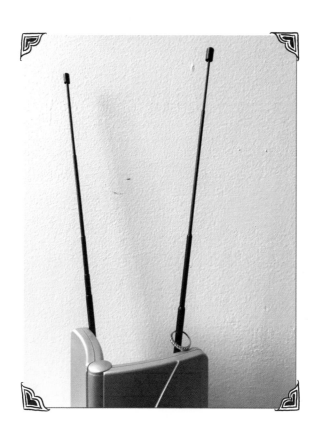

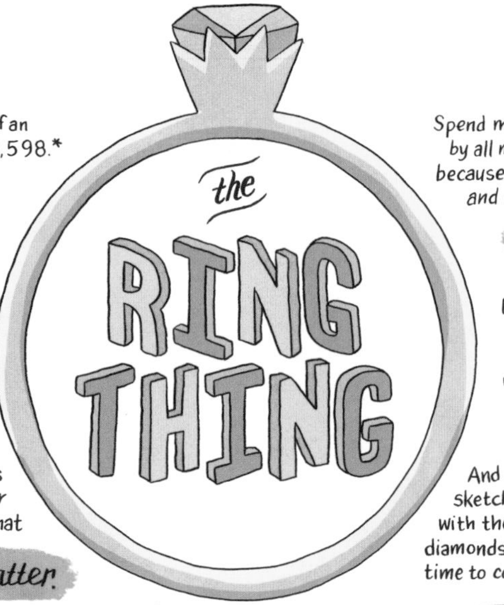

the RING THING

The average cost of an engagement ring is $5,598.*

There's also that ridiculous statistic about the percentage of income one is *obligated* to spend on an engagement ring.

oh, please.

It's exactly this thing—the implied "HAVE TO"—that makes people spend too much on their weddings, and often on stuff that

does not matter.

Spend money on what you want, by all means, but don't do it because of societal conventions and diamond lobbyists.

Gross.

Diamond engagement rings didn't even become a real "tradition" until 1938, when the De Beers diamond cartel began aggressively marketing them.

And considering the sketchy ethics associated with the mining and sale of diamonds and gold, perhaps it's time to consider some...

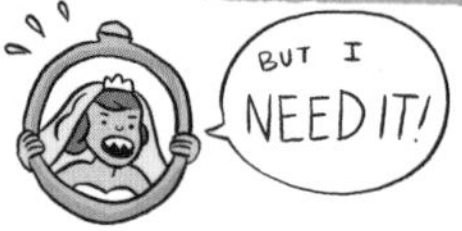
BUT I NEED IT!

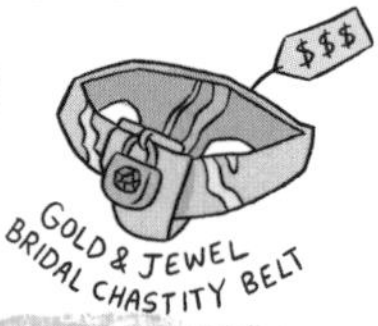
$$$
GOLD & JEWEL BRIDAL CHASTITY BELT

...Alternatives:

1. Go Vintage

There are an awful lot of old rings going unworn and unappreciated. You can snag an antique ring from a vintage shop or online, or better yet, track down an old ring from family members that you might use.

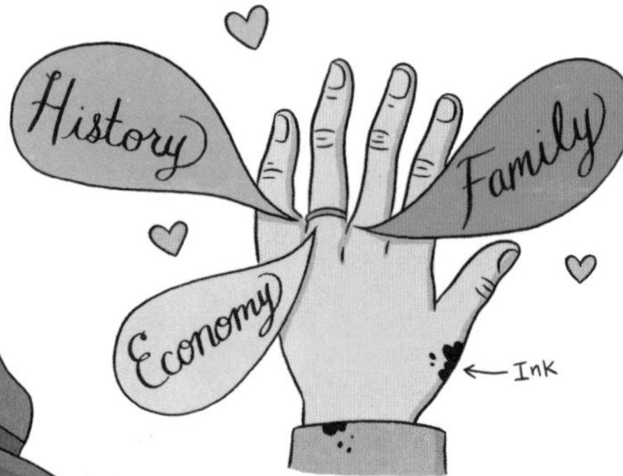
History
Family
Economy
Ink

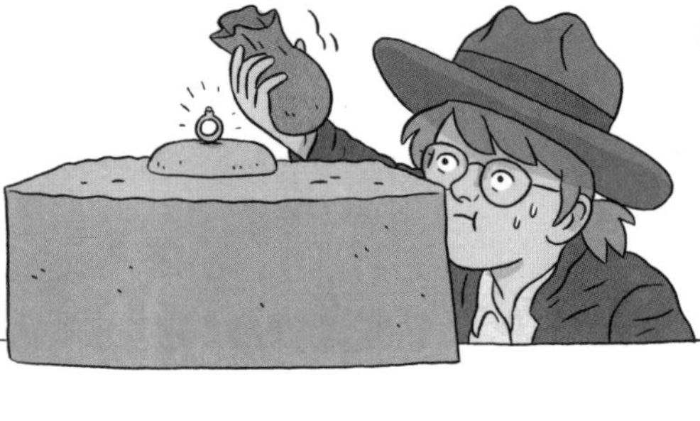

Mine belonged to John's Grandma Marsha. It was her wedding band, and suits me perfectly in its history and simplicity (and price, frankly. Who wants to wear $90,000 on the same hand they use to smudge paint and ink?).

*According to the 2013 Average Wedding Budget Breakdown from The Knot

2. Two For One

If you do want to pick a special ring, or have it made, perhaps one doesn't need another. One ring that serves as an engagement ring and wedding band can be elegant and simple. Bonus: then everyone in the marriage can wear the same number of rings—*Equality*!

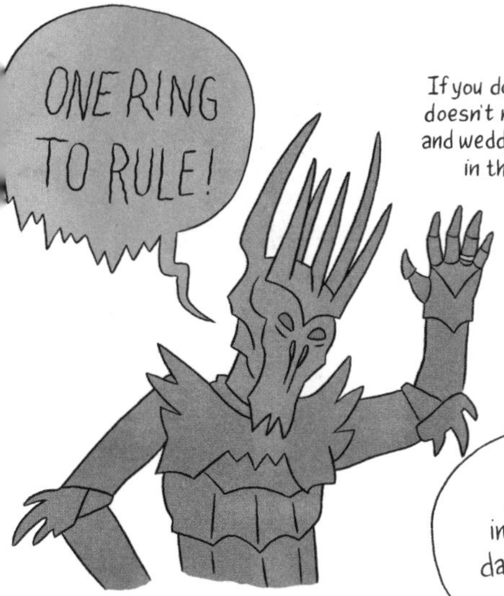

ONE RING TO RULE!

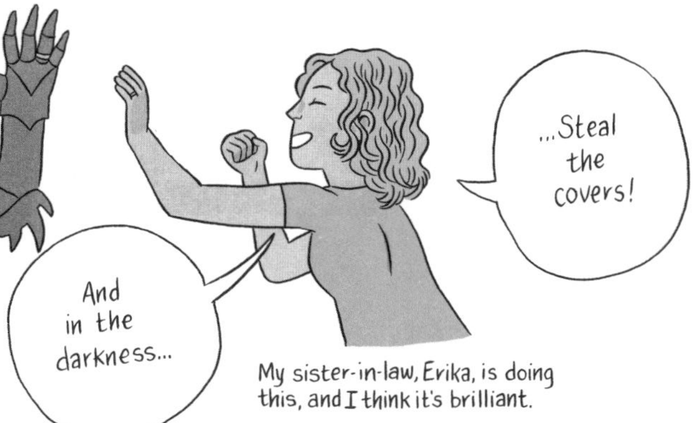

...Steal the covers!
And in the darkness...

My sister-in-law, Erika, is doing this, and I think it's brilliant.

3. No Ring at All

I have friends with wedding necklaces, wedding tattoos, and wedding earrings. Especially if you're not a ring person, remember there's no rule to say you *HAVE* to wear one. Perhaps some other trinket to signify your bond would better suit you.

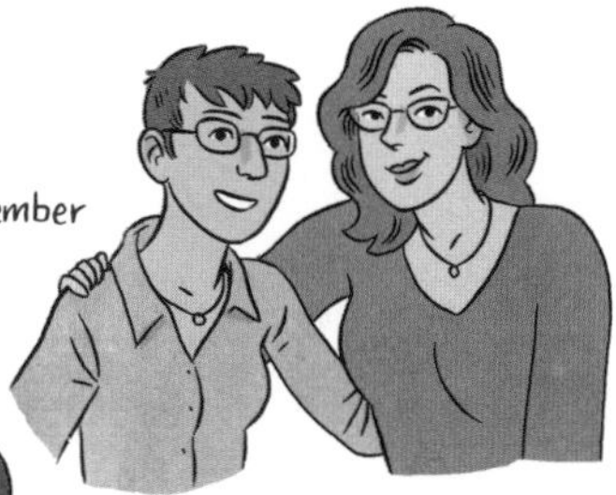

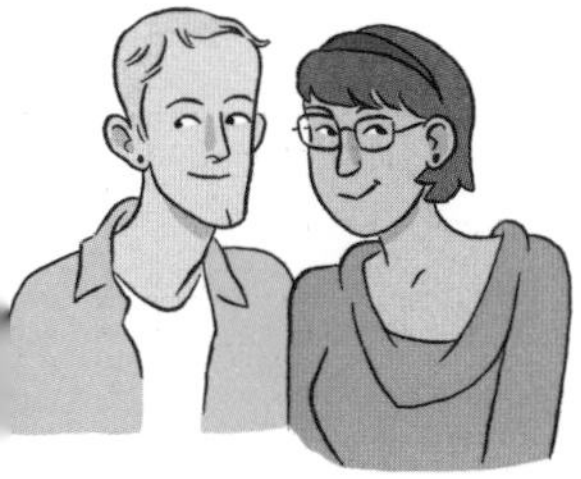

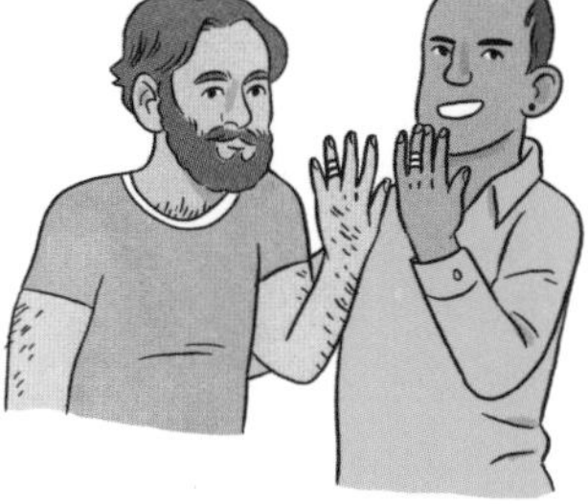

An Engagement Boa, perhaps?

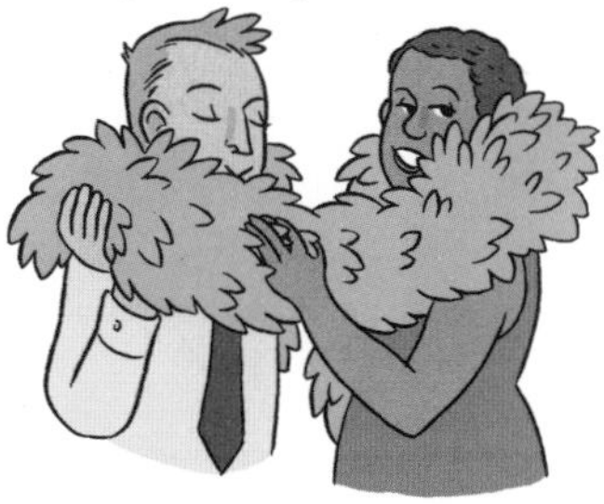

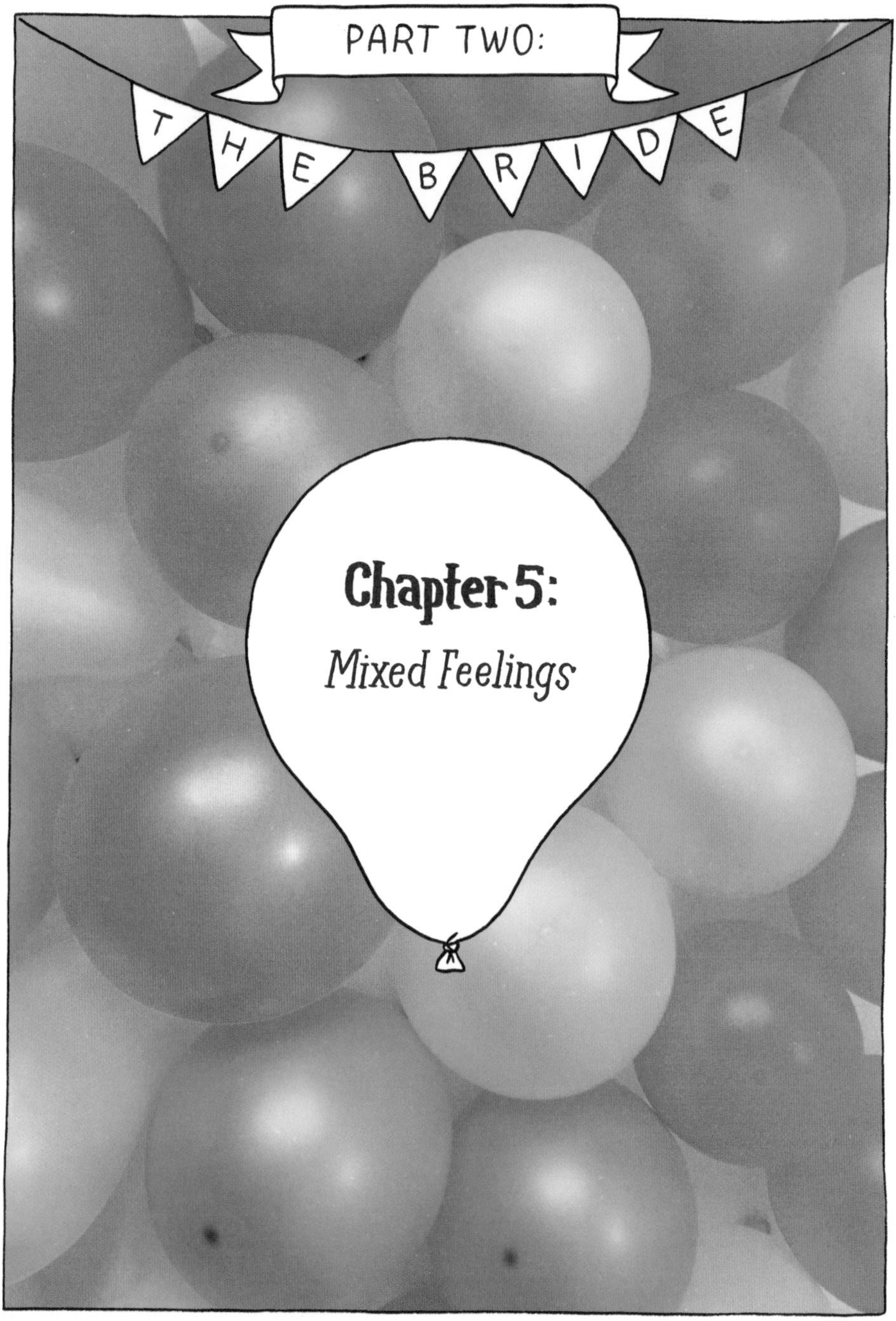
PART TWO:
THE BRIDE
Chapter 5:
Mixed Feelings

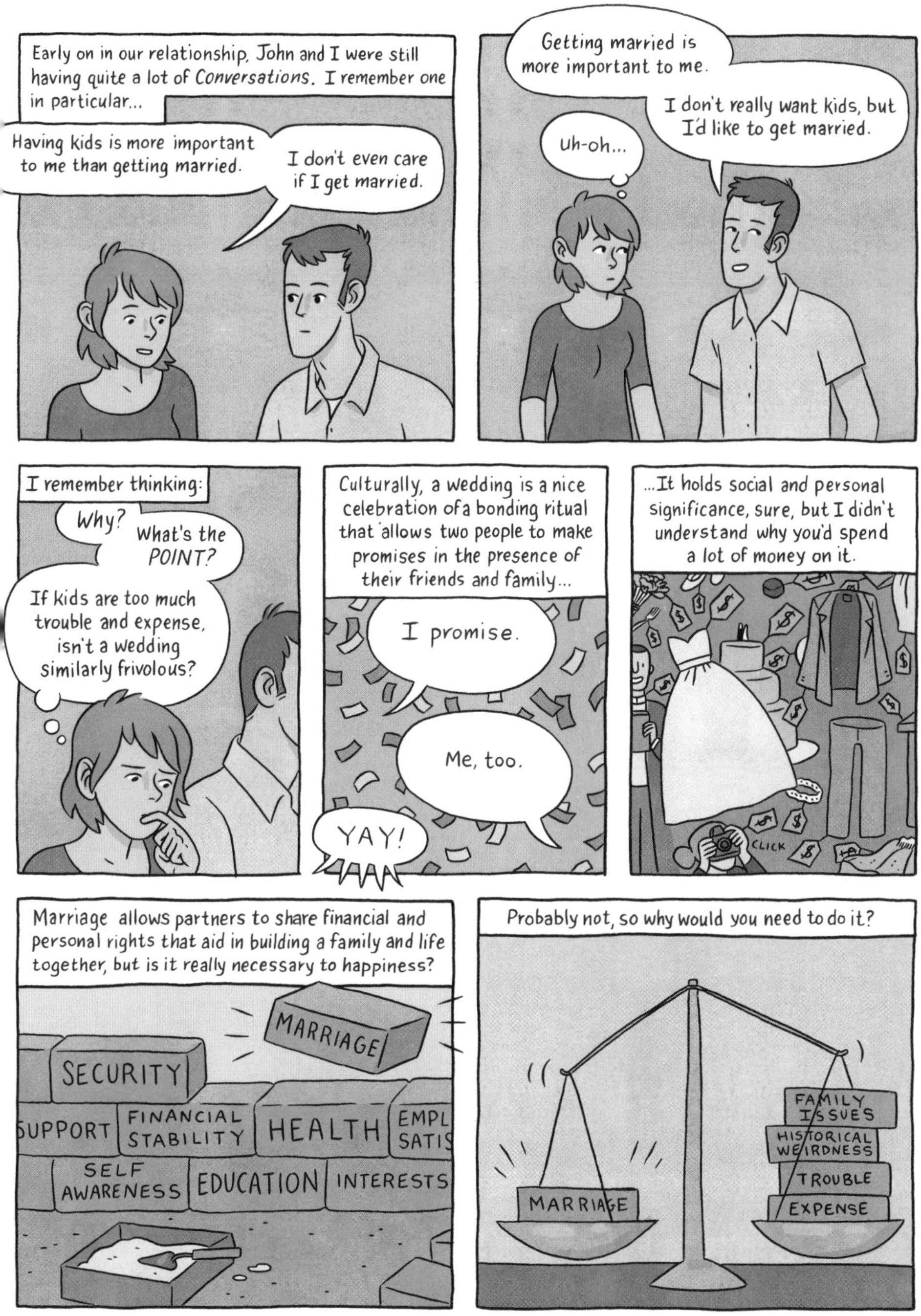

Early on in our relationship, John and I were still having quite a lot of *Conversations*. I remember one in particular...
Having kids is more important to me than getting married.
I don't even care if I get married.
Getting married is more important to me.
I don't really want kids, but I'd like to get married.
Uh-oh...
I remember thinking:
Why?
What's the *POINT?*
If kids are too much trouble and expense, isn't a wedding similarly frivolous?
Culturally, a wedding is a nice celebration of a bonding ritual that allows two people to make promises in the presence of their friends and family...
I promise.
Me, too.
YAY!
...It holds social and personal significance, sure, but I didn't understand why you'd spend a lot of money on it.
CLICK
Marriage allows partners to share financial and personal rights that aid in building a family and life together, but is it really necessary to happiness?
MARRIAGE
SECURITY
SUPPORT
FINANCIAL STABILITY
HEALTH
EMPL SATIS
SELF AWARENESS
EDUCATION
INTERESTS
Probably not, so why would you need to do it?
MARRIAGE
FAMILY ISSUES
HISTORICAL WEIRDNESS
TROUBLE
EXPENSE

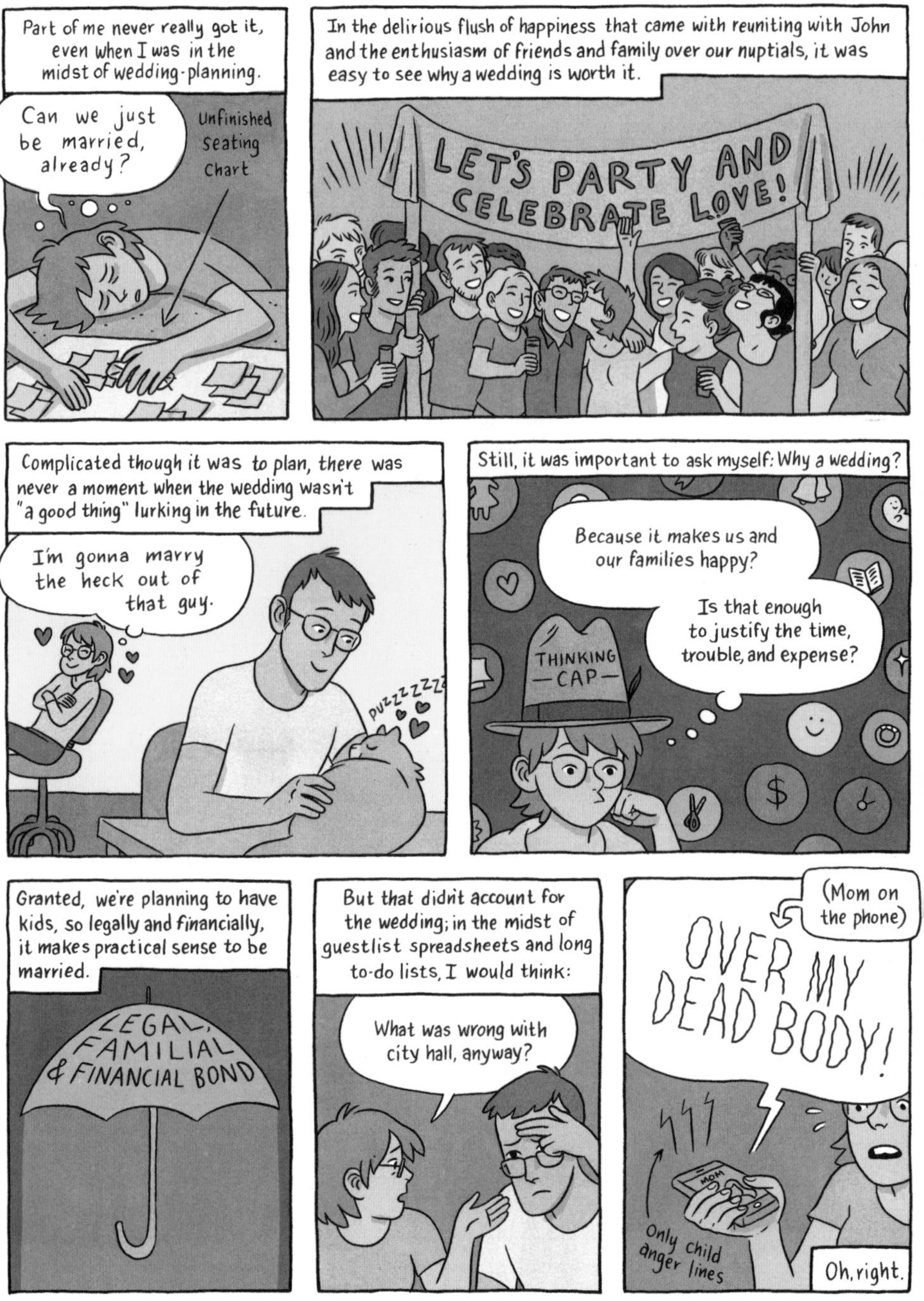
Part of me never really got it, even when I was in the midst of wedding-planning.
Can we just be married, already?
Unfinished seating chart
In the delirious flush of happiness that came with reuniting with John and the enthusiasm of friends and family over our nuptials, it was easy to see why a wedding is worth it.
LET'S PARTY AND CELEBRATE LOVE!
Complicated though it was to plan, there was never a moment when the wedding wasn't "a good thing" lurking in the future.
I'm gonna marry the heck out of that guy.
PUZZZZZZ
Still, it was important to ask myself: Why a wedding?
Because it makes us and our families happy?
Is that enough to justify the time, trouble, and expense?
THINKING CAP
Granted, we're planning to have kids, so legally and financially, it makes practical sense to be married.
LEGAL, FAMILIAL & FINANCIAL BOND
But that didn't account for the wedding; in the midst of guestlist spreadsheets and long to-do lists, I would think:
What was wrong with city hall, anyway?
(Mom on the phone)
OVER MY DEAD BODY!
MOM
Only child anger lines
Oh, right.

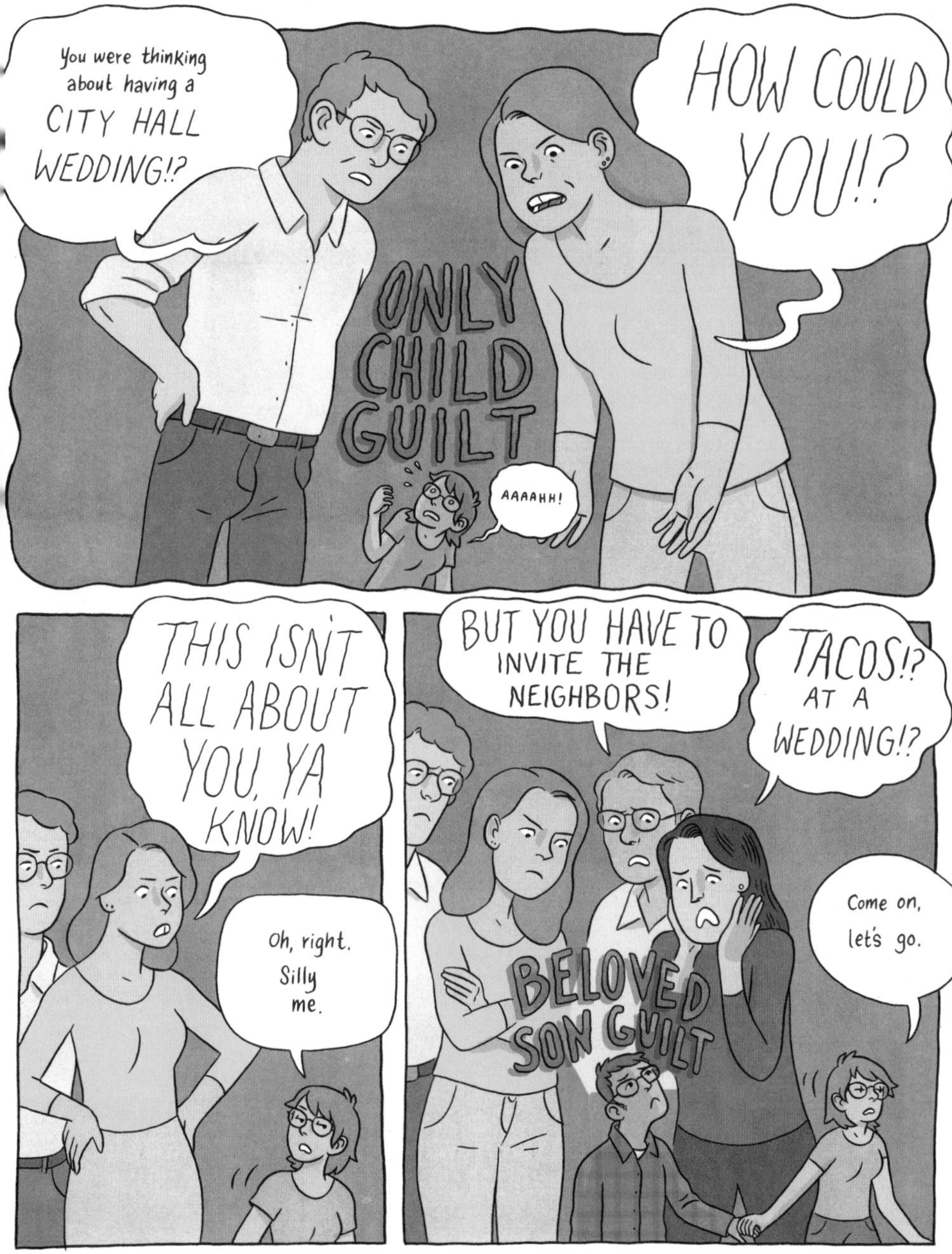
You were thinking about having a CITY HALL WEDDING!?
HOW COULD YOU!?
ONLY CHILD GUILT
AAAAHH!
THIS ISN'T ALL ABOUT YOU, YA KNOW!
Oh, right. Silly me.
BUT YOU HAVE TO INVITE THE NEIGHBORS!
TACOS!? AT A WEDDING!?
BELOVED SON GUILT
Come on, let's go.

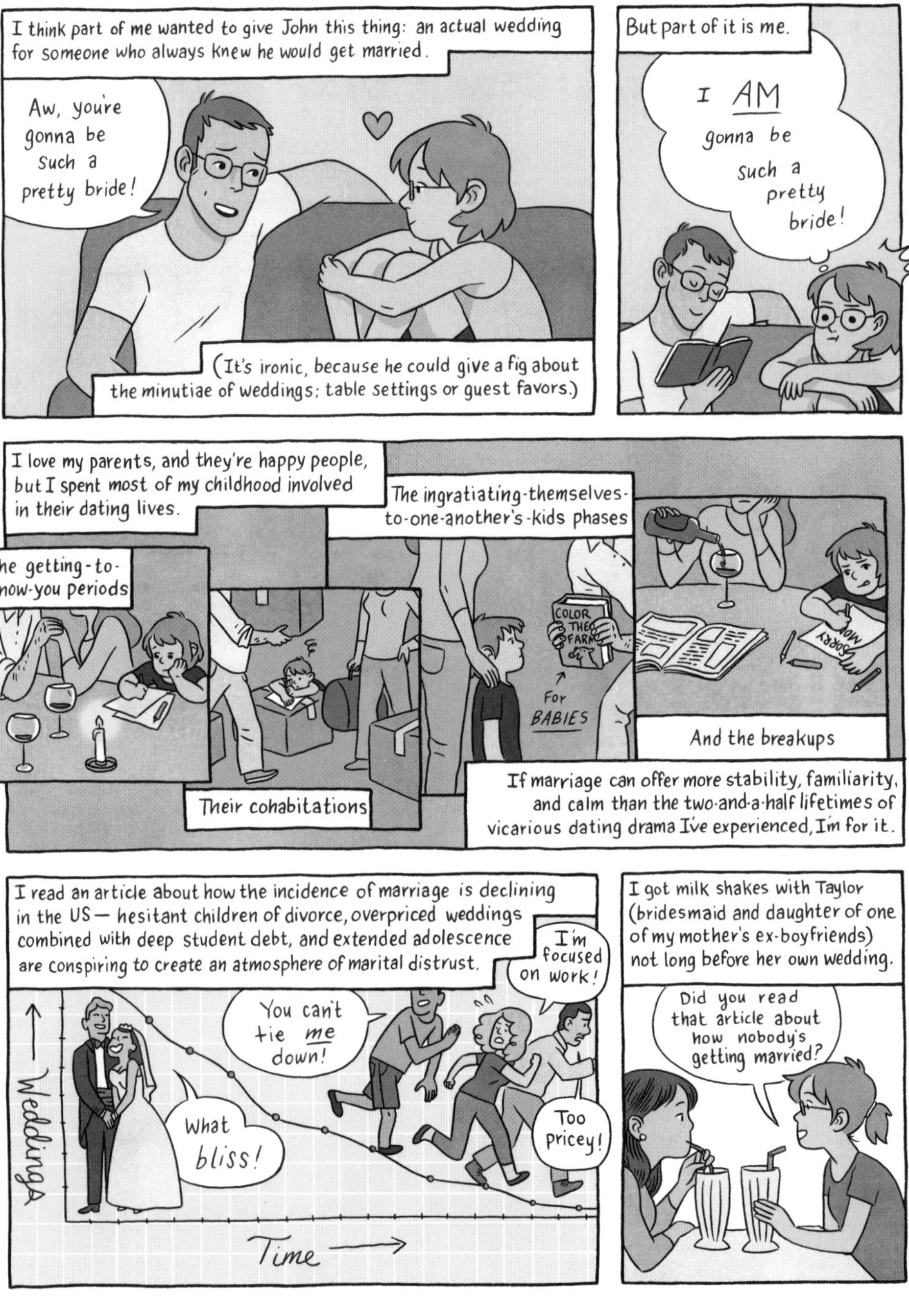
I think part of me wanted to give John this thing: an actual wedding for someone who always knew he would get married.
Aw, you're gonna be such a pretty bride!
(It's ironic, because he could give a fig about the minutiae of weddings; table settings or guest favors.)
But part of it is me.
I AM gonna be such a pretty bride!
I love my parents, and they're happy people, but I spent most of my childhood involved in their dating lives.
The getting-to-know-you periods
Their cohabitations
The ingratiating-themselves-to-one-another's-kids phases
COLOR THE FARM
For BABIES
And the breakups
SORRY MOM
If marriage can offer more stability, familiarity, and calm than the two-and-a-half lifetimes of vicarious dating drama I've experienced, I'm for it.
I read an article about how the incidence of marriage is declining in the US — hesitant children of divorce, overpriced weddings combined with deep student debt, and extended adolescence are conspiring to create an atmosphere of marital distrust.
Weddings
Time
What bliss!
You can't tie me down!
I'm focused on work!
Too pricey!
I got milk shakes with Taylor (bridesmaid and daughter of one of my mother's ex-boyfriends) not long before her own wedding.
Did you read that article about how nobody's getting married?

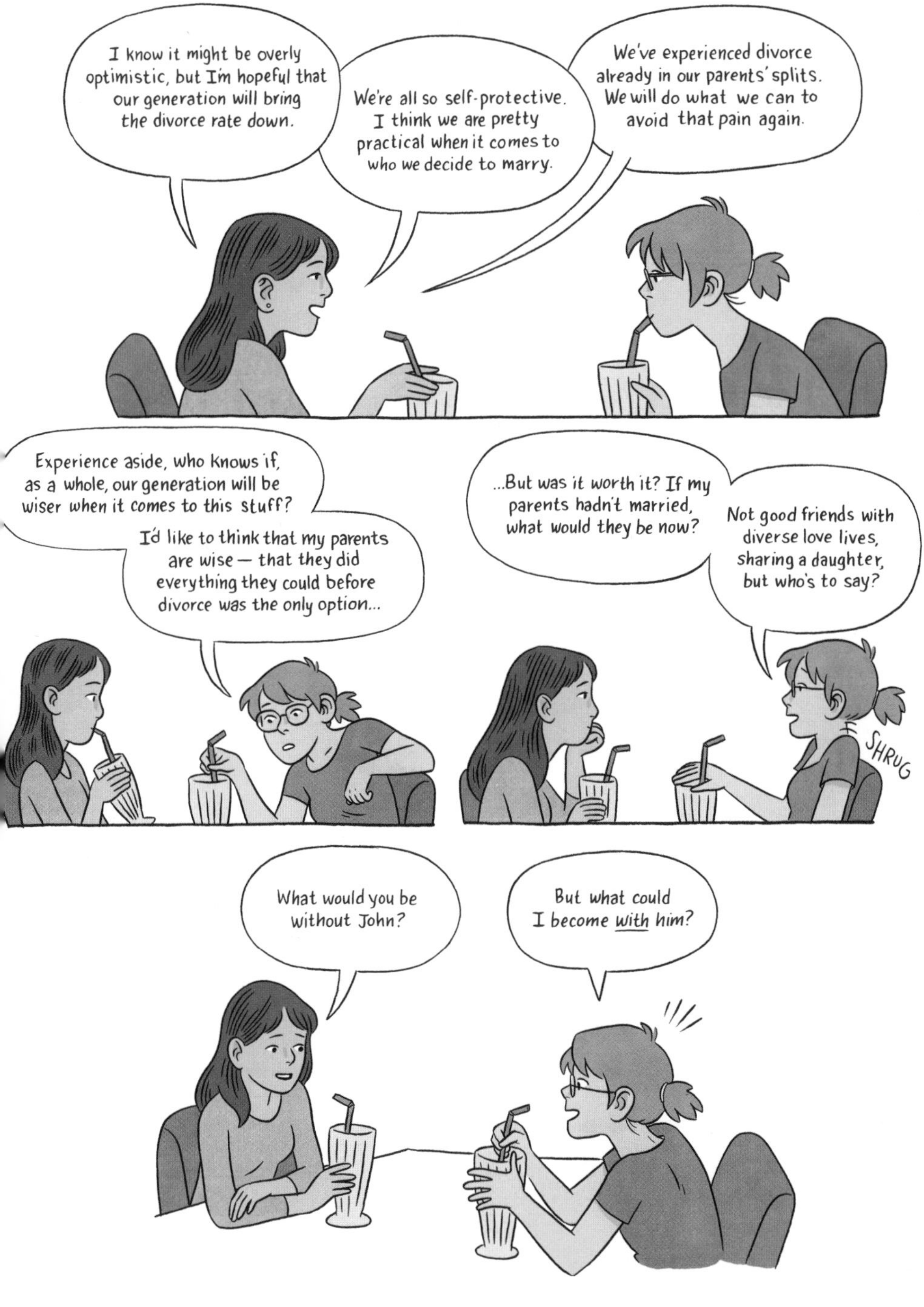
I know it might be overly optimistic, but I'm hopeful that our generation will bring the divorce rate down.
We're all so self-protective. I think we are pretty practical when it comes to who we decide to marry.
We've experienced divorce already in our parents' splits. We will do what we can to avoid that pain again.
Experience aside, who knows if, as a whole, our generation will be wiser when it comes to this stuff?
I'd like to think that my parents are wise — that they did everything they could before divorce was the only option...
...But was it worth it? If my parents hadn't married, what would they be now?
Not good friends with diverse love lives, sharing a daughter, but who's to say?
SHRUG
What would you be without John?
But what could I become with him?

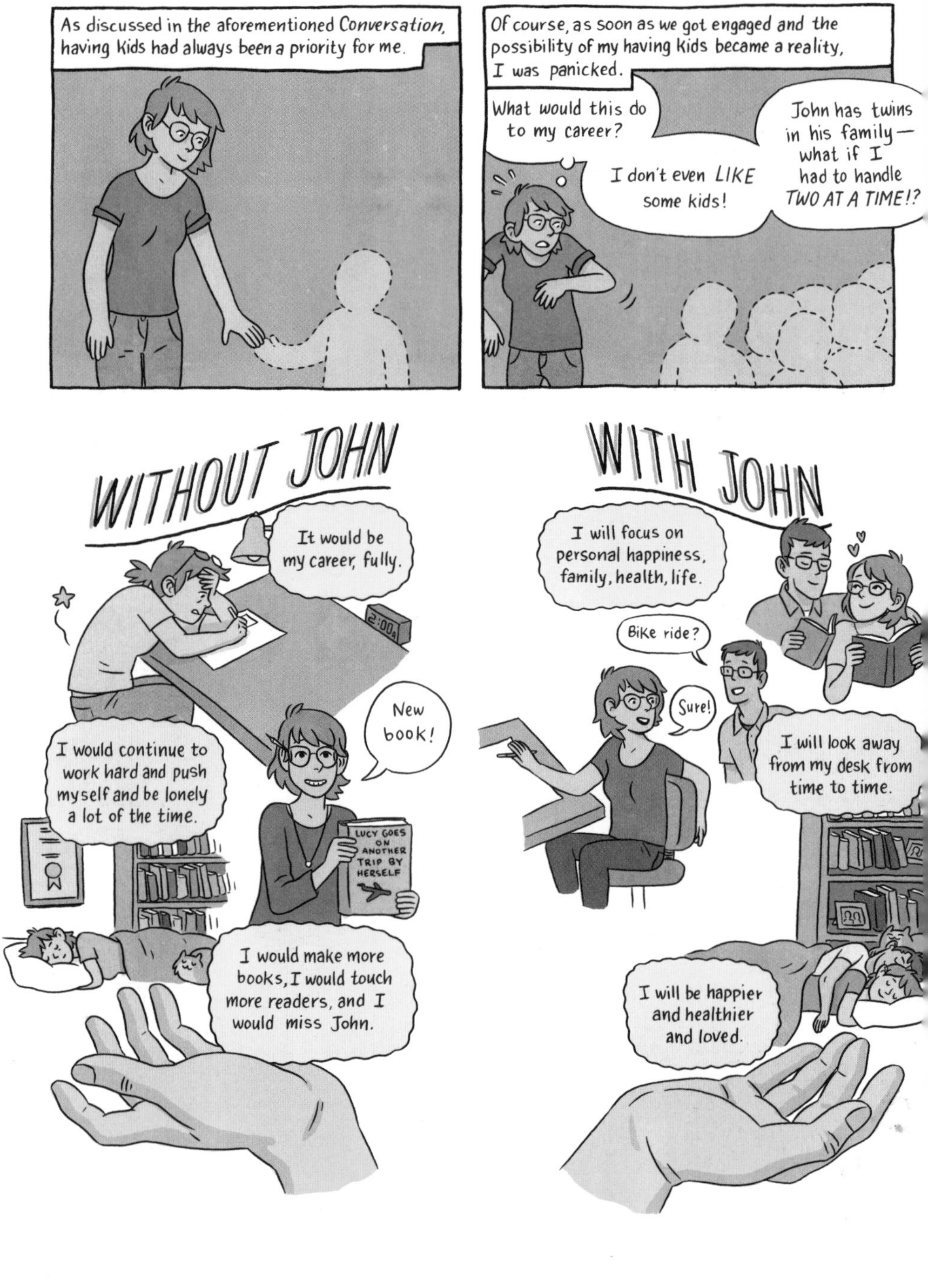
As discussed in the aforementioned Conversation, having kids had always been a priority for me.
Of course, as soon as we got engaged and the possibility of my having kids became a reality, I was panicked.
What would this do to my career?
I don't even LIKE some kids!
John has twins in his family— what if I had to handle TWO AT A TIME!?
WITHOUT JOHN
It would be my career, fully.
2:00
I would continue to work hard and push myself and be lonely a lot of the time.
New book!
LUCY GOES ON ANOTHER TRIP BY HERSELF
I would make more books, I would touch more readers, and I would miss John.
WITH JOHN
I will focus on personal happiness, family, health, life.
Bike ride?
Sure!
I will look away from my desk from time to time.
I will be happier and healthier and loved.

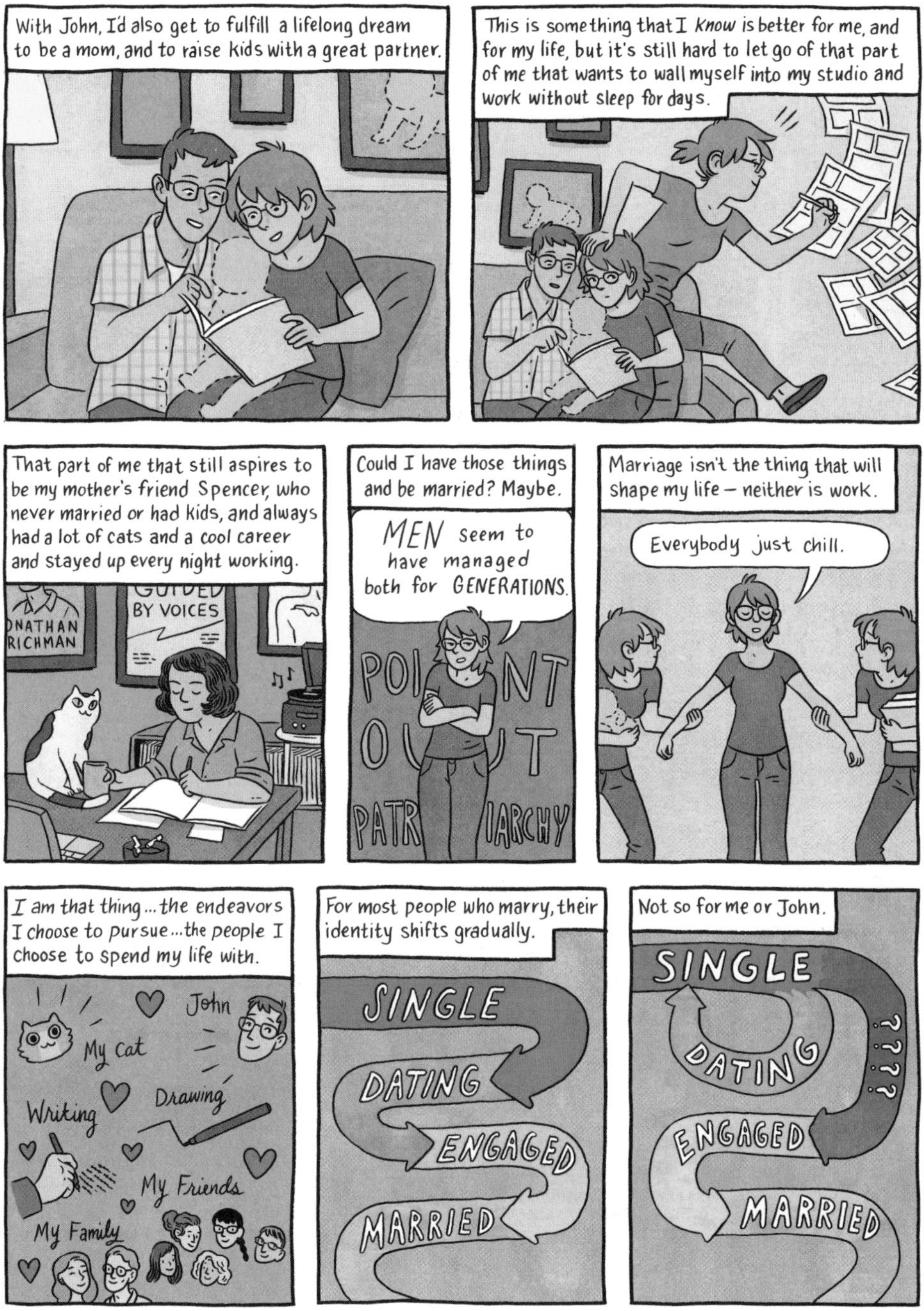

With John, I'd also get to fulfill a lifelong dream to be a mom, and to raise kids with a great partner.
This is something that I *know* is better for me, and for my life, but it's still hard to let go of that part of me that wants to wall myself into my studio and work without sleep for days.
That part of me that still aspires to be my mother's friend Spencer, who never married or had kids, and always had a lot of cats and a cool career and stayed up every night working.
GUIDED BY VOICES
JONATHAN RICHMAN
Could I have those things and be married? Maybe.
MEN seem to have managed both for GENERATIONS.
POINT OUT PATRIARCHY
Marriage isn't the thing that will shape my life — neither is work.
Everybody just chill.
I am that thing... the endeavors I choose to pursue... the people I choose to spend my life with.
John
My Cat
Drawing
Writing
My Friends
My Family
For most people who marry, their identity shifts gradually.
SINGLE
DATING
ENGAGED
MARRIED
Not so for me or John.
SINGLE
DATING
???
???
ENGAGED
MARRIED

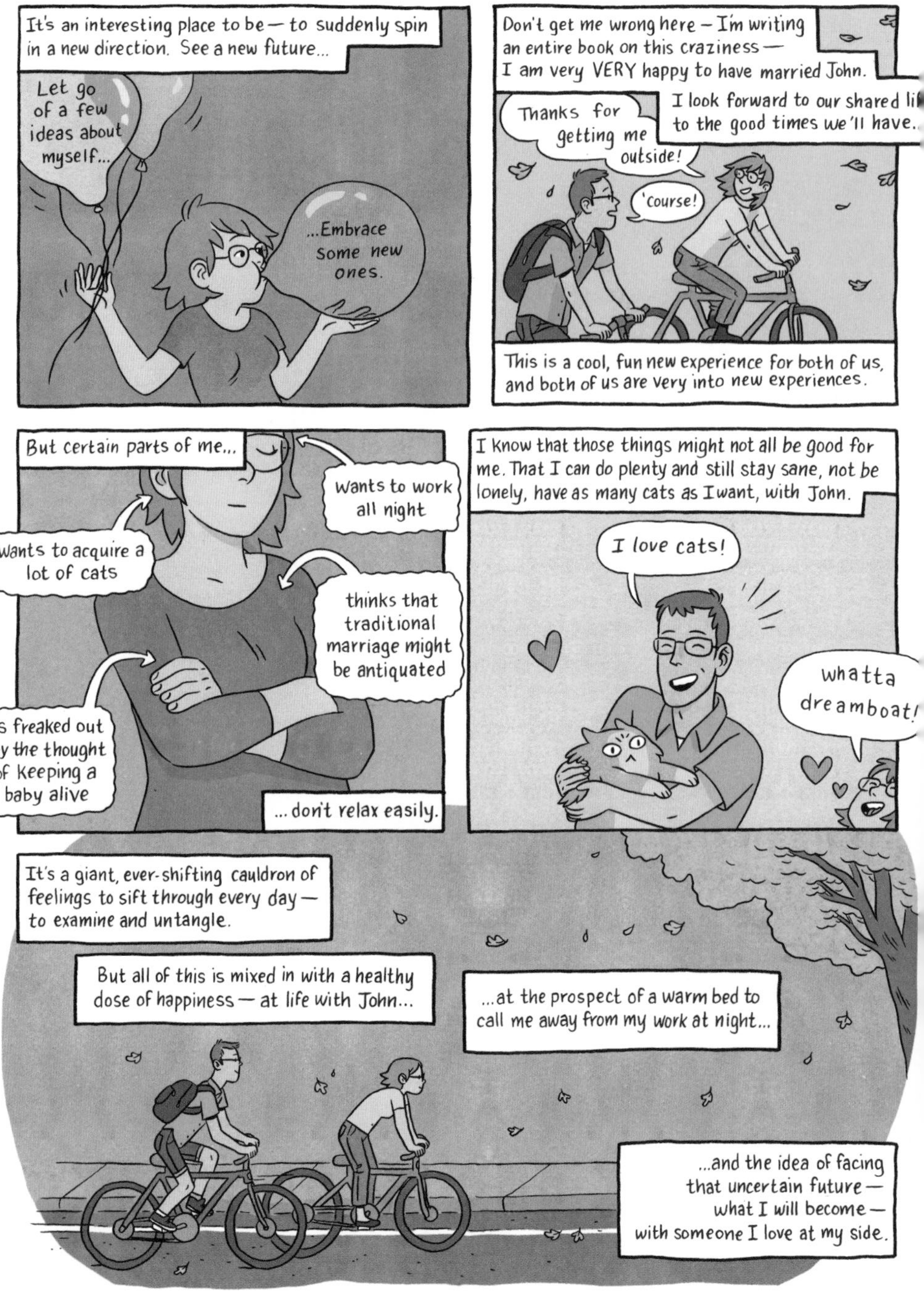

It's an interesting place to be — to suddenly spin in a new direction. See a new future...
Let go of a few ideas about myself...
...Embrace some new ones.
Don't get me wrong here — I'm writing an entire book on this craziness — I am very VERY happy to have married John.
I look forward to our shared li
to the good times we'll have.
Thanks for getting me outside!
'Course!
This is a cool, fun new experience for both of us, and both of us are very into new experiences.
But certain parts of me...
wants to work all night
wants to acquire a lot of cats
thinks that traditional marriage might be antiquated
is freaked out by the thought of keeping a baby alive
...don't relax easily.
I know that those things might not all be good for me. That I can do plenty and still stay sane, not be lonely, have as many cats as I want, with John.
I love cats!
whatta dreamboat!
It's a giant, ever-shifting cauldron of feelings to sift through every day — to examine and untangle.
But all of this is mixed in with a healthy dose of happiness — at life with John...
...at the prospect of a warm bed to call me away from my work at night...
...and the idea of facing that uncertain future — what I will become — with someone I love at my side.

🐱 + 🧑 4EVR

WEIRD WEDDING FACTS

Princess Mary (later known as "Bloody Mary") was promised in marriage at age two and given an engagement ring.

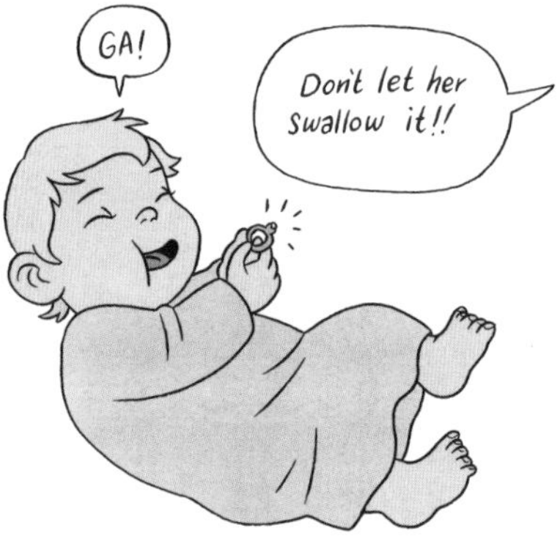
GA!
Don't let her swallow it!!

Pachelbel's Canon in D is the most popular song used in weddings, surpassing the wedding- and bridal-march themes.

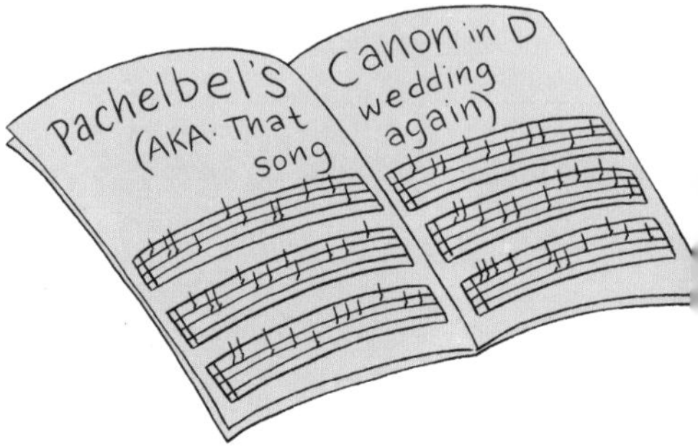
Pachelbel's Canon in D
(AKA: That song wedding again)

The reason the bride carries a bouquet stems from ancient Roman tradition, where the smell of an herbal sachet was to ward away trolls and evil spirits. That's why flowers with strong scents are still commonly used today.

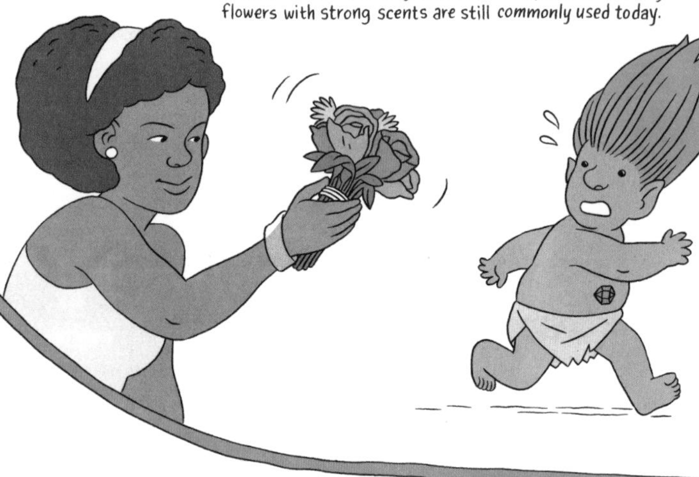

PART 1: EMOTION EDITION

In Morocco, brides typically bathe in milk to purify themselves for the wedding.

After a Korean wedding, there is a tradition where the groom's shoes and socks are removed, he is bound at the feet, and then those feet are beaten with a dead fish. This is supposed to prepare him for married life.

Speaking of feet, in parts of India, the groom takes off his shoes at the altar, and the bride's family is supposed to attempt to steal them, while the groom's family protects them from theft. If the bride's family succeeds in shoe-napping, they hold them hostage for a ransom.

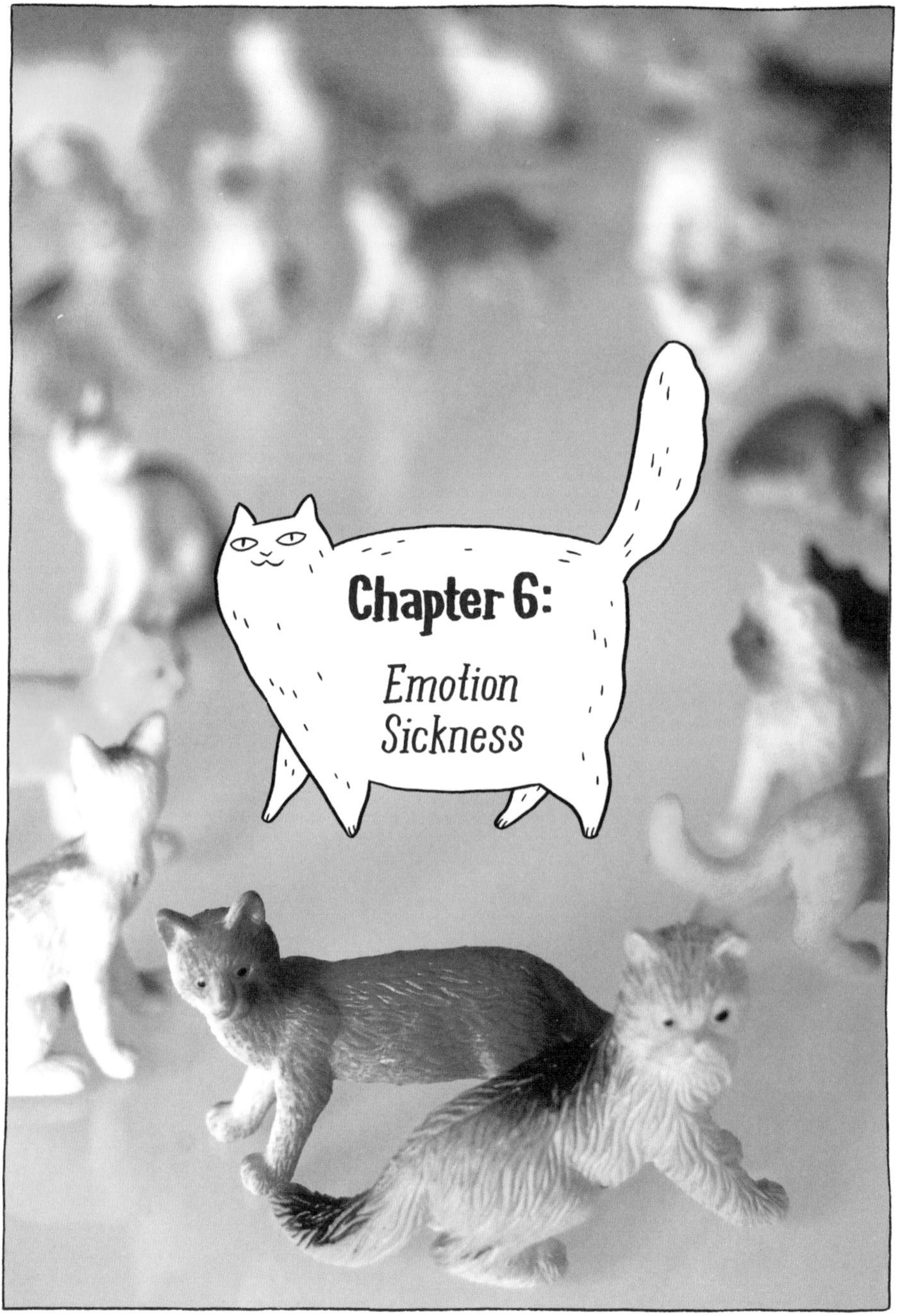
Chapter 6:
Emotion Sickness

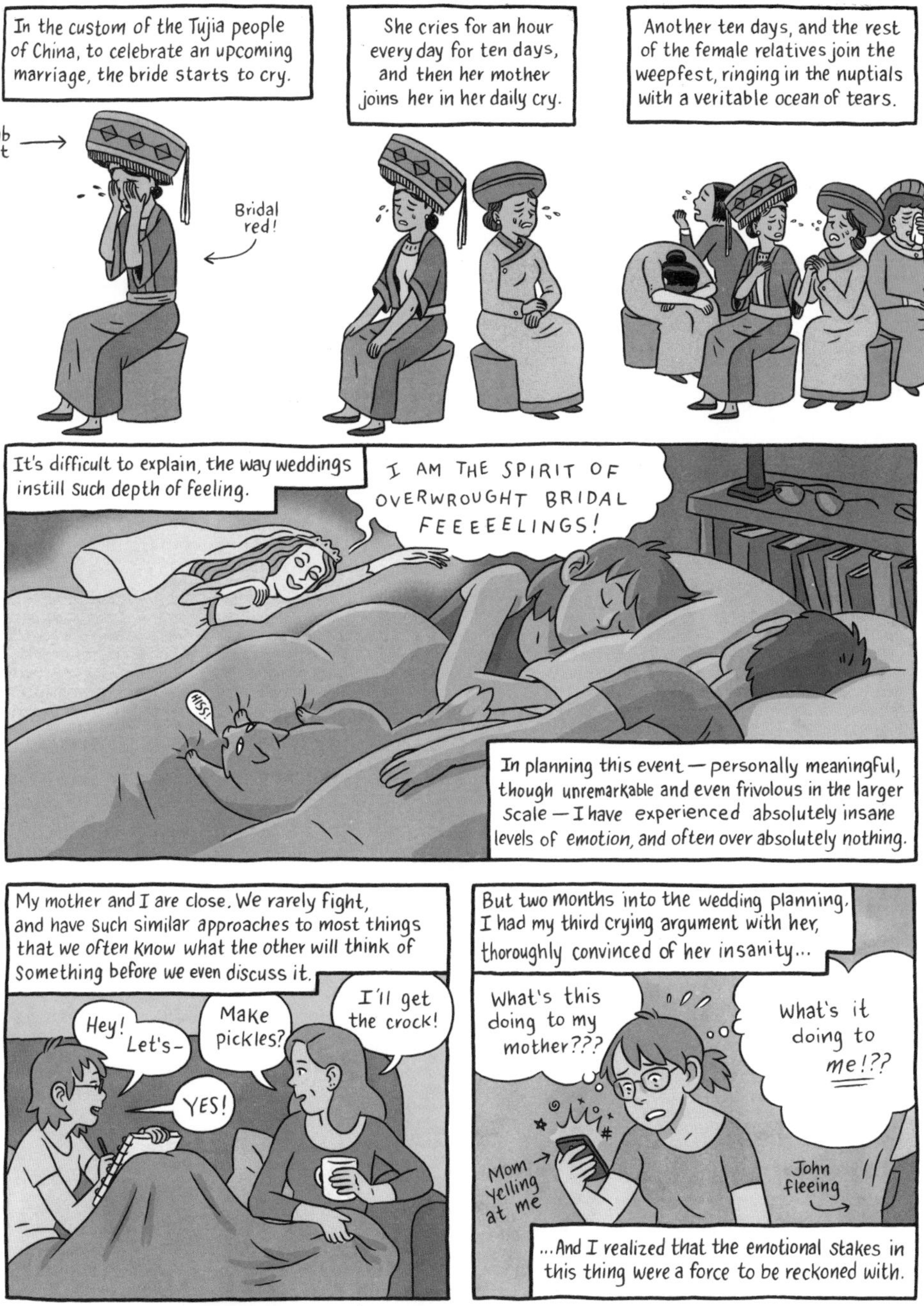
In the custom of the Tujia people of China, to celebrate an upcoming marriage, the bride starts to cry.
Bridal red!
She cries for an hour every day for ten days, and then her mother joins her in her daily cry.
Another ten days, and the rest of the female relatives join the weepfest, ringing in the nuptials with a veritable ocean of tears.
It's difficult to explain, the way weddings instill such depth of feeling.
I AM THE SPIRIT OF OVERWROUGHT BRIDAL FEEEEELINGS!
HISS!
In planning this event — personally meaningful, though unremarkable and even frivolous in the larger scale — I have experienced absolutely insane levels of emotion, and often over absolutely nothing.
My mother and I are close. We rarely fight, and have such similar approaches to most things that we often know what the other will think of something before we even discuss it.
Hey! Let's-
Make pickles?
YES!
I'll get the crock!
But two months into the wedding planning, I had my third crying argument with her, thoroughly convinced of her insanity...
What's this doing to my mother???
What's it doing to me!??
Mom yelling at me
John fleeing
...And I realized that the emotional stakes in this thing were a force to be reckoned with.

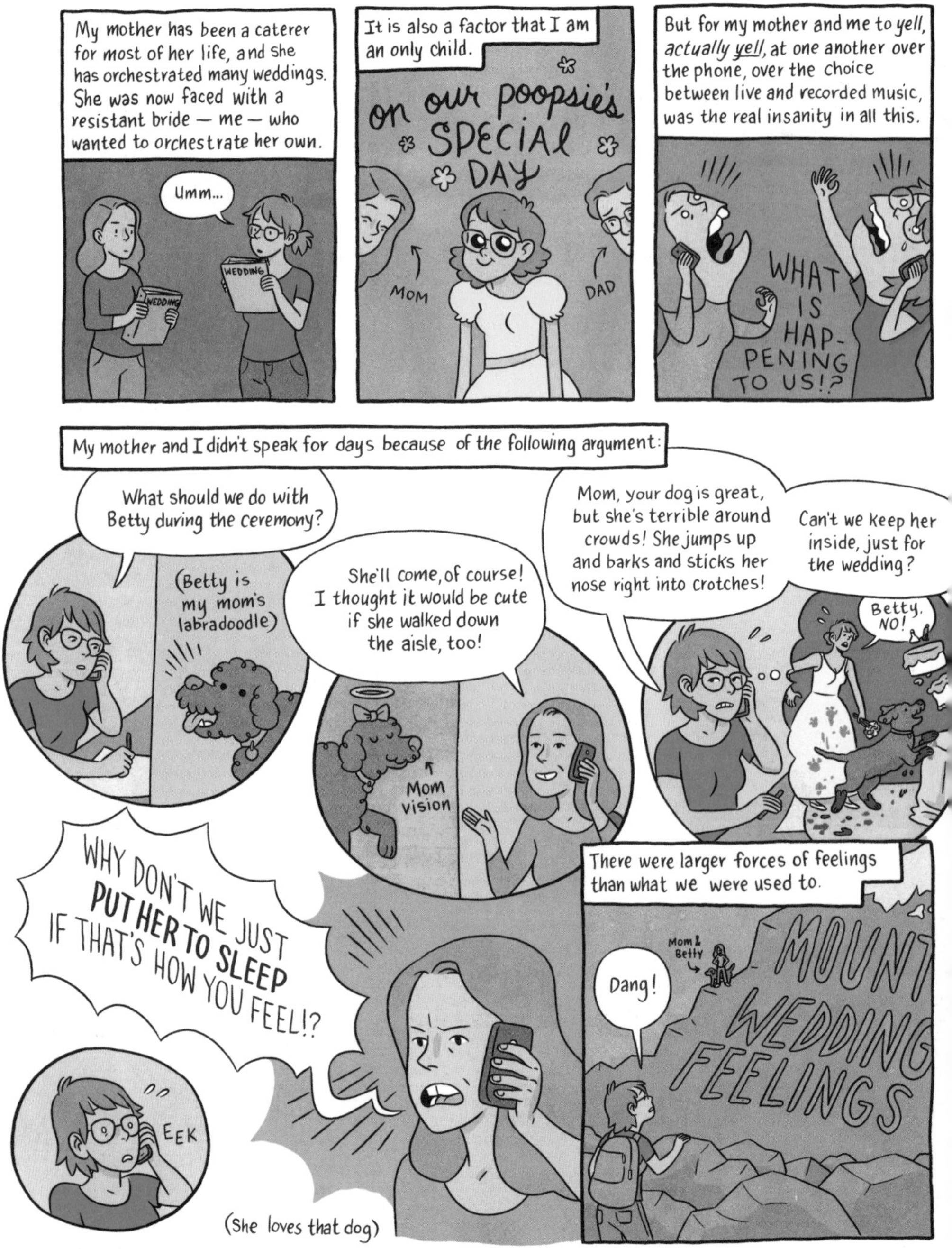

My mother has been a caterer for most of her life, and she has orchestrated many weddings. She was now faced with a resistant bride — me — who wanted to orchestrate her own.
Umm...
WEDDING
WEDDING
It is also a factor that I am an only child.
on our poopsie's SPECIAL DAY
MOM
DAD
But for my mother and me to *yell*, *actually yell*, at one another over the phone, over the choice between live and recorded music, was the real insanity in all this.
WHAT IS HAP-PENING TO US!?
My mother and I didn't speak for days because of the following argument:
What should we do with Betty during the ceremony?
(Betty is my mom's labradoodle)
She'll come, of course! I thought it would be cute if she walked down the aisle, too!
Mom vision
Mom, your dog is great, but she's terrible around crowds! She jumps up and barks and sticks her nose right into crotches!
Can't we keep her inside, just for the wedding?
Betty, NO!
WHY DON'T WE JUST PUT HER TO SLEEP IF THAT'S HOW YOU FEEL!?
EEK
(She loves that dog)
There were larger forces of feelings than what we were used to.
Mom & Betty
Dang!
MOUNT WEDDING FEELINGS

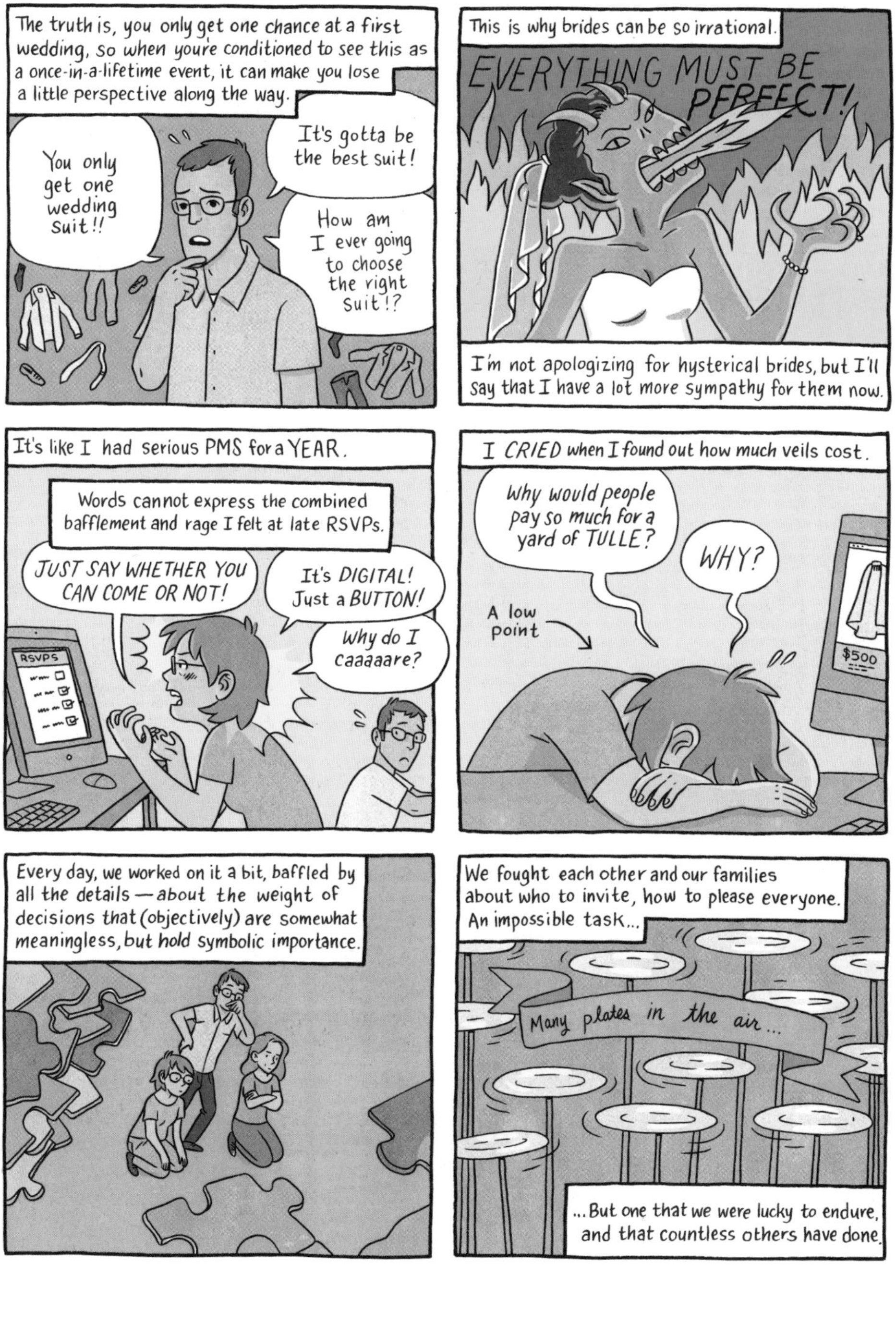

The truth is, you only get one chance at a first wedding, so when you're conditioned to see this as a once-in-a-lifetime event, it can make you lose a little perspective along the way.
You only get one wedding suit!!
It's gotta be the best suit!
How am I ever going to choose the right suit!?
This is why brides can be so irrational.
EVERYTHING MUST BE PERFECT!
I'm not apologizing for hysterical brides, but I'll say that I have a lot more sympathy for them now.
It's like I had serious PMS for a YEAR.
Words cannot express the combined bafflement and rage I felt at late RSVPs.
JUST SAY WHETHER YOU CAN COME OR NOT!
It's DIGITAL! Just a BUTTON!
Why do I caaaaare?
RSVPS
I CRIED when I found out how much veils cost.
Why would people pay so much for a yard of TULLE?
WHY?
A low point
$500
Every day, we worked on it a bit, baffled by all the details—about the weight of decisions that (objectively) are somewhat meaningless, but hold symbolic importance.
We fought each other and our families about who to invite, how to please everyone. An impossible task...
Many plates in the air...
...But one that we were lucky to endure, and that countless others have done.

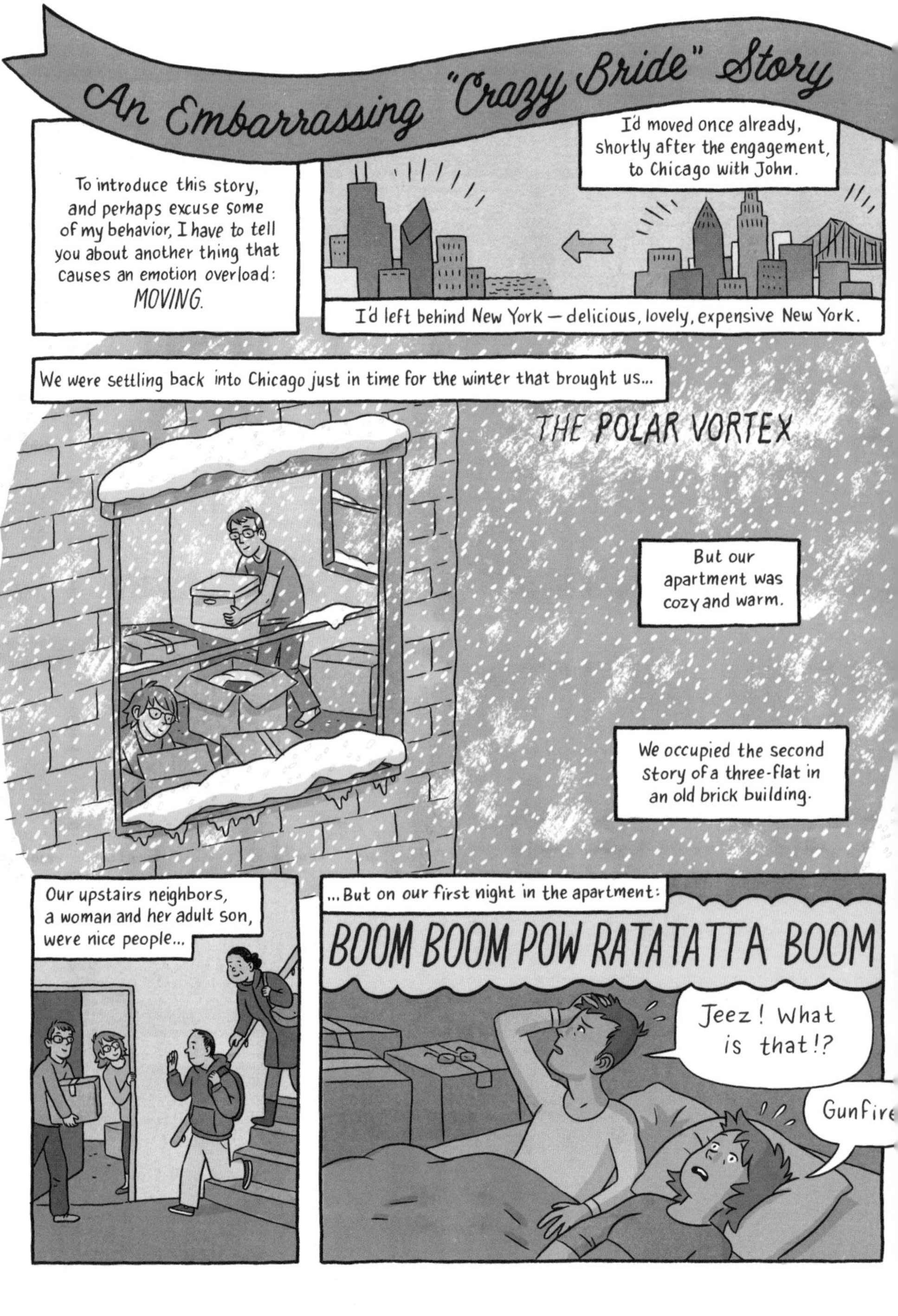
An Embarrassing "Crazy Bride" Story
To introduce this story, and perhaps excuse some of my behavior, I have to tell you about another thing that causes an emotion overload: MOVING.
I'd moved once already, shortly after the engagement, to Chicago with John.
I'd left behind New York — delicious, lovely, expensive New York.
We were settling back into Chicago just in time for the winter that brought us...
THE POLAR VORTEX
But our apartment was cozy and warm.
We occupied the second story of a three-flat in an old brick building.
Our upstairs neighbors, a woman and her adult son, were nice people...
...But on our first night in the apartment:
BOOM BOOM POW RATATATTA BOOM
Jeez! What is that!?
Gunfire

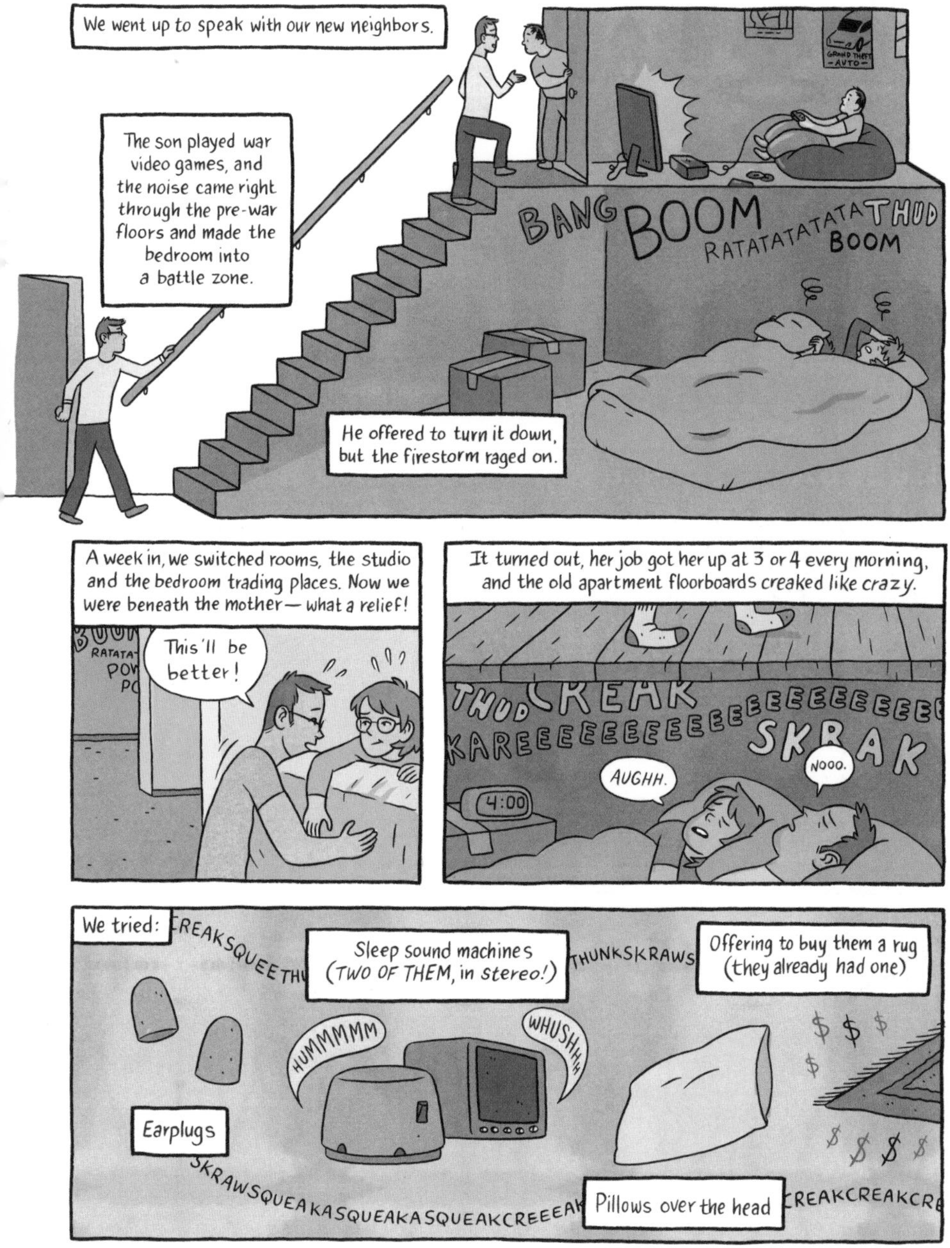
We went up to speak with our new neighbors.
The son played war video games, and the noise came right through the pre-war floors and made the bedroom into a battle zone.
GRAND THEFT AUTO
BANG BOOM RATATATATATATA THUD BOOM
He offered to turn it down, but the firestorm raged on.
A week in, we switched rooms, the studio and the bedroom trading places. Now we were beneath the mother— what a relief!
This'll be better!
It turned out, her job got her up at 3 or 4 every morning, and the old apartment floorboards creaked like crazy.
THUD CREAK
KAREEEEEEEEEEEEEEEEEEEEEE
SKRAK
AUGHH.
NOOO.
4:00
We tried:
CREAKSQUEETHU
Sleep sound machines (TWO OF THEM, in stereo!)
THUNKSKRAWS
Offering to buy them a rug (they already had one)
HUMMMMM
WHUSHHH
Earplugs
SKRAWSQUEAKASQUEAKASQUEAKCREEEAK
Pillows over the head
CREAKCREAKCRE

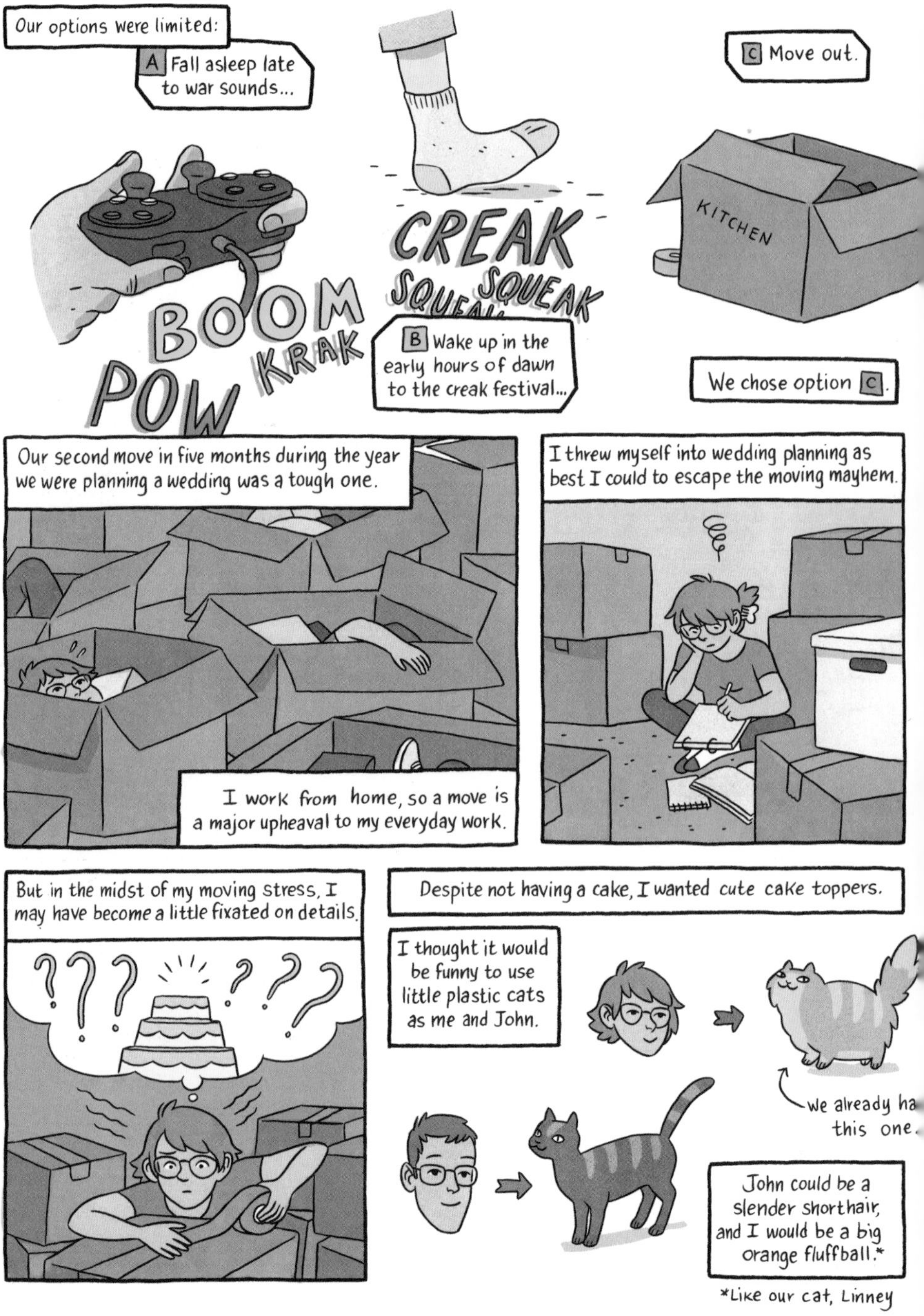
Our options were limited:
A Fall asleep late to war sounds...
BOOM
POW
KRAK
CREAK
SQUEAK
B Wake up in the early hours of dawn to the creak festival...
C Move out.
KITCHEN
We chose option C.
Our second move in five months during the year we were planning a wedding was a tough one.
I work from home, so a move is a major upheaval to my everyday work.
I threw myself into wedding planning as best I could to escape the moving mayhem.
But in the midst of my moving stress, I may have become a little fixated on details.
Despite not having a cake, I wanted cute cake toppers.
I thought it would be funny to use little plastic cats as me and John.
we already ha this one.
John could be a slender shorthair, and I would be a big orange fluffball.*
*Like our cat, Linney

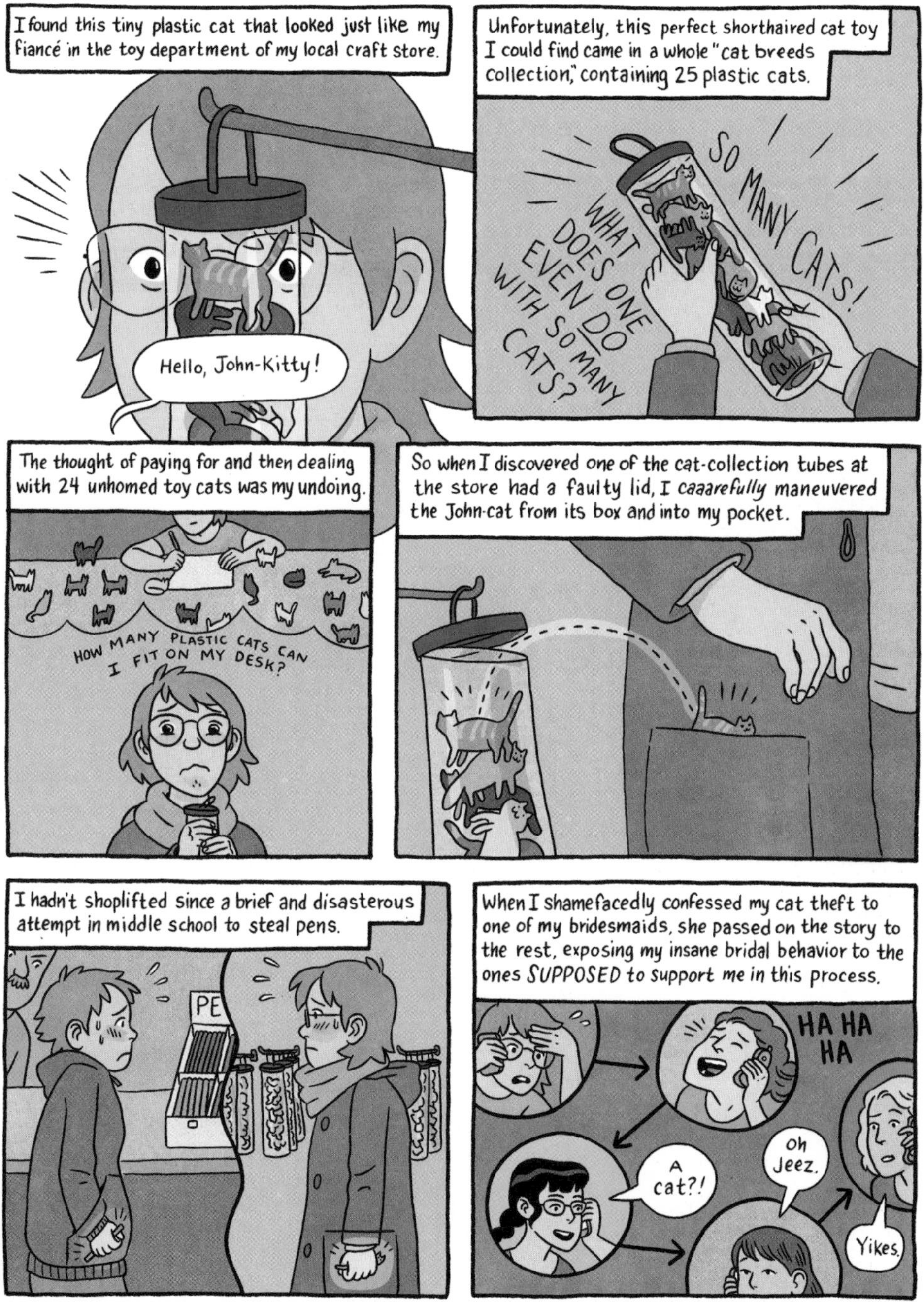
I found this tiny plastic cat that looked just like my fiancé in the toy department of my local craft store.
Hello, John-Kitty!
Unfortunately, this perfect shorthaired cat toy I could find came in a whole "cat breeds collection," containing 25 plastic cats.
WHAT DOES ONE EVEN DO WITH SO MANY CATS?
SO MANY CATS!
The thought of paying for and then dealing with 24 unhomed toy cats was my undoing.
HOW MANY PLASTIC CATS CAN I FIT ON MY DESK?
So when I discovered one of the cat-collection tubes at the store had a faulty lid, I caaarefully maneuvered the John-cat from its box and into my pocket.
I hadn't shoplifted since a brief and disasterous attempt in middle school to steal pens.
PE
When I shamefacedly confessed my cat theft to one of my bridesmaids, she passed on the story to the rest, exposing my insane bridal behavior to the ones SUPPOSED to support me in this process.
HA HA HA
A cat?!
Oh Jeez.
Yikes.

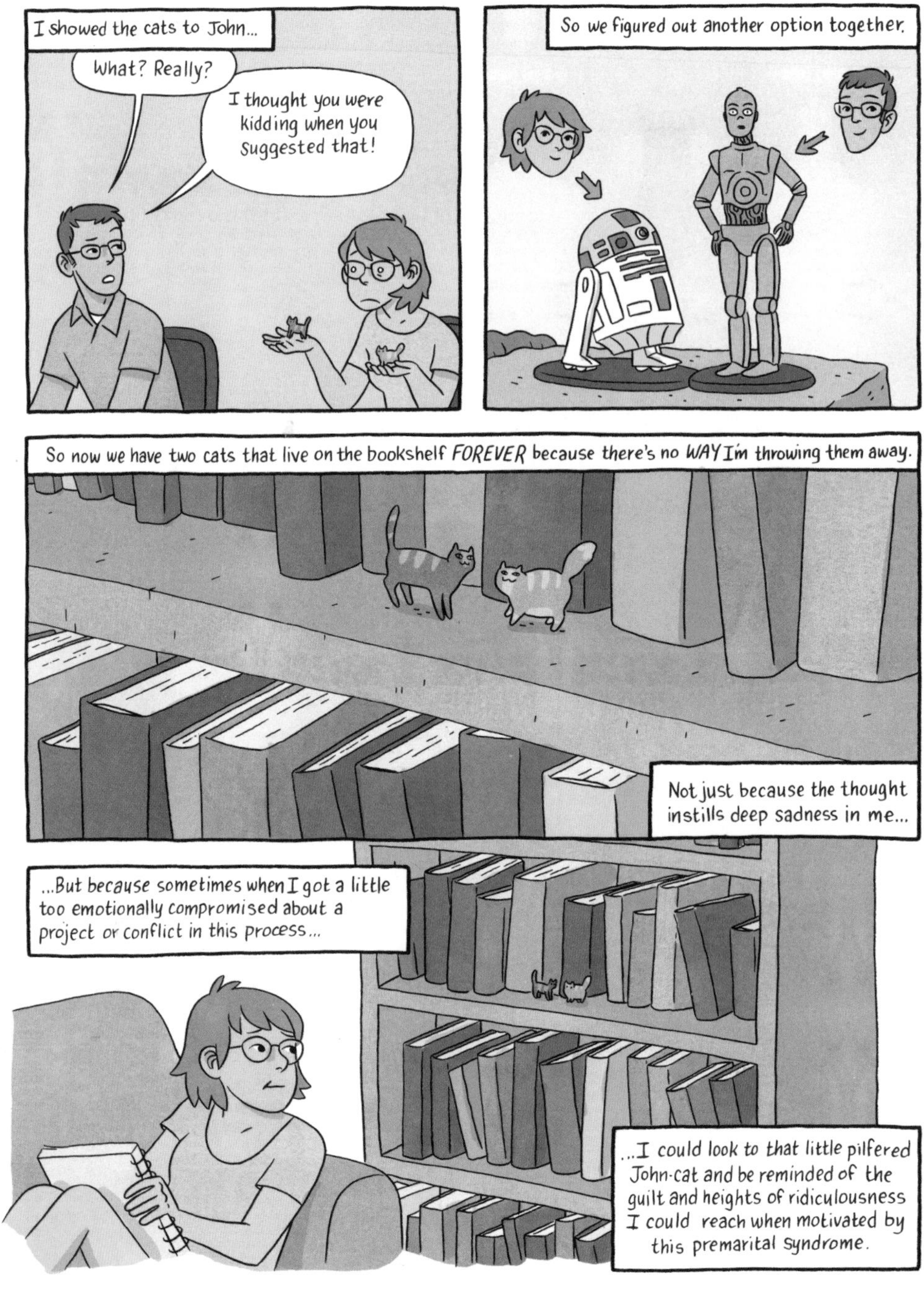
I showed the cats to John...
What? Really?
I thought you were kidding when you suggested that!
So we figured out another option together.
So now we have two cats that live on the bookshelf FOREVER because there's no WAY I'm throwing them away.
Not just because the thought instills deep sadness in me...
...But because sometimes when I got a little too emotionally compromised about a project or conflict in this process...
...I could look to that little pilfered John-cat and be reminded of the guilt and heights of ridiculousness I could reach when motivated by this premarital syndrome.

FILM STUDIES

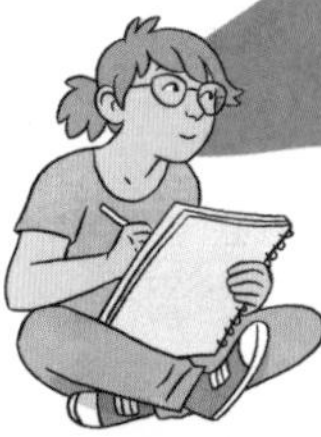

Before my wedding, I felt it was important to study the cultural significance of weddings in the most scholarly and journalistic form of research materials: *MOVIES*.

Here are a few wedding movies I watched during my engagement, and the lessons I took away from these studies that I applied to planning my own wedding.

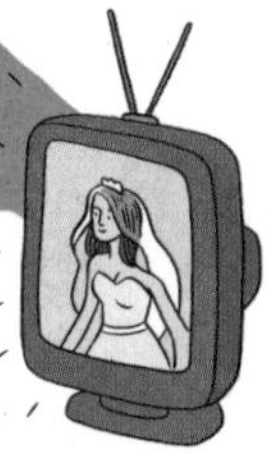

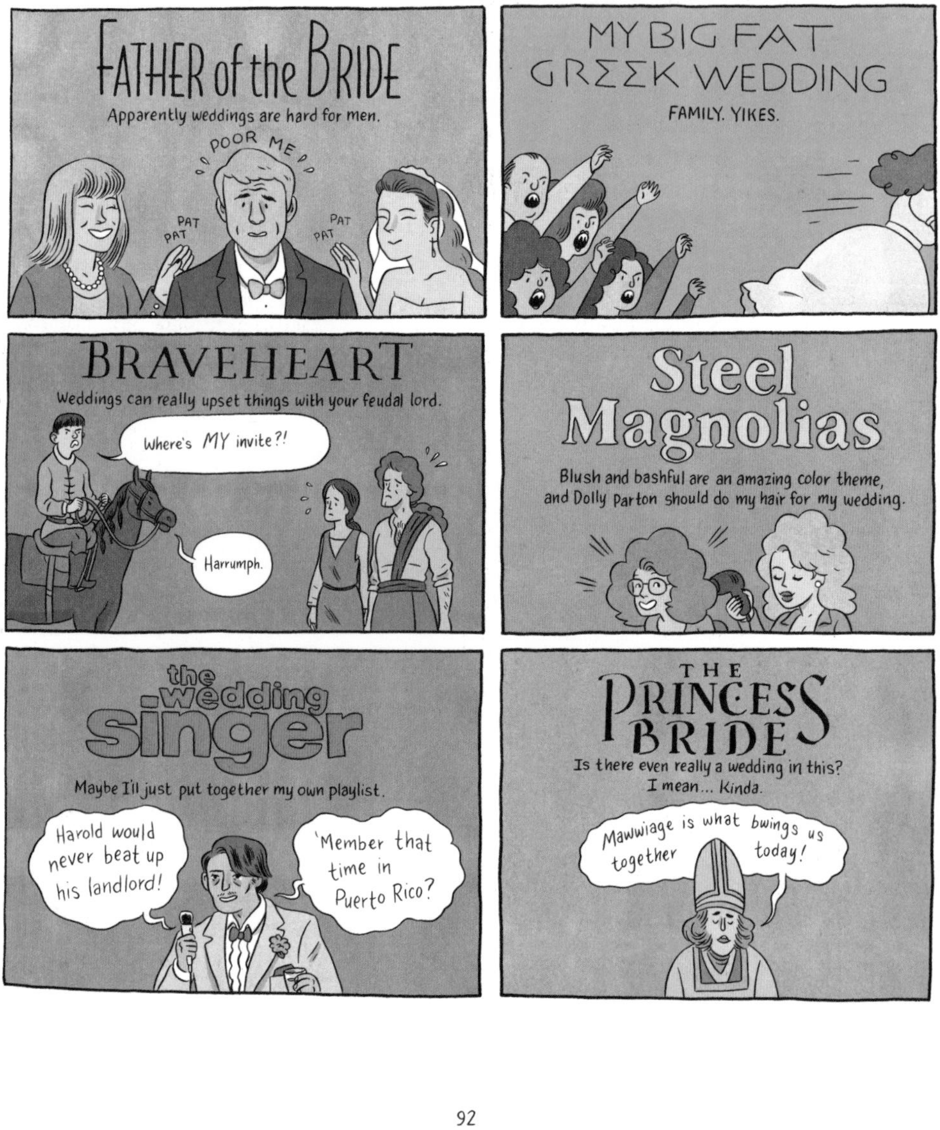
FATHER of the BRIDE
Apparently weddings are hard for men.
POOR ME
PAT PAT
PAT PAT
MY BIG FAT GREEK WEDDING
FAMILY. YIKES.
BRAVEHEART
Weddings can really upset things with your feudal lord.
Where's MY invite?!
Harrumph.
Steel Magnolias
Blush and bashful are an amazing color theme, and Dolly Parton should do my hair for my wedding.
the wedding singer
Maybe I'll just put together my own playlist.
Harold would never beat up his landlord!
'Member that time in Puerto Rico?
THE PRINCESS BRIDE
Is there even really a wedding in this? I mean... Kinda.
Mawwiage is what bwings us together today!

MY BEST FRIEND'S *Wedding*

I want Rupert Everett to come to my wedding.

KILL BILL

I'm not listening to my friend Mark's wedding movie suggestions anymore.

CLICK

CHOKE GASP

Sixteen Candles

Brides basically don't even have to be coherent, I guess.

BRIDES MAIDS

Light meals only, before any dress-fitting appointments.

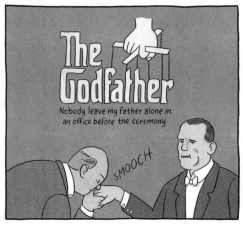

The Godfather

Nobody leave my father alone in an office before the ceremony.

SMOOCH

THE SOUND OF MUSIC

Nuns make the best bridesmaids!

HI-5!

93

Chapter 7:

Motivations

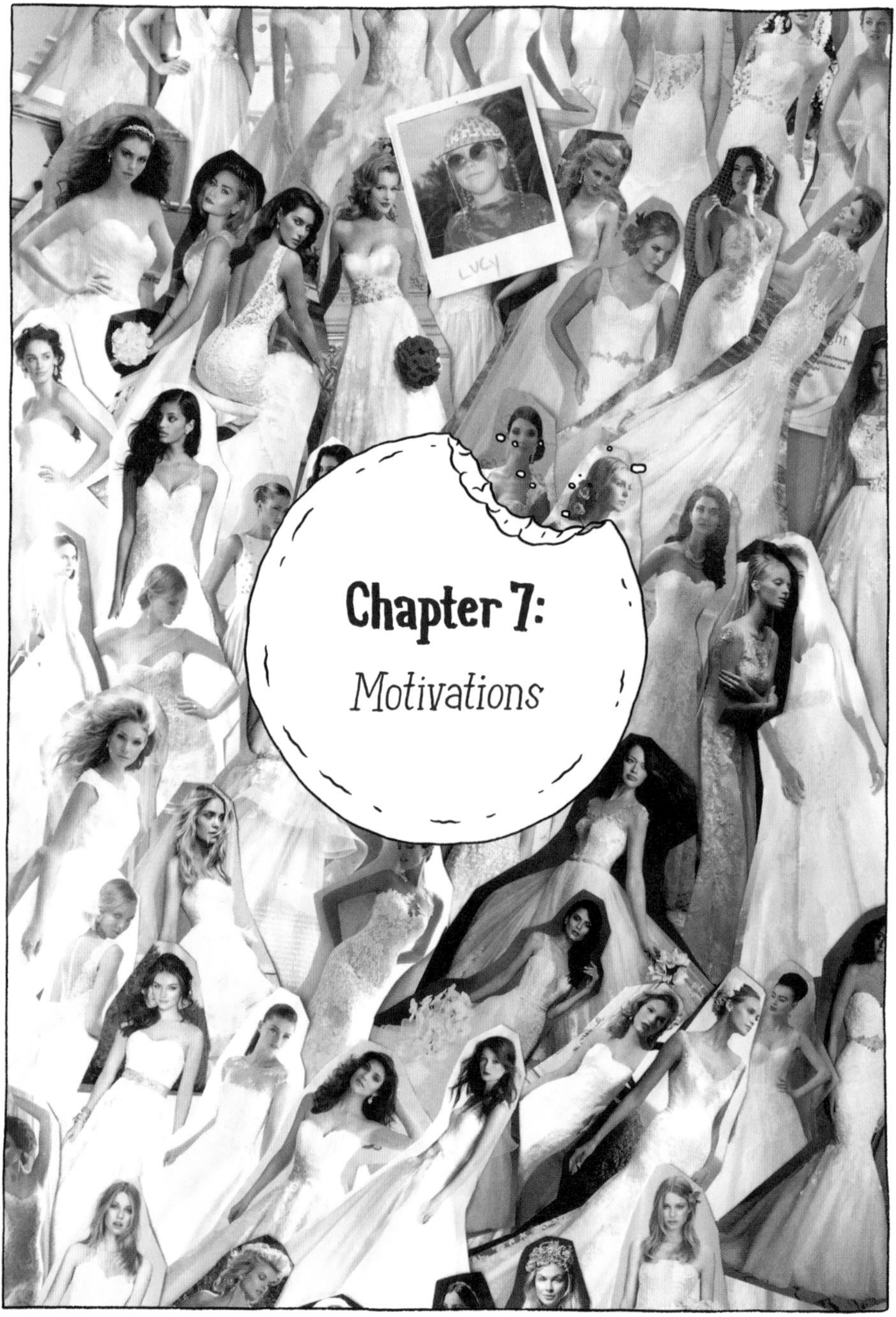
LUCY

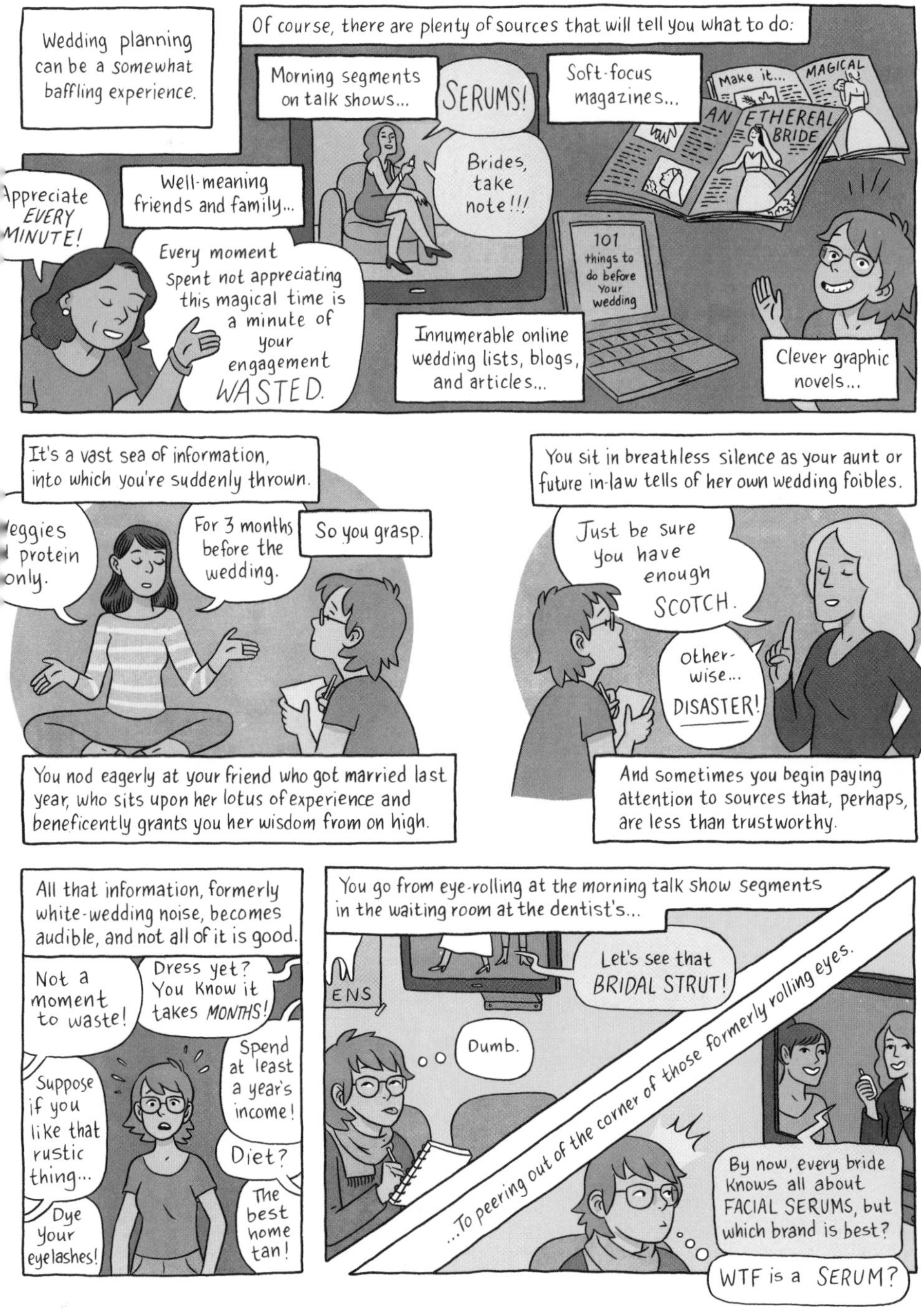
Wedding planning can be a somewhat baffling experience.
Of course, there are plenty of sources that will tell you what to do:
Morning segments on talk shows...
SERUMS!
Brides, take note!!!
Soft-focus magazines...
Make it...
MAGICAL
AN ETHEREAL BRIDE
Well-meaning friends and family...
Appreciate EVERY MINUTE!
Every moment spent not appreciating this magical time is a minute of your engagement WASTED.
101 things to do before your wedding
Innumerable online wedding lists, blogs, and articles...
Clever graphic novels...
It's a vast sea of information, into which you're suddenly thrown.
Veggies protein only.
For 3 months before the wedding.
So you grasp.
You nod eagerly at your friend who got married last year, who sits upon her lotus of experience and beneficently grants you her wisdom from on high.
You sit in breathless silence as your aunt or future in-law tells of her own wedding foibles.
Just be sure you have enough SCOTCH.
Other-wise... DISASTER!
And sometimes you begin paying attention to sources that, perhaps, are less than trustworthy.
All that information, formerly white-wedding noise, becomes audible, and not all of it is good.
Not a moment to waste!
Dress yet? You know it takes MONTHS!
Spend at least a year's income!
Suppose if you like that rustic thing...
Diet?
Dye your eyelashes!
The best home tan!
You go from eye-rolling at the morning talk show segments in the waiting room at the dentist's...
Let's see that BRIDAL STRUT!
ENS
Dumb.
...To peering out of the corner of those formerly rolling eyes.
By now, every bride knows all about FACIAL SERUMS, but which brand is best?
WTF is a SERUM?

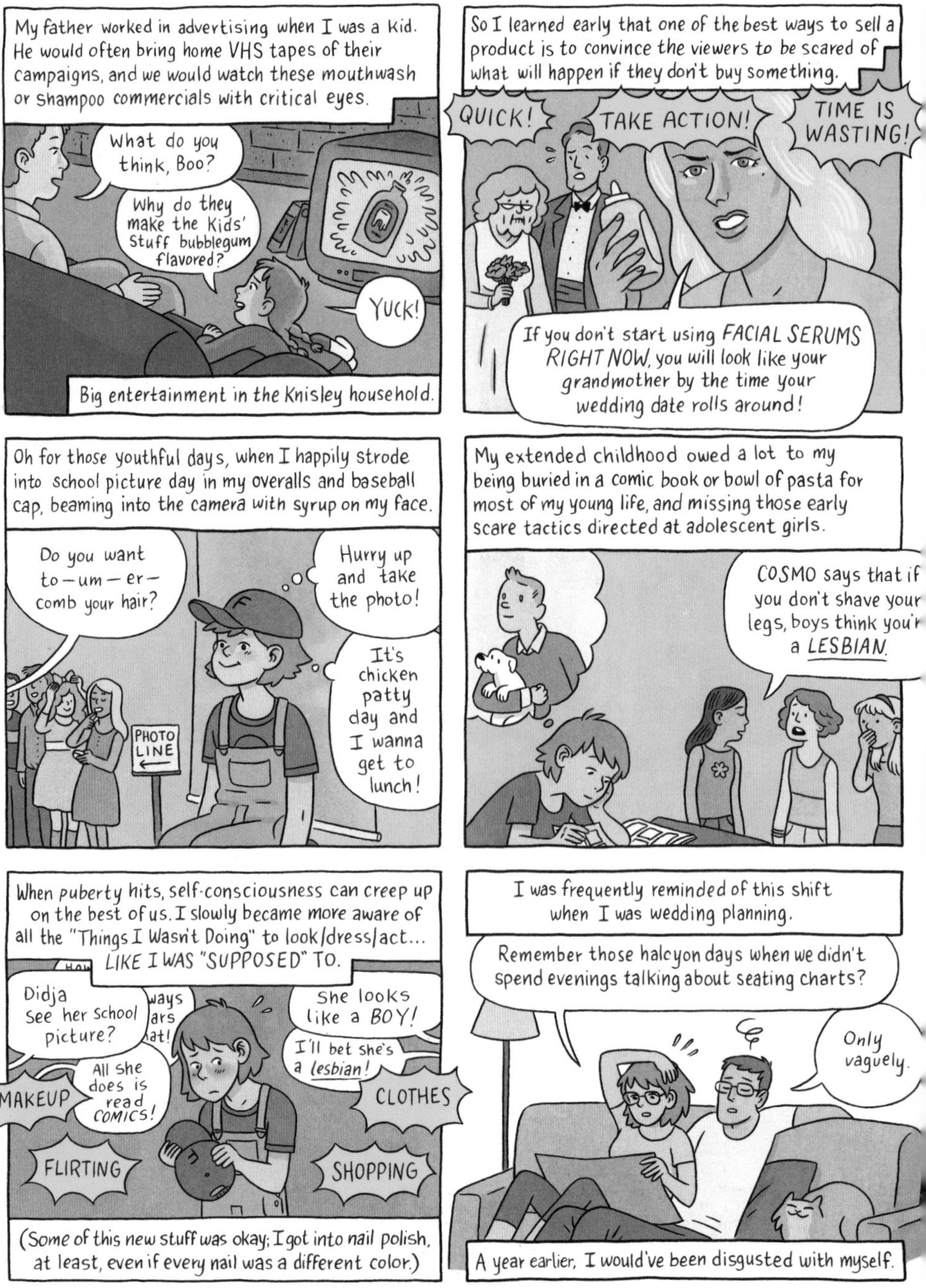

My father worked in advertising when I was a kid. He would often bring home VHS tapes of their campaigns, and we would watch these mouthwash or shampoo commercials with critical eyes.
What do you think, Boo?
Why do they make the Kids' Stuff bubblegum flavored?
YUCK!
Big entertainment in the Knisley household.
So I learned early that one of the best ways to sell a product is to convince the viewers to be scared of what will happen if they don't buy something.
QUICK!
TAKE ACTION!
TIME IS WASTING!
If you don't start using FACIAL SERUMS RIGHT NOW, you will look like your grandmother by the time your wedding date rolls around!
Oh for those youthful days, when I happily strode into school picture day in my overalls and baseball cap, beaming into the camera with syrup on my face.
Do you want to—um—er—comb your hair?
Hurry up and take the photo!
It's chicken patty day and I wanna get to lunch!
PHOTO LINE
My extended childhood owed a lot to my being buried in a comic book or bowl of pasta for most of my young life, and missing those early scare tactics directed at adolescent girls.
COSMO says that if you don't shave your legs, boys think you'r a LESBIAN.
When puberty hits, self-consciousness can creep up on the best of us. I slowly became more aware of all the "Things I Wasn't Doing" to look/dress/act... LIKE I WAS "SUPPOSED" TO.
Didja see her school picture?
She looks like a BOY!
I'll bet she's a lesbian!
All she does is read COMICS!
MAKEUP
CLOTHES
FLIRTING
SHOPPING
(Some of this new stuff was okay; I got into nail polish, at least, even if every nail was a different color.)
I was frequently reminded of this shift when I was wedding planning.
Remember those halcyon days when we didn't spend evenings talking about seating charts?
Only vaguely.
A year earlier, I would've been disgusted with myself.

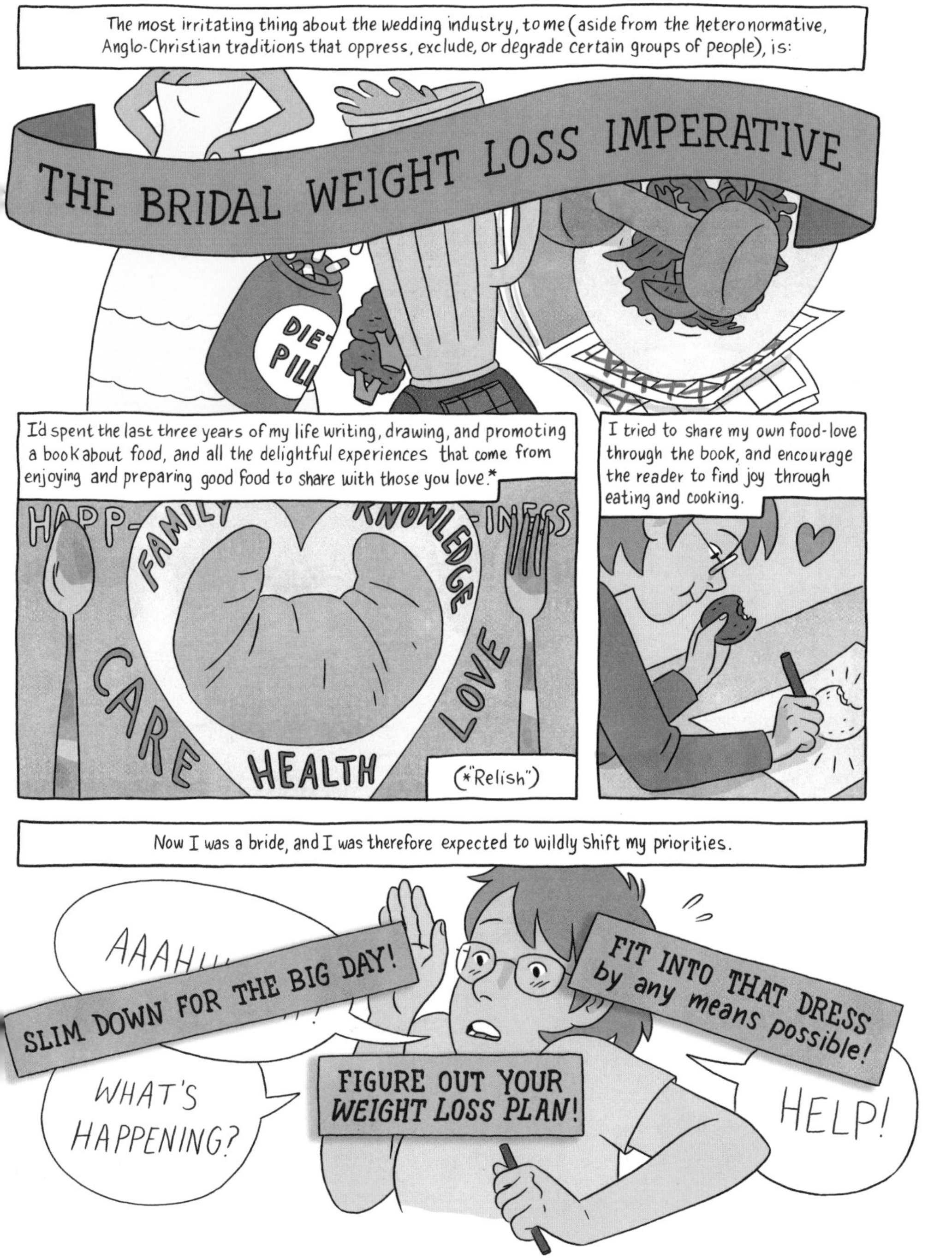

The most irritating thing about the wedding industry, to me (aside from the heteronormative, Anglo-Christian traditions that oppress, exclude, or degrade certain groups of people), is:
THE BRIDAL WEIGHT LOSS IMPERATIVE
DIET PILL
I'd spent the last three years of my life writing, drawing, and promoting a book about food, and all the delightful experiences that come from enjoying and preparing good food to share with those you love.*
HAPP-
FAMILY
KNOWLEDGE
-INESS
CARE
LOVE
HEALTH
(*"Relish")
I tried to share my own food-love through the book, and encourage the reader to find joy through eating and cooking.
Now I was a bride, and I was therefore expected to wildly shift my priorities.
AAAH
SLIM DOWN FOR THE BIG DAY!
FIT INTO THAT DRESS by any means possible!
FIGURE OUT YOUR WEIGHT LOSS PLAN!
WHAT'S HAPPENING?
HELP!

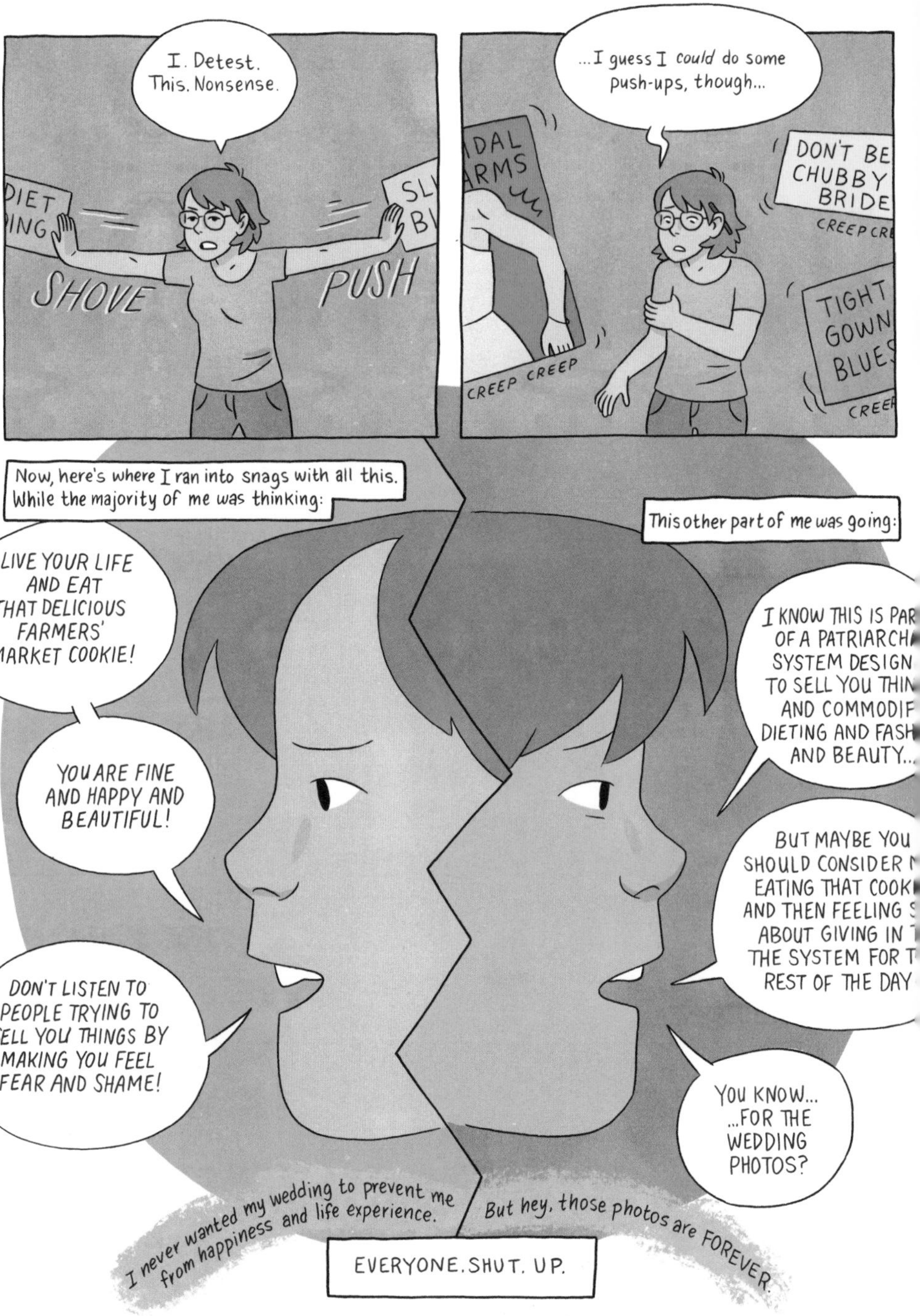

I. Detest. This. Nonsense.
DIET
SHOVE
PUSH
...I guess I *could* do some push-ups, though...
DON'T BE CHUBBY BRIDE
CREEP CREEP
TIGHT GOWN BLUES
CREEP CREEP
Now, here's where I ran into snags with all this. While the majority of me was thinking:
This other part of me was going:
LIVE YOUR LIFE AND EAT THAT DELICIOUS FARMERS' MARKET COOKIE!
YOU ARE FINE AND HAPPY AND BEAUTIFUL!
DON'T LISTEN TO PEOPLE TRYING TO SELL YOU THINGS BY MAKING YOU FEEL FEAR AND SHAME!
YOU KNOW... ...FOR THE WEDDING PHOTOS?
I never wanted my wedding to prevent me from happiness and life experience.
But hey, those photos are FOREVER.
EVERYONE. SHUT. UP.

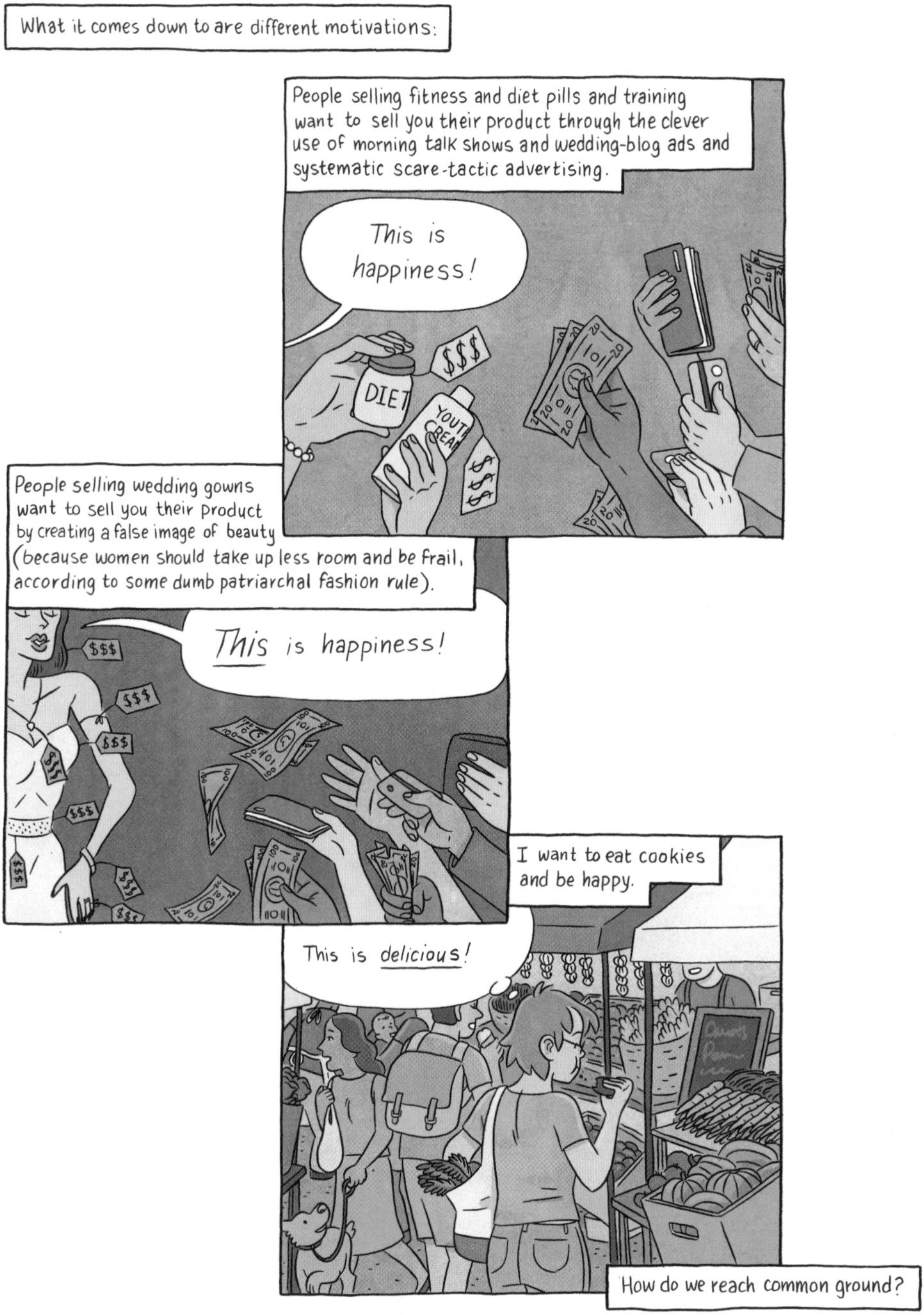
What it comes down to are different motivations:
People selling fitness and diet pills and training want to sell you their product through the clever use of morning talk shows and wedding-blog ads and systematic scare-tactic advertising.
This is happiness!
$$$
DIET
People selling wedding gowns want to sell you their product by creating a false image of beauty (because women should take up less room and be frail, according to some dumb patriarchal fashion rule).
This is happiness!
I want to eat cookies and be happy.
This is delicious!
How do we reach common ground?

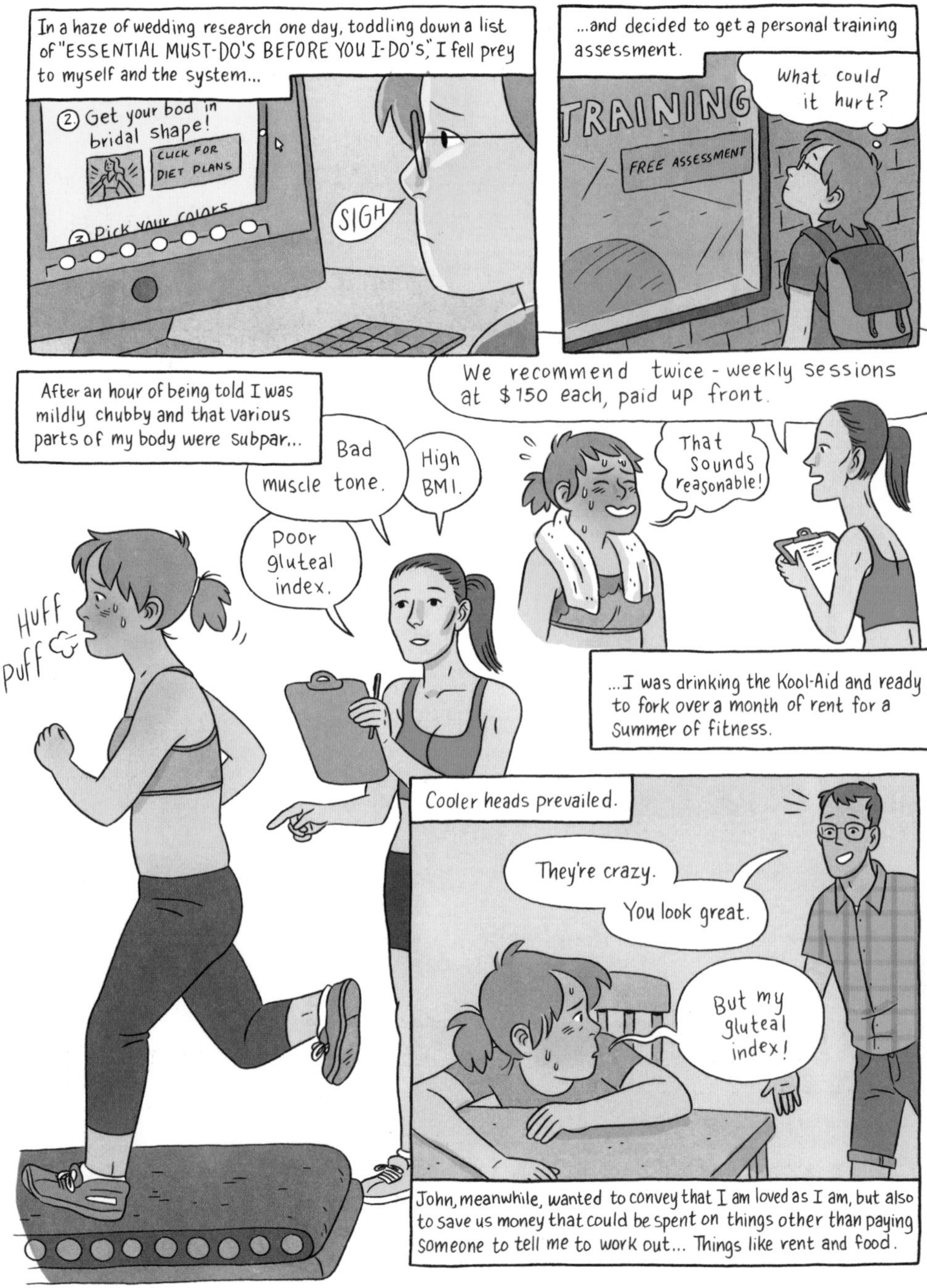
In a haze of wedding research one day, toddling down a list of "ESSENTIAL MUST-DO'S BEFORE YOU I-DO'S," I fell prey to myself and the system...
2. Get your bod in bridal shape!
CLICK FOR DIET PLANS
SIGH
...and decided to get a personal training assessment.
TRAINING
FREE ASSESSMENT
What could it hurt?
After an hour of being told I was mildly chubby and that various parts of my body were subpar...
Bad muscle tone.
High BMI.
Poor gluteal index.
HUFF
PUFF
We recommend twice-weekly sessions at $150 each, paid up front.
That sounds reasonable!
...I was drinking the Kool-Aid and ready to fork over a month of rent for a summer of fitness.
Cooler heads prevailed.
They're crazy.
You look great.
But my gluteal index!
John, meanwhile, wanted to convey that I am loved as I am, but also to save us money that could be spent on things other than paying someone to tell me to work out... Things like rent and food.

I think it's just a matter of finding one's own path. Perhaps that path includes pricey training and special diets — live your life, friend, as long as it's safe and healthy.

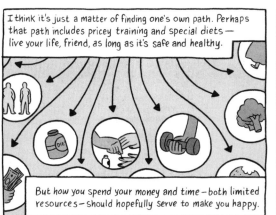

But how you spend your money and time — both limited resources — should hopefully serve to make you happy.

For me, happiness was better achieved through spending my time and money not on my body, but on making presents for my bridesmaids and tasting a variety of wedding desserts.

Bridesmaids' goodies

Color-coded to their dresses

LUCY'S PLAN FOR PRE-WEDDING HAPPINESS:

It was summer — I swam as often as I could, which I love to do anyway.

I did a few of those push-ups I kept talking about.

Ten!

Some of this stuff is actually supposed to be fun, remember?

I wore sunscreen, because sunburns make me very unhappy, and tanning is not an option for those of us of the more gingery persuasion.

I kept eating healthy and well, while choosing to take the opportunity to eat delicious farmers' market cookies when I got the chance.

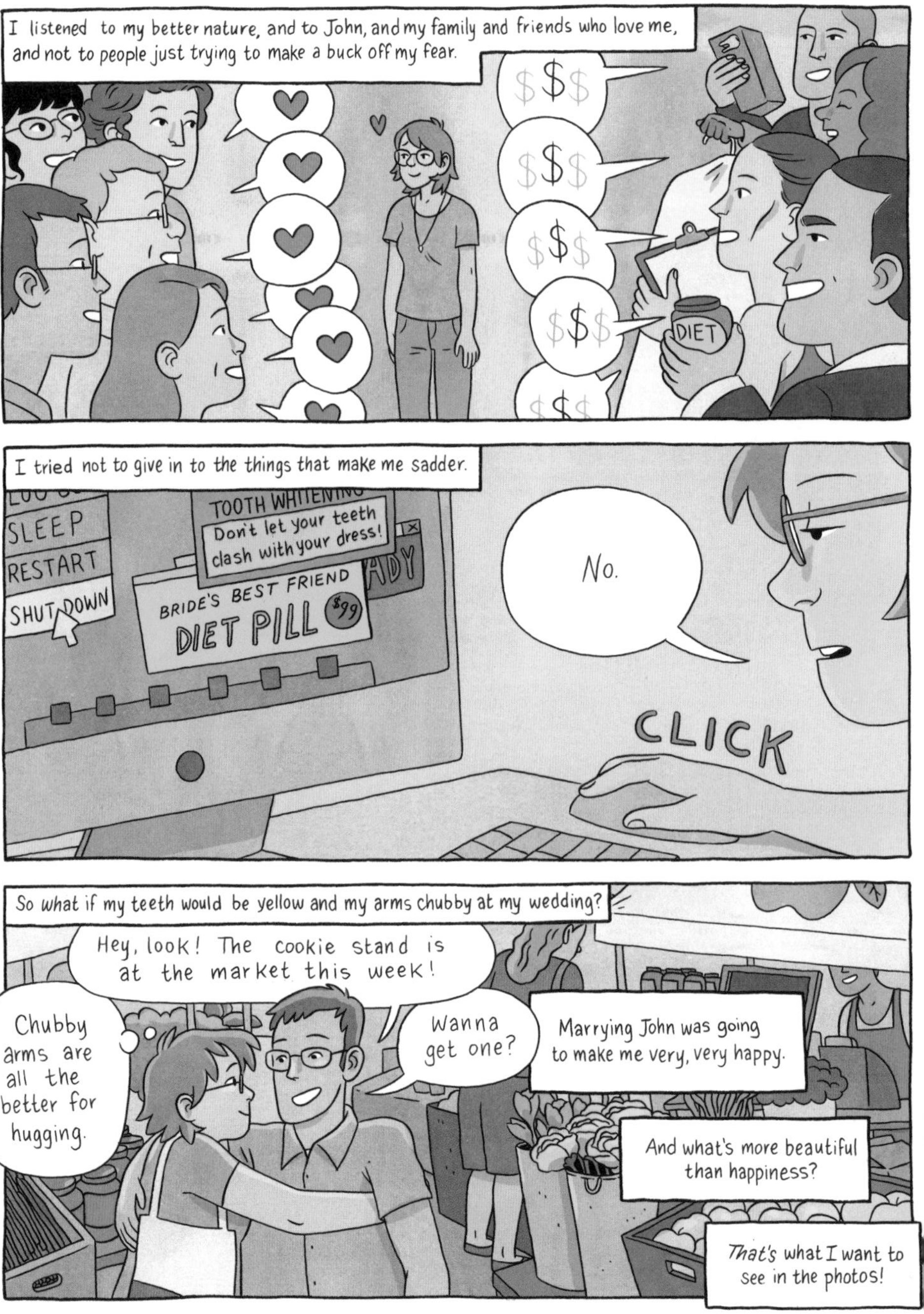

I listened to my better nature, and to John, and my family and friends who love me, and not to people just trying to make a buck off my fear.
I tried not to give in to the things that make me sadder.
SLEEP
RESTART
SHUT DOWN
TOOTH WHITENING
Don't let your teeth clash with your dress!
BRIDE'S BEST FRIEND
DIET PILL
$99
DIET
No.
CLICK
So what if my teeth would be yellow and my arms chubby at my wedding?
Hey, look! The cookie stand is at the market this week!
Chubby arms are all the better for hugging.
Wanna get one?
Marrying John was going to make me very, very happy.
And what's more beautiful than happiness?
That's what I want to see in the photos!

Let's enjoy some

BRIDAL MARKETING SCHEMES:

Can you tell the real from the fake?

CUSTOM ENGRAVED WEDDING BULLETS

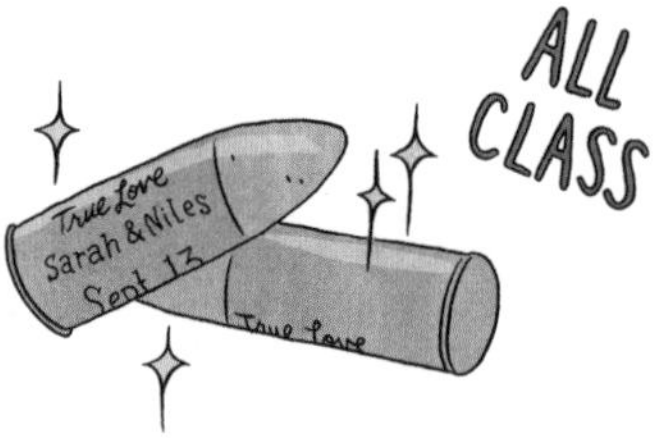
ALL CLASS
True Love
Sarah & Niles
Sept 13
True Love

RING BEARER PILLOW IN THE SHAPE OF A FOOTBALL

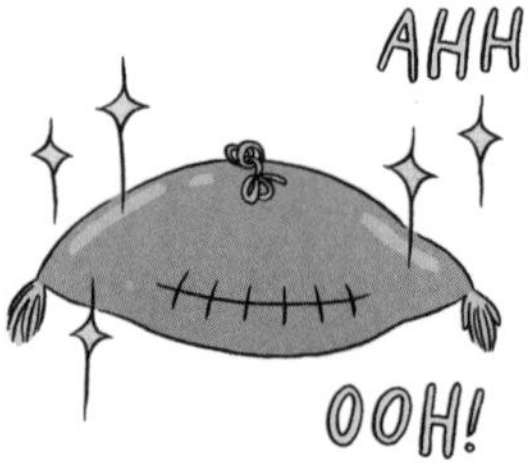
AHH!
OOH!

SENSUAL WEDDING NIGHT MEMORY-MAKING KIT

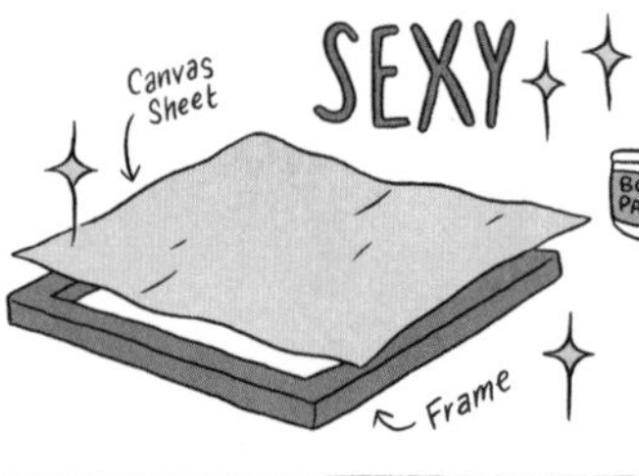
Canvas Sheet
SEXY
BODY PAINT
Frame

BRIDAL ARM-SKIN REJUVENATION

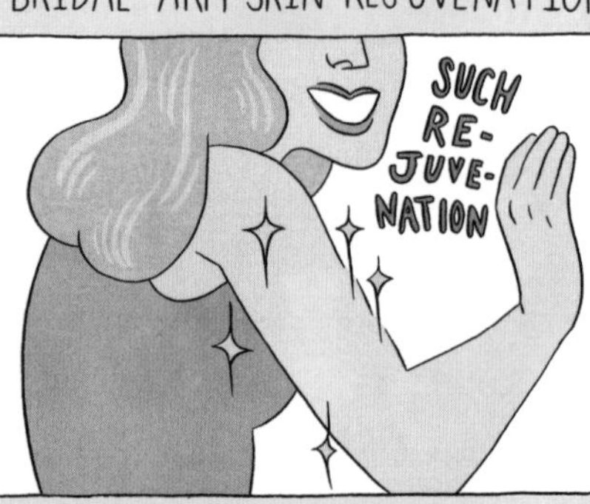
SUCH RE-JUVE-NATION

HEART-SHAPED MEASURING SPOONS FOR BAKING YOUR WEDDING CAKE

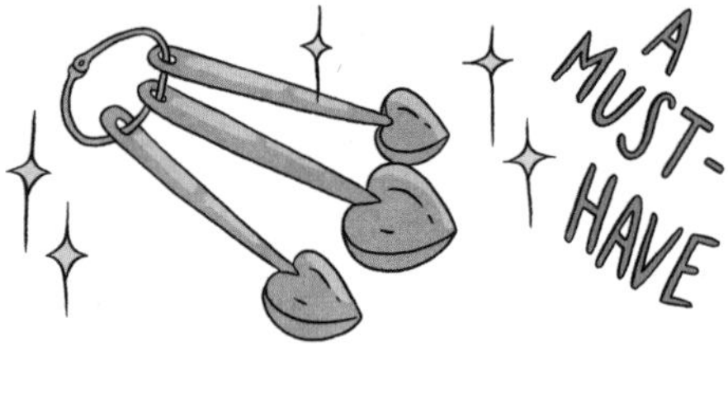
A MUST-HAVE

PLASTIC SHELLS (FOR BEACH WEDDING)

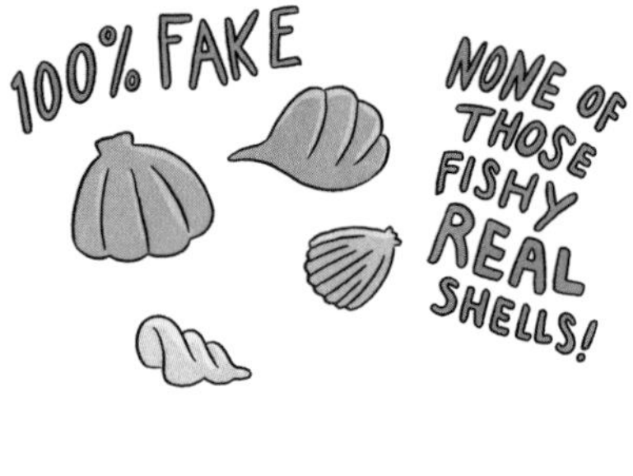
100% FAKE
NONE OF THOSE FISHY REAL SHELLS!

RING BEARER AND FLOWER GIRL MINK-TRIM VELVET CAPES

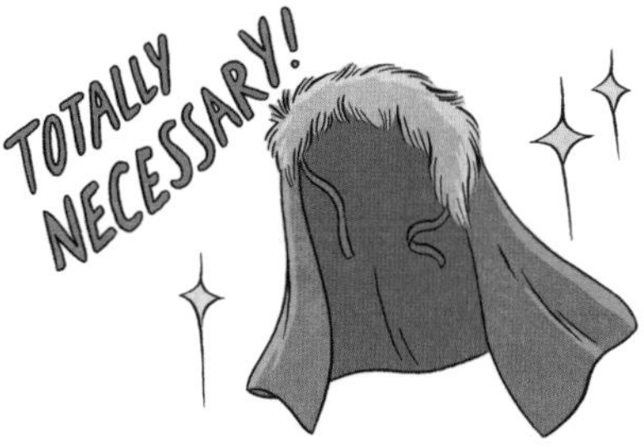
TOTALLY NECESSARY!

SILVER SHOE TREES FOR YOUR WEDDING SHOES

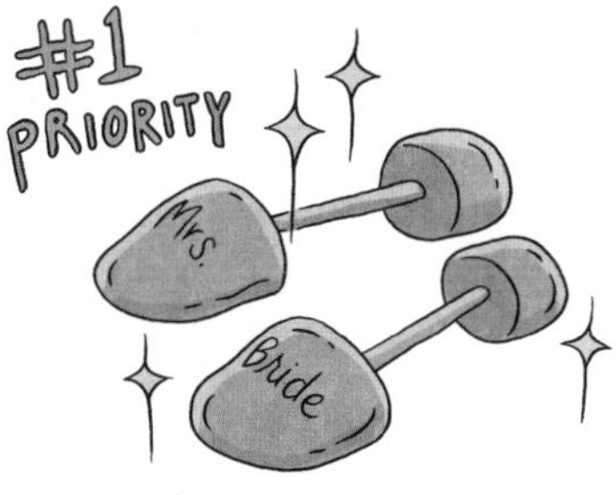
#1 PRIORITY
Mrs.
Bride

WEDDING GOLDFISH CENTERPIECES

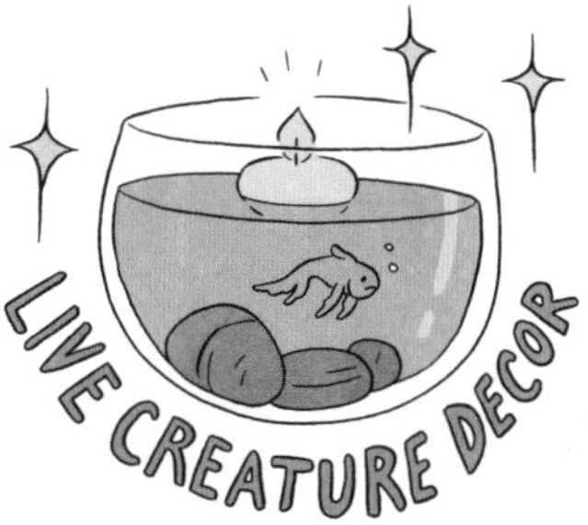
LIVE CREATURE DECOR

"WITH THIS RING" WEDDING STATUE

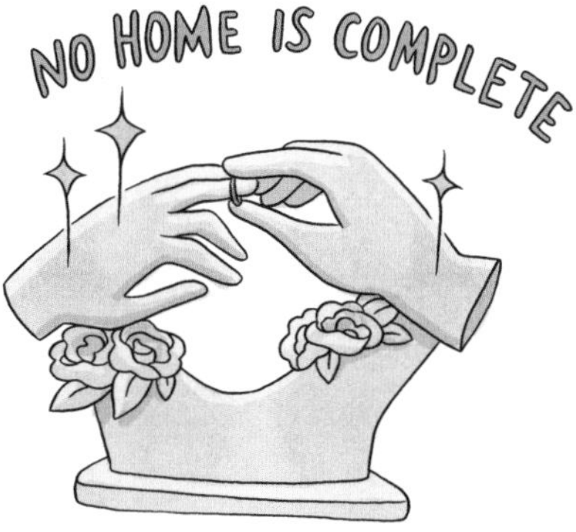
NO HOME IS COMPLETE

PLASTIC CEREMONIAL DRINKING HORN

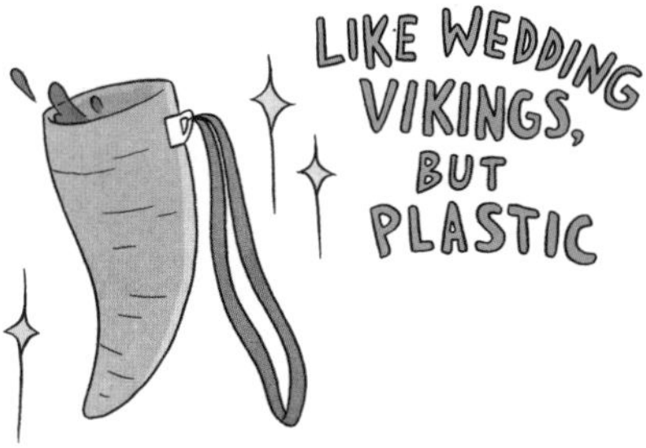
LIKE WEDDING VIKINGS, BUT PLASTIC

BRIDAL ICE BUCKET

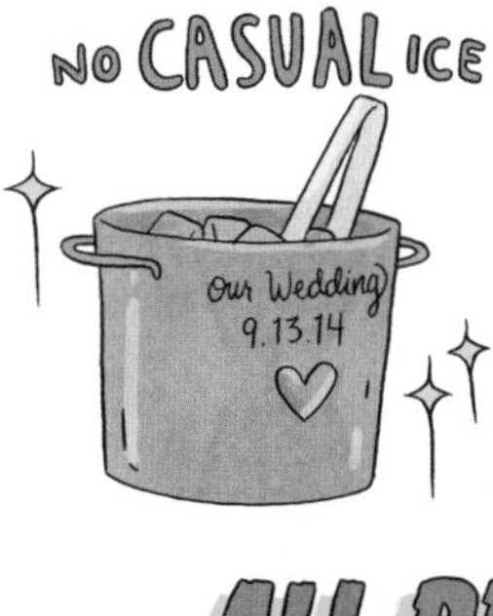
NO CASUAL ICE
Our Wedding
9.13.14

Just kidding! These are **ALL REAL.**

Chapter 8: My Feminist Party

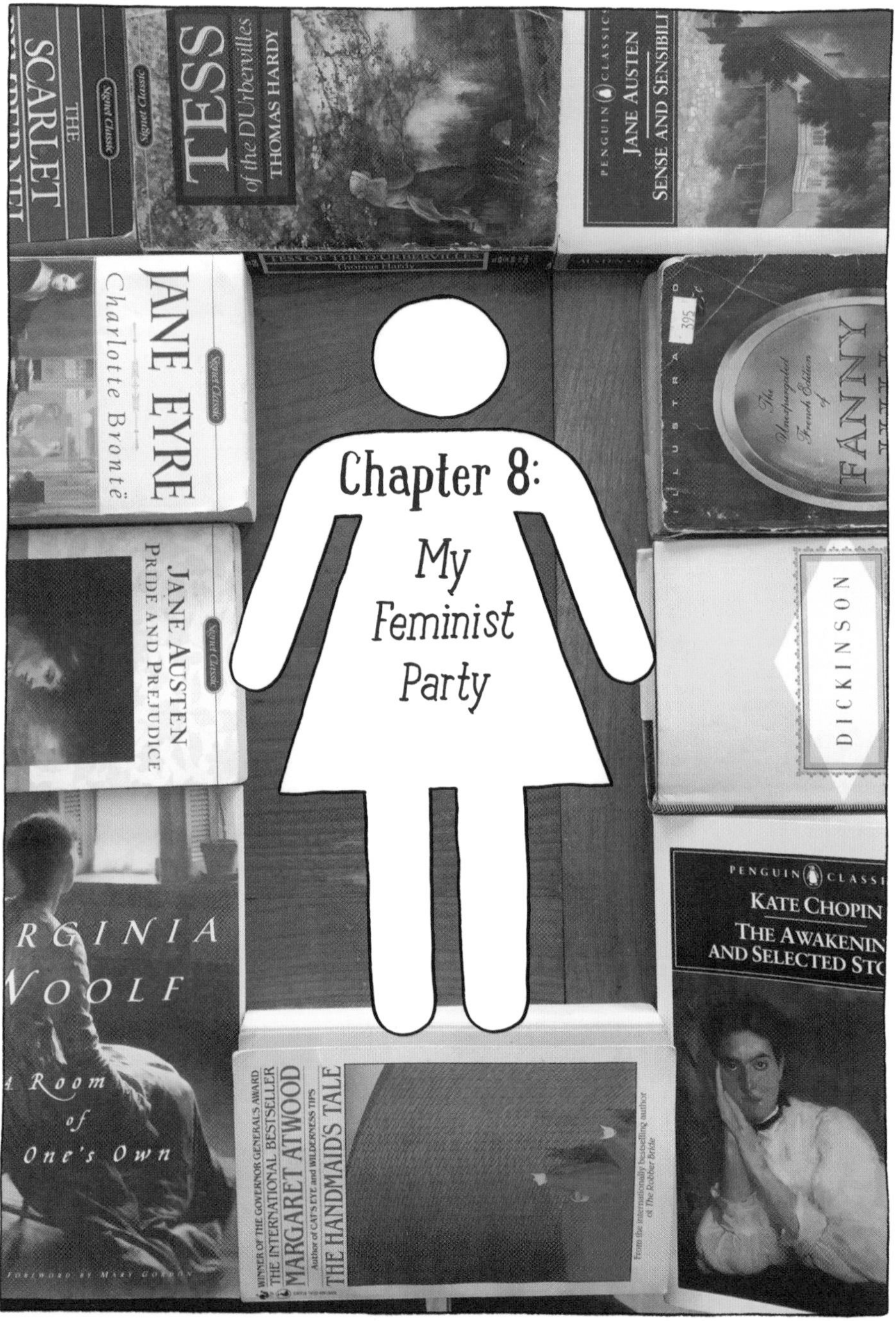
THE SCARLET
Signet Classic
TESS of the D'Urbervilles
THOMAS HARDY
TESS OF THE D'URBERVILLES Thomas Hardy
PENGUIN CLASSICS
JANE AUSTEN
SENSE AND SENSIBILI
JANE EYRE
Charlotte Brontë
Signet Classic
The Unexpurgated French Edition of FANNY
395
JANE AUSTEN
PRIDE AND PREJUDICE
Signet Classic
DICKINSON
PENGUIN CLASSICS
KATE CHOPIN
THE AWAKENIN
AND SELECTED STO
RGINIA
WOOLF
A Room of One's Own
WINNER OF THE GOVERNOR GENERAL'S AWARD
THE INTERNATIONAL BESTSELLER
MARGARET ATWOOD
Author of CAT'S EYE and WILDERNESS TIPS
THE HANDMAID'S TALE
From the internationally bestselling author of The Robber Bride

Cohabitation is pretty handy for a cartoonist.

Secret sketching

With John as my live-in life model and writing consultant, I can rely on him to provide editorial and visual aid when necessary...

...And also to pry me from my desk when I have become a piece of furniture.

Hey— let's eat!

It also helps to have an outside perspective, even though I predominantly write about my own life.

What are you doing?

Getting a Johnny point of view.

I enjoy getting to compare my own to his point of view.

For example: when we switched our online relationship status.

Here goes!

Occupation Cart

Status:

Single

It's Complicated

CLICK gaged

Married

To a Relationship

Doing this has become the equivalent of announcing your engagement in the local paper, but a benefit of print media over digital is the decided lack of targeted marketing.

Knisley is a go.

Release the ads!

Excellent.

Within minutes of the status update, I was squinting at the encroaching ads beside my image searches and social media, noticing the increasingly floral and satiny embellishments.

EBOOK

my lunch today!

50%

going to fabulous.

SALE

feeling tough!

Huh?

WORLD WEDDINGS

Suddenly, online articles about global warming were accompanied by blinking ads imploring me to lose weight or choose a gown or book a venue.

AUGH!

BUY!
YES DRESS
DIET NO!
AFFO
IN YO
ARE
THE BIG DAY IS CLOSER THAN YOU THINK!

While I appreciated our computer overlords' thoughtfulness in directing my attention to my "bridal duties," I was disturbed at how suddenly my online experience shifted.

CARE ABOUT THIS, NOW.

?

SHOVE

SPEND $ AND BE HER!

DO IT

There are hundreds of magazines, guides, websites, and books about "how to bride," along with an enormous industry catering to this fantasy princess ideal.

Can I just be with John, please?

BUY DRESS!

WEDDING INDUSTRY

The internet makes it easier than ever for this industry to reach us.

Can I just watch this baby sloth video without being distracted by my bridal responsibilities?

WEDDING WEIGHT BLUES? CLICK HERE

The trouble is, targeted marketing is maddeningly effective.

Huh. Affordable wedding photographers in my area?

click

Well, I guess I could check...

POSTSE

SICK OF SPENDING $$$ ON YOUR WEDDING? CLICK HERE!

It's hard not to feed the beast, unwittingly inviting more ads to descend.

One doesn't want to fall down on the job, after all.

HAVE YOU COMPLETED YOUR WEDDING TO-DO LIST?

NOT EVEN CLOSE, SARGE!

But I began to wonder...

WHAT HAS CHANGED IN JOHN'S ONLINE EXPERIENCE?

Good thing he was right there to ask.

NOTHING! Look at this!

No "Slim down for the big day," no "Affordable wedding decor," NOTHING!

Your ads are for apps and mail-order shaving companies!

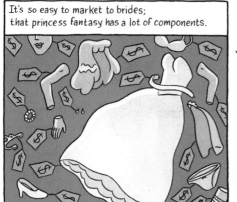

It's so easy to market to brides; that princess fantasy has a lot of components.

But what's the male equivalent of the princess fantasy?

PRINCE?

Why shouldn't men get to live out a pre-adolescent role-play through their weddings?

Maybe a superhero?

Should I wear a jetpack to the wedding?

Yes. Definitely.

And if my personal princess fantasy is a sassy Jane Austen heroine, why is it so hard to find a dress to fit this fantasy?

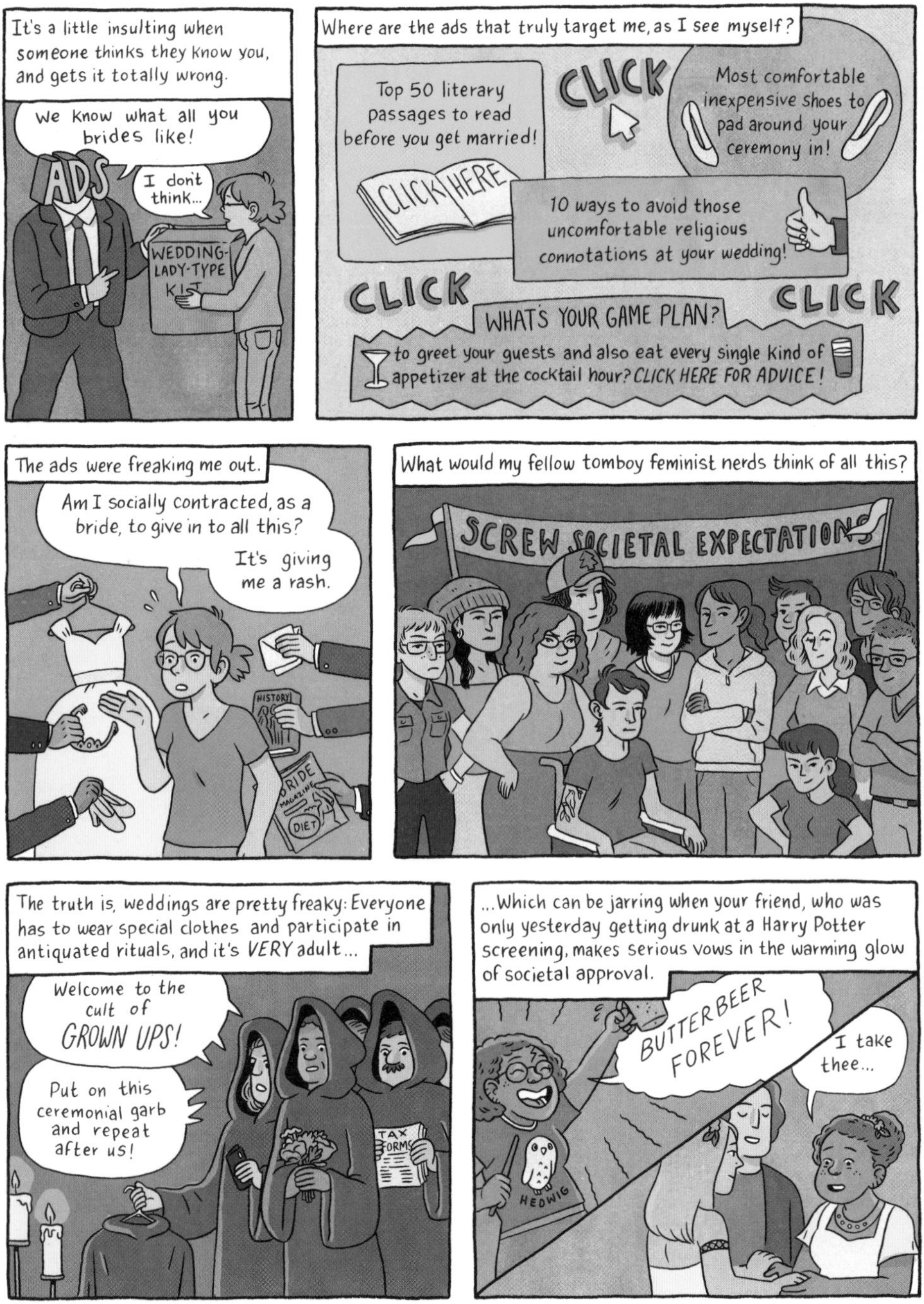

It's a little insulting when someone thinks they know you, and gets it totally wrong.
We know what all you brides like!
ADS
I don't think...
WEDDING-LADY-TYPE KIT
Where are the ads that truly target me, as I see myself?
Top 50 literary passages to read before you get married!
CLICK HERE
CLICK
Most comfortable inexpensive shoes to pad around your ceremony in!
10 ways to avoid those uncomfortable religious connotations at your wedding!
CLICK
CLICK
WHAT'S YOUR GAME PLAN?
to greet your guests and also eat every single kind of appetizer at the cocktail hour? CLICK HERE FOR ADVICE!
The ads were freaking me out.
Am I socially contracted, as a bride, to give in to all this?
It's giving me a rash.
HISTORY
BRIDE MAGAZINE
DIET
What would my fellow tomboy feminist nerds think of all this?
SCREW SOCIETAL EXPECTATIONS
The truth is, weddings are pretty freaky: Everyone has to wear special clothes and participate in antiquated rituals, and it's VERY adult...
Welcome to the cult of GROWN UPS!
Put on this ceremonial garb and repeat after us!
TAX FORMS
...Which can be jarring when your friend, who was only yesterday getting drunk at a Harry Potter screening, makes serious vows in the warming glow of societal approval.
BUTTERBEER FOREVER!
HEDWIG
I take thee...

Weddings are steeped in traditional gender roles and sexist implications like nothing else I've known.

She's subservient!

Yes, Father!

I'll take her!

(Because I, thankfully, live in the 21st century.)

As symbols, weddings smack of heteronormative conformity – rituals excluding those who have not been deemed acceptable by religious or governmental edict.

MEMBERS ONLY

Yucky stuff.

Of course, modern weddings can be anything...

SECULAR
RELIGIOUS
SMALL
MODERN
BIG
THEME
TRAD
SERIOUS
GRAB BAG

...Even, one hopes, enlightened beyond the confines of historically sexist traditions.

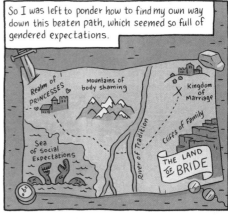

So I was left to ponder how to find my own way down this beaten path, which seemed so full of gendered expectations.

Realm of PRINCESSES
Mountains of body shaming
Kingdom of Marriage
Sea of Social Expectations
River of Tradition
Cliffs of Family
THE LAND OF BRIDE

And to deal with my own conflicted feelings about weddings.

How can I be a party to the conformist participation in a sexist ritual that promotes the role of a woman as chattel to a man?

Especially when there are still places in this country that don't allow people who love each other to legally wed!*

NERDY GLASSES PUSH

But I love John, and I want to throw a party and make some public promises to celebrate that love.

NERDY GLASSES DROOP

* This particular worry took place prior to the Supreme Court ruling of June 2015

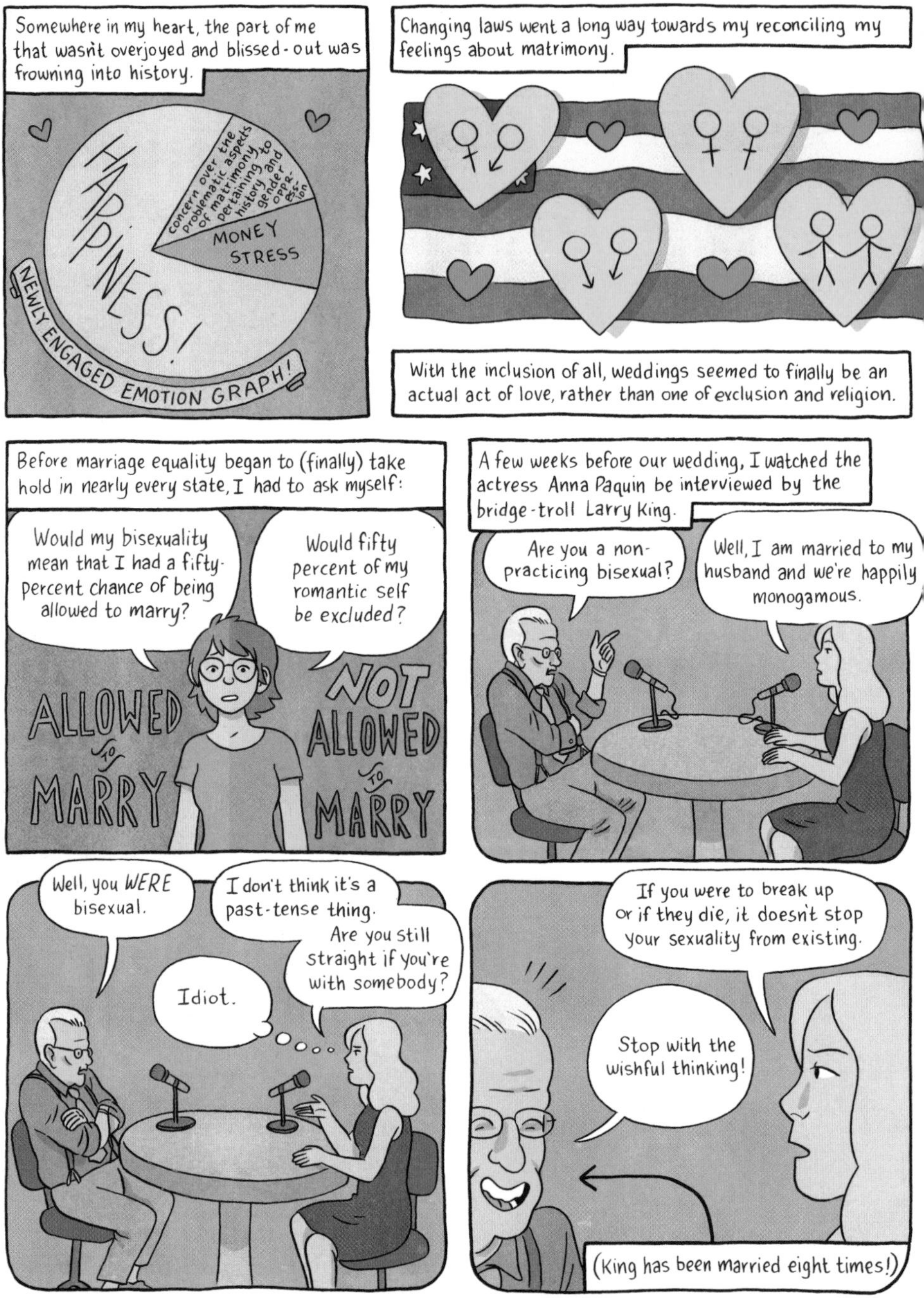
Somewhere in my heart, the part of me that wasn't overjoyed and blissed-out was frowning into history.
HAPPINESS!
concern over the problematic aspects of matrimony pertaining to history and gender oppression
MONEY STRESS
NEWLY ENGAGED EMOTION GRAPH!
Changing laws went a long way towards my reconciling my feelings about matrimony.
With the inclusion of all, weddings seemed to finally be an actual act of love, rather than one of exclusion and religion.
Before marriage equality began to (finally) take hold in nearly every state, I had to ask myself:
Would my bisexuality mean that I had a fifty-percent chance of being allowed to marry?
Would fifty percent of my romantic self be excluded?
ALLOWED to MARRY
NOT ALLOWED to MARRY
A few weeks before our wedding, I watched the actress Anna Paquin be interviewed by the bridge-troll Larry King.
Are you a non-practicing bisexual?
Well, I am married to my husband and we're happily monogamous.
Well, you WERE bisexual.
I don't think it's a past-tense thing.
Are you still straight if you're with somebody?
Idiot.
If you were to break up or if they die, it doesn't stop your sexuality from existing.
Stop with the wishful thinking!
(King has been married eight times!)

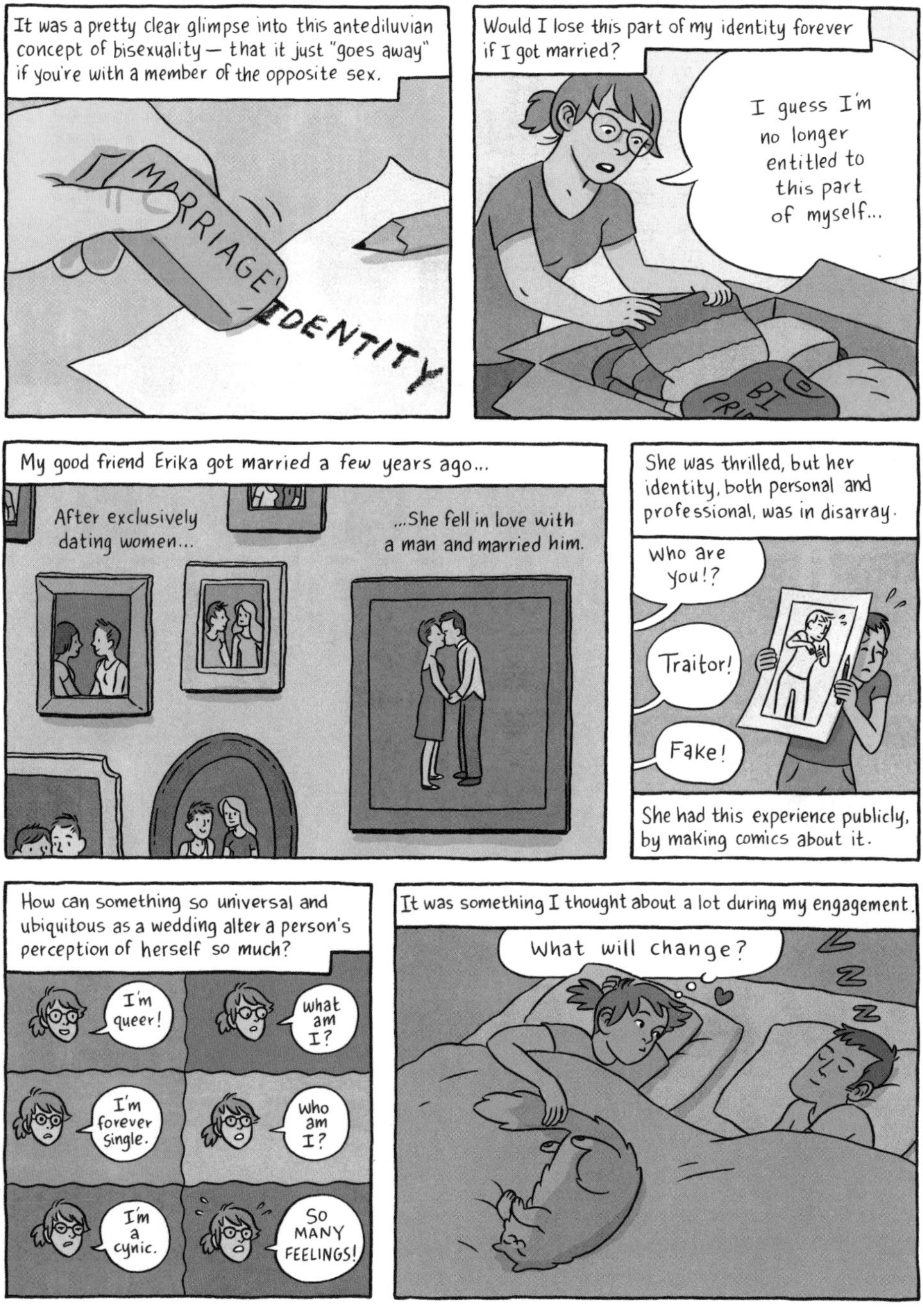

It was a pretty clear glimpse into this antediluvian concept of bisexuality — that it just "goes away" if you're with a member of the opposite sex.
MARRIAGE
IDENTITY
Would I lose this part of my identity forever if I got married?
I guess I'm no longer entitled to this part of myself...
My good friend Erika got married a few years ago...
After exclusively dating women...
...She fell in love with a man and married him.
She was thrilled, but her identity, both personal and professional, was in disarray.
Who are you!?
Traitor!
Fake!
She had this experience publicly, by making comics about it.
How can something so universal and ubiquitous as a wedding alter a person's perception of herself so much?
I'm queer!
What am I?
I'm forever single.
Who am I?
I'm a cynic.
So MANY FEELINGS!
It was something I thought about a lot during my engagement.
What will change?

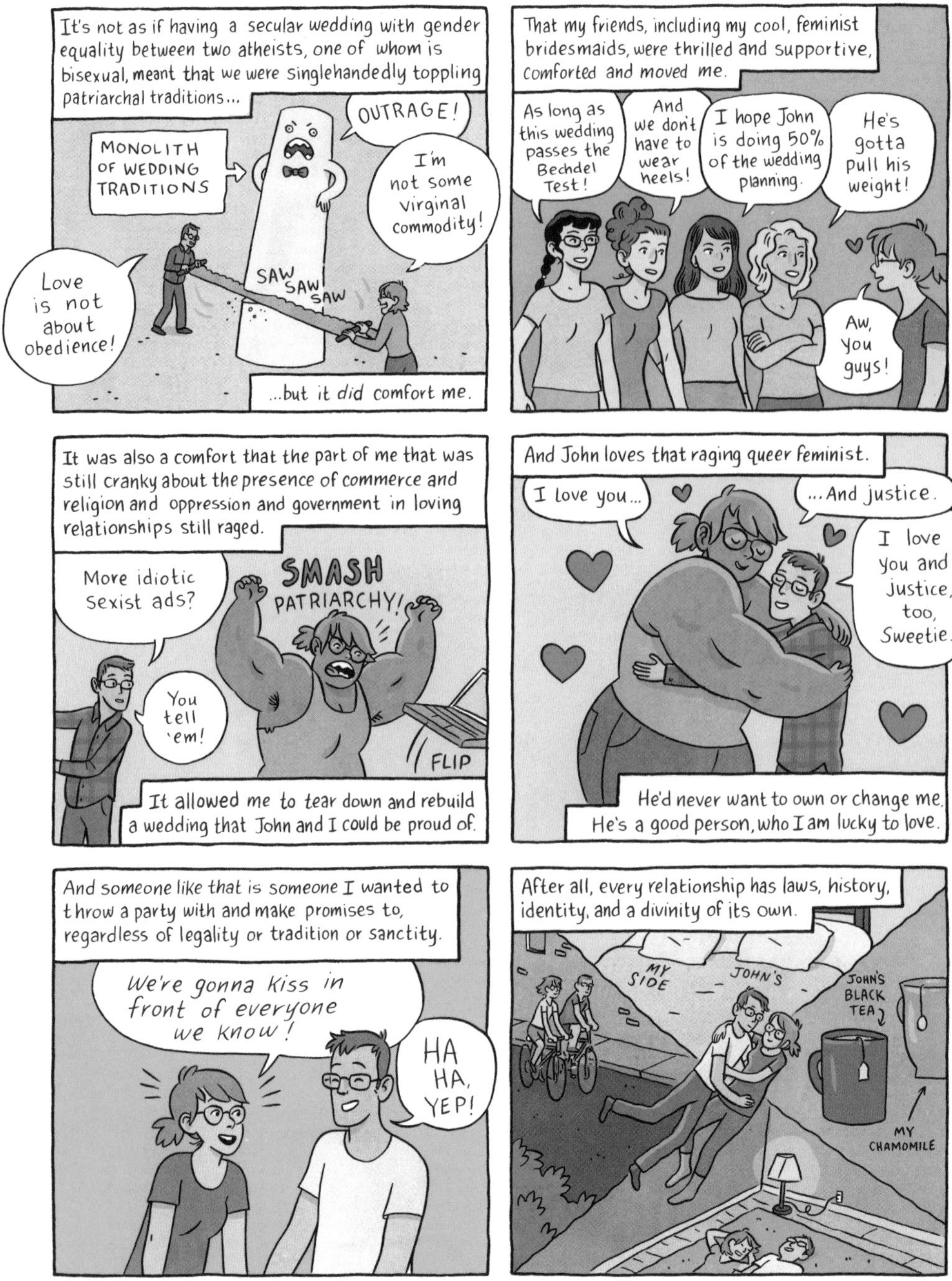

It's not as if having a secular wedding with gender equality between two atheists, one of whom is bisexual, meant that we were singlehandedly toppling patriarchal traditions...
MONOLITH OF WEDDING TRADITIONS
OUTRAGE!
I'm not some virginal commodity!
Love is not about obedience!
SAW SAW SAW
...but it did comfort me.
That my friends, including my cool, feminist bridesmaids, were thrilled and supportive, comforted and moved me.
As long as this wedding passes the Bechdel Test!
And we don't have to wear heels!
I hope John is doing 50% of the wedding planning.
He's gotta pull his weight!
Aw, you guys!
It was also a comfort that the part of me that was still cranky about the presence of commerce and religion and oppression and government in loving relationships still raged.
More idiotic sexist ads?
SMASH PATRIARCHY!
You tell 'em!
FLIP
It allowed me to tear down and rebuild a wedding that John and I could be proud of.
And John loves that raging queer feminist.
I love you...
...And justice.
I love you and justice, too, Sweetie.
He'd never want to own or change me. He's a good person, who I am lucky to love.
And someone like that is someone I wanted to throw a party with and make promises to, regardless of legality or tradition or sanctity.
We're gonna kiss in front of everyone we know!
HA HA, YEP!
After all, every relationship has laws, history, identity, and a divinity of its own.
MY SIDE
JOHN'S
JOHN'S BLACK TEA
MY CHAMOMILE

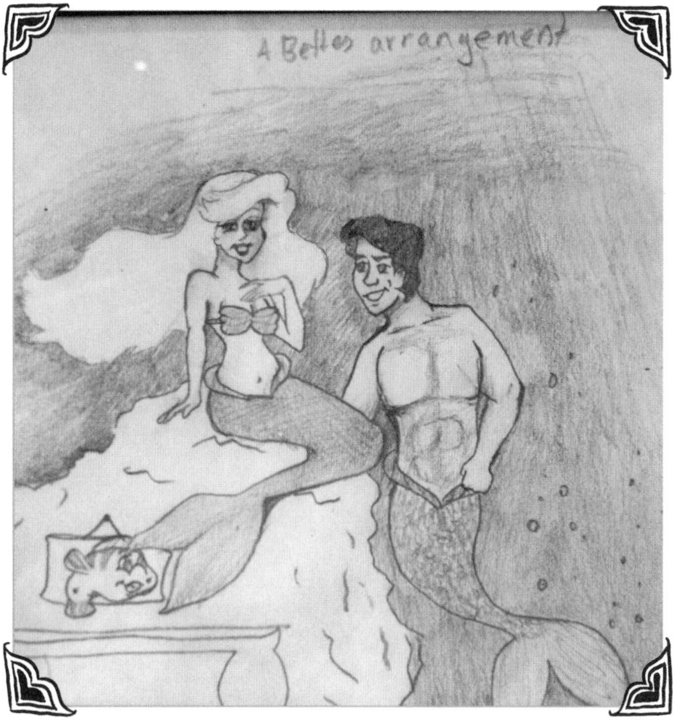
A Better arrangement

By Lucy, age 10

THE NAME

"Changing your name when you marry is **EASY!**..."

THE LAW

"...As long as you're a woman taking a man's last name."

IF YOU WANT ANOTHER OPTION, IT'S HARDER!

IN ORDER TO CHANGE YOUR MIDDLE NAME... (LIKE WE WANTED TO*)

*(To take one another's last names as our middle names)

1. Complete a "name change petition" in your home state and submit it to the court clerk. (You'll probably need to pay a court fee.)

Proof of residence

2. Publish your intent to change your name in a newspaper (good luck). You'll have to pay for this to run for at least two weeks.

Please, let us do this!!

The only print newspaper in existence

GAME

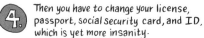

HELLO,
MY NAME IS:
?

3. Go to a court hearing where, if nobody has protested your intent, you can *maybe* get permission to move ahead.

4. Then you have to change your license, passport, social security card, and ID, which is yet more insanity.

BANG
BANG

ALTERNATIVELY:

You could do what
we did:

NOTHING.

It's combined laziness & cheapness.

We'll get around to it someday.

It would be cool to share a family name.

But for now...

You can't make changes to the account unless you share the same last name as your husband.

IT'S THE 21ST CENTURY!

CABLE CO.

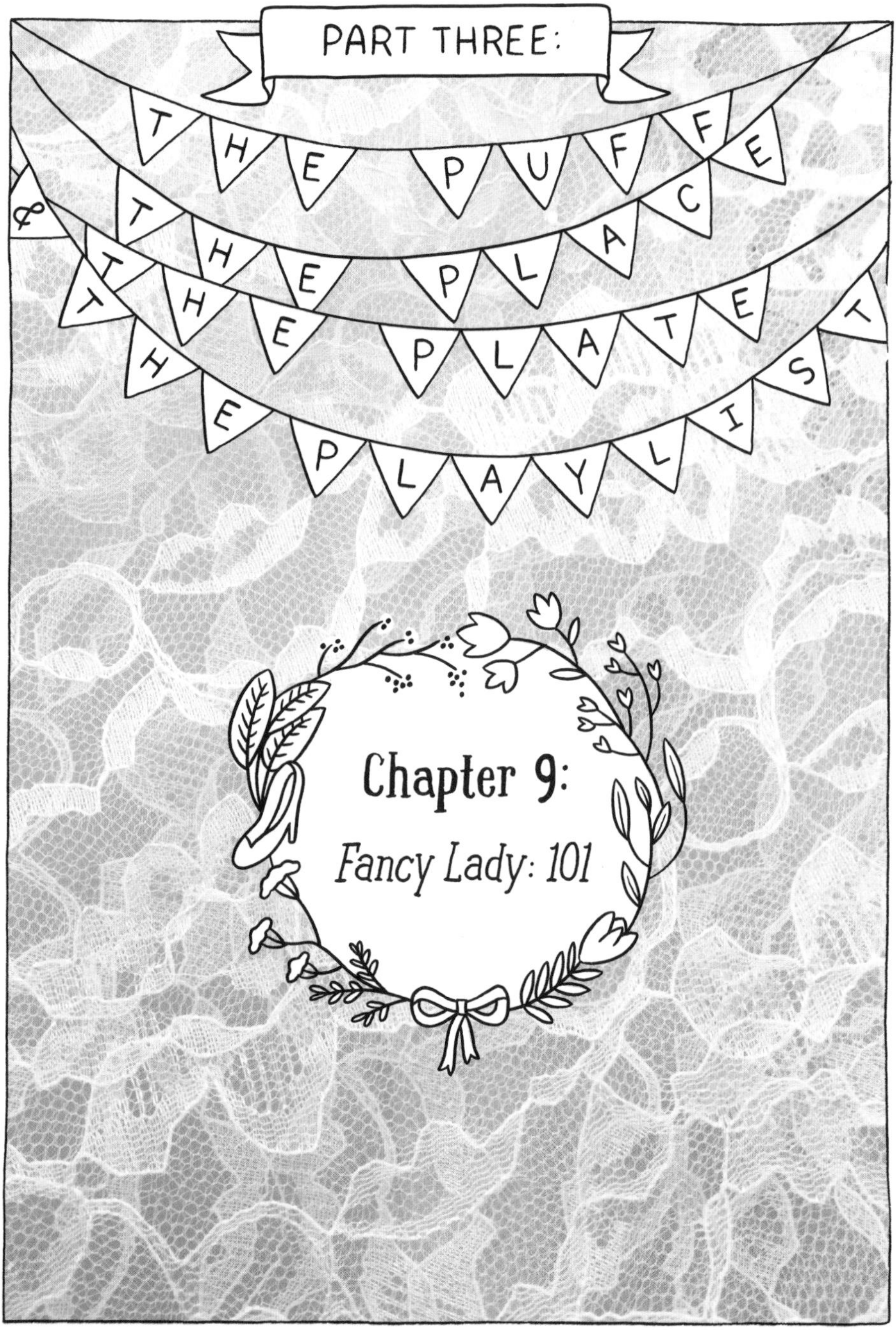
PART THREE:
THE PUFFE
& THE PLACE
& THE PLATE
& THE PLAYLIST
Chapter 9:
Fancy Lady: 101

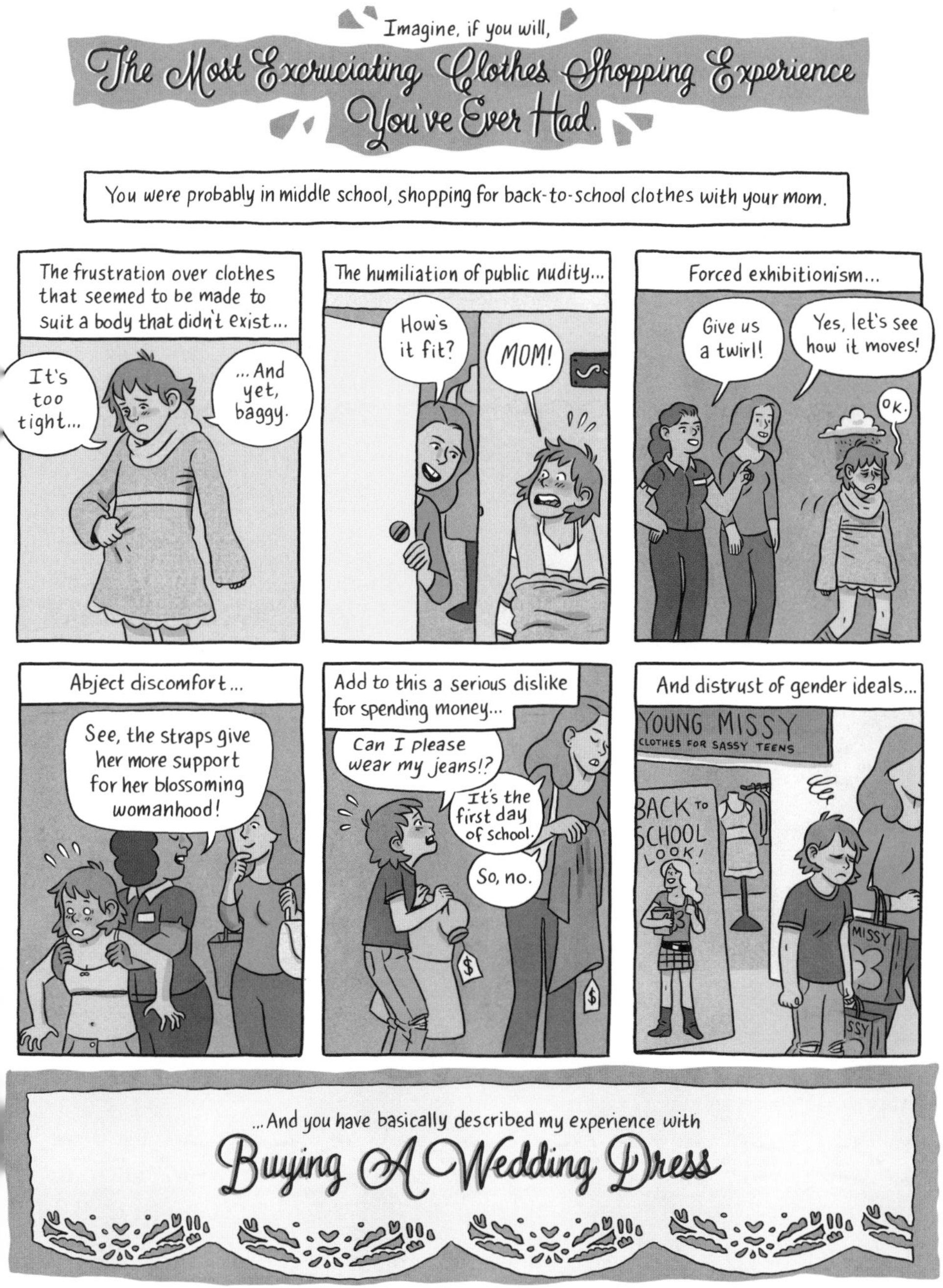
Imagine, if you will,
The Most Excruciating Clothes Shopping Experience You've Ever Had.
You were probably in middle school, shopping for back-to-school clothes with your mom.
The frustration over clothes that seemed to be made to suit a body that didn't exist...
It's too tight...
...And yet, baggy.
The humiliation of public nudity...
How's it fit?
MOM!
Forced exhibitionism...
Give us a twirl!
Yes, let's see how it moves!
OK.
Abject discomfort...
See, the straps give her more support for her blossoming womanhood!
Add to this a serious dislike for spending money...
Can I please wear my jeans!?
It's the first day of school.
So, no.
$
$
And distrust of gender ideals...
YOUNG MISSY
CLOTHES FOR SASSY TEENS
BACK TO SCHOOL LOOK!
MISSY
...And you have basically described my experience with
Buying A Wedding Dress

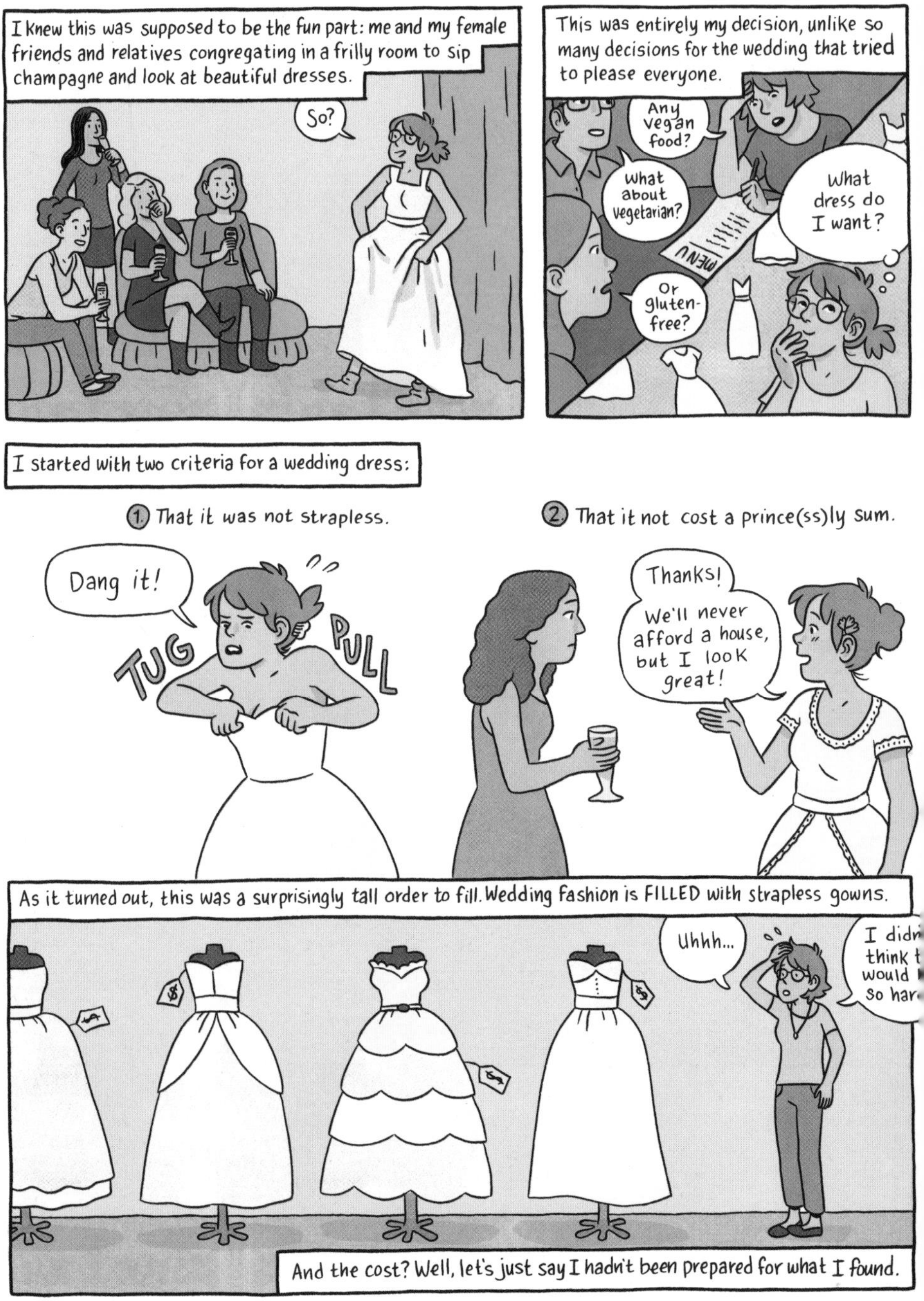
I knew this was supposed to be the fun part: me and my female friends and relatives congregating in a frilly room to sip champagne and look at beautiful dresses.
So?
This was entirely my decision, unlike so many decisions for the wedding that tried to please everyone.
Any vegan food?
What about vegetarian?
What dress do I want?
MENU
Or gluten-free?
I started with two criteria for a wedding dress:
1. That it was not strapless.
2. That it not cost a prince(ss)ly sum.
Dang it!
TUG
PULL
Thanks!
We'll never afford a house, but I look great!
As it turned out, this was a surprisingly tall order to fill. Wedding fashion is FILLED with strapless gowns.
Uhhh...
And the cost? Well, let's just say I hadn't been prepared for what I found.

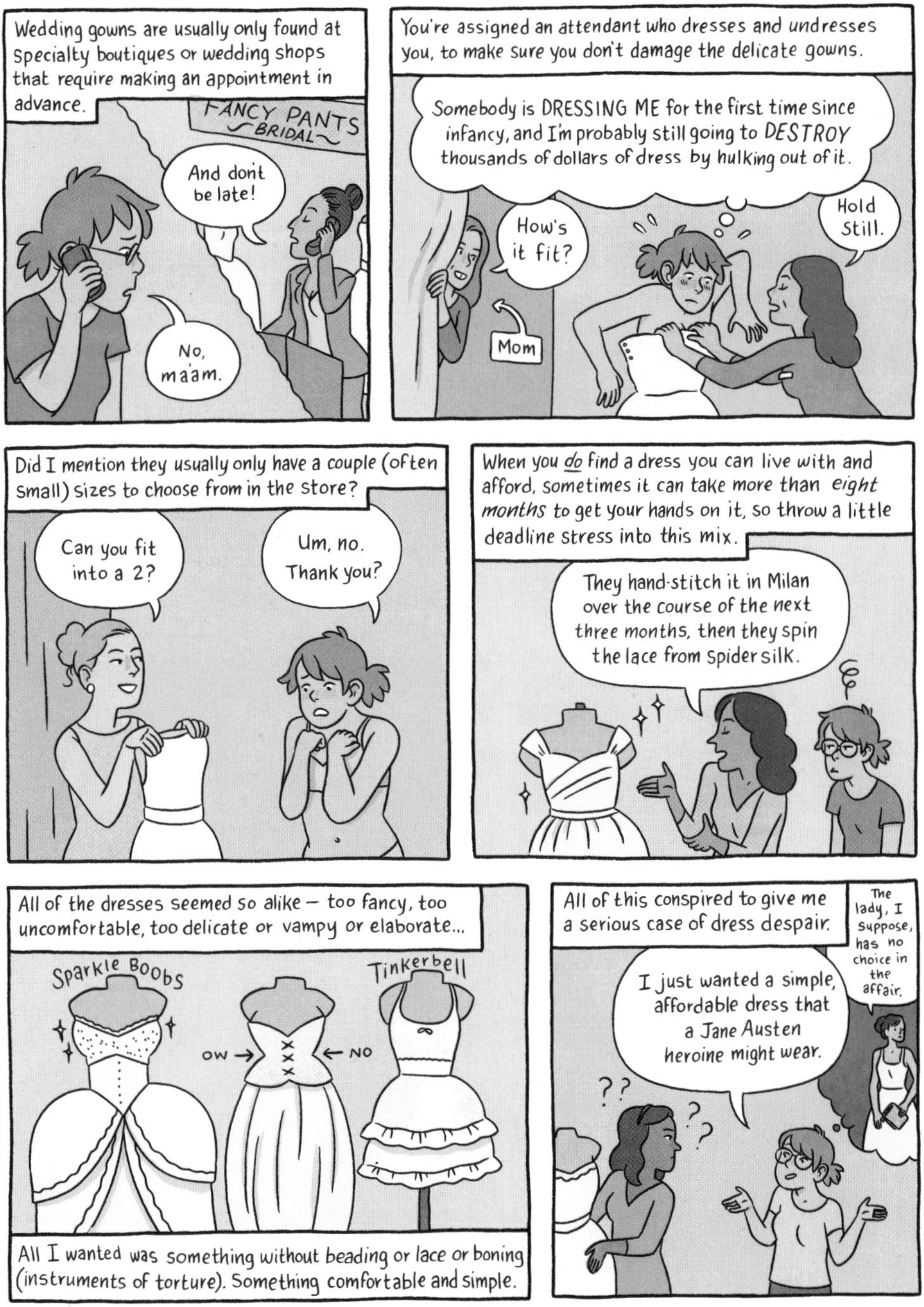
Wedding gowns are usually only found at specialty boutiques or wedding shops that require making an appointment in advance.
FANCY PANTS BRIDAL
And don't be late!
No, ma'am.
You're assigned an attendant who dresses and undresses you, to make sure you don't damage the delicate gowns.
Somebody is DRESSING ME for the first time since infancy, and I'm probably still going to DESTROY thousands of dollars of dress by hulking out of it.
How's it fit?
Mom
Hold Still.
Did I mention they usually only have a couple (often small) sizes to choose from in the store?
Can you fit into a 2?
Um, no. Thank you?
When you do find a dress you can live with and afford, sometimes it can take more than eight months to get your hands on it, so throw a little deadline stress into this mix.
They hand-stitch it in Milan over the course of the next three months, then they spin the lace from spider silk.
All of the dresses seemed so alike — too fancy, too uncomfortable, too delicate or vampy or elaborate...
Sparkle Boobs
OW →
← NO
Tinkerbell
All I wanted was something without beading or lace or boning (instruments of torture). Something comfortable and simple.
All of this conspired to give me a serious case of dress despair.
The lady, I suppose, has no choice in the affair.
I just wanted a simple, affordable dress that a Jane Austen heroine might wear.
??
??

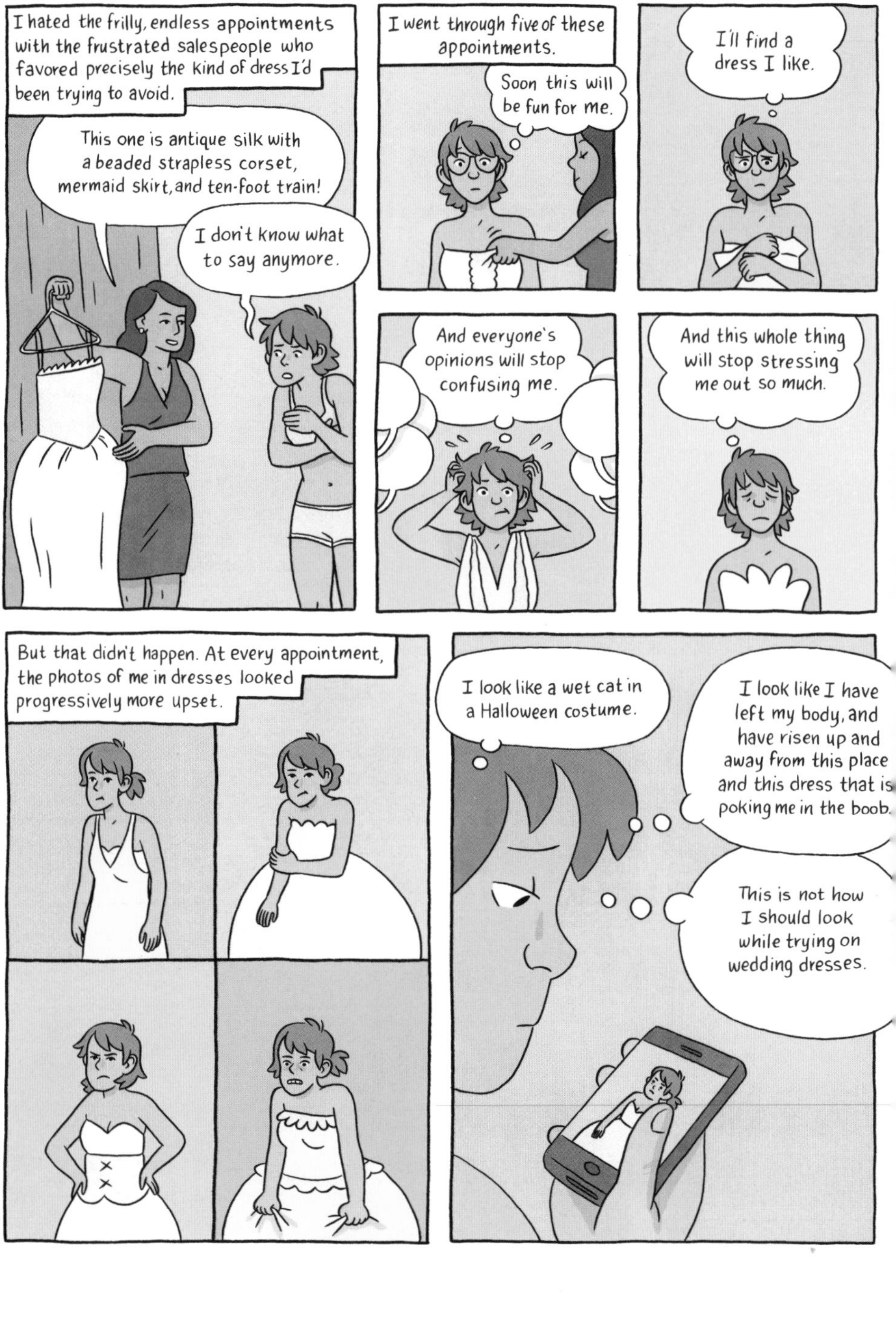

I hated the frilly, endless appointments with the frustrated salespeople who favored precisely the kind of dress I'd been trying to avoid.
This one is antique silk with a beaded strapless corset, mermaid skirt, and ten-foot train!
I don't know what to say anymore.
I went through five of these appointments.
Soon this will be fun for me.
I'll find a dress I like.
And everyone's opinions will stop confusing me.
And this whole thing will stop stressing me out so much.
But that didn't happen. At every appointment, the photos of me in dresses looked progressively more upset.
I look like a wet cat in a Halloween costume.
I look like I have left my body, and have risen up and away from this place and this dress that is poking me in the boob.
This is not how I should look while trying on wedding dresses.

I felt like I was missing something that everyone else seemed to already know...

How?

...Like I was taking a test for a class I'd never gone to.

The final is TODAY!?

But I didn't even know I was enrolled!!

Final Exam
Use your accumulated fashion & beauty know-how to pick a dress that wil... define you as a bride and refl... your perso... as a w... in o...

...Like I'd missed "Fancy Lady 101," and now I was expected to know how to transform myself into a princess through mysterious hair/makeup/dress-appointment means that were totally beyond me.

Ok, class, today I'm going to cover how to put your hair in a bun so it actually looks nice, and not like you made a hair pile on your head.

I would have taken that class, had I found it on offer!

My mother is a hippie who rarely wears makeup and favors peasant skirts and T-shirts.

FASHION STYLE

I grew up in sneakers and ripped jeans, and recently upped my lady game to include comfortable skirts.

I know all of two hairstyles, and cannot do makeup for the life of me.

I look like a raccoon.

There *were* some alternatives to this wedding dress gauntlet...

Handmade dresses: nice, but didn't remove the fuss or expense of the experience.

YIKES!

Vintage dresses might have worked, but my mother's was lost to the ages, and I didn't want to buy something online without seeing it in person.

So I kept making dress appointments, and wet-catting my way through them.
But after five appointments, I gave up.

I guess I should just get one of these.

They're all just as expensive and high-maintenance and uncomfortable as the rest.

I don't wanna be ~NAKED~ at my wedding, so I might as well choose the lesser evil.

So I went downtown to make a deposit on "The Lesser-Evil Gown."

At least this one has arms...
...Sorta.

CTA

It was an obscene sum of money, but more affordable than most of the dresses I'd seen, at least.

URK.

It would take six months to be made, which was down to the wire, and would allow little alteration time.

TIC
TIC

WEDDING

I'm an average height, so I'd probably need about four feet cut from the length...

...because that's how fashion is.

And it was *not* **comfortable.**

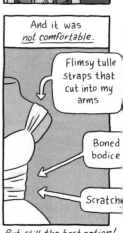

Flimsy tulle straps that cut into my arms

Boned bodice

Scratch

But still the best option!

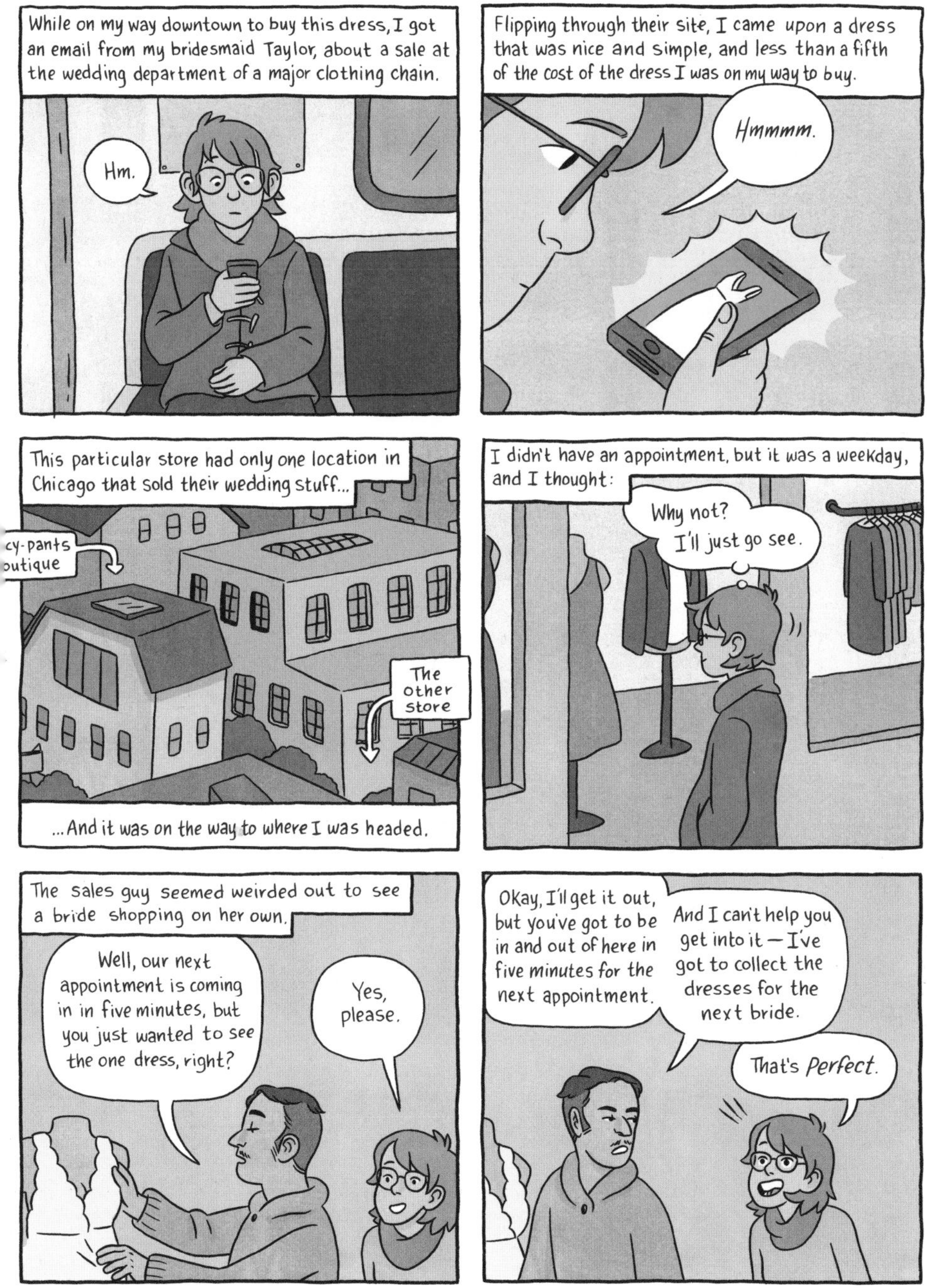
While on my way downtown to buy this dress, I got an email from my bridesmaid Taylor, about a sale at the wedding department of a major clothing chain.
Hm.
Flipping through their site, I came upon a dress that was nice and simple, and less than a fifth of the cost of the dress I was on my way to buy.
Hmmmm.
This particular store had only one location in Chicago that sold their wedding stuff...
cy-pants outique
The other store
...And it was on the way to where I was headed.
I didn't have an appointment, but it was a weekday, and I thought:
Why not? I'll just go see.
The sales guy seemed weirded out to see a bride shopping on her own.
Well, our next appointment is coming in in five minutes, but you just wanted to see the one dress, right?
Yes, please.
Okay, I'll get it out, but you've got to be in and out of here in five minutes for the next appointment.
And I can't help you get into it — I've got to collect the dresses for the next bride.
That's *Perfect*.

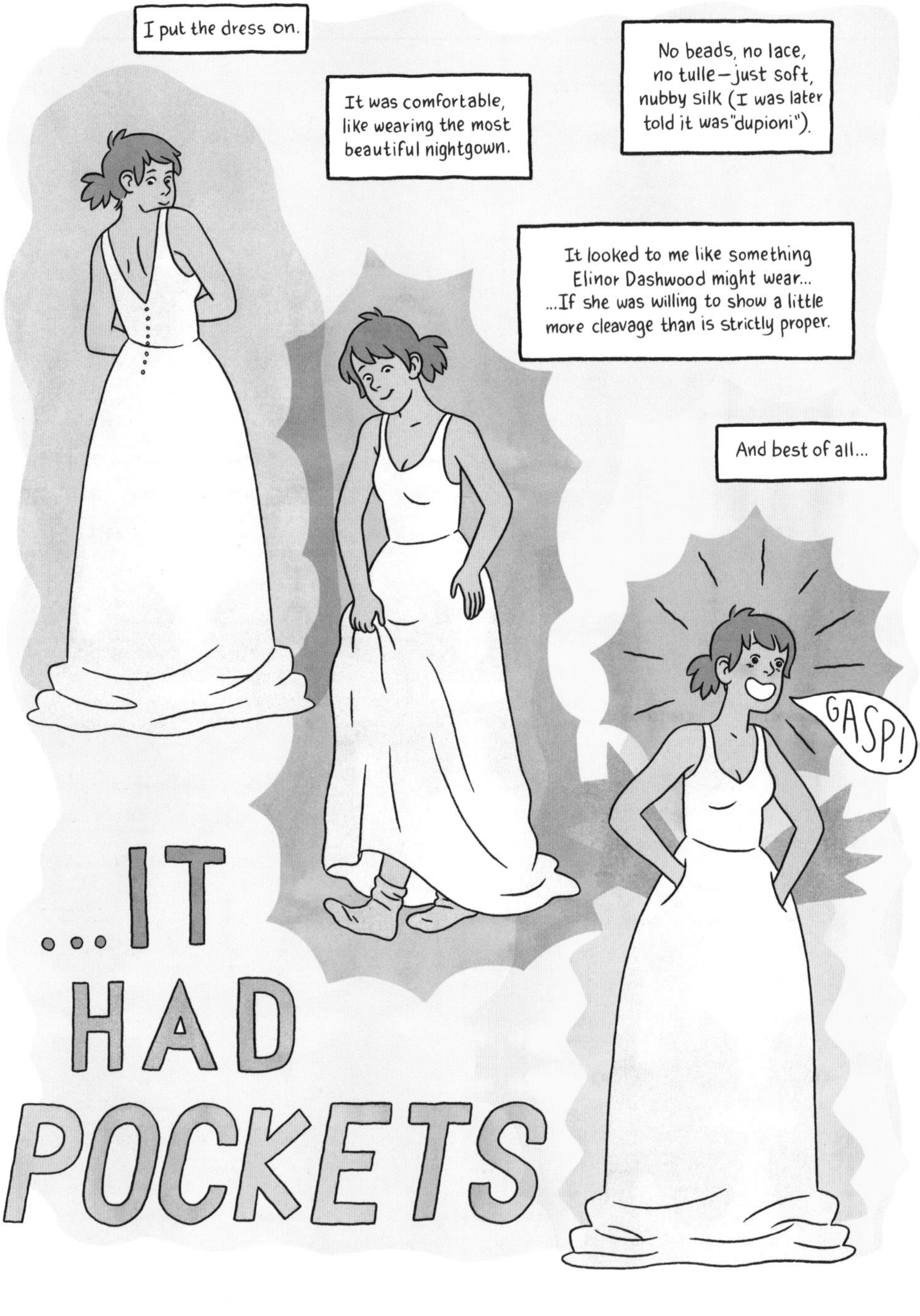

I put the dress on.
It was comfortable, like wearing the most beautiful nightgown.
No beads, no lace, no tulle—just soft, nubby silk (I was later told it was "dupioni").
It looked to me like something Elinor Dashwood might wear... ...If she was willing to show a little more cleavage than is strictly proper.
And best of all...
GASP!
...IT HAD POCKETS

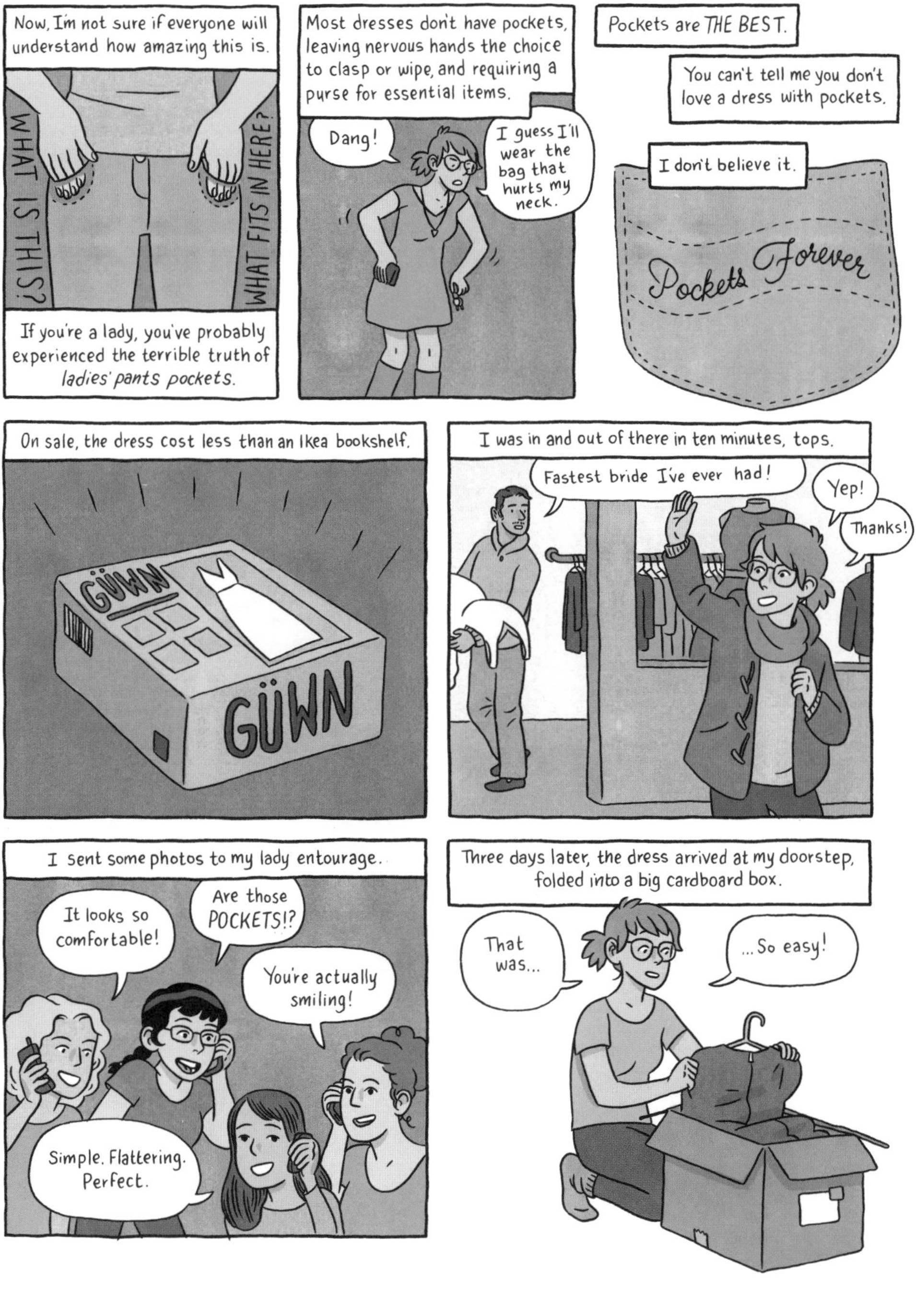
Now, I'm not sure if everyone will understand how amazing this is.
WHAT IS THIS?
WHAT FITS IN HERE?
If you're a lady, you've probably experienced the terrible truth of *ladies' pants pockets.*
Most dresses don't have pockets, leaving nervous hands the choice to clasp or wipe, and requiring a purse for essential items.
Dang!
I guess I'll wear the bag that hurts my neck.
Pockets are *THE BEST.*
You can't tell me you don't love a dress with pockets.
I don't believe it.
Pockets Forever
On sale, the dress cost less than an Ikea bookshelf.
GÜWN
GÜWN
I was in and out of there in ten minutes, tops.
Fastest bride I've ever had!
Yep!
Thanks!
I sent some photos to my lady entourage.
It looks so comfortable!
Are those POCKETS!?
You're actually smiling!
Simple. Flattering. Perfect.
Three days later, the dress arrived at my doorstep, folded into a big cardboard box.
That was...
...So easy!

I still had to have about four feet lopped off the end.

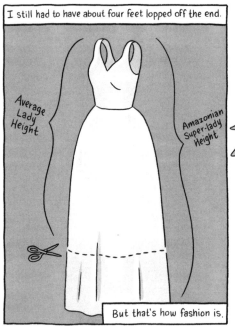

Average Lady Height

Amazonian Super-lady Height

But that's how fashion is.

I wore it with comfy flats, and a bracelet and earrings from Etsy.

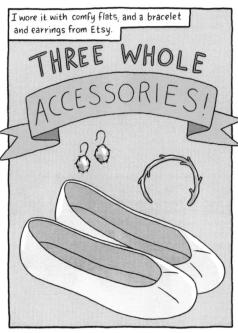

THREE WHOLE ACCESSORIES!

When I found out what veils cost, and that I had to go back to the boutiques to get one, I made my own out of tulle, a comb, and a lace ribbon.

1 yard of white tulle

Sew to comb

Gather

Cost: $10

Average veil cost: $200

GLUE

Craft glue

Lace ribbon

In my pockets, during the wedding, I kept lipstick, a handkerchief, and (up until the ceremony) John's ring.

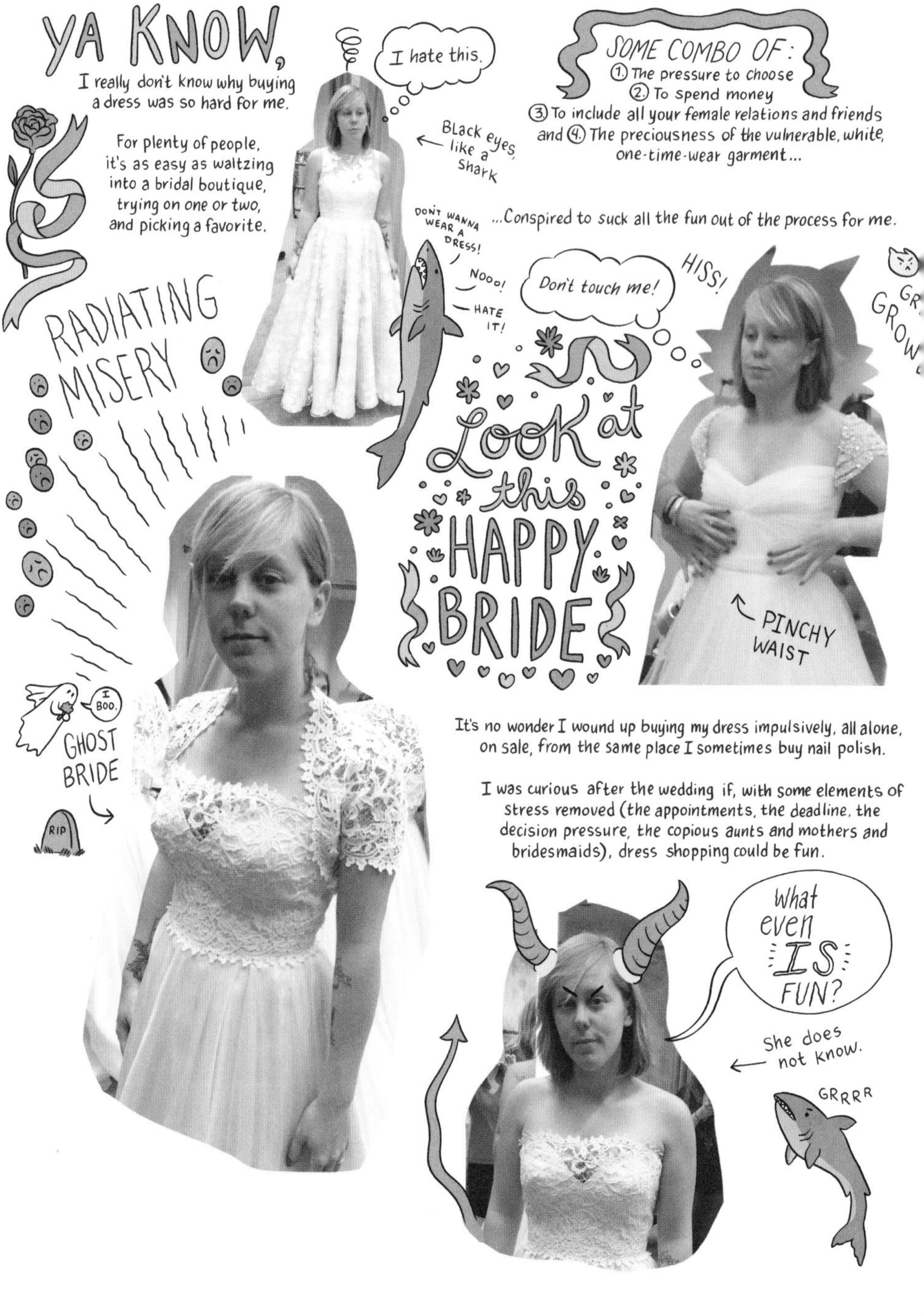
YA KNOW,
I really don't know why buying a dress was so hard for me.
For plenty of people, it's as easy as waltzing into a bridal boutique, trying on one or two, and picking a favorite.
I hate this.
Black eyes, like a shark
DON'T WANNA WEAR A DRESS!
NOOO!
HATE IT!
SOME COMBO OF:
① The pressure to choose
② To spend money
③ To include all your female relations and friends and ④ The preciousness of the vulnerable, white, one-time-wear garment...
...Conspired to suck all the fun out of the process for me.
RADIATING MISERY
Don't touch me!
HISS!
GROWL
Look at this HAPPY BRIDE
PINCHY WAIST
I BOO.
GHOST BRIDE
RIP
It's no wonder I wound up buying my dress impulsively, all alone, on sale, from the same place I sometimes buy nail polish.
I was curious after the wedding if, with some elements of stress removed (the appointments, the deadline, the decision pressure, the copious aunts and mothers and bridesmaids), dress shopping could be fun.
What even IS FUN?
She does not know.
GRRRR

As an experiment, months after the wedding, my friend and bridesmaid Nora agreed to go on a

DRESS SAFARI.

We would walk into a wedding boutique with no appointment and ask to see the dresses. If they let us, we'd pick the silliest (me) or prettiest (her) dresses we could find, and both try them on.

WHAT I LEARNED:

1. It helps to not be the only one trying on dresses. I experienced something a little like stage fright when it was only me, pressured to perform as a dutiful bride for an audience...

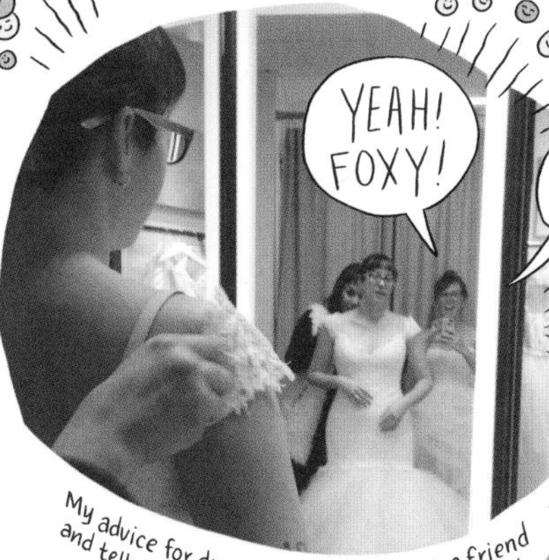
YEAH! FOXY!
WOO!

My advice for dress shopping: Go with a friend and tell the salespeople you're BOTH engaged. That way, you can see how dresses look from all angles, on someone else. You can also hear ONE outside opinion, from someone you trust.

2. Even the silliest, poofiest, most uncomfortable wedding dresses are actually very pretty.

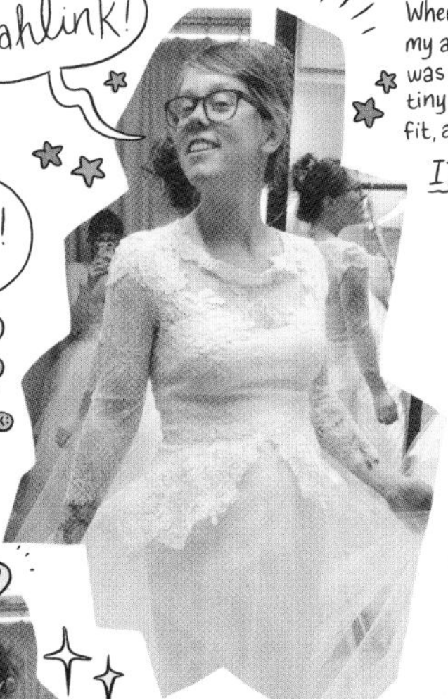
Dahlink!

When shopping for my actual dress, it was easy to see one tiny flaw, or a weird fit, and think: NO! IT'S HORRIBLE!

When the pressure is off, it's easy to see how beautiful the dresses are, as works of art, or as emblematic of the hope and beauty of weddings.

Although, this one... YEESH.

3. There's something very stunning, even moving, to see your friend in wedding duds.

Nora is single and happy, with no plans to wed, but she looked lovely and graceful in those dresses.

Had I gone on a dress safari with a friend back when I was single, I might have had a better idea of what I wanted when it came time to choose through the haze of wedding madness.

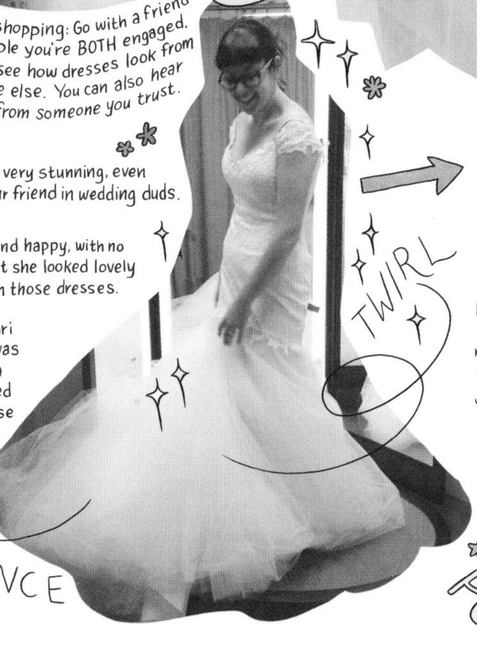
TWIRL
FLOUNCE

I suppose that applies to this whole process.

In hindsight, I wish I'd let myself dream a little more — rather than scoffed at single women who had "dream venues" or had picked "the dress." I'm not saying that planning out your whole wedding before you've even met a partner is a good idea. I'm just saying that, much like most things, it might not blindside you quite so much, if you just let yourself fantasize a little.

And yes, it can be fun.

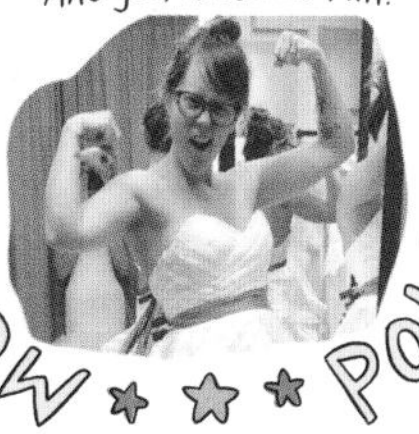
POW
POW

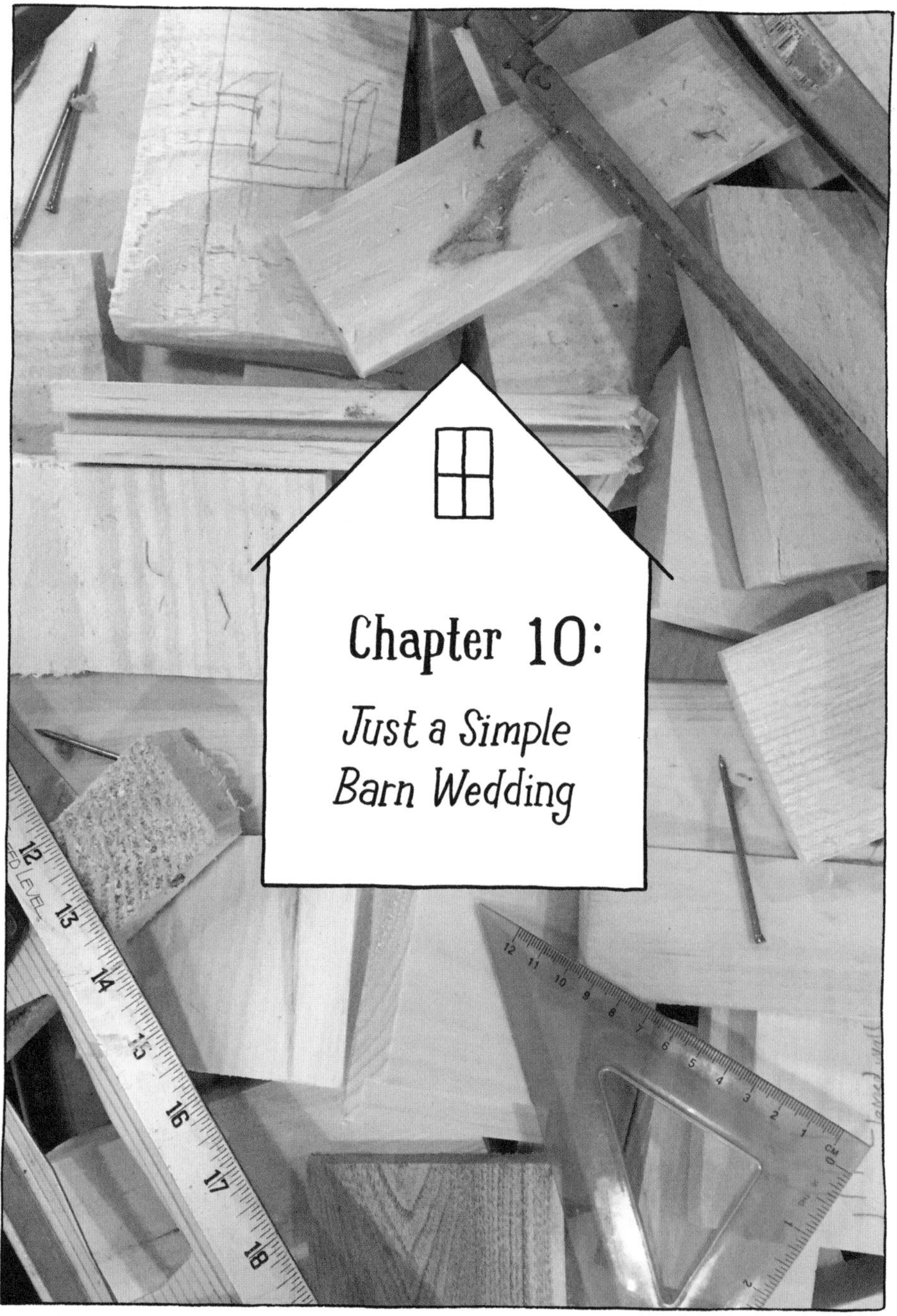

Chapter 10:

Just a Simple Barn Wedding

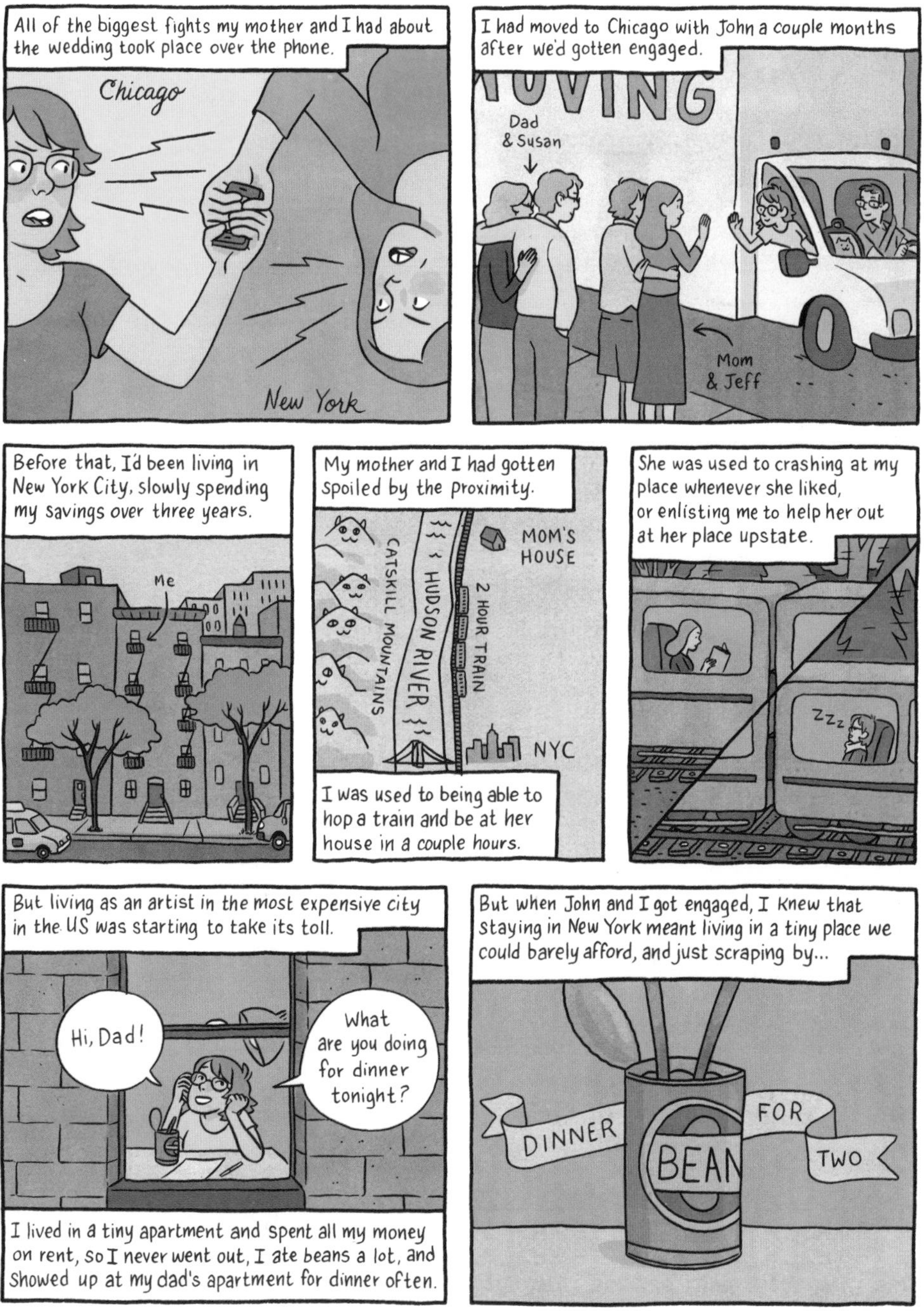

All of the biggest fights my mother and I had about the wedding took place over the phone.
Chicago
New York
I had moved to Chicago with John a couple months after we'd gotten engaged.
Dad & Susan
Mom & Jeff
Before that, I'd been living in New York City, slowly spending my savings over three years.
Me
My mother and I had gotten spoiled by the proximity.
CATSKILL MOUNTAINS
HUDSON RIVER
2 HOUR TRAIN
MOM'S HOUSE
NYC
I was used to being able to hop a train and be at her house in a couple hours.
She was used to crashing at my place whenever she liked, or enlisting me to help her out at her place upstate.
ZZZ
But living as an artist in the most expensive city in the US was starting to take its toll.
Hi, Dad!
What are you doing for dinner tonight?
I lived in a tiny apartment and spent all my money on rent, so I never went out, I ate beans a lot, and showed up at my dad's apartment for dinner often.
But when John and I got engaged, I knew that staying in New York meant living in a tiny place we could barely afford, and just scraping by...
DINNER
FOR
TWO
BEAN

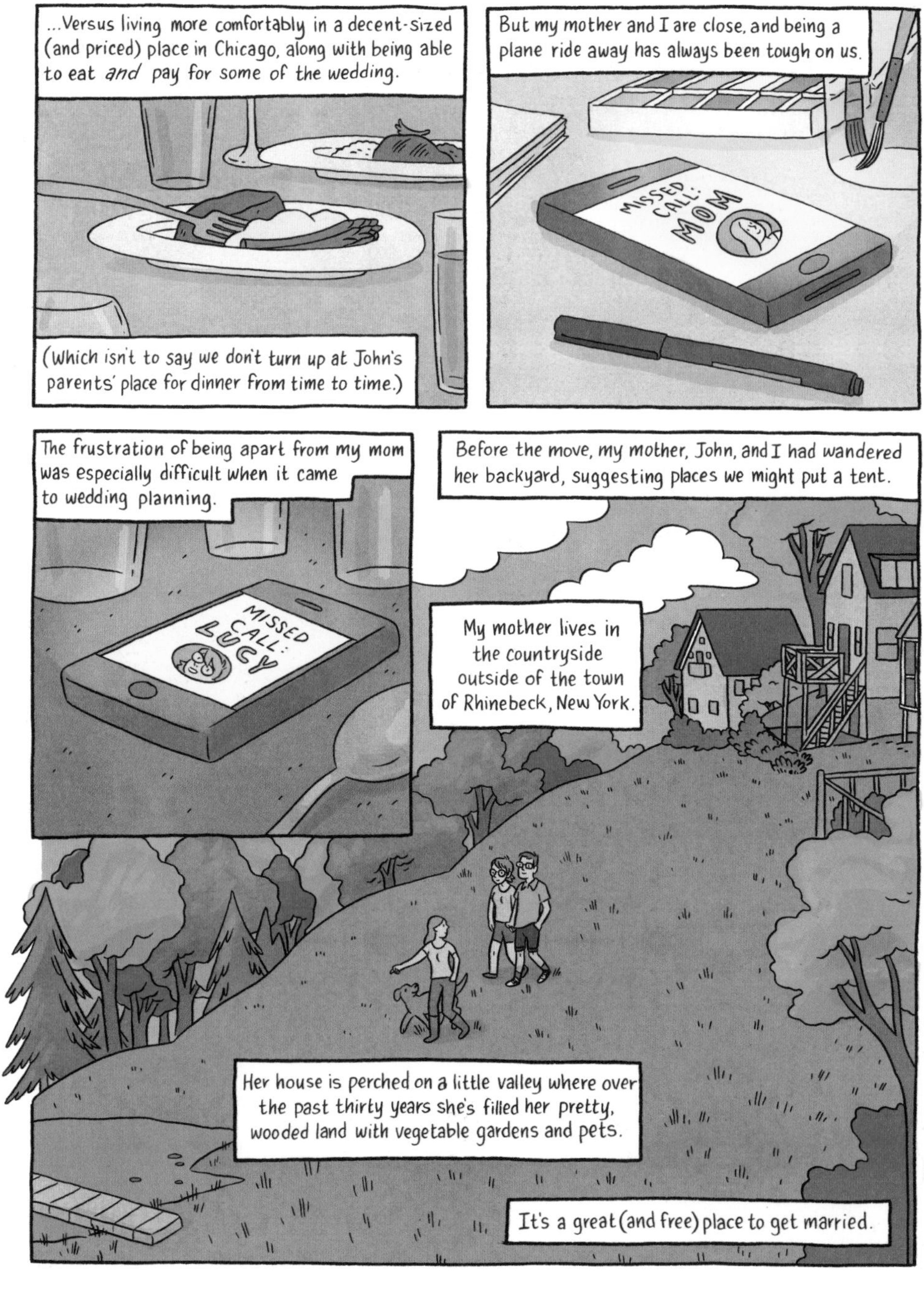
...Versus living more comfortably in a decent-sized (and priced) place in Chicago, along with being able to eat *and* pay for some of the wedding.
(Which isn't to say we don't turn up at John's parents' place for dinner from time to time.)
But my mother and I are close, and being a plane ride away has always been tough on us.
MISSED CALL: MOM
The frustration of being apart from my mom was especially difficult when it came to wedding planning.
MISSED CALL: LUCY
Before the move, my mother, John, and I had wandered her backyard, suggesting places we might put a tent.
My mother lives in the countryside outside of the town of Rhinebeck, New York.
Her house is perched on a little valley where over the past thirty years she's filled her pretty, wooded land with vegetable gardens and pets.
It's a great (and free) place to get married.

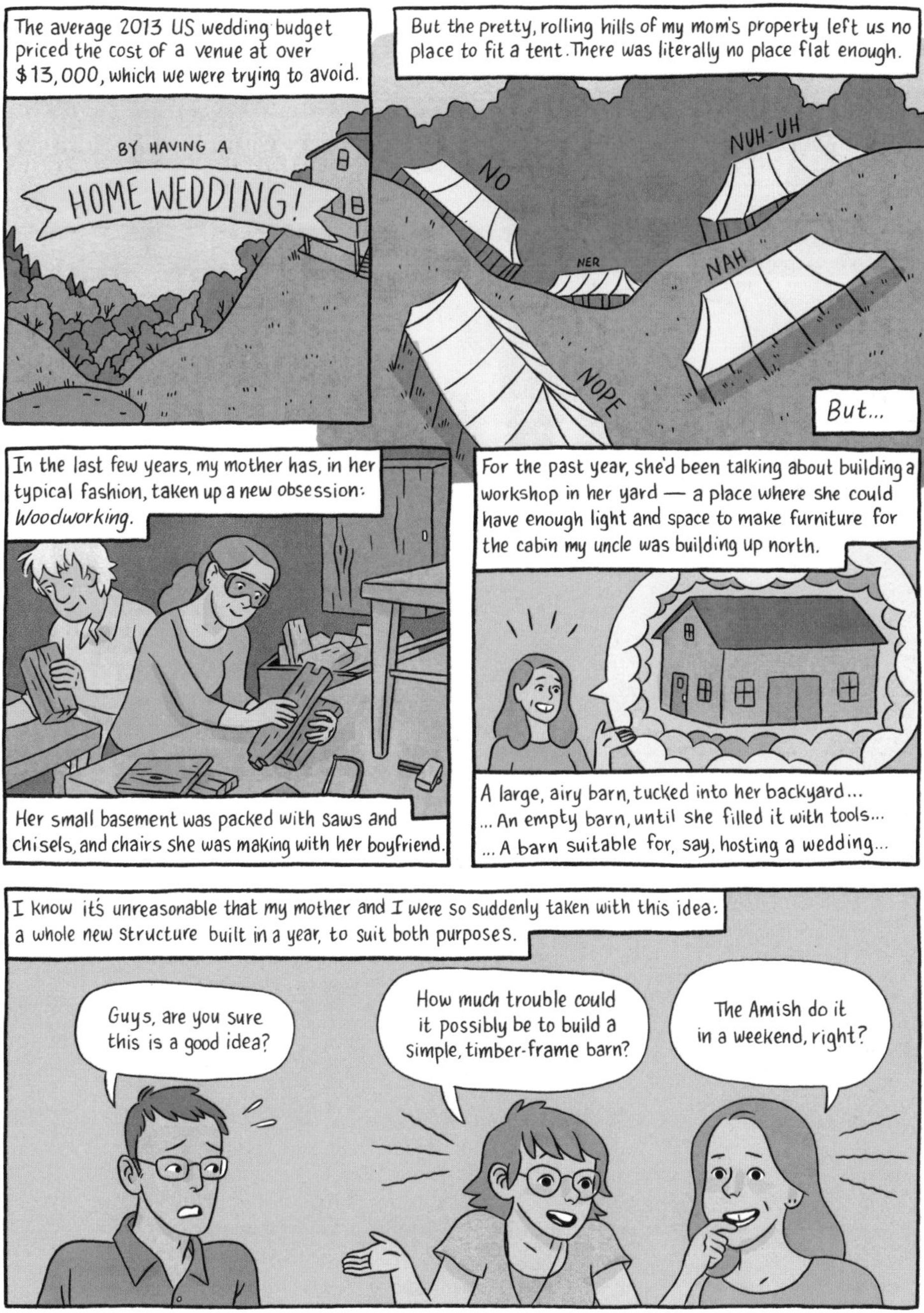
The average 2013 US wedding budget priced the cost of a venue at over $13,000, which we were trying to avoid.
BY HAVING A
HOME WEDDING!
But the pretty, rolling hills of my mom's property left us no place to fit a tent. There was literally no place flat enough.
NO
NUH-UH
NER
NAH
NOPE
But...
In the last few years, my mother has, in her typical fashion, taken up a new obsession: *Woodworking*.
Her small basement was packed with saws and chisels, and chairs she was making with her boyfriend.
For the past year, she'd been talking about building a workshop in her yard — a place where she could have enough light and space to make furniture for the cabin my uncle was building up north.
A large, airy barn, tucked into her backyard...
...An empty barn, until she filled it with tools...
...A barn suitable for, say, hosting a wedding...
I know it's unreasonable that my mother and I were so suddenly taken with this idea: a whole new structure built in a year, to suit both purposes.
Guys, are you sure this is a good idea?
How much trouble could it possibly be to build a simple, timber-frame barn?
The Amish do it in a weekend, right?

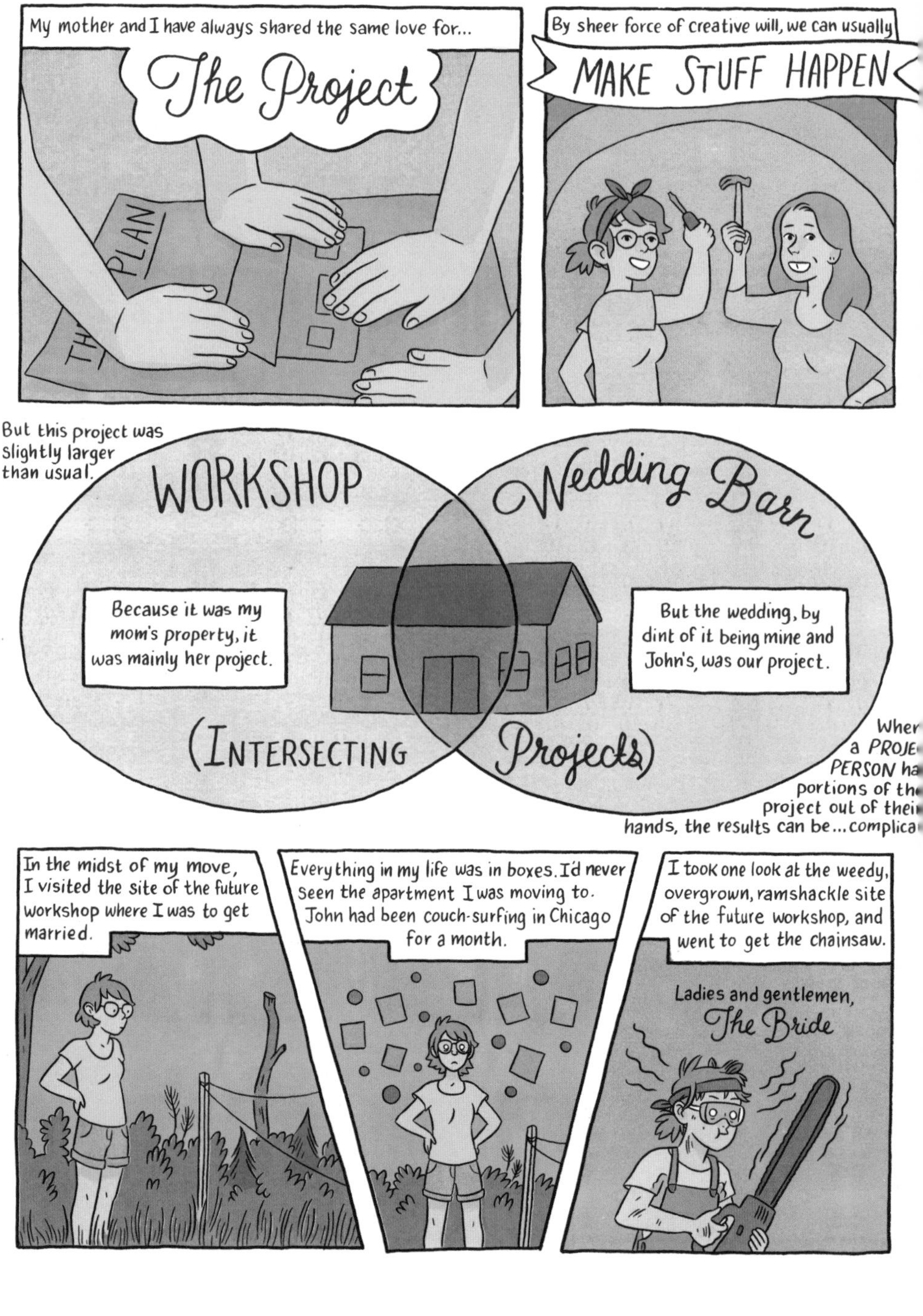
My mother and I have always shared the same love for...
The Project
THE PLAN
By sheer force of creative will, we can usually
MAKE STUFF HAPPEN
But this project was slightly larger than usual.
WORKSHOP
Wedding Barn
Because it was my mom's property, it was mainly her project.
But the wedding, by dint of it being mine and John's, was our project.
(INTERSECTING Projects)
When a PROJECT PERSON has portions of their project out of their hands, the results can be...complicated.
In the midst of my move, I visited the site of the future workshop where I was to get married.
Everything in my life was in boxes. I'd never seen the apartment I was moving to. John had been couch-surfing in Chicago for a month.
I took one look at the weedy, overgrown, ramshackle site of the future workshop, and went to get the chainsaw.
Ladies and gentlemen, The Bride

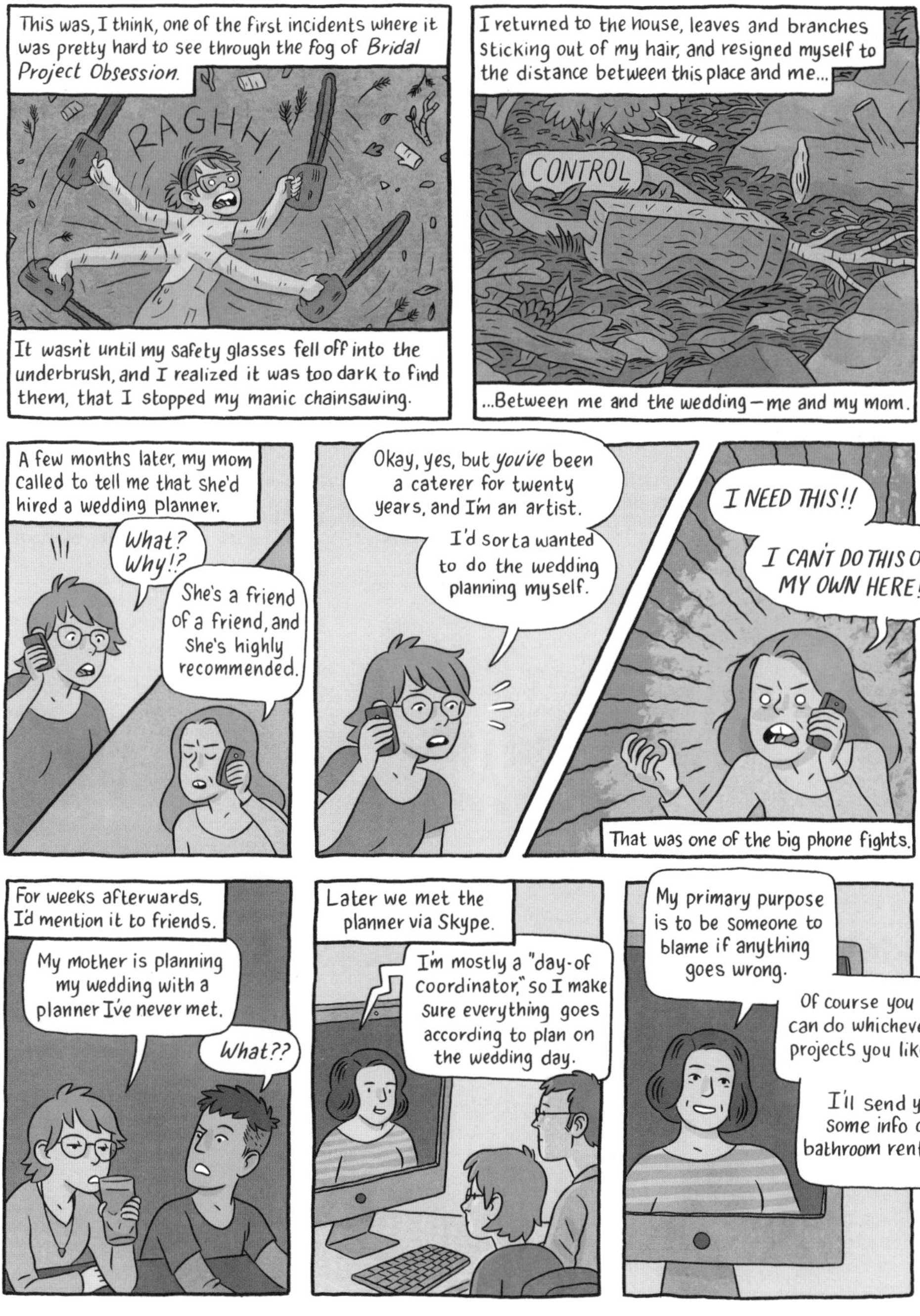
This was, I think, one of the first incidents where it was pretty hard to see through the fog of *Bridal Project Obsession*.
RAGHH
It wasn't until my safety glasses fell off into the underbrush, and I realized it was too dark to find them, that I stopped my manic chainsawing.
I returned to the house, leaves and branches sticking out of my hair, and resigned myself to the distance between this place and me...
CONTROL
...Between me and the wedding—me and my mom.
A few months later, my mom called to tell me that she'd hired a wedding planner.
What? Why!?
She's a friend of a friend, and she's highly recommended.
Okay, yes, but *you've* been a caterer for twenty years, and I'm an artist.
I'd sorta wanted to do the wedding planning myself.
I NEED THIS!!
I CAN'T DO THIS ON MY OWN HERE!!
That was one of the big phone fights.
For weeks afterwards, I'd mention it to friends.
My mother is planning my wedding with a planner I've never met.
What??
Later we met the planner via Skype.
I'm mostly a "day-of coordinator," so I make sure everything goes according to plan on the wedding day.
My primary purpose is to be someone to blame if anything goes wrong.
Of course you can do whichever projects you like.
I'll send you some info on bathroom rentals.

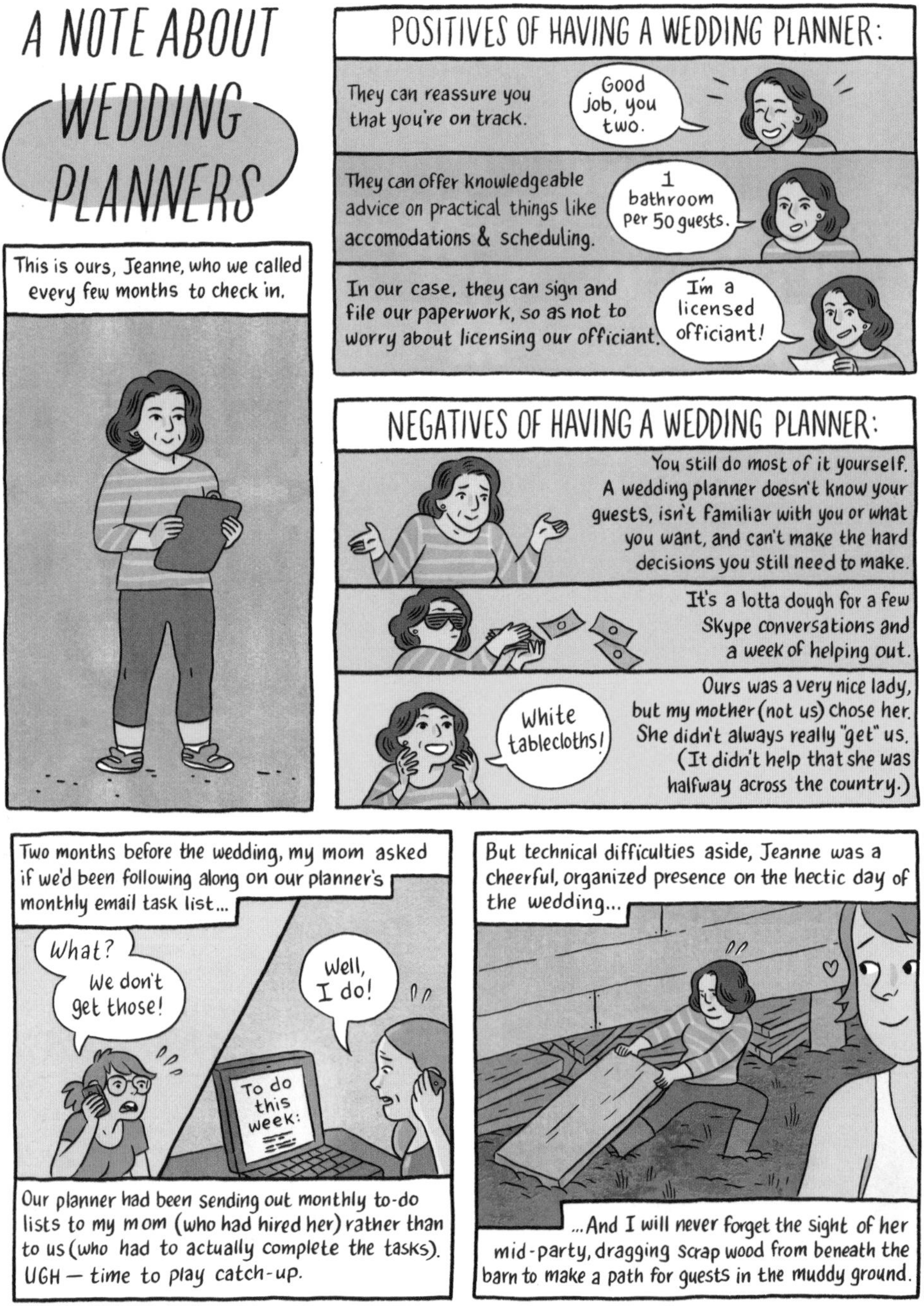
A NOTE ABOUT WEDDING PLANNERS
This is ours, Jeanne, who we called every few months to check in.
POSITIVES OF HAVING A WEDDING PLANNER:
They can reassure you that you're on track.
Good job, you two.
They can offer knowledgeable advice on practical things like accomodations & scheduling.
1 bathroom per 50 guests.
In our case, they can sign and file our paperwork, so as not to worry about licensing our officiant.
I'm a licensed officiant!
NEGATIVES OF HAVING A WEDDING PLANNER:
You still do most of it yourself. A wedding planner doesn't know your guests, isn't familiar with you or what you want, and can't make the hard decisions you still need to make.
It's a lotta dough for a few Skype conversations and a week of helping out.
Ours was a very nice lady, but my mother (not us) chose her. She didn't always really "get" us. (It didn't help that she was halfway across the country.)
White tablecloths!
Two months before the wedding, my mom asked if we'd been following along on our planner's monthly email task list...
What? We don't get those!
Well, I do!
To do this week:
Our planner had been sending out monthly to-do lists to my mom (who had hired her) rather than to us (who had to actually complete the tasks). UGH — time to play catch-up.
But technical difficulties aside, Jeanne was a cheerful, organized presence on the hectic day of the wedding...
...And I will never forget the sight of her mid-party, dragging scrap wood from beneath the barn to make a path for guests in the muddy ground.

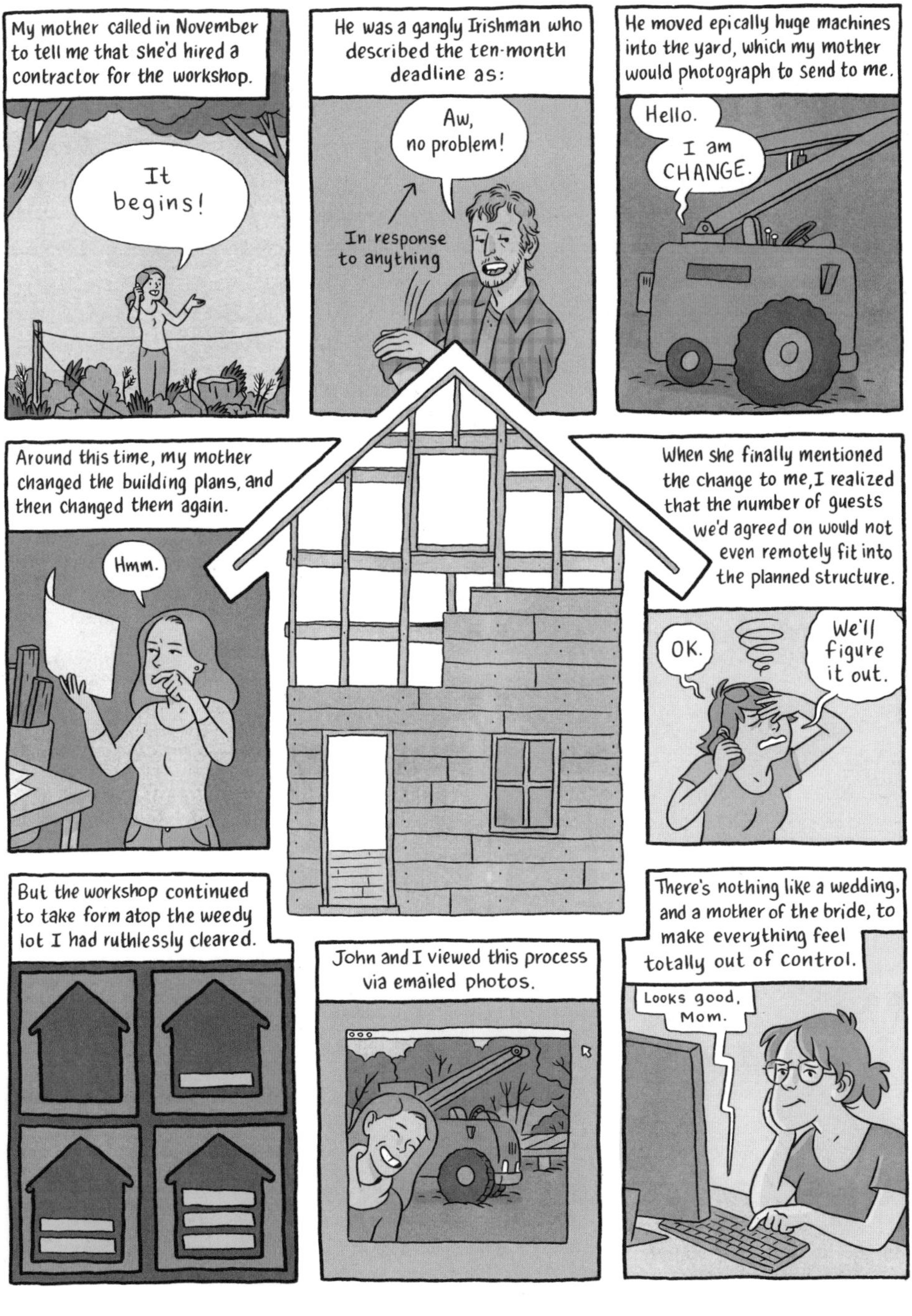
My mother called in November to tell me that she'd hired a contractor for the workshop.
It begins!
He was a gangly Irishman who described the ten-month deadline as:
Aw, no problem!
In response to anything
He moved epically huge machines into the yard, which my mother would photograph to send to me.
Hello.
I am CHANGE.
Around this time, my mother changed the building plans, and then changed them again.
Hmm.
When she finally mentioned the change to me, I realized that the number of guests we'd agreed on would not even remotely fit into the planned structure.
OK.
We'll figure it out.
But the workshop continued to take form atop the weedy lot I had ruthlessly cleared.
John and I viewed this process via emailed photos.
There's nothing like a wedding, and a mother of the bride, to make everything feel totally out of control.
Looks good, Mom.

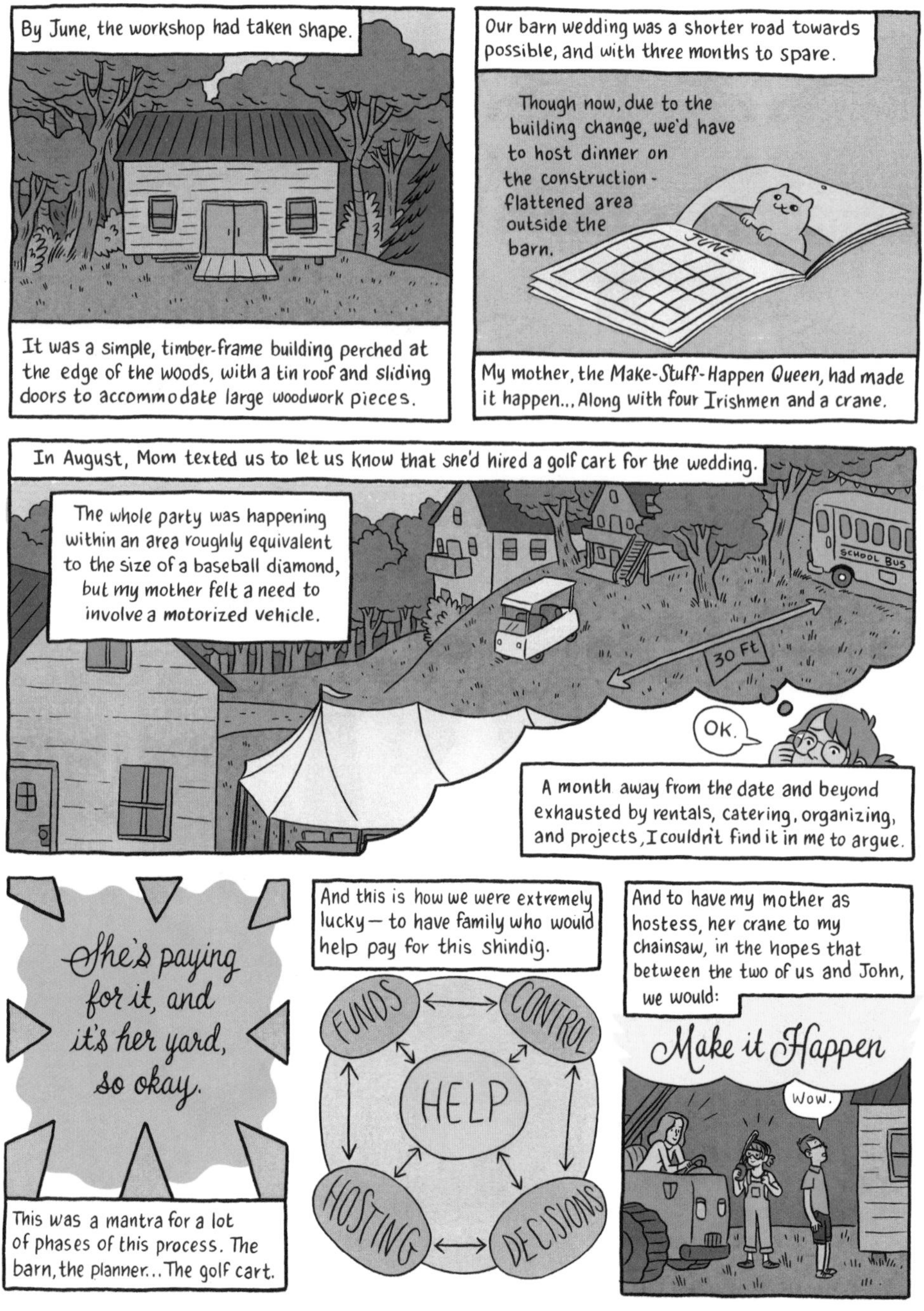
By June, the workshop had taken shape.
It was a simple, timber-frame building perched at the edge of the woods, with a tin roof and sliding doors to accommodate large woodwork pieces.
Our barn wedding was a shorter road towards possible, and with three months to spare.
Though now, due to the building change, we'd have to host dinner on the construction-flattened area outside the barn.
JUNE
My mother, the Make-Stuff-Happen Queen, had made it happen... Along with four Irishmen and a crane.
In August, Mom texted us to let us know that she'd hired a golf cart for the wedding.
The whole party was happening within an area roughly equivalent to the size of a baseball diamond, but my mother felt a need to involve a motorized vehicle.
SCHOOL BUS
30 Ft
OK.
A month away from the date and beyond exhausted by rentals, catering, organizing, and projects, I couldn't find it in me to argue.
She's paying for it, and it's her yard, so okay.
This was a mantra for a lot of phases of this process. The barn, the planner... The golf cart.
And this is how we were extremely lucky — to have family who would help pay for this shindig.
FUNDS
CONTROL
HELP
HOSTING
DECISIONS
And to have my mother as hostess, her crane to my chainsaw, in the hopes that between the two of us and John, we would:
Make it Happen
WOW.

WEIRD WEDDING FACTS

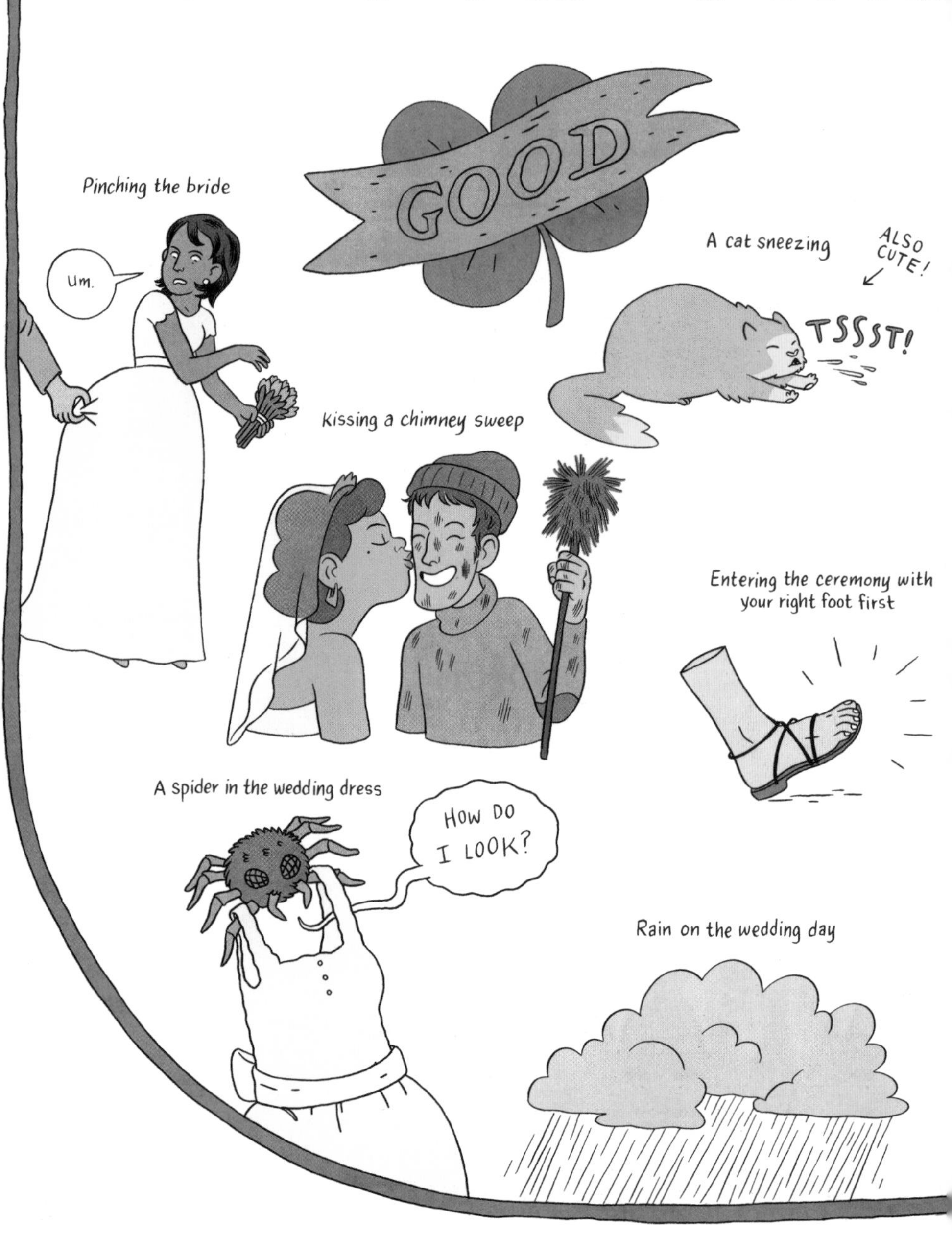
GOOD
Pinching the bride
Um.
A cat sneezing
ALSO CUTE!
TSSST!
Kissing a chimney sweep
Entering the ceremony with your right foot first
A spider in the wedding dress
HOW DO I LOOK?
Rain on the wedding day

PART 2: ALWAYS LUCK

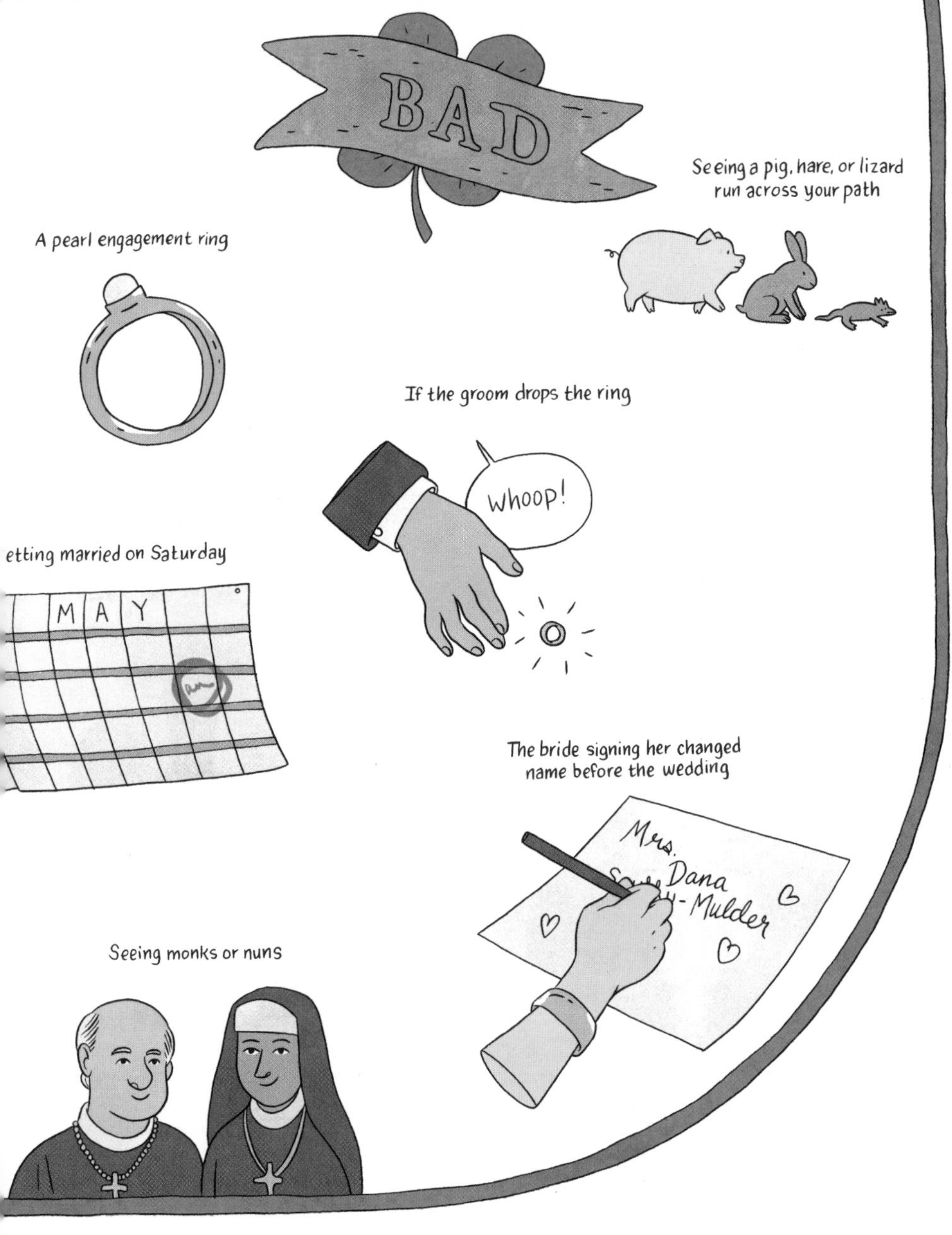

BAD
Seeing a pig, hare, or lizard run across your path
A pearl engagement ring
If the groom drops the ring
Whoop!
etting married on Saturday
MAY
The bride signing her changed name before the wedding
Mrs. Dana
-Mulder
Seeing monks or nuns

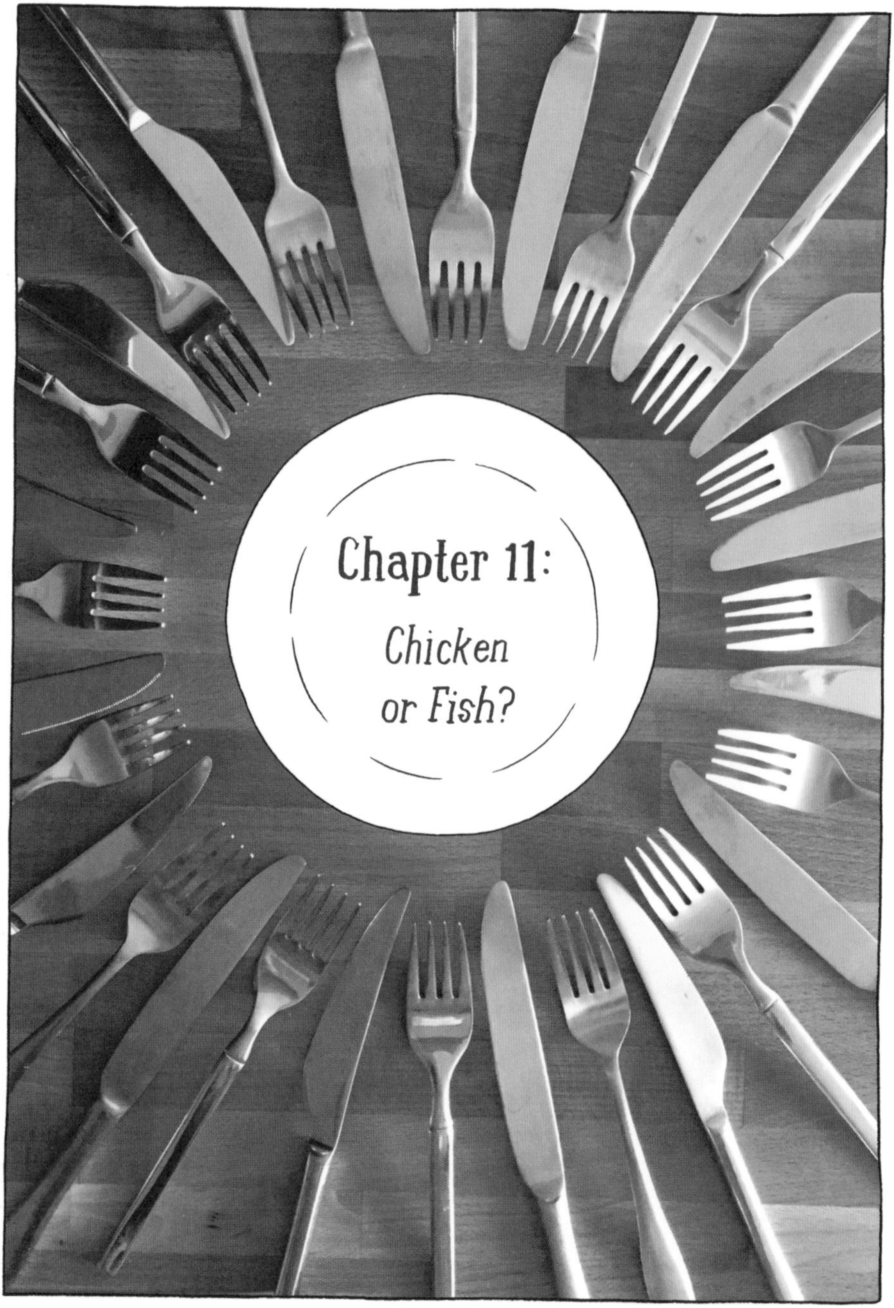
Chapter 11:
Chicken
or Fish?

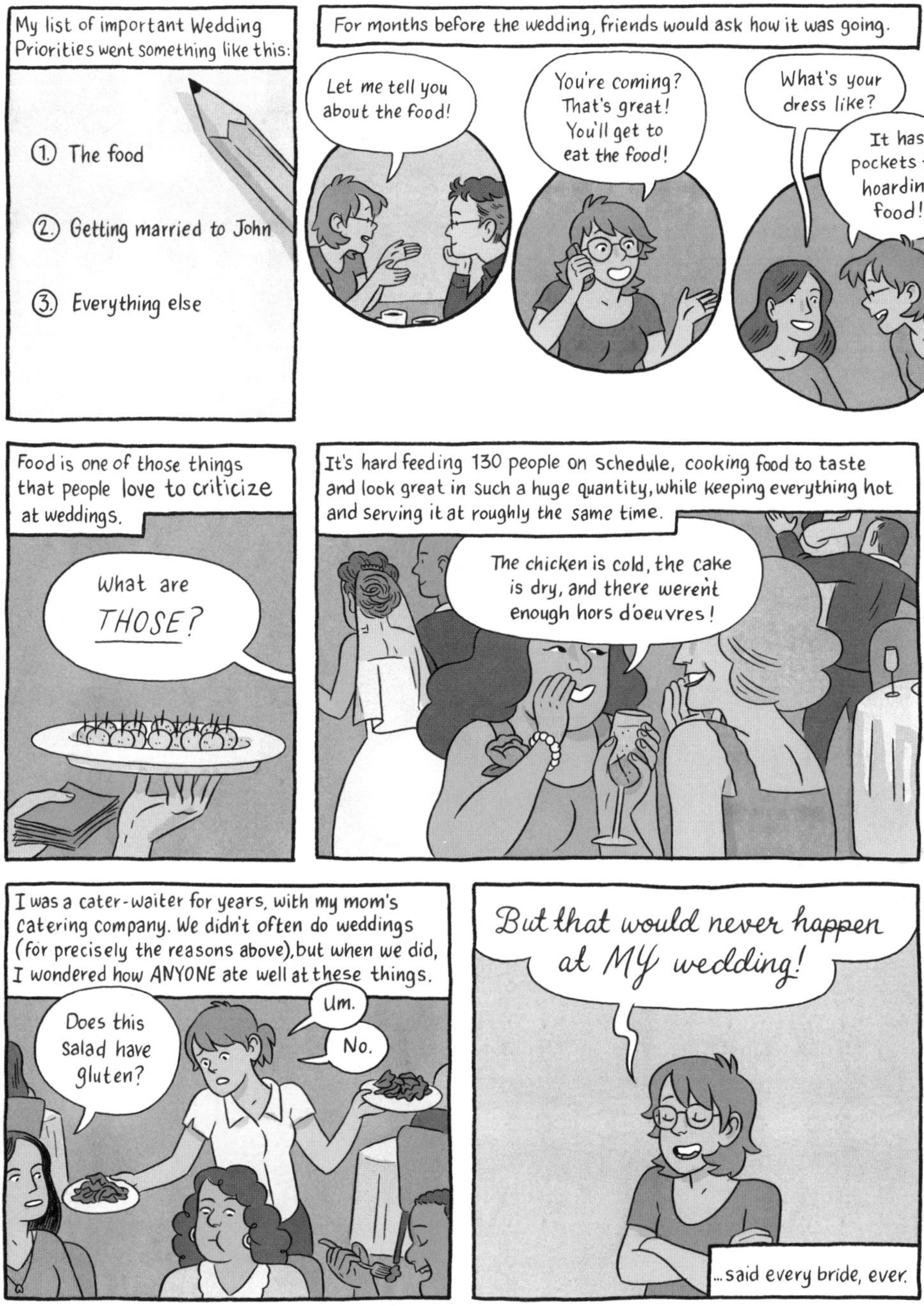

My list of important Wedding Priorities went something like this:
① The food
② Getting married to John
③ Everything else
For months before the wedding, friends would ask how it was going.
Let me tell you about the food!
You're coming? That's great! You'll get to eat the food!
What's your dress like?
It has pockets for hoarding food!
Food is one of those things that people love to criticize at weddings.
What are THOSE?
It's hard feeding 130 people on schedule, cooking food to taste and look great in such a huge quantity, while keeping everything hot and serving it at roughly the same time.
The chicken is cold, the cake is dry, and there weren't enough hors d'oeuvres!
I was a cater-waiter for years, with my mom's catering company. We didn't often do weddings (for precisely the reasons above), but when we did, I wondered how ANYONE ate well at these things.
Does this salad have gluten?
Um.
No.
But that would never happen at MY wedding!
...said every bride, ever.

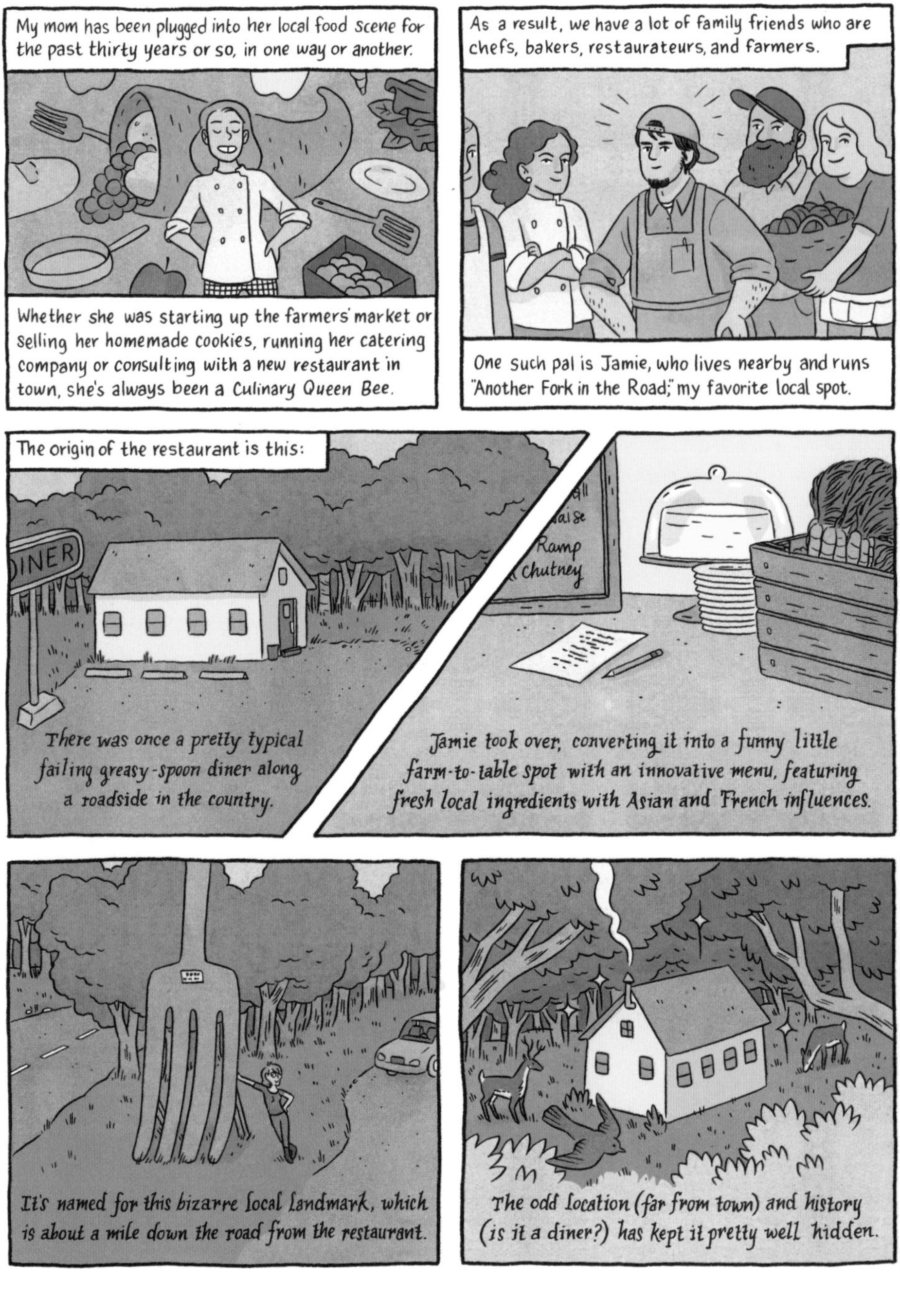
My mom has been plugged into her local food scene for the past thirty years or so, in one way or another.
Whether she was starting up the farmers' market or selling her homemade cookies, running her catering company or consulting with a new restaurant in town, she's always been a Culinary Queen Bee.
As a result, we have a lot of family friends who are chefs, bakers, restaurateurs, and farmers.
One such pal is Jamie, who lives nearby and runs "Another Fork in the Road," my favorite local spot.
The origin of the restaurant is this:
DINER
There was once a pretty typical failing greasy-spoon diner along a roadside in the country.
Ramp
chutney
Jamie took over, converting it into a funny little farm-to-table spot with an innovative menu, featuring fresh local ingredients with Asian and French influences.
It's named for this bizarre local landmark, which is about a mile down the road from the restaurant.
The odd location (far from town) and history (is it a diner?) has kept it pretty well hidden.

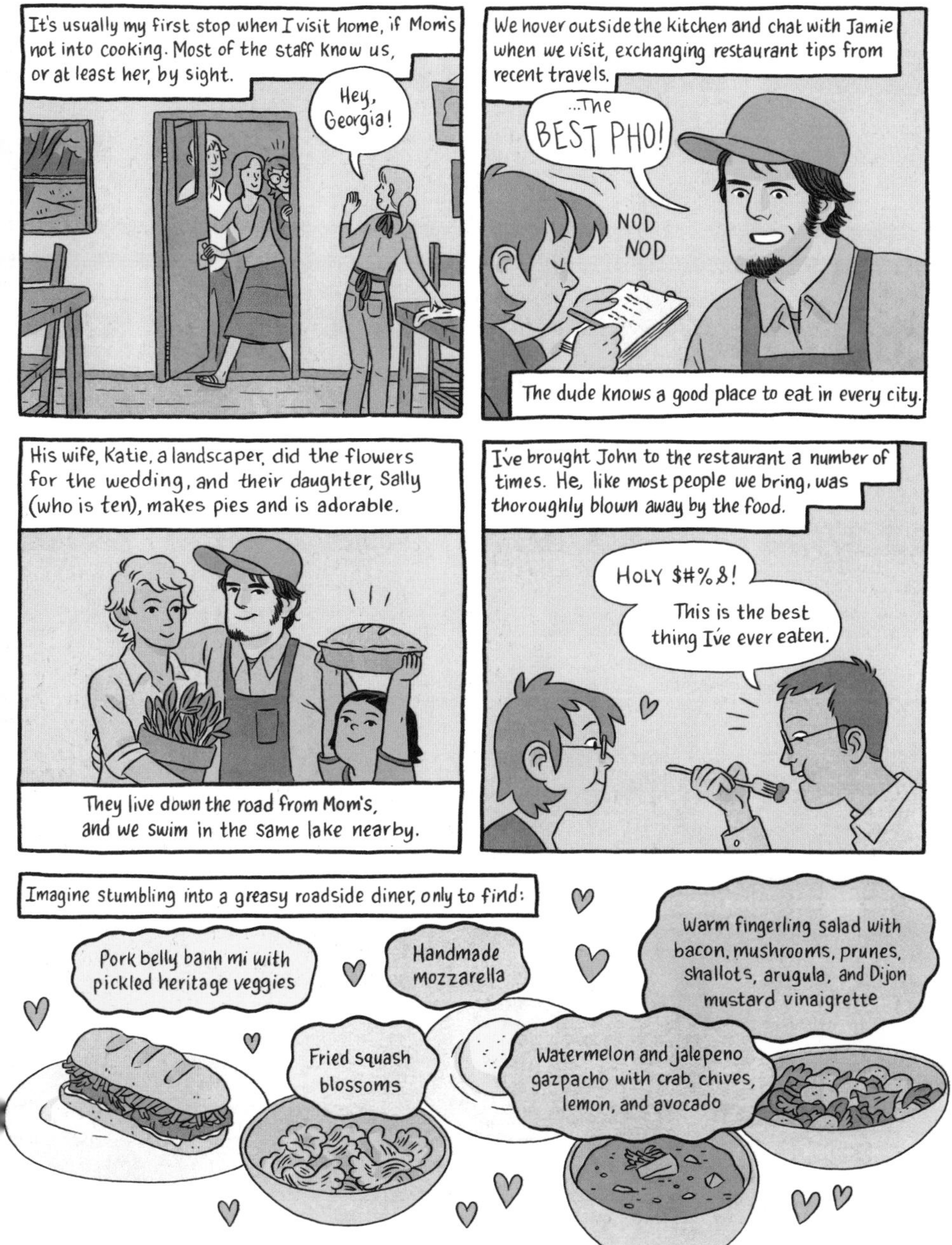
It's usually my first stop when I visit home, if Mom's not into cooking. Most of the staff know us, or at least her, by sight.
Hey, Georgia!
We hover outside the kitchen and chat with Jamie when we visit, exchanging restaurant tips from recent travels.
...The BEST PHO!
NOD NOD
The dude knows a good place to eat in every city.
His wife, Katie, a landscaper, did the flowers for the wedding, and their daughter, Sally (who is ten), makes pies and is adorable.
They live down the road from Mom's, and we swim in the same lake nearby.
I've brought John to the restaurant a number of times. He, like most people we bring, was thoroughly blown away by the food.
HOLY $#%&! This is the best thing I've ever eaten.
Imagine stumbling into a greasy roadside diner, only to find:
Pork belly banh mi with pickled heritage veggies
Handmade mozzarella
Warm fingerling salad with bacon, mushrooms, prunes, shallots, arugula, and Dijon mustard vinaigrette
Fried squash blossoms
Watermelon and jalepeno gazpacho with crab, chives, lemon, and avocado

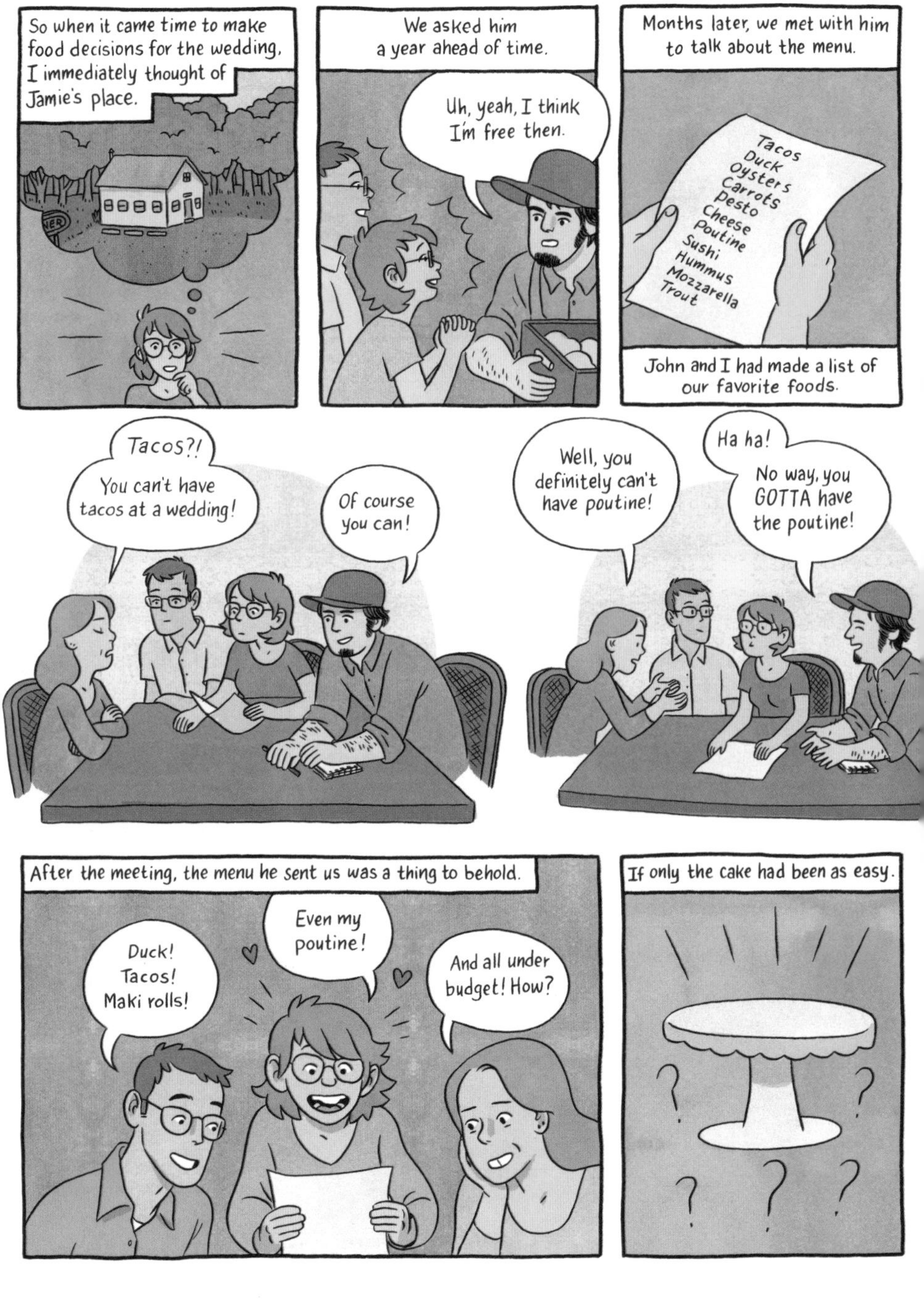
So when it came time to make food decisions for the wedding, I immediately thought of Jamie's place.
We asked him a year ahead of time.
Uh, yeah, I think I'm free then.
Months later, we met with him to talk about the menu.
Tacos
Duck
Oysters
Carrots
Pesto
Cheese
Poutine
Sushi
Hummus
Mozzarella
Trout
John and I had made a list of our favorite foods.
Tacos?!
You can't have tacos at a wedding!
Of course you can!
Well, you definitely can't have poutine!
Ha ha!
No way, you GOTTA have the poutine!
After the meeting, the menu he sent us was a thing to behold.
Duck! Tacos! Maki rolls!
Even my poutine!
And all under budget! How?
If only the cake had been as easy.

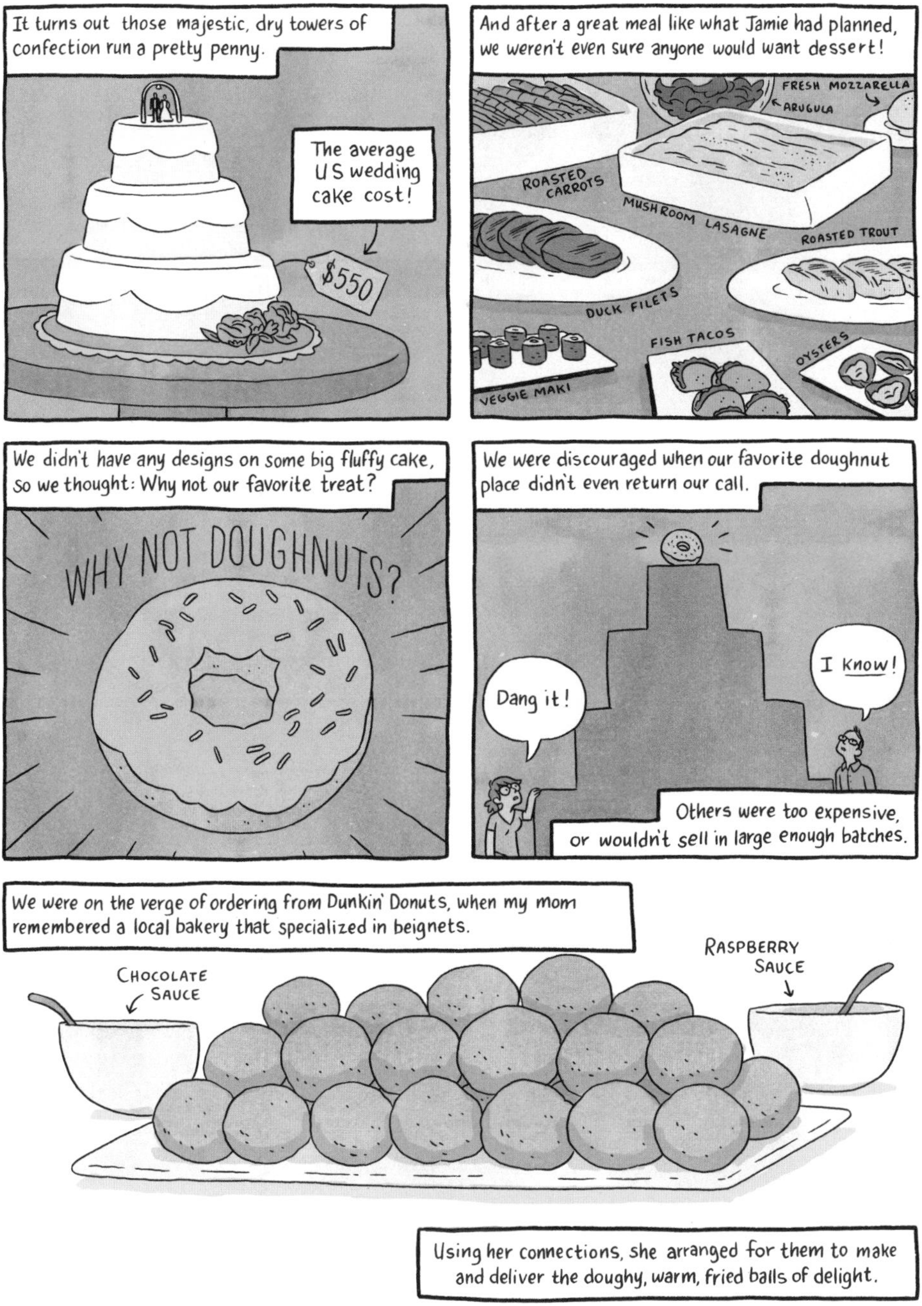
It turns out those majestic, dry towers of confection run a pretty penny.
The average US wedding cake cost!
$550
And after a great meal like what Jamie had planned, we weren't even sure anyone would want dessert!
FRESH MOZZARELLA
ARUGULA
ROASTED CARROTS
MUSHROOM LASAGNE
ROASTED TROUT
DUCK FILETS
FISH TACOS
OYSTERS
VEGGIE MAKI
We didn't have any designs on some big fluffy cake, so we thought: Why not our favorite treat?
WHY NOT DOUGHNUTS?
We were discouraged when our favorite doughnut place didn't even return our call.
Dang it!
I know!
Others were too expensive, or wouldn't sell in large enough batches.
We were on the verge of ordering from Dunkin' Donuts, when my mom remembered a local bakery that specialized in beignets.
CHOCOLATE SAUCE
RASPBERRY SAUCE
Using her connections, she arranged for them to make and deliver the doughy, warm, fried balls of delight.

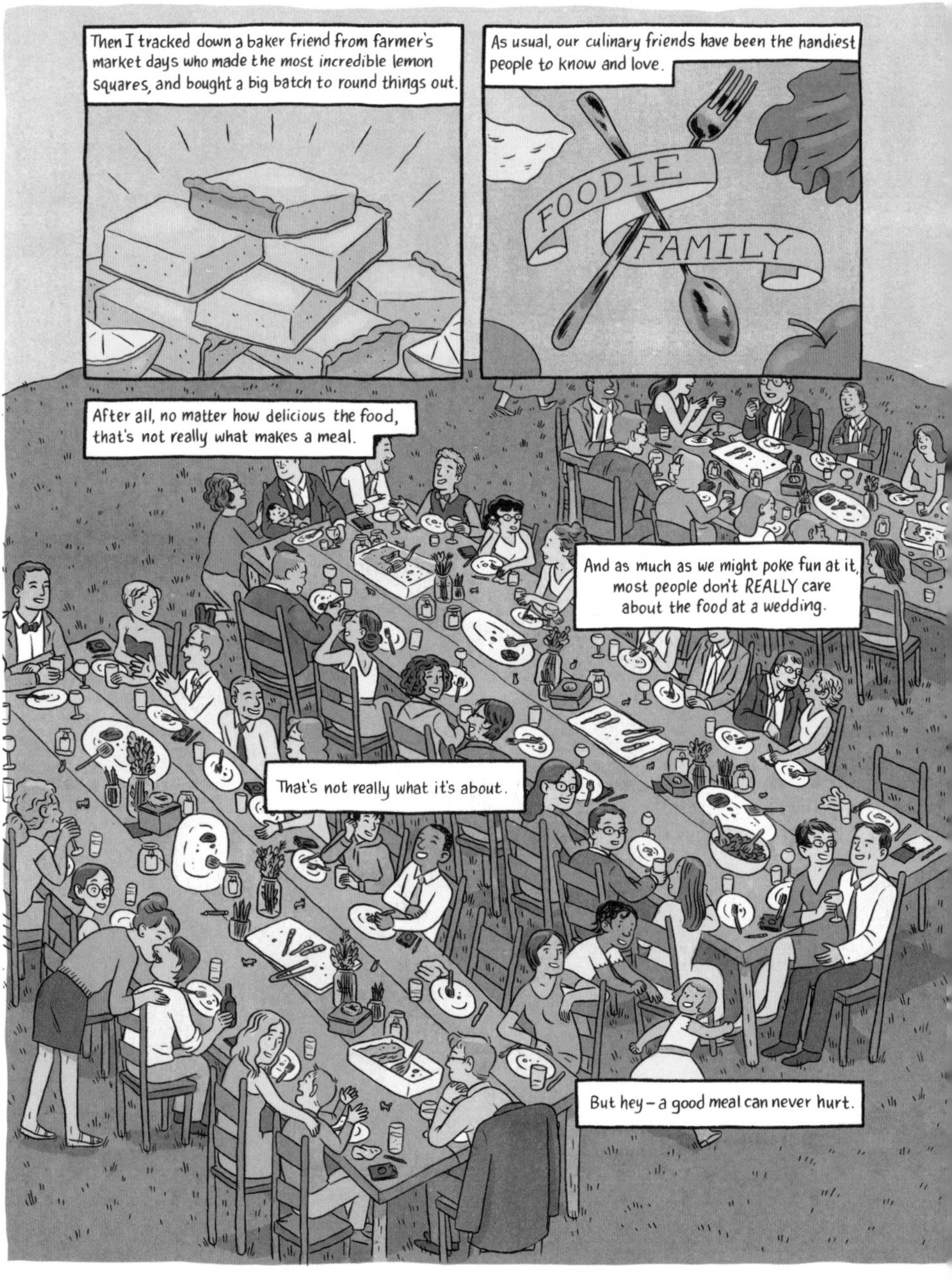
Then I tracked down a baker friend from farmer's market days who made the most incredible lemon squares, and bought a big batch to round things out.
As usual, our culinary friends have been the handiest people to know and love.
FOODIE FAMILY
After all, no matter how delicious the food, that's not really what makes a meal.
And as much as we might poke fun at it, most people don't REALLY care about the food at a wedding.
That's not really what it's about.
But hey – a good meal can never hurt.

A NOTE ABOUT POUTINE

(Because obviously that was the most important thing in the last chapter.)

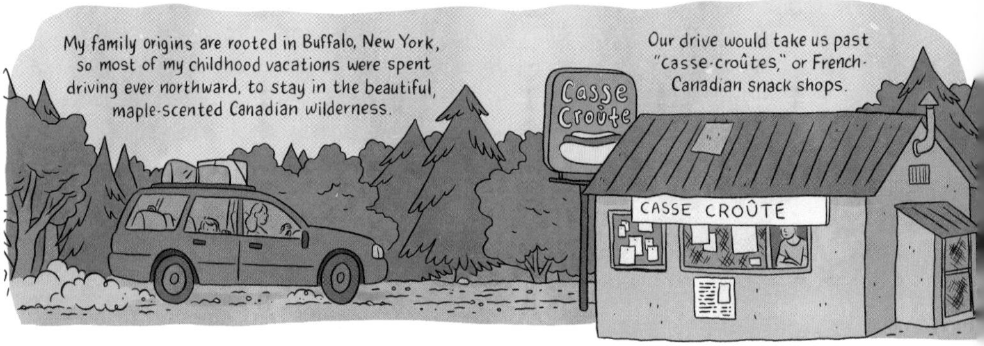
My family origins are rooted in Buffalo, New York, so most of my childhood vacations were spent driving ever northward, to stay in the beautiful, maple-scented Canadian wilderness.
Casse Croûte
Our drive would take us past "casse-croûtes," or French-Canadian snack shops.
CASSE CROÛTE

It was at one of these little locations that I first tried...

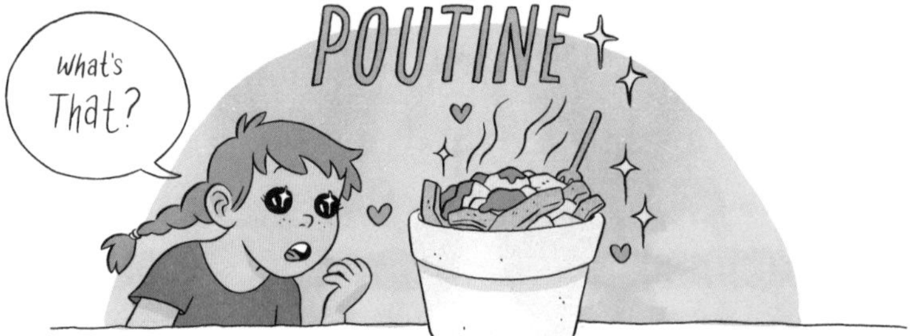
POUTINE
What's That?

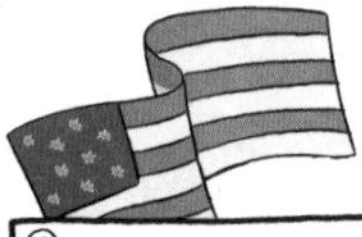

It is to the high casse-croûte standard that I hold all poutine. For an American, I'm something of a purist and have a pretty narrow definition of what I consider to be "real poutine."

The essentials are:

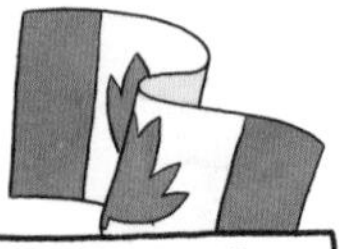

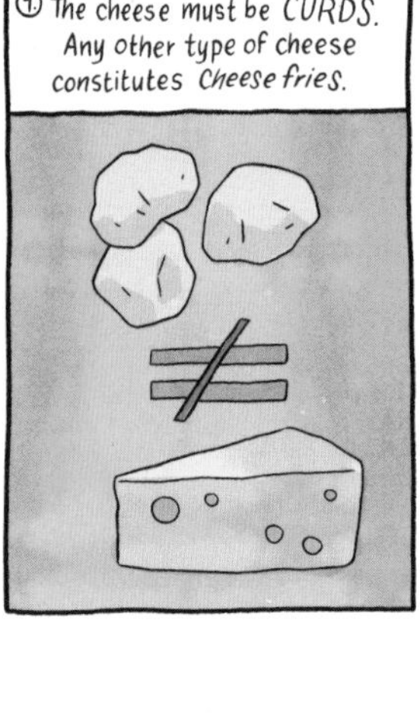
① The cheese must be CURDS. Any other type of cheese constitutes *Cheese fries*.

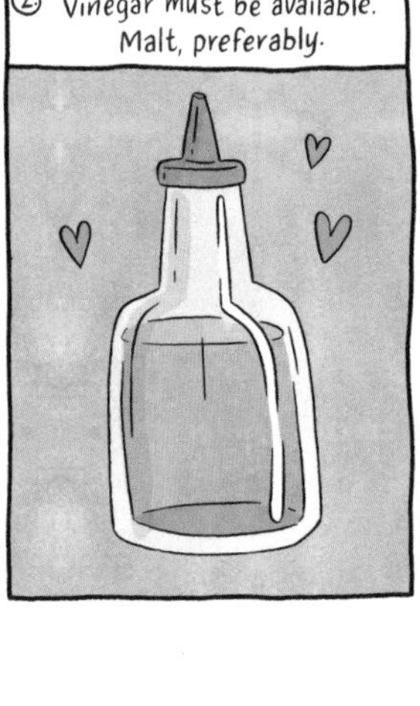
② Vinegar must be available. Malt, preferably.

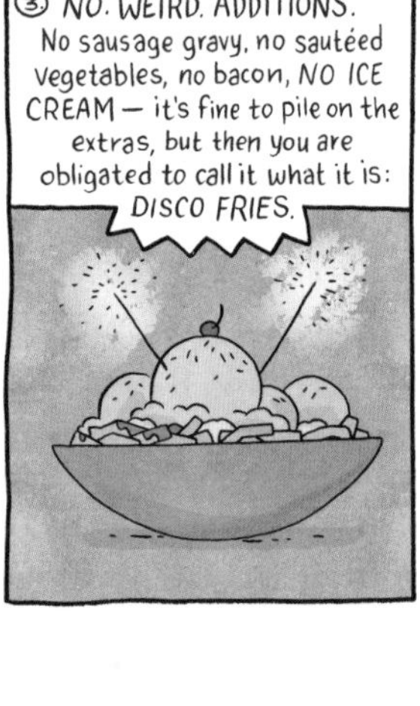
③ NO. WEIRD. ADDITIONS. No sausage gravy, no sautéed vegetables, no bacon, NO ICE CREAM — it's fine to pile on the extras, but then you are obligated to call it what it is:
DISCO FRIES.

It's impossible to truly re-create the glorious, mouth-scalding, vinegary mess from those casse-croûtes without actually driving two hours north of Ottawa into the woods. Making poutine at home lacks the greasy feel of the vinegar bottle, or the summery bliss of a once-a-year treat.

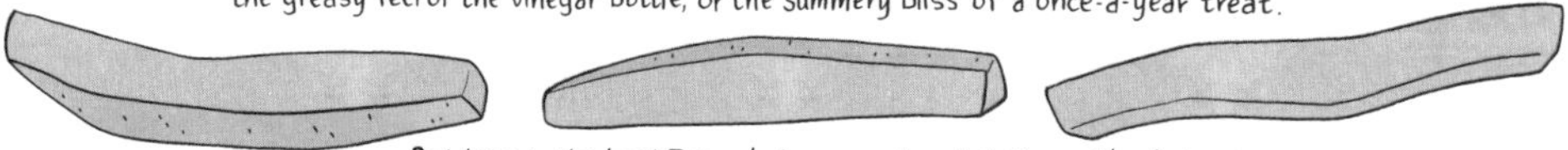

But here is the best I can do to re-create what I consider to be...

THE BEST POUTINE

Cut russet potatoes into strips and soak in water for an hour, then remove and pat dry.

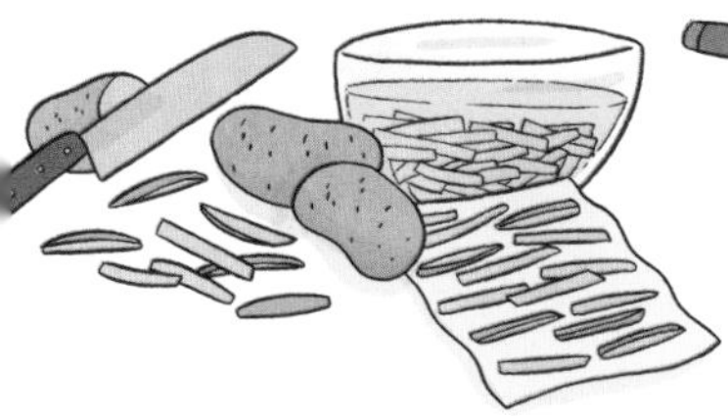

Pour enough peanut or canola oil to submerge fries into a big pot, and heat to 325°.

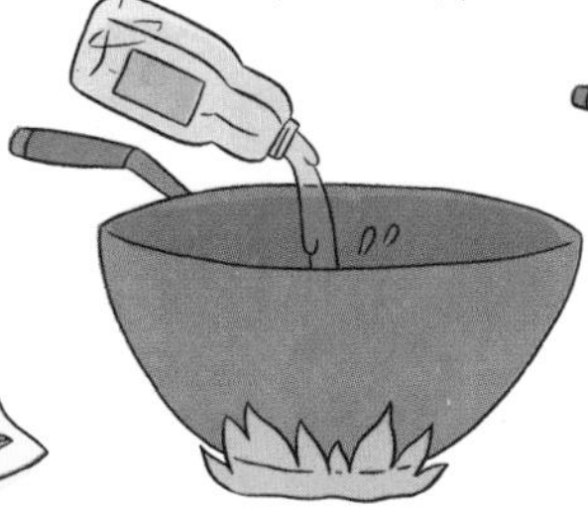

Fry the potatoes in the oil until golden brown, then place them on paper towels and add salt.

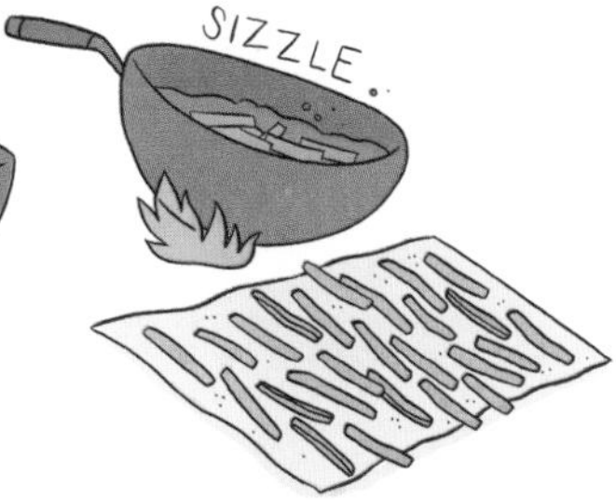
SIZZLE..

For the gravy:

Melt 4tsp butter in a pot over medium, and stir in a quarter cup of flour.

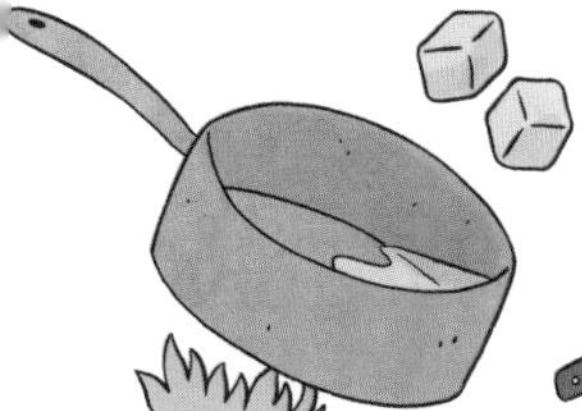

Add a minced garlic clove and minced shallot, and stir for about two min.

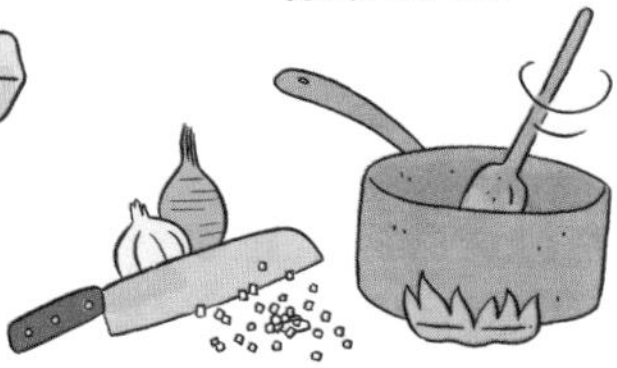

Add 4 cups of beef stock, 1 tsp of malt vinegar, and a squirt of Ketchup.

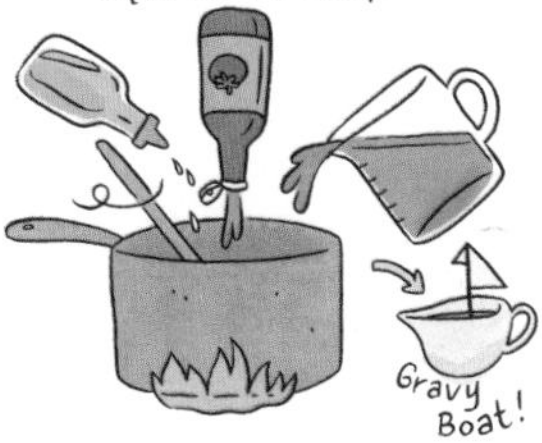
Gravy Boat!

Combine fries with cheese curds, warm in the oven to melt the curds a little, and pour gravy over the whole thing.

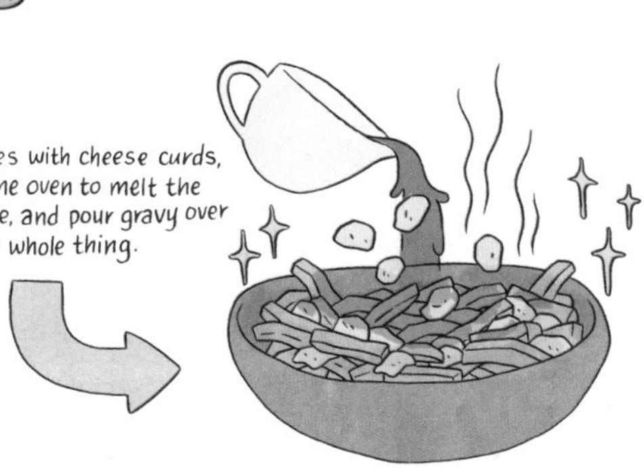

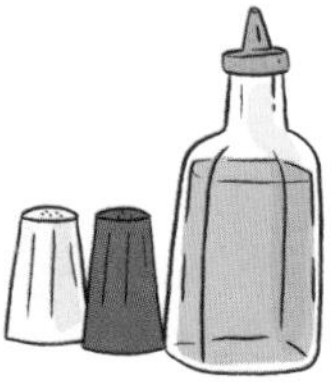

Serve with salt and pepper and malt vinegar, and eat outside in the sun.

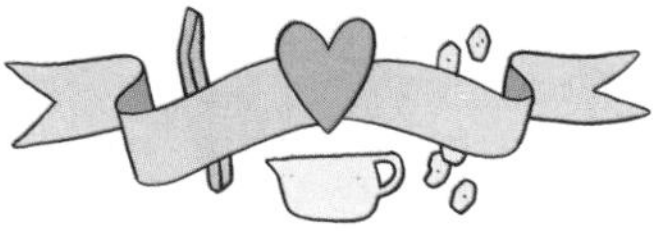

Chapter 12:

It's Electric

(Boogie Oogie Oogie)

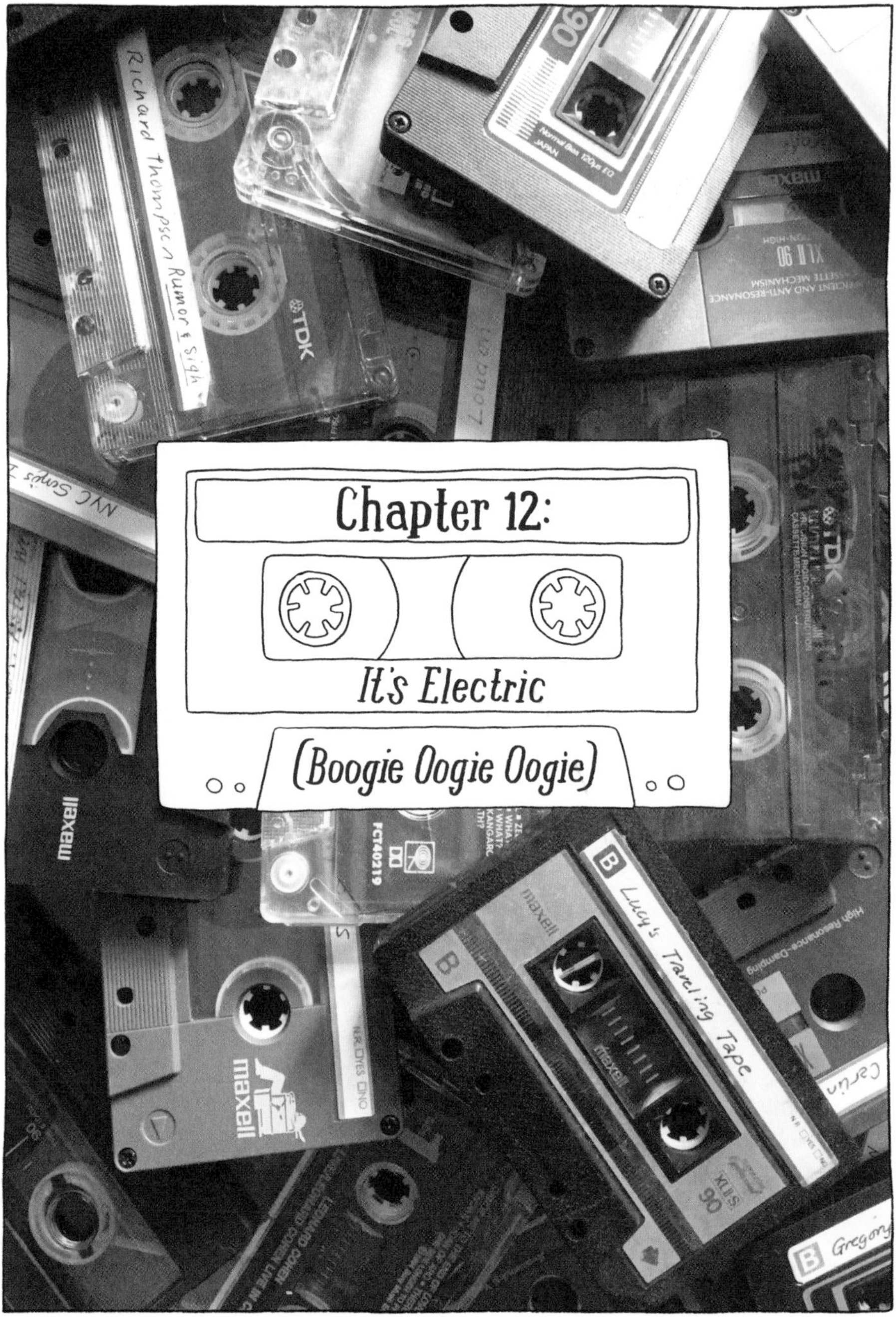

Richard Thompson Rumor & Sigh
TDK
maxell
Lucy's Traveling Tape
NYC Songs

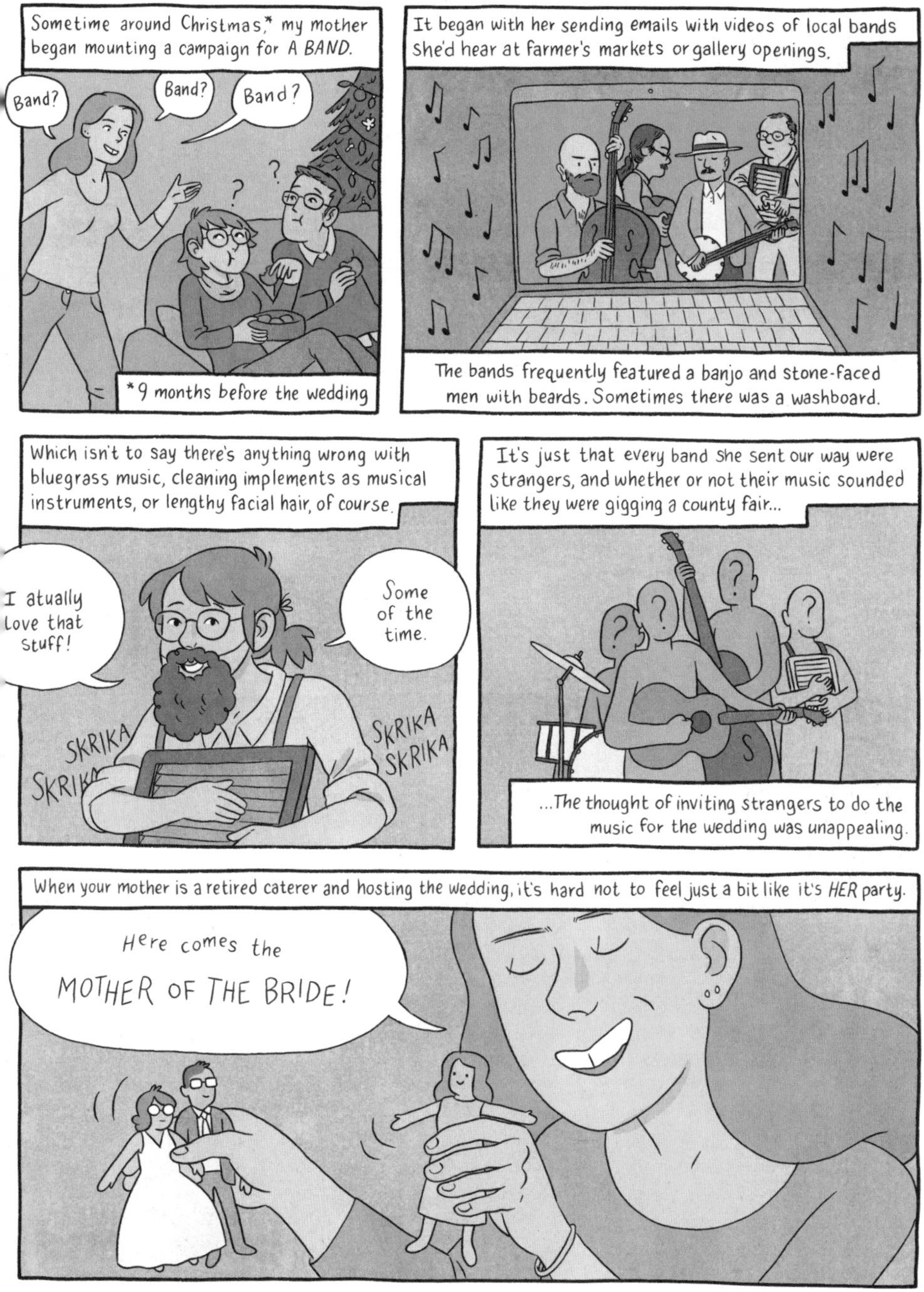
Sometime around Christmas,* my mother began mounting a campaign for A BAND.
Band?
Band?
Band?
?
?
*9 months before the wedding
It began with her sending emails with videos of local bands she'd hear at farmer's markets or gallery openings.
The bands frequently featured a banjo and stone-faced men with beards. Sometimes there was a washboard.
Which isn't to say there's anything wrong with bluegrass music, cleaning implements as musical instruments, or lengthy facial hair, of course.
I atually love that stuff!
Some of the time.
SKRIKA SKRIKA
SKRIKA SKRIKA
It's just that every band she sent our way were strangers, and whether or not their music sounded like they were gigging a county fair...
...The thought of inviting strangers to do the music for the wedding was unappealing.
When your mother is a retired caterer and hosting the wedding, it's hard not to feel just a bit like it's HER party.
Here comes the MOTHER OF THE BRIDE!

I'd thought about the music I wanted: songs with personal meaning to me and John, that came from our shared experience and featured musicians that we'd liked for years — who we felt we knew.

Mom, I want us to handle the music.

RECORDED?

But my mother insisted.

You HAVE to have live music! It's not a party without live music!

What I heard was:

It's not MY party without live music.

Moms & daughters, eh?

This power struggle was wearing me down. I'd given over control of the space (after all, it was my mother's barn), the wedding planner (my mother had insisted, and who could it hurt?), and a number of other decisions.

MOM'S PLATE

WEDDING DECISION PIE

MINE & JOHN'S ↓

My mother was there, on the proverbial ground, and I was far away in Chicago, trying to orchestrate things from there. It made sense to give way in the face of my mother's well-intentioned machinations.

CHICAGO

REMOTE WEDDING PLANNING

CATERER ON PHONE

RESEARCHING VOWS

NEW Y

DESIGNING BARN

DECIDING ON TENT

ORGANIZING LOCAL VENDORS & RENTALS

ARRANGIN PROPERT

But on the music, I refused to budge. Perhaps because it was something I could control from afar...

My mother was undeterred. She sent emails informing me that she'd hastily reserved the date with one band...

SIGH.

It's all arranged wit the Hill Street Count blues/rock band! I s them at market las week and I just kn perfect for the wedd Video below:

...Only to switch to another band and tell me she thought we should put down a deposit.

They're soooo much better, and I know you haven't made a decision—

But we HAVE.

ON A PLAYLIST.

Phone Calls ensued.

MOM.

CUT

IT

OUT

Please.

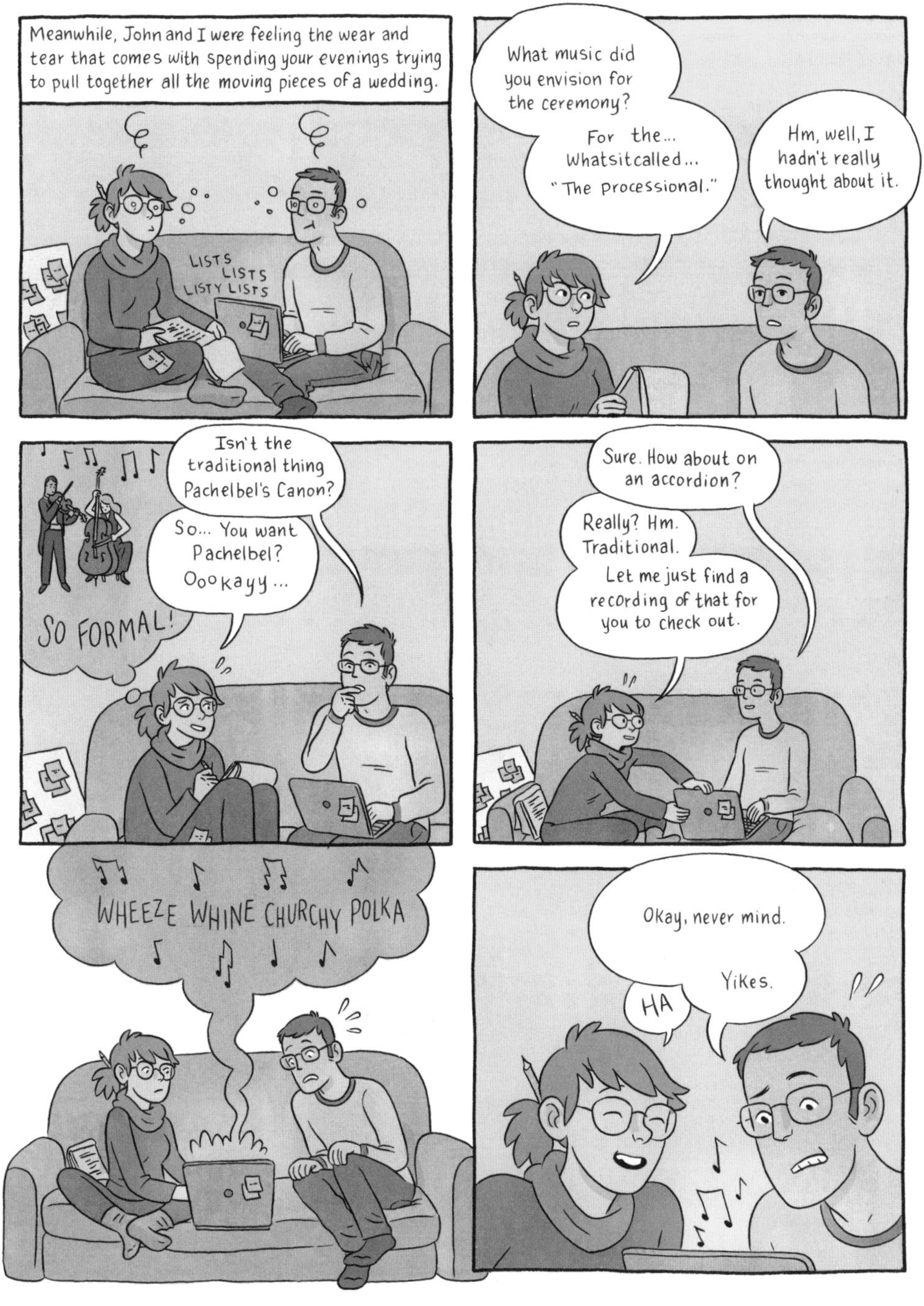
Meanwhile, John and I were feeling the wear and tear that comes with spending your evenings trying to pull together all the moving pieces of a wedding.
LISTS LISTS LISTY LISTS
What music did you envision for the ceremony?
For the... Whatsitcalled... "The Processional."
Hm, well, I hadn't really thought about it.
Isn't the traditional thing Pachelbel's Canon?
So... You want Pachelbel? Oookayy...
SO FORMAL!
Sure. How about on an accordion?
Really? Hm. Traditional.
Let me just find a recording of that for you to check out.
WHEEZE WHINE CHURCHY POLKA
Okay, never mind.
HA
Yikes.

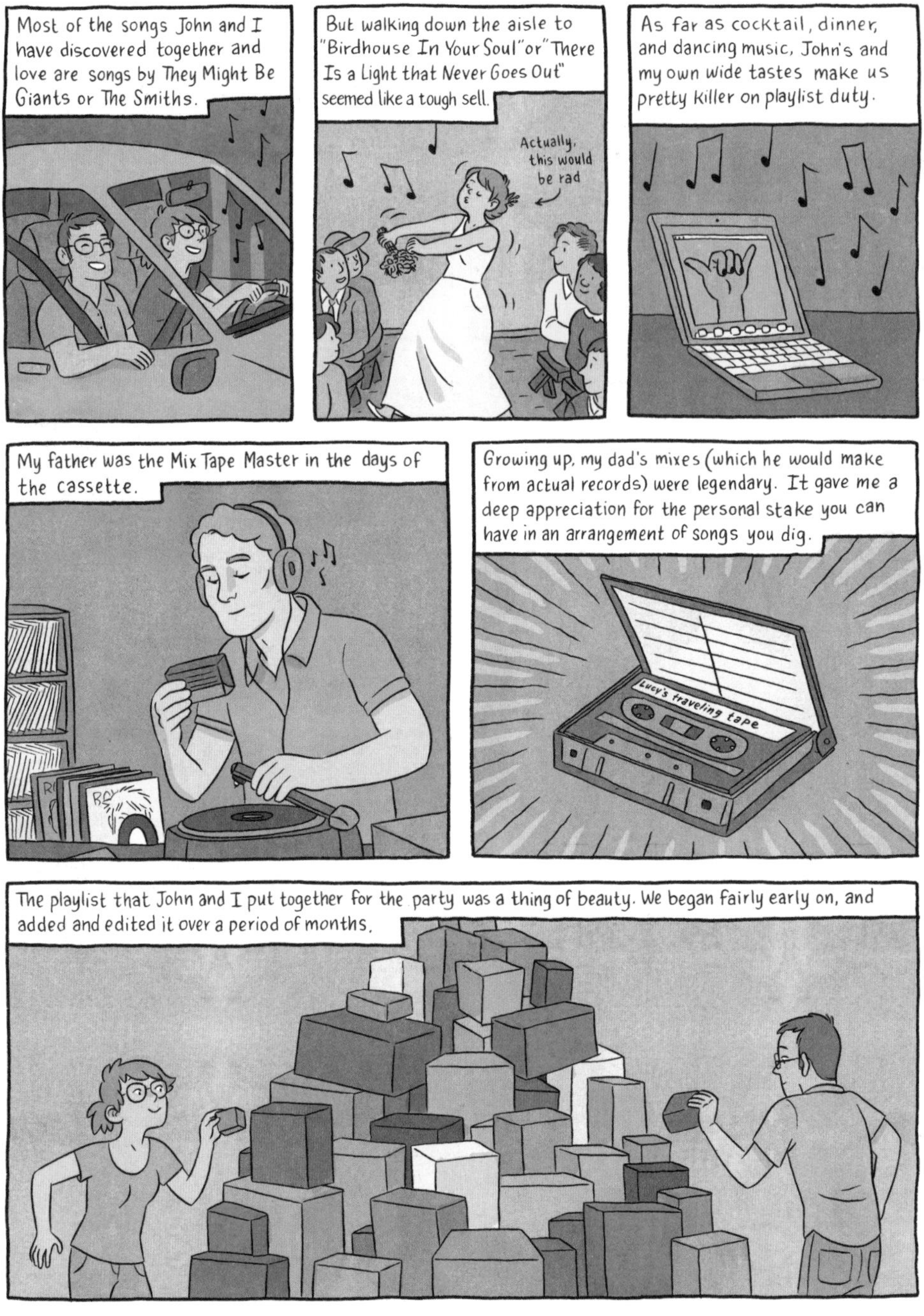
Most of the songs John and I have discovered together and love are songs by They Might Be Giants or The Smiths.
But walking down the aisle to "Birdhouse In Your Soul" or "There Is a Light that Never Goes Out" seemed like a tough sell.
Actually, this would be rad
As far as cocktail, dinner, and dancing music, John's and my own wide tastes make us pretty killer on playlist duty.
My father was the Mix Tape Master in the days of the cassette.
Growing up, my dad's mixes (which he would make from actual records) were legendary. It gave me a deep appreciation for the personal stake you can have in an arrangement of songs you dig.
Lucy's traveling tape
The playlist that John and I put together for the party was a thing of beauty. We began fairly early on, and added and edited it over a period of months.

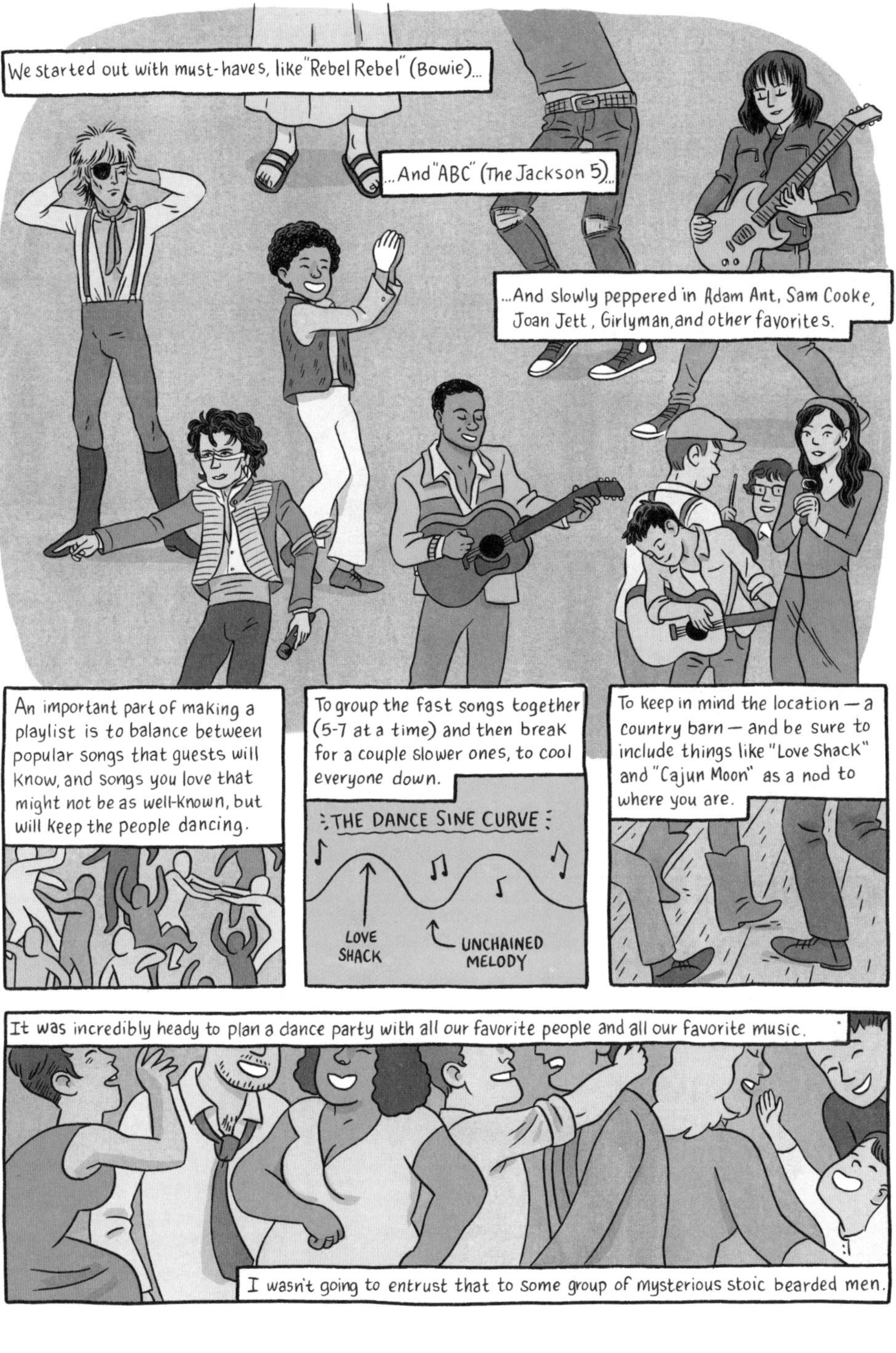
We started out with must-haves, like "Rebel Rebel" (Bowie)...
...And "ABC" (The Jackson 5)...
...And slowly peppered in Adam Ant, Sam Cooke, Joan Jett, Girlyman, and other favorites.
An important part of making a playlist is to balance between popular songs that guests will know, and songs you love that might not be as well-known, but will keep the people dancing.
To group the fast songs together (5-7 at a time) and then break for a couple slower ones, to cool everyone down.
THE DANCE SINE CURVE
LOVE SHACK
UNCHAINED MELODY
To keep in mind the location — a country barn — and be sure to include things like "Love Shack" and "Cajun Moon" as a nod to where you are.
It was incredibly heady to plan a dance party with all our favorite people and all our favorite music.
I wasn't going to entrust that to some group of mysterious stoic bearded men.

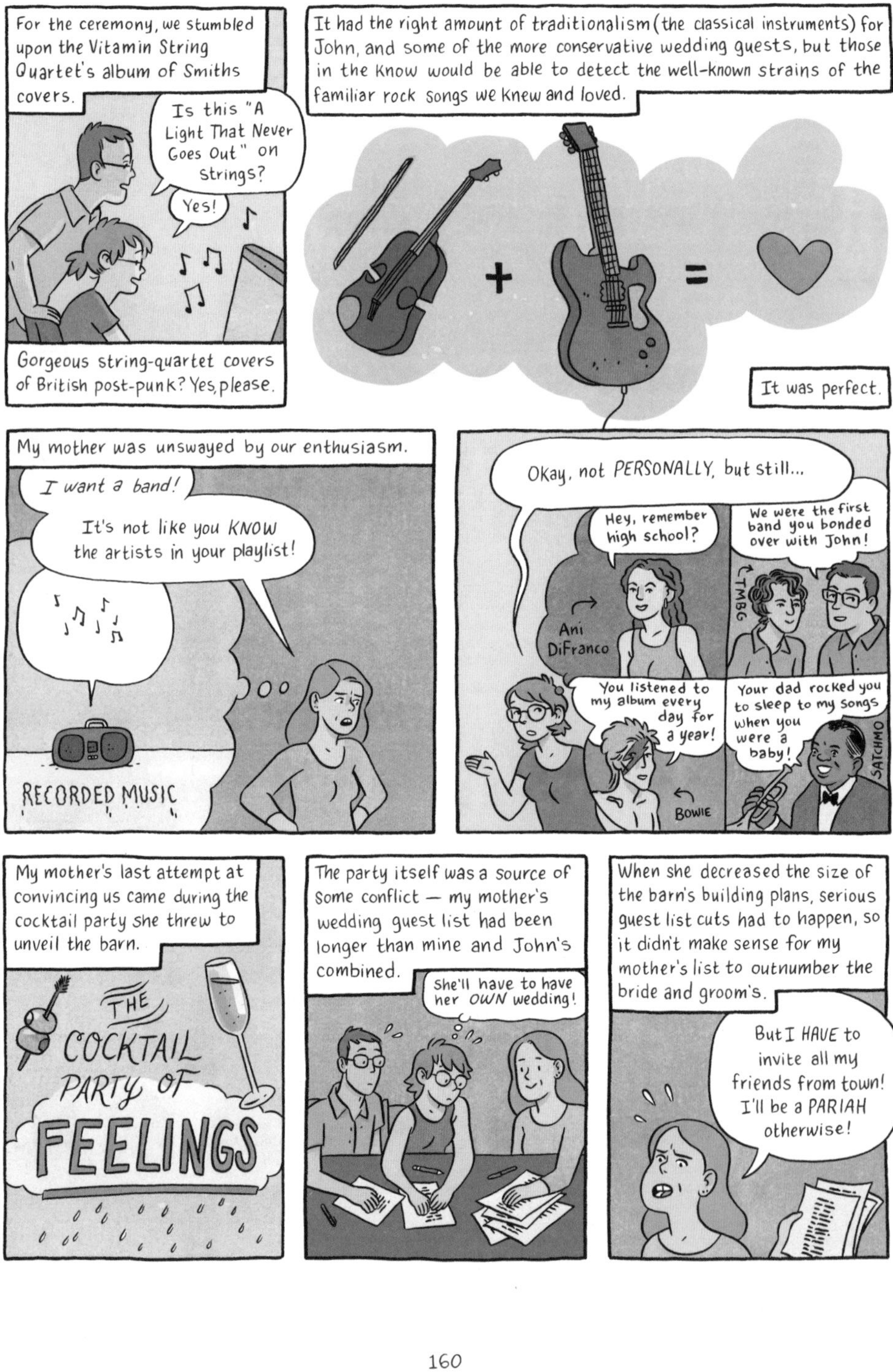
For the ceremony, we stumbled upon the Vitamin String Quartet's album of Smiths covers.
Is this "A Light That Never Goes Out" on strings?
Yes!
Gorgeous string-quartet covers of British post-punk? Yes, please.
It had the right amount of traditionalism (the classical instruments) for John, and some of the more conservative wedding guests, but those in the know would be able to detect the well-known strains of the familiar rock songs we knew and loved.
+
=
It was perfect.
My mother was unswayed by our enthusiasm.
I want a band!
It's not like you KNOW the artists in your playlist!
RECORDED MUSIC
Okay, not PERSONALLY, but still...
Hey, remember high school?
Ani DiFranco
We were the first band you bonded over with John!
TMBG
You listened to my album every day for a year!
BOWIE
Your dad rocked you to sleep to my songs when you were a baby!
SATCHMO
My mother's last attempt at convincing us came during the cocktail party she threw to unveil the barn.
THE COCKTAIL PARTY OF FEELINGS
The party itself was a source of some conflict — my mother's wedding guest list had been longer than mine and John's combined.
She'll have to have her OWN wedding!
When she decreased the size of the barn's building plans, serious guest list cuts had to happen, so it didn't make sense for my mother's list to outnumber the bride and groom's.
But I HAVE to invite all my friends from town! I'll be a PARIAH otherwise!

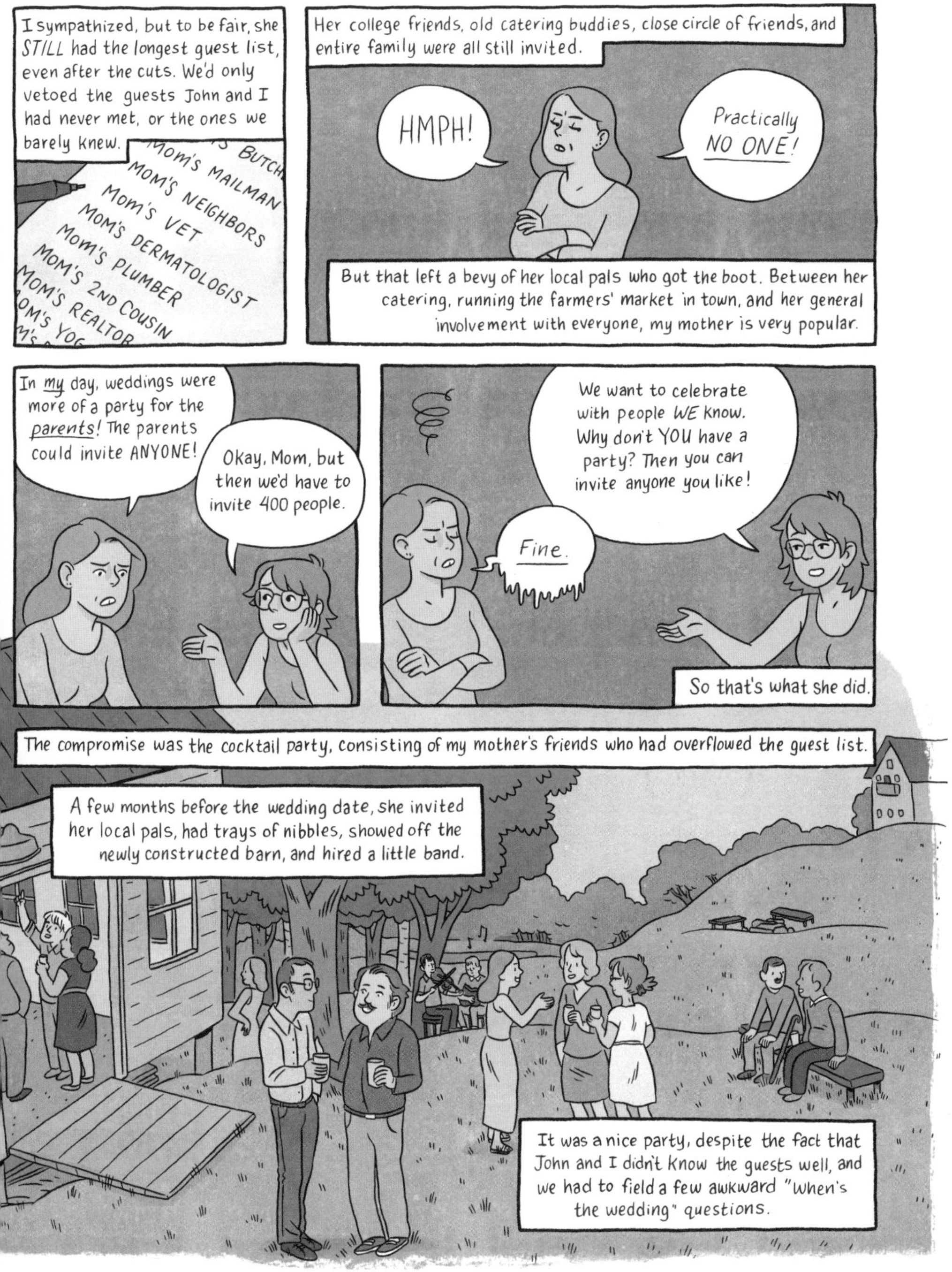
I sympathized, but to be fair, she STILL had the longest guest list, even after the cuts. We'd only vetoed the guests John and I had never met, or the ones we barely knew.
MOM'S MAILMAN
MOM'S NEIGHBORS
MOM'S VET
MOM'S DERMATOLOGIST
MOM'S PLUMBER
MOM'S 2ND COUSIN
MOM'S REALTOR
Her college friends, old catering buddies, close circle of friends, and entire family were all still invited.
HMPH!
Practically NO ONE!
But that left a bevy of her local pals who got the boot. Between her catering, running the farmers' market in town, and her general involvement with everyone, my mother is very popular.
In my day, weddings were more of a party for the parents! The parents could invite ANYONE!
Okay, Mom, but then we'd have to invite 400 people.
We want to celebrate with people WE know. Why don't YOU have a party? Then you can invite anyone you like!
Fine.
So that's what she did.
The compromise was the cocktail party, consisting of my mother's friends who had overflowed the guest list.
A few months before the wedding date, she invited her local pals, had trays of nibbles, showed off the newly constructed barn, and hired a little band.
It was a nice party, despite the fact that John and I didn't know the guests well, and we had to field a few awkward "When's the wedding" questions.

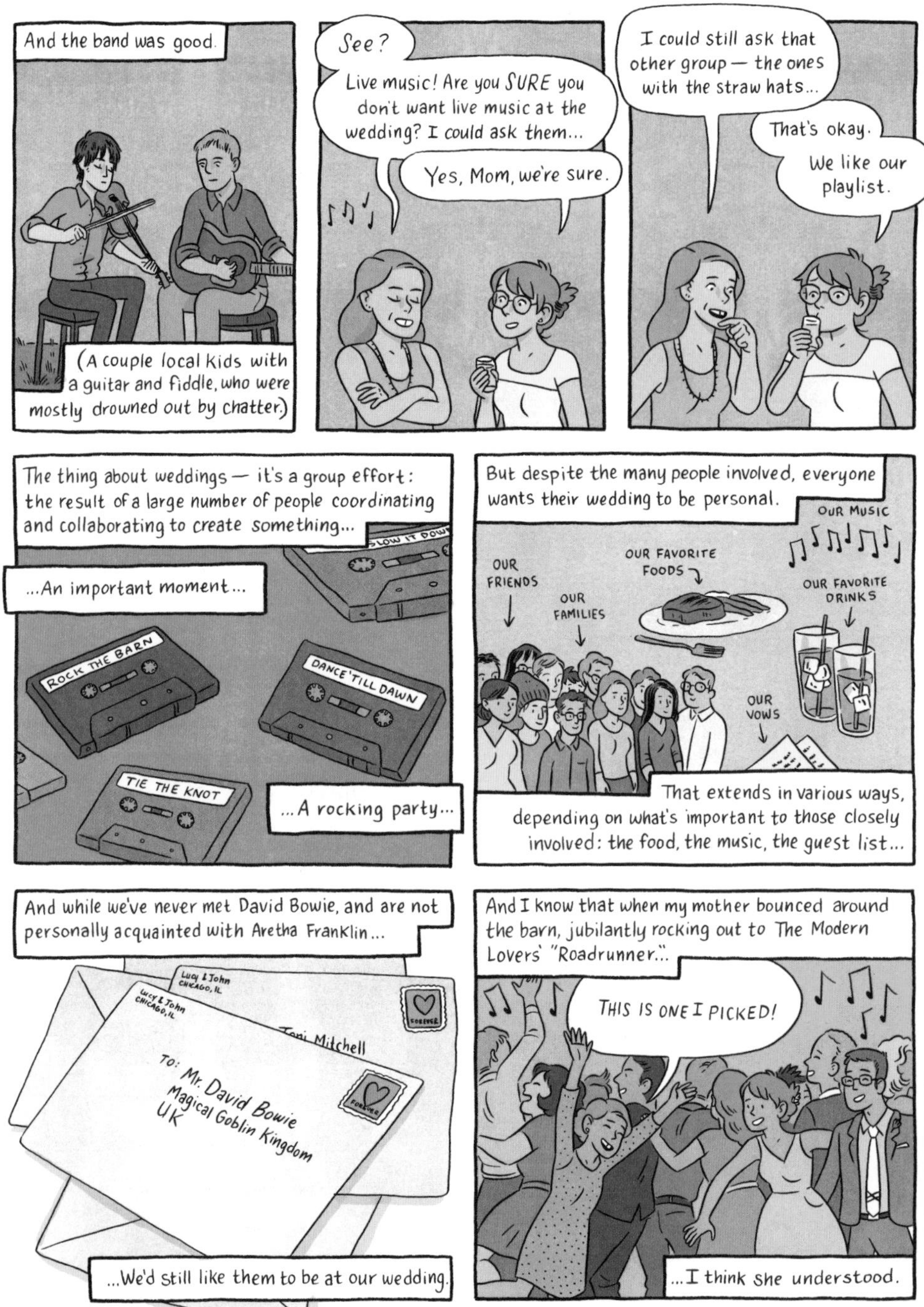
And the band was good.
(A couple local kids with a guitar and fiddle, who were mostly drowned out by chatter.)
See?
Live music! Are you SURE you don't want live music at the wedding? I could ask them...
Yes, Mom, we're sure.
I could still ask that other group — the ones with the straw hats...
That's okay.
We like our playlist.
The thing about weddings — it's a group effort: the result of a large number of people coordinating and collaborating to create something...
...An important moment...
ROCK THE BARN
DANCE 'TILL DAWN
TIE THE KNOT
...A rocking party...
But despite the many people involved, everyone wants their wedding to be personal.
OUR MUSIC
OUR FRIENDS
OUR FAMILIES
OUR FAVORITE FOODS
OUR FAVORITE DRINKS
OUR VOWS
That extends in various ways, depending on what's important to those closely involved: the food, the music, the guest list...
And while we've never met David Bowie, and are not personally acquainted with Aretha Franklin...
Lucy & John CHICAGO, IL
TO: Mr. David Bowie Magical Goblin Kingdom UK
...We'd still like them to be at our wedding.
And I know that when my mother bounced around the barn, jubilantly rocking out to The Modern Lovers' "Roadrunner"...
THIS IS ONE I PICKED!
...I think she understood.

Mom dancing with Cousin Ryan

WEIRD WEDDING FACTS

The Polterabend is part of the wedding traditions in Germany that consists of the wedding guests bringing old dishes or glasses to the bride and groom, and smashing them at their feet.

German brides carry a white ribbon (which is later tied to their car antennas), and the grooms carry grain in their pockets.

SMASH

Then the bride and groom have to clean it all up.

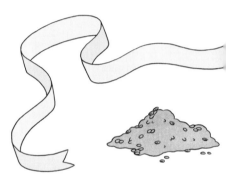

In Germany, the equivalent word for bachelor party is:

JUNGGESELLENABSCHIED

Awesome.

PART 3: GERMATRIMONY

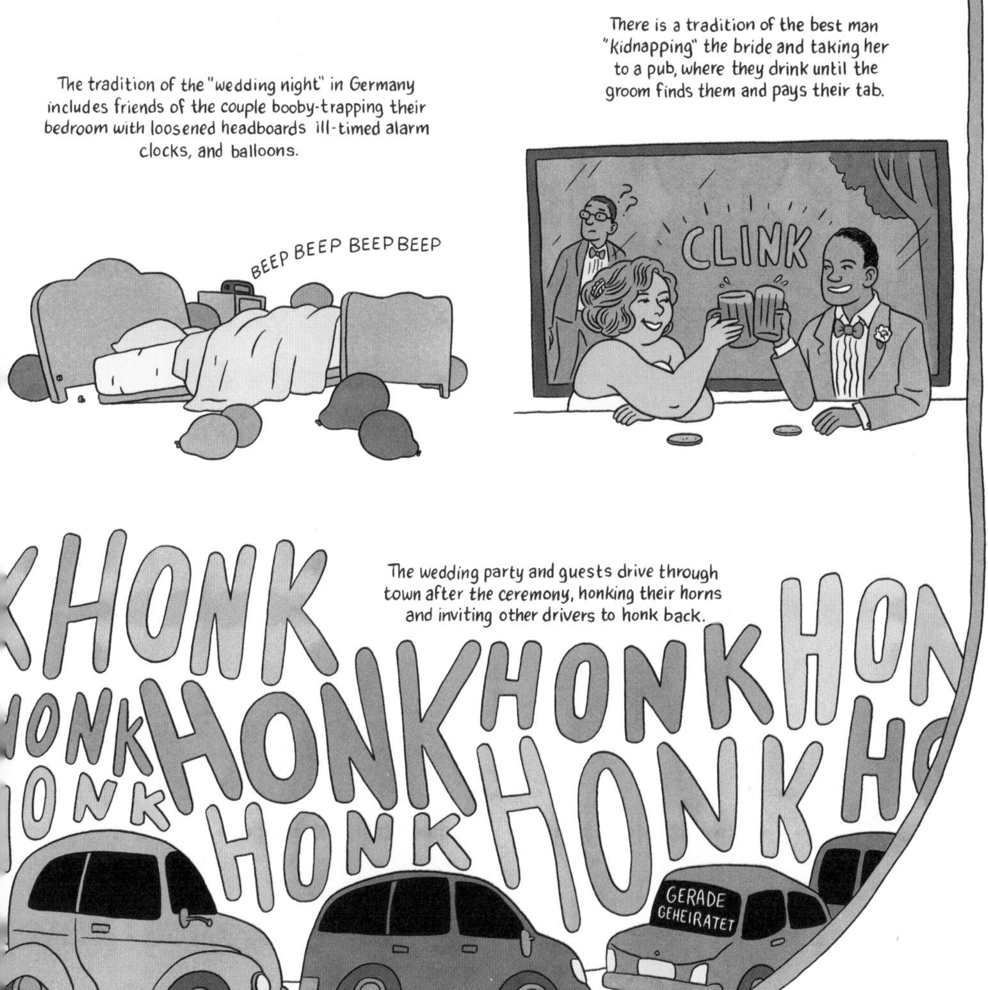
The tradition of the "wedding night" in Germany includes friends of the couple booby-trapping their bedroom with loosened headboards ill-timed alarm clocks, and balloons.
BEEP BEEP BEEP BEEP
There is a tradition of the best man "kidnapping" the bride and taking her to a pub, where they drink until the groom finds them and pays their tab.
CLINK
The wedding party and guests drive through town after the ceremony, honking their horns and inviting other drivers to honk back.
HONK HONK HONK HONK HONK HONK HONK HONK
GERADE GEHEIRATET

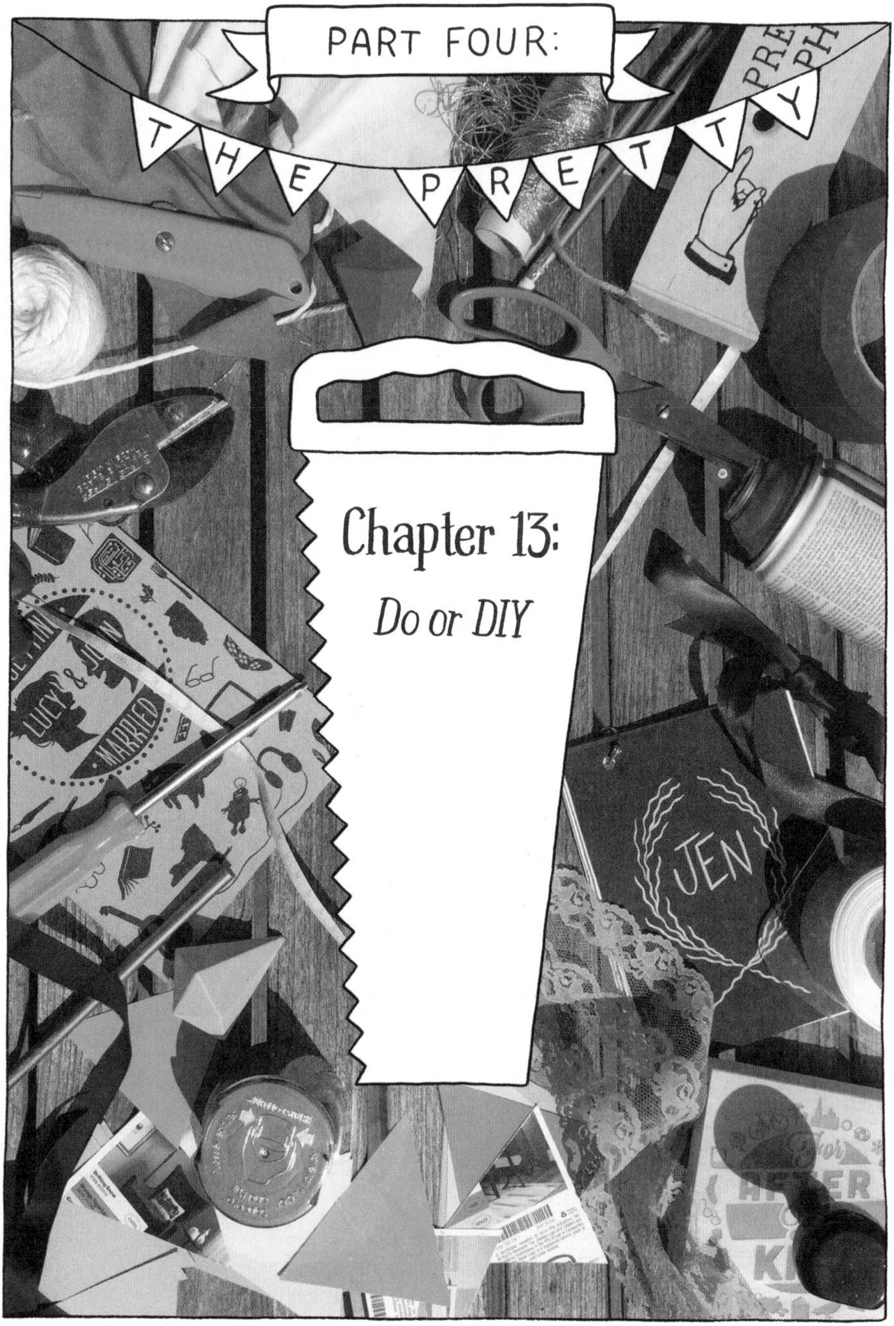
PART FOUR:
THE PRETTY
Chapter 13:
Do or DIY
LUCY & JEN
MARRIED
JEN

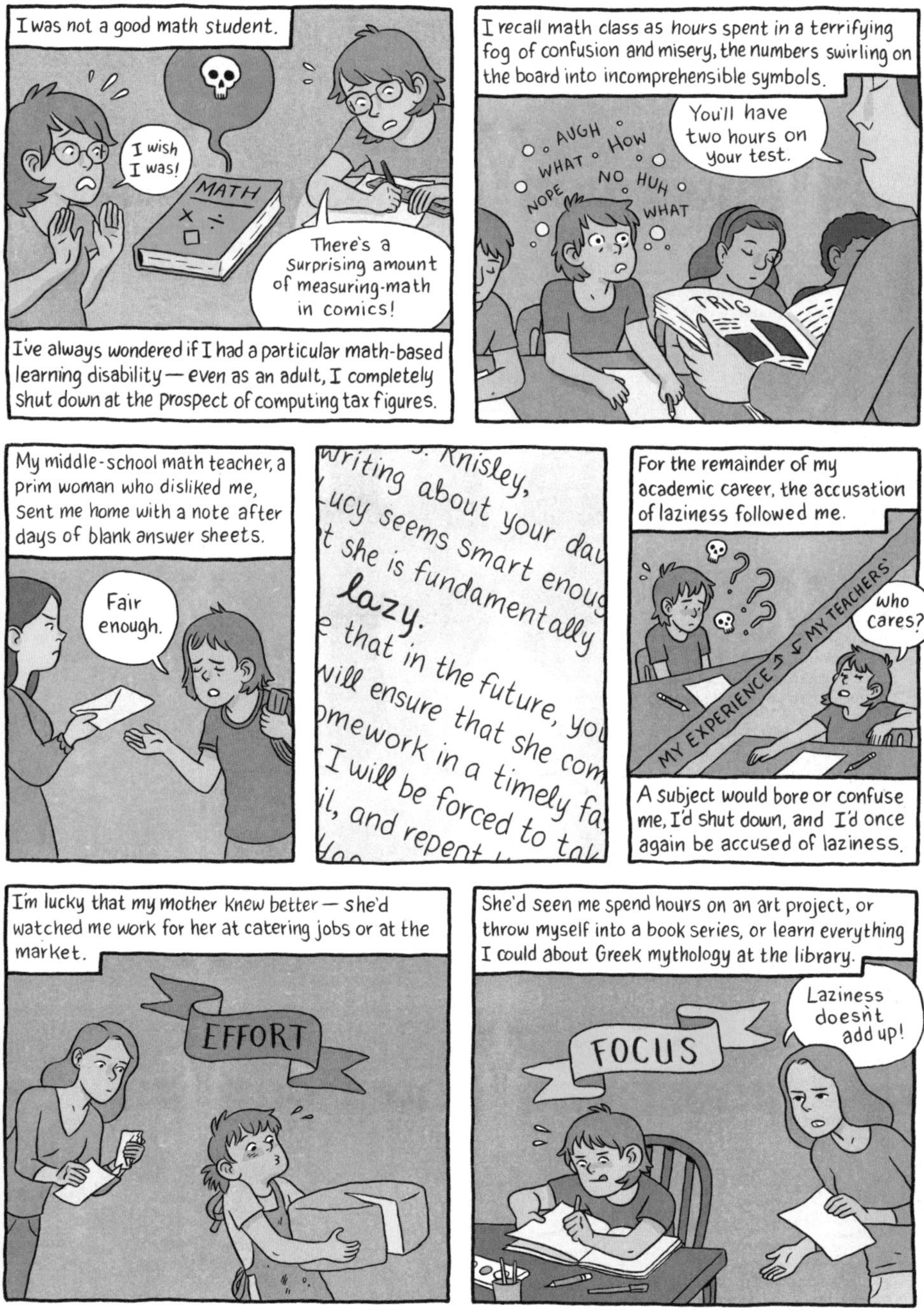
I was not a good math student.
I wish I was!
MATH
There's a surprising amount of measuring-math in comics!
I've always wondered if I had a particular math-based learning disability — even as an adult, I completely shut down at the prospect of computing tax figures.
I recall math class as hours spent in a terrifying fog of confusion and misery, the numbers swirling on the board into incomprehensible symbols.
AUGH
WHAT
HOW
NOPE
NO
HUH
WHAT
You'll have two hours on your test.
TRIG
My middle-school math teacher, a prim woman who disliked me, sent me home with a note after days of blank answer sheets.
Fair enough.
Knisley,
writing about your dau
Lucy seems smart enoug
t she is fundamentally
lazy.
e that in the future, you
will ensure that she com
omework in a timely fa
I will be forced to tak
il, and repent
For the remainder of my academic career, the accusation of laziness followed me.
MY EXPERIENCE
MY TEACHERS'
Who cares?
A subject would bore or confuse me, I'd shut down, and I'd once again be accused of laziness.
I'm lucky that my mother knew better — she'd watched me work for her at catering jobs or at the market.
EFFORT
She'd seen me spend hours on an art project, or throw myself into a book series, or learn everything I could about Greek mythology at the library.
FOCUS
Laziness doesn't add up!

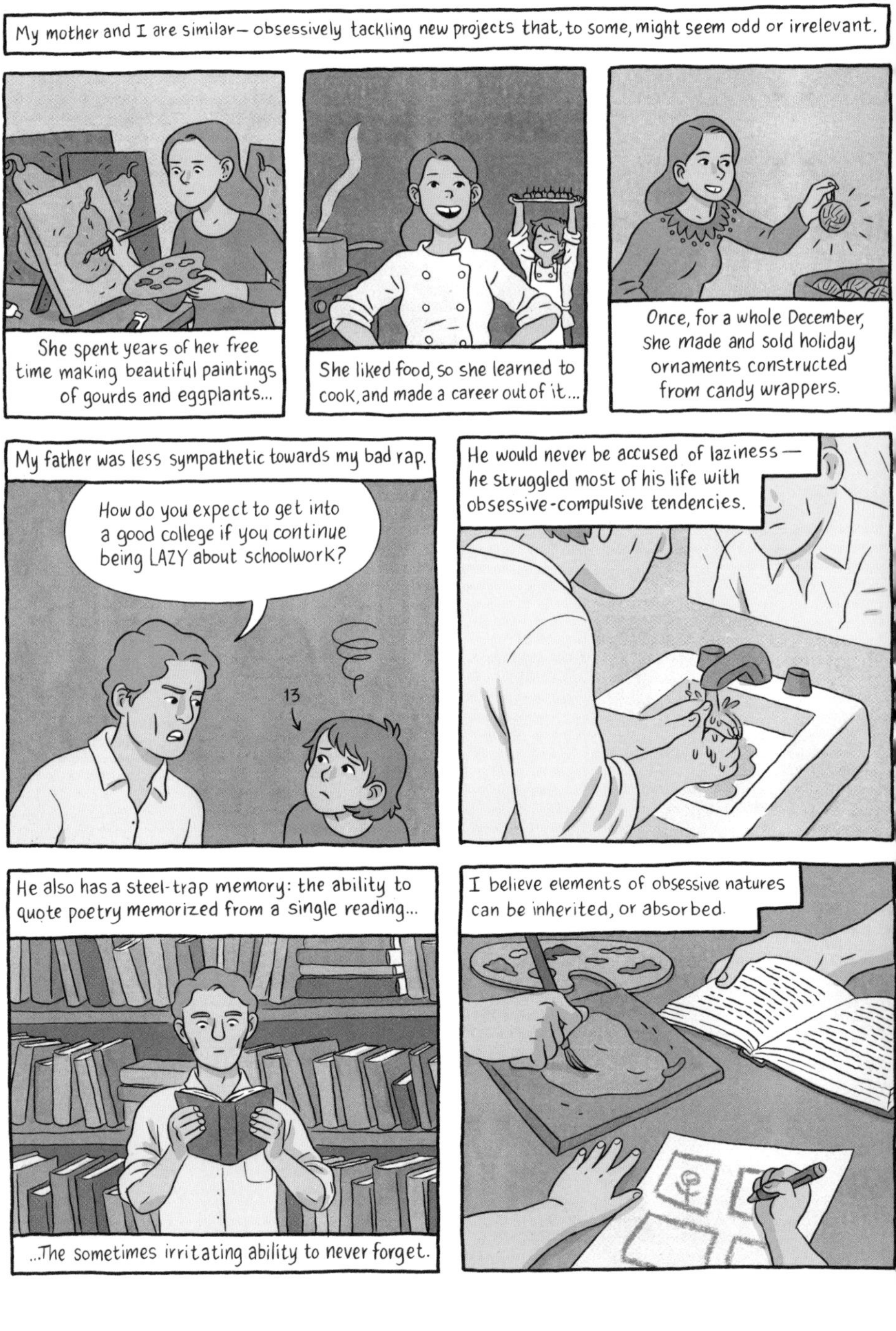
My mother and I are similar— obsessively tackling new projects that, to some, might seem odd or irrelevant.
She spent years of her free time making beautiful paintings of gourds and eggplants...
She liked food, so she learned to cook, and made a career out of it...
Once, for a whole December, she made and sold holiday ornaments constructed from candy wrappers.
My father was less sympathetic towards my bad rap.
How do you expect to get into a good college if you continue being LAZY about schoolwork?
13
He would never be accused of laziness— he struggled most of his life with obsessive-compulsive tendencies.
He also has a steel-trap memory: the ability to quote poetry memorized from a single reading...
...The sometimes irritating ability to never forget.
I believe elements of obsessive natures can be inherited, or absorbed.

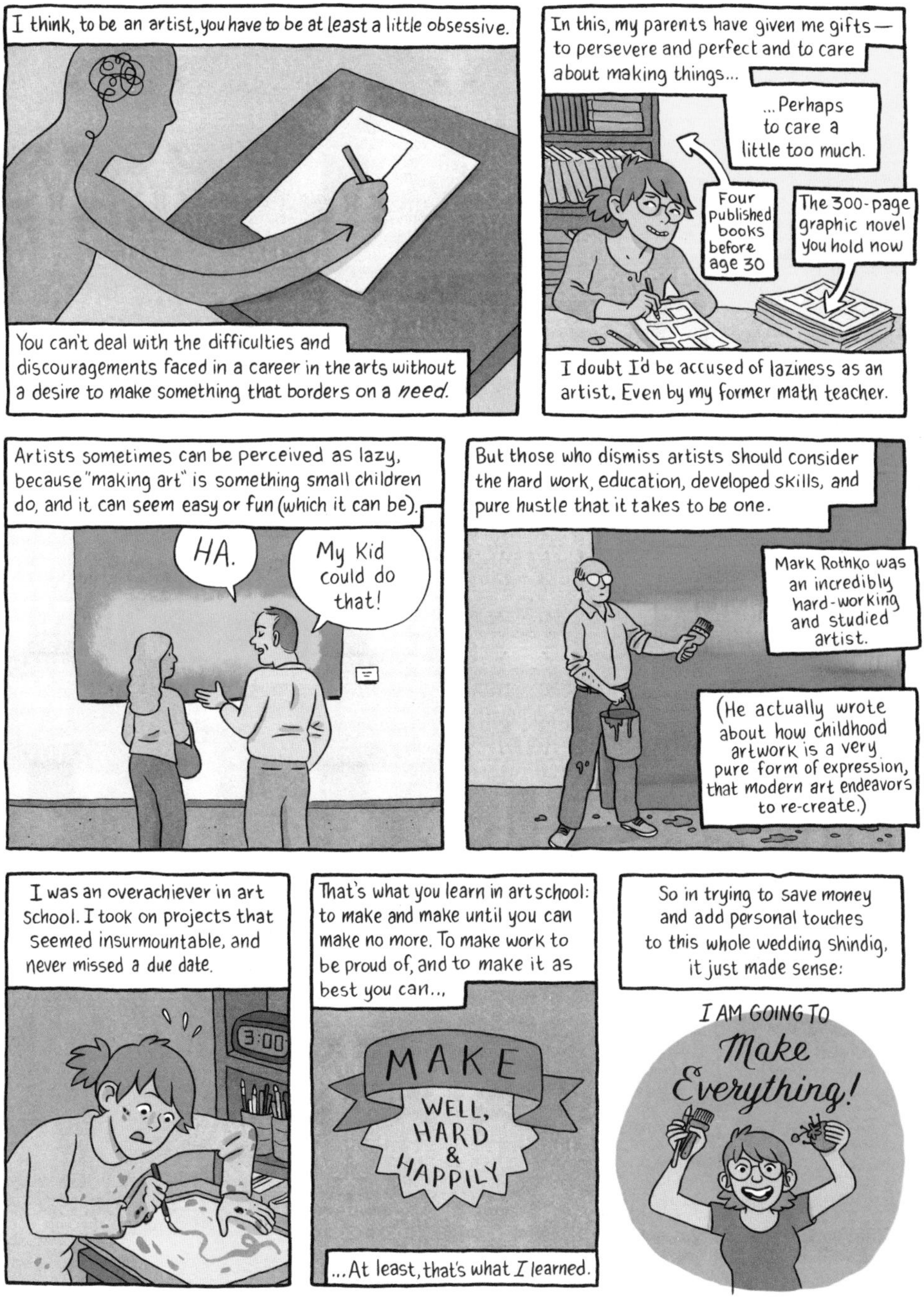

I think, to be an artist, you have to be at least a little obsessive.
You can't deal with the difficulties and discouragements faced in a career in the arts without a desire to make something that borders on a *need*.
In this, my parents have given me gifts — to persevere and perfect and to care about making things...
...Perhaps to care a little too much.
Four published books before age 30
The 300-page graphic novel you hold now
I doubt I'd be accused of laziness as an artist. Even by my former math teacher.
Artists sometimes can be perceived as lazy, because "making art" is something small children do, and it can seem easy or fun (which it can be).
HA.
My Kid could do that!
But those who dismiss artists should consider the hard work, education, developed skills, and pure hustle that it takes to be one.
Mark Rothko was an incredibly hard-working and studied artist.
(He actually wrote about how childhood artwork is a very pure form of expression, that modern art endeavors to re-create.)
I was an overachiever in art school. I took on projects that seemed insurmountable, and never missed a due date.
3:00
That's what you learn in art school: to make and make until you can make no more. To make work to be proud of, and to make it as best you can...
MAKE
WELL, HARD & HAPPILY
...At least, that's what *I* learned.
So in trying to save money and add personal touches to this whole wedding shindig, it just made sense:
I AM GOING TO Make Everything!

Lucy's Wedding-Project Rundown

Photobooth Backdrop

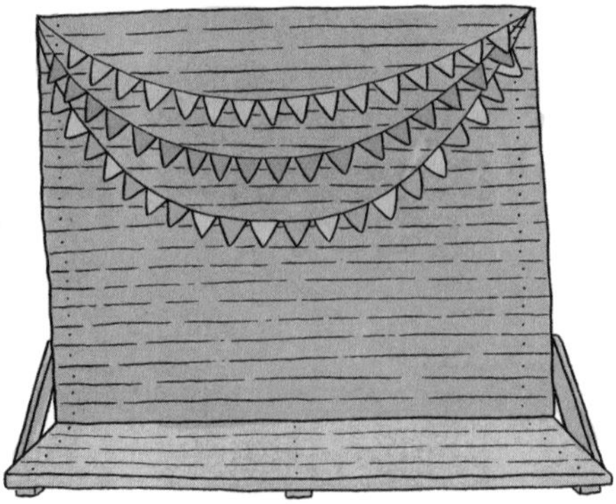

<u>Cost</u>: About $40

<u>Materials</u>: Pine furring strips, nails, paint
samples (swiped from a hardware store),
hot glue, string, 2x4s
<u>Tools</u>: Saw, nail gun, glue gun, scissors

<u>Time commitment</u>: About two afternoons

<u>Injuries sustained</u>: Dropped entire thing on
my head while trying to lift it myself...
Not recommended.

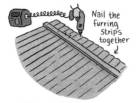
Nail the furring strips together

Affix upright using 2x4s

Cut paint samples into pennant triangles

Glue pennants to string and hang on the backdrop

Photobooth Mechanism

<u>Cost</u>: About $60 (already had the iPad, borrowed the camera

<u>Materials</u>: Scrap-wood box, table legs and leg attachments,
camera monopod, iPad and iPad mount, extension cord
camera, and camera-to-iPad cord, wired shutter
release, clip lights

<u>Tools</u>: Saw, drill

<u>Time commitment</u>: Much troubleshooting over the course
of a week of evenings

<u>Warning</u>: Camera battery dies quickly—Keep a replacement
battery around!

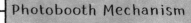

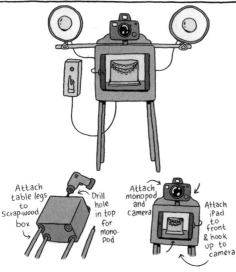

Attach
table legs
to
Scrap-wood
box

Drill
hole
in top
for
mono-
pod

Attach
monopod
and
camera

Attach
iPad
to
front
& hook
up to
camera

Hook up
camera to
Shutter
release
(I made a little
box for it)

Affix clip lights, and
test with fun pose!

Guest Sketchbooks/Place Cards

Cost: $50

Materials: Sketch paper, cover-paper, card board,
gold ink, book rings, customized pencils, gold string,
printed photos

Tools: Inking pen, printer for photos, 2-hole punch

Time commitment: A couple weeks of evenings

Note: Drawing decorative circles in gold ink can be
incredibly soothing to certain frazzled brides

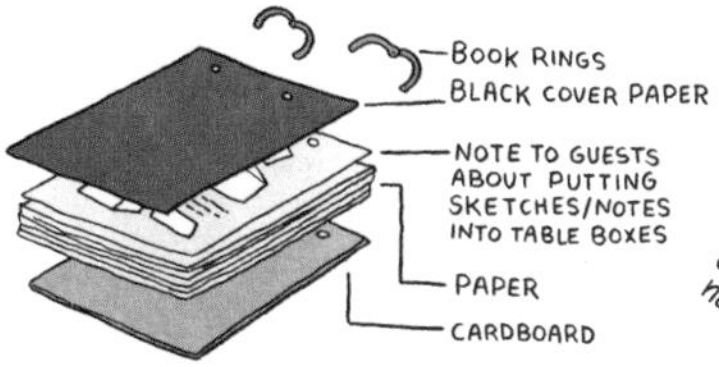

BOOK RINGS
BLACK COVER PAPER

NOTE TO GUESTS
ABOUT PUTTING
SKETCHES/NOTES
INTO TABLE BOXES

PAPER

CARDBOARD

Print out photos of you
& your guest

For "thank you"
- thank you
- brate with you! So
excited to cele-
On the back, write
Love, Lucy
a little welcome
note to guest

Tuck into
sketchbook

Draw circle and
guest's name in
gold ink

Tie closed
with
gold
string

Include
customized
pencil with
wedding
date

Lawn Games

BAGS AND BAGS BOARD:

Cost: $5   Materials: Scrap fabric, rice, scrap wood

Tools: Saw, nails & hammer, needle & thread

Recommended: Practice bag-toss accuracy
on sleeping fiancé's butt

Time: 2 hours

HORSESHOES:

Cost: $5   Materials: Lawn stakes, horseshoes

Tools: Spray paint, mallet   Time: 1 hour

Know This: Nobody will play these games if it rains

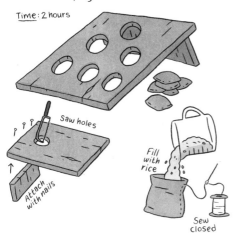

Saw holes

Fill
with
rice

Sew
closed

Attach
with nails

Spray-paint
horseshoes
to differentiate
teams

Hammer
stakes into
very rocky
ground

Veil

Cost: $10

Materials: 2 yards of tulle, lace ribbon, hair comb

Tools: Needle/thread, craft glue

Time commitment: A couple hours

Did You Know: They can charge THOUSANDS of DOLLARS for these things at boutiques!?

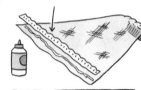

Pennant Flags

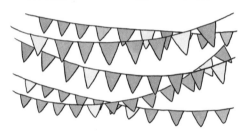

Cost: 10 bucks worth of string and glue

Materials: Jute string, scrap fabric, craft glue

Tools: Scissors, homemade triangle guide

Time commitment: A few afternoons

A thing my mom teased me about with this project: "It's like your wedding's at a used car lot!"

cut triangle guide from stiff paper

Cut triangles from scrap fabric

Glue flags to string

Hang 'em up!

Fabric can be found in craft shop scrap bins or thrift shops

PENCIL JARS:

Cost: $0 (if, like me, you have a lot of pencils and eat a lot of food in jars)

Materials: Jars you saved from the recycling bin over a six-month period, colored pencils from your lifelong art-supply-hoarding habit

Warning: Bugs really like to die in old jam or pickle jars

Table Stuff

GOLD ANIMALS:

Cost: $20

Materials: plastic toy animals, gold spray paint

Tip: Let the layers of paint dry between coats (otherwise you'll wind up with sticky animals)

PAPER TABLE RUNNERS:

Cost: $6

Materials: Permanent markers, roll of craft paper sawn in half, lengthwise

It helps if: You have a long table on hand to use as a drawing surface — otherwise, the floor works

GUEST-BOOK BOXES: *
*Actually my mom's project

Cost: $20

Materials: Scrap wood, glue, saws, items to use as handles

The function: of these pretty wooden boxes was to collect the notes and drawings from guests that they made in their sketchbooks/place cards. I don't have the woodworking know-how to make these, but my mom and her boyfriend do!

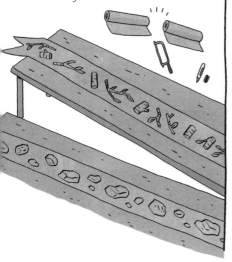

Groomsman Ties and Pocket Squares

Cost: $50   Materials: 1 yard of fabric per tie, lining fabric, iron-on interfacing, a tie pattern, fabric paint

Tools: Sewing machine, scissors, tie pattern guide, painting or screenprinting supplies, iron

Time: A few days   Big Help: A friend or bridesmaid who knows about sewing and screenprinting

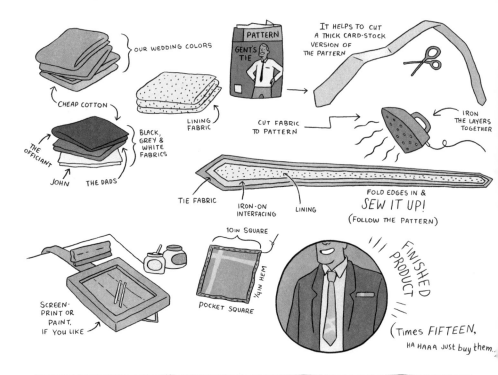

OUR WEDDING COLORS

CHEAP COTTON

THE OFFICIANT

JOHN   THE DADS

LINING FABRIC

BLACK, GREY & WHITE FABRICS

PATTERN
GENT'S TIE

IT HELPS TO CUT A THICK CARD-STOCK VERSION OF THE PATTERN

CUT FABRIC TO PATTERN

IRON THE LAYERS TOGETHER

TIE FABRIC   IRON-ON INTERFACING   LINING

FOLD EDGES IN & *SEW IT UP!*
(FOLLOW THE PATTERN)

SCREEN-PRINT OR PAINT, IF YOU LIKE

10 IN SQUARE

1/4 IN HEM

POCKET SQUARE

FINISHED PRODUCT

(Times *FIFTEEN*, HA HAAA just buy them.

Place ties and pocket squares in painted tie boxes, and include some matching socks, the groom's favorite book, a small portrait of the groomsman, and one of those switchblade combs (which will be explained later).

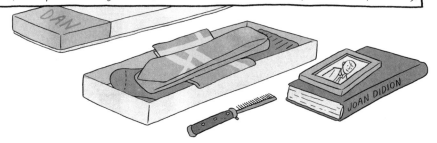

DAN

JOAN DIDION

Bridesmaid Color Kits

Materials: Toy cardboard suitcases, and numerous items, bought and made, that match in color

Requires: Color-matching skills, perseverance, enthusiasm! Cost: $100

Time: A long span of time during wedding prep Warning: Color-spotting may become addictive

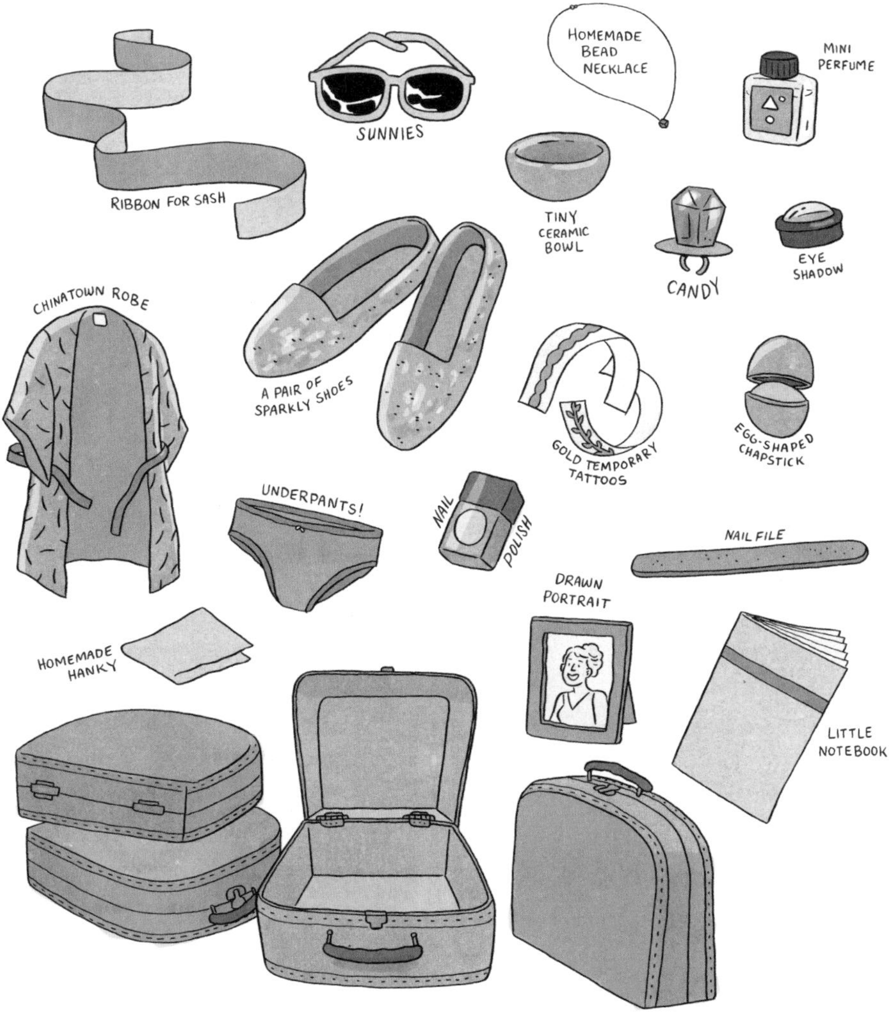

HOMEMADE BEAD NECKLACE
MINI PERFUME
SUNNIES
RIBBON FOR SASH
TINY CERAMIC BOWL
CANDY
EYE SHADOW
CHINATOWN ROBE
A PAIR OF SPARKLY SHOES
GOLD TEMPORARY TATTOOS
EGG-SHAPED CHAPSTICK
UNDERPANTS!
NAIL POLISH
NAIL FILE
DRAWN PORTRAIT
HOMEMADE HANKY
LITTLE NOTEBOOK

Mom Gifties

Materials: Gift boxes, a variety of things made and bought   Cost: $50

Time: A long span of time during wedding prep   Note: Don't forget about stepparents!

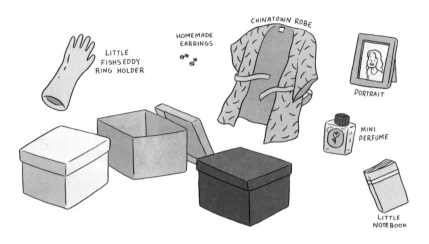

LITTLE FISHS EDDY RING HOLDER

HOMEMADE EARRINGS

CHINATOWN ROBE

PORTRAIT

MINI PERFUME

LITTLE NOTEBOOK

Flower Girl and Ring-Bearer Gifties

Materials: Gift boxes, boys' ties, fabric paint, and a variety of things made and bought   Cost: $30

Time: An afternoon   Note: Make sure, if you make the ties, to use a smaller tie pattern

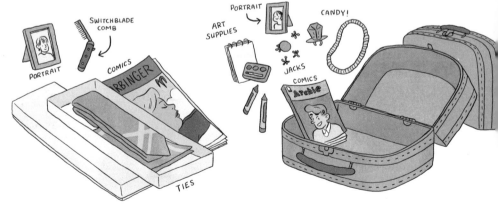

PORTRAIT

SWITCHBLADE COMB

COMICS

RBINGER

TIES

ART SUPPLIES

PORTRAIT

CANDY!

JACKS

COMICS

Archie

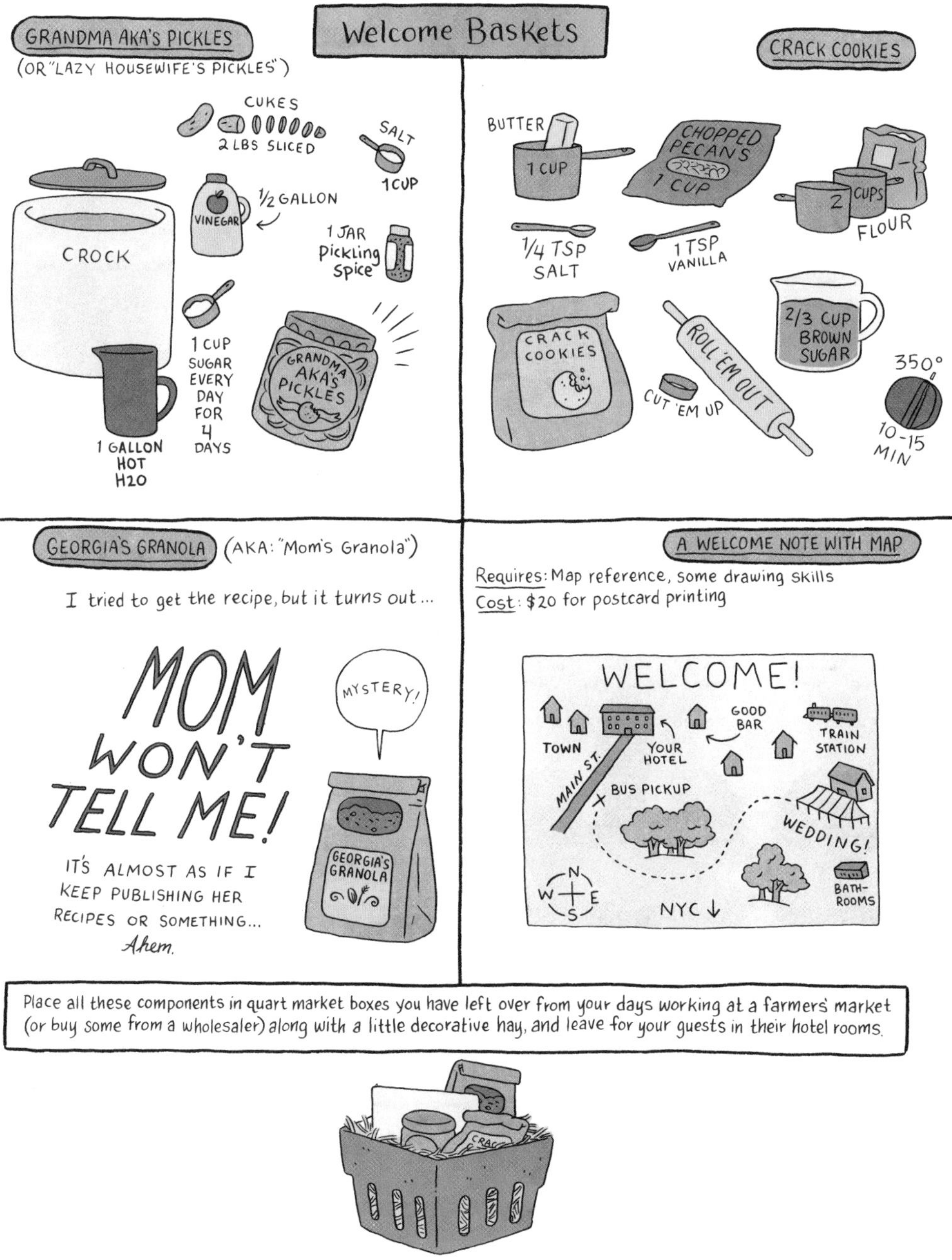
Welcome Baskets
GRANDMA AKA'S PICKLES
(OR "LAZY HOUSEWIFE'S PICKLES")
CUKES
2 LBS SLICED
SALT
1 CUP
1/2 GALLON
VINEGAR
CROCK
1 JAR
Pickling
Spice
1 CUP
SUGAR
EVERY
DAY
FOR
4
DAYS
1 GALLON
HOT
H2O
GRANDMA AKA'S PICKLES
CRACK COOKIES
BUTTER
1 CUP
CHOPPED PECANS
1 CUP
2 CUPS
FLOUR
1/4 TSP
SALT
1 TSP
VANILLA
CRACK COOKIES
ROLL 'EM OUT
CUT 'EM UP
2/3 CUP
BROWN
SUGAR
350°
10-15
MIN
GEORGIA'S GRANOLA
(AKA: "Mom's Granola")
I tried to get the recipe, but it turns out...
MOM WON'T TELL ME!
MYSTERY!
GEORGIA'S GRANOLA
IT'S ALMOST AS IF I
KEEP PUBLISHING HER
RECIPES OR SOMETHING...
Ahem.
A WELCOME NOTE WITH MAP
Requires: Map reference, some drawing skills
Cost: $20 for postcard printing
WELCOME!
GOOD
BAR
TRAIN
STATION
TOWN
YOUR
HOTEL
MAIN ST.
BUS PICKUP
WEDDING!
N
W
E
S
NYC ↓
BATH-
ROOMS
Place all these components in quart market boxes you have left over from your days working at a farmers' market (or buy some from a wholesaler) along with a little decorative hay, and leave for your guests in their hotel rooms.
CRAC

The Wedding Program

Cost: $100 for printing Requires: Some drawing and digital design skills, plus knowing a good print shop

Oof: This one took ages. Months of part-time work. Keep in mind that printing takes a while, so if there is time-sensitive content (like seating charts) and you're waiting on RSVPs, you may want to cut it.

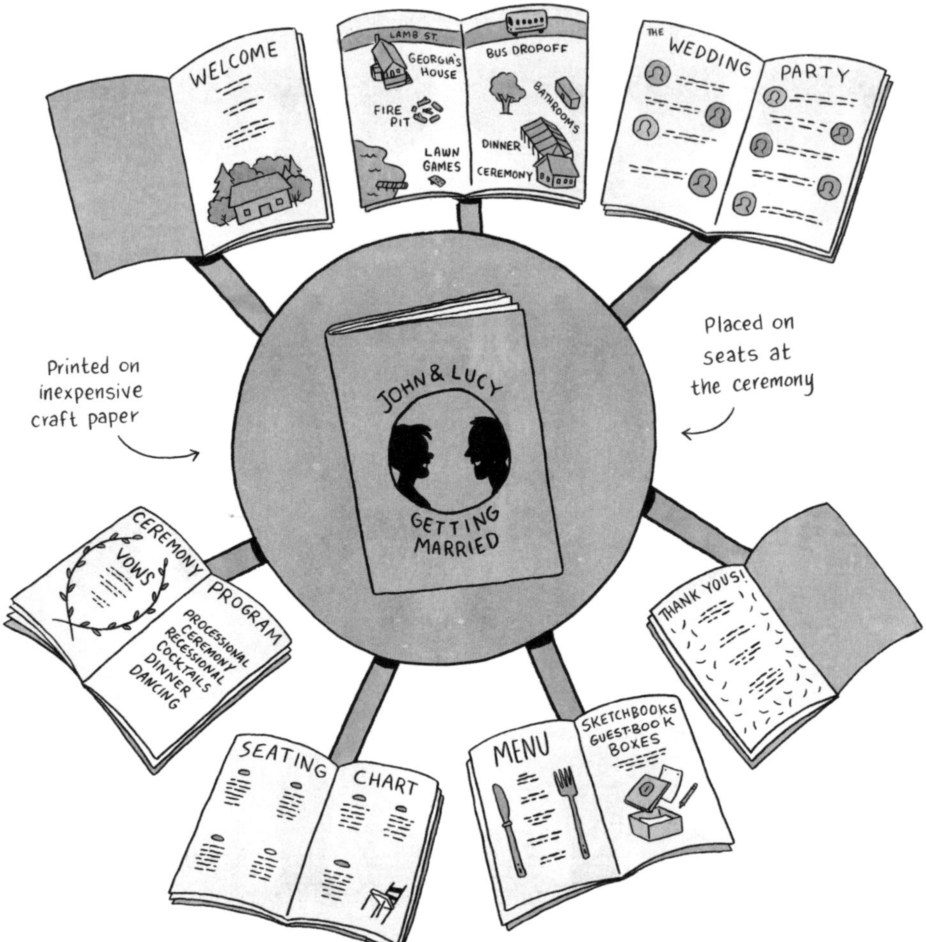

WELCOME
LAMB ST.
GEORGIA'S HOUSE
FIRE PIT
LAWN GAMES
BUS DROPOFF
BATHROOMS
DINNER
CEREMONY
THE WEDDING PARTY
Placed on seats at the ceremony
Printed on inexpensive craft paper
JOHN & LUCY
GETTING MARRIED
CEREMONY
VOWS
PROGRAM
PROCESSIONAL
CEREMONY
RECESSIONAL
COCKTAILS
DINNER
DANCING
THANK YOUS!
SEATING CHART
MENU
SKETCHBOOKS
GUEST-BOOK
BOXES

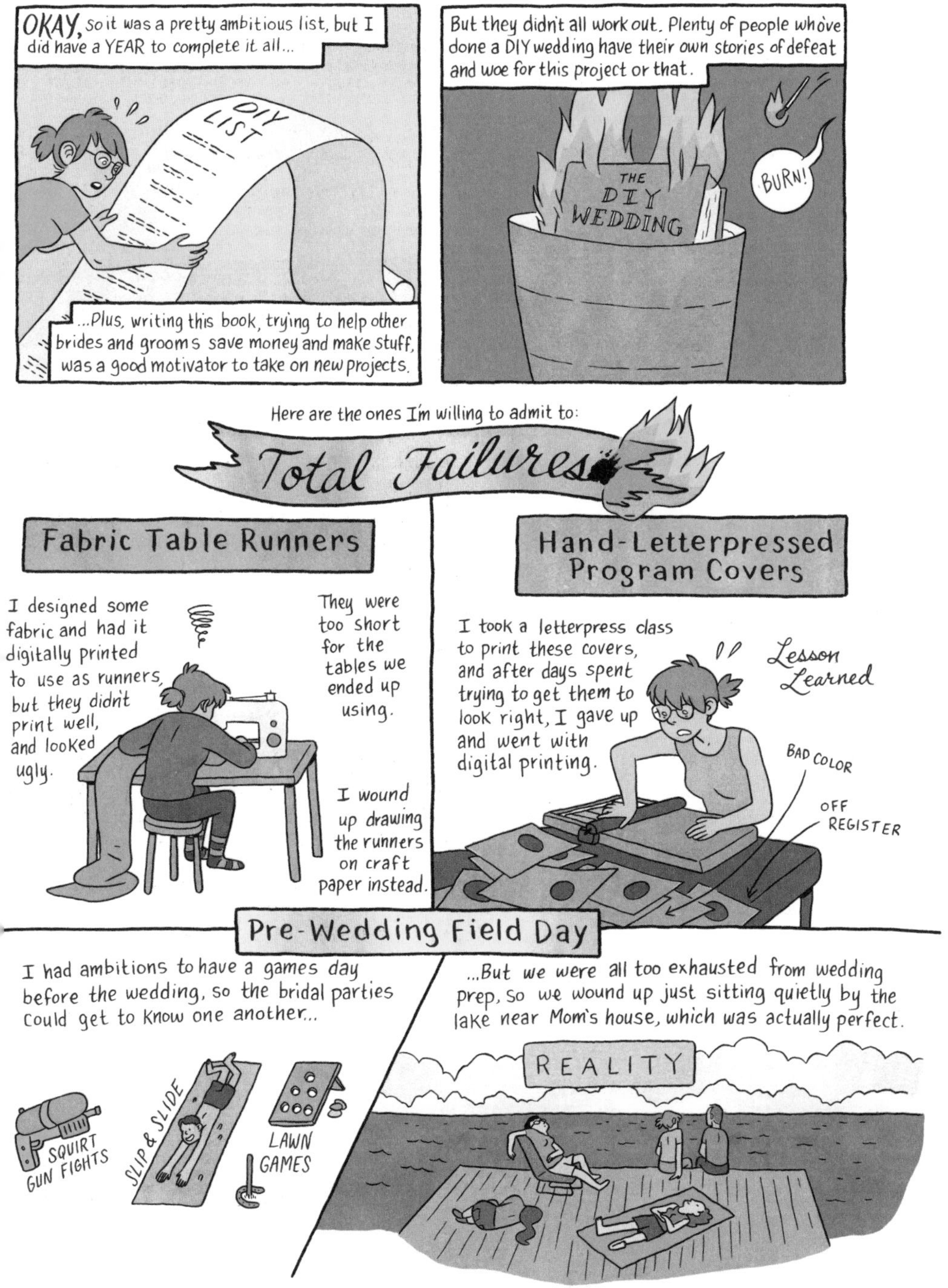

OKAY, so it was a pretty ambitious list, but I did have a YEAR to complete it all...
DIY LIST
...Plus, writing this book, trying to help other brides and grooms save money and make stuff, was a good motivator to take on new projects.
But they didn't all work out. Plenty of people who've done a DIY wedding have their own stories of defeat and woe for this project or that.
THE DIY WEDDING
BURN!
Here are the ones I'm willing to admit to:
Total Failures
Fabric Table Runners
I designed some fabric and had it digitally printed to use as runners, but they didn't print well, and looked ugly.
They were too short for the tables we ended up using.
I wound up drawing the runners on craft paper instead.
Hand-Letterpressed Program Covers
I took a letterpress class to print these covers, and after days spent trying to get them to look right, I gave up and went with digital printing.
Lesson Learned
BAD COLOR
OFF REGISTER
Pre-Wedding Field Day
I had ambitions to have a games day before the wedding, so the bridal parties could get to know one another...
SQUIRT GUN FIGHTS
SLIP & SLIDE
LAWN GAMES
...But we were all too exhausted from wedding prep, so we wound up just sitting quietly by the lake near Mom's house, which was actually perfect.
REALITY

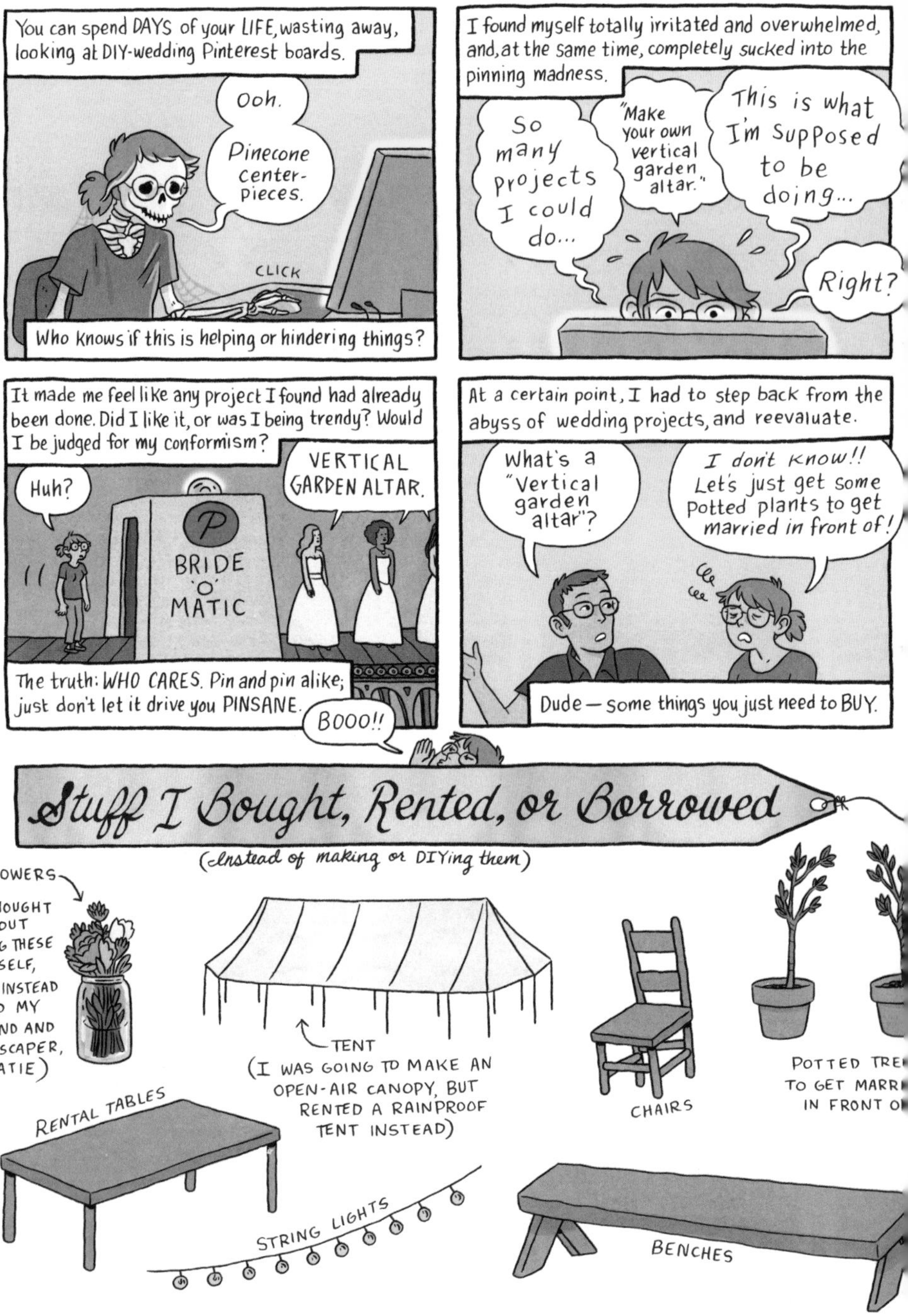
You can spend DAYS of your LIFE, wasting away, looking at DIY-wedding Pinterest boards.
Ooh.
Pinecone center-pieces.
CLICK
Who knows if this is helping or hindering things?
I found myself totally irritated and overwhelmed, and, at the same time, completely sucked into the pinning madness.
So many projects I could do...
"Make your own vertical garden altar."
This is what I'm supposed to be doing...
Right?
It made me feel like any project I found had already been done. Did I like it, or was I being trendy? Would I be judged for my conformism?
Huh?
VERTICAL GARDEN ALTAR.
P
BRIDE 'O' MATIC
The truth: WHO CARES. Pin and pin alike; just don't let it drive you PINSANE.
BOOO!!
At a certain point, I had to step back from the abyss of wedding projects, and reevaluate.
What's a "Vertical garden altar"?
I don't know!! Let's just get some potted plants to get married in front of!
Dude—some things you just need to BUY.
Stuff I Bought, Rented, or Borrowed
(Instead of making or DIYing them)
FLOWERS
(I THOUGHT ABOUT DOING THESE MYSELF, BUT INSTEAD HIRED MY FRIEND AND LANDSCAPER, KATIE)
TENT
(I WAS GOING TO MAKE AN OPEN-AIR CANOPY, BUT RENTED A RAINPROOF TENT INSTEAD)
CHAIRS
POTTED TRE
TO GET MARR
IN FRONT O
RENTAL TABLES
STRING LIGHTS
BENCHES

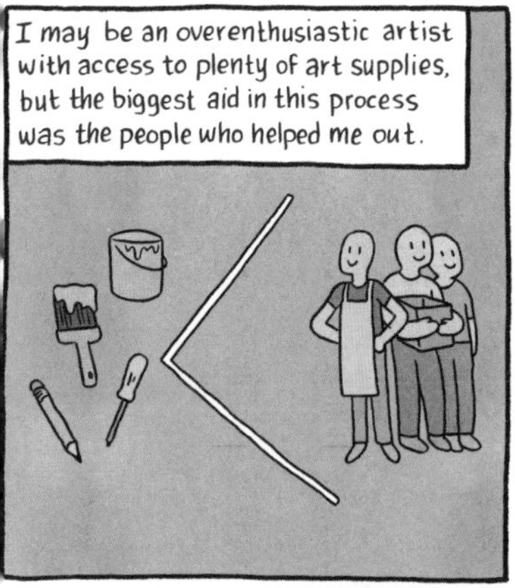
I may be an overenthusiastic artist with access to plenty of art supplies, but the biggest aid in this process was the people who helped me out.

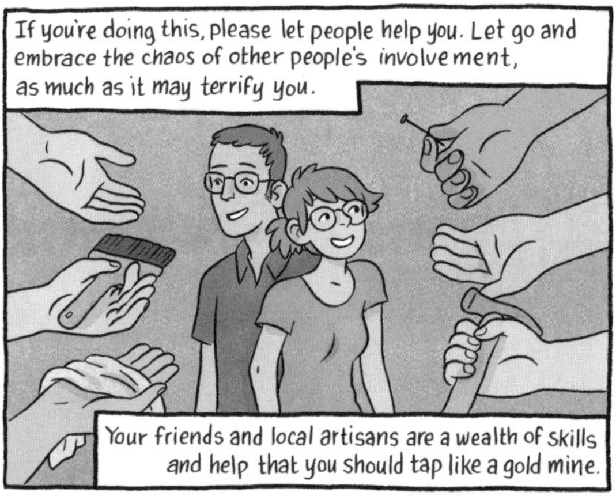
If you're doing this, please let people help you. Let go and embrace the chaos of other people's involvement, as much as it may terrify you.
Your friends and local artisans are a wealth of skills and help that you should tap like a gold mine.

Stuff I Straight-Up Farmed Out

THE HAIR

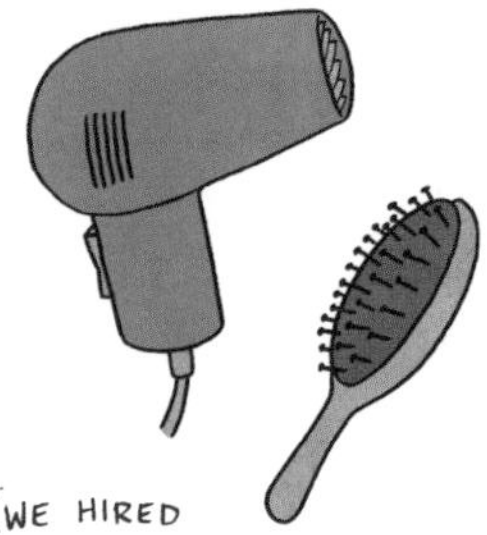

(WE HIRED MOM'S HAIRSTYLIST TO COME DO THE BRIDAL PARTY'S HAIR)

THE RINGS

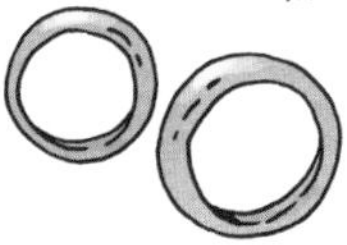

(WE COMMISSIONED A LOCAL JEWELRY MAKER TO MAKE OUR WEDDING BANDS)

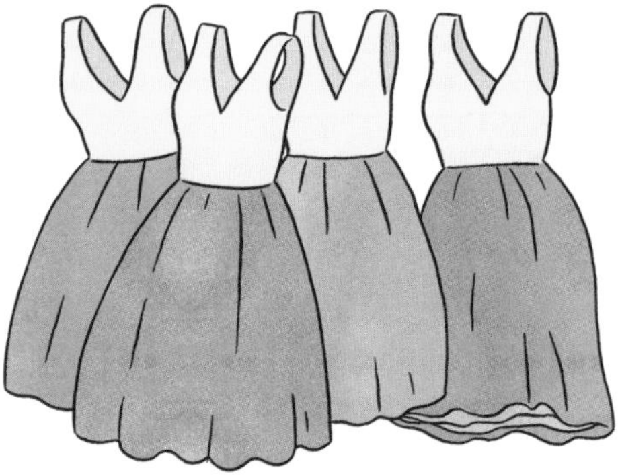

THE BRIDESMAIDS' DRESSES

(I HIRED NORA TO MAKE THESE)

MOM'S BOX CENTER-PIECES

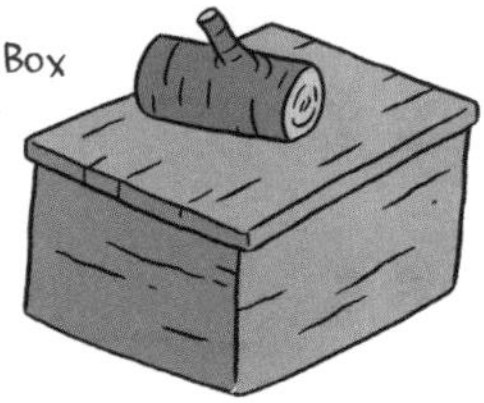

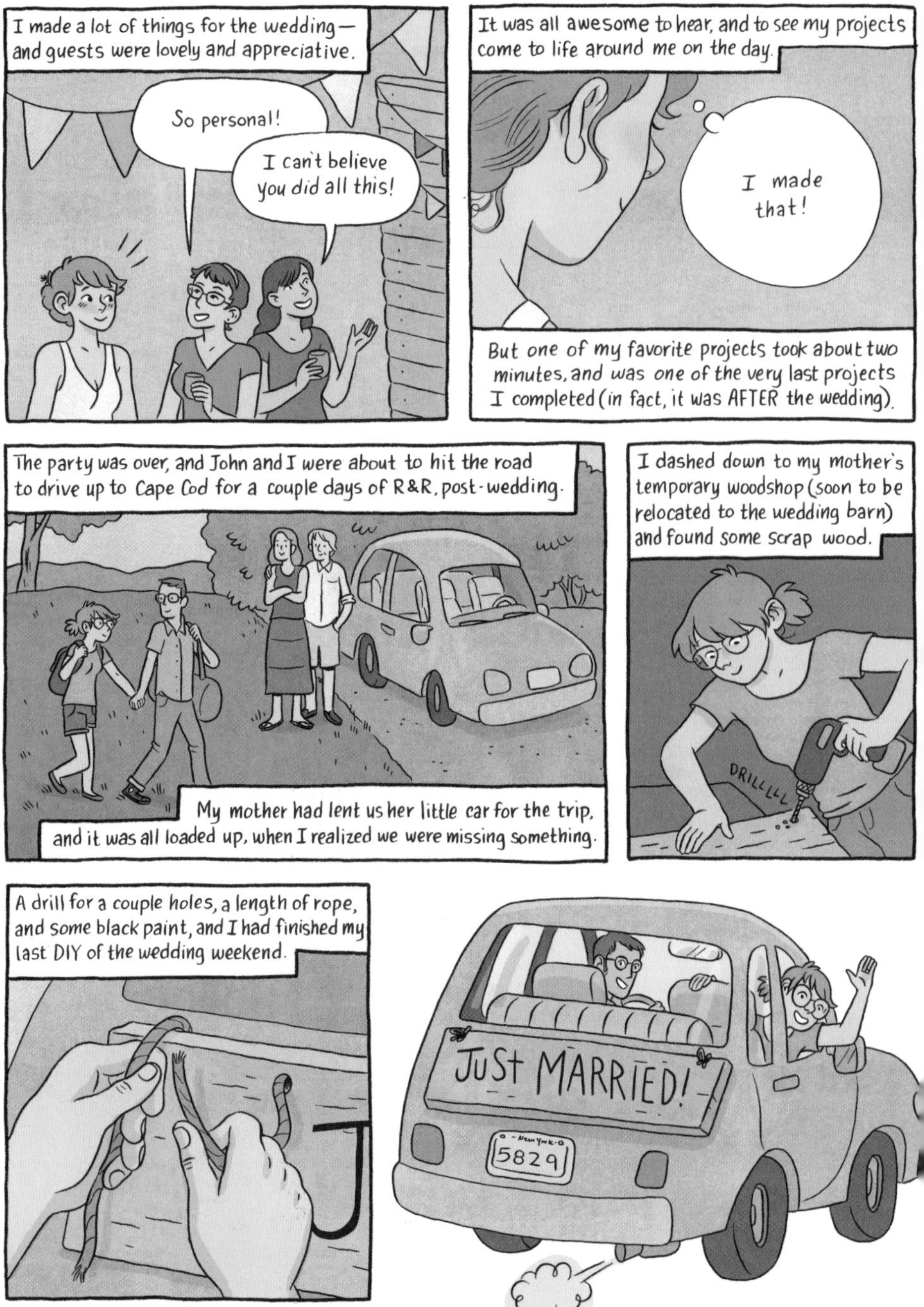
I made a lot of things for the wedding— and guests were lovely and appreciative.
So personal!
I can't believe you did all this!
It was all awesome to hear, and to see my projects come to life around me on the day.
I made that!
But one of my favorite projects took about two minutes, and was one of the very last projects I completed (in fact, it was AFTER the wedding).
The party was over, and John and I were about to hit the road to drive up to Cape Cod for a couple days of R&R, post-wedding.
My mother had lent us her little car for the trip, and it was all loaded up, when I realized we were missing something.
I dashed down to my mother's temporary woodshop (soon to be relocated to the wedding barn) and found some scrap wood.
DRILLLLL
A drill for a couple holes, a length of rope, and some black paint, and I had finished my last DIY of the wedding weekend.
JUST MARRIED!
5829

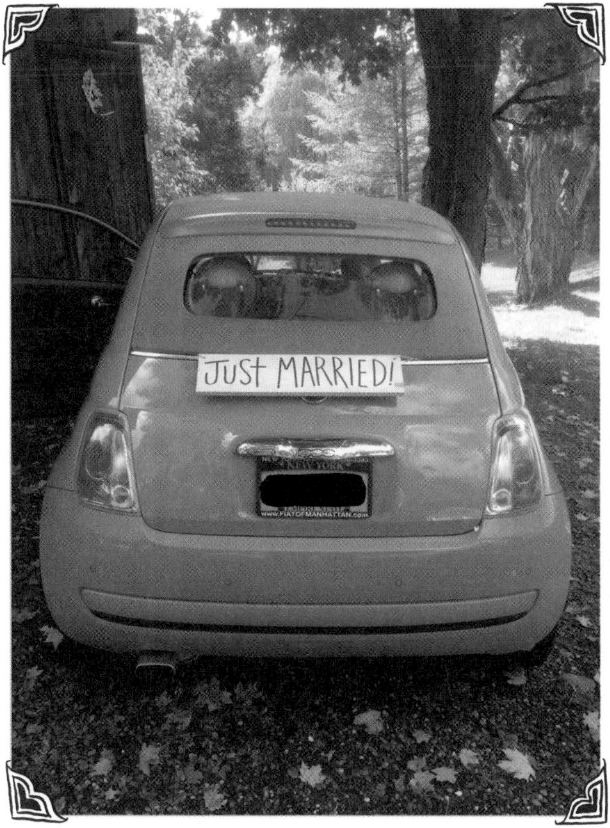
JUST MARRIED!
NEW YORK
www.FIATOFMANHATTAN.com

WEIRD WEDDING FACTS

THAT CREEPY GARTER-TOSS THING:

This is a remnant of when the bride and groom were expected to consummate the marriage directly after the ceremony, and everyone was creepily involved. Guests would help them on their way by assisting the bride in removing with her dress, going so far as to rip pieces of it from her body — especially undergarments.

CONSUMMATE!

JUST TAKE IT!

FLING

This (thankfully) eventually gave way to the act of removing the garter to toss to the crowd, to appease their creepy bloodlust. Ditto bouquet toss — literally tossing her flower. Gross.

To tie the bride to her family.

To symbolize her new life.

Meant to be from a married friend, to sneak some good fortune from their happy marriage.

SOMETHING OLD,
SOMETHING NEW,
SOMETHING BORROWED,
SOMETHING BLUE.

Blue traditionally sta for faithfulness, loyal and purity, due to its association with the Virgin Mary.

PART 4: SUPERSTITIONS EXPLAINED

NOT SEEING EACH OTHER ON THE WEDDING DAY:

This comes from the time when weddings were arranged, and it was thought that marrying couples would chicken out if they saw each other before it was too late to bolt. Swell.

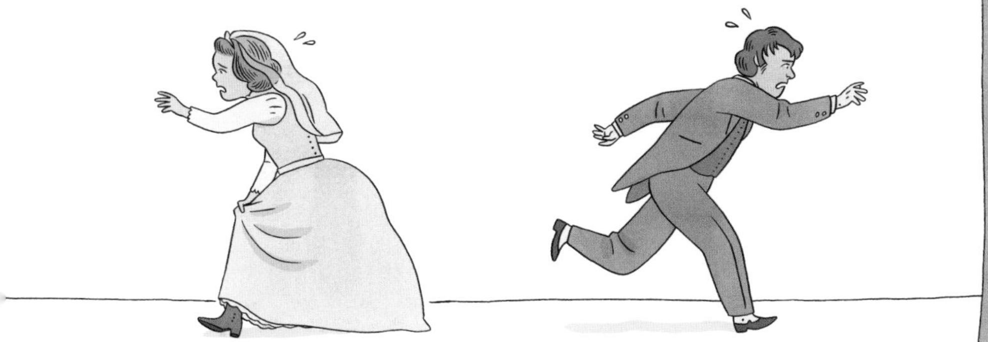

CARRIED OVER THE THRESHOLD:

Evil spirits reside in the ground and will come up and terrorize all brides, unless they are suspended above the demons' reach.

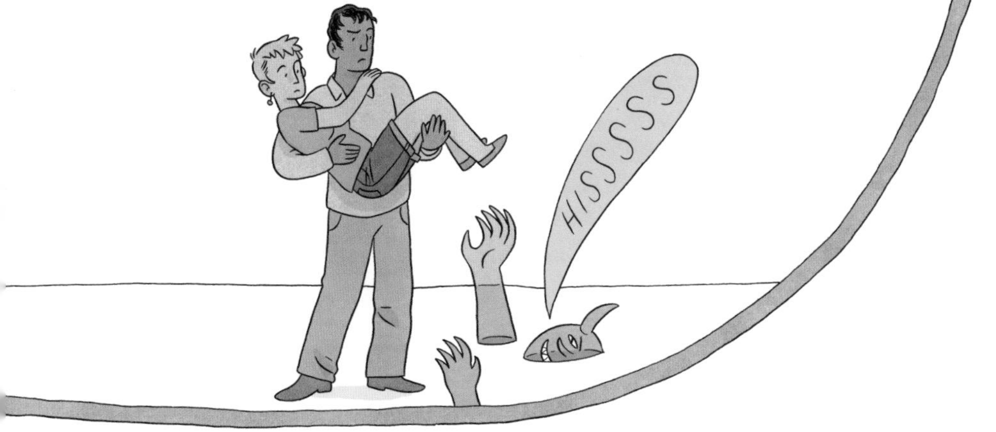
HISSSSS

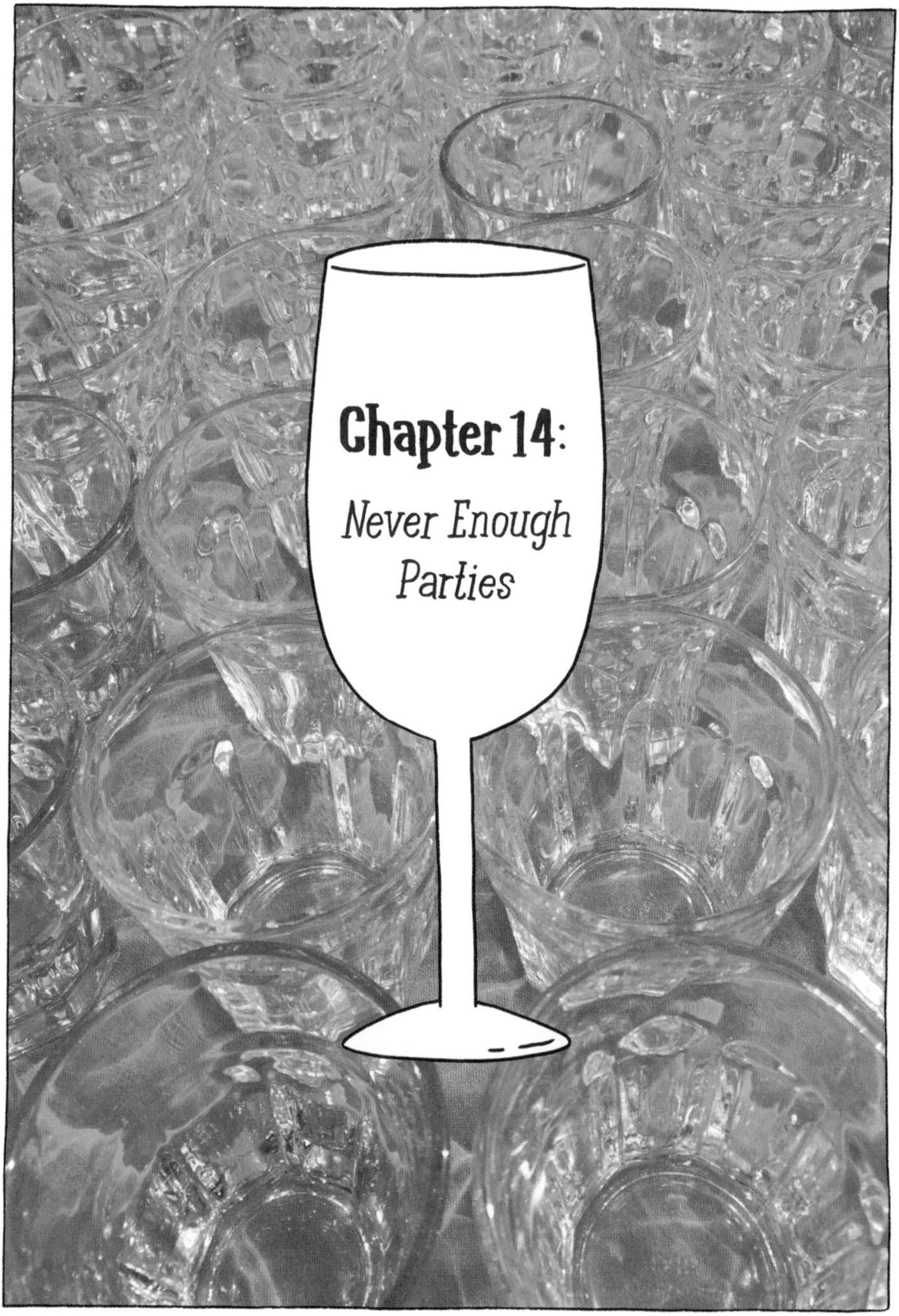
Chapter 14:
Never Enough Parties

I was about to move house for the second time that year, and was up to my ears in work, when my beloved aunt called.

Hullo?

So what's the theme?

I'm sorry?

For your shower! Lingerie, tea party..?

I just want to eat things and hang out.

That's not a theme.

Why not?

My poor aunt. Together with John's great-aunt and his best friend's mom, she was throwing me a wedding shower.

One weird thing about planning a wedding is that in the midst of the craziness, stress, and decision making, a fundamental truth remains:

THIS IS A VERY NICE THING AND WE ARE VERY LUCKY

GUEST LIST

SEATING C

To do

But this fact can sometimes get lost in the turmoil.

It's part of why people get annoyed by wedding talk.

Wedding planning is hard!

YOU'RE the ones who wanted to have some pageant to celebrate your conjoining!

Me, a year ago

I was very grateful to my family, but the thought of the shower was too much change and adulthood for me to handle at the moment.

MOVING

WEDDING

BOOK

TURNING 30

So I just carefully placed it in the "cannot control" area of my brain and went back to packing plates.

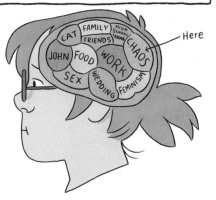

CAT FAMILY HIGH SCHOOL TRAUMA FRIENDS CHAOS JOHN FOOD WORK SEX WEDDING FEMINISM

Here

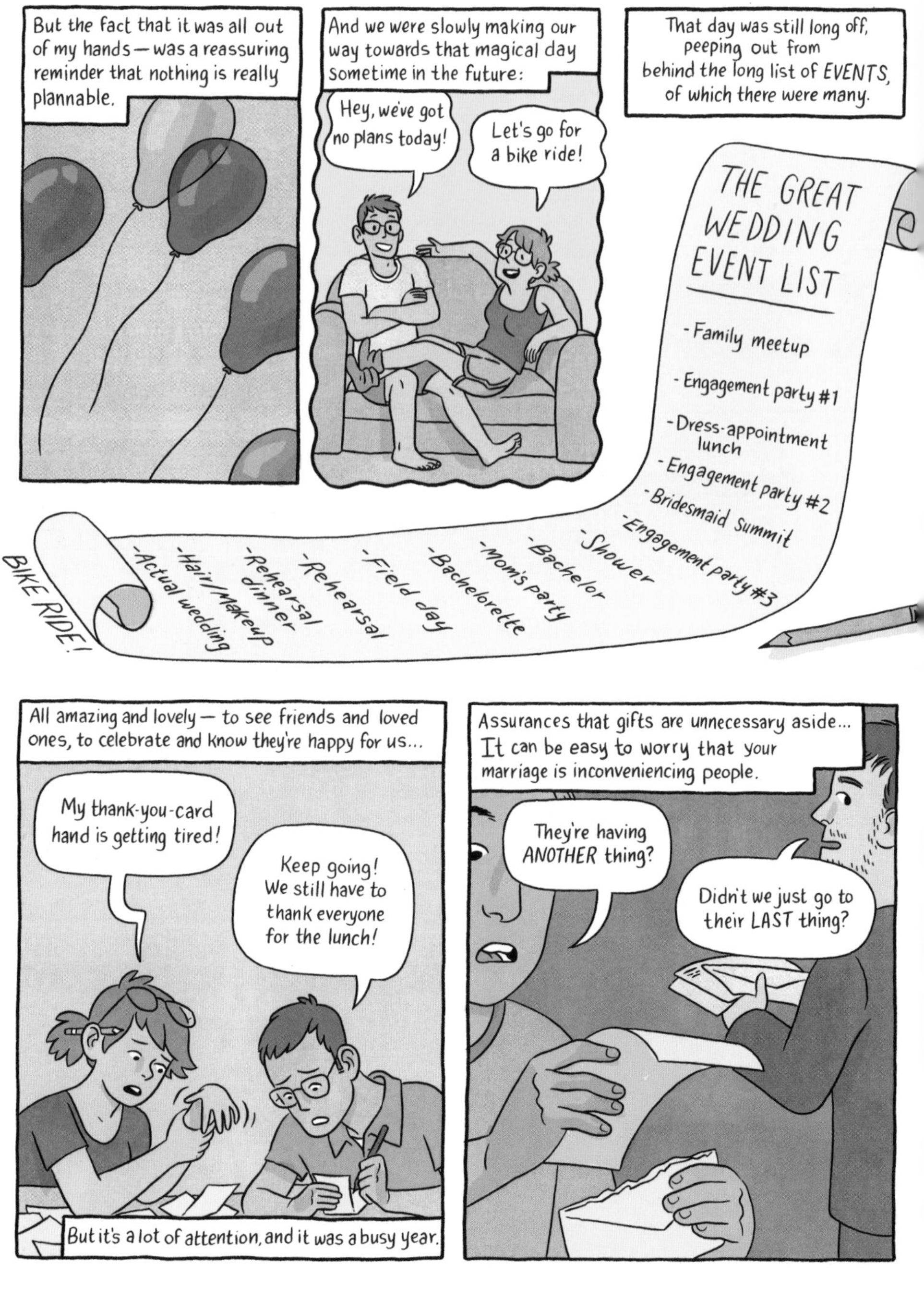

But the fact that it was all out of my hands — was a reassuring reminder that nothing is really plannable.
And we were slowly making our way towards that magical day sometime in the future:
Hey, we've got no plans today!
Let's go for a bike ride!
That day was still long off, peeping out from behind the long list of EVENTS, of which there were many.
THE GREAT WEDDING EVENT LIST
-Family meetup
-Engagement party #1
-Dress-appointment lunch
-Engagement party #2
-Bridesmaid Summit
-Engagement party #3
-Shower
-Bachelor
-Mom's party
-Bachelorette
-Field day
-Rehearsal
-Rehearsal dinner
-Hair/Makeup
-Actual wedding
BIKE RIDE!
All amazing and lovely — to see friends and loved ones, to celebrate and know they're happy for us...
My thank-you-card hand is getting tired!
Keep going! We still have to thank everyone for the lunch!
But it's a lot of attention, and it was a busy year.
Assurances that gifts are unnecessary aside... It can be easy to worry that your marriage is inconveniencing people.
They're having ANOTHER thing?
Didn't we just go to their LAST thing?

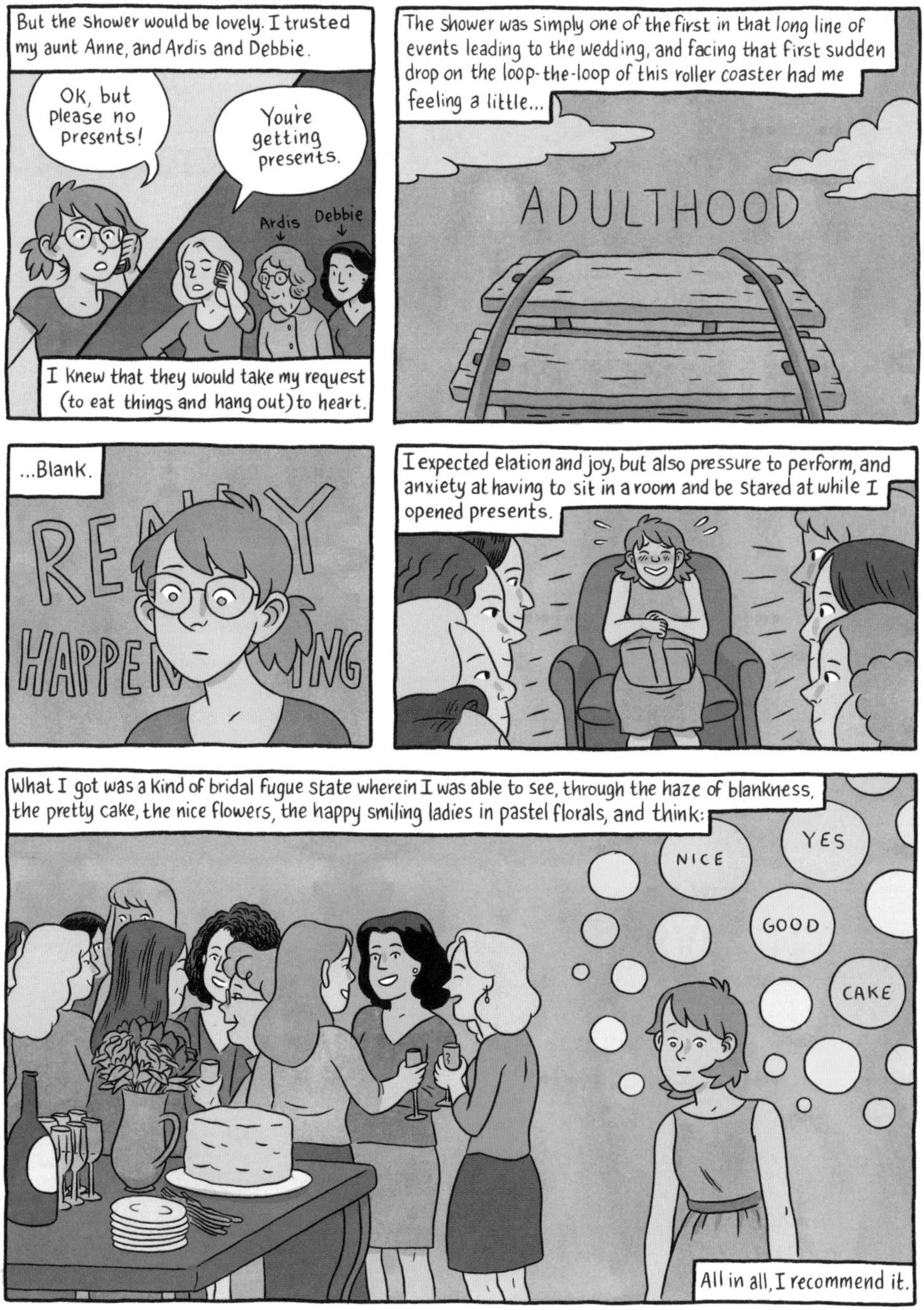
But the shower would be lovely. I trusted my aunt Anne, and Ardis and Debbie.
Ok, but please no presents!
You're getting presents.
Ardis
Debbie
I knew that they would take my request (to eat things and hang out) to heart.
The shower was simply one of the first in that long line of events leading to the wedding, and facing that first sudden drop on the loop-the-loop of this roller coaster had me feeling a little...
ADULTHOOD
...Blank.
I expected elation and joy, but also pressure to perform, and anxiety at having to sit in a room and be stared at while I opened presents.
What I got was a kind of bridal fugue state wherein I was able to see, through the haze of blankness, the pretty cake, the nice flowers, the happy smiling ladies in pastel florals, and think:
YES
NICE
GOOD
CAKE
All in all, I recommend it.

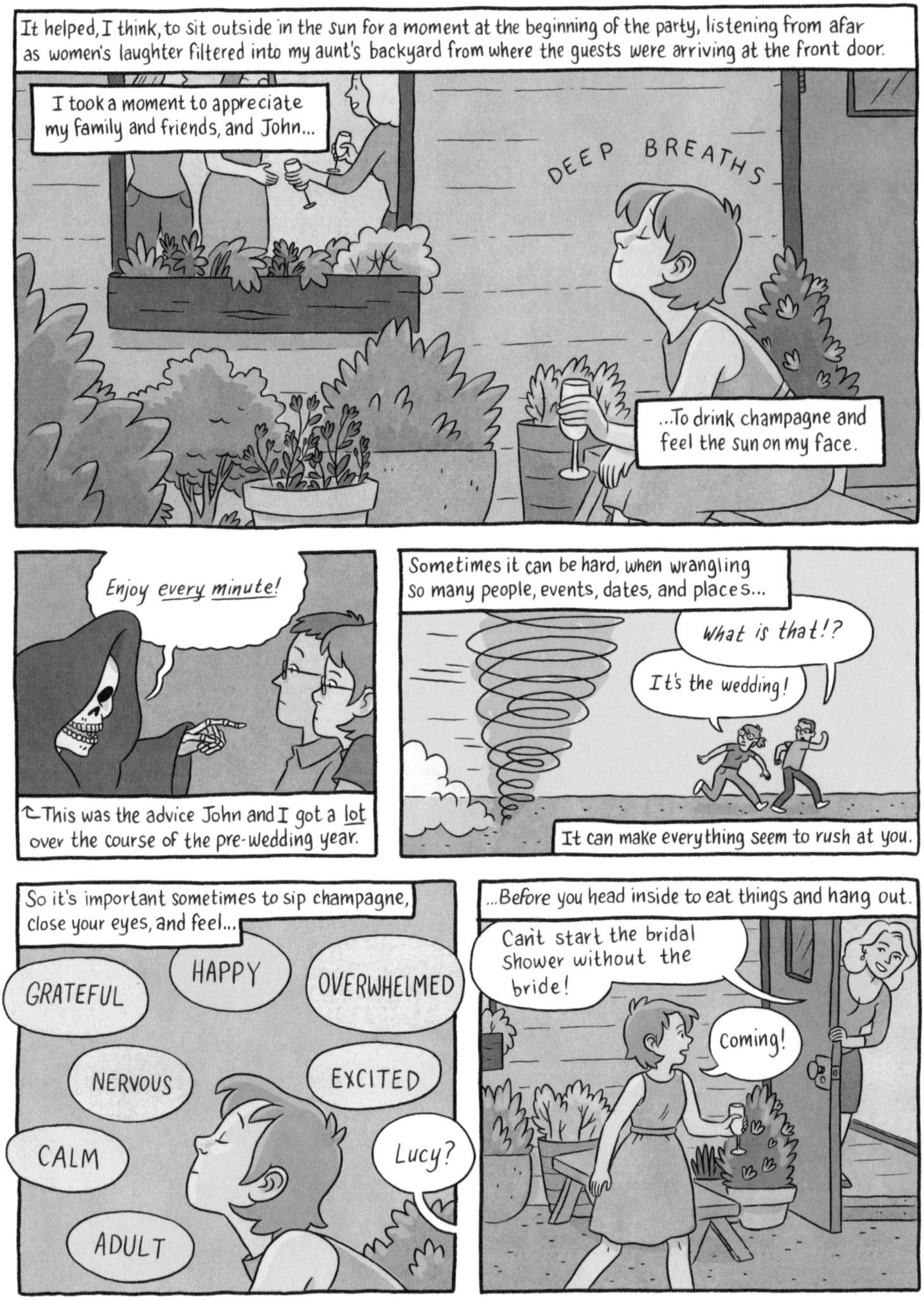
It helped, I think, to sit outside in the sun for a moment at the beginning of the party, listening from afar as women's laughter filtered into my aunt's backyard from where the guests were arriving at the front door.
I took a moment to appreciate my family and friends, and John...
DEEP BREATHS
...To drink champagne and feel the sun on my face.
Enjoy every minute!
↰This was the advice John and I got a lot over the course of the pre-wedding year.
Sometimes it can be hard, when wrangling so many people, events, dates, and places...
What is that!?
It's the wedding!
It can make everything seem to rush at you.
So it's important sometimes to sip champagne, close your eyes, and feel...
GRATEFUL
HAPPY
OVERWHELMED
NERVOUS
EXCITED
CALM
Lucy?
ADULT
...Before you head inside to eat things and hang out.
Can't start the bridal shower without the bride!
Coming!

My pink bridal-shower cake.

For months before the wedding, people would ask about the wedding's theme.
We didn't have one, though I'd argue that every wedding is "puffy, sparkly fluffkin" themed... Anyway...

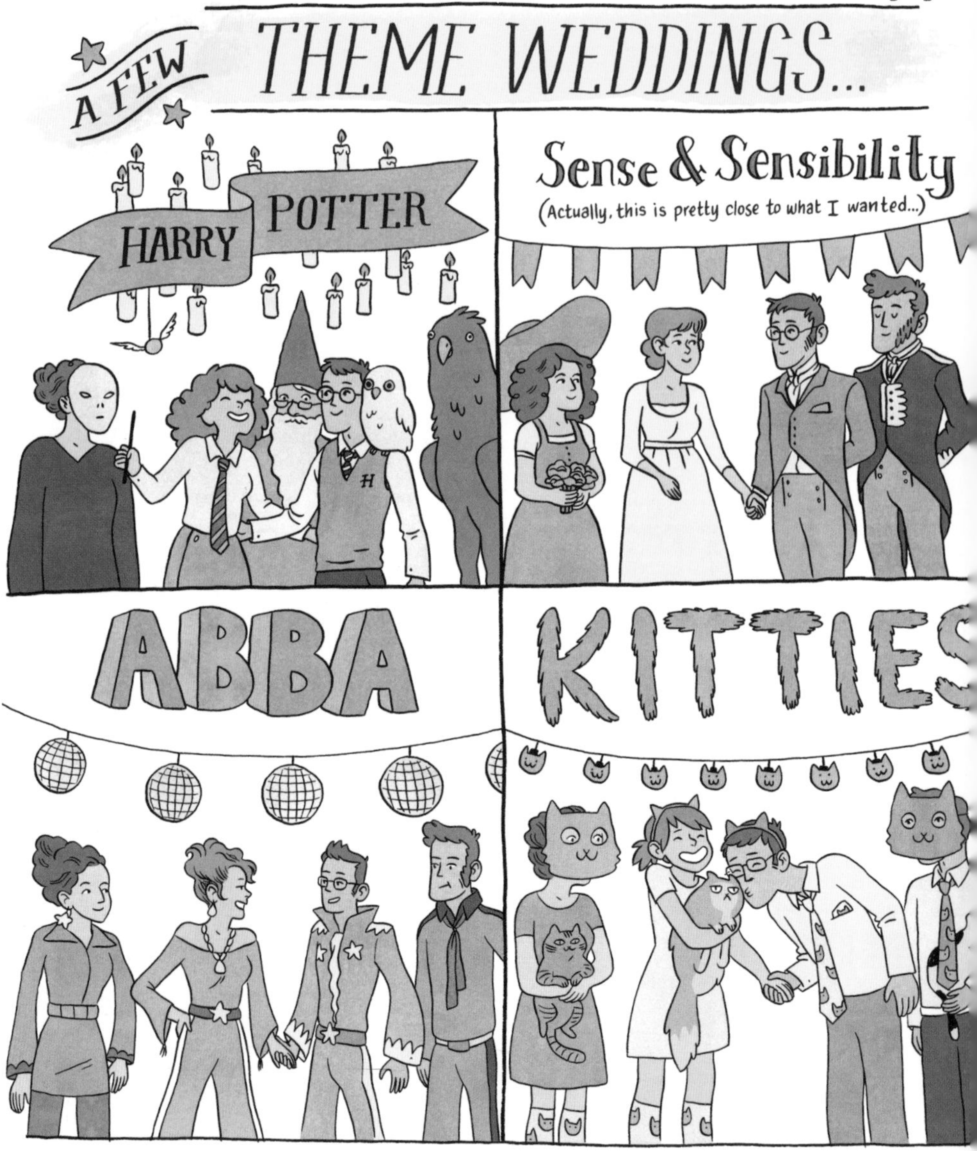
A FEW THEME WEDDINGS...
HARRY POTTER
Sense & Sensibility
(Actually, this is pretty close to what I wanted...)
ABBA
KITTIES

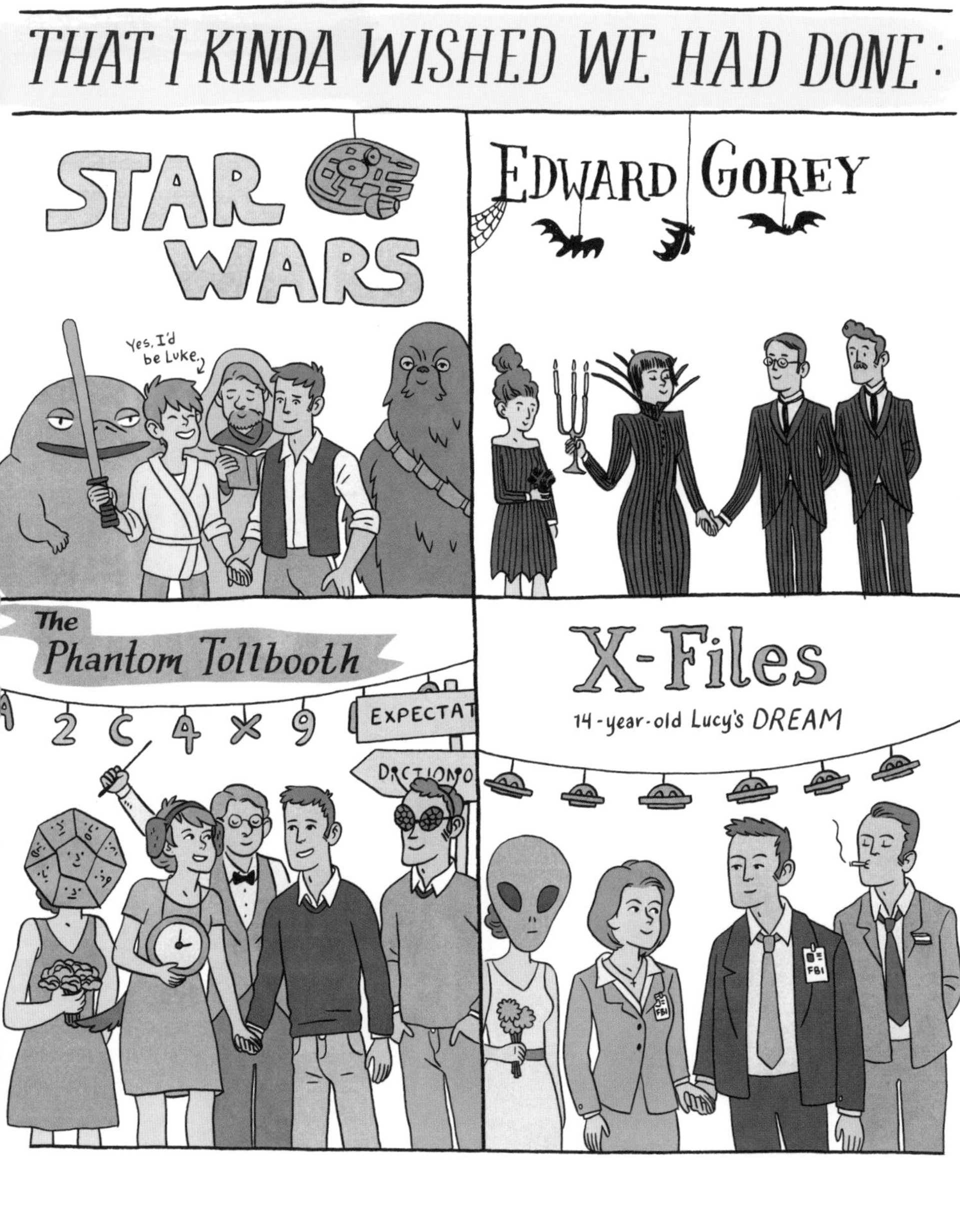
THAT I KINDA WISHED WE HAD DONE:
STAR WARS
Yes, I'd be Luke.
EDWARD GOREY
The Phantom Tollbooth
2 C 4 X 9
EXPECTAT
DICTIONO
X-Files
14-year-old Lucy's DREAM
FBI
FBI

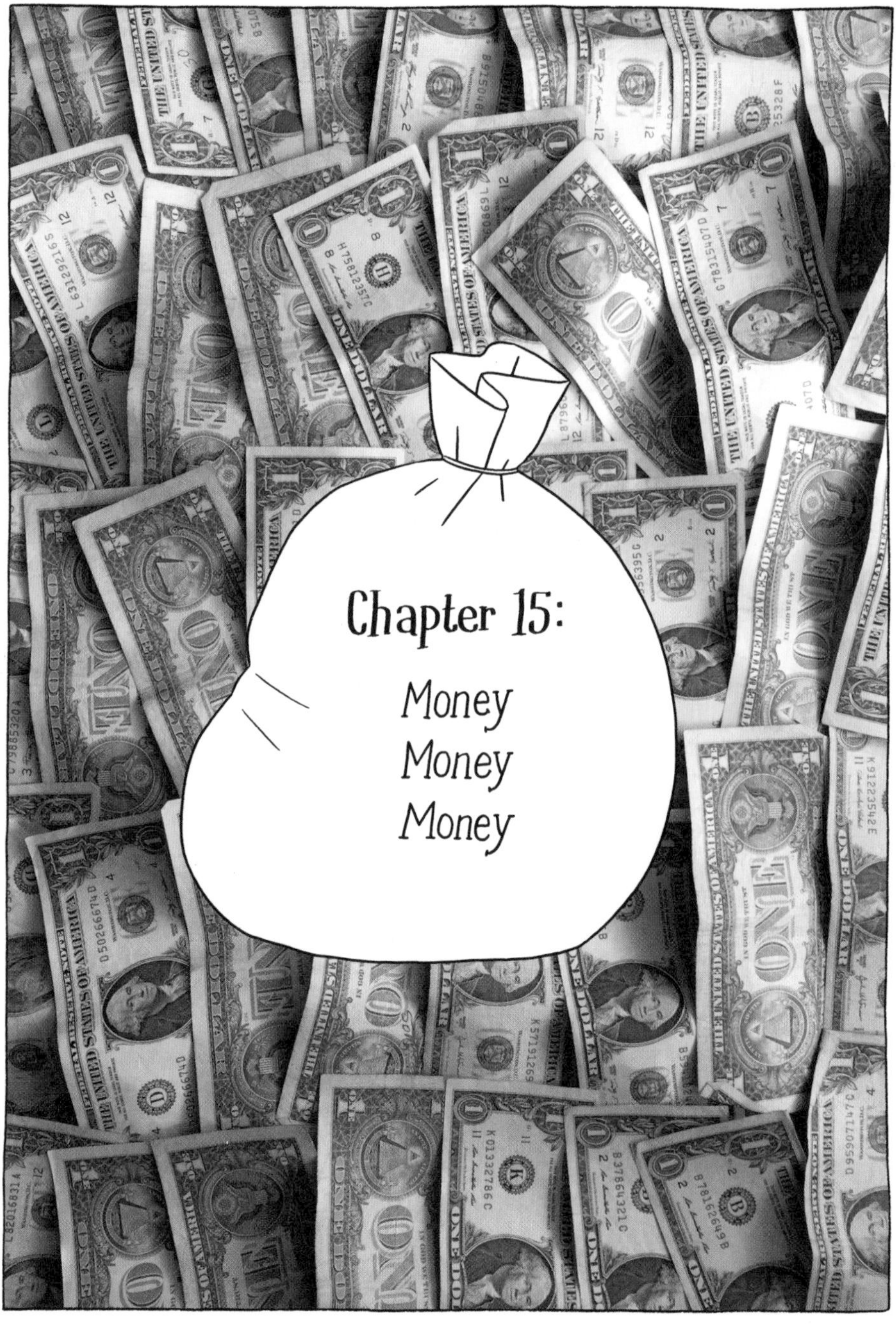
Chapter 15:
Money
Money
Money

In 2013, the average US wedding cost almost $30,000.

Which, the Wall Street Journal notes, is "well over half the median annual income in US households."

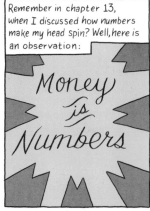

Remember in chapter 13, when I discussed how numbers make my head spin? Well, here is an observation:

Money is Numbers

So when I read that the average wedding cost almost $30,000, I had to sit down and conjure up some...

Visual Aids

That price is a year of fancy college...

...It's dining at the most expensive restaurant in Chicago 150 times...

...It's two years' rent...

...It's ten thousand of the pens I use, and almost 4,000 pads of the paper I like.

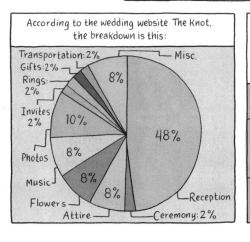

According to the wedding website The Knot, the breakdown is this:

Transportation: 2%
Gifts: 2%
Rings: 2%
Invites 2%
Misc.
8%
10%
Photos 8%
Music 8%
Flowers
Attire
8%
48%
Reception
Ceremony: 2%

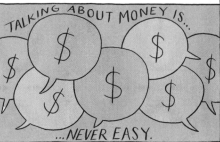

John and I, when deciding on a budget, talked things over with our parents. They offered their contributions, we tallied our own funds, and then we made a list of what was important, and estimated the costs with a little research.

TALKING ABOUT MONEY IS...

...NEVER EASY.

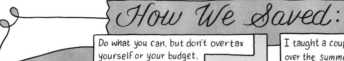

How We Saved:

Make Everything!*

*See chapter 13

Do what you can, but don't overtax yourself or your budget.

RMRMRMRMRMRMRN

I found ways to score free supplies, like a craft shop's scrap bin, to get material for making pennants and ties.

I taught a couple extra camp sessions over the summer to have access to studios with sewing and art supplies.

Art centers like where I teach can allow access to facilities for low fees.

Keep it Simple

The attire wound up costing little, due to our simple tastes and practical choices.

ON SALE OFF THE RACK

MADE BY ME

BRIDESMAID DRESSES MADE BY NORA

ON SALE

We didn't need a fountain or a flower canopy, so we wound up going light on the decor.

RENTED

MADE

FRIEND DID

HAD

MOM MADE

MADE

We skipped the DJ or live music and made a personal playlist ourselves, so we only had to rent a sound system.

Average DJ cost: $1,000

$200

We also didn't care about the big fancy cake, so our little lemon square and beignet dessert was way under the usual wedding sweets price tag.

$200

$130

Average cake cost: $550

I have a friend who had yummy sandwiches at her wedding, and saved a bundle on food.

Average cost of wedding catering: $66 per person

Also: CUPCAKES!

$200

$150

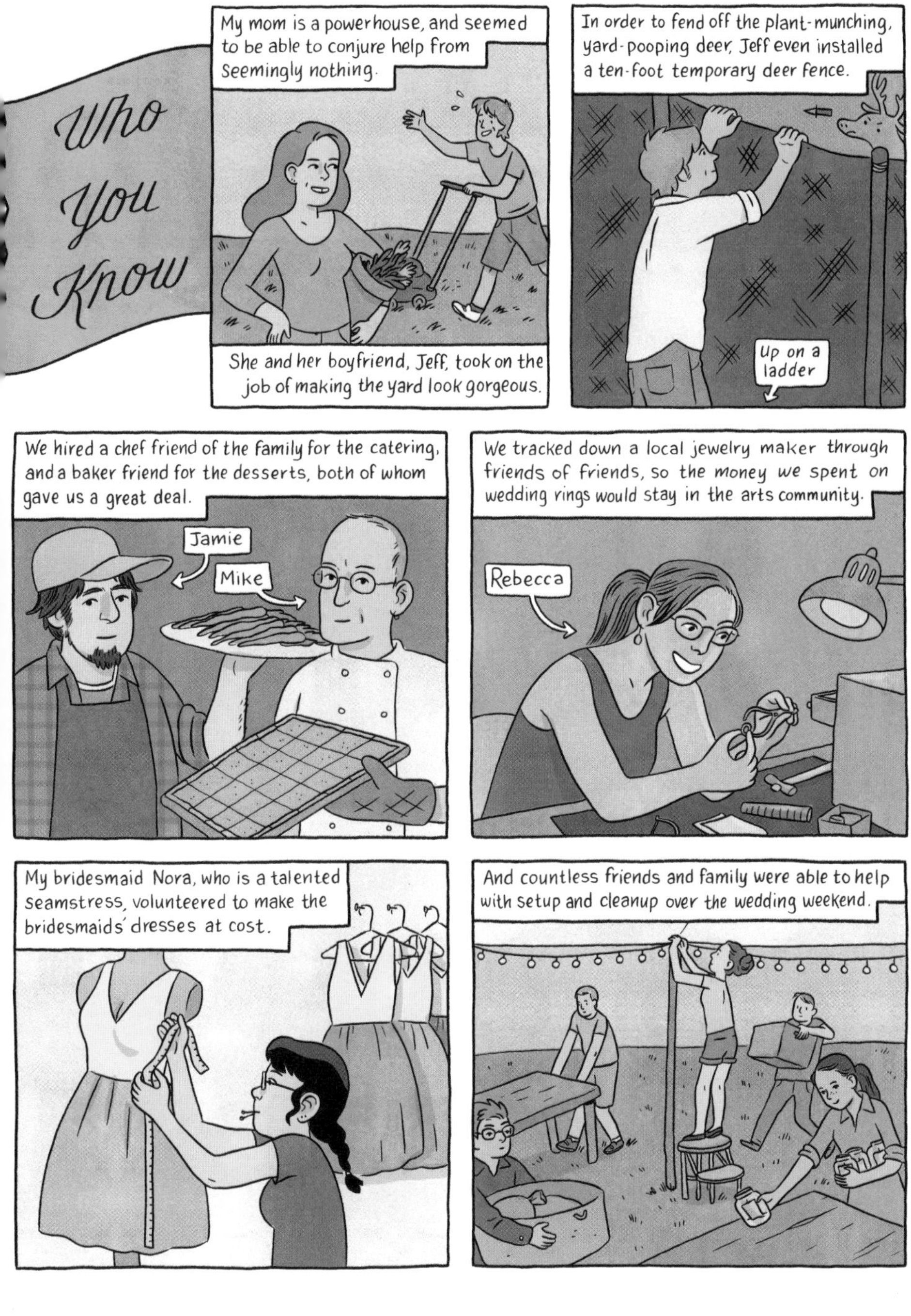
Who You Know
My mom is a powerhouse, and seemed to be able to conjure help from seemingly nothing.
She and her boyfriend, Jeff, took on the job of making the yard look gorgeous.
In order to fend off the plant-munching, yard-pooping deer, Jeff even installed a ten-foot temporary deer fence.
Up on a ladder
We hired a chef friend of the family for the catering, and a baker friend for the desserts, both of whom gave us a great deal.
Jamie
Mike
We tracked down a local jewelry maker through friends of friends, so the money we spent on wedding rings would stay in the arts community.
Rebecca
My bridesmaid Nora, who is a talented seamstress, volunteered to make the bridesmaids' dresses at cost.
And countless friends and family were able to help with setup and cleanup over the wedding weekend.

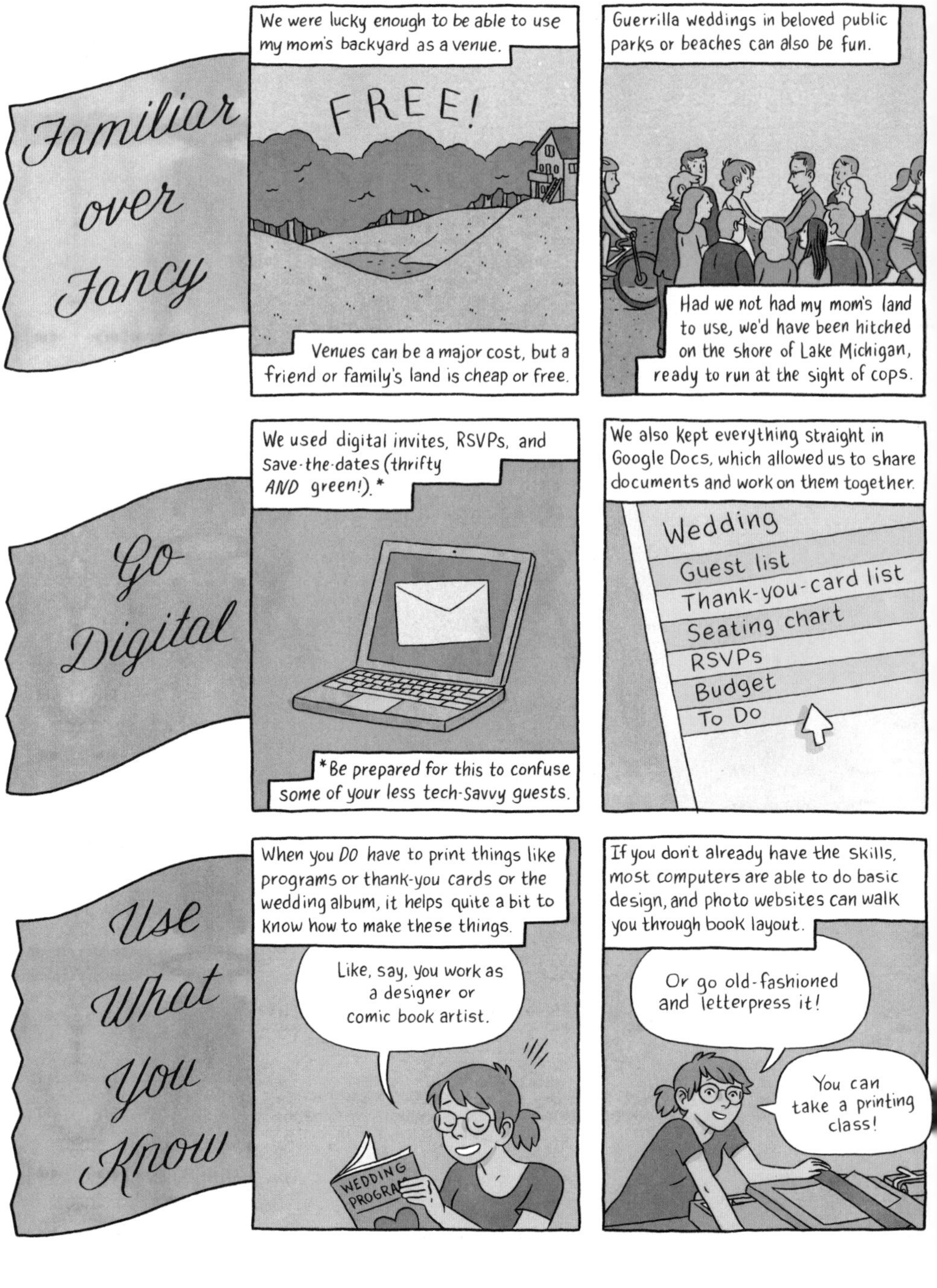
Familiar over Fancy
We were lucky enough to be able to use my mom's backyard as a venue.
FREE!
Venues can be a major cost, but a friend or family's land is cheap or free.
Guerrilla weddings in beloved public parks or beaches can also be fun.
Had we not had my mom's land to use, we'd have been hitched on the shore of Lake Michigan, ready to run at the sight of cops.
Go Digital
We used digital invites, RSVPs, and save-the-dates (thrifty AND green!).*
*Be prepared for this to confuse some of your less tech-savvy guests.
We also kept everything straight in Google Docs, which allowed us to share documents and work on them together.
Wedding
Guest list
Thank-you-card list
Seating chart
RSVPs
Budget
To Do
Use What You Know
When you DO have to print things like programs or thank-you cards or the wedding album, it helps quite a bit to know how to make these things.
Like, say, you work as a designer or comic book artist.
WEDDING PROGRA
If you don't already have the skills, most computers are able to do basic design, and photo websites can walk you through book layout.
Or go old-fashioned and letterpress it!
You can take a printing class!

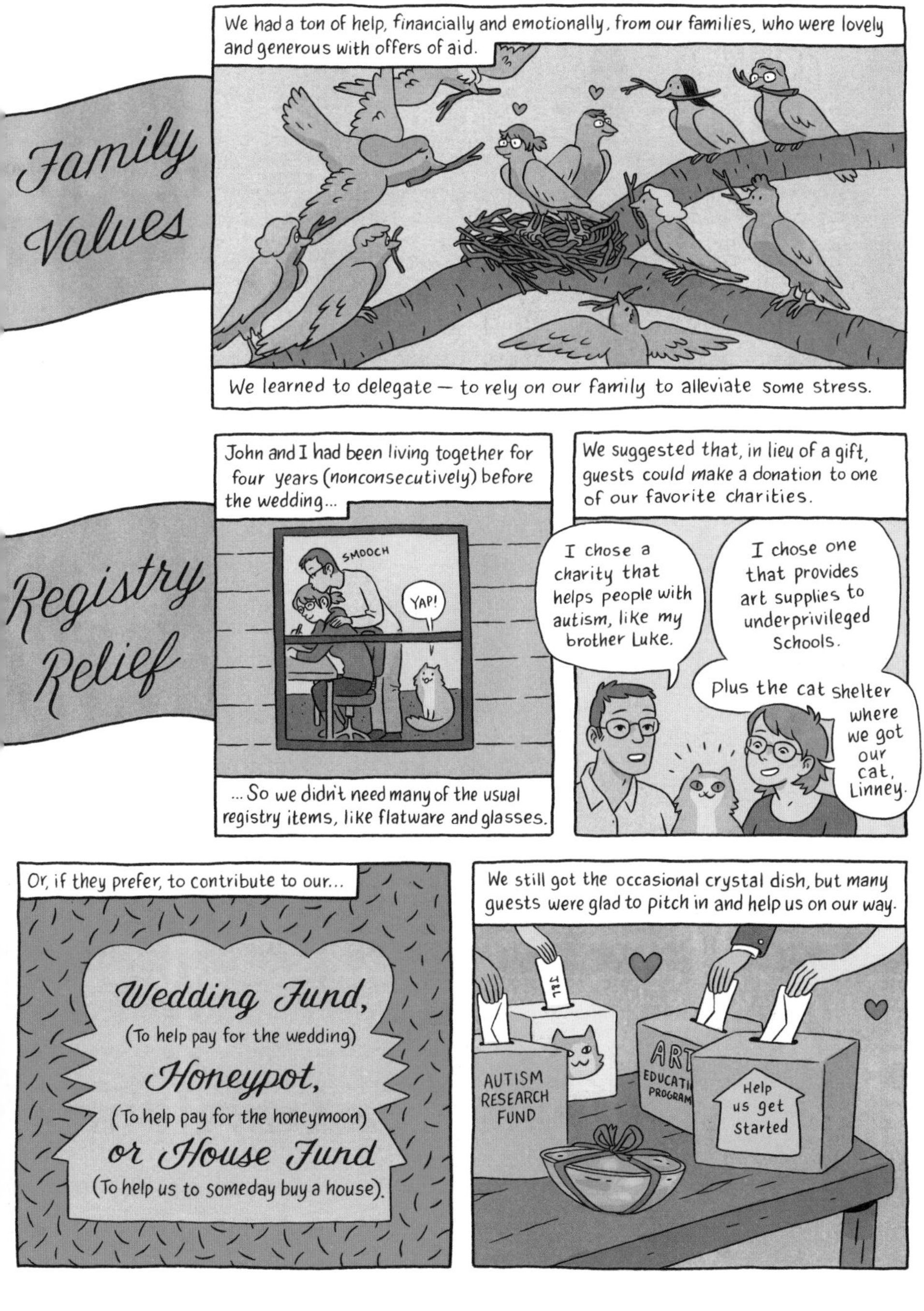

Family Values
We had a ton of help, financially and emotionally, from our families, who were lovely and generous with offers of aid.
We learned to delegate — to rely on our family to alleviate some stress.
Registry Relief
John and I had been living together for four years (nonconsecutively) before the wedding...
SMOOCH
YAP!
...So we didn't need many of the usual registry items, like flatware and glasses.
We suggested that, in lieu of a gift, guests could make a donation to one of our favorite charities.
I chose a charity that helps people with autism, like my brother Luke.
I chose one that provides art supplies to underprivileged schools.
Plus the cat shelter where we got our cat, Linney.
Or, if they prefer, to contribute to our...
Wedding Fund,
(To help pay for the wedding)
Honeypot,
(To help pay for the honeymoon)
or House Fund
(To help us to someday buy a house).
We still got the occasional crystal dish, but many guests were glad to pitch in and help us on our way.
J&L
AUTISM RESEARCH FUND
ART EDUCATI PROGRAM
Help us get started

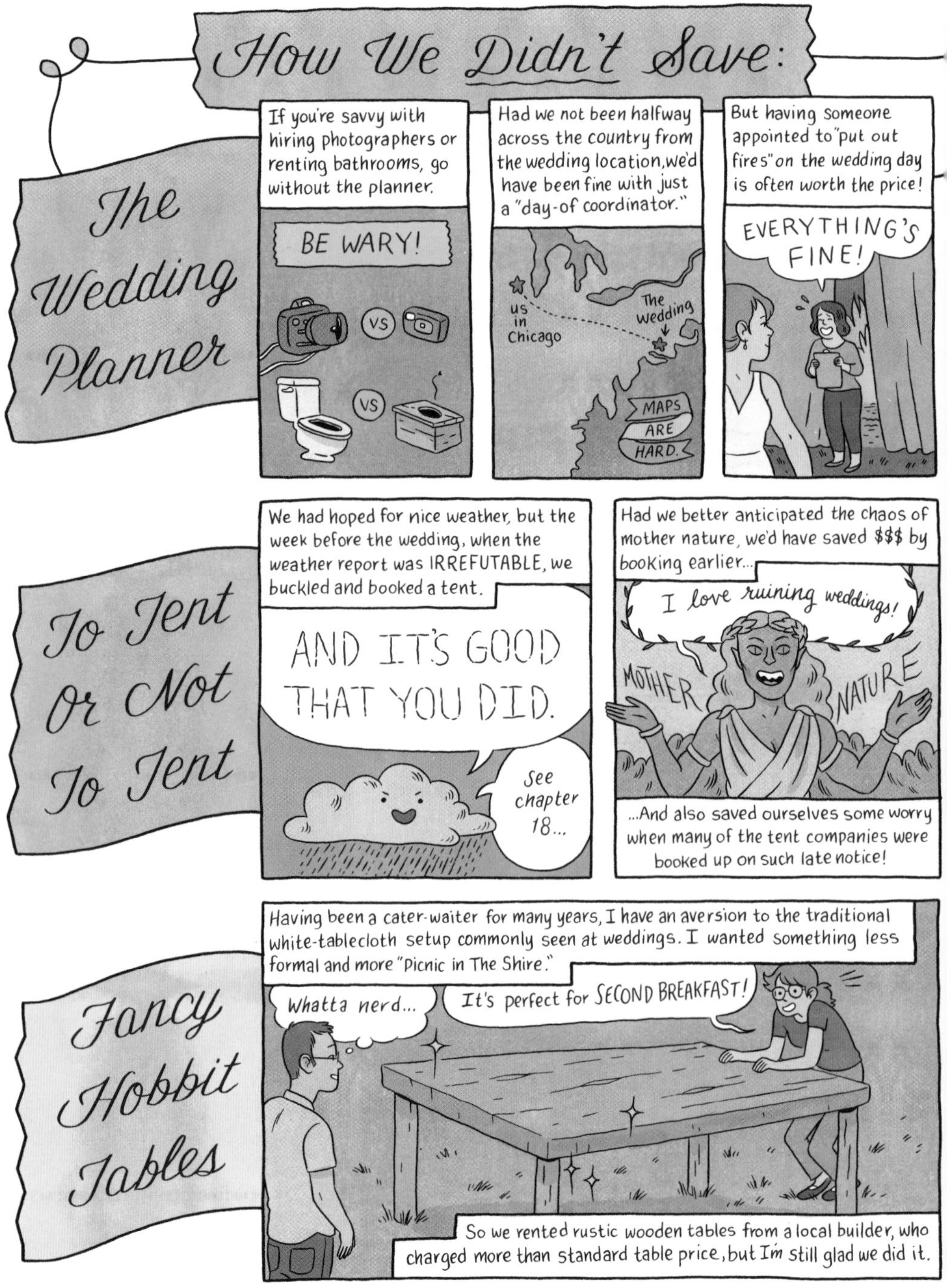
How We Didn't Save:
The Wedding Planner
If you're savvy with hiring photographers or renting bathrooms, go without the planner.
BE WARY!
VS
VS
Had we not been halfway across the country from the wedding location, we'd have been fine with just a "day-of coordinator."
us in Chicago
The wedding
MAPS ARE HARD.
But having someone appointed to "put out fires" on the wedding day is often worth the price!
EVERYTHING'S FINE!
To Tent Or Not To Tent
We had hoped for nice weather, but the week before the wedding, when the weather report was IRREFUTABLE, we buckled and booked a tent.
AND IT'S GOOD THAT YOU DID.
See chapter 18...
Had we better anticipated the chaos of mother nature, we'd have saved $$$ by booking earlier...
I love ruining weddings!
MOTHER NATURE
...And also saved ourselves some worry when many of the tent companies were booked up on such late notice!
Fancy Hobbit Tables
Having been a cater-waiter for many years, I have an aversion to the traditional white-tablecloth setup commonly seen at weddings. I wanted something less formal and more "Picnic in The Shire."
Whatta nerd...
It's perfect for SECOND BREAKFAST!
So we rented rustic wooden tables from a local builder, who charged more than standard table price, but I'm still glad we did it.

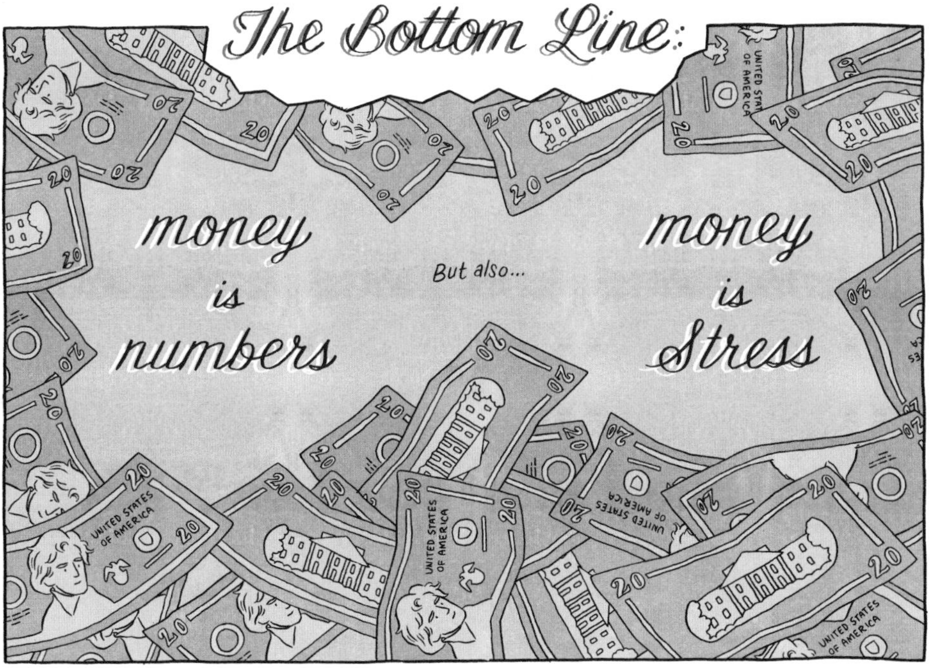
The Bottom Line:
money is numbers
But also...
money is Stress

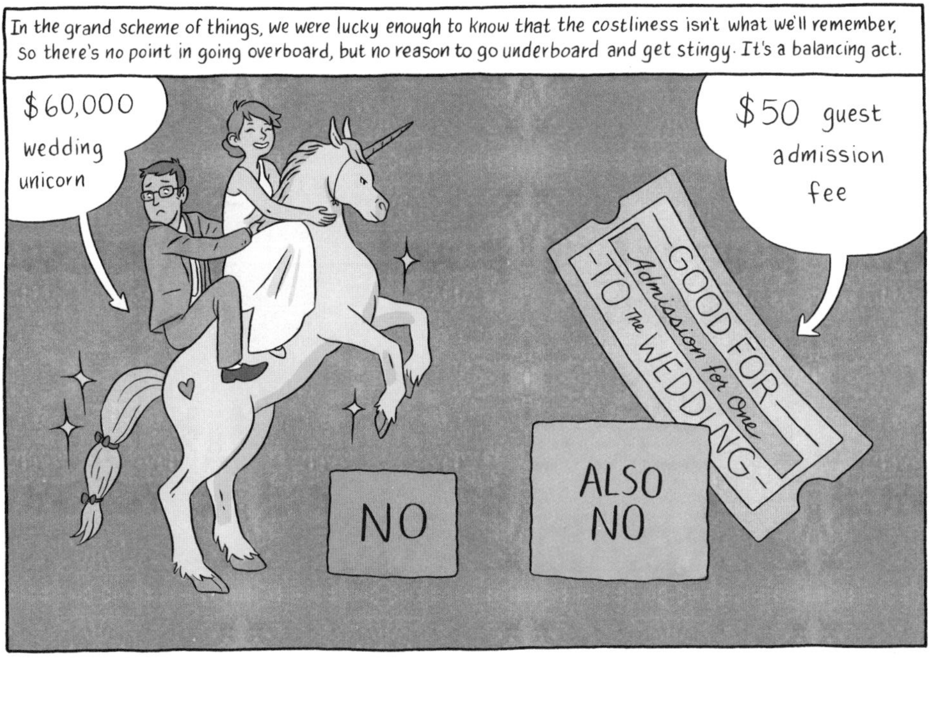
In the grand scheme of things, we were lucky enough to know that the costliness isn't what we'll remember, so there's no point in going overboard, but no reason to go underboard and get stingy. It's a balancing act.
$60,000 wedding unicorn
$50 guest admission fee
GOOD FOR
Admission for One
TO the WEDDING
NO
ALSO NO

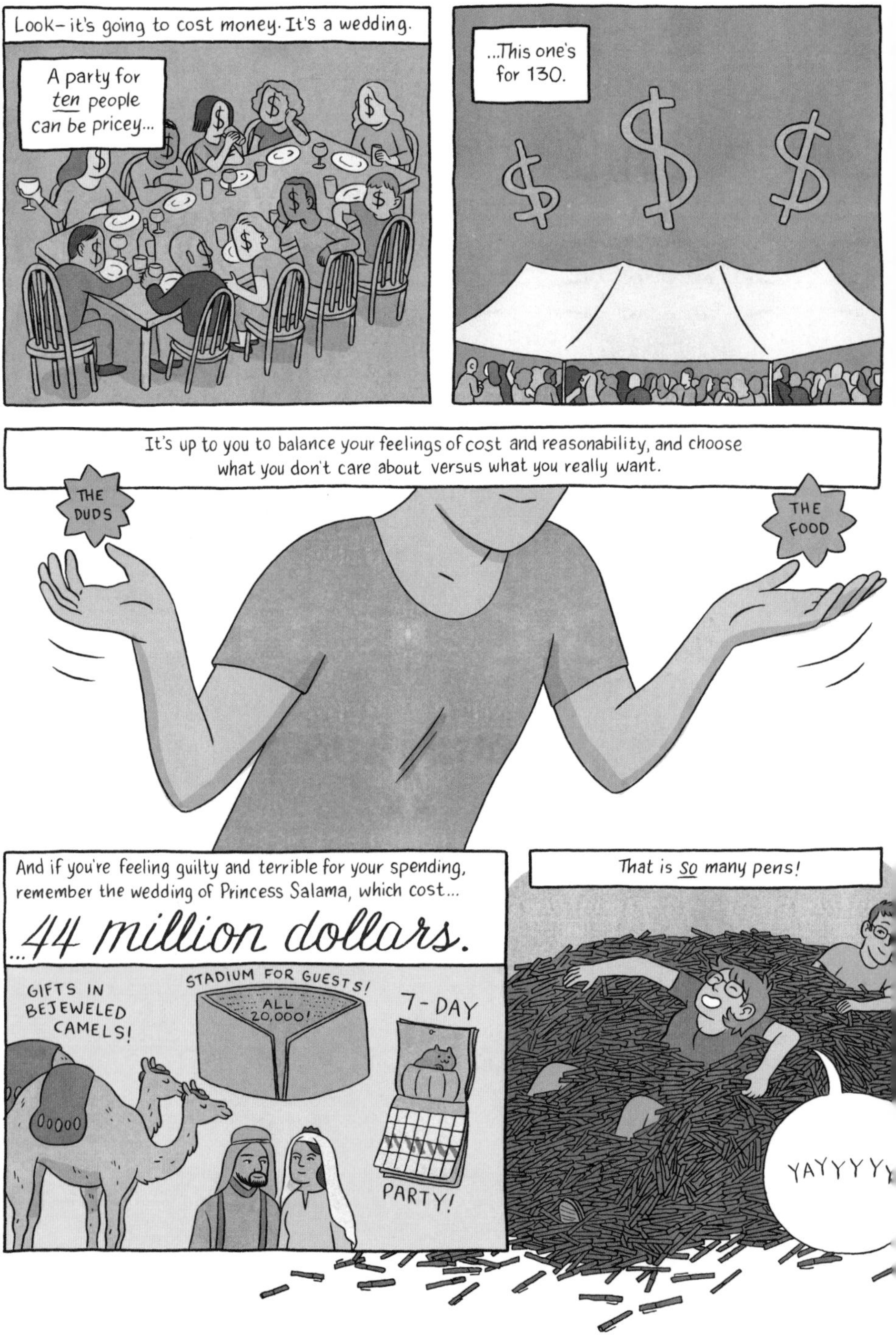
Look– it's going to cost money. It's a wedding.
A party for ten people can be pricey...
...This one's for 130.
It's up to you to balance your feelings of cost and reasonability, and choose what you don't care about versus what you really want.
THE DUDS
THE FOOD
And if you're feeling guilty and terrible for your spending, remember the wedding of Princess Salama, which cost...
...44 million dollars.
GIFTS IN BEJEWELED CAMELS!
STADIUM FOR GUESTS!
ALL 20,000!
7-DAY
PARTY!
That is so many pens!
YAYYYY

Buying the wedding booze with Mom.

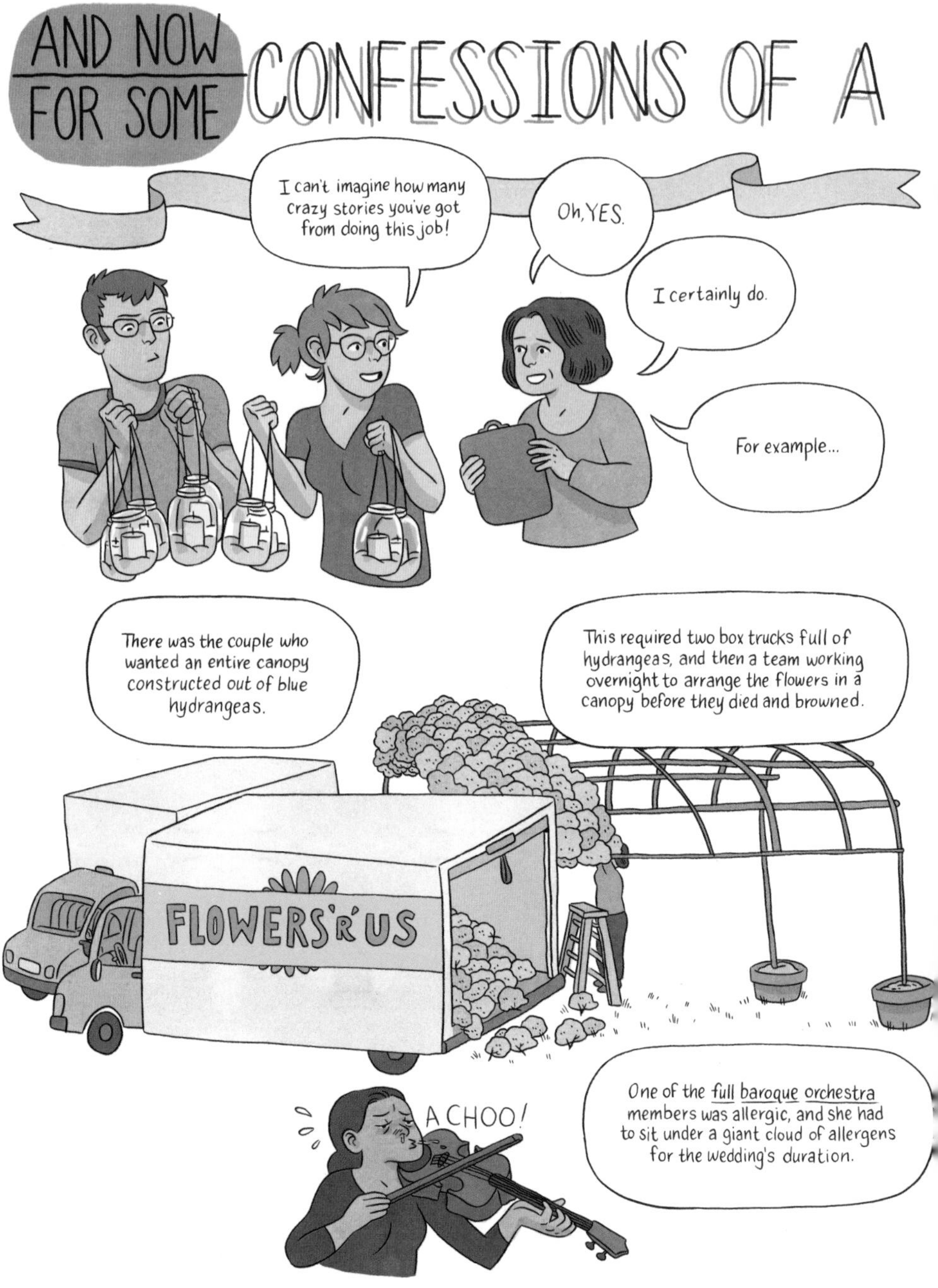
AND NOW FOR SOME
CONFESSIONS OF A
I can't imagine how many crazy stories you've got from doing this job!
Oh, YES.
I certainly do.
For example...
There was the couple who wanted an entire canopy constructed out of blue hydrangeas.
This required two box trucks full of hydrangeas, and then a team working overnight to arrange the flowers in a canopy before they died and browned.
FLOWERS'R'US
One of the full baroque orchestra members was allergic, and she had to sit under a giant cloud of allergens for the wedding's duration.
A CHOO!

WEDDING PLANNER—OH DO TELL!

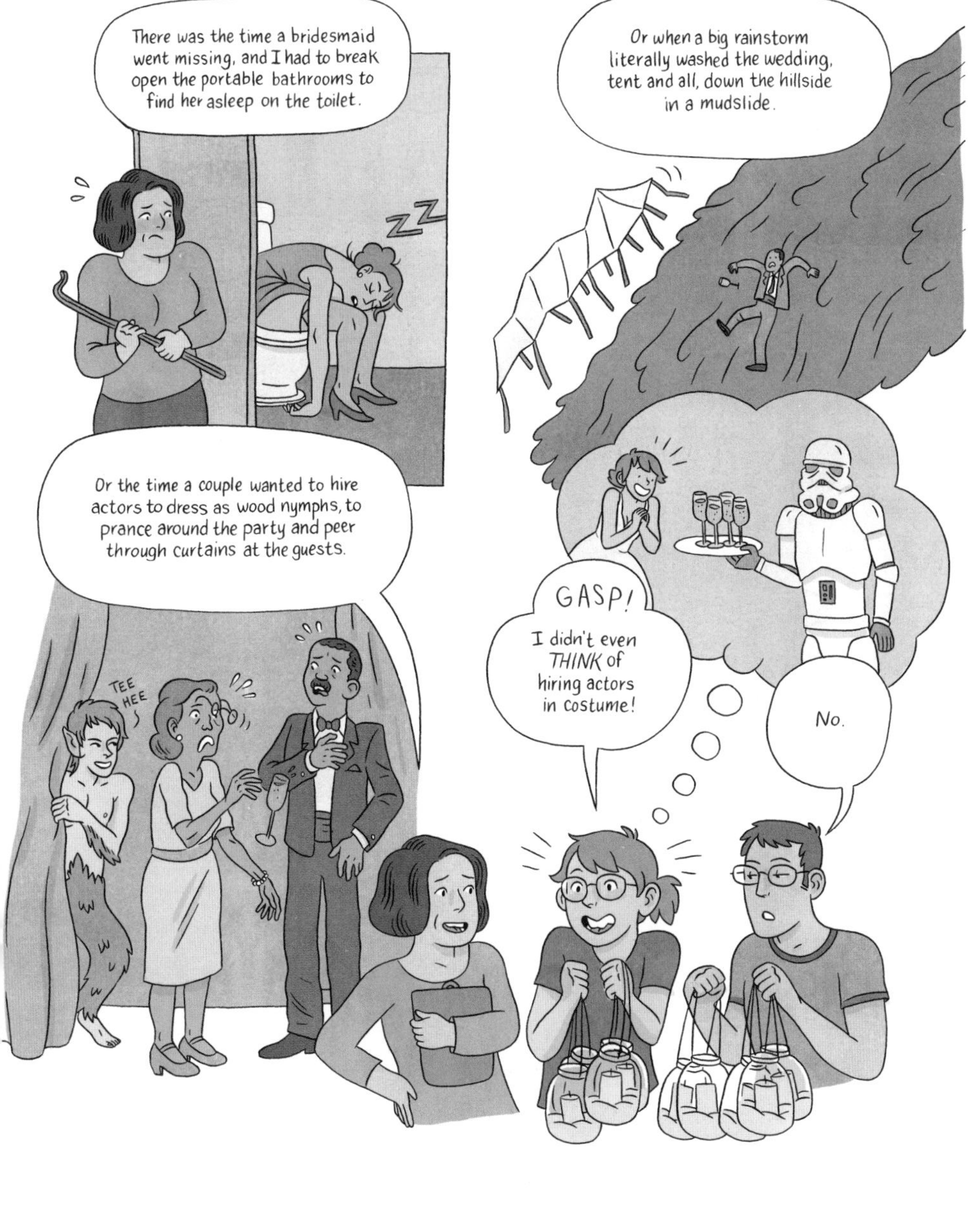
There was the time a bridesmaid went missing, and I had to break open the portable bathrooms to find her asleep on the toilet.
ZZZ
Or when a big rainstorm literally washed the wedding, tent and all, down the hillside in a mudslide.
Or the time a couple wanted to hire actors to dress as wood nymphs, to prance around the party and peer through curtains at the guests.
TEE HEE
GASP!
I didn't even *THINK* of hiring actors in costume!
No.

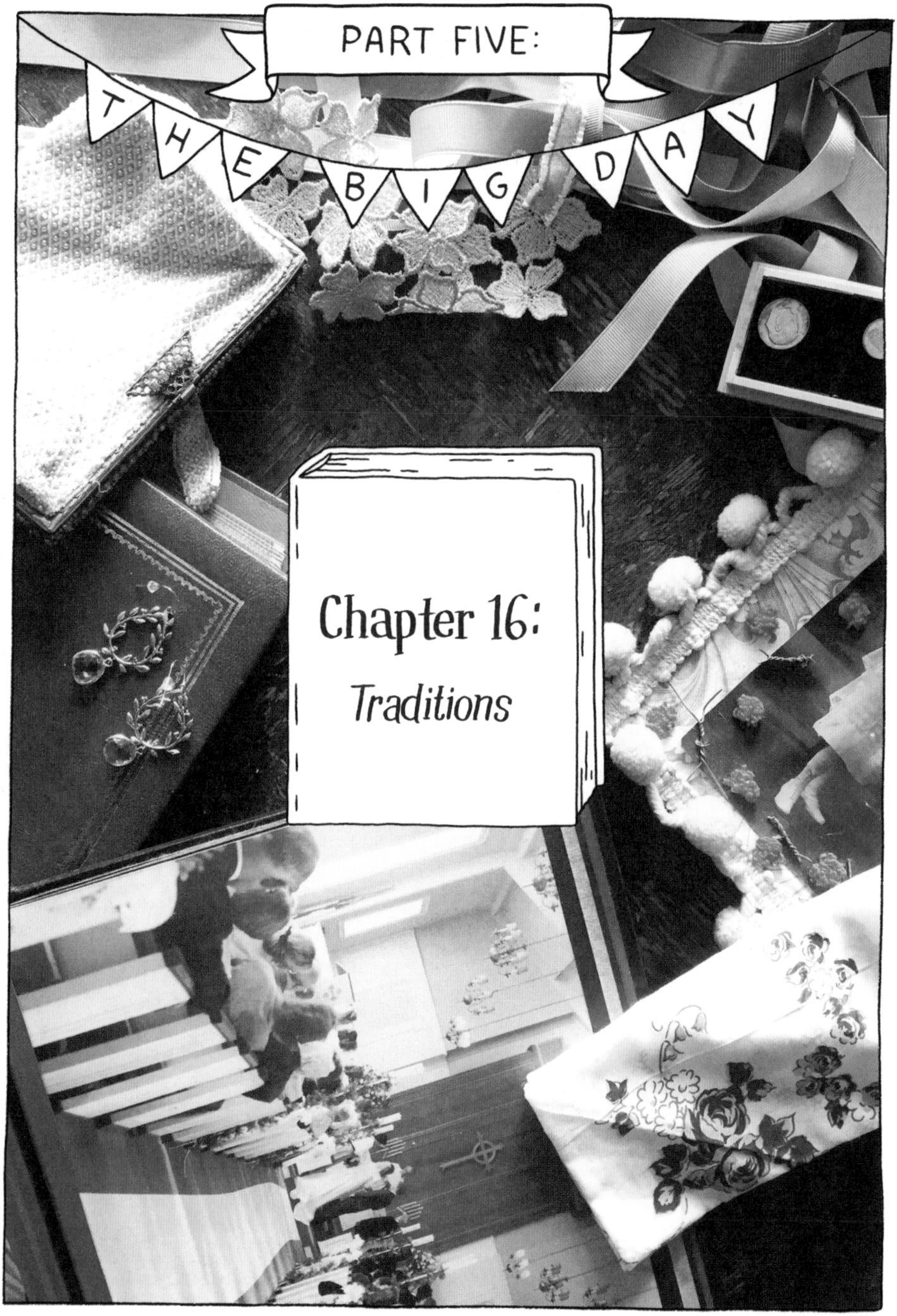
PART FIVE:
THE BIG DAY
Chapter 16:
Traditions

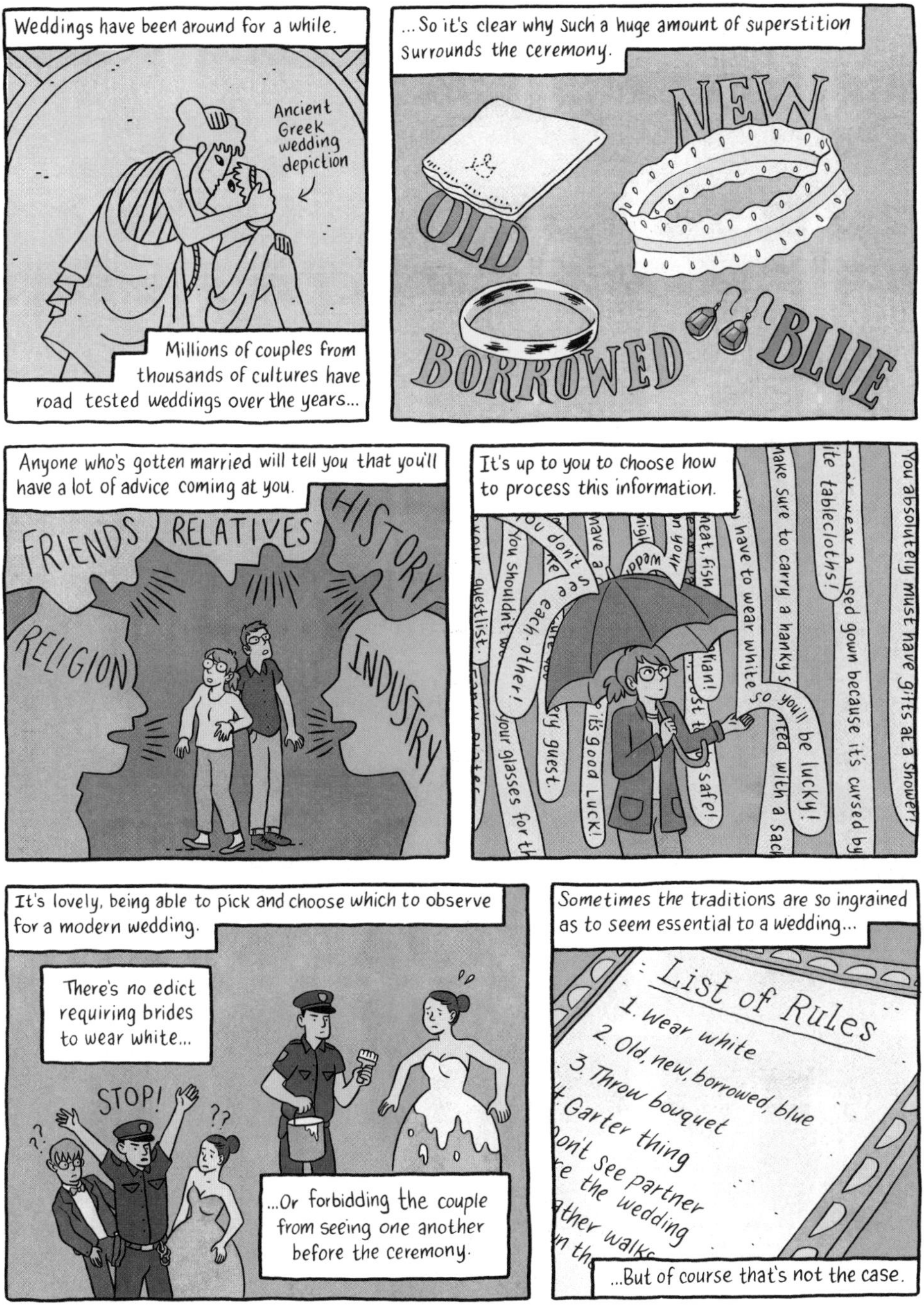
Weddings have been around for a while.
Ancient Greek wedding depiction
Millions of couples from thousands of cultures have road tested weddings over the years...
...So it's clear why such a huge amount of superstition surrounds the ceremony.
OLD
NEW
BORROWED
BLUE
Anyone who's gotten married will tell you that you'll have a lot of advice coming at you.
FRIENDS
RELATIVES
HISTORY
RELIGION
INDUSTRY
It's up to you to choose how to process this information.
You absolutely must have gifts at a shower!
it's good Luck!
safe!
It's lovely, being able to pick and choose which to observe for a modern wedding.
There's no edict requiring brides to wear white...
STOP!
??
??
...Or forbidding the couple from seeing one another before the ceremony.
Sometimes the traditions are so ingrained as to seem essential to a wedding...
List of Rules
1. Wear white
2. Old, new, borrowed, blue
3. Throw bouquet
4. Garter thing
...But of course that's not the case.

John and I aren't superstitious, but we do have an appreciation for sentiment and history.

(After all, we did get married.)

So how do two rational atheists who don't believe in "bad luck" design their wedding ceremony?

We were open to suggestions.

HISTORY A460-B30

How else do traditions begin?

We looked to cultural history. John and I both come from a mix of Nordic, British, and Germanic roots.

Swedish weddings are especially nice, with very simple traditions. Ceremonies tend to be very egalitarian between the genders, and fairly secular.

A Swedish bride wears coins in her shoes — one gold and one silver, given by the parents to show their support and love.

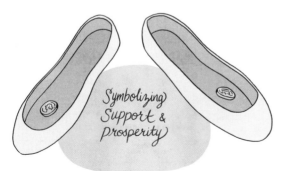

Symbolizing Support & Prosperity

The "coins in the shoes" tradition is actually present in other cultures. The rhyme most people are familiar with has an addendum in historical English tradition.

*Something old,
something new,
something borrowed,
something blue,
and a sixpence
for my shoe.*

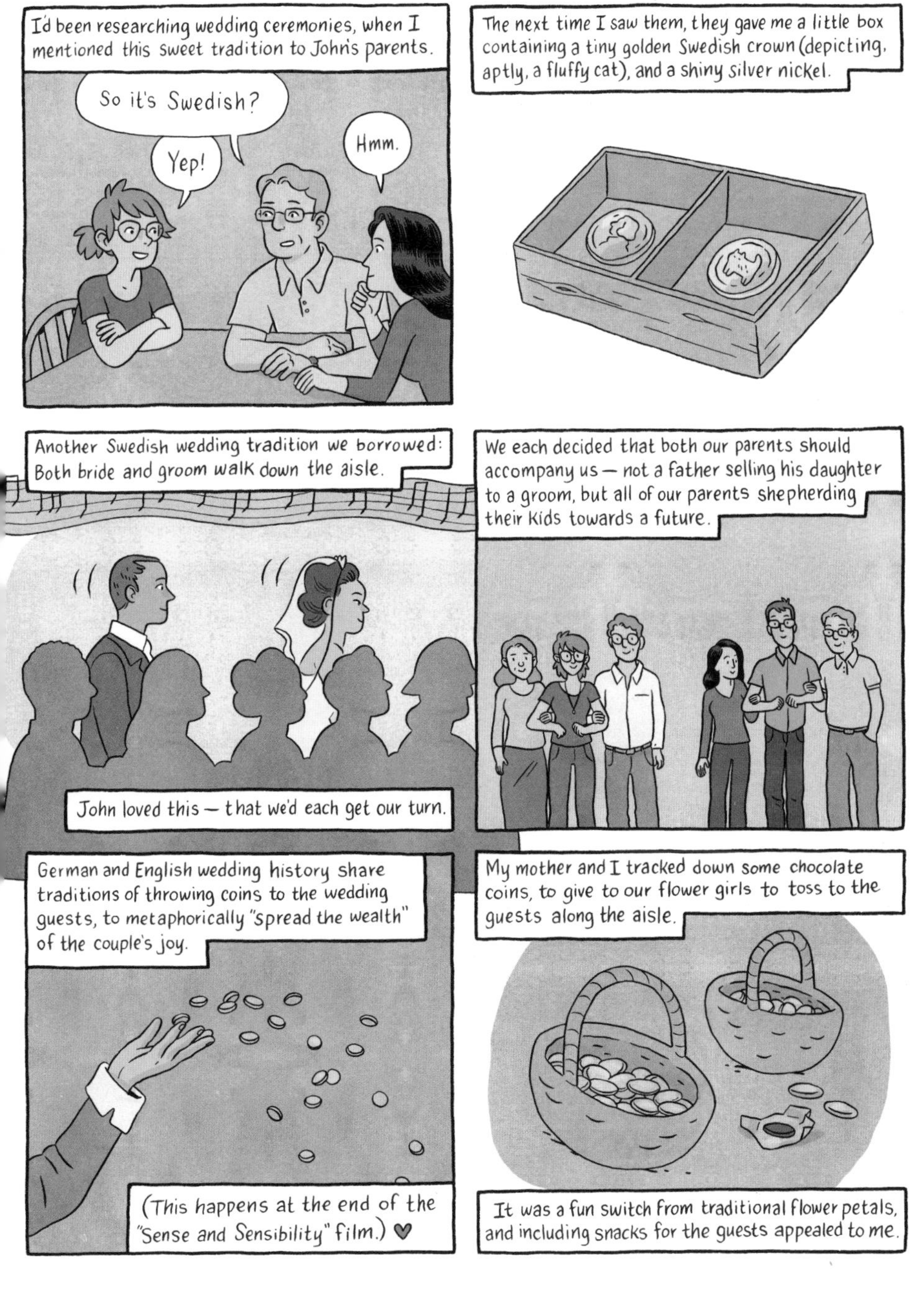
I'd been researching wedding ceremonies, when I mentioned this sweet tradition to John's parents.
So it's Swedish?
Yep!
Hmm.
The next time I saw them, they gave me a little box containing a tiny golden Swedish crown (depicting, aptly, a fluffy cat), and a shiny silver nickel.
Another Swedish wedding tradition we borrowed: Both bride and groom walk down the aisle.
John loved this — that we'd each get our turn.
We each decided that both our parents should accompany us — not a father selling his daughter to a groom, but all of our parents shepherding their kids towards a future.
German and English wedding history share traditions of throwing coins to the wedding guests, to metaphorically "spread the wealth" of the couple's joy.
(This happens at the end of the "Sense and Sensibility" film.) ♥
My mother and I tracked down some chocolate coins, to give to our flower girls to toss to the guests along the aisle.
It was a fun switch from traditional flower petals, and including snacks for the guests appealed to me.

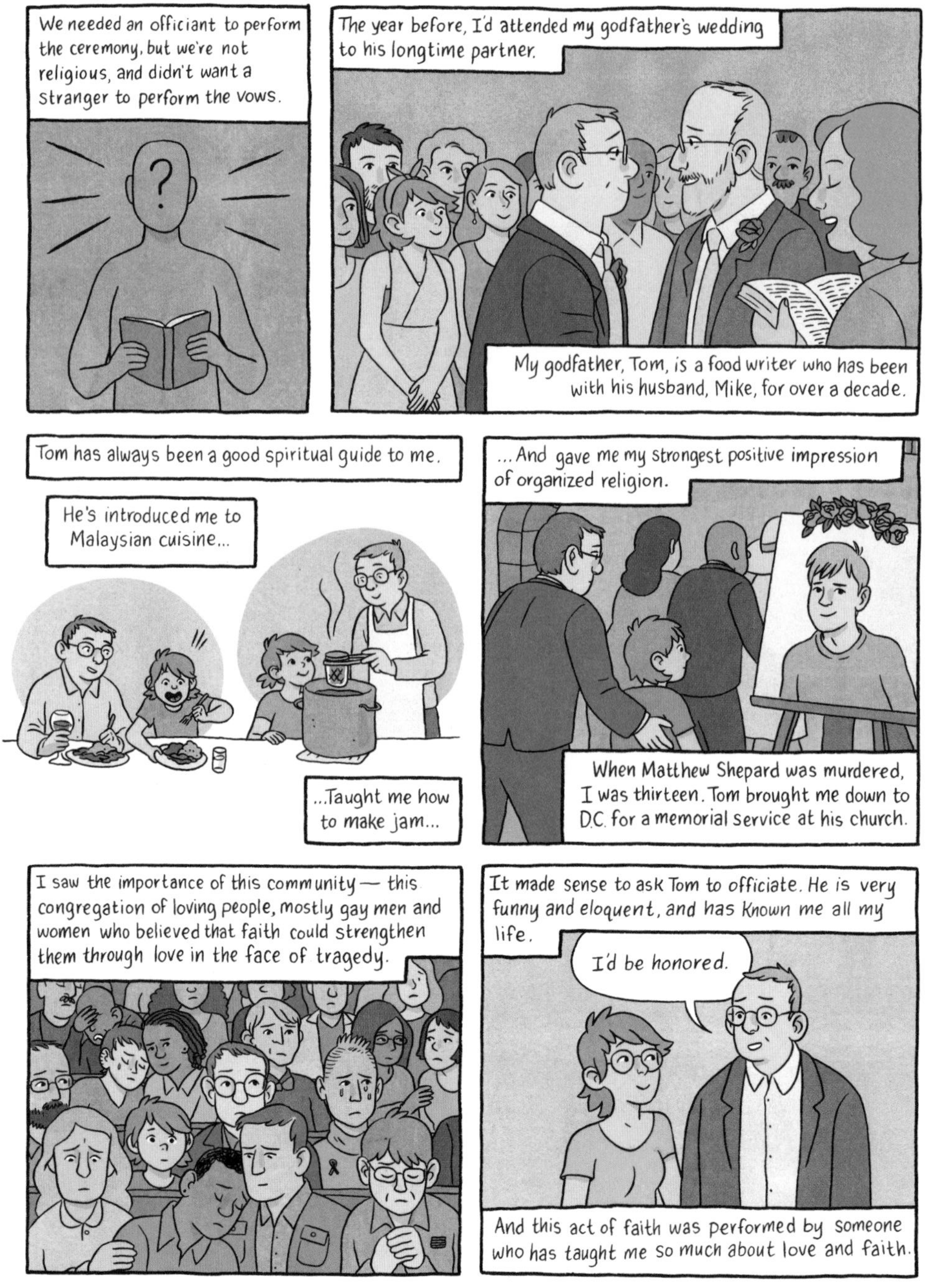
We needed an officiant to perform the ceremony, but we're not religious, and didn't want a stranger to perform the vows.
The year before, I'd attended my godfather's wedding to his longtime partner.
My godfather, Tom, is a food writer who has been with his husband, Mike, for over a decade.
Tom has always been a good spiritual guide to me.
He's introduced me to Malaysian cuisine...
...Taught me how to make jam...
...And gave me my strongest positive impression of organized religion.
When Matthew Shepard was murdered, I was thirteen. Tom brought me down to D.C. for a memorial service at his church.
I saw the importance of this community — this congregation of loving people, mostly gay men and women who believed that faith could strengthen them through love in the face of tragedy.
It made sense to ask Tom to officiate. He is very funny and eloquent, and has known me all my life.
I'd be honored.
And this act of faith was performed by someone who has taught me so much about love and faith.

That still left the vows themselves. None of the traditional wedding wording seemed right for us.

We made a plan: Each of us would write a list of what we felt were the ten most important elements in a marriage.

5. That you always draw me handsome!

Of course!

When we compared the list, we found most of the same things, worded slightly differently.

These combined lists became our vows, which we edited and added to over a few months.

Agreeing on word choice was a little tense at times, but the talks we had about the vows were good pre-marriage chats.

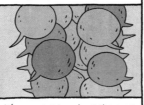

We were talking about the vows, but we were also discussing what we felt was important, and what we wanted out of marriage.

We agreed that these vows would always be a working document — that they'd keep growing along with us over the years.

We kept it succinct. Neither of us wanted a long ceremony, and the plan was to recite them from memory, so neither of us wanted a lengthy tome to memorize.

Uhhhhh...

We had most of the summer to get the vows down pat.

JULY

memorize vows!

Other traditions—like not seeing one another on the day—were easily discarded.

But the **BAD LUCK!**

Actually, the tradition has to do with desertion of arranged marriages, not luck.

John and I live together — we wanted to wake up together on the wedding day.

We'd spend most of the day apart, getting ready and greeting our wedding party, so seeing each other that morning was a nice pre-chaos moment.

Happy wedding day!

MORNING PERSON

My mom had called a few weeks before the wedding to politely inquire whether John and I would need *privacy* on our wedding night.

It's just that *traditionally* you two would have a hotel room, but you're planning to stay in your childhood bedroom, so perhaps Jeff and I could leave...

Mom, you are aware that we <u>live together</u>, right?

Besides, we're gonna be exhausted.

Some wedding traditions just don't fit. Example: When a wedding is over in Korea, groomsmen beat the groom's feet with a fish, to prepare him for married life* I can do without that one.

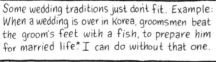

Why!?

While other traditions *seem* to make a wedding *a wedding*—unique among other parties.

I want to get married in my favorite color...

...White.

Queen Victoria started the Western world's white-dress tradition back in 1840.

*I mentioned this on page 81, but it's just so awesome, I had to bring it up again.

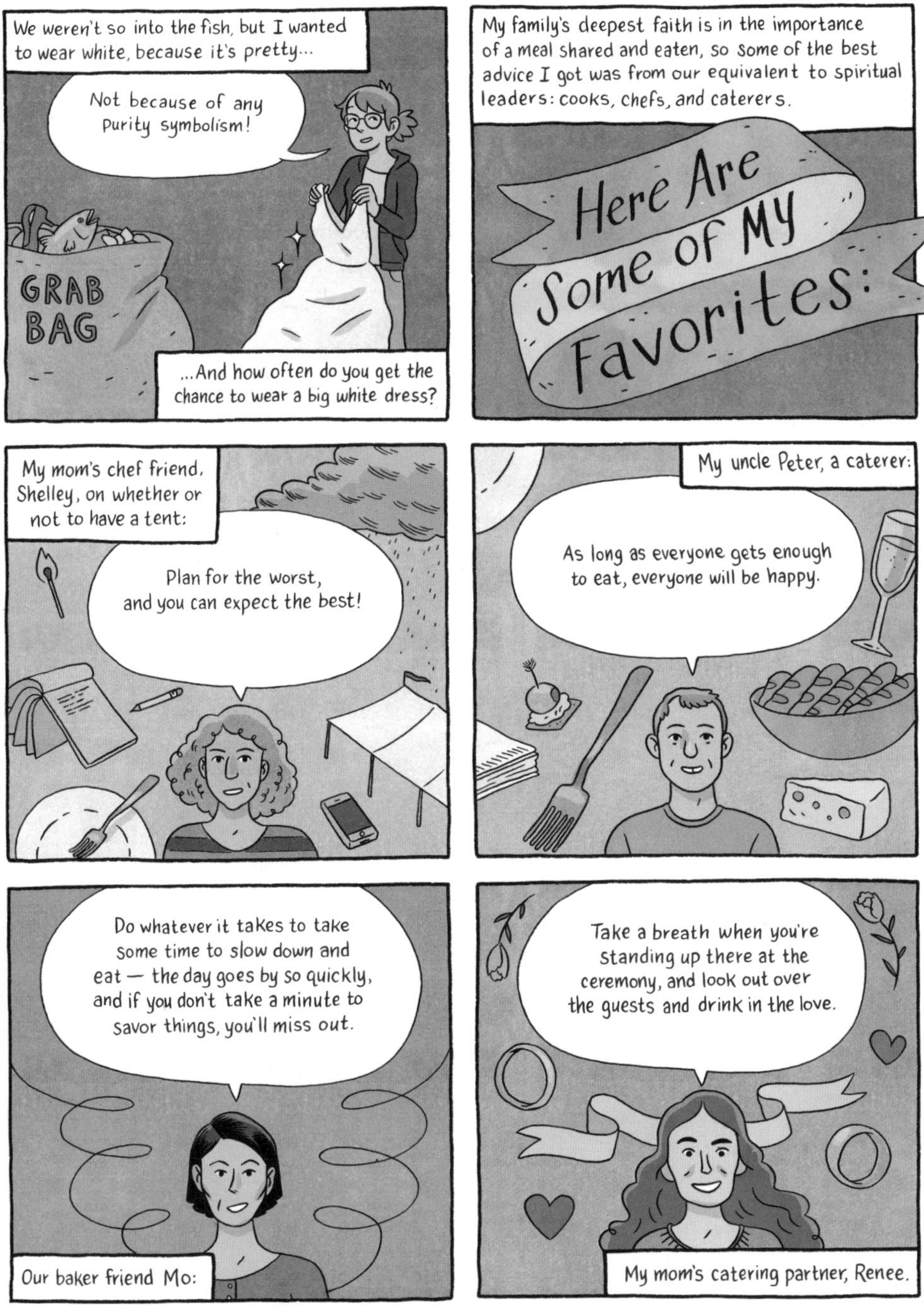

We weren't so into the fish, but I wanted to wear white, because it's pretty...
Not because of any purity symbolism!
GRAB BAG
...And how often do you get the chance to wear a big white dress?
My family's deepest faith is in the importance of a meal shared and eaten, so some of the best advice I got was from our equivalent to spiritual leaders: cooks, chefs, and caterers.
Here Are Some of My Favorites:
My mom's chef friend, Shelley, on whether or not to have a tent:
Plan for the worst, and you can expect the best!
My uncle Peter, a caterer:
As long as everyone gets enough to eat, everyone will be happy.
Do whatever it takes to take some time to slow down and eat — the day goes by so quickly, and if you don't take a minute to savor things, you'll miss out.
Our baker friend Mo:
Take a breath when you're standing up there at the ceremony, and look out over the guests and drink in the love.
My mom's catering partner, Renee.

All the research, the traditions, the advice, and the planning can never fully prepare you, of course, but it's nice to have a few connectors, tethering you to people and to history, to be beacons through the day.

A moment with my new mother-in-law, putting the coins in my shoes.

A moment with John and Tom, looking out over the guests.

A moment to consider the fact that this wedding is at once totally new...

Fiona

Tia

Chocolate!

How unusual!

...And also a part of millions of other weddings throughout history.

Good wishes for you and your lady, my lord!

My blessings, well-wishers!

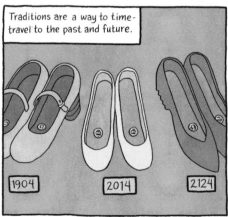

Traditions are a way to time-travel to the past and future.

1904

2014

2124

In our research of wedding traditions, there was one other German wedding custom we decided to keep:

The newlyweds stay at the party until the last guest goes home.

We might not be *awake*, but we'll close that shindig *DOWN*.

AGREED!

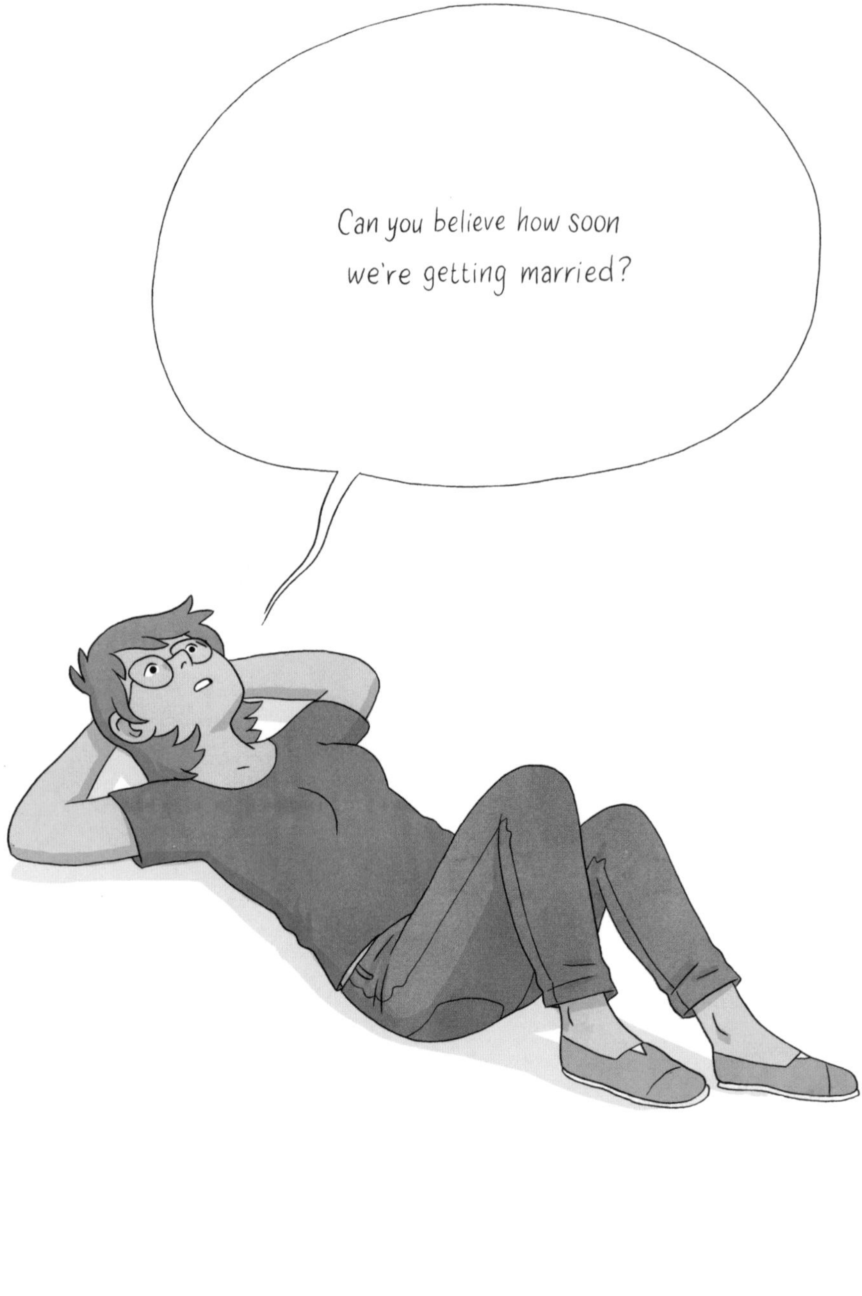
Can you believe how soon we're getting married?

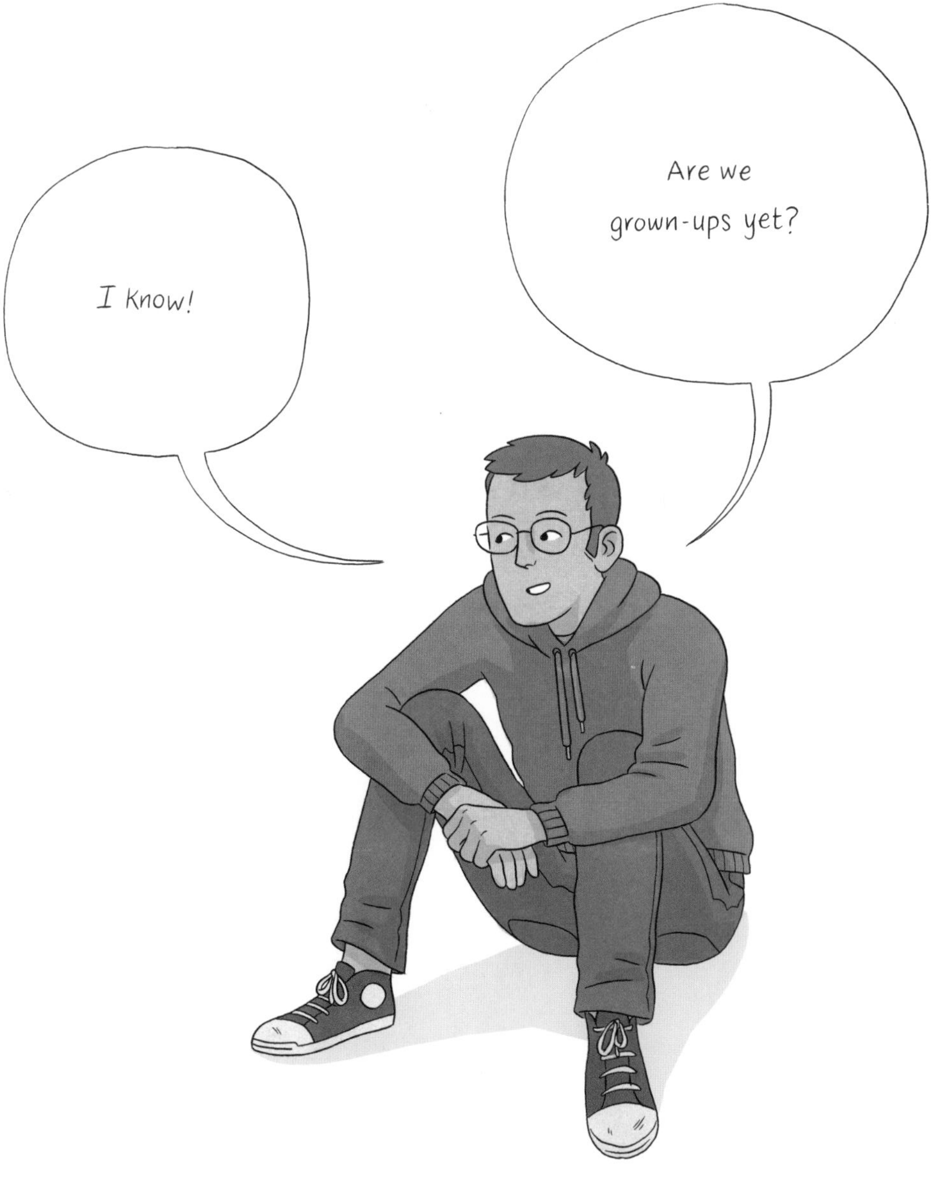
I Know!
Are we grown-ups yet?

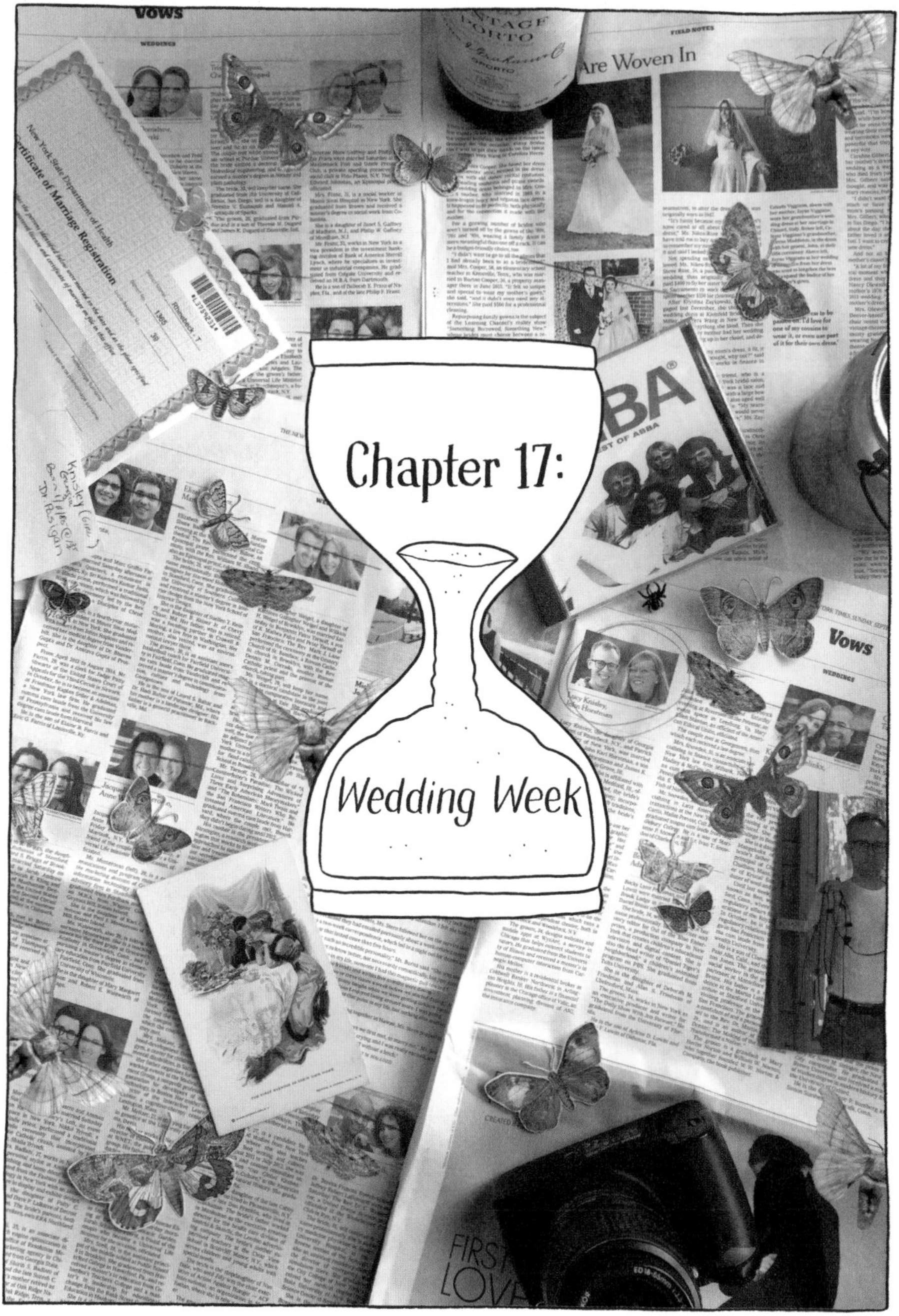
Vows
Are Woven In
Certificate of Marriage Registration
Vows
FIRST LOVE

Chapter 17:

Wedding Week

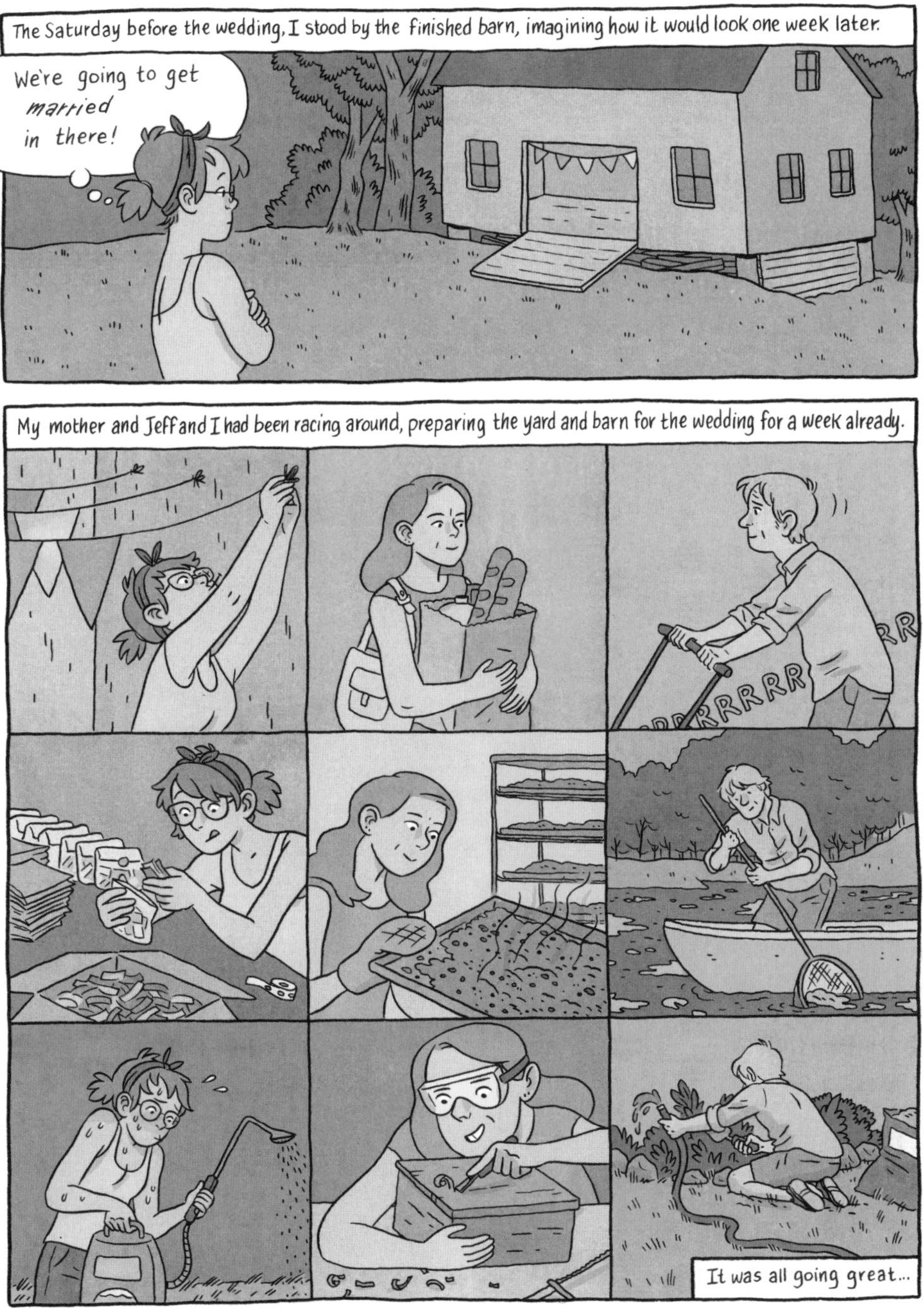
The Saturday before the wedding, I stood by the finished barn, imagining how it would look one week later.
We're going to get *married* in there!
My mother and Jeff and I had been racing around, preparing the yard and barn for the wedding for a week already.
RRRRRRRR
It was all going great...

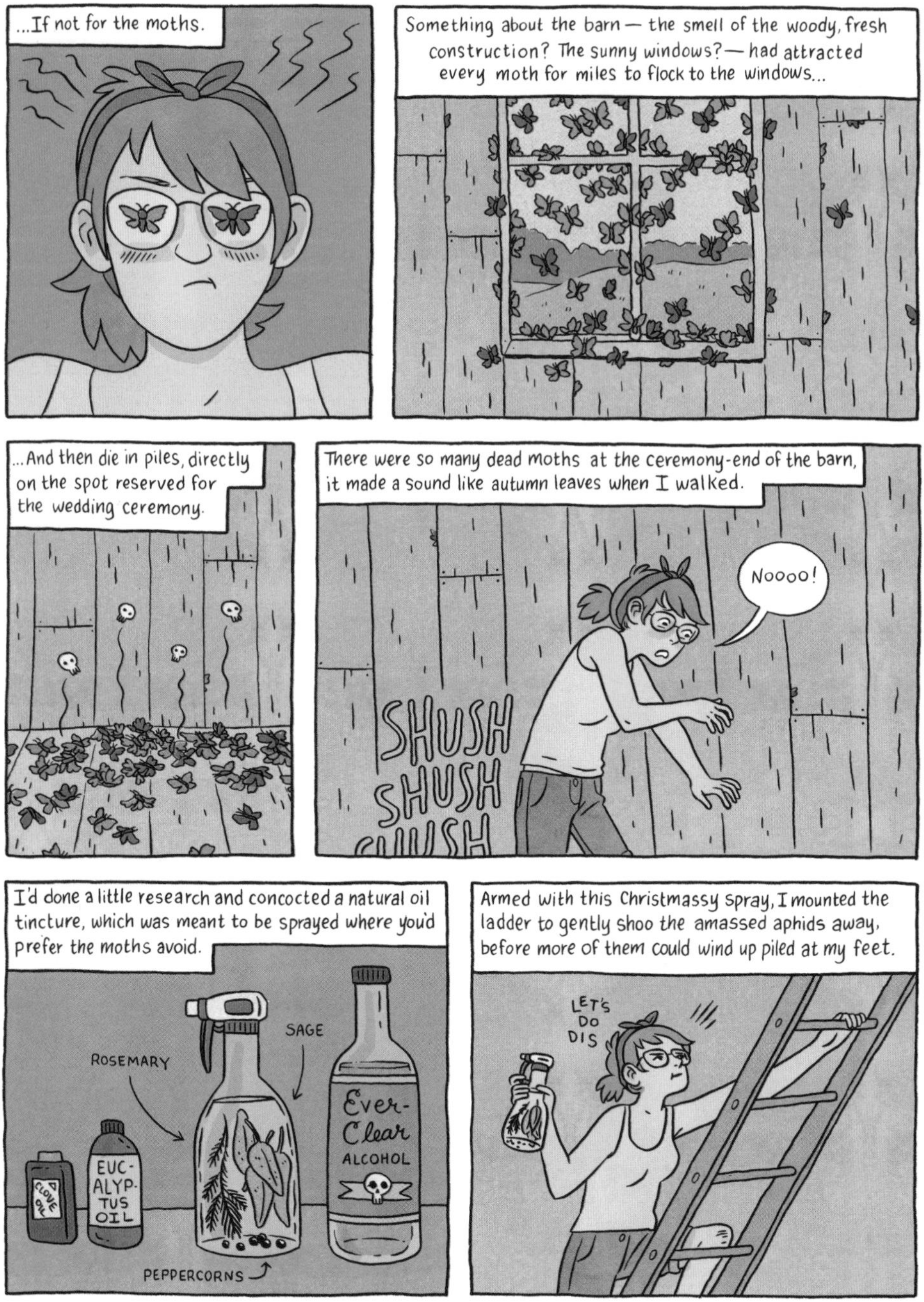
...If not for the moths.
Something about the barn — the smell of the woody, fresh construction? The sunny windows? — had attracted every moth for miles to flock to the windows...
...And then die in piles, directly on the spot reserved for the wedding ceremony.
There were so many dead moths at the ceremony-end of the barn, it made a sound like autumn leaves when I walked.
Noooo!
SHUSH
SHUSH
I'd done a little research and concocted a natural oil tincture, which was meant to be sprayed where you'd prefer the moths avoid.
ROSEMARY
SAGE
CLOVE OIL
EUC-ALYP-TUS OIL
Ever-Clear
ALCOHOL
PEPPERCORNS
Armed with this Christmassy spray, I mounted the ladder to gently shoo the amassed aphids away, before more of them could wind up piled at my feet.
LET'S DO DIS

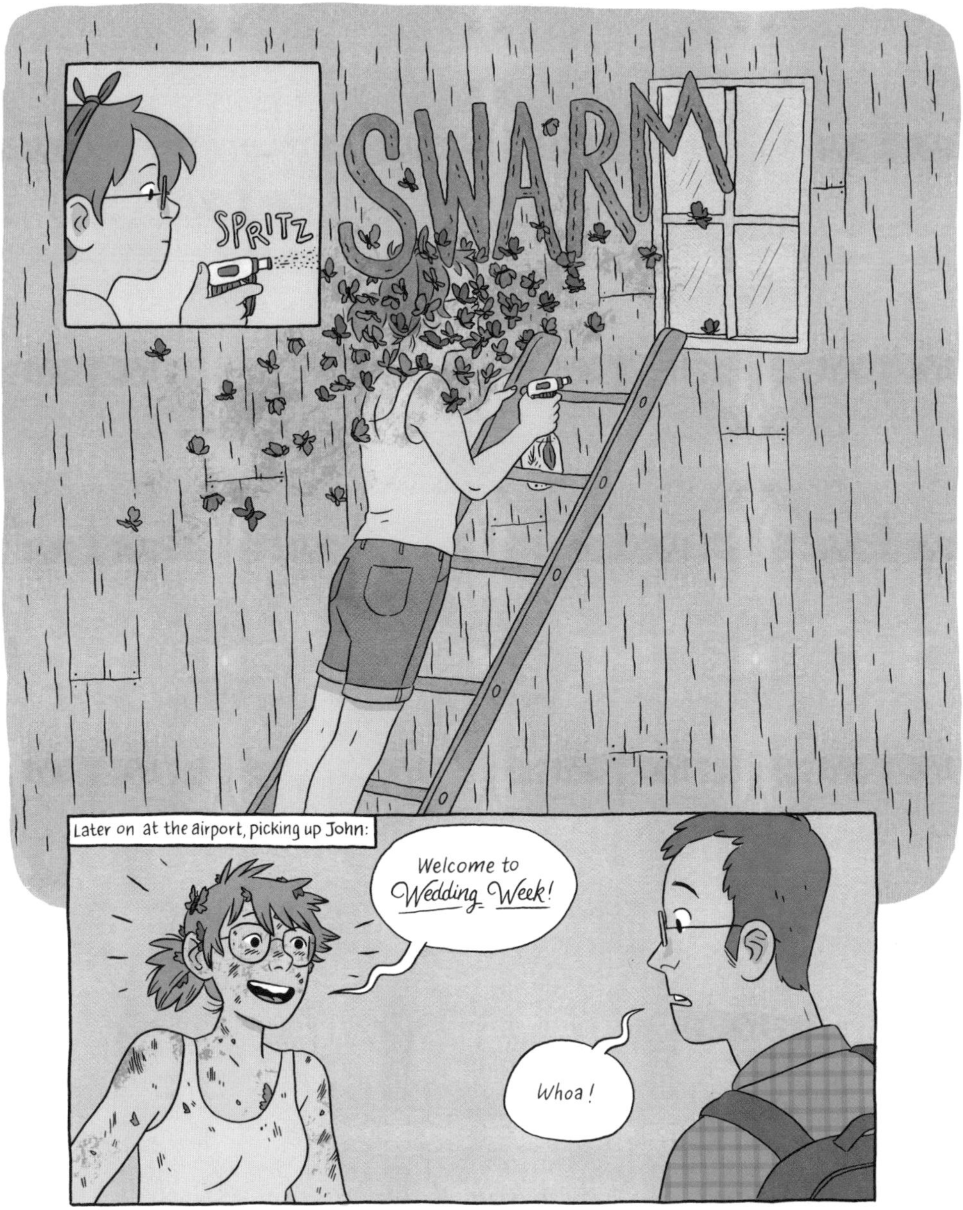
SPRITZ
SWARM
Later on at the airport, picking up John:
Welcome to Wedding Week!
Whoa!

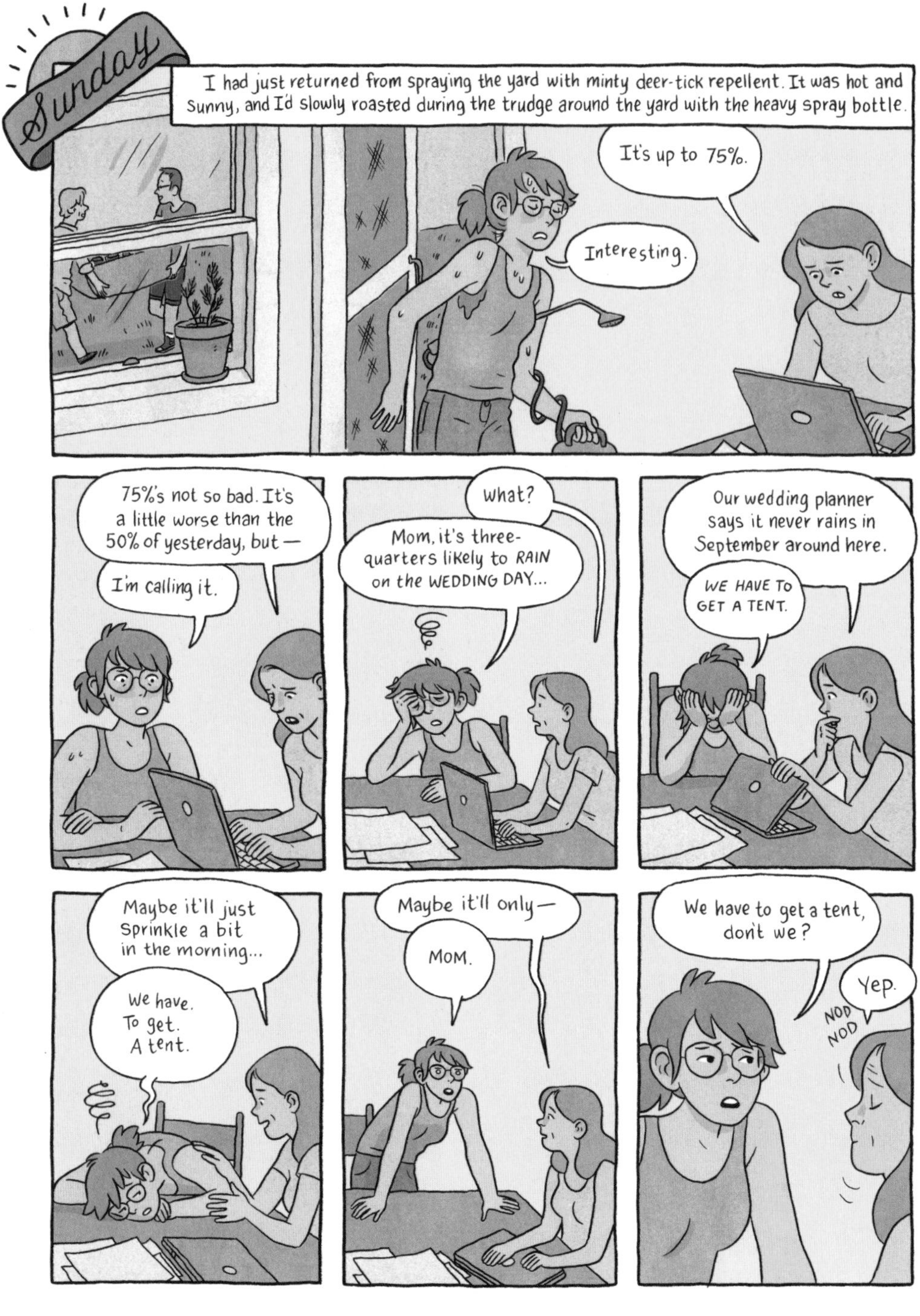
Sunday
I had just returned from spraying the yard with minty deer-tick repellent. It was hot and sunny, and I'd slowly roasted during the trudge around the yard with the heavy spray bottle.
It's up to 75%.
Interesting.
75%'s not so bad. It's a little worse than the 50% of yesterday, but—
I'm calling it.
What?
Mom, it's three-quarters likely to RAIN on the WEDDING DAY...
Our wedding planner says it never rains in September around here.
WE HAVE TO GET A TENT.
Maybe it'll just sprinkle a bit in the morning...
We have. To get. A tent.
Maybe it'll only—
MOM.
We have to get a tent, don't we?
Yep.
NOD NOD

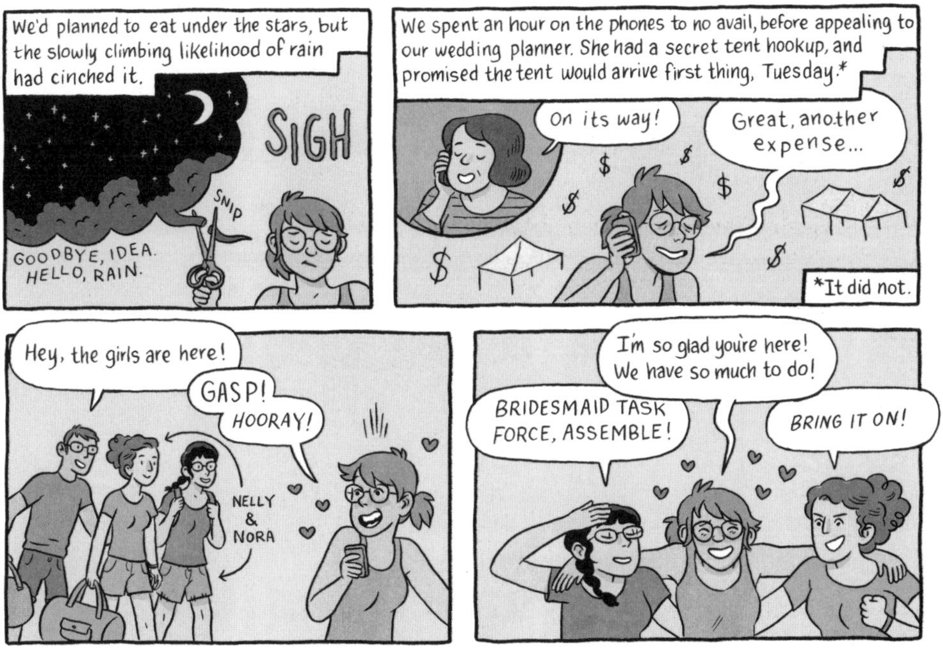
We'd planned to eat under the stars, but the slowly climbing likelihood of rain had cinched it.
SIGH
SNIP
GOODBYE, IDEA. HELLO, RAIN.
We spent an hour on the phones to no avail, before appealing to our wedding planner. She had a secret tent hookup, and promised the tent would arrive first thing, Tuesday.*
On its way!
Great, another expense...
*It did not.
Hey, the girls are here!
GASP! HOORAY!
NELLY & NORA
I'm so glad you're here! We have so much to do!
BRIDESMAID TASK FORCE, ASSEMBLE!
BRING IT ON!

We worked on the

MAGICAL WOODLAND GROTTO

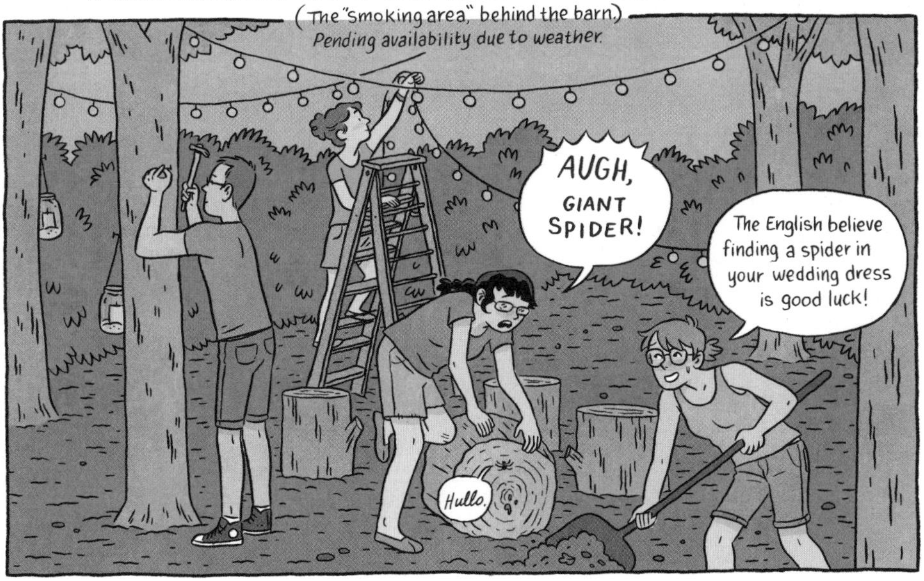
(The "smoking area," behind the barn.)
Pending availability due to weather.
AUGH, GIANT SPIDER!
The English believe finding a spider in your wedding dress is good luck!
Hullo.

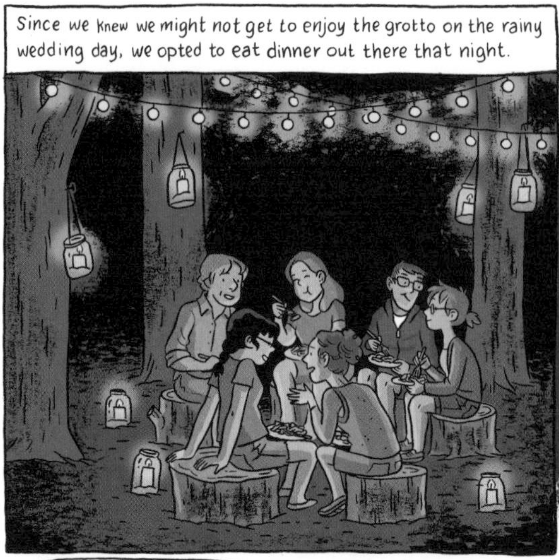
Since we knew we might not get to enjoy the grotto on the rainy wedding day, we opted to eat dinner out there that night.

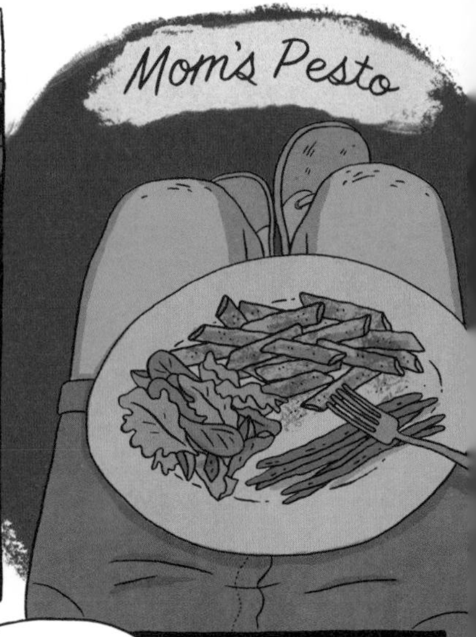
Mom's Pesto

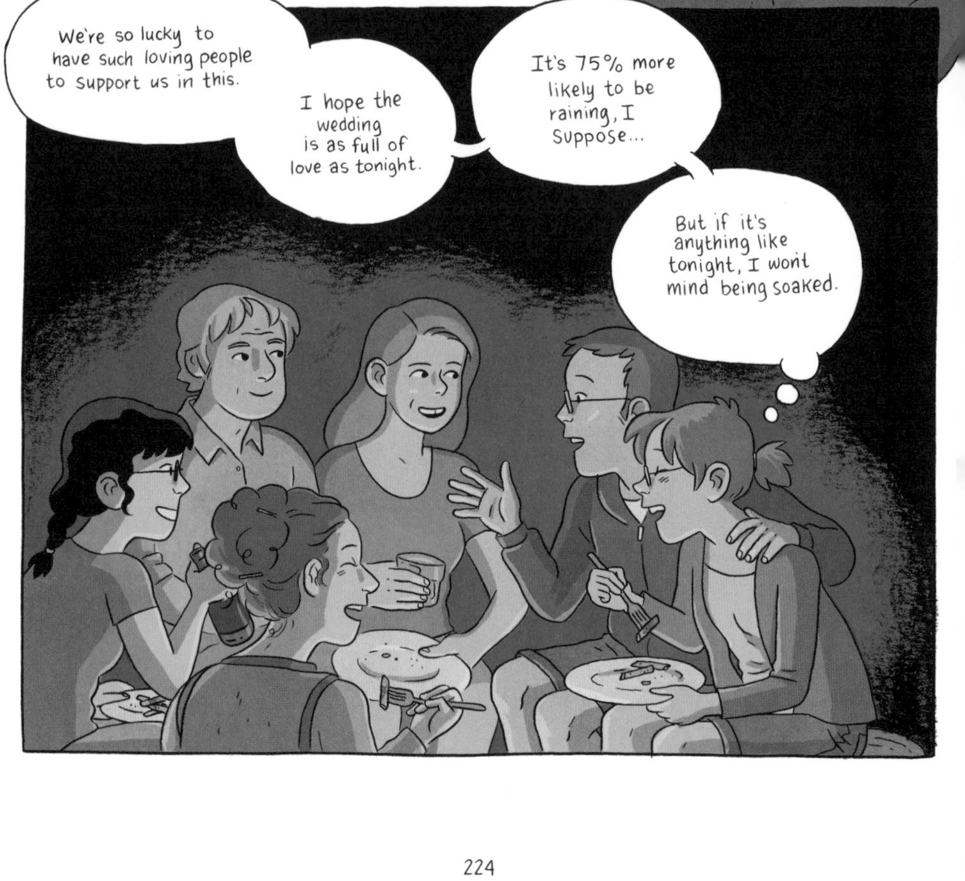
We're so lucky to have such loving people to support us in this.
I hope the wedding is as full of love as tonight.
It's 75% more likely to be raining, I suppose...
But if it's anything like tonight, I won't mind being soaked.

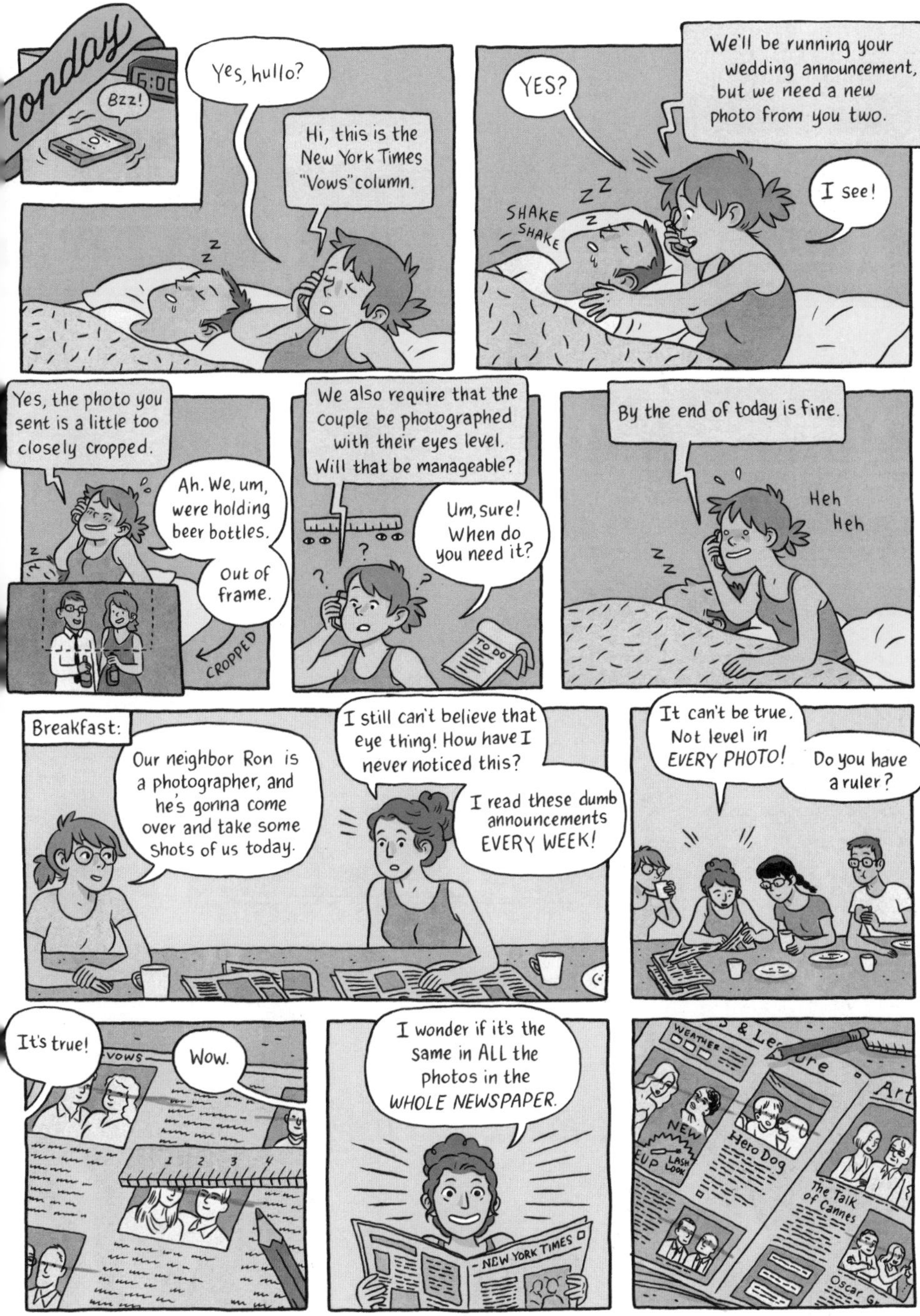
Monday
Bzz!
6:00
Yes, hullo?
Hi, this is the New York Times "Vows" column.
YES?
We'll be running your wedding announcement, but we need a new photo from you two.
SHAKE SHAKE
I see!
Yes, the photo you sent is a little too closely cropped.
Ah. We, um, were holding beer bottles.
Out of frame.
CROPPED
We also require that the couple be photographed with their eyes level. Will that be manageable?
Um, sure! When do you need it?
TO DO
By the end of today is fine.
Heh Heh
Breakfast:
Our neighbor Ron is a photographer, and he's gonna come over and take some shots of us today.
I still can't believe that eye thing! How have I never noticed this?
I read these dumb announcements EVERY WEEK!
It can't be true. Not level in EVERY PHOTO!
Do you have a ruler?
It's true!
Wow.
VOWS
I wonder if it's the same in ALL the photos in the WHOLE NEWSPAPER.
NEW YORK TIMES
WEATHER
NEW
LASH LOOK
Hero Dog
The Talk of Cannes
Art

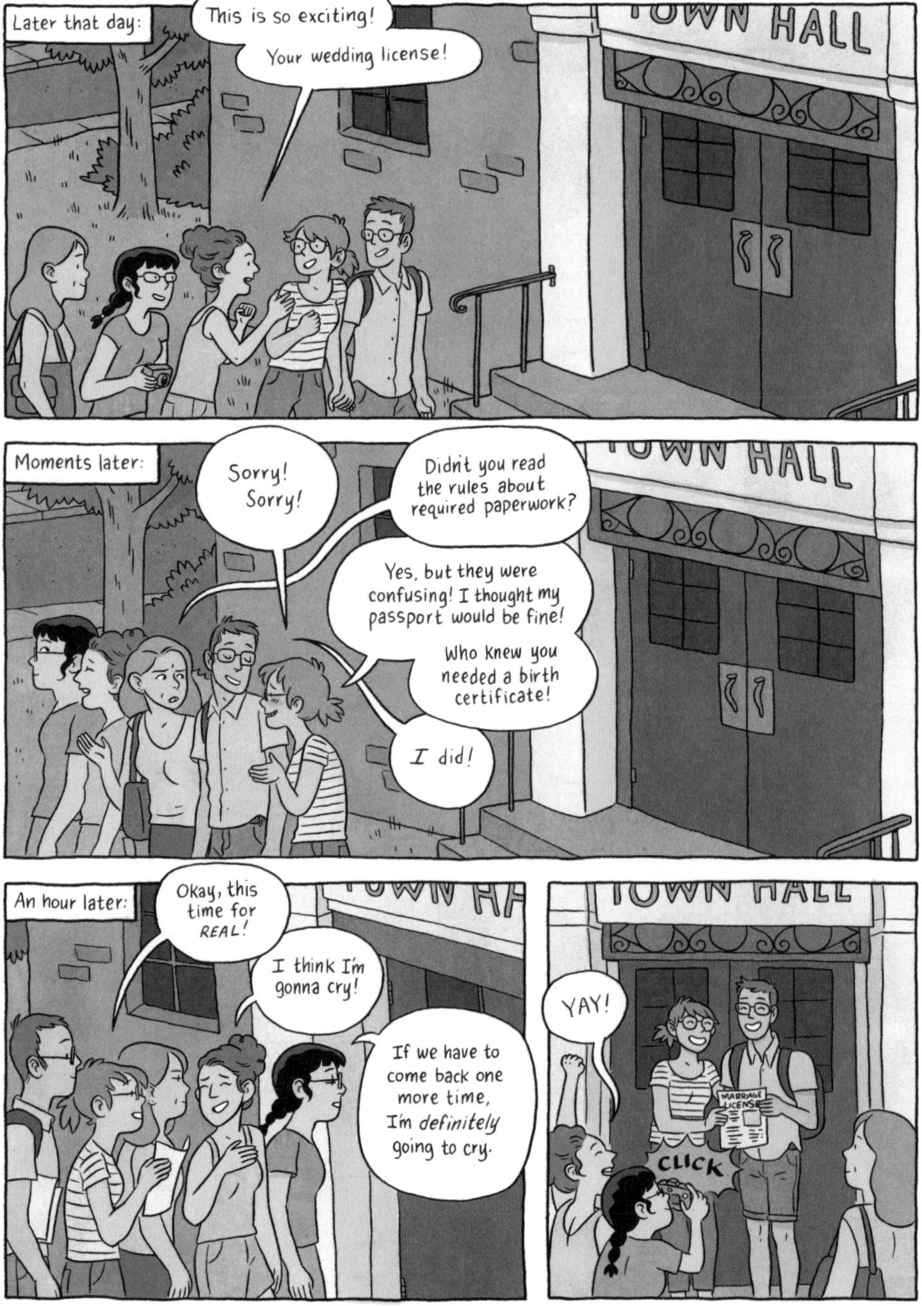
Later that day:
This is so exciting!
Your wedding license!
TOWN HALL
Moments later:
Sorry! Sorry!
Didn't you read the rules about required paperwork?
Yes, but they were confusing! I thought my passport would be fine!
Who knew you needed a birth certificate!
I did!
TOWN HALL
An hour later:
Okay, this time for REAL!
I think I'm gonna cry!
If we have to come back one more time, I'm definitely going to cry.
TOWN HALL
YAY!
MARRIAGE LICENSE
CLICK

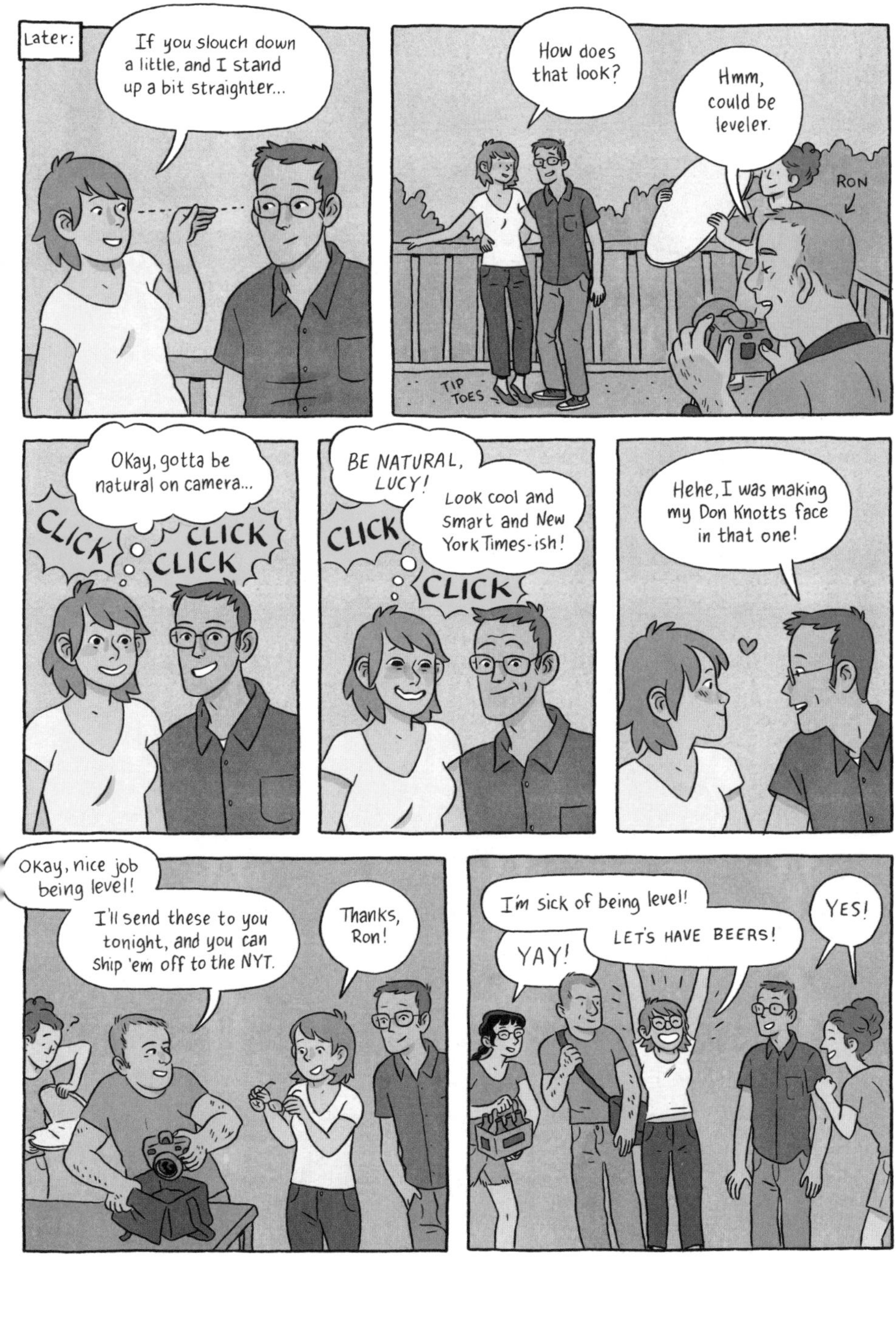
Later:
If you slouch down a little, and I stand up a bit straighter...
How does that look?
Hmm, could be leveler.
RON
TIP TOES
Okay, gotta be natural on camera...
CLICK
CLICK
CLICK
BE NATURAL, LUCY!
Look cool and smart and New York Times-ish!
CLICK
CLICK
Hehe, I was making my Don Knotts face in that one!
Okay, nice job being level!
I'll send these to you tonight, and you can ship 'em off to the NYT.
Thanks, Ron!
I'm sick of being level!
LET'S HAVE BEERS!
YAY!
YES!

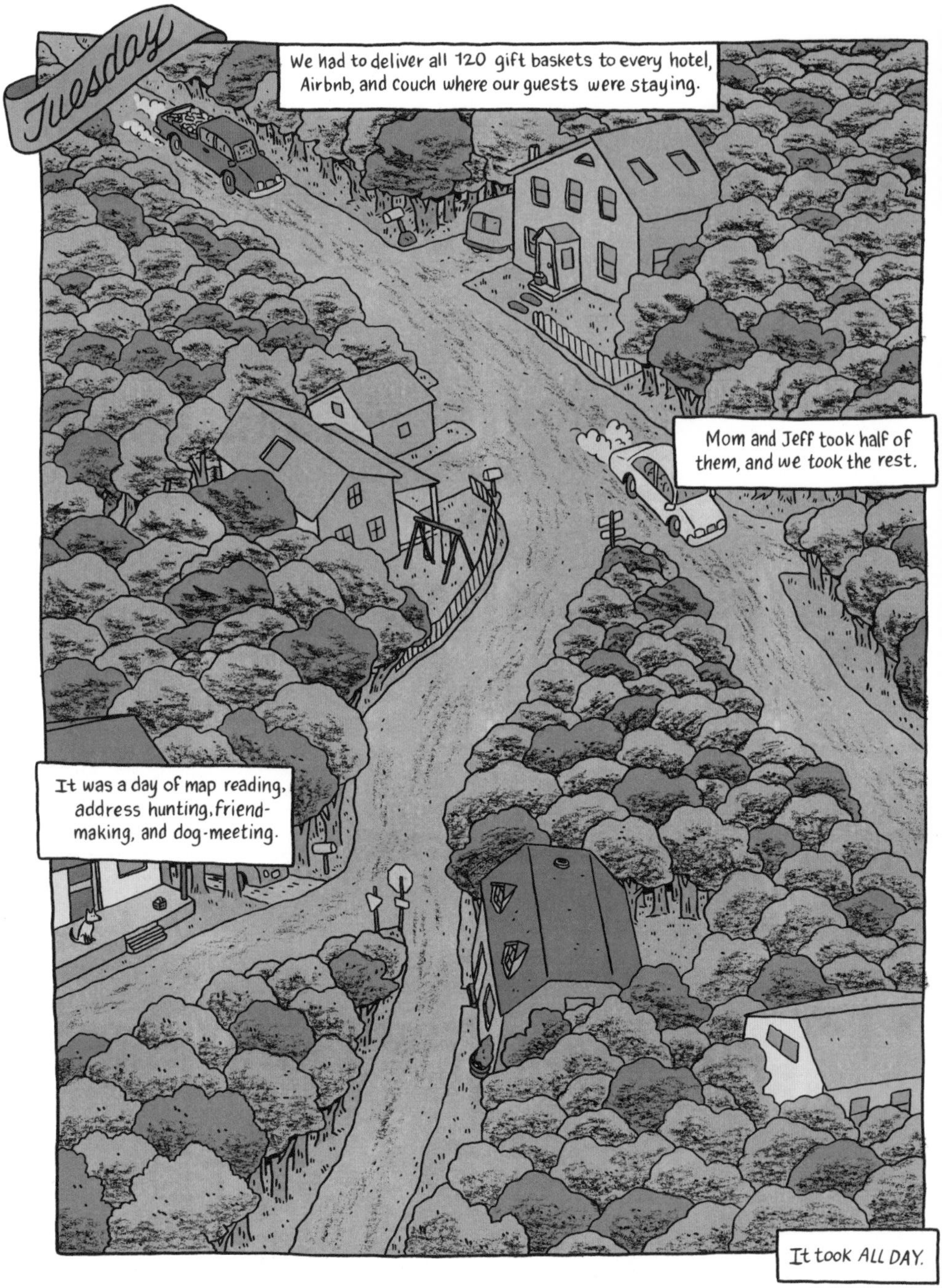
Tuesday
We had to deliver all 120 gift baskets to every hotel, Airbnb, and couch where our guests were staying.
Mom and Jeff took half of them, and we took the rest.
It was a day of map reading, address hunting, friend-making, and dog-meeting.
It took ALL DAY.

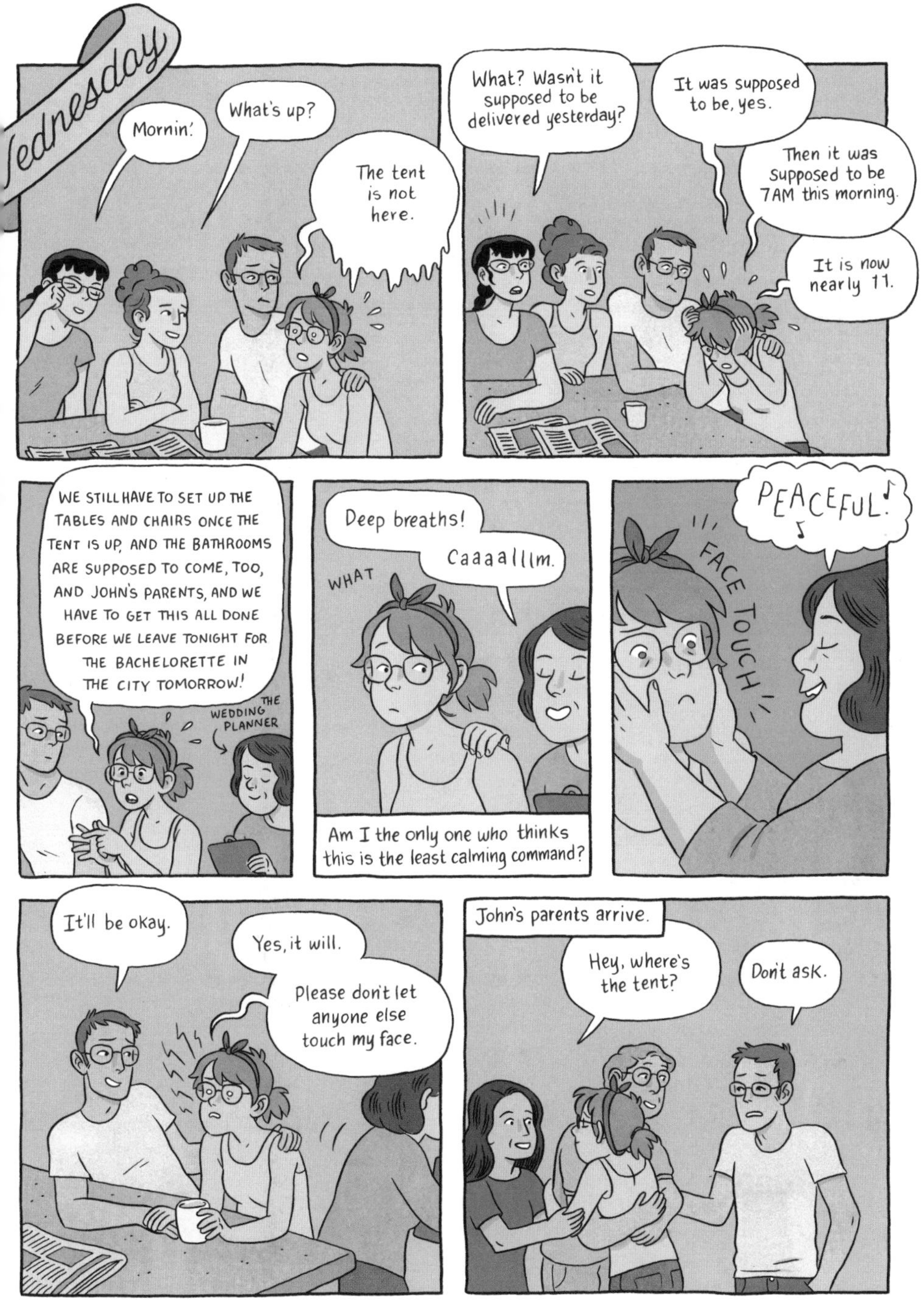
Wednesday
Mornin'.
What's up?
The tent is not here.
What? Wasn't it supposed to be delivered yesterday?
It was supposed to be, yes.
Then it was supposed to be 7AM this morning.
It is now nearly 11.
WE STILL HAVE TO SET UP THE TABLES AND CHAIRS ONCE THE TENT IS UP, AND THE BATHROOMS ARE SUPPOSED TO COME, TOO, AND JOHN'S PARENTS, AND WE HAVE TO GET THIS ALL DONE BEFORE WE LEAVE TONIGHT FOR THE BACHELORETTE IN THE CITY TOMORROW!
THE WEDDING PLANNER
Deep breaths!
Caaaalllm.
WHAT
Am I the only one who thinks this is the least calming command?
PEACEFUL!
FACE TOUCH
It'll be okay.
Yes, it will.
Please don't let anyone else touch my face.
John's parents arrive.
Hey, where's the tent?
Don't ask.

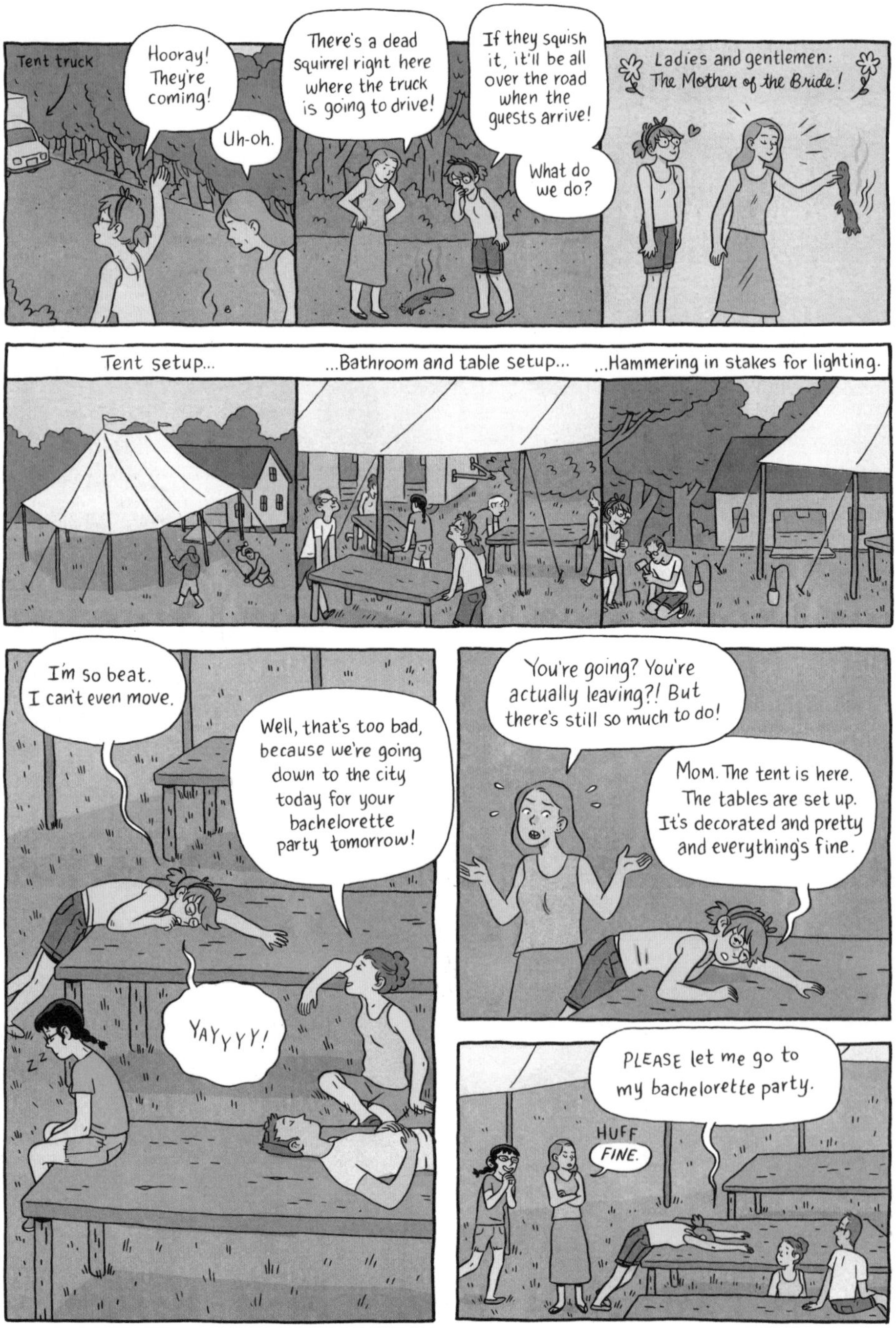
Tent truck
Hooray! They're coming!
Uh-oh.
There's a dead squirrel right here where the truck is going to drive!
If they squish it, it'll be all over the road when the guests arrive!
What do we do?
Ladies and gentlemen: The Mother of the Bride!
Tent setup...
...Bathroom and table setup...
...Hammering in stakes for lighting.
I'm so beat. I can't even move.
Well, that's too bad, because we're going down to the city today for your bachelorette party tomorrow!
YAYYYY!
You're going? You're actually leaving?! But there's still so much to do!
MOM. The tent is here. The tables are set up. It's decorated and pretty and everything's fine.
PLEASE let me go to my bachelorette party.
HUFF
FINE.

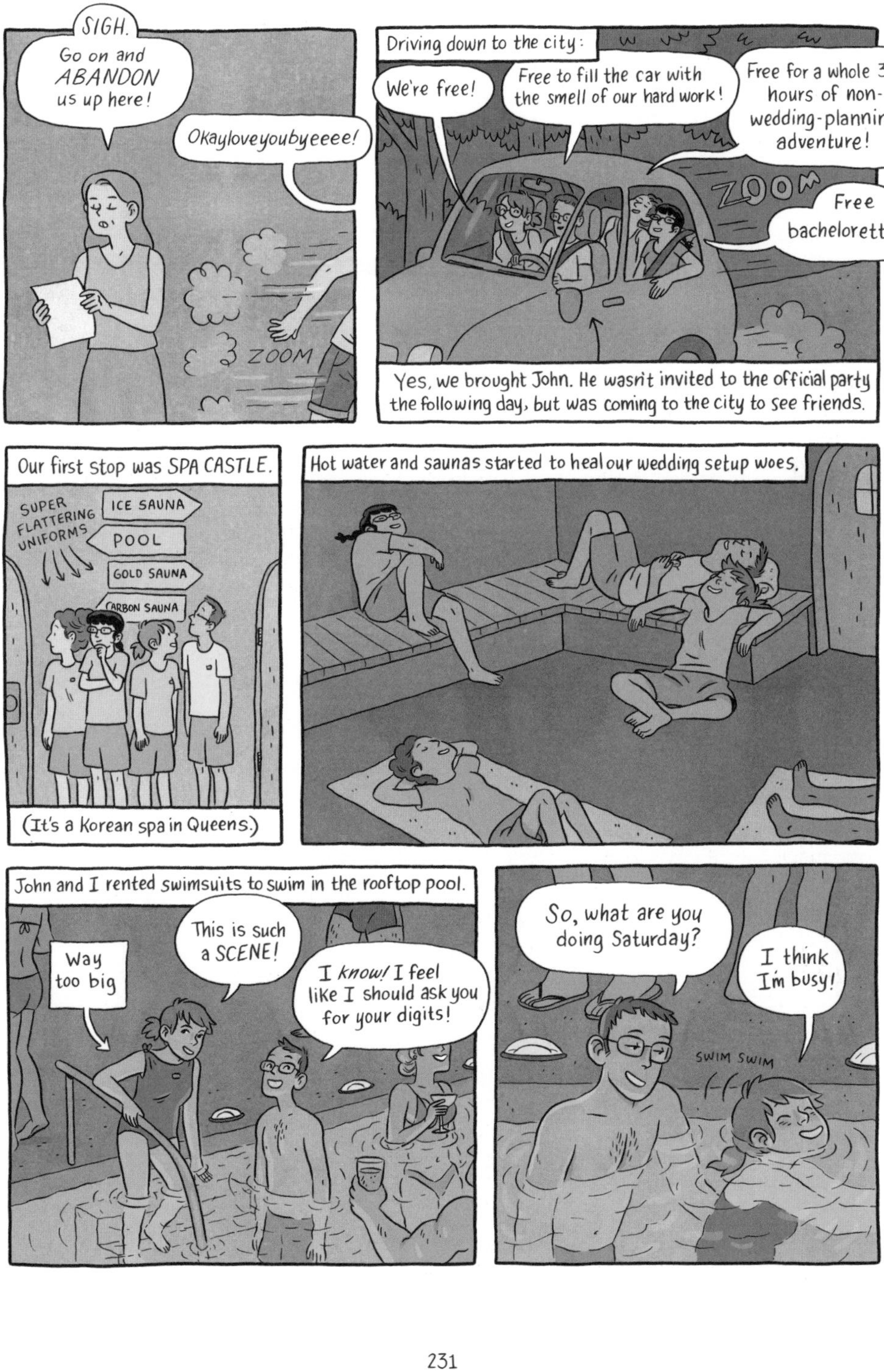
SIGH.
Go on and ABANDON us up here!
Okayloveyoubyeeee!
ZOOM
Driving down to the city:
We're free!
Free to fill the car with the smell of our hard work!
Free for a whole 36 hours of non-wedding-planning adventure!
ZOOM
Free bachelorettes!
Yes, we brought John. He wasn't invited to the official party the following day, but was coming to the city to see friends.
Our first stop was SPA CASTLE.
SUPER FLATTERING UNIFORMS
ICE SAUNA
POOL
GOLD SAUNA
CARBON SAUNA
(It's a Korean spa in Queens.)
Hot water and saunas started to heal our wedding setup woes.
John and I rented swimsuits to swim in the rooftop pool.
Way too big
This is such a SCENE!
I know! I feel like I should ask you for your digits!
So, what are you doing Saturday?
I think I'm busy!
SWIM SWIM

Close to midnight:

Clean, Relaxed, Exhausted

AHHH!

SPA

Swinging by the airport to pick up Erika (John's sister, my bridesmaid) from her late-night flight:

ARRIVALS

YAY!
Bachelorette Eve!

Driving over the bridge to Manhattan to my dad's place, the city looked beautiful and dark...

The wedding is in *three days.*

But when we arrived: (2 AM)

The Key's not working!

We could just sleep here...

Whimperrr...

Hello, everyone. Come on in.

Dad →

YAAAAAAAYYYY!

All Asleep in Moments.

ZZZZZZZ

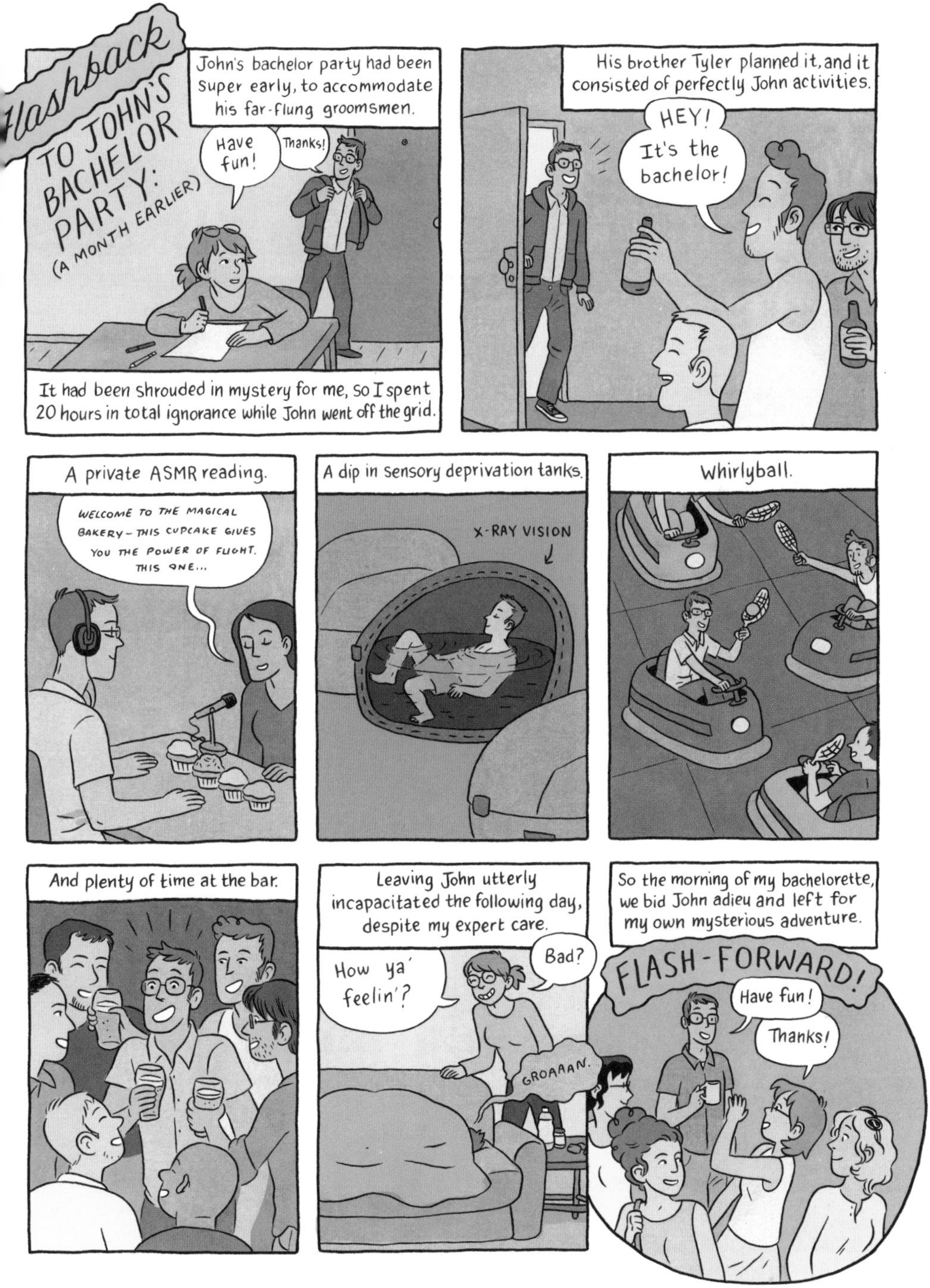
Flashback
TO JOHN'S BACHELOR PARTY:
(A MONTH EARLIER)
John's bachelor party had been super early, to accommodate his far-flung groomsmen.
Have fun!
Thanks!
It had been shrouded in mystery for me, so I spent 20 hours in total ignorance while John went off the grid.
His brother Tyler planned it, and it consisted of perfectly John activities.
HEY! It's the bachelor!
A private ASMR reading.
WELCOME TO THE MAGICAL BAKERY – THIS CUPCAKE GIVES YOU THE POWER OF FLIGHT. THIS ONE...
A dip in sensory deprivation tanks.
X-RAY VISION
Whirlyball.
And plenty of time at the bar.
Leaving John utterly incapacitated the following day, despite my expert care.
How ya' feelin'?
Bad?
GROAAAN.
So the morning of my bachelorette, we bid John adieu and left for my own mysterious adventure.
FLASH-FORWARD!
Have fun!
Thanks!

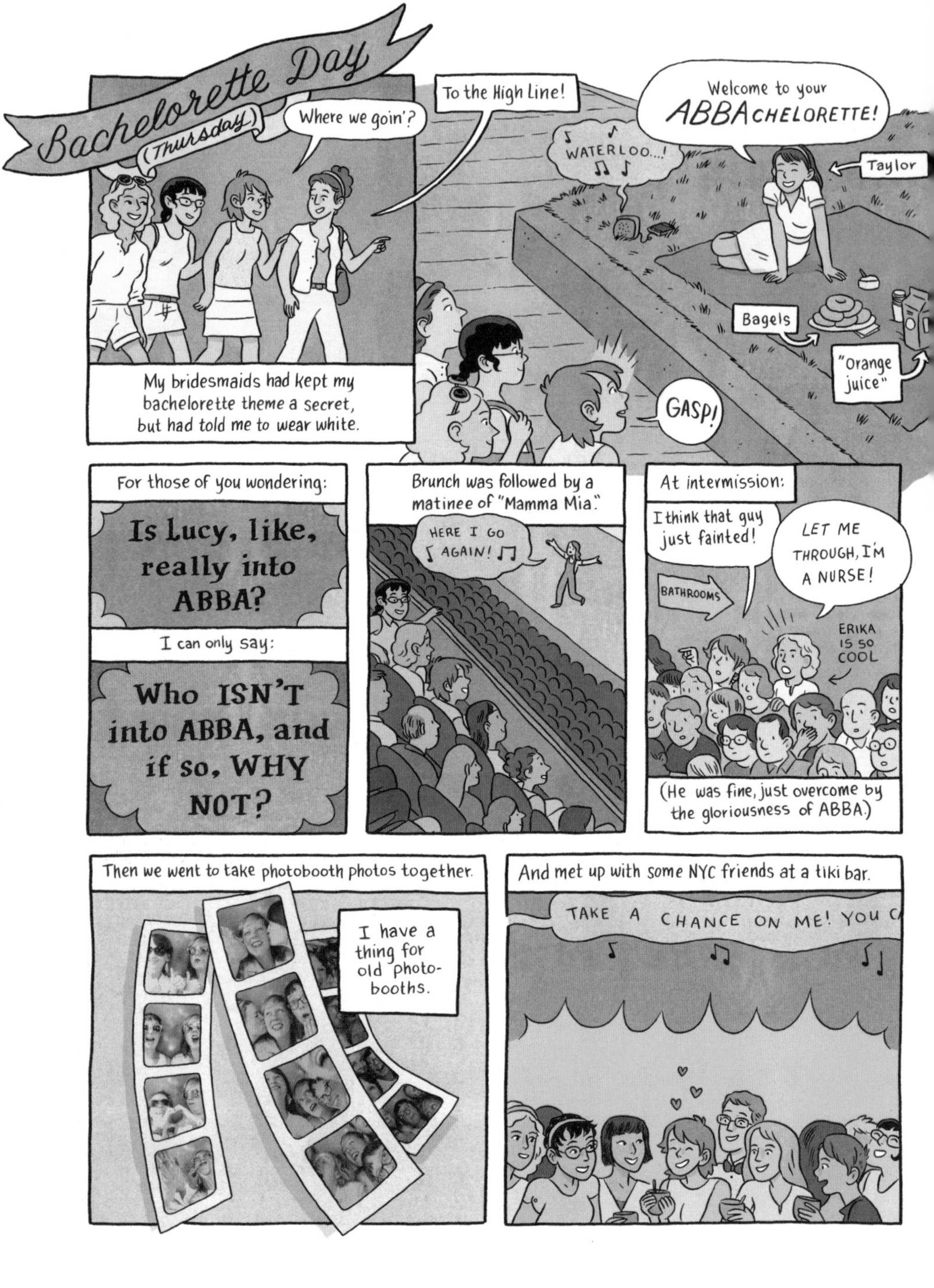
Bachelorette Day
(Thursday)
Where we goin'?
My bridesmaids had kept my bachelorette theme a secret, but had told me to wear white.
To the High Line!
WATERLOO...!
Welcome to your ABBACHELORETTE!
Taylor
Bagels
"Orange juice"
GASP!
For those of you wondering:
Is Lucy, like, really into ABBA?
I can only say:
Who ISN'T into ABBA, and if so, WHY NOT?
Brunch was followed by a matinee of "Mamma Mia."
HERE I GO AGAIN!
At intermission:
I think that guy just fainted!
BATHROOMS
LET ME THROUGH, I'M A NURSE!
ERIKA IS SO COOL
(He was fine, just overcome by the gloriousness of ABBA.)
Then we went to take photobooth photos together.
I have a thing for old photo-booths.
And met up with some NYC friends at a tiki bar.
TAKE A CHANCE ON ME! YOU C

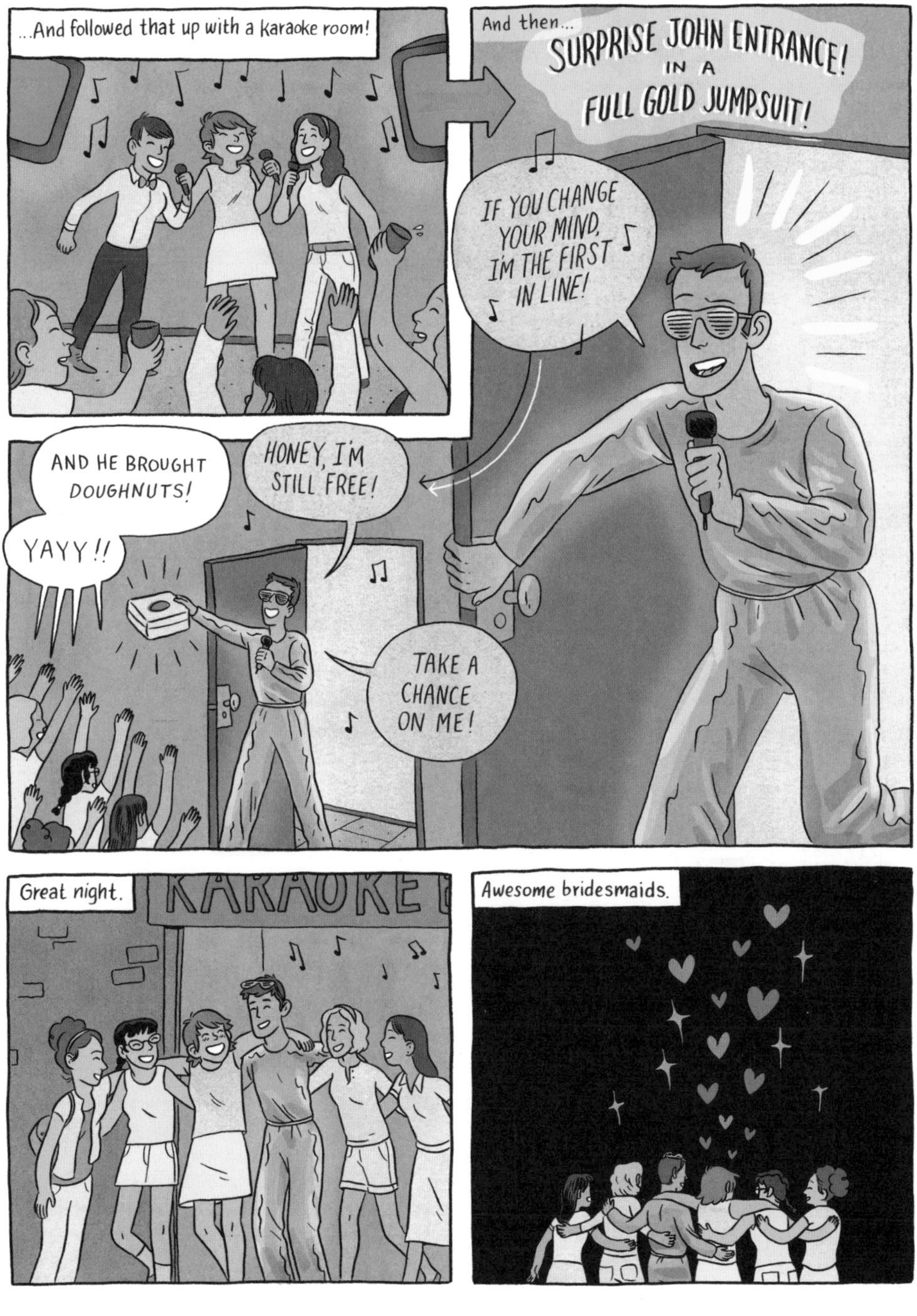
...And followed that up with a karaoke room!
And then...
SURPRISE JOHN ENTRANCE! IN A FULL GOLD JUMPSUIT!
IF YOU CHANGE YOUR MIND, I'M THE FIRST IN LINE!
AND HE BROUGHT DOUGHNUTS!
YAYY!!
HONEY, I'M STILL FREE!
TAKE A CHANCE ON ME!
Great night.
KARAOKE
Awesome bridesmaids.

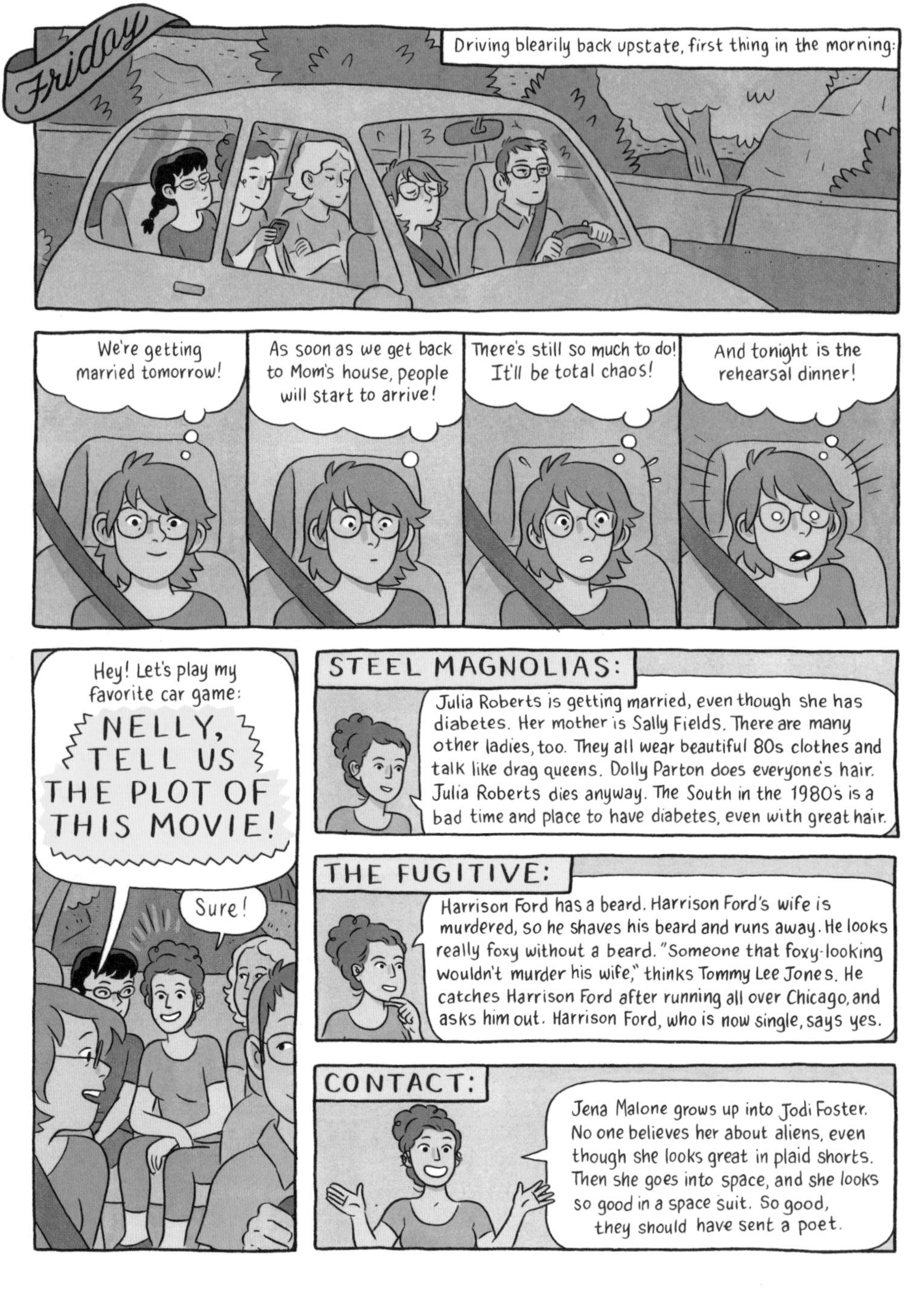
Friday
Driving blearily back upstate, first thing in the morning:
We're getting married tomorrow!
As soon as we get back to Mom's house, people will start to arrive!
There's still so much to do! It'll be total chaos!
And tonight is the rehearsal dinner!
Hey! Let's play my favorite car game:
NELLY, TELL US THE PLOT OF THIS MOVIE!
Sure!
STEEL MAGNOLIAS:
Julia Roberts is getting married, even though she has diabetes. Her mother is Sally Fields. There are many other ladies, too. They all wear beautiful 80s clothes and talk like drag queens. Dolly Parton does everyone's hair. Julia Roberts dies anyway. The South in the 1980's is a bad time and place to have diabetes, even with great hair.
THE FUGITIVE:
Harrison Ford has a beard. Harrison Ford's wife is murdered, so he shaves his beard and runs away. He looks really foxy without a beard. "Someone that foxy-looking wouldn't murder his wife," thinks Tommy Lee Jones. He catches Harrison Ford after running all over Chicago, and asks him out. Harrison Ford, who is now single, says yes.
CONTACT:
Jena Malone grows up into Jodi Foster. No one believes her about aliens, even though she looks great in plaid shorts. Then she goes into space, and she looks so good in a space suit. So good, they should have sent a poet.

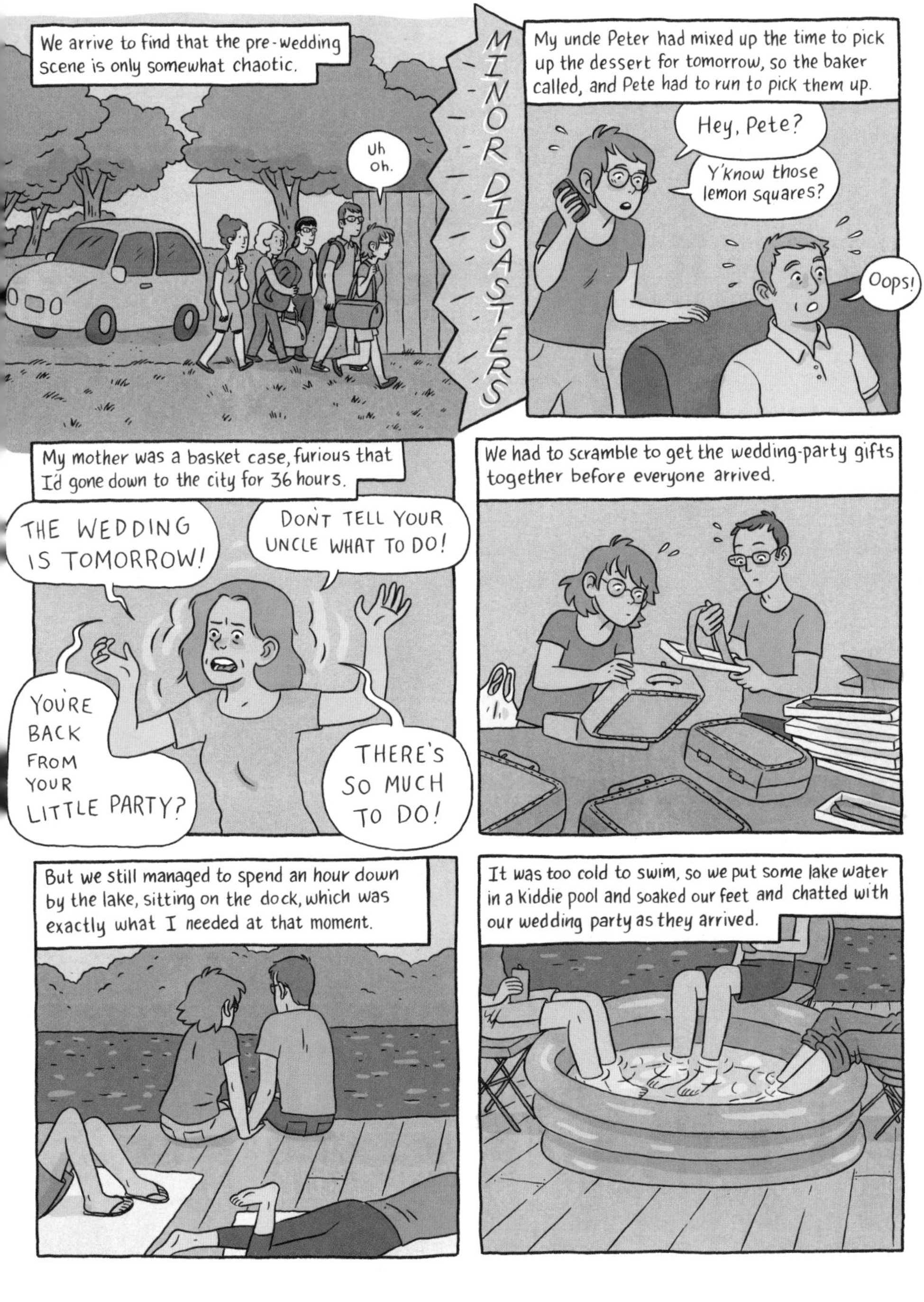
We arrive to find that the pre-wedding scene is only somewhat chaotic.
Uh oh.
MINOR DISASTERS
My uncle Peter had mixed up the time to pick up the dessert for tomorrow, so the baker called, and Pete had to run to pick them up.
Hey, Pete?
Y'know those lemon squares?
Oops!
My mother was a basket case, furious that I'd gone down to the city for 36 hours.
THE WEDDING IS TOMORROW!
DON'T TELL YOUR UNCLE WHAT TO DO!
YOU'RE BACK FROM YOUR LITTLE PARTY?
THERE'S SO MUCH TO DO!
We had to scramble to get the wedding-party gifts together before everyone arrived.
But we still managed to spend an hour down by the lake, sitting on the dock, which was exactly what I needed at that moment.
It was too cold to swim, so we put some lake water in a kiddie pool and soaked our feet and chatted with our wedding party as they arrived.

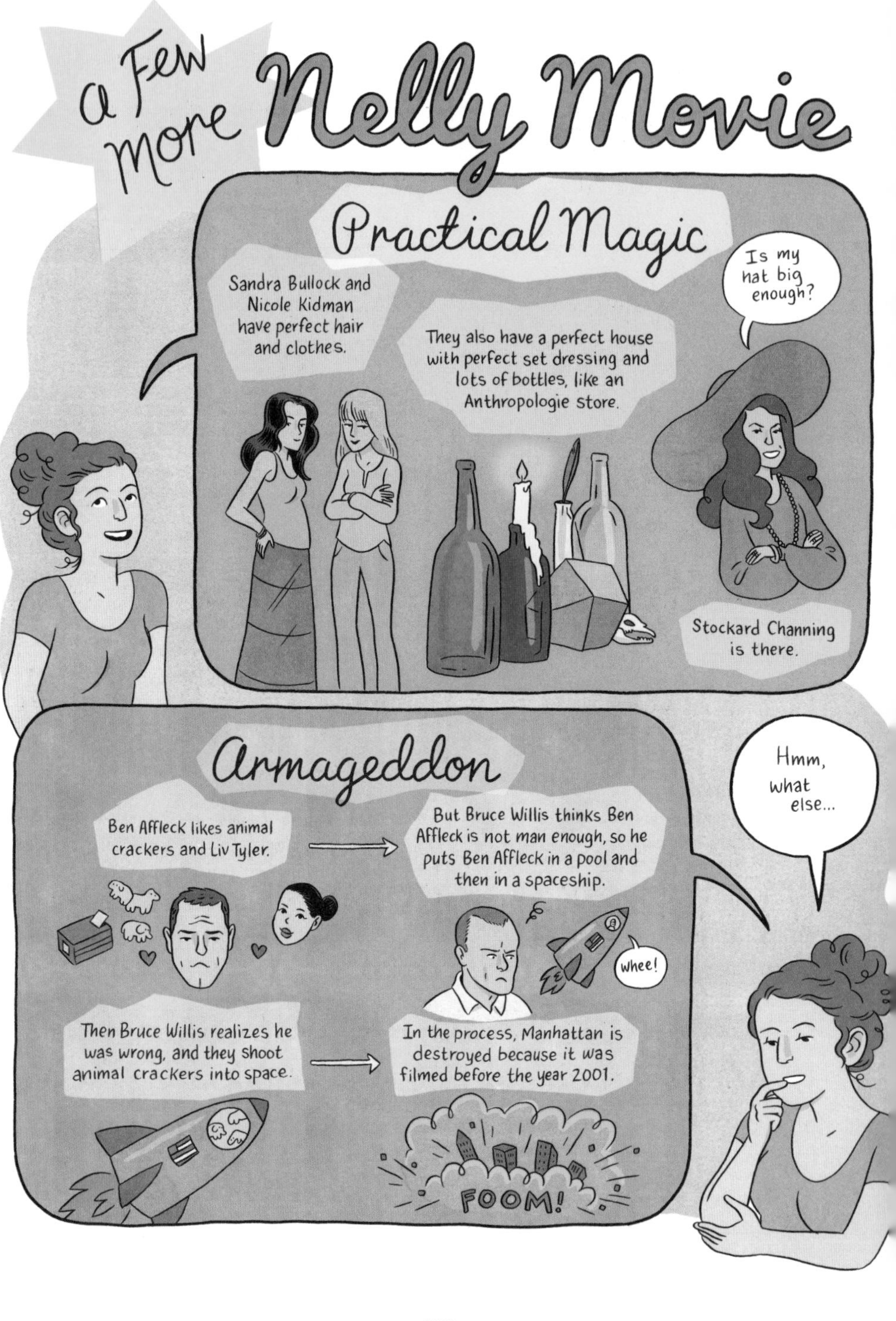
a Few more Nelly Movie
Practical Magic
Sandra Bullock and Nicole Kidman have perfect hair and clothes.
They also have a perfect house with perfect set dressing and lots of bottles, like an Anthropologie store.
Is my hat big enough?
Stockard Channing is there.
Armageddon
Ben Affleck likes animal crackers and Liv Tyler.
But Bruce Willis thinks Ben Affleck is not man enough, so he puts Ben Affleck in a pool and then in a spaceship.
whee!
Hmm, what else...
Then Bruce Willis realizes he was wrong, and they shoot animal crackers into space.
In the process, Manhattan is destroyed because it was filmed before the year 2001.
FOOM!

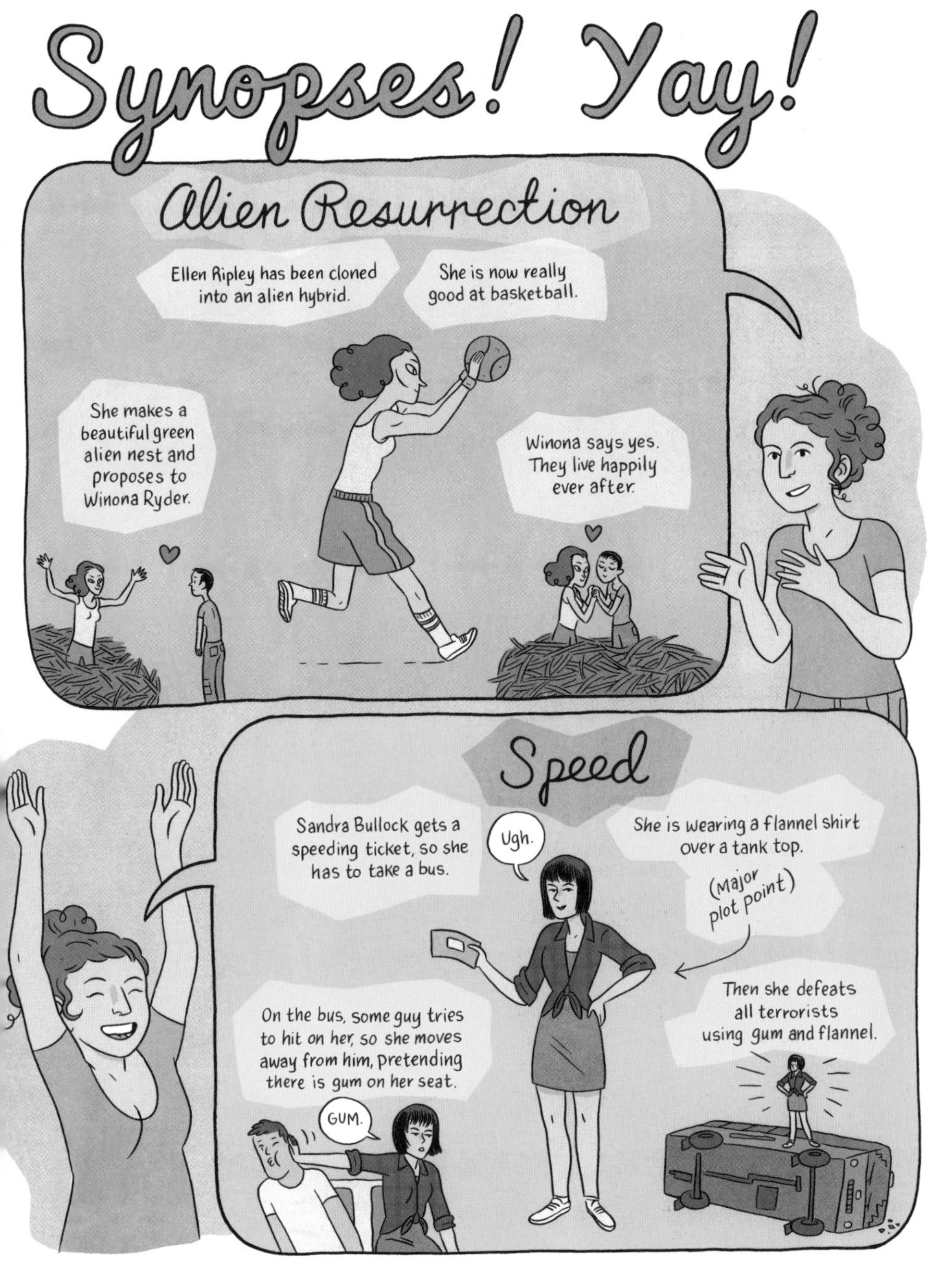
Synopses! Yay!
Alien Resurrection
Ellen Ripley has been cloned into an alien hybrid.
She is now really good at basketball.
She makes a beautiful green alien nest and proposes to Winona Ryder.
Winona says yes. They live happily ever after.
Speed
Sandra Bullock gets a speeding ticket, so she has to take a bus.
Ugh.
She is wearing a flannel shirt over a tank top.
(Major plot point)
On the bus, some guy tries to hit on her, so she moves away from him, pretending there is gum on her seat.
GUM.
Then she defeats all terrorists using gum and flannel.

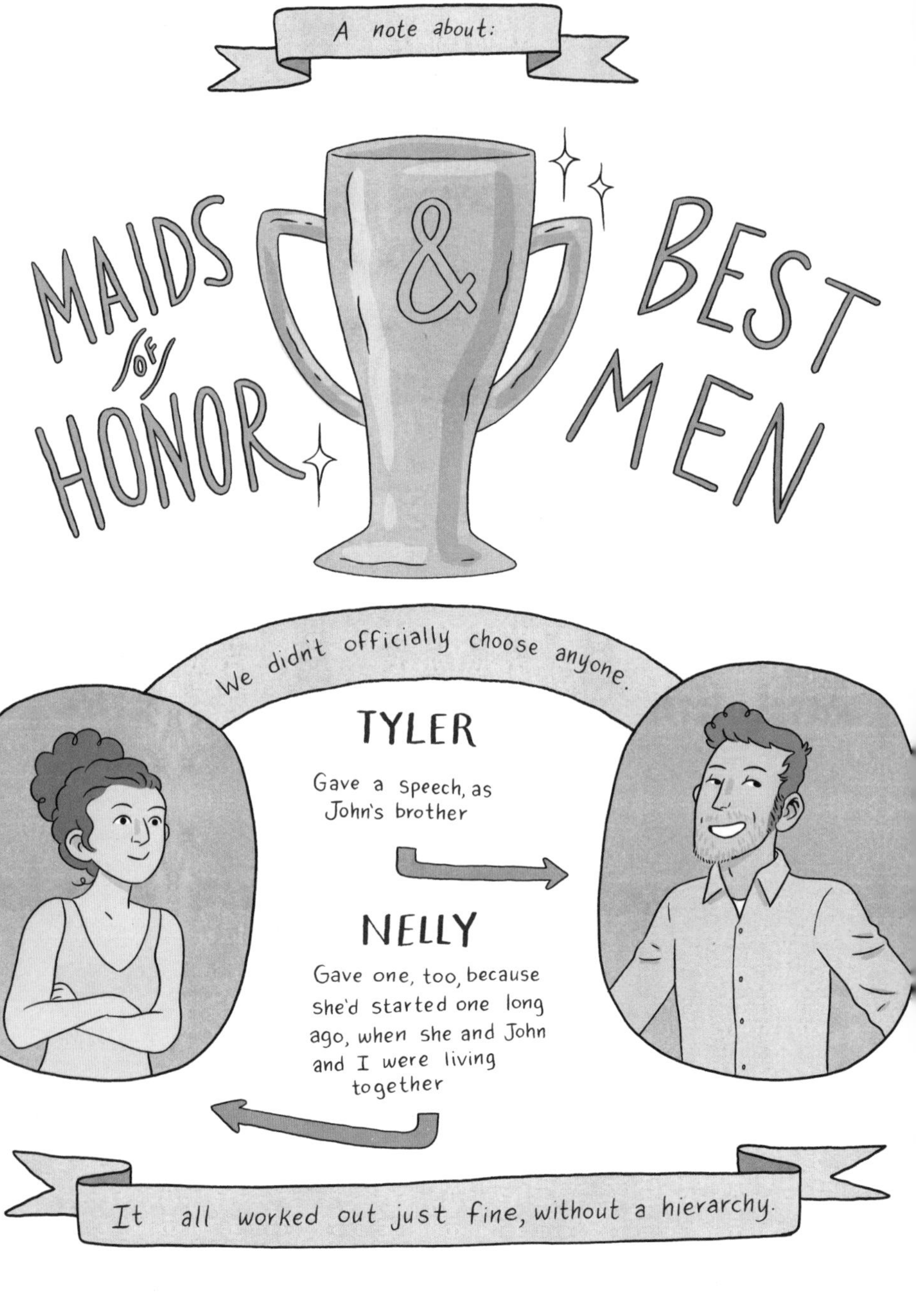
A note about:
MAIDS of HONOR & BEST MEN
We didn't officially choose anyone.
TYLER
Gave a speech, as John's brother
NELLY
Gave one, too, because she'd started one long ago, when she and John and I were living together
It all worked out just fine, without a hierarchy.

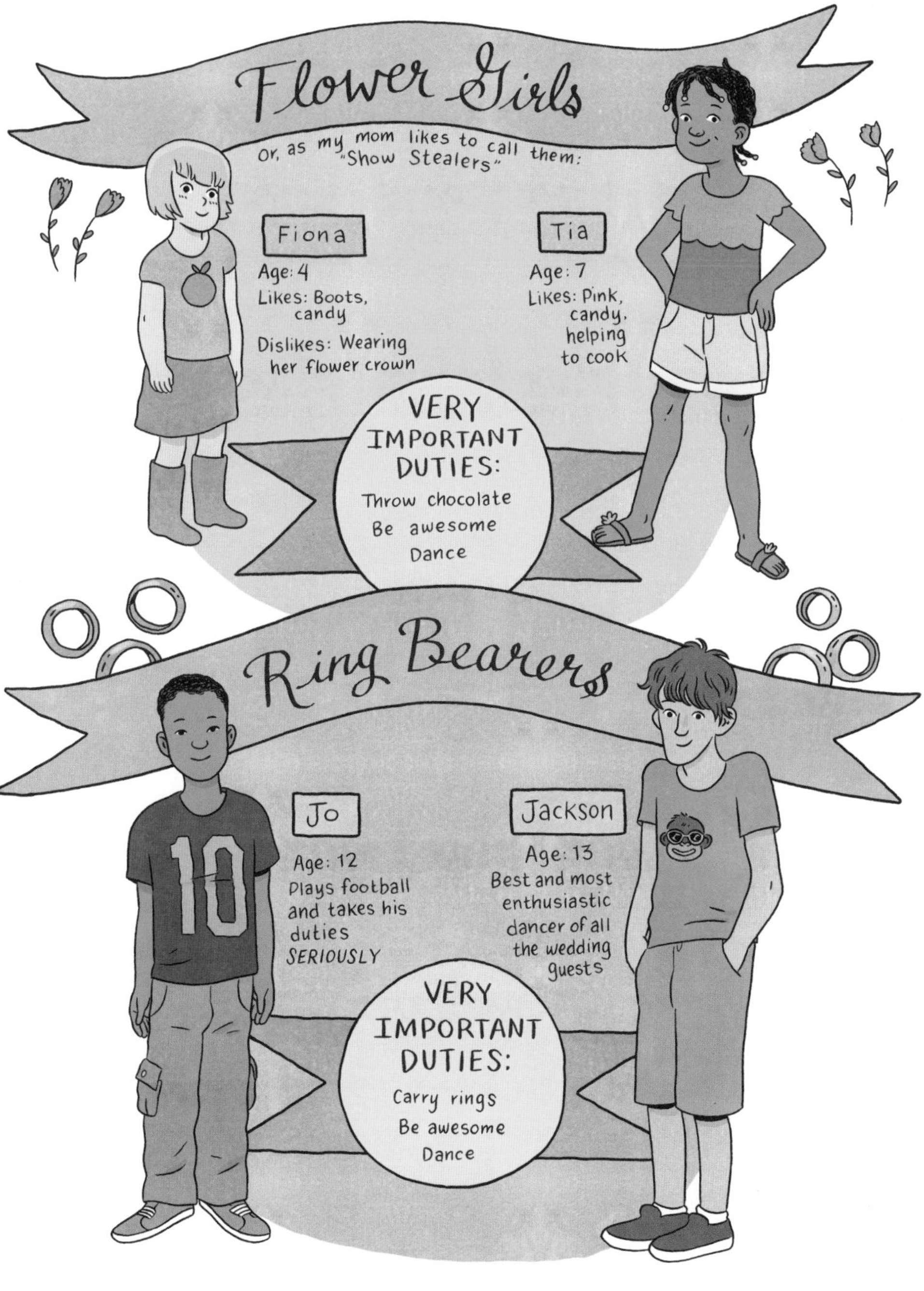
Flower Girls
Or, as my mom likes to call them: "Show Stealers"
Fiona
Age: 4
Likes: Boots, candy
Dislikes: Wearing her flower crown
Tia
Age: 7
Likes: Pink, candy, helping to cook
VERY IMPORTANT DUTIES:
Throw chocolate
Be awesome
Dance
Ring Bearers
Jo
Age: 12
Plays football and takes his duties SERIOUSLY
Jackson
Age: 13
Best and most enthusiastic dancer of all the wedding guests
VERY IMPORTANT DUTIES:
Carry rings
Be awesome
Dance

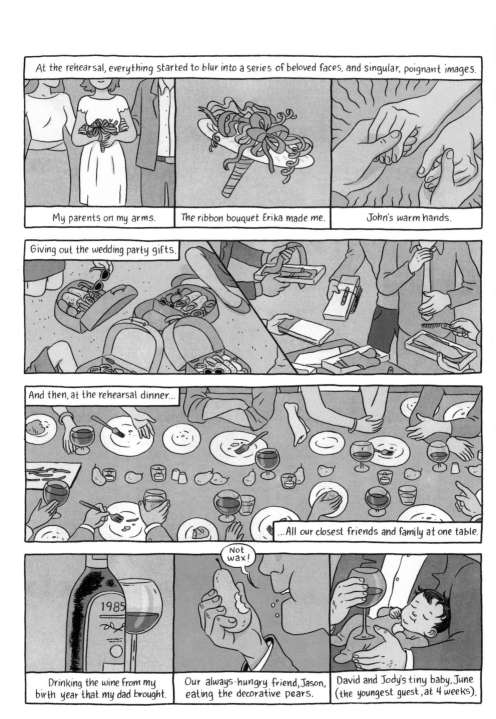

At the rehearsal, everything started to blur into a series of beloved faces, and singular, poignant images.

My parents on my arms.

The ribbon bouquet Erika made me.

John's warm hands.

Giving out the wedding party gifts.

And then, at the rehearsal dinner...

...All our closest friends and family at one table.

Not wax!

Drinking the wine from my birth year that my dad brought.

Our always-hungry friend, Jason, eating the decorative pears.

David and Jody's tiny baby, June (the youngest guest, at 4 weeks).

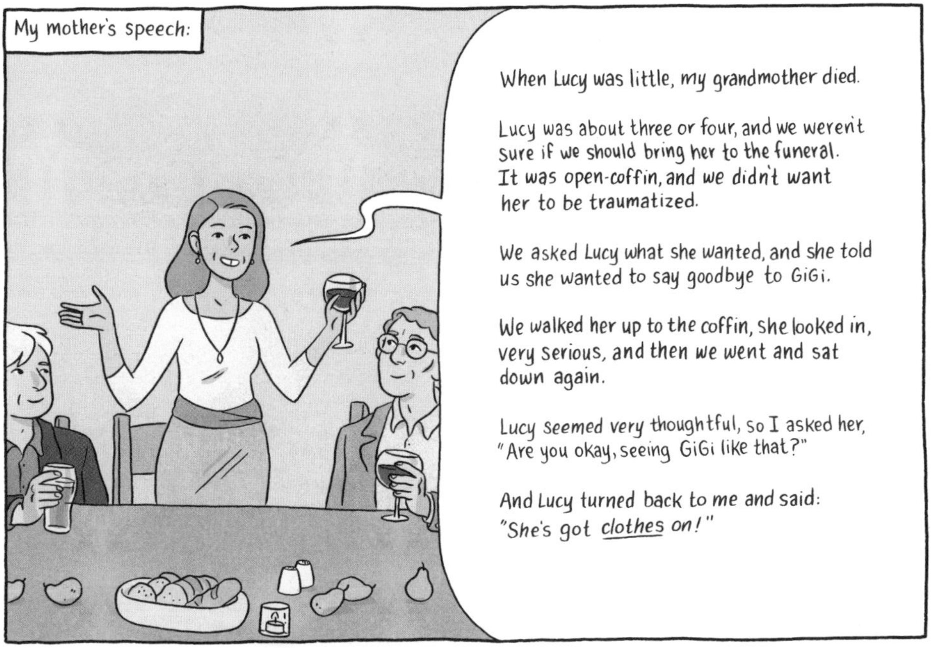
My mother's speech:
When Lucy was little, my grandmother died.
Lucy was about three or four, and we weren't sure if we should bring her to the funeral. It was open-coffin, and we didn't want her to be traumatized.
We asked Lucy what she wanted, and she told us she wanted to say goodbye to GiGi.
We walked her up to the coffin, she looked in, very serious, and then we went and sat down again.
Lucy seemed very thoughtful, so I asked her, "Are you okay, seeing GiGi like that?"
And Lucy turned back to me and said: "She's got clothes on!"

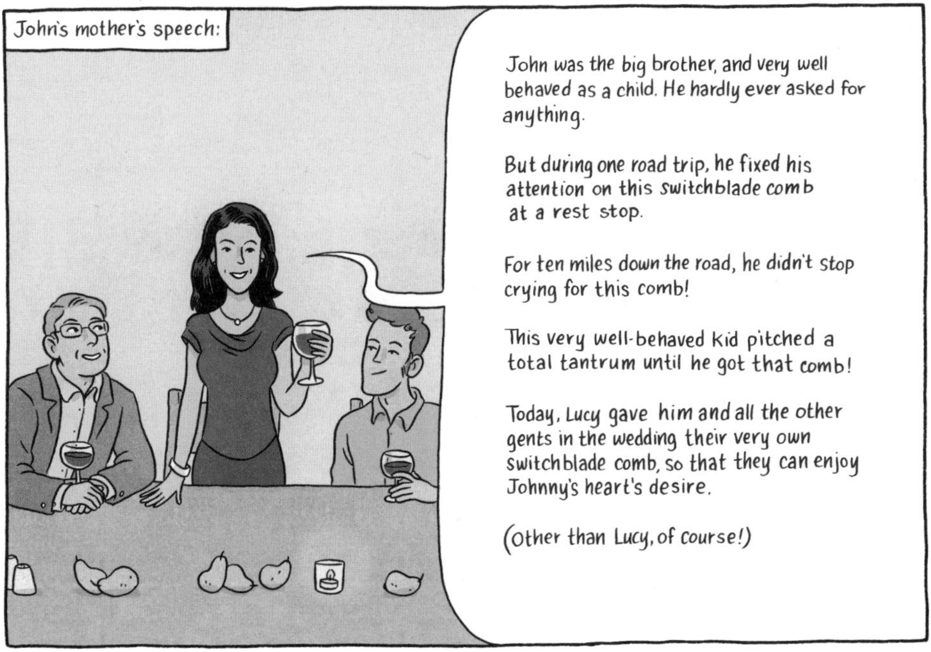
John's mother's speech:
John was the big brother, and very well behaved as a child. He hardly ever asked for anything.
But during one road trip, he fixed his attention on this switchblade comb at a rest stop.
For ten miles down the road, he didn't stop crying for this comb!
This very well-behaved kid pitched a total tantrum until he got that comb!
Today, Lucy gave him and all the other gents in the wedding their very own switchblade comb, so that they can enjoy Johnny's heart's desire.
(Other than Lucy, of course!)

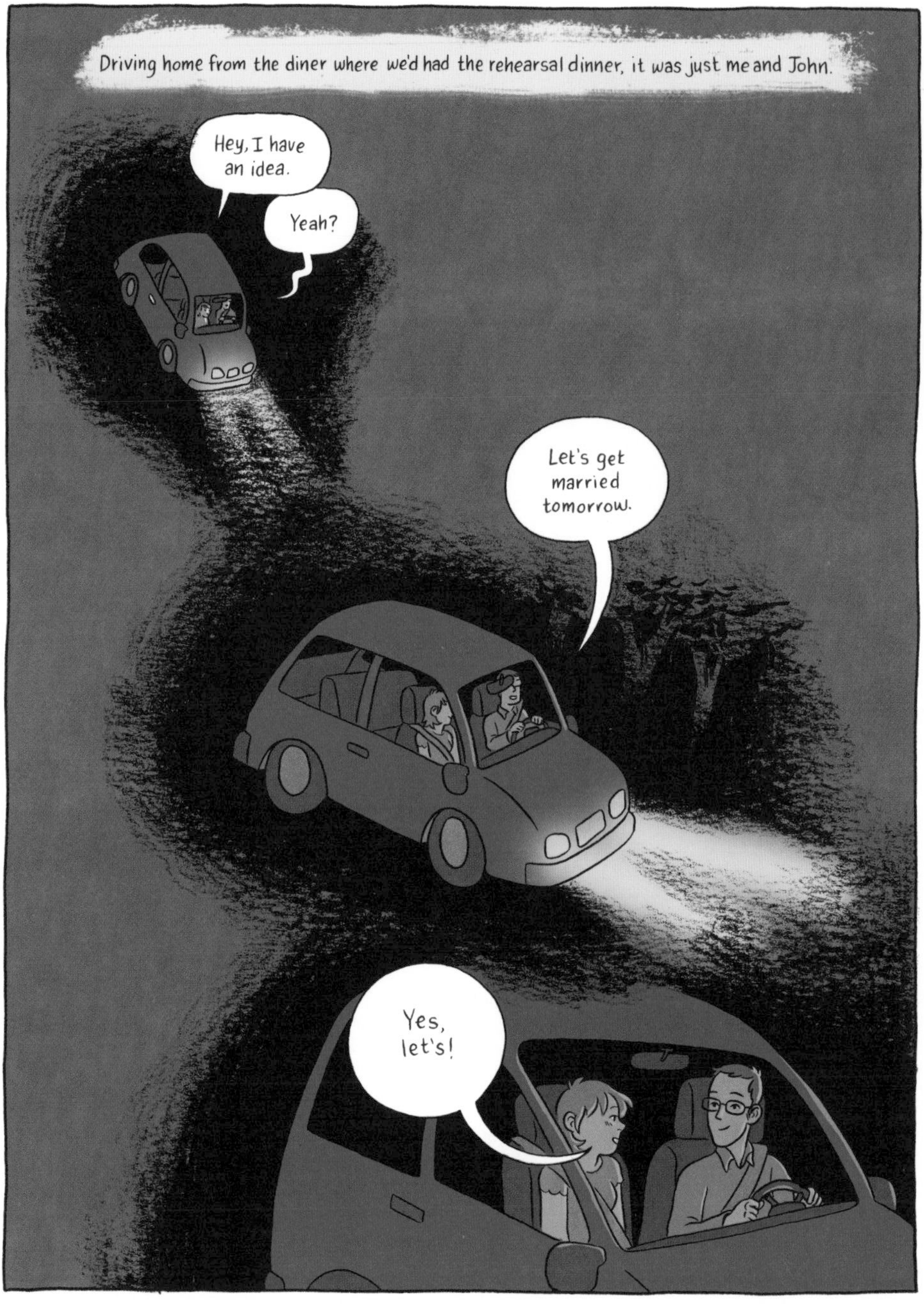
Driving home from the diner where we'd had the rehearsal dinner, it was just me and John.
Hey, I have an idea.
Yeah?
Let's get married tomorrow.
Yes, let's!

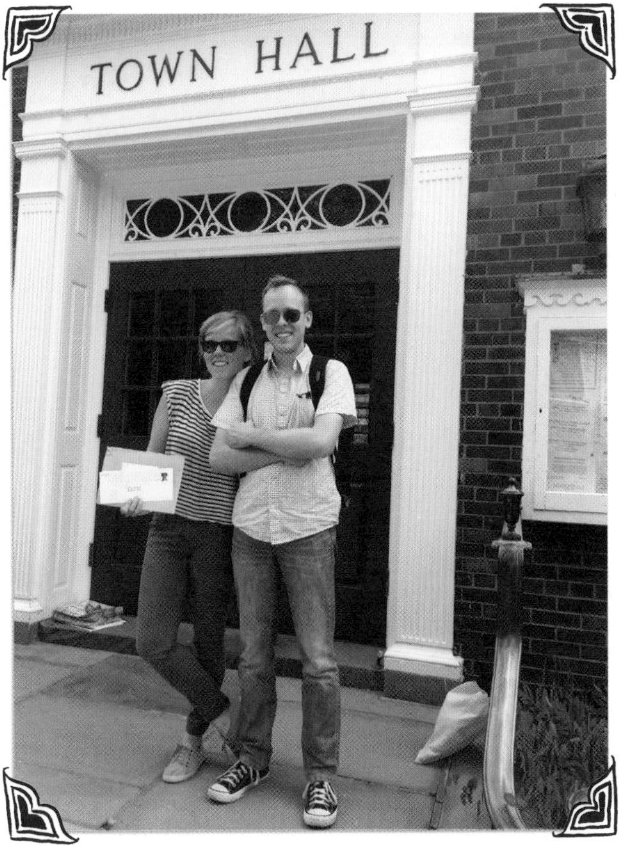
TOWN HALL

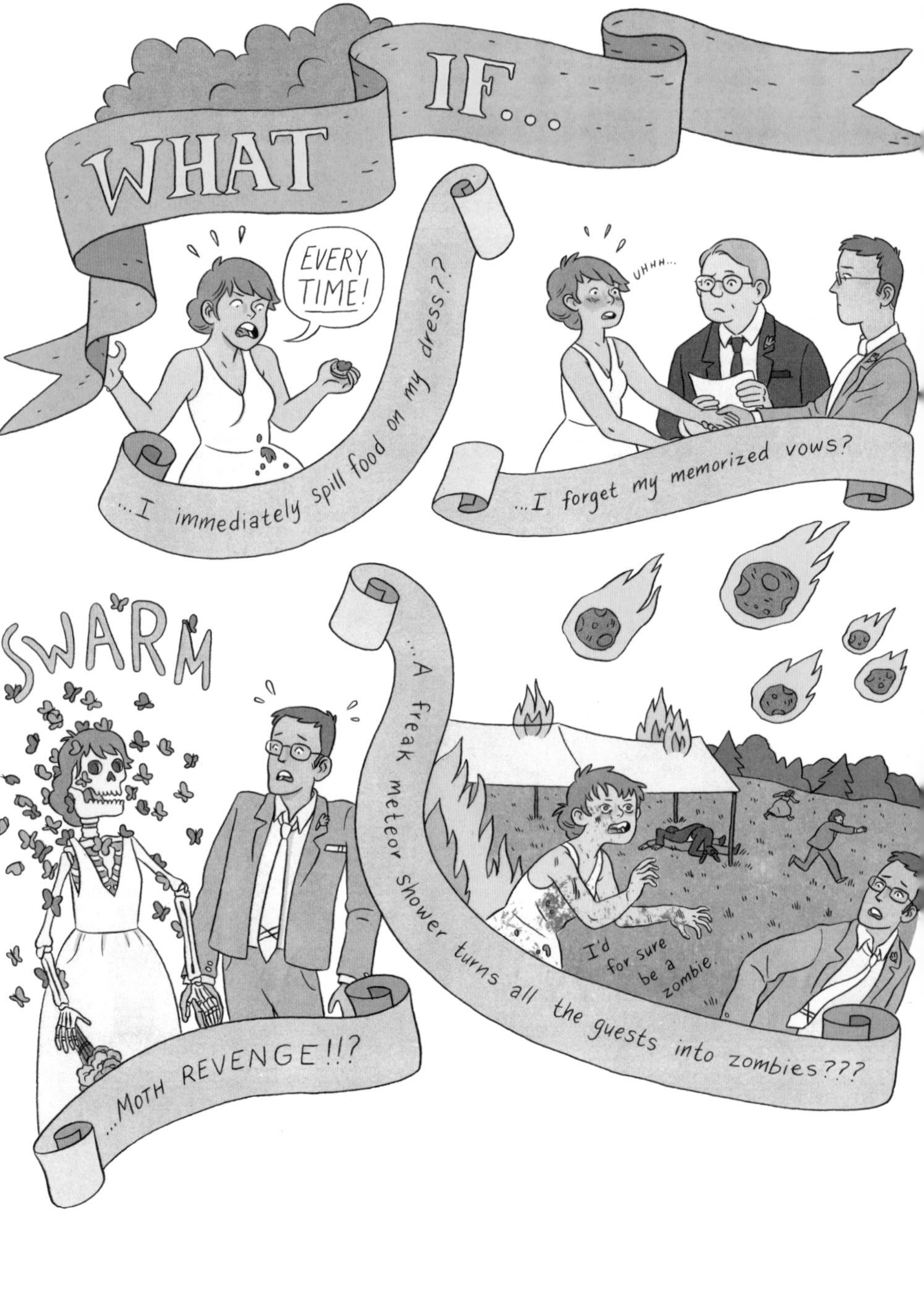
WHAT IF...
EVERY TIME!
...I immediately spill food on my dress??
UHHH...
...I forget my memorized vows?
SWARM
...MOTH REVENGE!!?
...A freak meteor shower turns all the guests into zombies???
I'd for sure be a zombie.

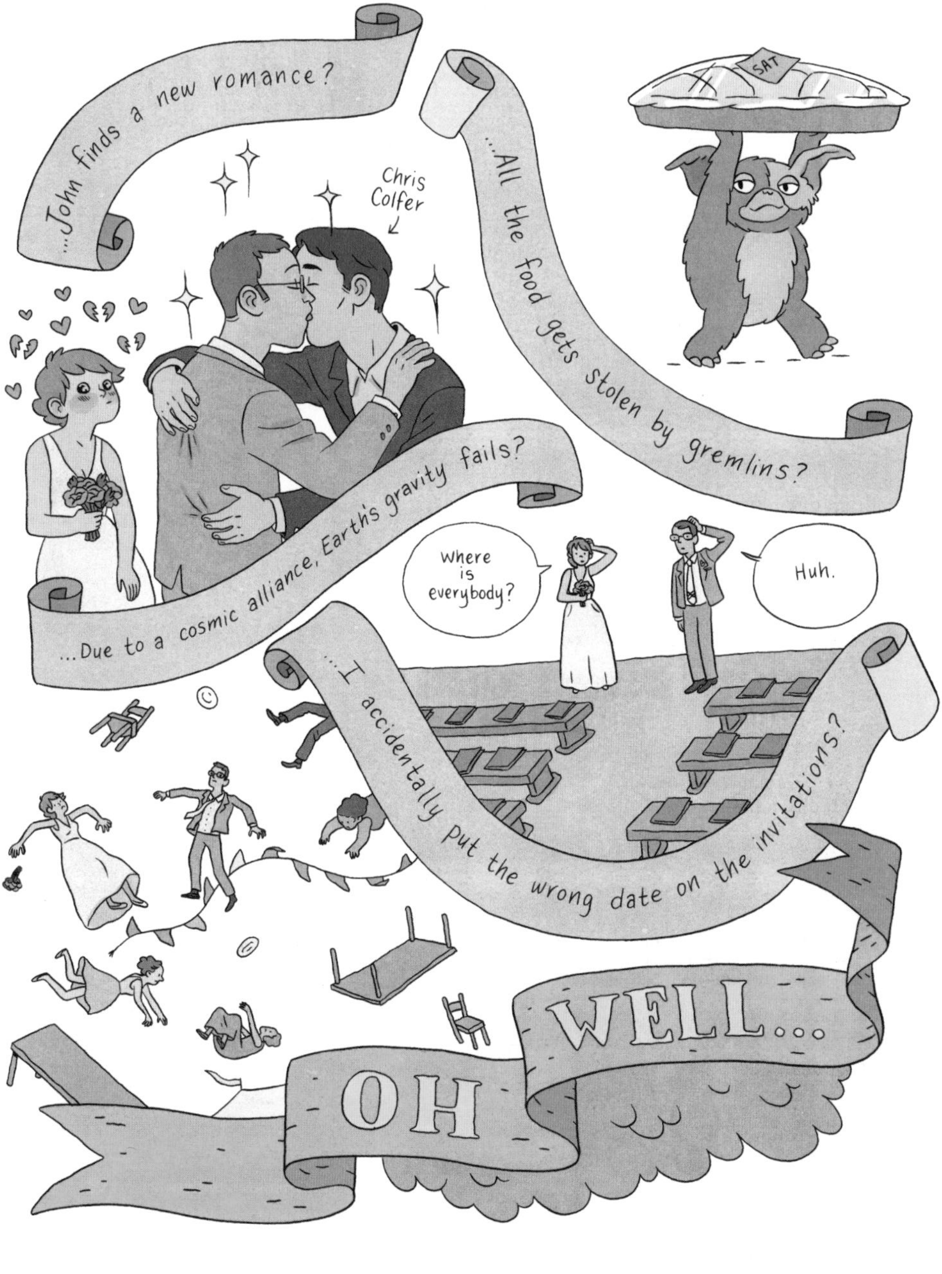

...John finds a new romance?
Chris Colfer
...All the food gets stolen by gremlins?
SAT
...Due to a cosmic alliance, Earth's gravity fails?
Where is everybody?
Huh.
...I accidentally put the wrong date on the invitations?
OH WELL...

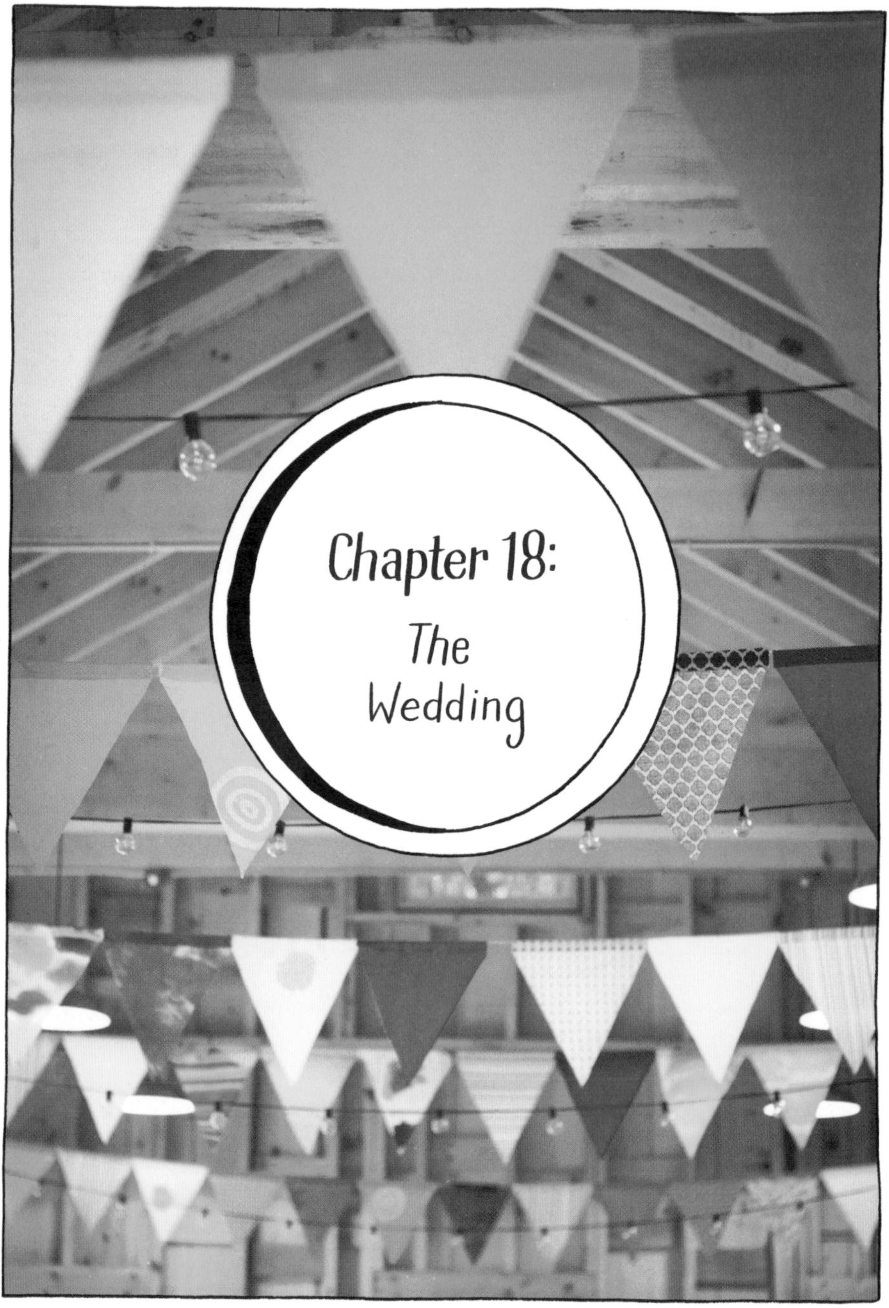
Chapter 18:
The Wedding

There are two main reasons why rain is considered good luck on a wedding day:

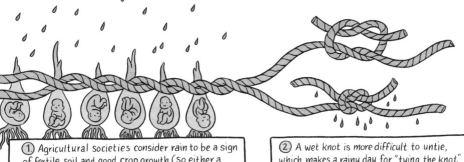

① Agricultural societies consider rain to be a sign of fertile soil and good crop growth (so either a literal good harvest, or a harvest of babies).

② A wet knot is more difficult to untie, which makes a rainy day for "tying the knot" more auspicious for a lasting marriage.

But I mainly think it was dreamed up to reassure a newly wakened bride who is staring out the window and watching everything at her wedding get slowly drenched and muddy.

WAKE UP, WEDDING PEOPLE! Look who's in the New York Times!

Wow!

Our eyes must've been level enough to pass the test!

Lucy Knisley and John Horstman

Georg

That's right. Couple of level-eyed folks right here.

Dad calling from town to congratulate us on being sufficiently level.

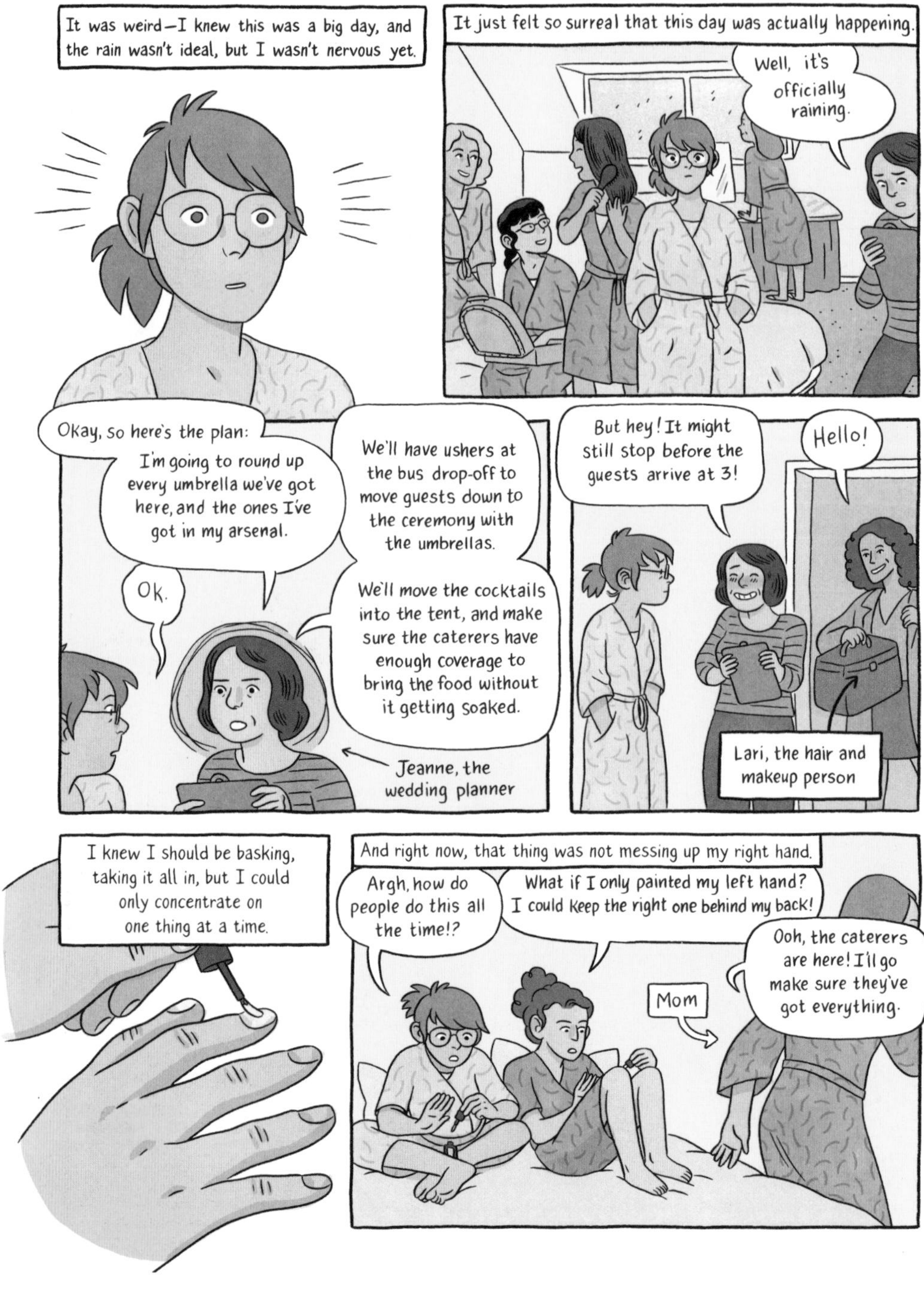

It was weird—I knew this was a big day, and the rain wasn't ideal, but I wasn't nervous yet.
It just felt so surreal that this day was actually happening.
Well, it's officially raining.
Okay, so here's the plan:
I'm going to round up every umbrella we've got here, and the ones I've got in my arsenal.
We'll have ushers at the bus drop-off to move guests down to the ceremony with the umbrellas.
Ok.
We'll move the cocktails into the tent, and make sure the caterers have enough coverage to bring the food without it getting soaked.
Jeanne, the wedding planner
But hey! It might still stop before the guests arrive at 3!
Hello!
Lari, the hair and makeup person
I knew I should be basking, taking it all in, but I could only concentrate on one thing at a time.
And right now, that thing was not messing up my right hand.
Argh, how do people do this all the time!?
What if I only painted my left hand? I could keep the right one behind my back!
Ooh, the caterers are here! I'll go make sure they've got everything.
Mom

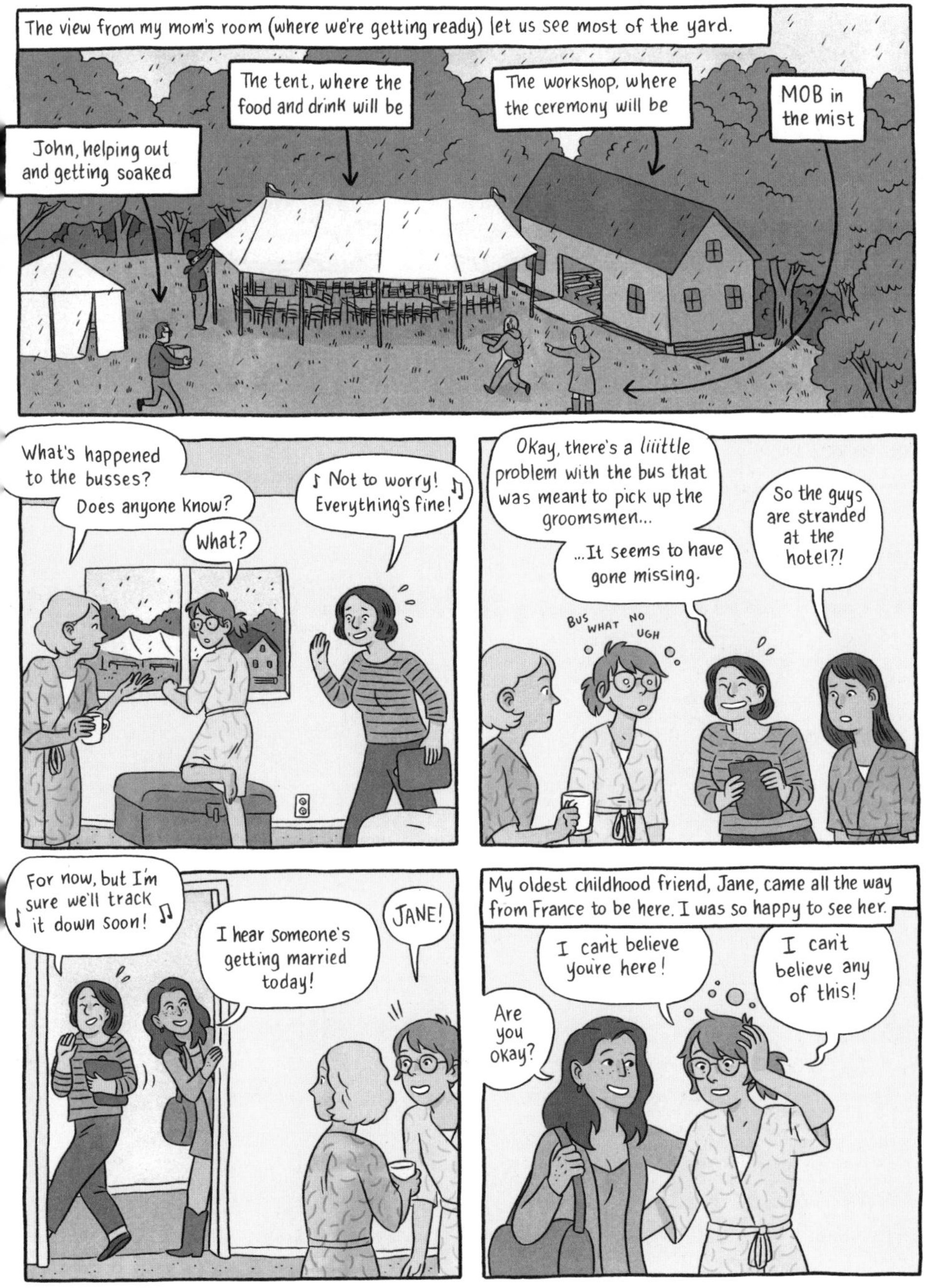
The view from my mom's room (where we're getting ready) let us see most of the yard.
John, helping out and getting soaked
The tent, where the food and drink will be
The workshop, where the ceremony will be
MOB in the mist
What's happened to the busses?
Does anyone know?
What?
♪ Not to worry! Everything's fine! ♫
Okay, there's a liiittle problem with the bus that was meant to pick up the groomsmen...
...It seems to have gone missing.
BUS WHAT NO UGH
So the guys are stranded at the hotel?!
For now, but I'm sure we'll track it down soon! ♫
I hear someone's getting married today!
JANE!
My oldest childhood friend, Jane, came all the way from France to be here. I was so happy to see her.
Are you okay?
I can't believe you're here!
I can't believe any of this!

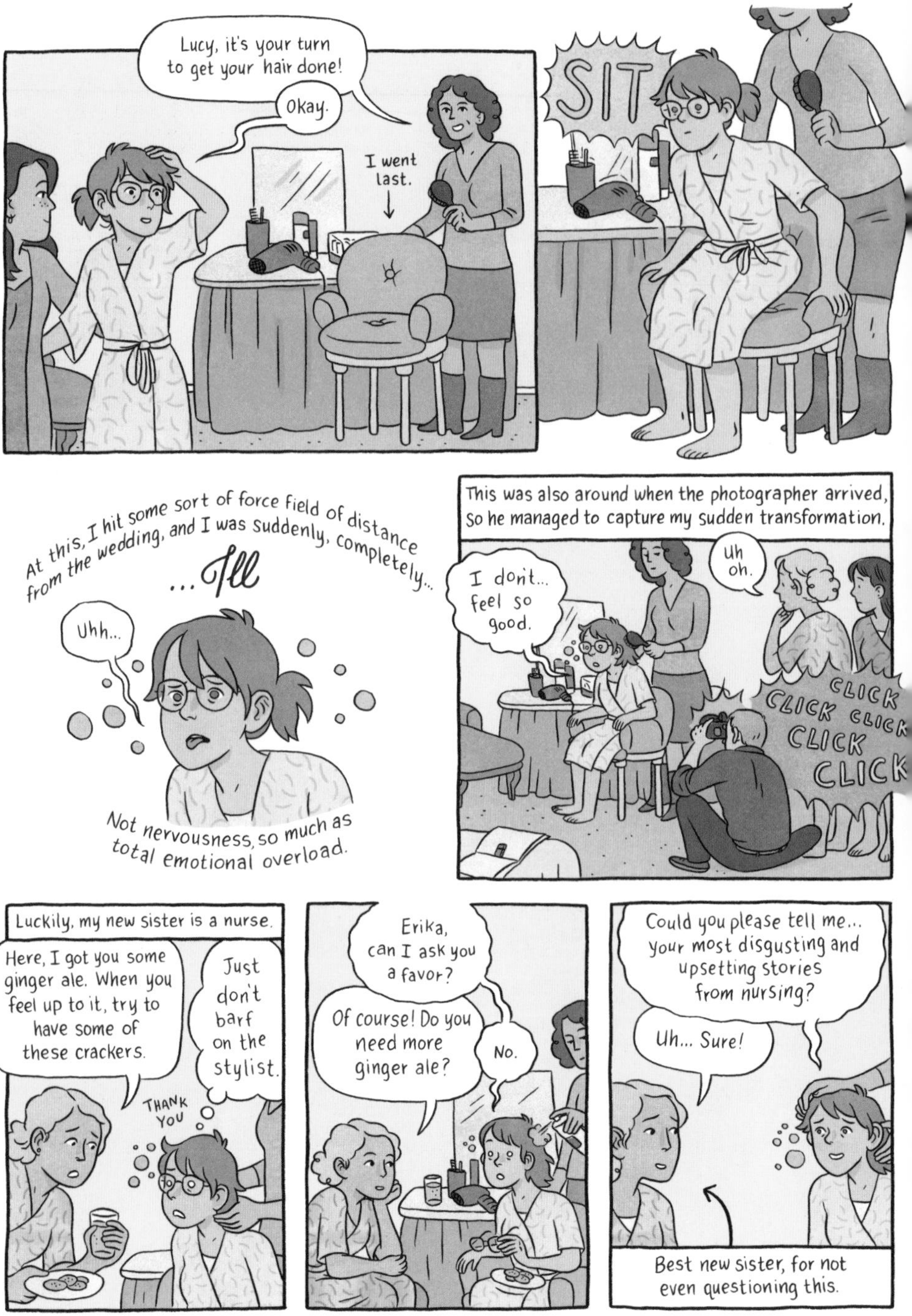

Lucy, it's your turn to get your hair done!
Okay.
I went last.
SIT
At this, I hit some sort of force field of distance from the wedding, and I was suddenly, completely...
...Ill
Uhh...
Not nervousness, so much as total emotional overload.
This was also around when the photographer arrived, so he managed to capture my sudden transformation.
I don't... feel so good.
Uh oh.
CLICK CLICK CLICK CLICK CLICK
Luckily, my new sister is a nurse.
Here, I got you some ginger ale. When you feel up to it, try to have some of these crackers.
Just don't barf on the stylist.
THANK YOU
Erika, can I ask you a favor?
Of course! Do you need more ginger ale?
No.
Could you please tell me... your most disgusting and upsetting stories from nursing?
Uh... Sure!
Best new sister, for not even questioning this.

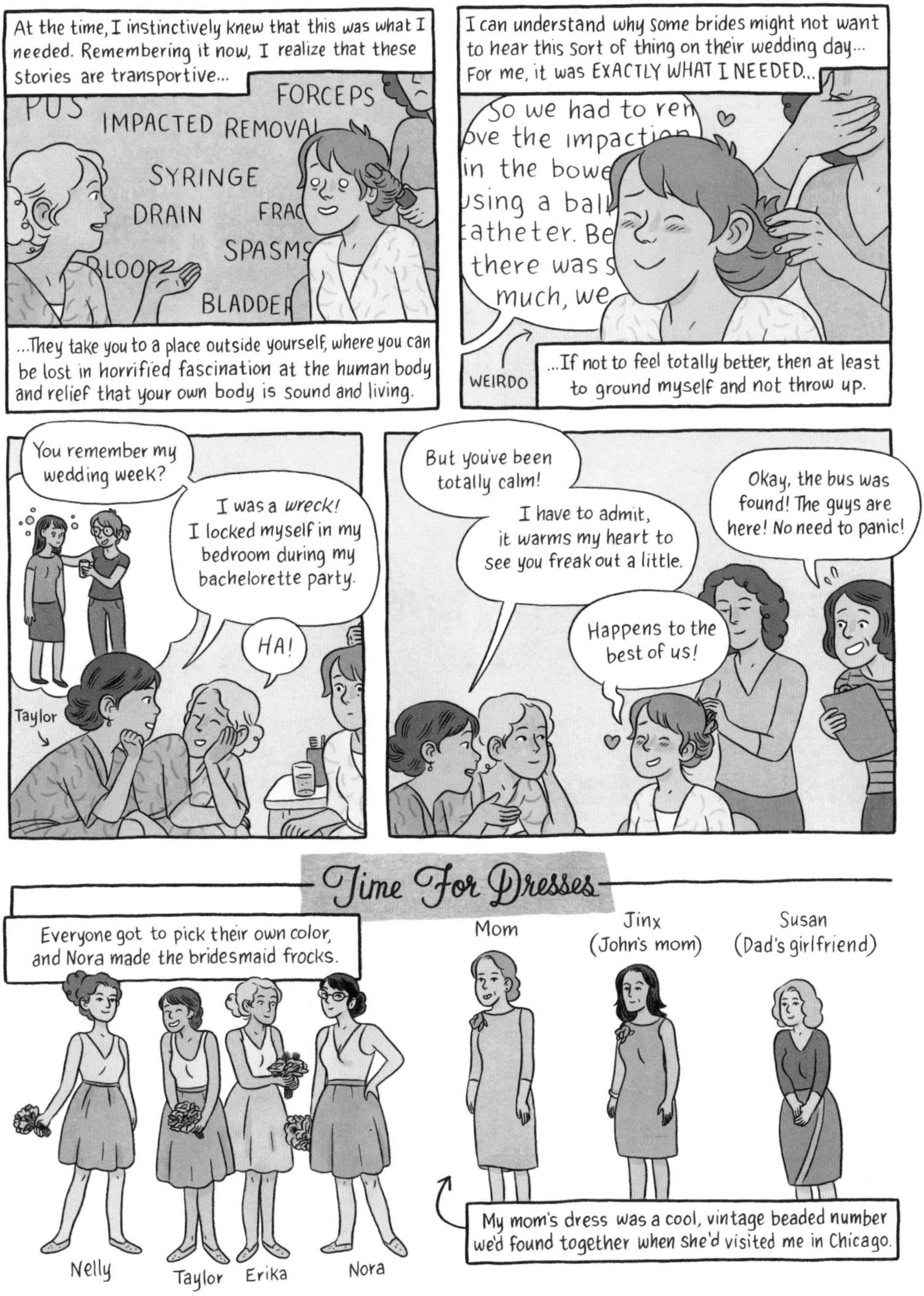
At the time, I instinctively knew that this was what I needed. Remembering it now, I realize that these stories are transportive...
PUS
FORCEPS
IMPACTED REMOVAL
SYRINGE
DRAIN
FRAC
SPASMS
BLOOD
BLADDER
...They take you to a place outside yourself, where you can be lost in horrified fascination at the human body and relief that your own body is sound and living.
I can understand why some brides might not want to hear this sort of thing on their wedding day... For me, it was EXACTLY WHAT I NEEDED...
So we had to re ove the impacti in the bowe using a ball atheter. Be there was s much, we
WEIRDO
...If not to feel totally better, then at least to ground myself and not throw up.
You remember my wedding week?
I was a *wreck!* I locked myself in my bedroom during my bachelorette party.
HA!
Taylor
But you've been totally calm!
I have to admit, it warms my heart to see you freak out a little.
Okay, the bus was found! The guys are here! No need to panic!
Happens to the best of us!
Time For Dresses
Everyone got to pick their own color, and Nora made the bridesmaid frocks.
Nelly
Taylor
Erika
Nora
Mom
Jinx (John's mom)
Susan (Dad's girlfriend)
My mom's dress was a cool, vintage beaded number we'd found together when she'd visited me in Chicago.

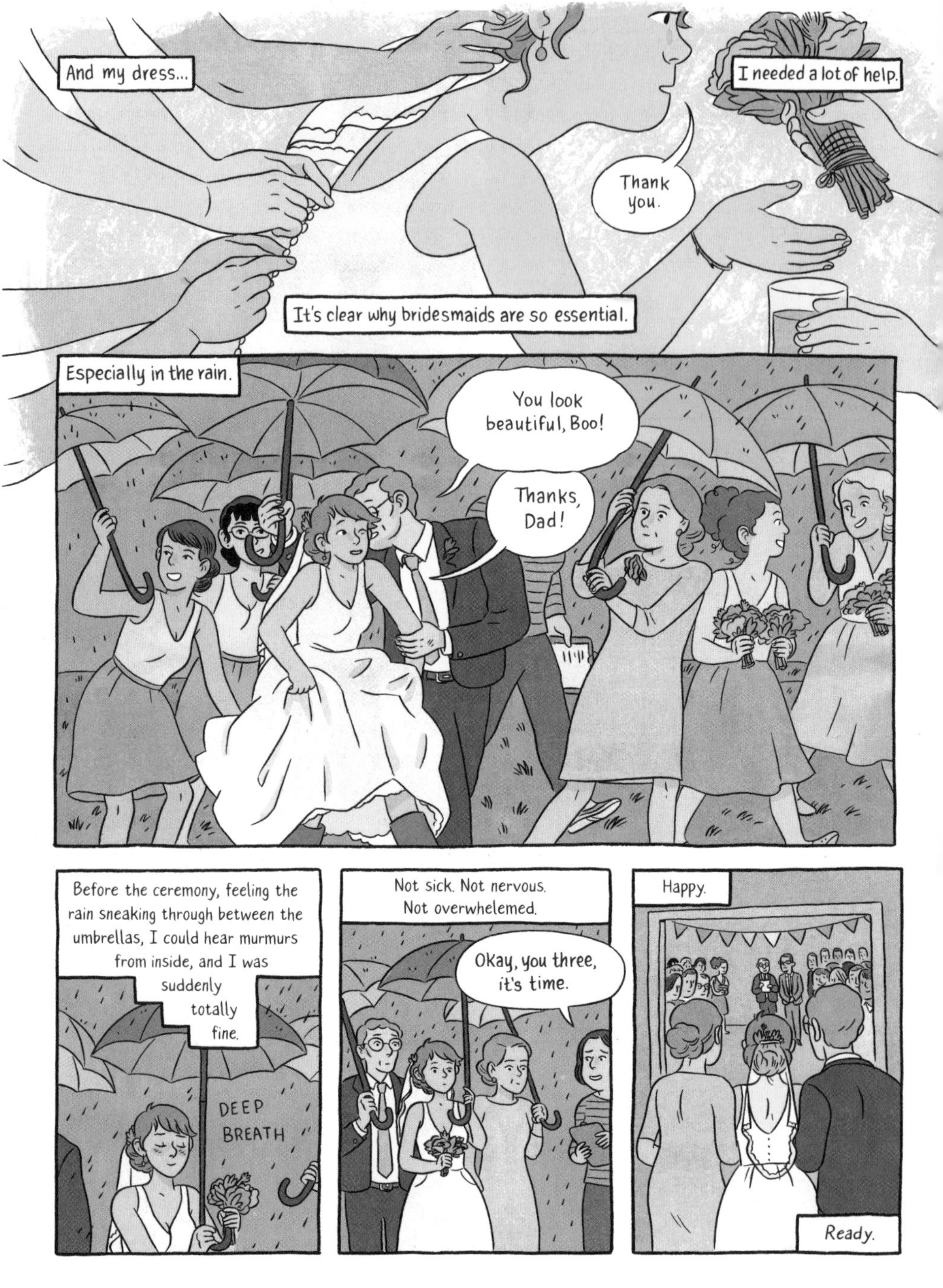
And my dress...
I needed a lot of help.
Thank you.
It's clear why bridesmaids are so essential.
Especially in the rain.
You look beautiful, Boo!
Thanks, Dad!
Before the ceremony, feeling the rain sneaking through between the umbrellas, I could hear murmurs from inside, and I was suddenly totally fine.
DEEP BREATH
Not sick. Not nervous. Not overwhelemed.
Okay, you three, it's time.
Happy.
Ready.

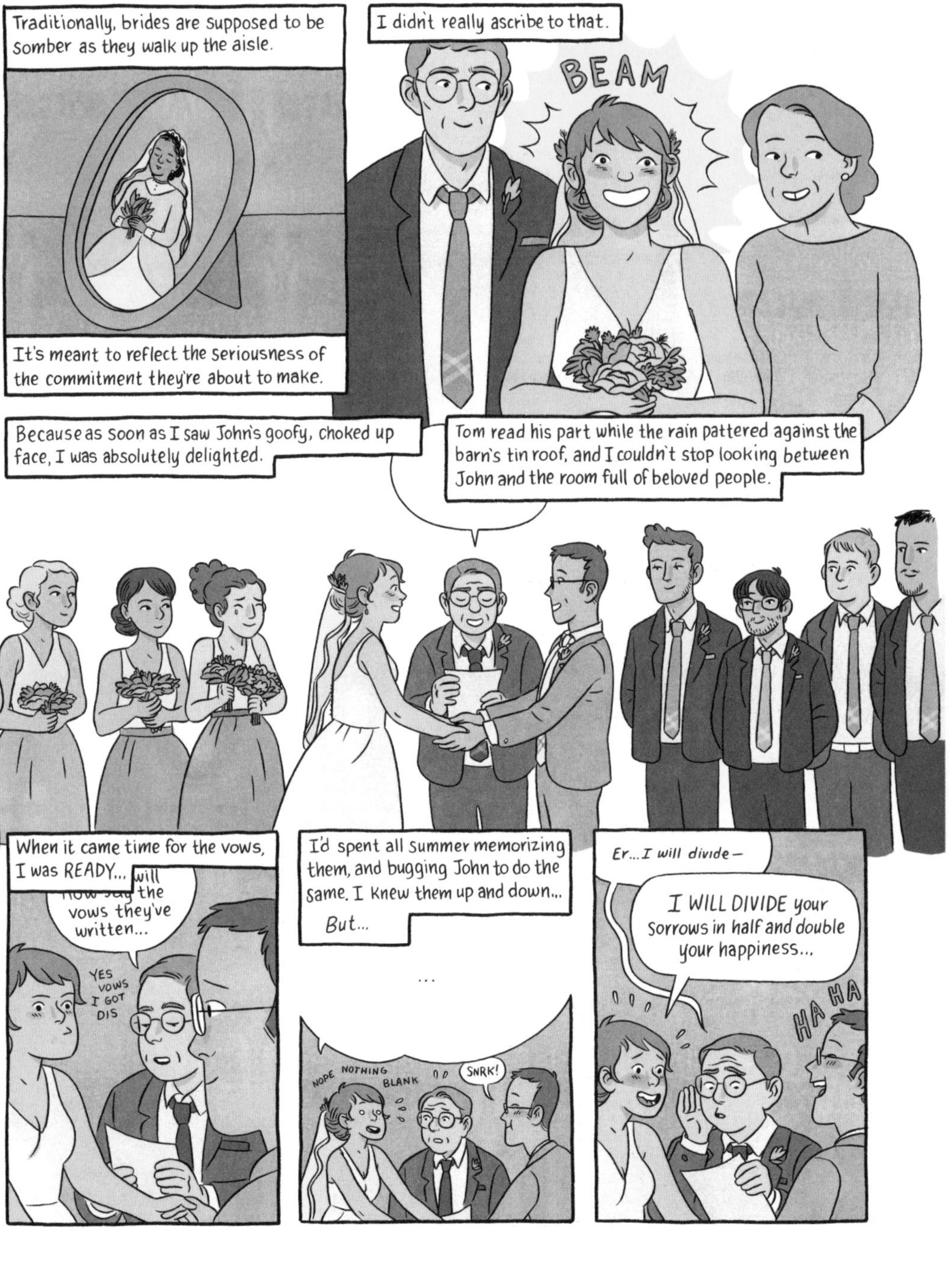

Traditionally, brides are supposed to be somber as they walk up the aisle.
It's meant to reflect the seriousness of the commitment they're about to make.
I didn't really ascribe to that.
BEAM
Because as soon as I saw John's goofy, choked up face, I was absolutely delighted.
Tom read his part while the rain pattered against the barn's tin roof, and I couldn't stop looking between John and the room full of beloved people.
When it came time for the vows, I was READY...
will
the vows they've written...
YES VOWS I GOT DIS
I'd spent all summer memorizing them, and bugging John to do the same. I knew them up and down...
But...
...
NOPE NOTHING BLANK
SNRK!
Er... I will divide –
I WILL DIVIDE your sorrows in half and double your happiness...
HA HA

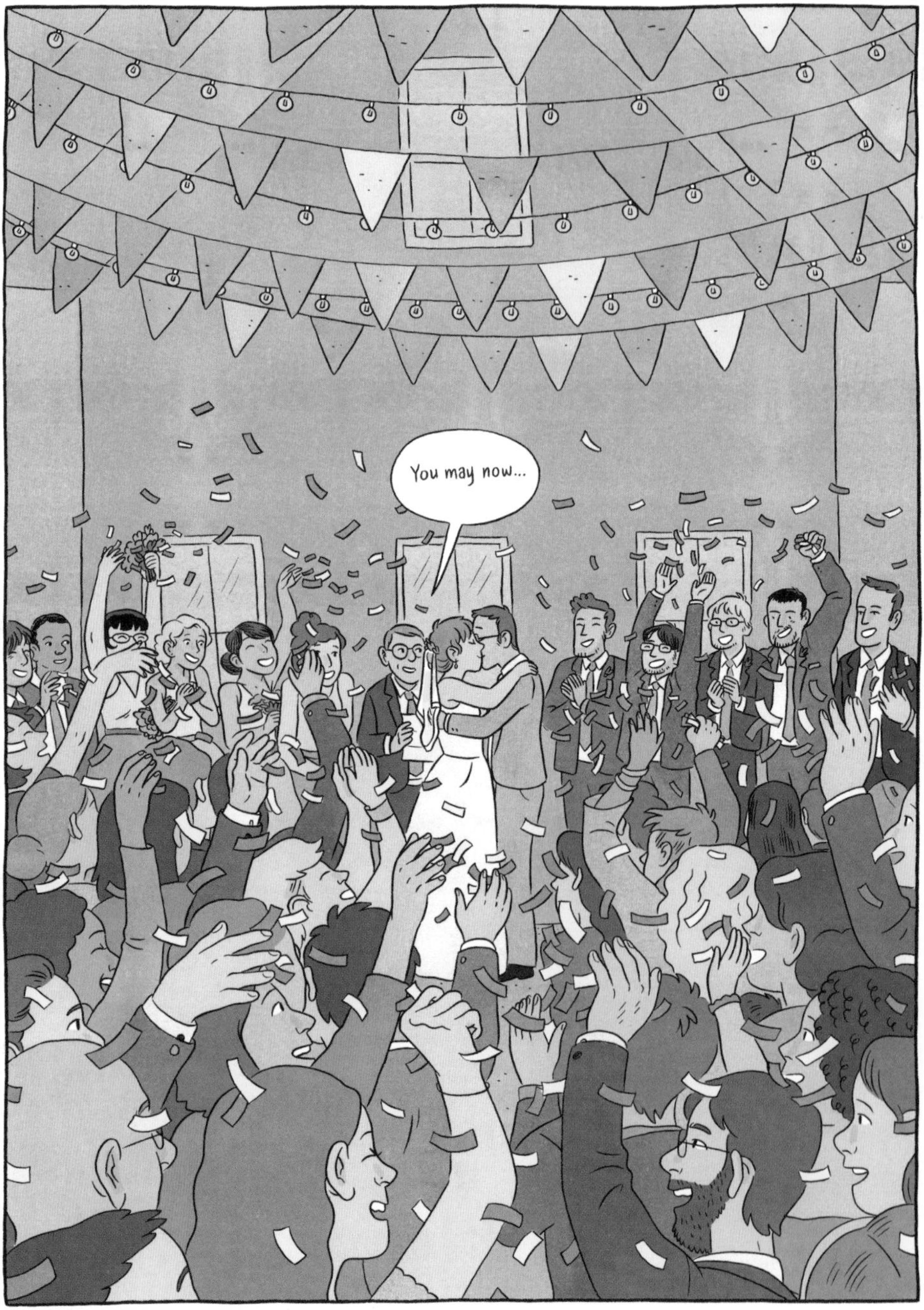
You may now...

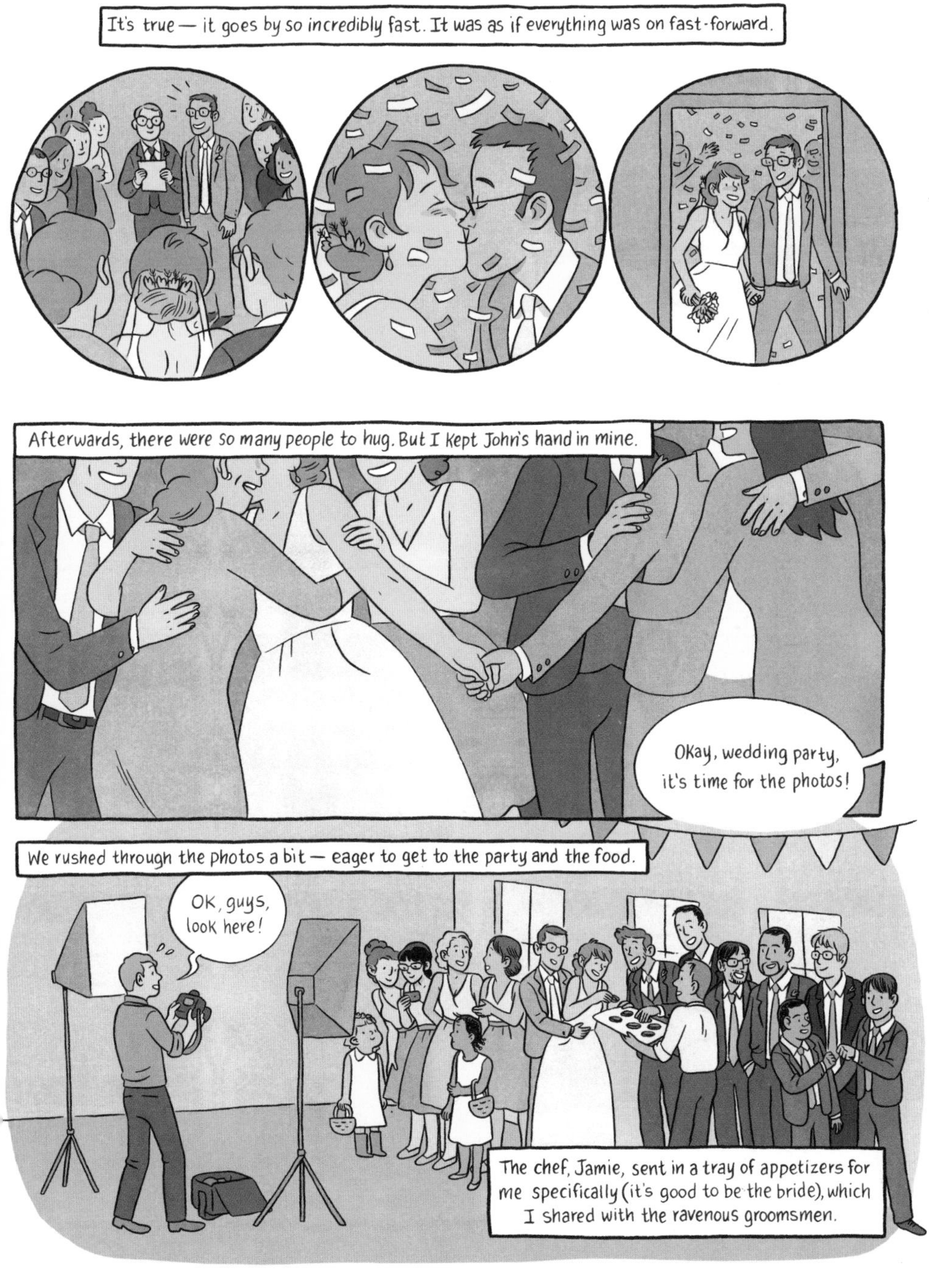
It's true — it goes by so incredibly fast. It was as if everything was on fast-forward.
Afterwards, there were so many people to hug. But I kept John's hand in mine.
Okay, wedding party, it's time for the photos!
We rushed through the photos a bit — eager to get to the party and the food.
OK, guys, look here!
The chef, Jamie, sent in a tray of appetizers for me specifically (it's good to be the bride), which I shared with the ravenous groomsmen.

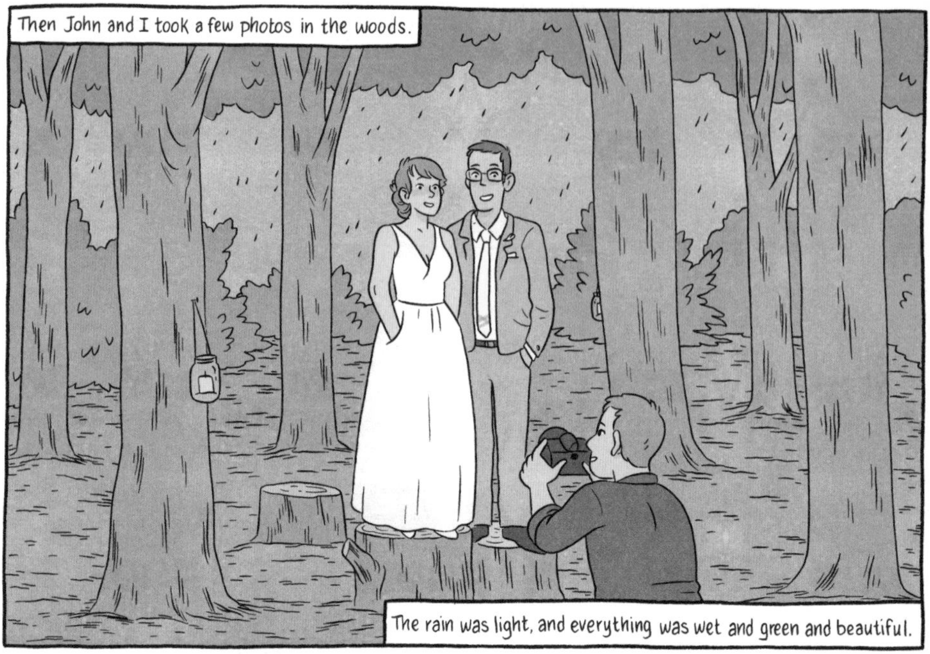
Then John and I took a few photos in the woods.
The rain was light, and everything was wet and green and beautiful.

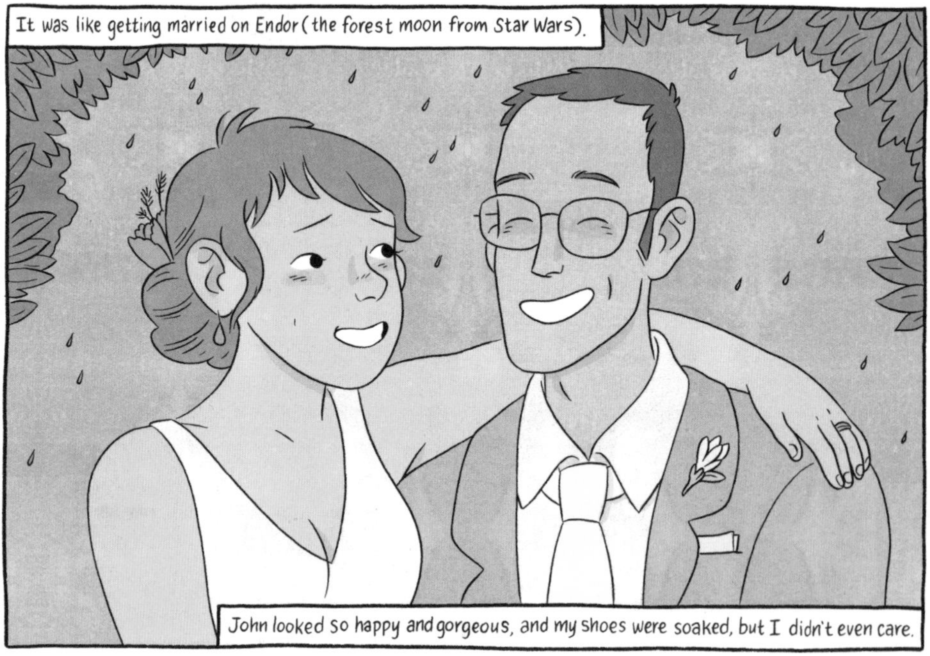
It was like getting married on Endor (the forest moon from Star Wars).
John looked so happy and gorgeous, and my shoes were soaked, but I didn't even care.

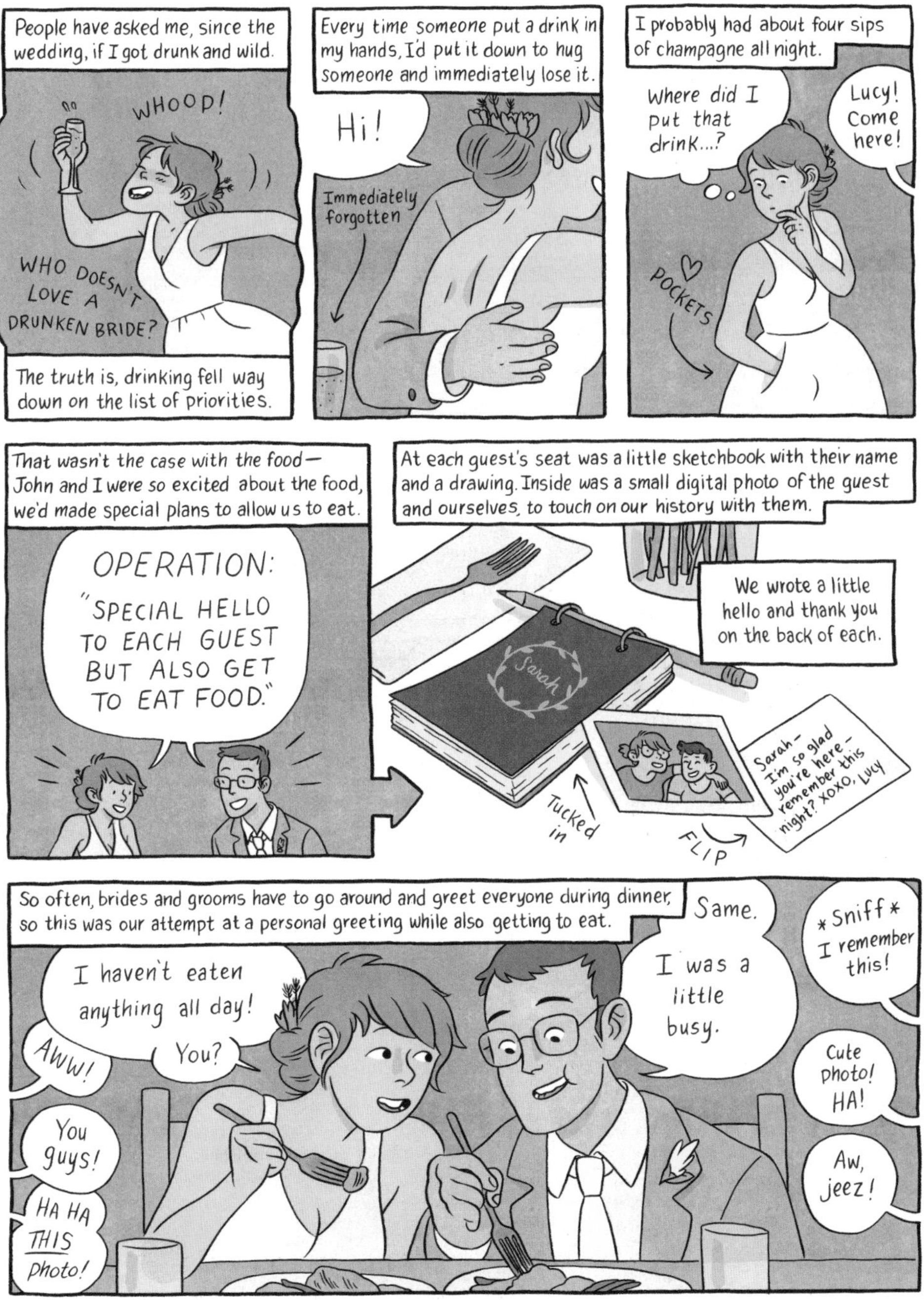
People have asked me, since the wedding, if I got drunk and wild.
WHOOP!
WHO DOESN'T LOVE A DRUNKEN BRIDE?
The truth is, drinking fell way down on the list of priorities.
Every time someone put a drink in my hands, I'd put it down to hug someone and immediately lose it.
Hi!
Immediately forgotten
I probably had about four sips of champagne all night.
Where did I put that drink...?
Lucy! Come here!
POCKETS
That wasn't the case with the food— John and I were so excited about the food, we'd made special plans to allow us to eat.
OPERATION: "SPECIAL HELLO TO EACH GUEST BUT ALSO GET TO EAT FOOD."
At each guest's seat was a little sketchbook with their name and a drawing. Inside was a small digital photo of the guest and ourselves, to touch on our history with them.
We wrote a little hello and thank you on the back of each.
Sarah
Tucked in
FLIP
Sarah— I'm so glad you're here— remember this night? XOXO, Lucy
So often, brides and grooms have to go around and greet everyone during dinner, so this was our attempt at a personal greeting while also getting to eat.
I haven't eaten anything all day!
You?
Same.
I was a little busy.
Sniff I remember this!
AWW!
Cute photo! HA!
You guys!
Aw, jeez!
HA HA THIS photo!

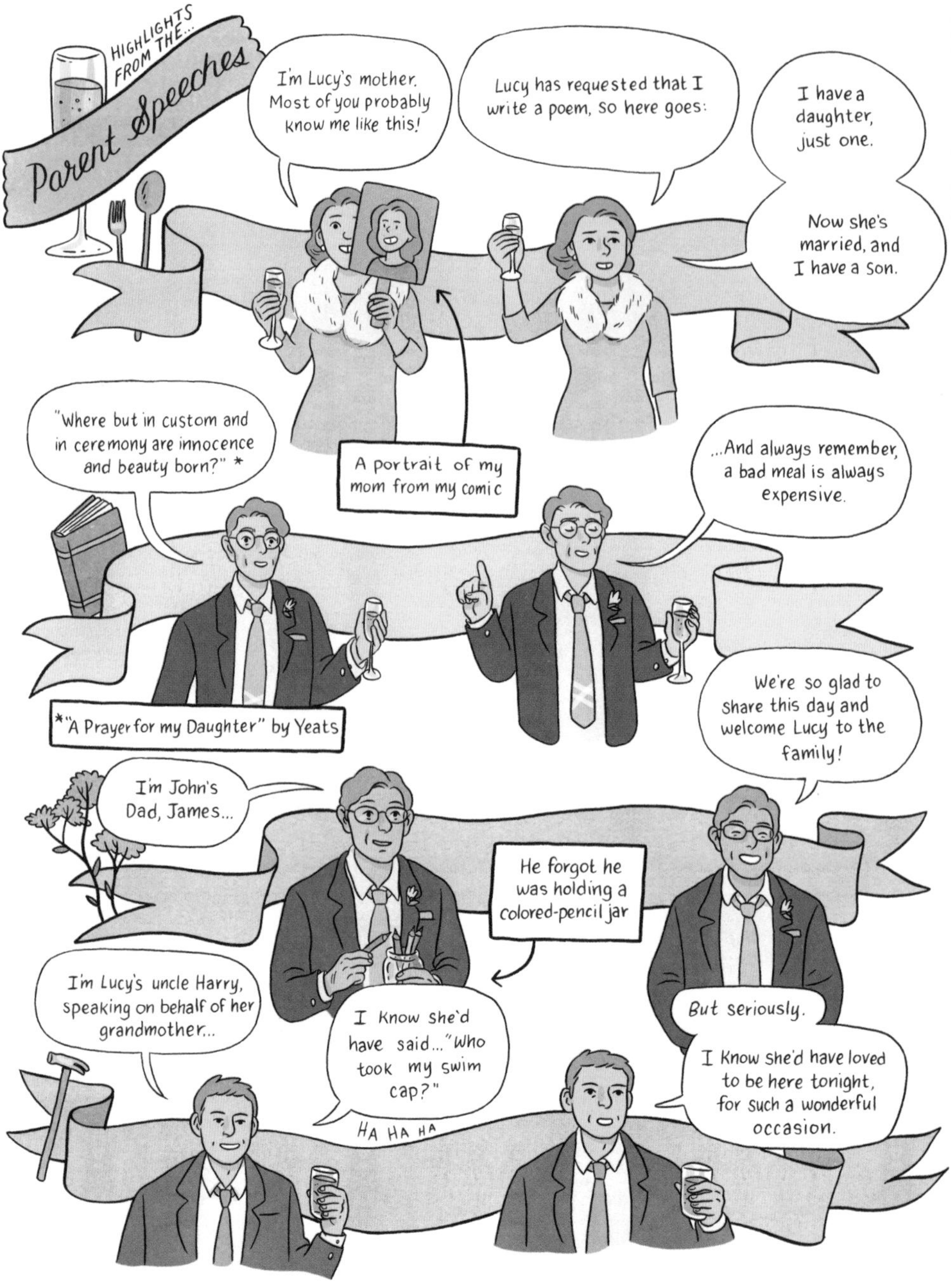

HIGHLIGHTS FROM THE...
Parent Speeches
I'm Lucy's mother. Most of you probably know me like this!
Lucy has requested that I write a poem, so here goes:
I have a daughter, just one.
Now she's married, and I have a son.
A portrait of my mom from my comic
"Where but in custom and in ceremony are innocence and beauty born?" *
...And always remember, a bad meal is always expensive.
*"A Prayer for my Daughter" by Yeats
We're so glad to share this day and welcome Lucy to the family!
I'm John's Dad, James...
He forgot he was holding a colored-pencil jar
I'm Lucy's uncle Harry, speaking on behalf of her grandmother...
I know she'd have said..."Who took my swim cap?"
HA HA HA
But seriously.
I know she'd have loved to be here tonight, for such a wonderful occasion.

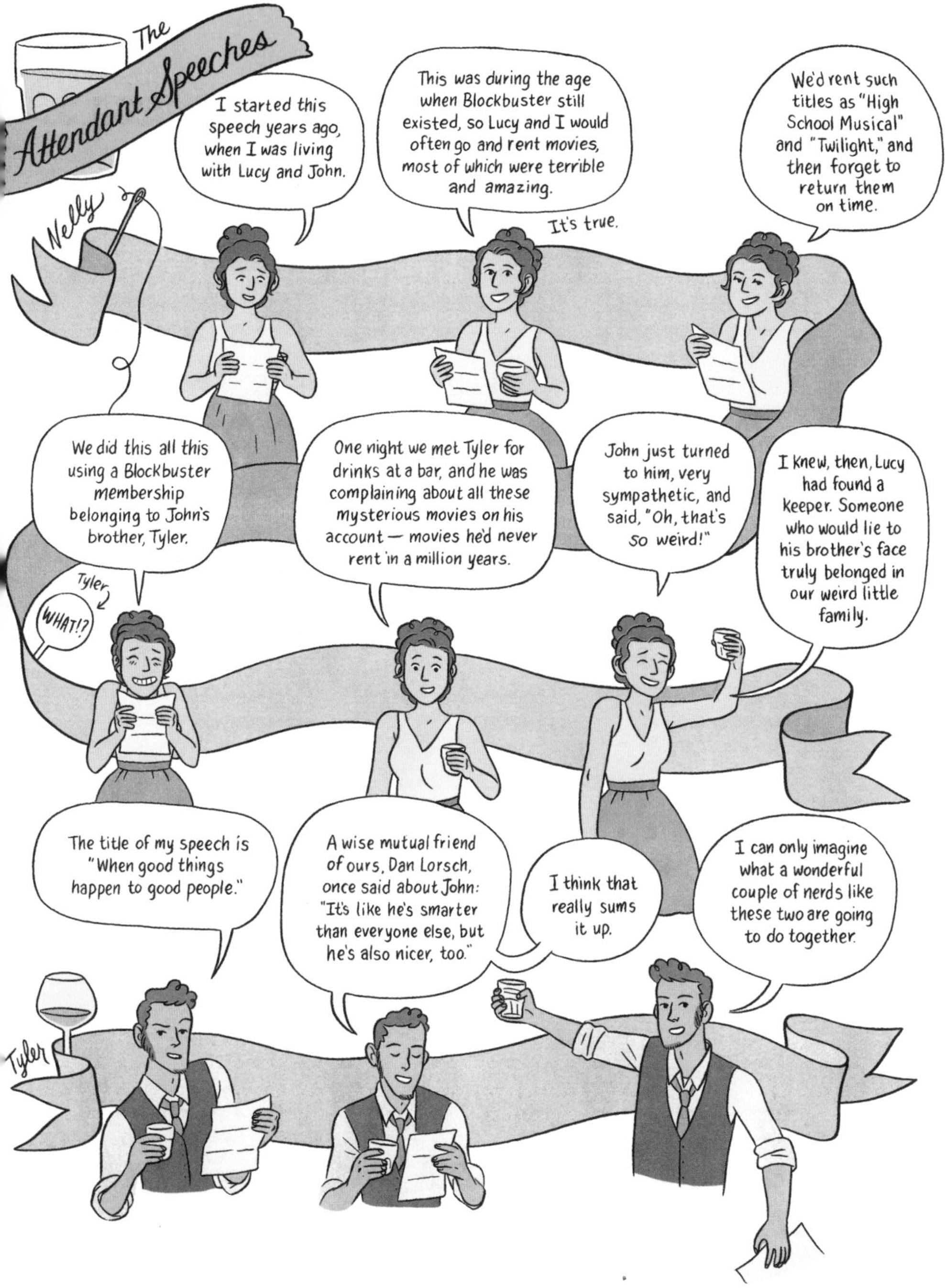

The Attendant Speeches
Nelly
I started this speech years ago, when I was living with Lucy and John.
This was during the age when Blockbuster still existed, so Lucy and I would often go and rent movies, most of which were terrible and amazing.
It's true.
We'd rent such titles as "High School Musical" and "Twilight," and then forget to return them on time.
We did this all this using a Blockbuster membership belonging to John's brother, Tyler.
Tyler
WHAT!?
One night we met Tyler for drinks at a bar, and he was complaining about all these mysterious movies on his account — movies he'd never rent in a million years.
John just turned to him, very sympathetic, and said, "Oh, that's so weird!"
I knew, then, Lucy had found a keeper. Someone who would lie to his brother's face truly belonged in our weird little family.
Tyler
The title of my speech is "When good things happen to good people."
A wise mutual friend of ours, Dan Lorsch, once said about John: "It's like he's smarter than everyone else, but he's also nicer, too."
I think that really sums it up.
I can only imagine what a wonderful couple of nerds like these two are going to do together.

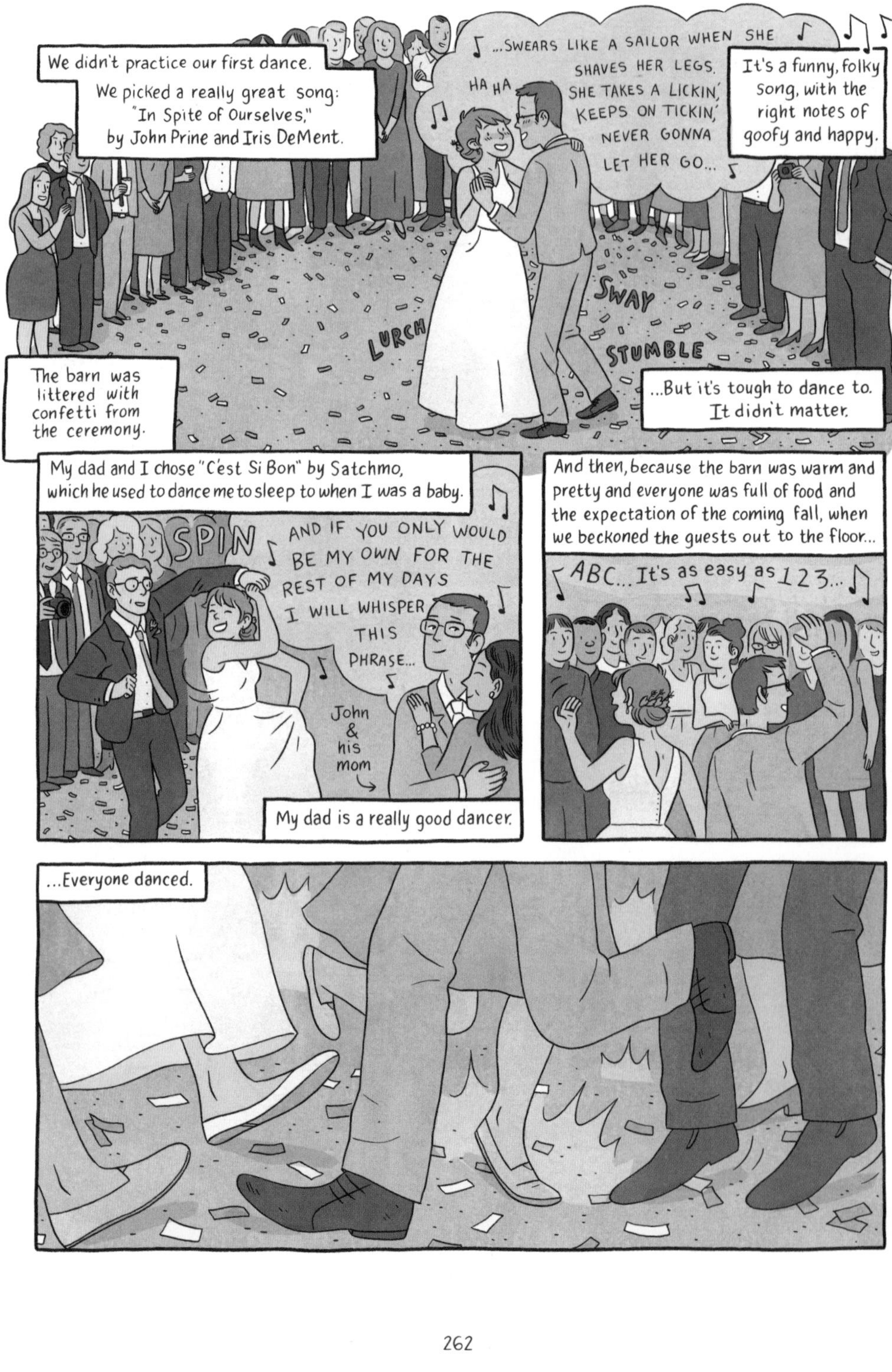
We didn't practice our first dance.
We picked a really great song: "In Spite of Ourselves," by John Prine and Iris DeMent.
...SWEARS LIKE A SAILOR WHEN SHE SHAVES HER LEGS. SHE TAKES A LICKIN', KEEPS ON TICKIN', NEVER GONNA LET HER GO...
HA HA
It's a funny, folky song, with the right notes of goofy and happy.
LURCH
SWAY
STUMBLE
The barn was littered with confetti from the ceremony.
...But it's tough to dance to. It didn't matter.
My dad and I chose "C'est Si Bon" by Satchmo, which he used to dance me to sleep to when I was a baby.
SPIN
AND IF YOU ONLY WOULD BE MY OWN FOR THE REST OF MY DAYS I WILL WHISPER THIS PHRASE...
John & his mom
My dad is a really good dancer.
And then, because the barn was warm and pretty and everyone was full of food and the expectation of the coming fall, when we beckoned the guests out to the floor...
ABC... It's as easy as 123...
...Everyone danced.

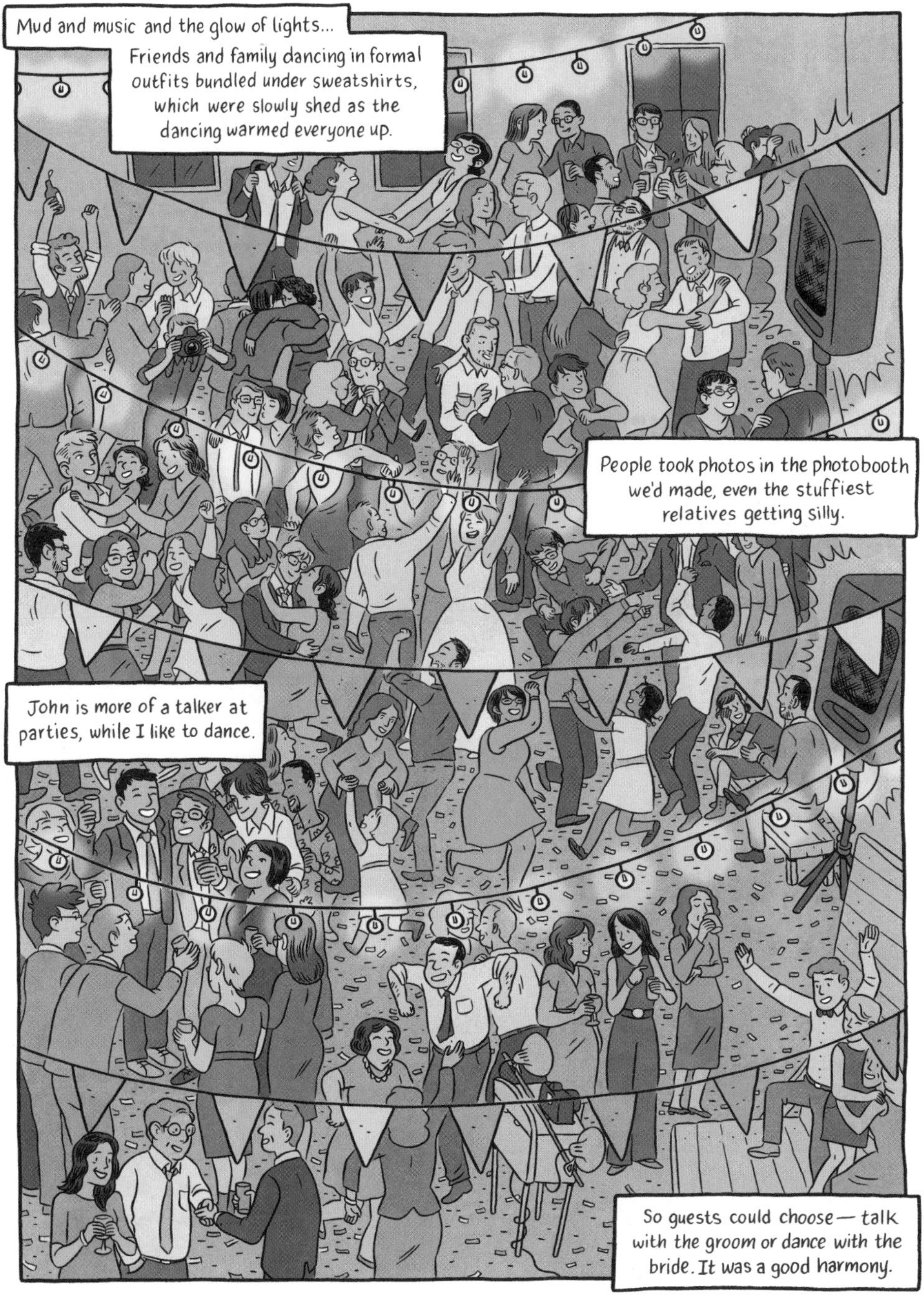
Mud and music and the glow of lights...
Friends and family dancing in formal outfits bundled under sweatshirts, which were slowly shed as the dancing warmed everyone up.
People took photos in the photobooth we'd made, even the stuffiest relatives getting silly.
John is more of a talker at parties, while I like to dance.
So guests could choose— talk with the groom or dance with the bride. It was a good harmony.

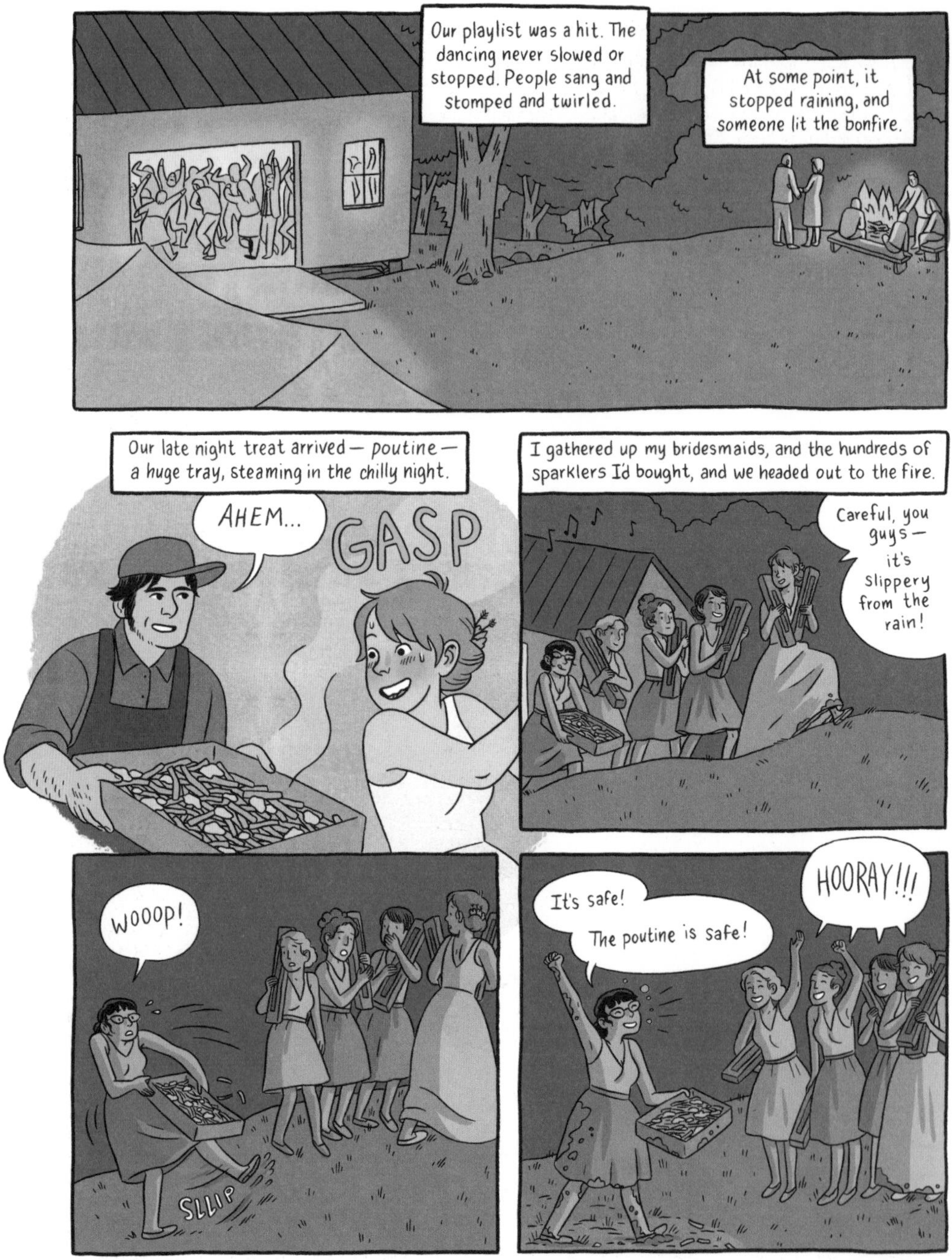
Our playlist was a hit. The dancing never slowed or stopped. People sang and stomped and twirled.
At some point, it stopped raining, and someone lit the bonfire.
Our late night treat arrived — poutine — a huge tray, steaming in the chilly night.
AHEM...
GASP
I gathered up my bridesmaids, and the hundreds of sparklers I'd bought, and we headed out to the fire.
Careful, you guys — it's slippery from the rain!
WOOOP!
SLLIP
It's safe!
The poutine is safe!
HOORAY!!!

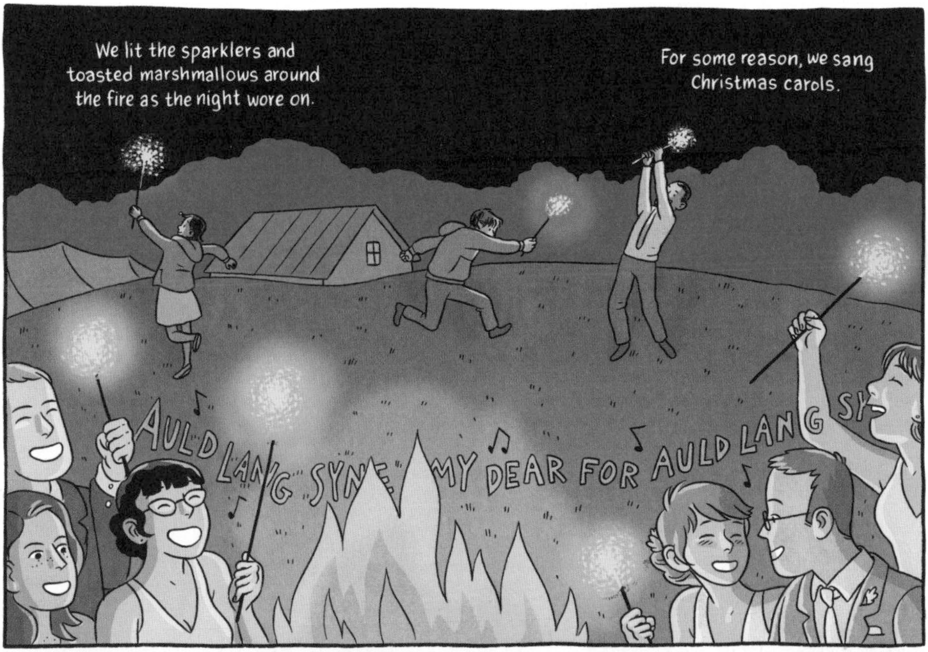
We lit the sparklers and toasted marshmallows around the fire as the night wore on.
For some reason, we sang Christmas carols.
AULD LANG SYNE MY DEAR FOR AULD LANG SY

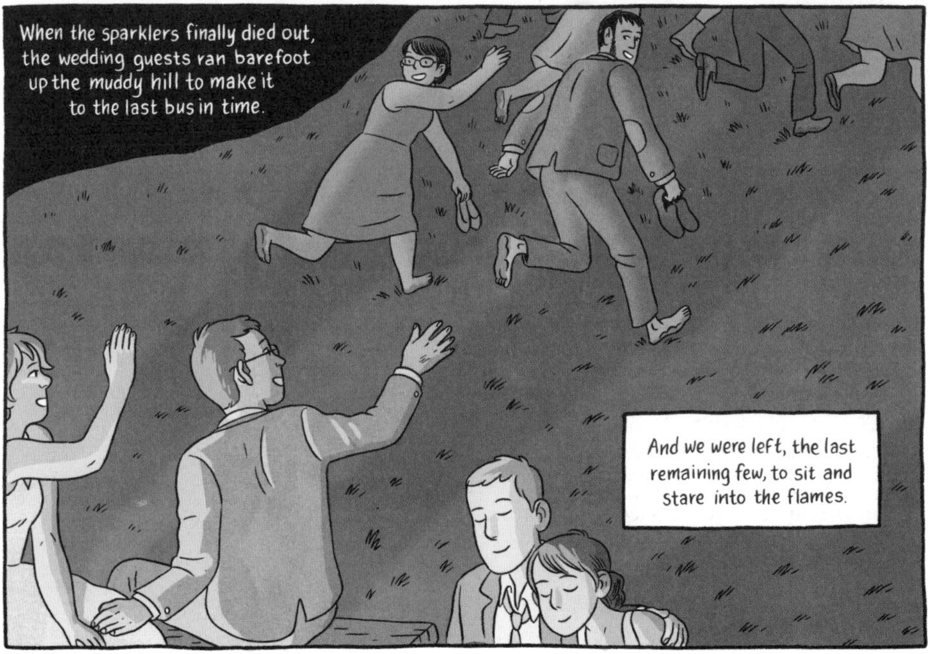
When the sparklers finally died out, the wedding guests ran barefoot up the muddy hill to make it to the last bus in time.
And we were left, the last remaining few, to sit and stare into the flames.

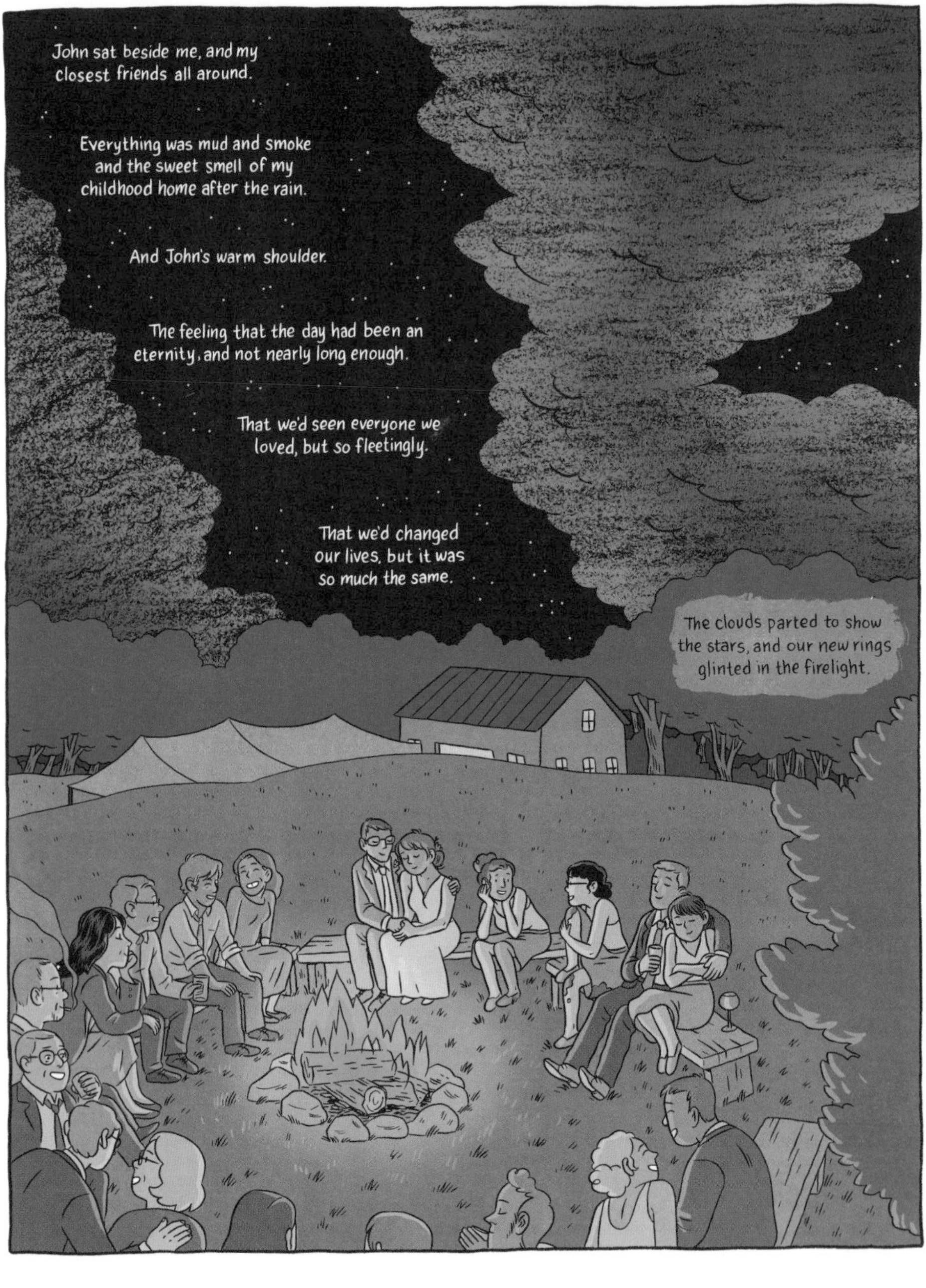
John sat beside me, and my closest friends all around.
Everything was mud and smoke and the sweet smell of my childhood home after the rain.
And John's warm shoulder.
The feeling that the day had been an eternity, and not nearly long enough.
That we'd seen everyone we loved, but so fleetingly.
That we'd changed our lives, but it was so much the same.
The clouds parted to show the stars, and our new rings glinted in the firelight.

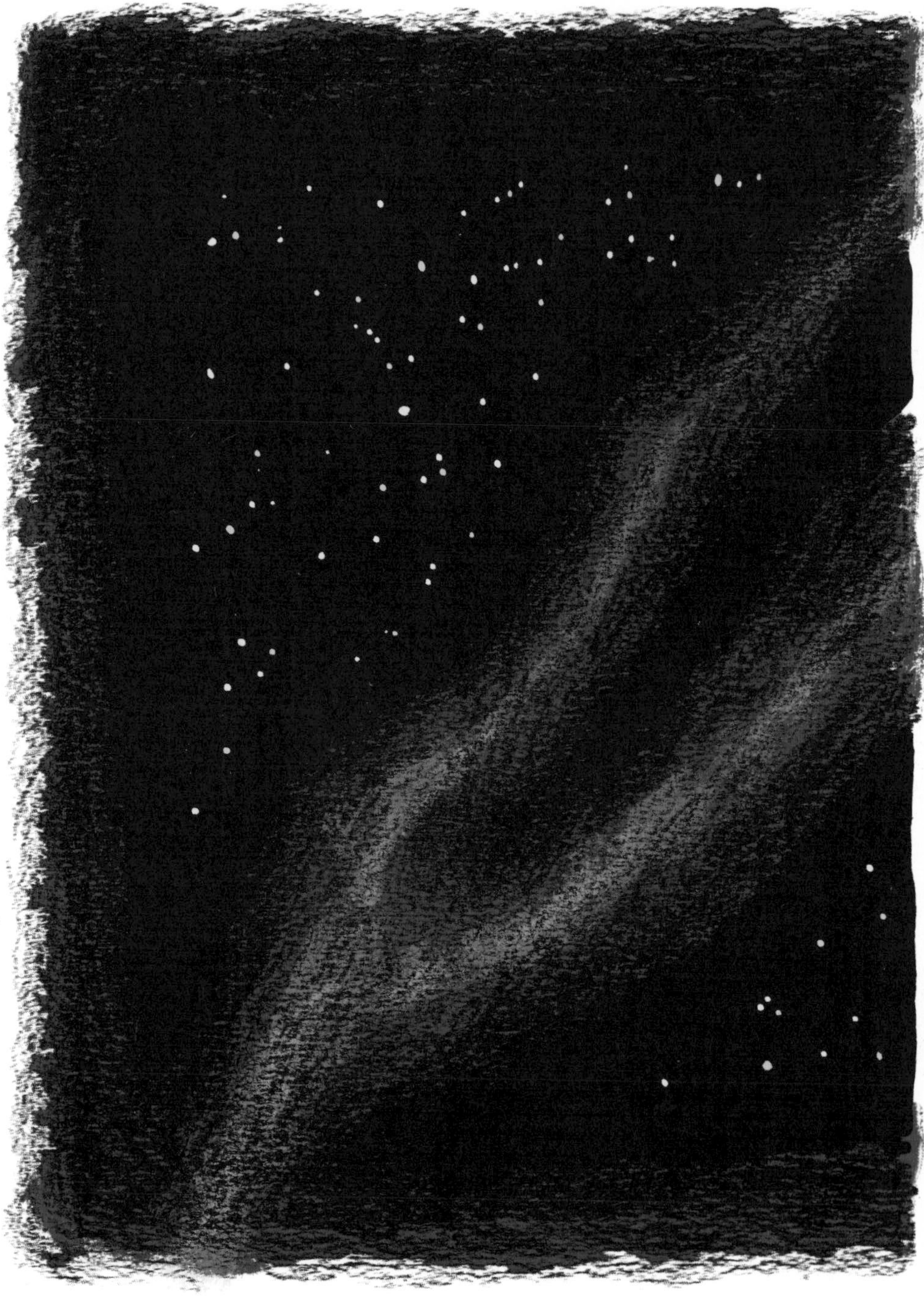

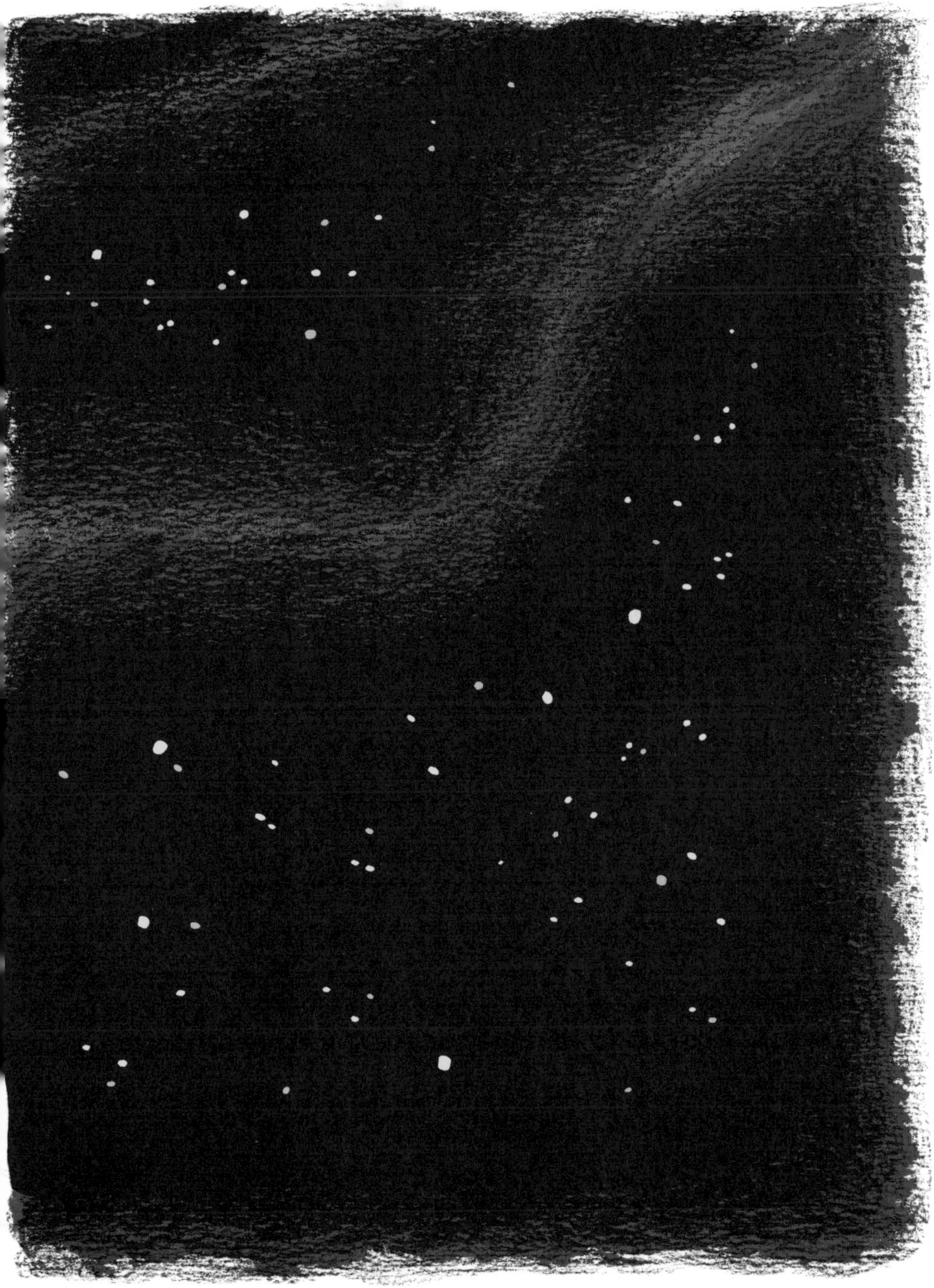

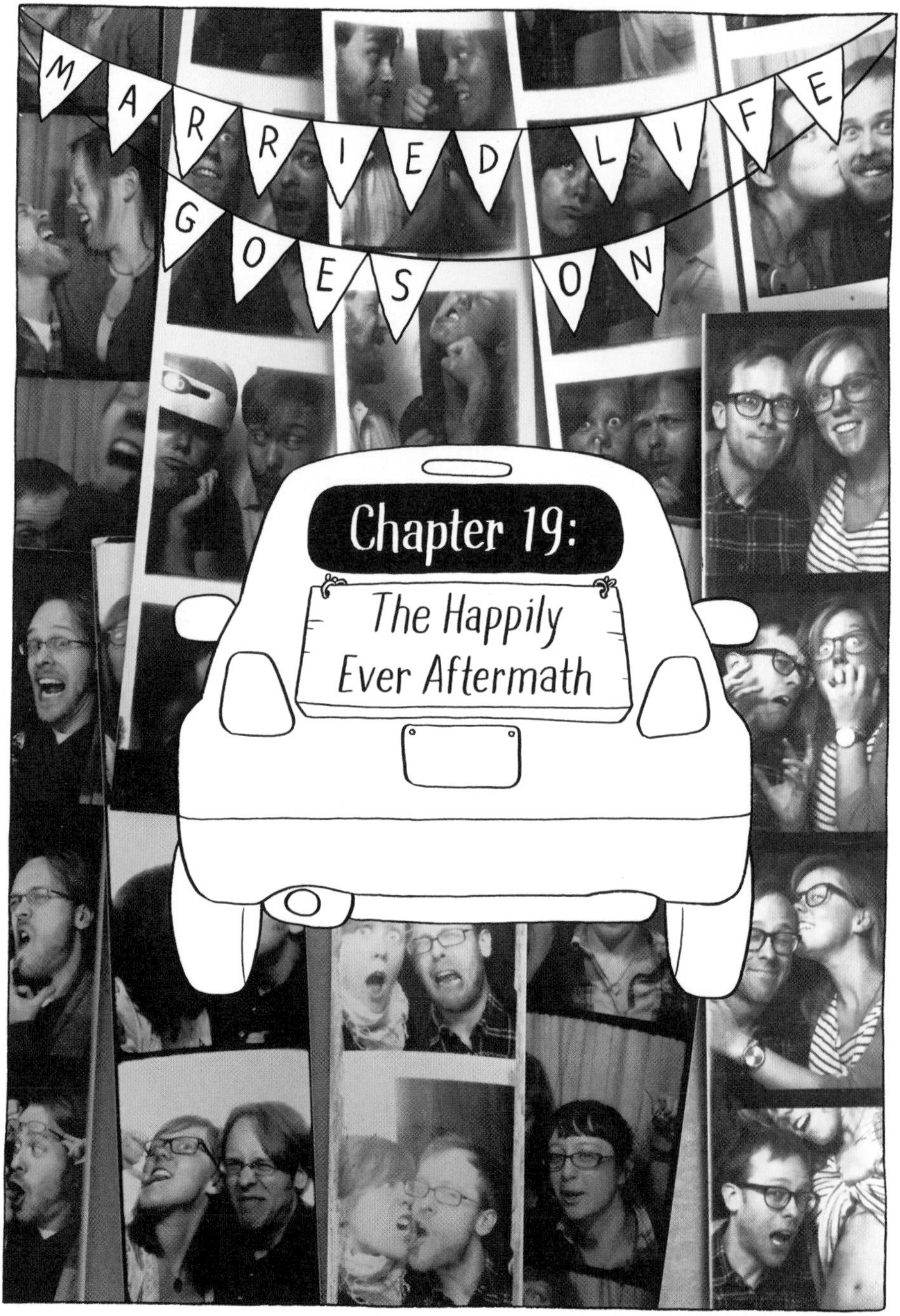
MARRIED LIFE
GOES ON
Chapter 19:
The Happily Ever Aftermath

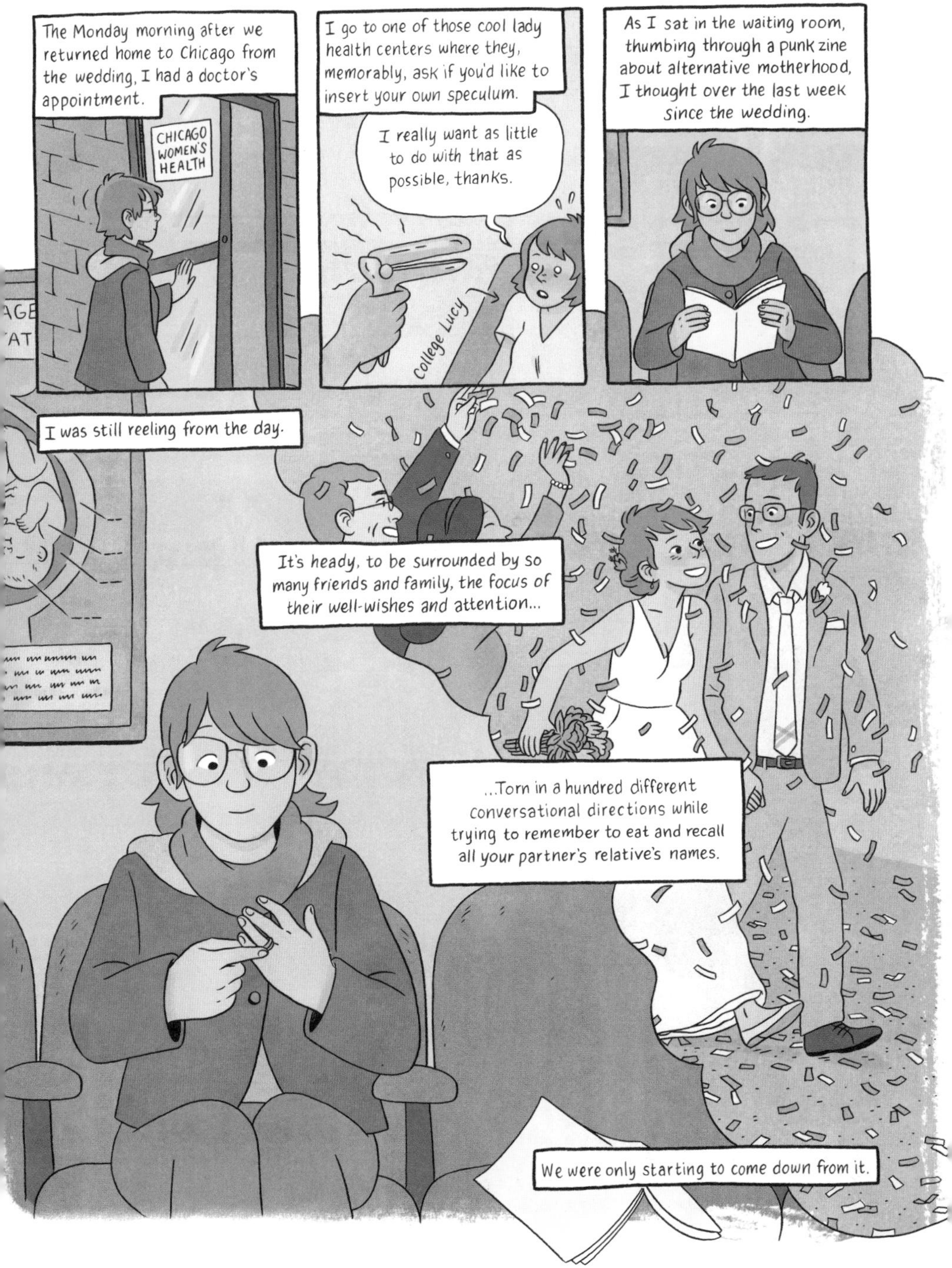

The Monday morning after we returned home to Chicago from the wedding, I had a doctor's appointment.
CHICAGO WOMEN'S HEALTH
I go to one of those cool lady health centers where they, memorably, ask if you'd like to insert your own speculum.
I really want as little to do with that as possible, thanks.
College Lucy
As I sat in the waiting room, thumbing through a punk zine about alternative motherhood, I thought over the last week since the wedding.
I was still reeling from the day.
It's heady, to be surrounded by so many friends and family, the focus of their well-wishes and attention...
...Torn in a hundred different conversational directions while trying to remember to eat and recall all your partner's relative's names.
We were only starting to come down from it.

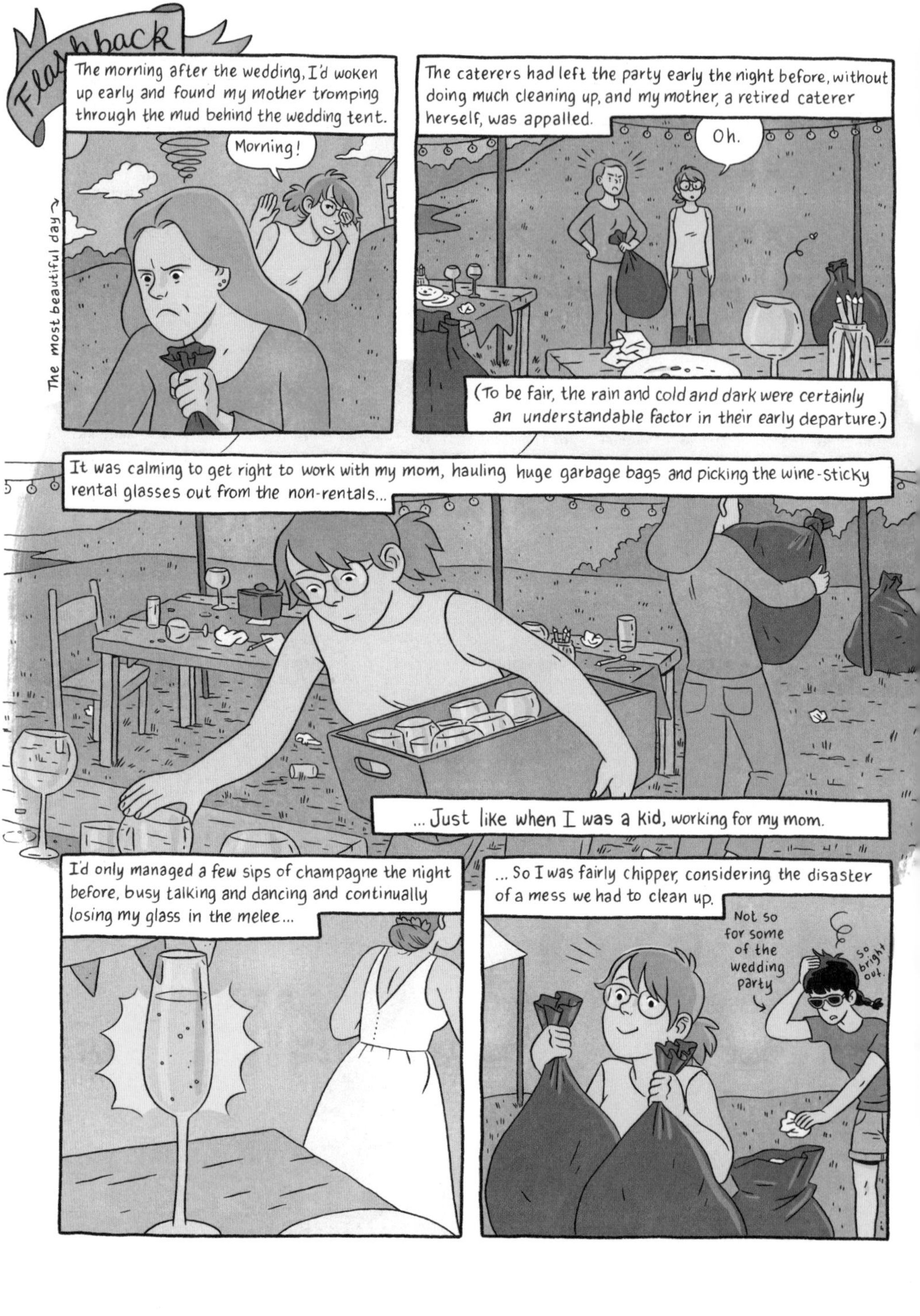
Flashback
The morning after the wedding, I'd woken up early and found my mother tromping through the mud behind the wedding tent.
Morning!
The most beautiful day
The caterers had left the party early the night before, without doing much cleaning up, and my mother, a retired caterer herself, was appalled.
Oh.
(To be fair, the rain and cold and dark were certainly an understandable factor in their early departure.)
It was calming to get right to work with my mom, hauling huge garbage bags and picking the wine-sticky rental glasses out from the non-rentals...
...Just like when I was a kid, working for my mom.
I'd only managed a few sips of champagne the night before, busy talking and dancing and continually losing my glass in the melee...
...So I was fairly chipper, considering the disaster of a mess we had to clean up.
Not so for some of the wedding party
So bright out.

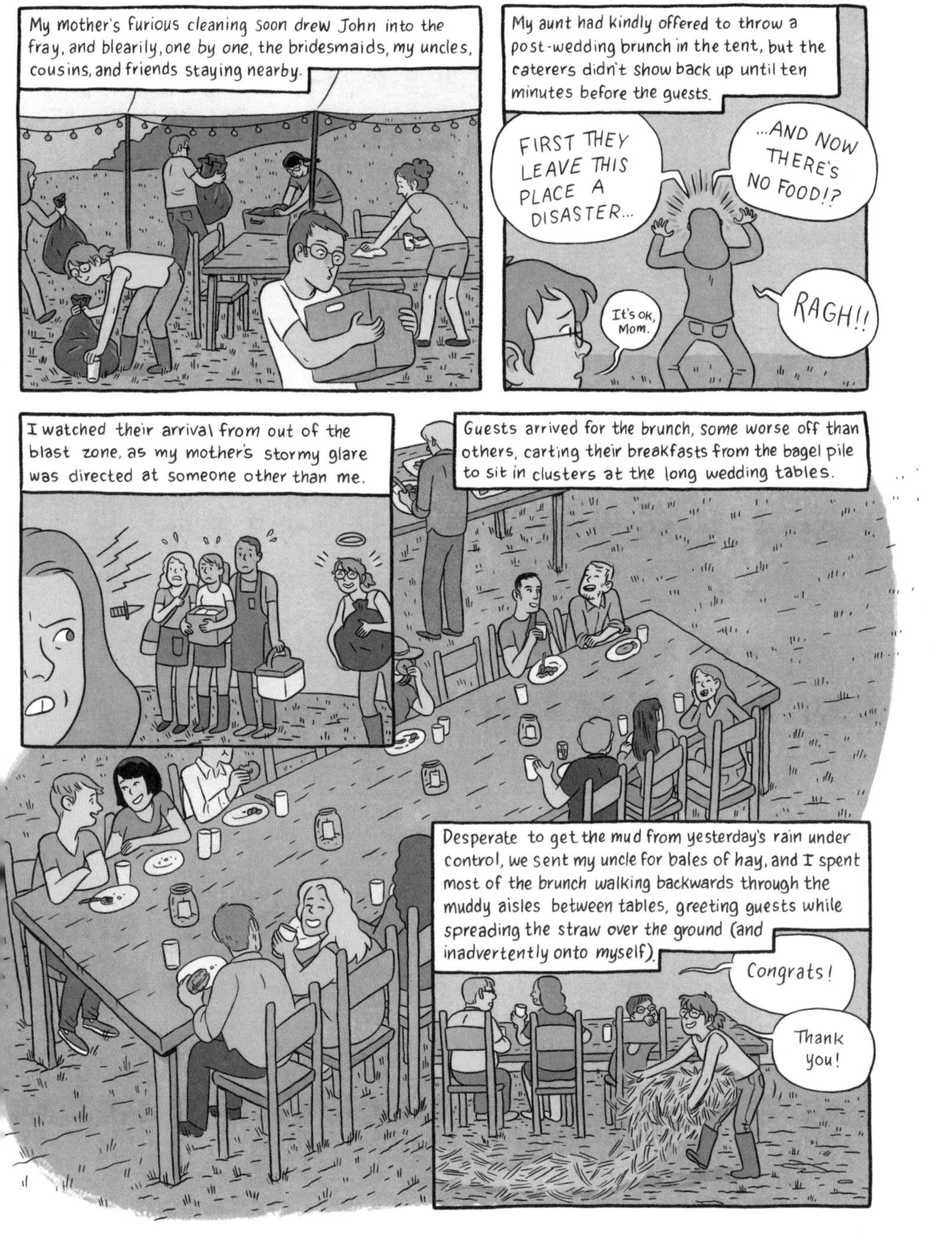
My mother's furious cleaning soon drew John into the fray, and blearily, one by one, the bridesmaids, my uncles, cousins, and friends staying nearby.
My aunt had kindly offered to throw a post-wedding brunch in the tent, but the caterers didn't show back up until ten minutes before the guests.
FIRST THEY LEAVE THIS PLACE A DISASTER...
...AND NOW THERE'S NO FOOD!?
It's OK, Mom.
RAGH!!
I watched their arrival from out of the blast zone, as my mother's stormy glare was directed at someone other than me.
Guests arrived for the brunch, some worse off than others, carting their breakfasts from the bagel pile to sit in clusters at the long wedding tables.
Desperate to get the mud from yesterday's rain under control, we sent my uncle for bales of hay, and I spent most of the brunch walking backwards through the muddy aisles between tables, greeting guests while spreading the straw over the ground (and inadvertently onto myself).
Congrats!
Thank you!

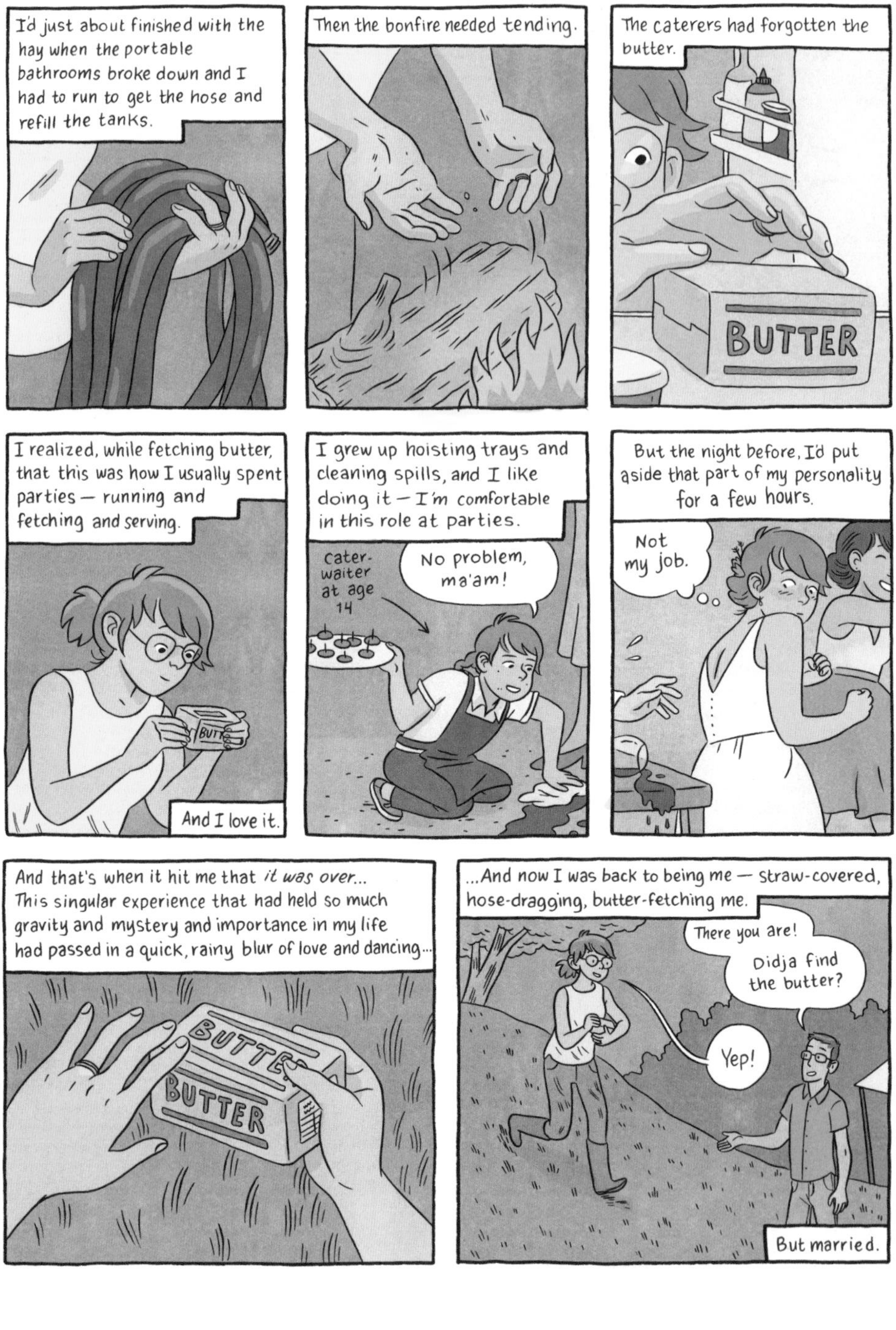
I'd just about finished with the hay when the portable bathrooms broke down and I had to run to get the hose and refill the tanks.
Then the bonfire needed tending.
The caterers had forgotten the butter.
BUTTER
I realized, while fetching butter, that this was how I usually spent parties — running and fetching and serving.
And I love it.
I grew up hoisting trays and cleaning spills, and I like doing it — I'm comfortable in this role at parties.
cater-waiter at age 14
No problem, ma'am!
But the night before, I'd put aside that part of my personality for a few hours.
Not my job.
And that's when it hit me that *it was over*... This singular experience that had held so much gravity and mystery and importance in my life had passed in a quick, rainy blur of love and dancing...
BUTTER
BUTTER
...And now I was back to being me — straw-covered, hose-dragging, butter-fetching me.
There you are!
Didja find the butter?
Yep!
But married.

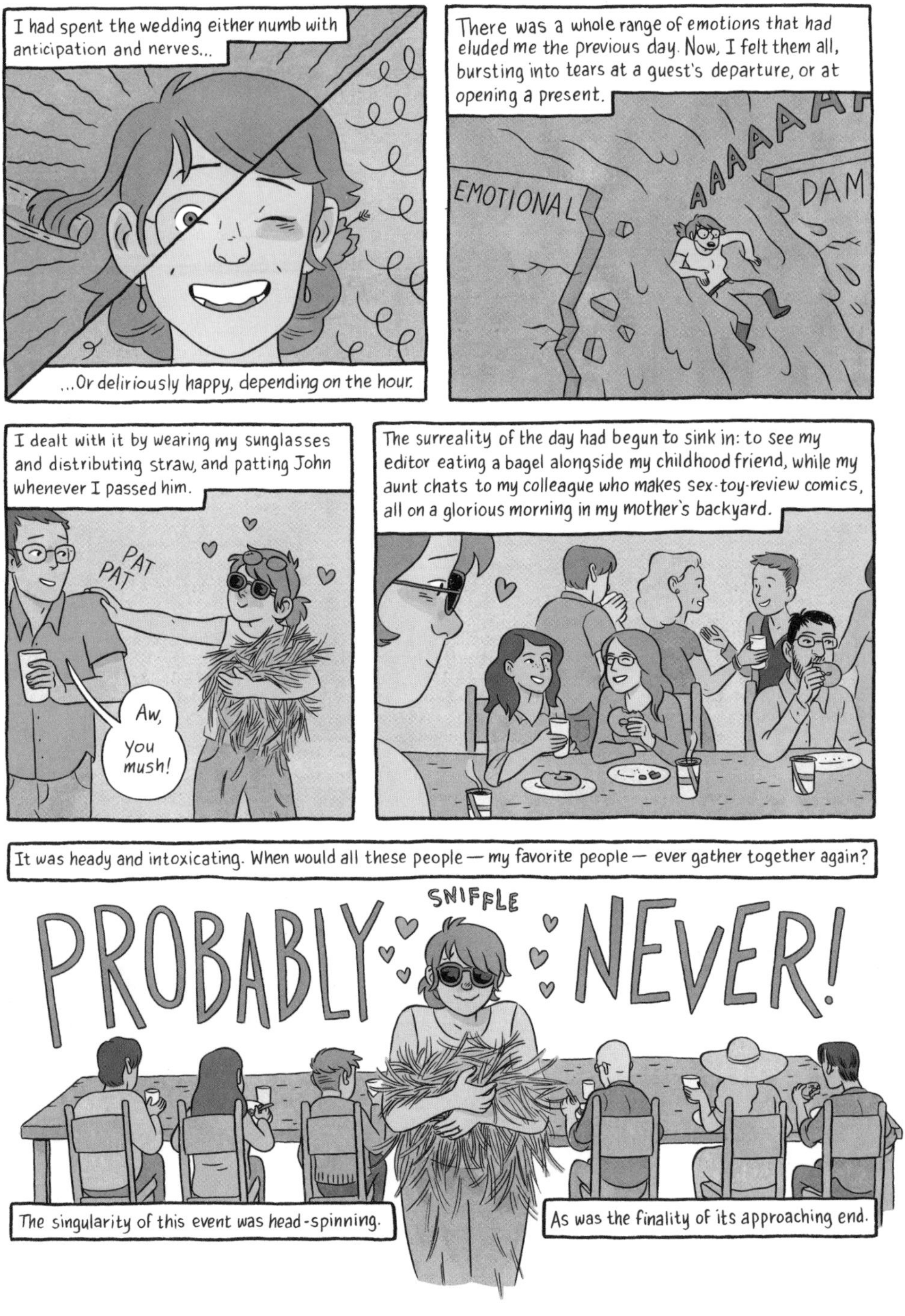
I had spent the wedding either numb with anticipation and nerves...
...Or deliriously happy, depending on the hour.
There was a whole range of emotions that had eluded me the previous day. Now, I felt them all, bursting into tears at a guest's departure, or at opening a present.
AAAAAAAH
EMOTIONAL
DAM
I dealt with it by wearing my sunglasses and distributing straw, and patting John whenever I passed him.
PAT PAT
Aw, you mush!
The surreality of the day had begun to sink in: to see my editor eating a bagel alongside my childhood friend, while my aunt chats to my colleague who makes sex-toy-review comics, all on a glorious morning in my mother's backyard.
It was heady and intoxicating. When would all these people — my favorite people — ever gather together again?
SNIFFLE
PROBABLY NEVER!
The singularity of this event was head-spinning.
As was the finality of its approaching end.

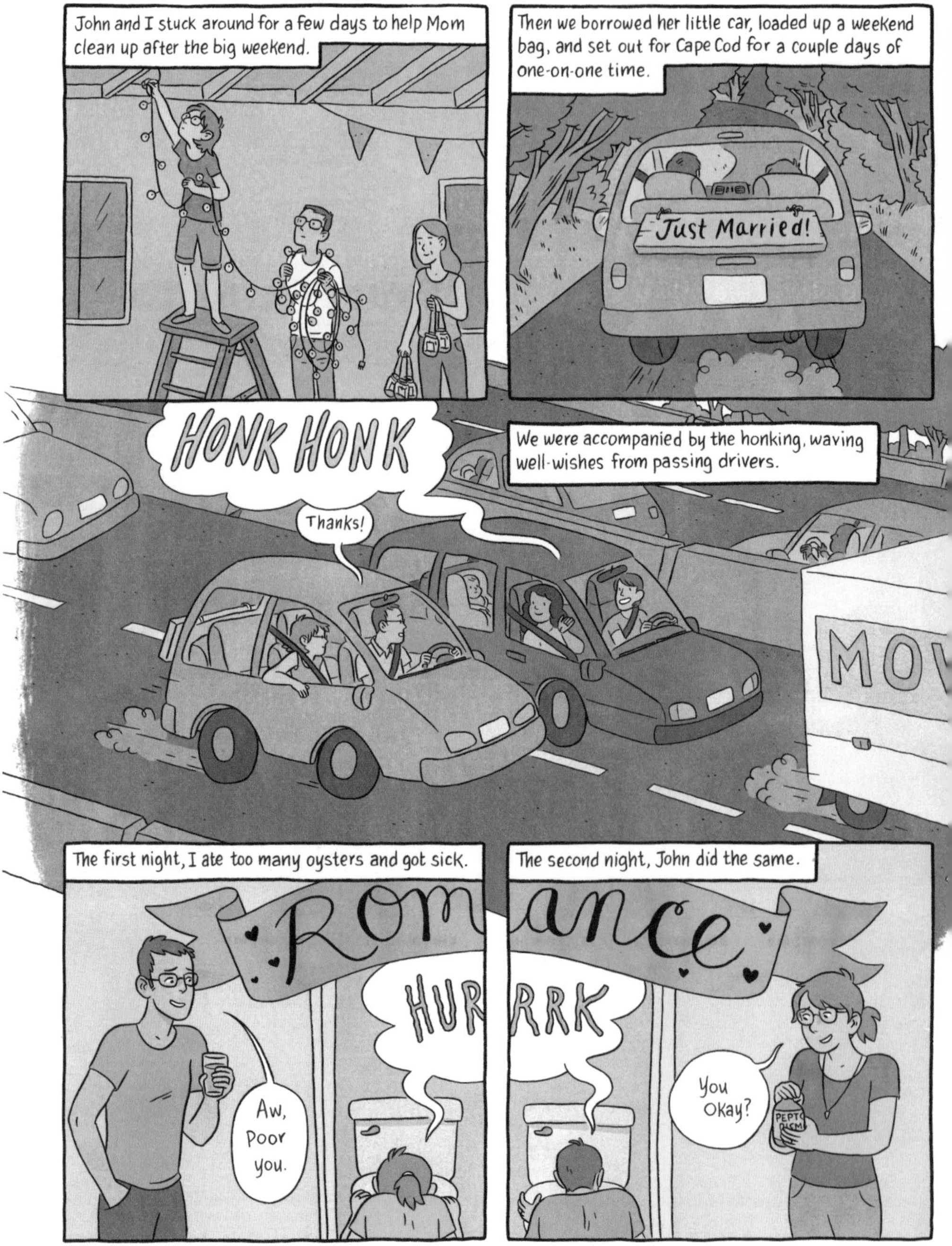
John and I stuck around for a few days to help Mom clean up after the big weekend.
Then we borrowed her little car, loaded up a weekend bag, and set out for Cape Cod for a couple days of one-on-one time.
Just Married!
HONK HONK
We were accompanied by the honking, waving well-wishes from passing drivers.
Thanks!
MOV
The first night, I ate too many oysters and got sick.
The second night, John did the same.
Romance
HURRRK
Aw, Poor you.
You Okay?

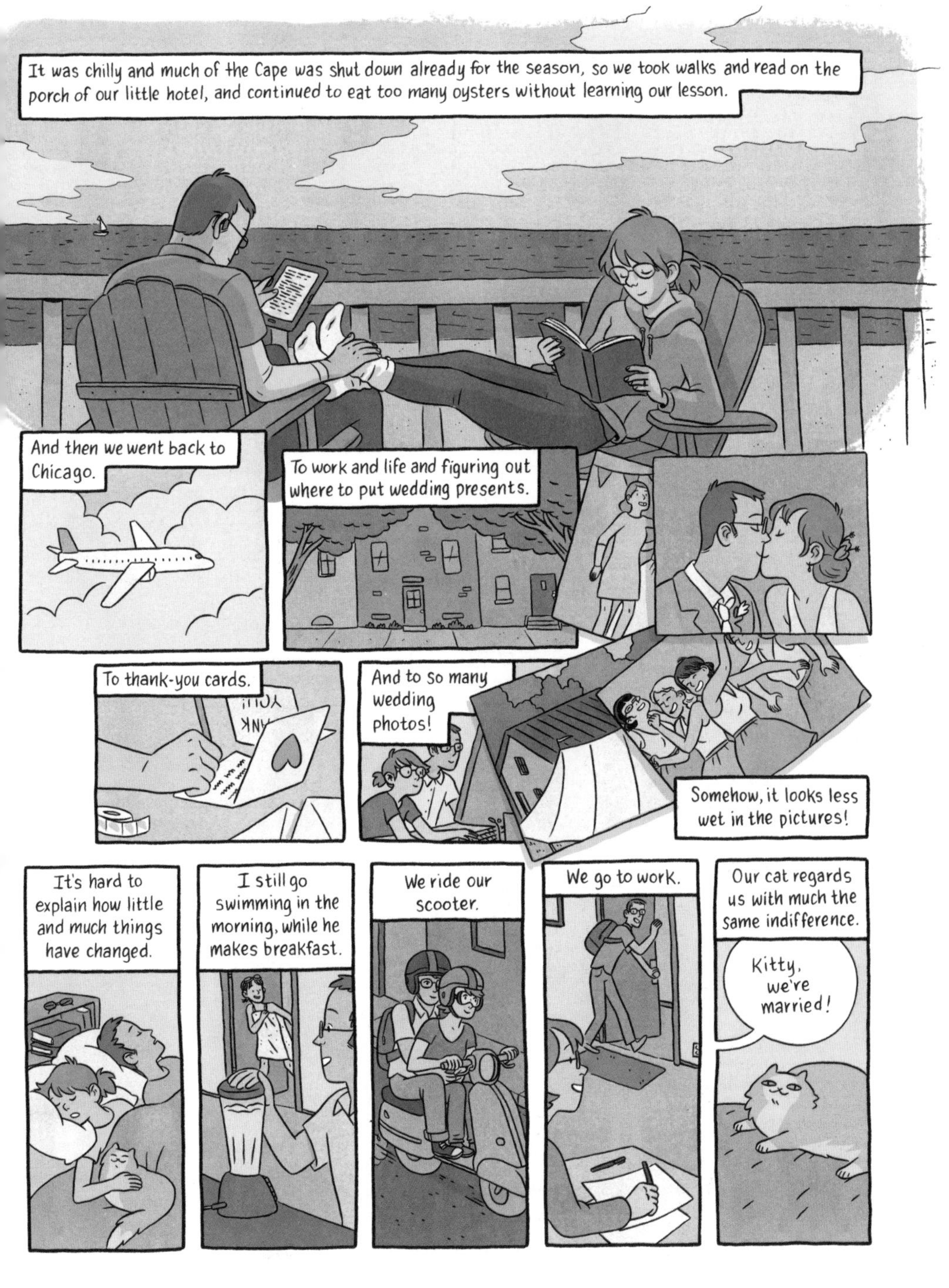
It was chilly and much of the Cape was shut down already for the season, so we took walks and read on the porch of our little hotel, and continued to eat too many oysters without learning our lesson.
And then we went back to Chicago.
To work and life and figuring out where to put wedding presents.
To thank-you cards.
And to so many wedding photos!
Somehow, it looks less wet in the pictures!
It's hard to explain how little and much things have changed.
I still go swimming in the morning, while he makes breakfast.
We ride our scooter.
We go to work.
Our cat regards us with much the same indifference.
Kitty, we're married!

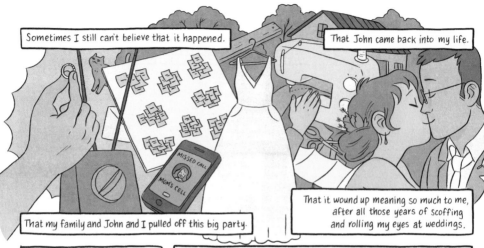

Sometimes I still can't believe that it happened.

That John came back into my life.

That my family and John and I pulled off this big party.

That it wound up meaning so much to me, after all those years of scoffing and rolling my eyes at weddings.

Two weeks after the wedding, it was a perfect, glorious Saturday, so John and I went down to the lakeshore.

We sat on the grass by the Adler Planetarium, which boasts one of the best views of the Chicago skyline.

While we sat, a limo pulled up, and a wedding party piled out in torrents of finery.

They lined up for photos along the water's edge.

Nice day for it.

I guess! If you LIKE this sort of weather for a wedding.

I realized my feelings about weddings had shifted. It stirred up memories of my own — joyful and fun and singular — just to look at that happy party.

Aww, you mush.

Sniffle

It had been a long and crazy year.

AND HERE IS WHAT I LEARNED:

I know, marriage is supposed to be hard work — and it is, as is any relationship, but... In marriage, we make our own rules.

It's about making *two* people happy, rather than 120.

The work is done while we don't notice it — don't schedule time for it — don't make a seating chart.

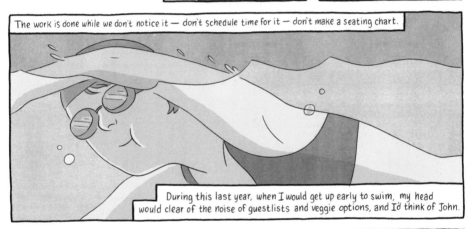

During this last year, when I would get up early to swim, my head would clear of the noise of guestlists and veggie options, and I'd think of John.

I'd come home and he would have made breakfast, and we would eat it while standing at the kitchen counter, making plans for the day — grocery lists and wedding tasks and making sure he wears sunscreen.

ACK!

HEH HEH

You're all wet!

279

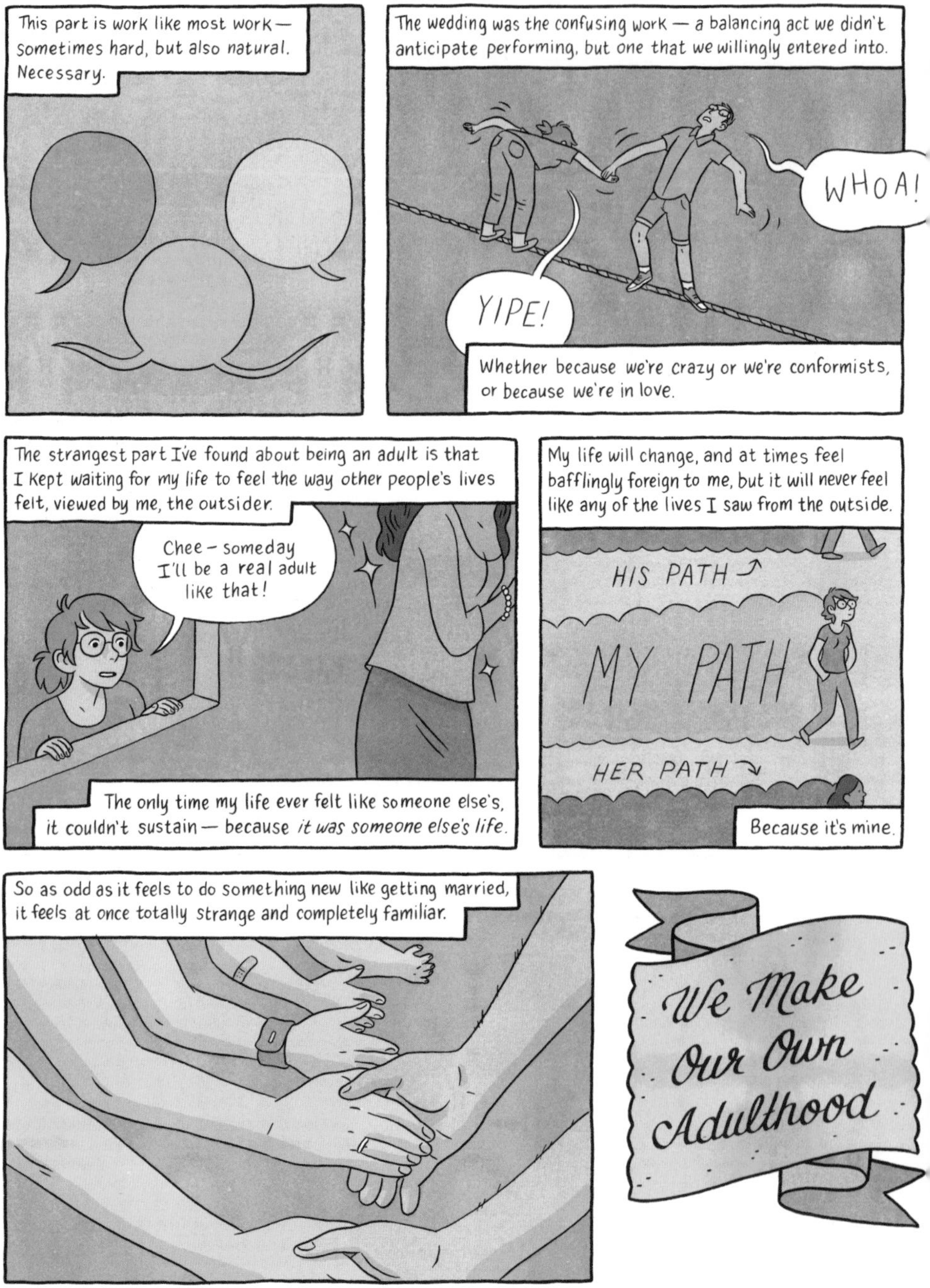
This part is work like most work — sometimes hard, but also natural. Necessary.
The wedding was the confusing work — a balancing act we didn't anticipate performing, but one that we willingly entered into.
WHOA!
YIPE!
Whether because we're crazy or we're conformists, or because we're in love.
The strangest part I've found about being an adult is that I kept waiting for my life to feel the way other people's lives felt, viewed by me, the outsider.
Chee — someday I'll be a real adult like that!
The only time my life ever felt like someone else's, it couldn't sustain — because *it was someone else's life*.
My life will change, and at times feel bafflingly foreign to me, but it will never feel like any of the lives I saw from the outside.
HIS PATH
MY PATH
HER PATH
Because it's mine.
So as odd as it feels to do something new like getting married, it feels at once totally strange and completely familiar.
We Make Our Own Adulthood

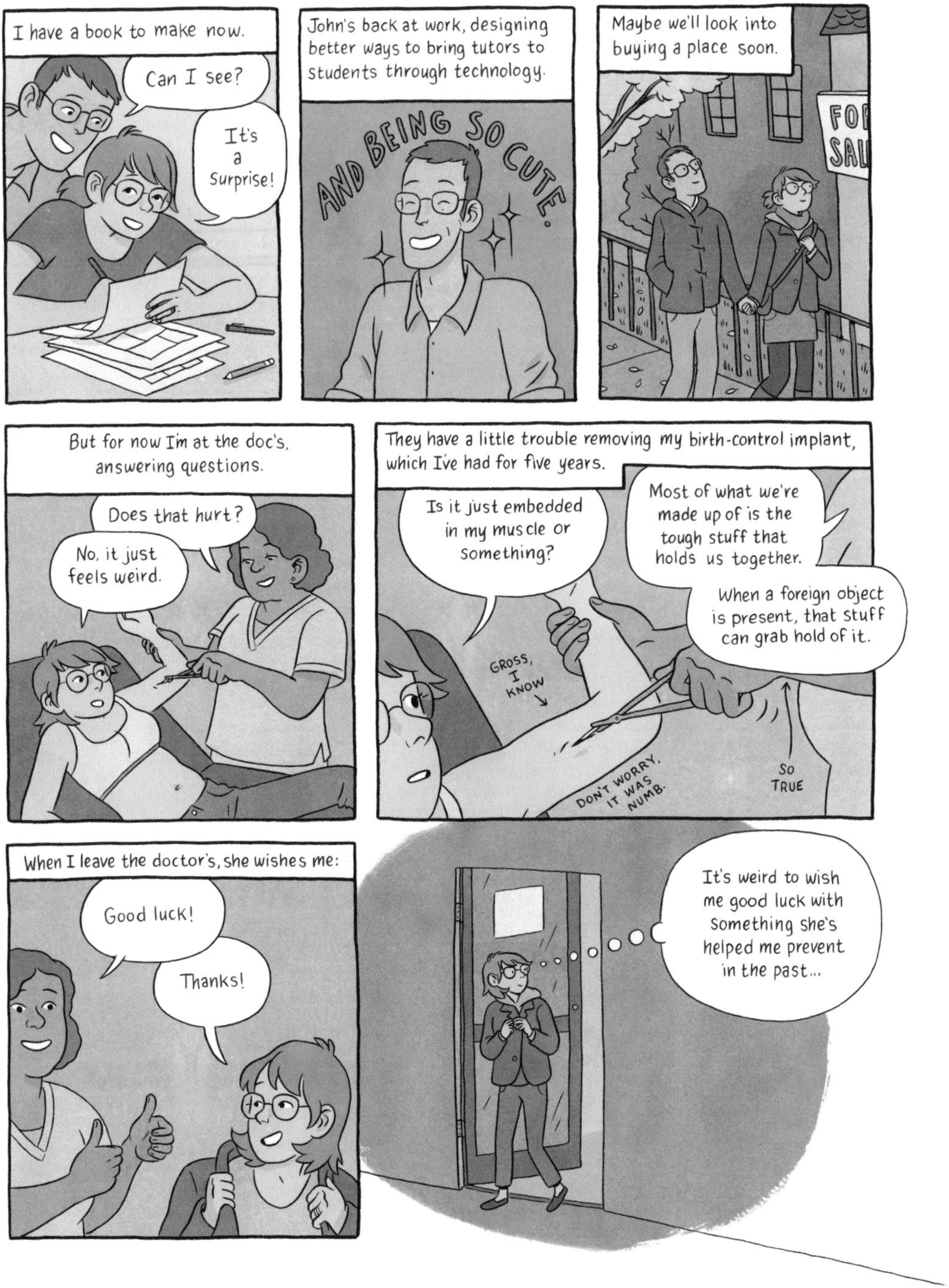

I have a book to make now.
Can I see?
It's a surprise!
John's back at work, designing better ways to bring tutors to students through technology.
AND BEING SO CUTE.
Maybe we'll look into buying a place soon.
But for now I'm at the doc's, answering questions.
Does that hurt?
No, it just feels weird.
They have a little trouble removing my birth-control implant, which I've had for five years.
Is it just embedded in my muscle or something?
Most of what we're made up of is the tough stuff that holds us together.
When a foreign object is present, that stuff can grab hold of it.
GROSS, I KNOW
DON'T WORRY, IT WAS NUMB.
SO TRUE
When I leave the doctor's, she wishes me:
Good luck!
Thanks!
It's weird to wish me good luck with something she's helped me prevent in the past...

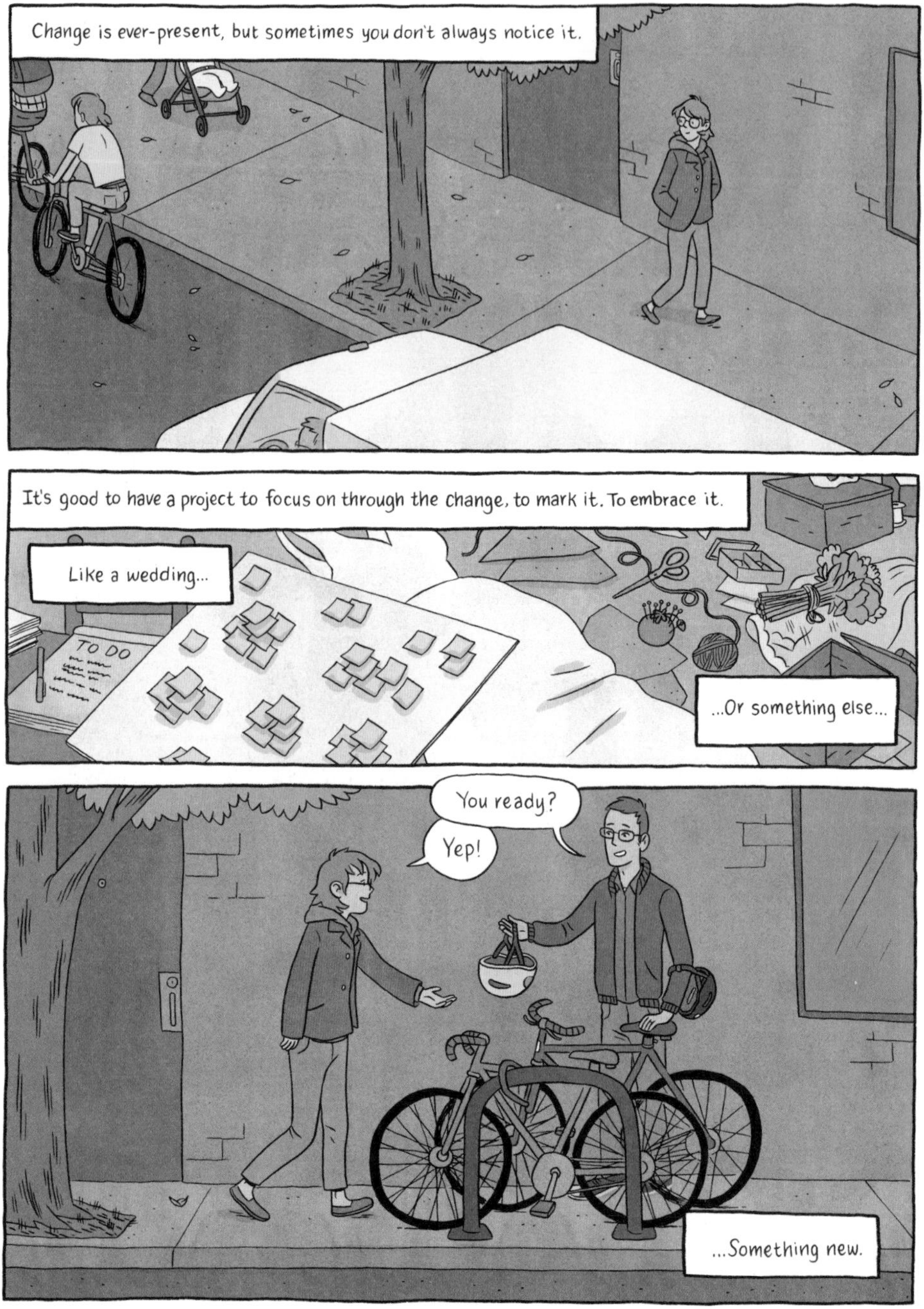
Change is ever-present, but sometimes you don't always notice it.
It's good to have a project to focus on through the change, to mark it. To embrace it.
Like a wedding...
TO DO
...Or something else...
You ready?
Yep!
...Something new.

THE END

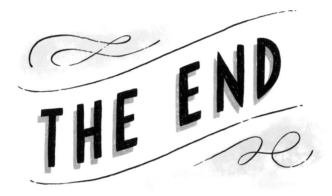

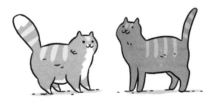

AN AFTERWORD FROM
John

Weddings are daunting enough on their own; the thought of planning one with a creative powerhouse like Lucy had me thoroughly intimidated.

There was plenty to be happy about, of course: She has excellent taste, a formidable work ethic, and a willingness to tackle any project and see it through to the end, no matter how grueling or imposing.

(That third quality can be a mixed blessing. For example, I admired Lucy's ambition in making the wedding party's neckties from scratch, but I must admit that I questioned her decision when I considered the time she could've saved by screenprinting a few cheap ties from H&M.)

They didn't have the right color ties!

Before I got married, I assumed that the details of a couple's wedding were all the outcome of conscious decisions. As a result, I was surprised that so many couples had generic, seemingly identical weddings — didn't these people care about expressing themselves?

I envisioned my own wedding as a precise representation of my personal aesthetic and sensibilities.

Now that I've been in the trenches, my perspective has changed, and I understand lots of people simply don't have the endurance or interest in personalizing the minutiae of their wedding, after using up their energy battling societal expectations, family drama, and wedding costs.

This absolutely makes sense to me. I was exhausted by the endless list of decisions, and I was lucky to have a partner whose attention to detail is even more fanatical than my own.

People ask me what it's like to be married to someone who publishes true stories about our life. Does it make me nervous, or do I feel exposed?

Frankly, I love it. By now, I know that I can count on Lucy's work to be true to life without revealing anything that would break our trust. It's a unique privilege to see my wedding recorded in honest detail by such a thoughtful scribe, the only other person as intimately involved in the planning as I was myself.

So, while Lucy is a tough act to follow, there's one last wedding story I'd like to add to this book.

By February, Chicago winters have worn down even the hardiest Midwest residents. The temperatures are low, the snow is high, and cabin fever is rampant. Luckily, Lucy & I had planned the perfect respite: a honeymoon in Costa Rica, five months after our September wedding.

Costa Rica was beautiful, tropical, exotic — it was a very honeymoon-ish place to honeymoon. We spent entire afternoons swimming in the warm ocean and then drying off on a lounge chair on the beach with a book, repeating the process several times.

On one such afternoon, we had spread our towels on the sand to take a seat and watch the sun set into the surf. We enjoyed a few minutes of peace before spotting a large black SUV driving towards us along the beach. It was the only car on a long beach otherwise filled only with humans and hermit crabs. The SUV pulled to a stop directly in front of us, blocking our view of the aforementioned sunset and surf. The beach was a few miles long and populated by maybe 50 people, so this choice of parking space seemed oddly specific to the two of us.

A man exited the SUV with a camera around his neck, followed by a conspicuously attractive young bride and groom wearing decidedly non-beach outfits. The man was dressed old-fashioned classy, like a member of Mumford & Sons, and the woman was dressed to match in a white, rustic-chic dress. There was an awkwardness between them, and it gradually became clear that they weren't a couple, but instead models on a wedding fashion shoot.

The man with the camera began barking orders at the couple: Stand over there, smile at each other, loosen up, have fun, be in love. The couple complied, assuming casual poses and staging spontaneous displays of affection. The lighting from the sunset was flawless – not that we could see much of it past the giant car blocking our view.

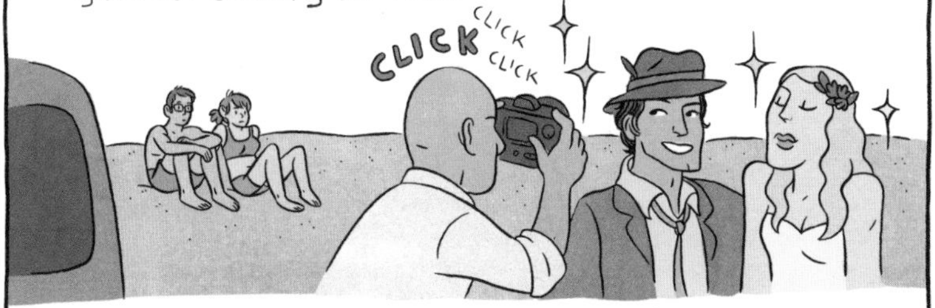
CLICK
CLICK
CLICK

The scene was a wedding-magazine photo come to life. We'd seen a thousand variations of this in advertisements, blog posts, and Pinterest boards: a fake perfect couple sharing a loving gaze against a fantasy backdrop, leaving the viewer to wonder if their own marriage will ever measure up.

Lucy and I remained planted in the sand and watched the scene unfold. The wedding-industry assault we'd endured for months had followed us all the way to our honeymoon.

By now our own wedding was well behind us and we'd gained a few months of perspective. On the beach in Costa Rica, we reflected on that period when the pressures of wedding planning and societal expectations felt inescapable. We reminisced and laughed for a while, then picked up our beach towels to return to our hotel.

That night, my wife and I shared a dinner of fruit, beans, and rice, and fell asleep to the sound of the ocean.

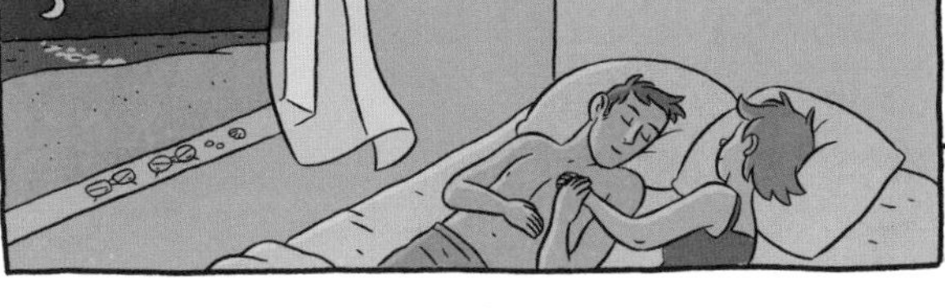

·· THANK YOU ·♥

A few weeks after John and I got engaged, I was sitting in the office of my editor, Calista, recounting some of the insane elements I'd already encountered in the wedding-industry madness. She, like me and so many others before us, had been blindsided by the fact that, to get married, you're expected to care about the symmetry of wedding centerpieces, navigate antiquated gender norms, comply with tradition, and make everything! Through this chat about our mutual befuddlement, this book was born — a wedding story about how nuts weddings are, but, at the same time, how great.

I'm so glad to get to work with someone who lights my fire like Calista does, and who rides the same nerdy, feminist wavelength. She and my publicist, Gina, and the First Second family have been wonderful to work with. One of my biggest bummers about moving out of New York has been that I can no longer drop in on them like I used to, any time it struck my fancy, to whine about deadlines or drop off pages and ride the fancy Flatiron elevators.

(Calista and her hubby in the photobooth)

(Holly and her wife and daughter in the photobooth)

Sometimes when I'm trying to decide what to wear to a thing, I want to call my agent and pal, Holly Bemiss. She has been an amazing, supportive, and helpful friend to me, offering advice on my career and on being a grown-up, all while buying me nachos and kicking ass on my behalf for the last (wow) eight years now. I know I never would have made the work I've made without her help and guidance, and the unwavering support she always lends, often over nachos.

This book was on a tight deadline. We wanted to keep it immediate, so much of it was written over the course of the months before the wedding, and then drawn in the months following. In the midst of a panic over how I'd get this 300-page book written, drawn, and colored in time, I sent out a plea for help, and Luke Healy answered that call. Luke churned out the color-flats for the pages at a superhuman rate, laying the groundwork to make my life far easier, and breezing through the technical specs and my inability to close my lines. I lucked out, big-time, with that dude.

As the book mentioned, the wedding was a group effort. My wedding party pulled through magnificently — with advice, yard-work, bride-soothing,and, in Nora's case, actual garment construction. Nora, Nelly, Taylor, and Erika were instrumental in this wedding. Our groomsmen (Tyler, Dan, Kevin, Troy, and Jason) and ushers (Greg, David, Mark, and Andrew —yeah, there were a lot of dudes in this wedding) handled a rainy, muddy situation, and turned it into a party.

photo by Peter Demuth

My family, new and old, not only made our wedding a blast, but put up with me turning the whole thing into a comic book. Jinx, James, Erika, and Tyler: I know you might not have specifically chosen to have a daughter/sister-in-law who compulsively draws the events and people around her, including you, but I'm so lucky that you bear it with such grace.

My parents, Patrick, Susan, Jeff, and (especially) Georgia, worked hard to make the day better than I could have hoped.

We had a lot of professional help, from Jamie and Katie, who fed and flowered us; from Jeanne, who kept us all on schedule and everything together; Lari, who beautified us; and Peter and Ron, who made sure the whole thing was captured for posterity.

And endless, endless thanks to John, for not only marrying me and encouraging this craziness, but for rubbing my sore inking hand and bringing home hot dogs, and feeding the cat, and making breakfast every day, writing (and inking) his wonderful afterword, and always telling me my work is brilliant, even (and especially) when I hate it and want to quit. What a guy. Marrying such a wonderful person is worth a hundred graphic novels, but I hope this one will do.

And Mom, thank you again for moving that squirrel.

291

Most of the photos
in this book were taken by me, but
a few were used with permission
from friends and family:
Ashley Van Buren
Georgia Dent
Ron Reeves
Ben Chont
Tiffany Hands
Nora Renick Rinehart
Taylor Reiss-Gouge
& Peter Demuth Photography

Thank you!